EYEWITNESS TRAVEL

THE
NETHERLANDS

MAIN CONTRIBUTOR: GERARD M.L.   NS

LONDON, NEW YORK,
MELBOURNE, MUNICH AND DELHI
www.dk.com

Produced by Van Reemst Uitgeverij/Unieboek bv

MAIN CONTRIBUTOR Gerard M.L. Harmans
DESIGN Studio Putto, De Rijp ART EDITOR Dick Polman
EDITORIAL (DUTCH ORIGINAL) de Redactie, boekverzorgers, Amsterdam

PHOTOGRAPHERS
Max Alexander, ANWB Audiovisuele Dienst
(Thijs Tuurenhout), George Burggraaff, Jurjen Drenth,
Rubert Horrox, Kim Sayer, Herman Scholten

ILLUSTRATORS
Hilbert Bolland, Jan Egas, Gieb van Enckevort,
Nick Gibbard, Mark Jurriëns, Maltings Partnership,
Derrick Stone, Khoobie Verwer, Martin Woodward

CARTOGRAPHY
Jane Hanson, Armand Haye, Lovell Johns Limited
(Oxford, UK), Phil Rose, Jennifer Skelley, Peter de Vries

PICTURE RESEARCHER Harry Bunk
PRODUCTION Sarah Dodd

ENGLISH-LANGUAGE ADAPTATION PRODUCED BY
International Book Productions Inc.,
25A Morrow Ave, Toronto, Ontario M6R 2H9, Canada
MANAGING EDITOR Barbara Hopkinson
EDITOR Judy Phillips
DTP DESIGNERS Dietmar Kokemohr, Sean Gaherty

Reproduced in Singapore by Colourscan
Printed and bound by L.Rex Printing Company Limited

First published in Great Britain in 2003
by Dorling Kindersley Limited
80 Strand, London WC2R 0RL

11 12 13 14 10 9 8 7 6 5 4 3 2 1

Reprinted with revisions 2005, 2008, 2011

Front cover main image: Tulip fields with windmill in background, Netherlands

MIX
Paper from
responsible sources
FSC
www.fsc.org FSC™ C018179

**The information in this
DK Eyewitness Travel Guide is checked regularly.**
Every effort has been made to ensure that this book is as up-to-date
as possible at the time of going to press. Some details, however, such
as telephone numbers, opening hours, prices, gallery hanging
arrangements and travel information are liable to change. The
publishers cannot accept responsibility for any consequences arising
from the use of this book, nor for any material on third party
websites, and cannot guarantee that any website address in this book
will be a suitable source of travel information. We value the views
and suggestions of our readers very highly. Please write to: Publisher,
DK Eyewitness Travel Guides, Dorling Kindersley, 80 Strand, London
WC2R 0RL, Great Britain, or email: travelguides@dk.com.

CONTENTS

HOW TO USE
THIS GUIDE **6**

Zeeland's coat of arms

INTRODUCING
THE NETHERLANDS

DISCOVERING THE
NETHERLANDS **12**

PUTTING THE
NETHERLANDS
ON THE MAP **10**

A PORTRAIT OF THE
NETHERLANDS **16**

Girl with a Pearl Earring (1665)
by Johannes Vermeer

THE NETHERLANDS
THROUGH
THE YEAR **32**

THE HISTORY OF
THE NETHERLANDS **38**

◁ **A typical Dutch landscape with cows, pastures and windmills – here near the little town of Woudrichem**

The 15th-century Koppelpoort by Amersfoort

Thialf fans *(see p300)*

The imposing Sint Jan in 's-Hertogenbosch

HOW TO USE THIS GUIDE

This guide helps you get the most from your stay in the Netherlands. The first section, *Introducing the Netherlands,* places the country on the map and puts it in its historical and cultural context. Chapters on the provinces and the capital, Amsterdam, describe the most important sights and places of interest. Features cover topics from architecture to tulip growing. They are accompanied by detailed and helpful illustrations. *Travellers' Needs* gives specifics on where to stay and where to eat and drink, while the *Survival Guide* contains practical information on everything from the public telephone system to transport and personal safety.

AMSTERDAM

Amsterdam is divided into five tourist areas. The corresponding chapters all begin with a list of numbered sights and places of interest, which are plotted on the Area Map. The information for each sight follows this numerical order, making sights easy to locate within the chapter.

Sights at a Glance groups the sights by category: historical buildings and monuments, streets, squares and gardens, museums and churches.

All pages about Amsterdam are marked in red.

1 Area Map
This map is numbered to show the most important attractions. They are also given in the Street Finder section on pages 150–9.

A locator map places the district in the context of the rest of the city.

A recommended route covers the most interesting streets in the area.

2 Street-by-Street Map
This map gives a detailed summary of the heart of the five main tourist areas of the city.

Stars indicate sights that should not be missed.

3 Detailed Information
All main attractions are described individually, including their addresses, opening hours and other practical information. Keys to the symbols used are on the rear flap of this book.

1 Introduction

The scenery, history and character of each province are outlined here, showing how the area has changed through the centuries, and what it has to offer today's visitor.

THE NETHERLANDS AREA BY AREA

The Netherlands is divided into 12 provinces. Each of these provinces, Amsterdam and the Wadden Islands are dealt with in separate chapters. The most interesting towns, villages and places are shown on the Regional Map.

2 Regional Map

This map shows the main roads and the main tourist attractions of an area, and also gives useful information about driving and rail travel.

Each province is colour-coded for easy reference.

3 Detailed Information

Major sights and attractions are described in detail in the order in which they are numbered on the Regional Map. Within each entry is detailed information on buildings, parks, museums and other sights.

Story boxes explore specific topics.

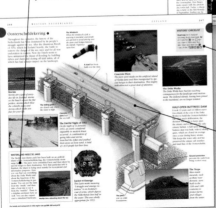

The Visitors' Checklist gives practical information to help you plan your visit.

4 The Top Sights

These sights are described on two or more pages. Cutaway illustrations and floor plans show the most important buildings, museums and other sights.

INTRODUCING THE NETHERLANDS

DISCOVERING THE NETHERLANDS

From the Frisian Islands in the north to Zeeland in the south, the Netherlands packs quite a punch for such a small country, with its fine sandy beaches, picturesque villages and vibrant, progressive cities. This mix becomes more remarkable when you consider that one-third of their present

Avocet wading bird

land was reclaimed from the sea. "God may have created the earth, but the Dutch created the Netherlands", as the popular saying goes. Water and trade shaped its history, and as any visitor will soon discover, this friendly, outward-looking nation is adept at managing both.

AMSTERDAM

- Beautiful waterways
- Golden Age mansions
- Rijksmuseum art gems
- Cosy "brown" cafés

For one of the world's great cultural centres, Amsterdam wears its riches with remarkable ease. It has a wealth of art gems and handsome buildings in an old centre bathed by beautiful waterways. Lined with elms and spanned by hump-backed bridges, the canals frame the gabled mansions built for Dutch merchants and bankers (*see pp62–3*). In the 17th century, they frequently commissioned artists such as Rembrandt van Rijn, whose celebrated *Nightwatch* can be seen in the **Rijksmuseum** (*see pp122–3*). This repository of Old Masters includes works by Johannes Vermeer, Frans Hals and Jan Steen. It is located near the unmissable **Van Gogh Museum** (*see pp126–7*), which has over

200 paintings on display, the largest collection of the artist's paintings in the world. The **Stedelijk Museum** (*see pp128–9*) has a rich collection of modern art. The city has museums galore, from the moving displays of the **Anne Frank Huis** (*see pp108–9*) to ones devoted to sex, tulips and hemp. Wondrous architecture is seen everywhere, from the elaborate **Westerkerk** (*see p110*) to the designer offices on the IJ riverside. From the 14th century, sailors sought more transient pleasures in the **Red Light District** (*see p74*), today a mish-mash of bars, brothels and neon-lit sex shops, though the council has started a clean-up campaign. The Dutch have a strong café culture (*see pp68–9*). It is arguably cosiest in the renowned "brown" cafés, some 400 years old, named for their dark, cosy, wood-panelled interiors. Many are hidden in the tiny lanes of the **Jordaan**, the popular former workers' district (*see pp106–7*).

Transporting cheeses at Alkmaar cheese market, North Holland

NORTH HOLLAND

- Rich heritage of Haarlem
- Windmills at Zaanse Schans
- Traditional cheese markets
- The past comes to life at Enkhuizen

A short distance from Amsterdam you'll find charms that rival any the capital has to offer. The historic city of **Haarlem** has a well-preserved old centre, anchored by the vast **Grote Kerk** and buildings in classic Dutch and Art Deco style (*see pp182–5*). Here the **Frans Hals Museum** (*see pp186–7*) is a must for lovers of fine art. To the north lies **Zaanse Schans** with its picture-book windmills (*see p175*). The old ports of **Hoorn** (*see p178*) and **Monnickendam** (*see p174*) along the coast of the IJsselmeer exude an old-time prosperity. On the West Frisian peninsula, the one-

Elegant houses lining Amsterdam's canals

◁ *View of Delft* (c.1660) – a masterpiece by Johannes Vermeer

Colourful planting at the Keukenhof gardens, South Holland

time fishing village of Enkhuizen is home to the intriguing **Zuiderzeemuseum**, an open-air museum depicting village life of yesteryear *(see pp176–7)*. Of all the traditional Dutch cheese markets, the most famous is held in **Alkmaar** *(see p181)*.

UTRECHT

- **Towering glory of the Dom**
- **Innovative Rietveld house**
- **Witch scales at Oudewater**

The river **Vecht** weaves lazily through this petite province, where many landed gentry kept their summer estates *(see p198)*. The church bishops of **Utrecht** city once wielded enormous power, and their influence is still palpable in this merry university town. Its soaring **Domtoren**, or cathedral tower, is the country's tallest *(see p202)*. A milestone of the De Stijl movement, the fascinating architecture of the **Rietveld Schröderhuis** features moveable walls *(see p204)*. Superstition is the thing in sleepy **Oudewater**, which still has a set of witches' scales *(see p197)*.

SOUTH HOLLAND

- **Radiant tulip fields**
- **Old Master paintings in Mauritshuis**
- **Daring Rotterdam designs**

The most densely populated region of the country is home to the Dutch government and the industrial heartland, yet vast areas are chocolate-box pretty, with verdant meadows, windmills and grazing cattle. Come springtime, the **bulb fields** erupt into a riot of colours, an event choreographed at **Keukenhof** gardens *(see p212)*. **Leiden** is famous for its university, the country's oldest, and the exotic gardens of **Hortus Botanicus** *(see pp216)*. An air of refined elegance pervades **The Hague**, where French was once the *lingua franca* of the upper class *(see pp218–21)*. Due to a compromise with Holland's trading elite, the city became the seat of Dutch parliament but never the capital. Its impressive **Mauritshuis** contains Vermeer's masterpiece, *Girl with a Pearl Earring (see pp222–3)*. Weaving and brewing put it on the map, but **Delft** is known best for its distinctive

blue-and-white pottery *(see p229)*. The busiest port in the world, **Rotterdam** boasts an abundance of unusual architecture *(see pp230–33)* and art collections such as the **Museum Boijmans Van Beuningen** *(see pp234–5)*.

ZEELAND

- **Zeeuws Abbey in Middelburg**
- **Mighty Delta flood barrier**
- **Historic houses of Zierikzee**

Of all the watery Dutch provinces, none experiences Neptune's wrath more than tiny Zeeland. Lakes and river estuaries slice the landscape into islands and peninsulas, giving its communities an isolated feel. It was a fitting spot for monks, as chronicled at the **Zeeuws Abbey Museum** in **Middelburg** *(see p250)*. Nowadays the sea is checked by the **Delta Works**, a marvel of Dutch engineering *(see p247)*. Hundreds of listed buildings, some of them from the Middle Ages, can be admired in historic **Zierikzee** *(see p252)*.

WEST FRISIAN ISLANDS

- **Bird-filled wetlands**
- **Dark forests of Texel**
- **Wild, windswept dunes**

This necklace of sandy isles offers some of the most alluring and remote terrain in

Dunes and clear skies in the West Frisian Islands

Europe. The shores of the Waddenzee have wetlands favoured by breeding and migratory birds *(see pp268–9)*. A curious local pastime is *wadlopen*, or walking through the mud-flats when the tide goes out *(see p271)*. The largest and most diverse island is **Texel**, with its wide beaches, dark pine forests and sleepy villages *(see p272)*. **Schiermonnikoog** is perfect for hiking, and entirely car-free *(see p275)*. The smallest island, **Vlieland**, consists only of dunes *(see p273)*.

Spritsail barges in Sneek, Friesland

GRONINGEN

- **Lively Groningen city**
- **Seal nursery at Pieterburen**
- **Star fortress of Bourtange**

In the Middle Ages this northerly province grew rich through farming, and later through its links to the Hanseatic League of trading cities. Agriculture is still big, but the region is also noted for its windmills, castles and *terps*, or ancient knobs of elevated land. Historic **Groningen** is the provincial capital, a lively university town with the cutting-edge **Groninger Museum** of art, archaeology and history *(see pp284–5)*. The **seal nursery** at Pieterburen attracts visitors from around the country *(see p287)*. The geometric beauty

of **Bourtange**, a star-shaped fortress commissioned by William of Orange, is now an open-air museum *(see p289)*.

FRIESLAND

- **Frisian pomp in Leeuwarden**
- **Skating hub Thialfstadion**
- **Sailor's paradise at Sneek**

The Frisians are known for their singularity thanks to a distinct language, sports like *fierljeppen* (ditch-polevaulting) and an unmistakable breed of black-and-white cow. Its hub, **Leeuwarden**, was home to World War I femme fatale Mata Hari as well as the House of Orange-Nassau, a branch of the Dutch Royal Family, and its generous parks, courtyards and

gardens bear their royal stamp *(see p296)*. The region produces champion ice-skaters who race at the **Thialfstadion** in Heerenveen *(see p300)*. In summer, **Sneek** comes alive with boaters in their sailbarges on the glistening lakes *(see p299)*.

DRENTHE

- **Lush peatlands and heath**
- **Mysterious megaliths**

The Netherlands' prehistoric roots run deepest in this sparsely-populated region that has always lived off the land. Woodlands, heath and peat bogs ooze a primeval atmosphere and the province is peppered with **megaliths** that mark ancient burial grounds *(pp307–9)*. The largest concentration of megaliths can be found at **Emmen** *(see p311)*.

OVERIJSSEL

- **Hanseatic trading towns**
- **Canals of Giethoorn**

This eastern province has a long and fascinating history marked by clashes in religion and dialect among its competing towns. The picturesque river port of **Zwolle** belonged to the Hanseatic League, which dominated trade with England and the Baltic states *(see p316)*. It was later joined by

Windmills dot the Groningen landscape

Kampen and Deventer, both pretty towns with fortifications *(see p316, p320)*. Girded by ponds, lakes and tiny canals, Giethoorn is an impossibly quaint village *(see pp318–19)*.

FLEVOLAND

- 17th-century frigate *Batavia*
- Age-old fishing villages

Consisting solely of reclaimed land, this is the youngest Dutch province, established only in 1986. Its star turn is the *Batavia*, a reconstruction of a 17th-century Dutch frigate that sank on its maiden voyage to the East Indies *(see p327)*. The former island villages of Urk and Schokland have fishermen's cottages, churches and monuments to those lost at sea *(see p326)*. The Oostervaardersplassen is a marshland reserve that lures bird-watchers *(p328)*.

GELDERLAND

- Magnificent Paleis Het Loo
- Hoge Veluwe National Park
- Kröller-Müller art museum

This former duchy is known for its medieval buildings, castles and fortified towns. Its royal pedigree led the House of Orange to build the fabulous Paleis Het Loo, where Queen Wilhelmina lived until 1962 *(see pp334–5)*. The rambling Nationaal Park De Hoge

The waterways of Giethoorn, Overijssel

Veluwe is the biggest in the country. It contains the acclaimed Kröller-Müller Museum with its major works by Van Gogh *(see pp338–9)*. Pummelled in a fierce battle in World War II, Arnhem has several monuments restored to their pre-war splendour *(see p340)*.

NORTH BRABANT

- Prosperous Den Bosch
- Gothic Sint Jan cathedral
- Imposing castles and bastions

This southern province bears many hallmarks of its medieval heyday. Towns flourished along key trading routes, including 's-Hertogenbosch, also called Den Bosch, a wealthy town founded by the Dukes of Brabant *(see pp358–9)*. The old centre is dominated by the Gothic-style Sint Jan Cathedral, which has many religious treasures *(see pp360–61)*. There are plenty of castles to be admired in towns like Breda and Heeze *(see pp362–5)*. North Brabant is also renowned for the natural beauty of areas such as the Biesbosch National Park and the Loonse dunes, which teem with wildlife *(see pp356–7)*.

LIMBURG

- Cosmopolitan Maastricht
- Gentle rolling hillscapes
- Fortified town Valkenburg

Perched on a spit of land with Belgium and Germany on either side, Limburg is multilingual and easy-going. The cosmopolitan town of Maastricht, which was founded in Roman times, has several fine museums,

Romanesque Onze-Lieve-Vrouwebasiliek in Maastricht

limestone caves, a splendid basilica and some of the country's best restaurants *(see pp372–3)*. Its Bonnefantenmuseum has an outstanding gallery of modern art *(see pp374–5)*. In contrast to the northern flatlands, the gently rolling hills of the Heuvelland are dotted with woodlands and fruit orchards *(see pp380–81)*. Situated in an area replete with castles, the old fortified town of Valkenburg has a 13th-century Romanesque church, catacombs and a cable car *(see p379)*.

Magestic Sint Jan cathedral, North Brabant

Putting the Netherlands on the Map

The Netherlands is situated in Western Europe, bordering Belgium to the south and Germany to the east. To its north and west is the North Sea. The country is popularly known as Holland, although the provinces of North and South Holland form only part of the Netherlands in reality. Since the completion of the Deltawerken (Delta Works), the coastline is some 800 km (500 miles) in length. The country's major waterways and excellent road and rail systems make it an important gateway to the rest of Europe, and to Germany in particular. Approximately one-sixth of its total area is covered with water. The Netherlands has a population of about 16 million.

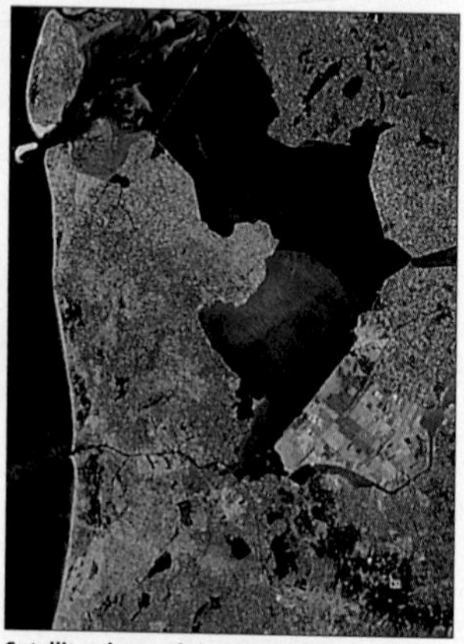

Satellite photo of the northern part of the western Netherlands with the IJsselmeer

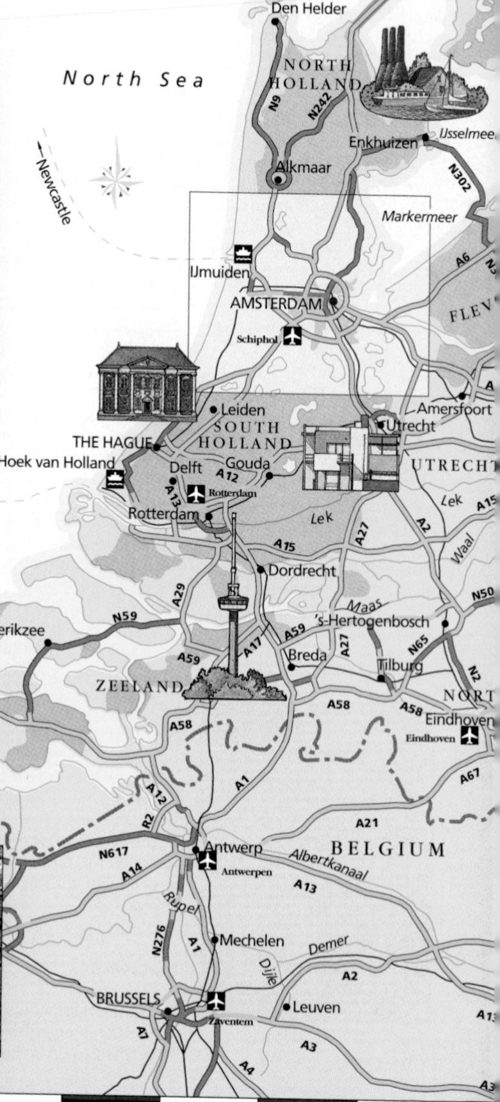

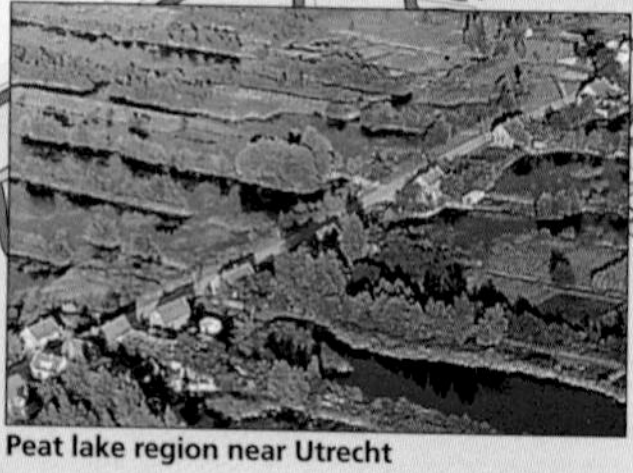

0 kilometres 20

0 miles 20

Peat lake region near Utrecht

WEST FRISIAN ISLANDS

Waddenzee

North Sea

Newcastle

Hull, Harwich

Den Helder

NORTH HOLLAND

Enkhuizen · IJsselmeer

Alkmaar

Markermeer

IJmuiden

AMSTERDAM

Schiphol

FLEVO

Leiden

Amersfoort

SOUTH HOLLAND

Utrecht

THE HAGUE

Hoek van Holland Delft Gouda

UTRECHT

Rotterdam Lek

Lek

Dordrecht

Waal

Zierikzee

Maas

's-Hertogenbosch

N50

Breda Tilburg

ZEELAND

Middelburg

A58 Eindhoven

NORT

Antwerp Albertkanaal

BELGIUM

Antwerpen

Mechelen Demer

BRUSSELS Zaventem Leuven

Rupel Dijle

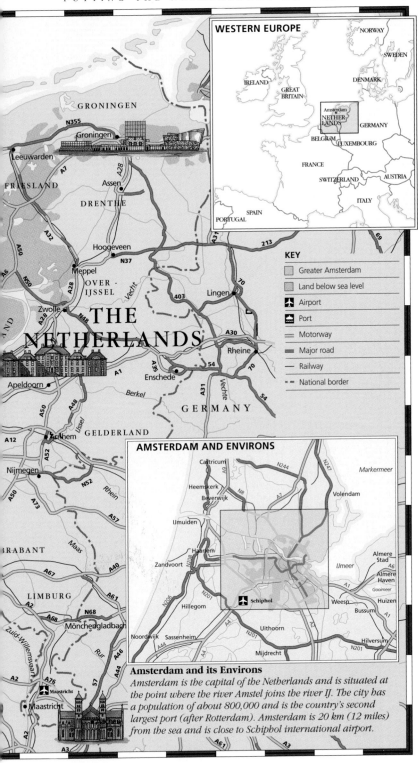

WESTERN EUROPE

NORWAY
SWEDEN
IRELAND
GREAT BRITAIN
DENMARK
Amsterdam
NETHER-LANDS
GERMANY
BELGIUM LUXEMBOURG
FRANCE
SWITZERLAND
AUSTRIA
ITALY
SPAIN
PORTUGAL

GRONINGEN
Groningen
N355
Leeuwarden
A7
A28
Assen
FRIESLAND
DRENTHE
A32
A50
N50
A6
Hoogeveen
Meppel
N37
OVER-IJSSEL
Vecht
403
Lingen
A28
N68
Zwolle
THE NETHERLANDS
A1
A30
Rheine
A35
Enschede
A31
Vechte
Apeldoorn
Berkel
GERMANY
A50
IJssel
A48
A12
Arnhem
GELDERLAND
A52
Nijmegen
N52
Rhein
A50
A73
A57
BRABANT
Maas
A67
A40
A61
LIMBURG
A2
N68
A68
Mönchengladbach
Rur
A46
Zuid-Willemsvaart
A2
A76
Maastricht
A3
A61
A3

213
70
54
70
54
69
A31

KEY

Greater Amsterdam
Land below sea level
✈ Airport
⚓ Port
Motorway
Major road
Railway
National border

AMSTERDAM AND ENVIRONS

Castricum
N244
N247
Markermeer
Heemskerk
N8
A7
Volendam
Beverwijk
IJmuiden
A9
Almere Stad
Haarlem
IJmeer
A6
Zandvoort
N208
Almere Haven
Goolmeer
N201
Huizen
Hillegom
✈ Schiphol
Weesp
A1
Bussum
A1
Noordwijk Sassenheim
A4
Uithoorn
A2
Hilversum
N201
A44
N201
Mijdrecht
N201

Amsterdam and its Environs

Amsterdam is the capital of the Netherlands and is situated at the point where the river Amstel joins the river IJ. The city has a population of about 800,000 and is the country's second largest port (after Rotterdam). Amsterdam is 20 km (12 miles) from the sea and is close to Schiphol international airport.

A PORTRAIT OF
THE NETHERLANDS

From the Frisian Islands in the north to Zeeland in the south, the Netherlands is a place of contrasts, with fine sandy beaches, picturesque villages and vibrant towns with multilingual and outward-looking people. The mighty river Rhine bisects the country, bringing trade and prosperity from far and wide.

The landscape of what is now the Netherlands has changed considerably over the past 2,000 years. Since Roman times, large tracts of land have been swallowed up by the sea in areas such as Zeeland and the former Zuiderzee. Old maps show that during the Middle Ages almost half of today's provinces of North Holland and South Holland were under water. Since then, large parts of this land have been reclaimed. The constant battle with the sea reached its height with the Delta Works. This massive hydraulic engineering achievement *(see pp246–7)* was designed to protect the southwestern part of the country against flooding. The project was started after the disastrous floods of 1953, in which more than 1,800 people died.

Typical cottage in Marken

The Netherlands covers an area of 41,547 sq km (16,040 sq miles), about one-tenth the size of California. With some 16 million inhabitants, this means a population density of around 380 per sq km (1,000 per sq mile), making it the third most densely populated country in Europe after Monaco and Malta. However, this is not something that is readily noticeable to visitors outside the main cities, as the flat landscape seems anything but crowded.

Dutch people are friendly, outgoing and direct. They care about social issues and the environment and almost everyone speaks English, many fluently. They live in a country that is neat and tidy, where there is excellent public transport and where visitors find it easy to get around.

The pier, the focus of social life on the beach at Scheveningen

◁ Bulb-grower in his tulip field near Ursem in North Holland

Holland's dunes, a natural barrier against the sea and an important water catchment area

INTRODUCING THE NETHERLANDS

Although the Netherlands is this country's official name, most of the rest of the world call it Holland. However, Holland actually comprises only 2 of the 13 Dutch provinces. North and South Holland contain the country's three main cities of Amsterdam, Rotterdam and Den Haag (The Hague), which together with the cities of Dordrecht, Utrecht, Leiden and Haarlem form a horseshoe-shaped conurbation known as the Randstad, literally, "rim city" *(see pp166–7)*.

When people ask, "What is the capital of the Netherlands?", the smiling Dutch tend to reply: "Our capital is Amsterdam, and the government sits in The Hague." Amsterdam is the most cosmopolitan of these three cities, as well as the the country's centre for cultural life. Rotterdam, home to the Europoort, one of the world's largest ports, is the Netherlands' industrial centre. The Hague is the seat of government and quarters many prestigious institutions, including the International Court of Justice. With its neighbouring seaside resort of Scheveningen, The Hague is where most of the foreign embassies and consulates are situated.

Holland can be roughly divided into the Protestant north and Catholic south, separated by the great rivers flowing into the North Sea: the Rhine, the Waal and the Maas (Meuse). The people in the north of the country tend to be more sober and matter-of-fact, whereas those of the south tend to be much more flamboyant in their lifestyles.

Shoppers at the Albert Cuypmarkt in Amsterdam

SOCIETY AND POLITICS

Social life in the Netherlands was for many years based on the idea of *verzuiling*, wherein society lay on four pillars *(zuilen)* on which different sections of society rested their beliefs: Protestantism, Catholicism, liberalism and socialism. At one time, these groups had almost no contact with one another. Catholics would always vote for the *Katholieke Volkspartij*, join

Catholic trade unions, base their social lives on Catholic societies and send their children to Catholic schools. The Protestant "pillar", on the other hand, was formed of two main factions: the Dutch Reformed Church and the Calvinist Church. Both had their own political parties, their own trades unions and their own schools and societies. As for socialism and liberalism, the division was less explicit, though the gap between the world of the "workers" and that of the "entrepreneurs" was huge.

View of picturesque Dordrecht marina

A major step towards unity came in 1980, when the three largest religion-based political parties united in the CDA, a Christian Democratic alliance that went on to dominate government coalitions for the next 20 years. The gap between the other parties closed in 1994, when the Labour Party (PvdA) and the small D66 formed a coalition with the conservative Liberal Party (VVD). This resulted in a tripartite "purple" cabinet, which appeared so successful that the coalition was continued in 1998.

A hollow post mill in the polder landscape

The Dutch elections of May 2002 surprised everybody as the country moved to the right of the political spectrum. The assassination, nine days before, of the popular, flamboyant and openly gay Pim Fortuyn had shocked the entire country. With his unyielding views on Muslims and immigration, and his criticism of the establishment, Fortuyn was the antithesis of the Dutch tradition of consensual politics. Despite the loss of their charismatic leader, LPF became the second largest party in the Lower House; only the Christian Democrats (CDA) did better. The coalition parties of the former government lost

The de Geul river at Epen in Zuid Limburg

Football fans sporting orange costumes

43 seats between them, making this the biggest shake-up in Dutch politics since World War II.

The 2010 elections revealed dissatisfaction with another eight years of coalition between the PvDA, CDA and conservative Christen Unie. The PvDA and CDA lost many seats, seeing gains for the VVD and Geert Wilders' Party for Freedom (PVV). Most other parties balked at forming a coalition with Wilders, known for his criticism of Islam. In October 2010 a right-wing coalition was finally formed between the VVD, CDA and PVV parties, changing the Dutch political climate completely.

Dutch beer, fresh from the tap

LANGUAGE AND CULTURE

Dutch, a Germanic language, is used by more than 20 million people in Holland, Flanders and parts of the former Dutch colonies. Afrikaans, a lan-

A herring stall in Amsterdam

guage of South Africa closely related to Dutch, is a separate language, as is Frisian, which is spoken by more than 400,000 people in the province of Friesland. Dutch has many dialects, each of which has numerous regional differences. However, these differences are gradually disappearing because of the far-reaching influences of radio and television.

Culturally, Holland has plenty to offer. The country's colourful history is reflected in its many old buildings and large number of valuable museum collections. Exhibits range from those with local themes to world-famous art such as the collections in Amsterdam's Rijksmuseum *(see pp122–5)* and the Mauritshuis in The Hague *(see pp222–3)*. In addition to the major museums of the cities, contemporary art can be seen in galleries all over the country, and in the profusion of works displayed in the streets and at numerous local markets. As for the performing arts, more variety is available today than ever before. Holland boasts a number of renowned orchestras and is an established name in ballet. Stage and theatre have recently marked a shift from experimental to more conventional performances.

THE DUTCH WAY OF LIFE

The German poet Heinrich Heine (1797–1856) described Holland as a place where "everything happens 50 years later than anywhere else". But today, anyone who reflects on the tolerant Dutch attitude towards drugs, the country's relaxed laws regarding euthanasia and the popular opposition to the deployment of nuclear weapons will come away with a different picture. In fact, the Netherlands was the first country to legalize gay marriages, regulate prostitution, officially sanction euthanasia and tolerate the over-the-counter sale of marijuana. Even the attitude of the Dutch towards their monarchy is modern – they are regarded with an affection more commonly extended to family members than to rulers.

Since the depredations of the

Second World War, much has changed in the way the Dutch live their lives. Thrift and moderation, the two traditional virtues of Calvinism, are no longer writ large in society. A measure of flamboyance is slowly but surely making its way into the Dutch lifestyle. Today the Dutch eat out enthusiastically as well as often. Restaurant and cooking columns are now featured in newspapers and magazines, and there are also many cookery programmes aired on television.

A Dutch production of *The Three Musketeers*

Dutch drinking habits have also changed. On fine-weather days, people throng the pavement cafés to end the working day with a beer or a glass of wine. They also drink a great deal more wine with meals than once was the case. As well, the renowned Dutch gin, *jenever*, with its various types *(see p428)*, is still popular. Nevertheless, overall per capita alcohol consumption is reasonable.

As soon as they have spare time, Dutch people head outdoors, often on bicycles, which are enormously popular. Love of the environment is a strong Dutch characteristic. Outdoors, there are hundreds of organized rambling and cycling tours, funfairs and theme parks, as well as a wide assortment of festivals and other events held throughout the year *(see pp32–5)*. And wherever you are, you will always find a flea market – with items ranging from flowers to antiques for sale – not far away.

The new-found *joie de vivre* of the Dutch reflects the general trend evident in Western European countries. This is the result of a new leisure culture, one which is more "sensory". Less time is devoted to reading and contemplation as food, drink, sport and the arts all take on increasingly prominent roles. Politically, socially and culturally, the Dutch are embracing the 21st century with confidence.

De Waalkade, the promenade of Nijmegen

Holding Back the Water

Recent floods in the Netherlands' river valleys, particularly the one which occurred in 1995, when 200,000 people needed to be evacuated from the area, have shown what a threat water continues to pose to the Netherlands. The only way the sea can be held back is by dams, but in order to contain rivers at high tide, the country is adopting a new approach, that of "controlled flooding".

Flooded farm in Gelderland (1995)

Since the 11th century, *increasing areas of land have been reclaimed from the sea. Countless dykes were built over the centuries using elementary tools, such as spades and "burries", a kind of stretcher. The illustration shows a breached dyke being filled.*

At the Hook of Holland, the sea is not held back by dunes, as it is along the entire coast of North Holland and South Holland, but by a dyke.

The lowest point in Holland is the Zuidplaspolder at Gouda, 6.74 m (22 ft) below sea level.

At Krimpen, the IJssel discharges into the Nieuwe Maas.

The Krimpenerwaard, between the IJssel and the Lek, consists of high-quality hayfields and pasture.

The River Lek

KEY

☐ Above sea level

☐ Below sea level

A large part of the Netherlands *(blue on the map) is below sea level. These areas have been called "laag-Nederland", or the "low Netherlands", and have only come into being over the past 10,000 years.*

CROSS-SECTION OF THE NETHERLANDS

This cross-section of the Netherlands follows a straight line from the Hook of Holland to Achterhoek (see Locator Map) and shows clearly how low much of the land is. Only some 65 km (40 miles) inland, at Neder-Betuwe, does the ground rise above sea level. The lowest point in the Netherlands is the Zuidplaspolder, which is more than 6.74 m (22 ft) below sea level. Comparatively elevated areas like the Betuwe have nothing to fear from the sea, but this does not mean that they are not at risk of flooding: the Waal River, which runs more or less parallel to this cross-section, may flood at unusually high tides or after a heavy rainfall.

Floods in the river valleys *in 1993 and 1995 led to the implementation of large-scale dyke reinforcement projects, known as the "delta plan for the large rivers". Old flood channels were also repaired as a matter of priority to allow more water to drain off.*

THE STORY OF HANS BRINKER

The tale of the little boy who held his finger in a leak in a dyke to hold back the sea is not a figure from Dutch folklore but probably originated in the book *Hans Brinker, or, The Silver Skates*, by American writer Mary Mapes Dodge (1831–1905). It tells the story of a poverty-stricken boy who helps his ailing father. Hans and the doctor in the book (Boerhaave) are historical figures. The story was published in over 100 editions in Dodge's lifetime.

Statue of Hans Brinker in Spaarndam

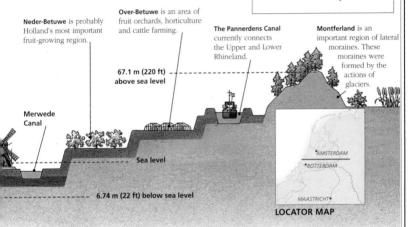

Neder-Betuwe is probably Holland's most important fruit-growing region.

Over-Betuwe is an area of fruit orchards, horticulture and cattle farming.

The Pannerdens Canal currently connects the Upper and Lower Rhineland.

Montferland is an important region of lateral moraines. These moraines were formed by the actions of glaciers.

67.1 m (220 ft) above sea level

Merwede Canal

Sea level

6.74 m (22 ft) below sea level

LOCATOR MAP

AMSTERDAM
ROTTERDAM
MAASTRICHT

CROSS-SECTION OF A MODERN RIVER DYKE

Blocks of boulder clay protect the dyke from the wash of the river. The water seeps through the water-resistant clay layer slowly, draining off quickly only once it reaches the sand layer. This way the body of the dyke stays dry and hard.

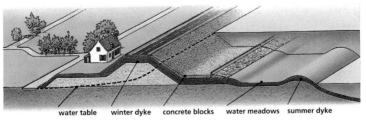

water table   winter dyke   concrete blocks   water meadows   summer dyke

Farmhouses and Windmills

In the mainly flat landscape of the Netherlands , farmhouses always stand in the shelter of trees. Windmills, on the other hand, needing as much wind as they can get, usually stand in very exposed areas. Both are highly valued because they are so picturesque, and it is easy to forget that they actually belong in the category of functional architecture. How a windmill works is explained on page 179.

In the farmhouses *of North Holland, the barn, threshing-floor and house are all tunder one pyramidal roof.*

This Drenthe farmhouse *is a modern version of what has been known since the Middle Ages as a* los hoes *(detached house).*

THE ZUID LIMBURG FARMHOUSES

The traditional farmhouses of Zuid Limburg have a distinctive inner yard, enclosed by the house and farm buildings. In the inner yard, ducks, chickens and pigs once roamed, rummaging in the dunghill. The picture may have been lively but was not particularly hygienic.

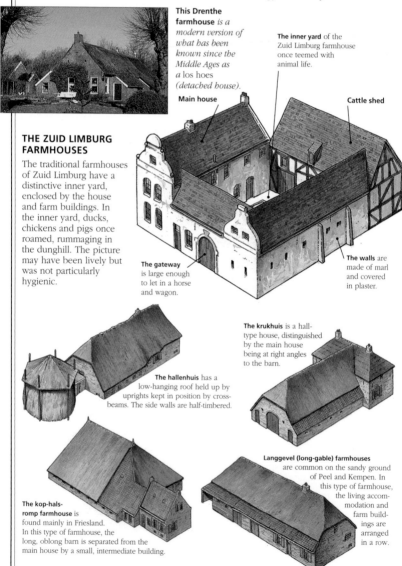

The inner yard of the Zuid Limburg farmhouse once teemed with animal life.

Main house

Cattle shed

The gateway is large enough to let in a horse and wagon.

The walls are made of marl and covered in plaster.

The hallenhuis has a low-hanging roof held up by uprights kept in position by cross-beams. The side walls are half-timbered.

The krukhuis is a hall-type house, distinguished by the main house being at right angles to the barn.

The kop-hals-romp farmhouse is found mainly in Friesland. In this type of farmhouse, the long, oblong barn is separated from the main house by a small, intermediate building.

Langgevel (long-gable) farmhouses are common on the sandy ground of Peel and Kempen. In this type of farmhouse, the living accommodation and farm buildings are arranged in a row.

PALTROK MILLS

Paltrok, or smock, mills were developed for use as sawmills around 1600. They were so called because of their resemblance to the paltrok, a smock that was commonly worn at the time. These windmills were mounted on a circular track, allowing them to rotate in their entirety. Generally, smock mills were used to saw *wagenschot* – entire oak trunks that had been split in two.

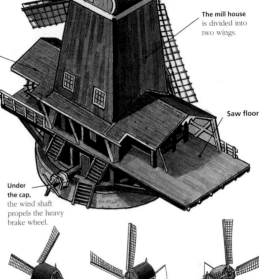

Sail

Wheels allow the windmill to rotate on its axis.

Ridge post

Underneath the porch is a crane for lifting the tree trunks from the water.

The mill house is divided into two wings.

Saw floor

Under the cap, the wind shaft propels the heavy brake wheel.

Belt or berg mills
have an extra-high body because of surrounding buildings or trees. A mound (berg) made at the base of the mill provides access to the sails.

Toren mills (tower mills)
have a brick cylindrical body and a cap that can be rotated from inside. Only four survive in Holland today. The oldest one can be seen at Achterhoek near Zeddam.

Stander (post) mills
are the oldest type of mill in Holland. The entire wooden body rotates on a central wooden post. Most post mills were used to grind corn.

Wipmolen are a later version of the stander mills and were designed to pump water. The smaller body rotates on a fixed, pyramidal base.

Stellingmolen, like the belt mill, has an extra-tall body. This type was used to produce dye, oil or paper. An encircling platform halfway up the body enables the mill to be rotated and the sails to be reefed on the wings.

The tjasker was used to drain small areas of water. It consisted of a sloping axle with sails at one end and an Archimedes' screw at the other.

The Dutch Masters

The proliferation of painting in the Netherlands during the 17th century – the country's Golden Age – corresponded with the great demand for paintings among newly rich townspeople. The lack of major royal and ecclesiastic patrons meant that there was no official school of painting, which left artists free to specialize in particular fields, such as historical subjects, portraits, landscapes and still life, as well as genre painting.

Willem Heda *(1594–1680) was one of the masters of still life. The painter's simple compositions reflect his signature use of sober colours.*

Frans Hals *(c.1580–1666) left an oeuvre of some 200 portraits and more than 50 genre paintings. He painted not only regents and wealthy townsmen but also peasants, soldiers, fishermen, publicans and drunkards. No sketches for his paintings are known, and it is assumed that he painted* alla prima, *that is, straight onto the canvas without sketches.* The Fool, *shown above, dates from around 1623.*

REMBRANDT VAN RIJN

Rembrandt van Rijn is regarded by many as the greatest Dutch painter of all time. He was born in Leiden in 1606 but lived in Amsterdam from 1632 until his death in 1669. Rembrandt was a master in the use of light and shadow. *The Jewish Bride* (painted around 1665) is regarded as one of the best portraits of his later period.

Jacob van Ruisdael *(1628–82) was an unrivalled landscape painter. In his* View of Haarlem *depicted here, the low horizon is dwarfed by an imposing sky with clouds.*

The silversmith Adam van Vianen
*(1569–1627) was famous for his
ornamental style, which was
known as* kwabstijl, *or "flabby
style", and distinguished by
flowing ornamentation and the
use of various fantasy elements.
This gilded silver jug is an example
of his style. Much of the silver work
from this time has been lost because
pieces have been melted down in
order to trade in the metal for cash.*

Jan Steen *(1625–79) was a prolific painter with
a variety of works, 800 of which survive today.
They include everything from altar pieces to
landscape paintings to works with mythological
themes. However, Steen is known primarily for
his genre painting, which gives a detailed,
humorous picture of 17th-century society. The*
Family Scene, *shown above, is a typical "Jan Steen
household" – one in disarray. Tavern scenes were
another of the artist's favourite subjects.*

Gerard van Honthorst *(1590–1656) was
greatly influenced by the works of Caravaggio.
As well as historical scenes and portraits, he
painted genre pieces such as* The Merry
Fiddler *(above). His famous nocturnal scenes
lit by candle-light led to his being nicknamed
"Gherardo delle Notte" in Italy.*

Johannes Vermeer *(1632–75) spent his entire life
in Delft. Only 40 of his works are known today, but
even this modest oeuvre plays a prominent role in
the history of painting. His balanced compositions
appear very modern. Long before the Impressionists,
Vermeer succeeded in conveying light through
colour. The street depicted in* View of Houses in
Delft *(c.1658), left, has become known as
"Vermeer's street".*

Pottery and Tiles

When in 1620 exports of porcelain from China to Europe fell because of the troubles in China, Dutch potters seized the opportunity and started to produce their own wares, imitating the Chinese style on a large scale. The quality of the Dutch blue-white pottery was excellent. The city of Delft became one of the prime centres for the production of this china, which reached its height between 1660 and 1725. During the Art Nouveau and Art Deco periods, Dutch potters regained their international renown. The best known of them was TAC Colenbrander.

Tulip vase

Stylized flowers reflect the Italian majolica tradition.

De Porceleyne Fles *is the only Delftware shop which has managed to survive throughout the centuries. The business was bought in 1876 and revived by Joost Thooft, whose initials can still be seen on the workshop's mark. The exquisite painting on the porcelain continues to be done by hand, although the rest of the manufacturing process no longer involves the craft's traditional methods.*

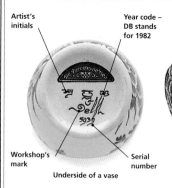

Artist's initials

Year code – DB stands for 1982

Workshop's mark

Serial number

Underside of a vase

DELFTWARE

Although tin-glazed earthenware was also made in other parts of the Netherlands, "Delft" came to describe almost all earthenware made in the Netherlands during this period. Any piece made after 1650 will always have a workshop mark. Later, the glazer's initials, as well as a code denoting the year and a serial number, were added.

This set of four tiles *features a pattern of pomegranates, grapes, rosettes and lilies.*

The first Dutch porcelain *was made in 1759 in the North Holland town of Weesp. At the time, it was second in quality only to Meissen porcelain. However, production was halted after 10 years because of financial difficulties. In 1774, a new factory was opened in Loosdrecht, which was moved to Ouder-Amstel in 1784. This large vase from 1808 is a typical example of the Amstel china that was produced there.*

Delft design *is used here to decorate a plane tail. The artist Hugo Kaagman decorated the tails of four British Airways' aircraft with blue Delft designs.*

TILES

Majolica wall tiles – decorated earthenware on a tin-glazed background – were made for the first time in the Netherlands during the 16th century, with production reaching its peak in the 17th century. Until 1625, polychrome decoration predominated, after which the majority of tiles were painted in blue on white. Major centres were Makkum – where in the 17th century the Tichelaar family firm, which operates to this day, was established – as well as Harlingen, Delft, Gouda, Amsterdam, Utrecht and Haarlem. The tiles depicted here are from Haarlem. See also page 427.

The lily often features as a corner motif on Dutch tiles.

TAC COLENBRANDER

One of the biggest names in Art Nouveau pottery is TAC Colenbrander (1841–1930). Originally an architect, he became known for his fanciful floral-based designs for the Rozenburg earthenware and porcelain factory in The Hague, where he was chief designer from 1884 to 1889. As celebrated as his designs were, the ceramics had limited commercial success. One reason for this was their expense, a reflection of the labour-intensive production. In 1912–13, Colenbrander worked for the Zuid-Holland pottery in Gouda. In addition to pottery, he designed wallpaper and carpets, and worked as a graphic and interior designer.

The Art Nouveau plate *by WP Hartgring was made in 1904, the same year as this master potter won a gold medal at the world exhibition at the St Louis World's Fair. Hartgring worked for 20 years at the Rozenburg factory in The Hague and for 10 years at the Zuid-Holland pottery. His works reflect the Japanese style.*

"Day and Night" set by Colenbrander, 1885

The Netherlands in Bloom

Orchid

The Dutch love affair with flowers began rather unromantically in homes during the 17th century, when flowers were used to keep bad smells at bay. The aesthetic aspect soon developed, and today the Netherlands is one of the world's most important flower-growing countries. It has an unrivalled distribution system, keeping Holland ahead of competition from countries such as Israel, Spain, Colombia, Kenya, Zimbabwe and Zambia. The Netherlands has a 92 per cent share of the world market for flowers.

Fields of flowers *are not confined to the west of the country. These rose fields are outside Lottum in the north of the southern province of Limburg, where every year a special rose competition is held.*

Tulips *were introduced to Holland from Turkey in the 17th century. They became the subject of an unparalleled speculative bubble which has become known as "tulip mania". Today the tulip is considered a quintessentially Dutch product, with innumerable varieties.*

The annual flower competition (bloemen corso) *in the bulb-growing region is a grand event* (see p32).

CUT FLOWERS FROM DUTCH NURSERIES

As consumers have become increasingly demanding, the number of flower species and varieties is constantly on the rise. Consumer tastes vary from place to place: in France, gladioli are very popular, whereas in Great Britain, it is lilies and carnations. In Asia, tulips are in great demand. A small sample of the flowers grown commercially in the Netherlands is shown here.

The iris *(Iris) flower and bulb are in demand.*

The chrysanthemum *(Chrysanthemum)* originated in China.

The sandy soil *in the high areas behind the dunes of Holland is known as "geest soil" and is very well suited for cultivating bulbs.*

Not all daffodil bulbs can survive the winter.

Crocus bulbs should be planted in September.

Hyacinth bulbs range in colour from violet red to white.

Tulip bulbs are highly resistant to disease and pests.

Iris bulbs should be dug up after flowering.

FLOWER SELLERS

Flower sellers are part and parcel of the Netherlands' street scene. They can also be found indoors, in places such as stations or office buildings. In most countries, cut flowers are considered a luxury. In the Netherlands, however, they are practically a daily shopping item. The Netherlands is indeed the land of flowers *par excellence*.

Dahlias *(Dahlia)* come in 20,000 varieties.

The lilac *(Syringa)* is often bought for its fragrance.

The carnation *(Dianthus)* is loved as a spray.

The rose *(Rosa)* is known as "the queen of flowers".

THE NETHERLANDS THROUGH THE YEAR

The Netherlands has much to offer in the way of holidays, festivals and other events. The choice of cultural events is greatest in summer – several cities host theatre festivals in June. Some festivals, such as Leiden's 3-Oktoberfeesten, have deep historical roots, whereas others, such as the multicultural

Festival float

Zomercarnaval in Rotterdam, are much more modern. Many of the events are held to honour navigation and fishing, such as Flag Day (Vlaggetjesdag), held each May in Scheveningen. Music, too, plays a prominent role. The world-renowned North Sea Jazz festival brings the genre's greats to Rotterdam.

SPRING

In March, daffodils and crocuses burst into bloom in the country's towns and villages. From mid-April onwards, when the tulips are in flower, the bulb fields along the Dutch coast are a spectacular sight to see.

MARCH

Foto Biënnale *(mid-Mar to mid-Apr)*, Rotterdam. This biannual international photography exhibition takes place in odd-numbered years.
Meezing Matthäus *(Easter)*, Amsterdam and elsewhere. Concert-goers are welcome to sing along during many

A young street musician on Queen's Day in Amsterdam

performances of Bach's *St Matthew's Passion*.
Keukenhof *(end Mar to mid-May)*, near Lisse. These 32 ha (79 acres) of landscape gardens demonstrate the best of all the flowers Holland has to offer. This open air exhibition was started in 1949, and has become internationally renowned.

Blossoming fruit tree in de Betuwe

APRIL

First of April Celebrations, Brielle. Dressed in 16th-century-style clothing, the inhabitants of Brielle (Den Briel) re-create the 1572 recovery of the city from the Spaniards.
Bloemen Corso (Flower Competition) *(late Apr)*, Bollenstreek. Floats with floral sculptures travel a 40-km (25-mile) route through Haarlem, Hillegom, Lisse and Noordwijk.
Koninginnedag (Queen's Day) *(30 Apr)*. The birthday of the former queen, Juliana, sees festivities throughout the land; the biggest event is held in Amsterdam.

MAY

Landelijke Fietsmaand (National Cycling Month) *(all month)*. Cycling activities throughout the country.
Nationale Moldendag (National Windmill Day) *(second Sat in May)*. Some 600 of the 1,000 windmills

in the country are opened up to the public.
Vlaggetjesdag (Flag Day) *(May)*, Scheveningen. The arrival of the first herring catch of the season is celebrated with demonstrations of traditional fishing-related crafts, music and a race.
Aspergerie Primeur (Ascension Day), Venlo. In a festive atmosphere on a re-created old-time village green, visitors can tuck into deliciously cooked asparagus.
Keidagen *(around Ascension Day)*, Lochem. Five days of music, funfairs, street fairs and performances by international artists.

Flag Day, the start of the new herring fishing season

Sloepenrace (Boat Regatta). A regatta from Harlingen to Terschelling.
Jazz in Duketown *(around Whitsun)*, 's-Hertogenbosch. Four days of open-air high-quality jazz and blues bands at various venues in town. The beer flows freely.

SUMMER

Summer in the Netherlands is a time of major cultural events. These include the Holland Festival in Amsterdam, the Theater a/d Werf in Utrecht, the Rotterdam Parade and the Haagse Zomer in The Hague. And if theatre is not your favourite pastime, there are plenty of other activities to keep you entertained.

JUNE

Holland Festival *(3 weeks of Jun)*, venues throughout Amsterdam and major cities. A varied programme of concerts, plays, opera and ballet.
Aaltjesdag (Eel Day) *(second Sat in Jun)*, Harderwijk. Major fishing celebration in this former harbour on the Zuider Zee.
Oerol Festival *(mid-Jun)*, Terschelling. This alternative cultural festival lasts for ten days, with clowns, street theatre, acrobats, pop concerts and music from around the world.
Poetry International *(mid-Jun)*, Rotterdam.

Herring-eating by hand

Prestigious poetry festival featuring an international programme, in Rotterdam's Doelen district.
Pasar Malam Besar *(second half of Jun)*, The Hague. This festival of Indonesian music and dance, shadow puppets, cooking demonstrations and colourful eastern market takes place at Malieveld in The Hague.
Nationale Vlootdagen (Navy days) *(end Jun/early*

The increasingly popular boat race to Terschelling

Jul), Den Helder. A chance to see frigates, submarines, torpedo boats and mine

Caribbean scenes during the Zomercarnaval in Rotterdam

hunters belonging to the Netherlands Navy, with spectacular shows put on by the Netherlands Marines.

JULY

Oud Limburgs Schuttersfeest (Marksman's Festival) *(first Sun in Jul)*. Annual tournament by the marksmen of Limburg is a colourful folk event held in the hometown of the previous year's winner.
North Sea Jazz *(mid-Jul)*, Rotterdam. A three-day spectacle widely acknowledged as the world's largest jazz festival, with performances by the biggest names in jazz.
Tilburgse kermis (Tilburg Fair) *(end Jul)*. One of the biggest and most exuberant fairs in Holland, with a special gay Pink Monday.
Zomercarnaval (Summer Carnival) *(last Sat in Jul)*, Rotterdam. A lively Caribbean carnival with exotic music, plenty to eat and drink and a swirling procession.

North Sea Jazz, one of the world's major jazz events

The Nijmegen Fair, a popular tradition dating back centuries

AUGUST

Gay Pride *(first weekend in Aug)*, Amsterdam. One of the very best Prides in the world; the highlight is the Canal Parade.

Mosselfeesten (Mussel Festivals) *(third Sat in Aug)*, Yerseke; *(last weekend in Aug)*, Philippine. Harvest festival presenting the new crops of Zeeland.

Preuvenemint *(last weekend in Aug)*, Maastricht. Flamboyant festival of food and drink at the historical Vrijthof.

Uitmarkt *(last weekend in Aug)*, Amsterdam. Festive opening of the theatre season with performances and information booths. There is also a book fair, where literary publishers are represented with their own stalls.

An elaborate fruit sculpture at the Tiel Fruitcorso

AUTUMN

As the cold weather starts slowly but surely to set in, indoor events become more prominent. In autumn, the theatres are full in the evenings, and museums are routinely busy. However, open-air events are still held, the golden light of dusk and magnificent clouds adding to the atmosphere.

SEPTEMBER

Monumentendag (Monument Day) *(second Sat in Sep)*. Private historic buildings open to the public.

Fruitcorso *(second weekend in Sep)*, Tiel. Spectacular parade of floats with gigantic fruit sculptures.

Vliegerfeest (Kite Festival) *(mid-Sep)*, Scheveningen. For two days, hundreds of strange creations hover over the beach.

Jordaanfestival *(second and third weeks in Sep)*, Amsterdam. Fairs, street parties, talent contests and live music are held in the southern part of the picturesque former working-class district of Jordaan.

Prinsjesdag *(third Tue in Sep)*, The Hague. Accompanied by high-ranking government officials and with a guard of honour, the queen rides in her golden carriage from Noordeinde Palace to the Binnenhof (Parliament Building), where she makes her Royal Speech in the Ridderzaal (Hall of the Knights) in order to open the Dutch Parliament.

Queen Beatrix delivering the Royal Speech on Prinsjesdag

Nijmeegse kermis (Nijmegen fair) *(end Sep/early Oct)*. Held every year since the 13th century, the fair stretches ribbon-like through the centre of the city. On Mondays and Tuesdays are the "piekdagen", when children can visit the attractions for the entrance price of 50 cents.

OCTOBER

3-Oktoberfeesten, Leiden. A large public festival to commemorate the relief of Leiden from its siege on 3 October 1574.

Permanent fixtures in the festivities are the distribution of herring and white bread to the townspeople, as well as the procession and funfair.

The distribution of white bread in celebration of the relief of Leiden

Eurospoor *(mid- to late Oct)*, Utrecht. Europe's biggest model train show takes place in the Jaarbeues.

NOVEMBER

Sint-Maarten *(11 Nov)*, Western and Northern Netherlands. In the early evening, children equipped with lanterns walk from door to door, singing songs, for which they are given sweets.

Intocht van Sinterklaas (arrival of St Nicholas) *(second or third week in Nov)*. St Nicholas is celebrated in every town and village in Holland. He arrives by ship near St Nicholasskerk *(see p91)* and then rides on his grey horse through town.

Until 5 December, children traditionally sing Nicholas carols in the evenings, and every morning find sweets in their shoes.

WINTER

December aside, there are not as many events in the winter calendar as there are for the rest of the year – perhaps to the relief of those who need January to recover from St Nicholas, Christmas and the New Year.

DECEMBER

Sinterklaasavond (St Nicholas' Day) *(5 Dec)*. St Nicholas ends with St Nicholas' Eve on 5 December. Both young and old are brought gifts, more often than not in person by (a hired) Santa Claus. Friends give poems caricaturing each other.

Cirque d'Hiver *(between Christmas and New Year's Eve)*, Roermond. Four days of world-class circus acts in the Oranjerie theatre hotel, in the historic town centre.

New Year's Eve *(31 Dec)*. The Dutch spend the last evening of the old year in festive surroundings at home or with friends. Fritters and apple turnovers are eaten and, in many houses, the champagne corks pop at midnight. Afterwards, people walk the streets to see in the New Year with organized firework displays.

JANUARY

Nieuwjaarsduik (New Year's Dip) *(1 Jan)*, Scheveningen. Every year, at noon on New Year's Day, a starting-gun is fired on the pier in Scheveningen, and hundreds of people in swimsuits run down the beach to take a dip in the ice-cold water.

New Year's fireworks display

Leidse Jazzweek *(mid-Jan)*, Leiden. Throughout the week, jazz of all styles is played in the halls and cafés of the old town.

FEBRUARY

Hiswa *(Feb or Mar)*, Amsterdam. Boat show in the RAI *(see p141)*, featuring all types of crafts, from dinghies to yachts.

The latest boats on display at the annual Hiswa

Carnival *(Feb or Mar)*. Officially three, but in practice five, days before Lent, the Catholic south celebrates wildly. There are processions with colourful floats, and costumed people sing and dance in the cafés and in the streets.

The arrival of St Nicholas, attracting a great deal of attention

The Climate in the Netherlands

The Netherlands has a maritime climate, characterized by cool summers and mild winters. In summer, the average maximum temperature is around 20°C (68°F), while in winter the average minimum temperature is around 0°C (32°F). It is slightly warmer south of the country's big rivers than north of them, and there are slightly more hours of sunshine on the coast than inland. Because of the temperature difference between the land and the sea, there is a constant westerly sea breeze on the coast in summer.

WEST FRISIAN
ISLANDS

Leeuwarden
FRIESLAN

NORTH
HOLLAND

Haarlem
AMSTERDAM

Lelystad
FLEVOLAND

The Hague
SOUTH
HOLLAND

Rotterdam

Utrecht
UTRECHT

Nijmeger

's-Hertogenbosch

NORTH BRABANT

Middelburg
ZEELAND

Eindhoven

Maas-
tricht

DEN HELDER

Month	Jan	Mar	May	Jul	Sep	Nov
°C (F)	5 (41)	7 (45)	14 (57)	19 (66)	18 (64)	9 (48)
	1 (34)	2 (36)	9 (48)	14 (57)	13 (55)	5 (41)
☀	48 hours	111 hours	227 hours	212 hours	145 hours	50 hours
☂	76 mm	45 mm	32 mm	67 mm	76 mm	79 mm

DE BILT

Month	Jan	Mar	May	Jul	Sep	Nov
°C (F)	5 (41)	9 (48)	17 (63)	21 (70)	19 (66)	9 (48)
	−1 (30)	1 (34)	7 (45)	12 (54)	10 (50)	3 (37)
☀	54 hours	118 hours	214 hours	191 hours	143 hours	53 hours
☂	76 mm	44 mm	43 mm	82 mm	73 mm	55 mm

Average maximum temperature

Average minimum temperature

Average hours of sunshine per month

Average rainfall per month

BEEK

Month	Jan	Mar	May	Jul	Sep	Nov
°C (F)	4 (39)	10 (50)	18 (64)	22 (72)	19 (66)	9 (48)
	−1 (30)	2 (36)	8 (46)	13 (55)	10 (50)	4 (39)
☀	44 hours	109 hours	202 hours	181 hours	145 hours	53 hours
☂	68 mm	45 mm	62 mm	89 mm	81 mm	62 mm

GRONINGEN

● Groningen

● Assen

DRENTHE

●Zwolle

OVERIJSSEL

Apeldoorn

Enschede

GELDERLAND

Arnhem

LIMBURG

EELDE						
°C (F)	4 (39) -1 (30)	8 (46) 0 (32)	16 (61) 6 (43)	21 (70) 12 (54)	18 (64) 9 (48)	8 (46) 3 (37)
☀	46 hours	104 hours	214 hours	183 hours	142 hours	50 hours
☂	72 mm	46 mm	53 mm	95 mm	72 mm	66 mm
Month	Jan	Mar	May	Jul	Sep	Nov

0 kilometres   20

0 miles   20

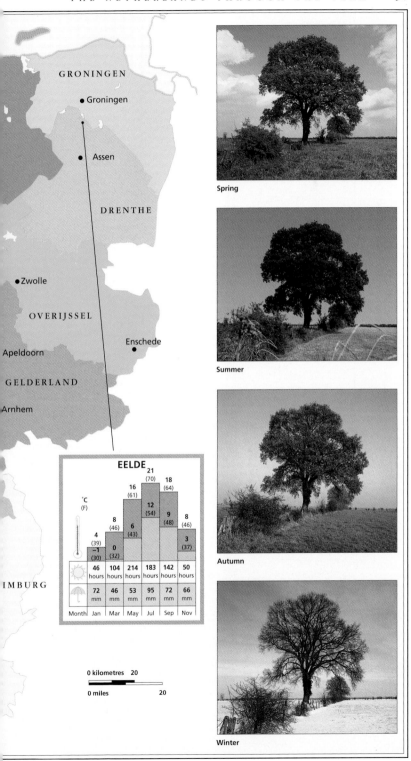

Spring

Summer

Autumn

Winter

THE HISTORY OF THE NETHERLANDS

In 12 BC, the Romans conquered southern Holland, and in AD 50 they declared the Rhine the northern border of their empire. The region north of this was conquered by the Frisians. At the end of the 4th century, the Romans withdrew from the Low Countries, which were taken over by the Frisians, Franks and Saxons. In the 8th century, the Franks ruled the region alone. The introduction of Christianity, begun by the missionary Willibrord in 695, was completed under Charlemagne.

After the disintegration of the Frankish Empire, the Netherlands fell under German rule. Actual power was exercized by the vassals, of whom the Bishop of Utrecht was the most powerful – until the Concordat of Worms in 1122, when the German king lost the right to appoint bishops. In the course of the 12th century, the Count of Holland was the most important figure in the region.

In the 14th and 15th centuries, the dispute between the two factions – the Hooks and the Cods – marked, in a certain sense, the end of the feudal age.

Model of a 17th-century merchant ship

When at the end of the 16th century the Northern Netherlands liberated itself from the Habsburg Duke Philip II, it enjoyed a period of unprecedented economic and cultural flowering. By the mid-17th century, it had become the greatest trading nation in the world, a status gradually relinquished during the 18th century.

The different independent regions making up the republic were joined together under Napoleon, with William I becoming king in 1815. However, unification with Belgium proved unsuccessful and was officially ended in 1839, although it had already ended *de facto* in 1830.

In the 20th century, Holland maintained neutrality during World War I, but suffered greatly during World War II. Invaded by the Nazis in May 1940, the country was not liberated entirely until May 1945. It subsequently developed into one of the most prosperous states within the European Union. Today, the country remains a constitutional monarchy, the royal family enjoying great popularity among the Dutch.

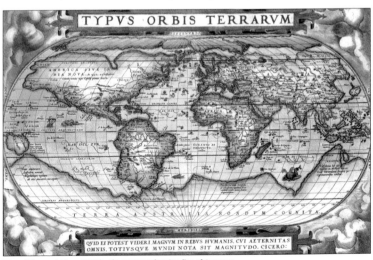

Map of the world from 1564 by the cartographer Ortelius of Antwerp

◁ *The IJ at Amsterdam, Viewed from the Mussel Quay*, painted by Ludolf Backhuysen (1631–1708)

Rulers of the Netherlands

Old coin with
image of
Queen Beatrix

In the Middle Ages, the Netherlands were run by local
feudal dukes, as well as by the counts of Holland
and the bishops of Utrecht. They were all officially
vassals of the German king. In the 15th century, the
region came under the rule of the House of Burgundy
through marriage alliances, after which it was
incorporated into the Habsburg Empire. In 1581,
the Northern Netherlands freed itself from the
Habsburgs. Since then – with some interruptions – the House
of Orange has ruled over parts of what are today called
Holland, initially as stadholders, but from 1815 as monarchs.

1417–1433
Jacoba of Bavaria

c. 685–719
Radboud,
King of the
Frisians

1152–1190
Frederik Barbarossa
(German king)

1342–1364
Jan IV van
Arkel, Bishop
of Utrecht

1312–1355
Jan III (Duke of
Brabant and
Limburg)

814–840
Louis the
Pious

**885–
889**
Gerulf,
Count
of
Holland

1404–1417
Willem VI,
Count of
Holland

1203–1222
Willem I,
Count of Holland

700	800	900	1000	1100	1200	1300	1400

BUR

700	800	900	1000	1100	1200	1300	1400

936–973
Otto I
(German
king)

1371–1402
Willem I,
Duke of Gelre
and Gulik

918–976
Balderik,
Bishop of
Utrecht

1345–1354
Margaretha
of Bavaria

1069–1090
Egbert II,
Count of
Friesland, last
of the
Brunonen

1271–1326
Reinald I,
Count of
Gelre

1433–1467
Philip the Good
(House of Burgundy)

1267–1294
Jan I, Duke of
Brabant (from
1288 also Duke
of Limburg)

1234–1256
Willem II (Count
of Holland)

1091–1121
Floris II, Count
of Holland

1128–1139
Andries van Kuik
(Bishop of Utrecht)

1256–1296
Floris V
(Count of Holland)

768–814
Charlemagne

FLORENT V. XVI Comte de H.

1585–1625
Maurits

1559–1567 and 1572–1584
William of Orange,
"The Silent" (stadholder
of Holland, Zeeland and
Utrecht, under Philip II
until 1581)

1806–1810
Louis Napoleon
(French viceroy,
king of Holland)

1815–1840
William I (king)

1567–1573
Ferdinand, Duke of
Alva (viceroy under
Philip II)

1625–1647
Frederick-Hendrik

1467–1477
Charles the Bold

1647–1650
William II

1477–1482
Maria of Burgundy

1672–1702
William III

1687–1711
Johan Willem
Friso, stadholder
of Friesland
(1696), Prince of
Orange (1702)

1890–1898
Emma (regent)

1898–1948
Wilhelmina

1482–1506
Philip the Handsome
(House of Habsburg)

	1500	1600	1700	1800	1900	2000
NDY	HABSBURG	HUIS VAN ORANJE				
	1500	1600	1700	1800	1900	2000

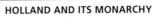

1849–1890
William III

1840–1849 William II

1795–1806 Batavian Republic

1751–1795
William V

1559–1567
Margaretha of Parma
(governor under Philip II)

1948–1980
Juliana

1506–1555
Charles V

1555–1581
Philip II

1747–1751
William IV

1980–present
Beatrix

HOLLAND AND ITS MONARCHY

The Dutch royal family is extremely
popular. The present queen, Beatrix,
is the fourth queen in a row. When
the crown passes to her son,
Willem Alexander, the country
will have its first king since 1890.

Prehistoric and Roman Times

About 13,000 years ago, the Low Countries emerged from under the ice of the last Ice Age. Temperatures gradually rose, turning the tundra into areas of forest and marshes, inhabited by nomadic hunters. In the Early Stone Age (4500–2000 BC), farming communities were established here and there. The megalith builders were the best known of these settled inhabitants. Around 600 BC, Germanic and Celtic tribes settled in the Low Countries. They were here when the Romans conquered the southern part of the region, in the 1st century BC. In AD 50, the Romans finally declared the Rhine as the Roman Empire's northern frontier, establishing Roman settlements in Utrecht and Maastricht.

Roman dagger

THE LOW COUNTRIES (AD 50)

☐ *Germanic peoples*

☐ *Roman territory*

— *Coastline in 3000 BC*

Megaliths
Between 3400 and 3200 BC, the inhabitants of the Drenthe plateau built some 100 megaliths. Of these, 54 have survived into the present (see pp306–7). These impressive tombs were once con-cealed beneath a mound of sand.

Urns
These urns date from 1150–800 BC.

The dark rings in this picture are of the ditches that originally surrounded the urn-mounds. The rings are interrupted at their southeastern edge, possibly to represent the symbolic entrance to the tomb.

TIMELINE

55,000 BC Small groups of Neanderthal people inhabit the surroundings of Hijken and Hoogersmilde. A few hand axes and two campsites have been found			**4500 BC** Farmers settle on the loess land of Zuid Limburg. They have been referred to as "Bandkeramikers", or the Linear Pottery Culture, after their striped pottery		**1900 BC** Start of the Bronze Age in the Low Countries
10,000 BC	**7500 BC**	**5000 BC**	**2500 BC**	**2000 BC**	
		3400–3200 BC Farmers of the Beaker Folk build megaliths at Drenthe, Overijssel and Groningen	*Wheel from 2700 BC*		
11,000 BC Reindeer hunters of the Hamburg Culture inhabit Drenthe					

The Simpelveld Sarcophagus
In the 1930s, a Roman burial urn was excavated at Simpelveld near Limburg. The interior of the urn is decorated with reliefs depicting the exterior and the furnishings of a Roman house.

WHERE TO SEE PREHISTORIC AND ROMAN HOLLAND

In addition to the mega-liths of Drenthe and the Someren urnfield, prehistoric graves have been discovered at Almere, Hilversum, Vaassen, Lunteren, Goirle and Rolde, and at Toterfout/Halfmijl in Brabant, where 16 burial mounds have been restored to their original condition, complete with trenches and rings of stakes. The urnfield on the Bosoverheide, a couple of kilometres west of the Weert, was, around 800 BC, one of the largest burial grounds in northwestern Europe. Roman finds can be seen in places like Oudheden in Leiden (see p217) and the Valkhof museum in Nijmegen (see p343). The Archeon archaeological theme park in Alphen a/d Rijn (see p434) is highly informative and entertaining, for adults and children alike.

THE URNFIELD

In 1991, an urnfield dating from 600 BC was discovered at Someren near Brabant. It had been ploughed under by farmers during the Middle Ages. The dead were cremated in southern Holland from 1500 BC, and in northern Holland from 1000 BC. The burial mounds of Someren were arranged closely together, and each contained its own urn.

Roman Mask
This mask was found near Nijmegen, which was once the camp of a Roman legion.

Glass Flasks
These Roman flasks from the 2nd century AD were excavated at Heerlen.

Farmer with Plough *The plough was used in the Iron Age.*

1500 BC	1000 BC	750 BC	500 BC	250 BC	AD 1

Bronze Age sacrificial dagger

750–400 BC First Iron Age in the Low Countries

450 BC Start of the Second Iron Age, or La Tène Age

55–10 BC Batavians settle in the river area, the Cananefates in the coastal area and the Frisians in the north

Roman temple in Elst

1300 BC The Exloo necklace is made from tin beads from England, Baltic amber and Egyptian pottery beads

300–100 BC The Germans expand southwards across the Rhine, clashing with Celtic tribes

57 BC Caesar conquers the Belgae, who inhabit present-day Belgium

AD 69–70 Batavian Uprising, followed by the re-establishment of Roman rule

Frisians, Franks and Saxons

When the Romans withdrew at the end of the 4th century, the Low Countries, like the rest of Europe, experienced a great migration of peoples. By around 500, the Frisians had spread their territory southwards to the great rivers, while the Saxons lived east of the IJssel and the Franks had settled in the area south of the great rivers. Approximately two centuries later, the Franks took over the whole region as far as the Lauwerszee. With the spread of Christianity and under Charlemagne, the entire area of the Netherlands became Christian. After Charlemagne's death, the region belonged first to the Middle Kingdom of Lothair, and then, from 925, to the German Empire.

Frisian cloak pin

THE LOW COUNTRIES (AD 700)

☐ Frisians

☐ Franks

☐ Saxons

THE LIFE OF ST BONIFACE

Two episodes in the life of the Anglo-Saxon missionary Boniface are illustrated here: on the left, he is shown baptizing a convert; on the right, his martyrdom is depicted. In 716 and 719, Boniface went on missionary expeditions to Friesland. He was subsequently made bishop and later archbishop. In 753, he embarked on a further missionary expedition to Friesland, which resulted in his death the following year.

Widukind
In 785, Charlemagne defeated the Saxons led by Widukind. This event led to the east of Holland finally being incorporated into Charlemagne's empire.

The staff is one of Boniface's constant possessions. He was reputed to have used it to make a spring well up.

Early Medieval Pottery
For the Frisians, pottery was an important barter good, along with cattle and dye.

A convert being baptized.

Fibula from Dorestad

TIMELINE

Relief showing a Roman galley

295
Constantius Chlorus defeats the Franks at the battle of the Rhine delta, but allows them to remain in the Betuwe, where they are used to defend the frontiers

600–700
Dorestad becomes an important trading settlement

AD 200	400	500	550	600	650

350–400
Romans leave the Low Countries

500
The territory of the Frisians stretches from the Zwin in Zeeland Flanders to the mouth of the Weser in Germany

Frankish denarii

Radboud, King of the Frisians
The Frisian king Radboud was forced to capitulate to the Frankish ruler Pippin II. He later regained the land he had lost, and with his army marched on Cologne. In 734, the Frisians under Count Bubo were again defeated at the de Boorne River, allowing Charles Martel to extend Frankish domain up to the Lauwerszee.

Boniface uses his Bible to protect himself from the sword.

Pagan ceremonial axe

DORESTAD

Situated at the confluence of the Lek and the Kromme Rijn (by present-day Wijk bij Duurstede, see p207), Dorestad was the most important trading settlement in northern Holland during the Early Middle Ages. It was the centre of Frisian trade in the 7th century and afterwards under the Merovingians and Carolingians. In the 9th century, Dorestad was repeatedly plundered by marauding Vikings, who sailed up the rivers in their longboats in search of booty. The settlement's decline, however, was due to the damming of the Rhine against flooding rather than because of the Viking raids. There is no reference in historical records to Dorestad after 863. During the 10th century, Dorestad's functions were taken over by Tiel, Deventer and Utrecht. In Wijk, the Museum Dorestad (tel. 0343-571448) gives an excellent idea of what life must have been like here during the Early Middle Ages through its various displays of archaeological finds from that period, as well as its informative diorama, complete with models of port houses.

Viking Sword
This sword, dubbed "Adalfriid's sword", was found in the Waal.

689 Pippin II defeats the Frisian king Radboud at Dorestad and gains the river region and Utrecht

768–814 Rule of Charlemagne. Holland is divided into *pagi* (cantons), each of which is ruled by a count

925 Holland is taken over by the German Empire

1007 Last Viking invasion of the Low Countries

700 **750** **800** **900** **1000**

695 Willibrord becomes bishop of Frisia and establishes his see in Utrecht

754 Boniface is killed at Dokkum by pagan looters

834–837 Dorestad plundered at various times by Vikings

Viking longboat

The Emergence of Towns

Pilgrim's badge

In the 13th century, towns started to acquire considerable economic power. At that time, the Low Countries were nominally under the rule of the German king, but in practice local nobles ran things themselves. In the north, the counts of Holland were the most powerful. In the mid-14th century, their territory fell into the hands of the House of Bavaria. Disunity between Margaretha of Bavaria and her son William marked the beginning of the dispute between the Hooks and the Cods, which split towns as well as noble families for one and a half centuries.

THE LOW COUNTRIES (1300)

☐ *German Empire*

☐ *France*

The Fulling Industry
During the 15th century, the cloth industry flourished in Leiden and 's-Hertogenbosch. This painting by IC Swanenburgh shows the fullers and dyers at work. In the background to the right, inspectors are checking the quality of the cloth.

Minting Coins
Minting rights lay not only with the sovereign. Local rulers, both church and secular, were entitled to mint coins.

Pilgrims who had visited Santiago de Compostela, well established as a place of pilgrimage by the 11th century, wore the scallop shell of the apostle St James on their hats.

The sheriff, with his distinctive chain of bells, was the representative of the sovereign. Here he is on the way to pronounce a death sentence, which is shown by the red pole, the "rod of justice", carried by an executioner.

TIMELINE

The coat of arms of 's-Hertogenbosch

c.1050
The first dykes are built

1185
's-Hertogenbosch is granted its town charter

1247
William II of Holland is appointed king of Germany by the pro-Papal party

1000	1050	1100	1150	1200	1250

1076–1122
Investiture dispute between the German king and the Pope on the right to appoint bishops

1165
Frederick Barbarossa places Friesland under the joint rule of the Bishop of Utrecht and the Count of Holland

Cruel Punishment

In the Middle Ages, barbaric punishments were often meted out. This cask on the wall of the waag in Deventer was once used to immerse counterfeiters in boiling oil.

Grain brought by farmers to the towns was inspected by officials. Produce in the meat and fish markets was also inspected daily. An excise tax was charged on the basis of the inspection.

A MEDIEVAL TOWN

Demands of trade and industry meant that towns were given all kinds of privileges from the 13th century onwards. Often important allies for the counts of Holland against local feudal lords, Dutch towns were more powerful than in other countries during this period because of the lack of a powerful central authority.

WHERE TO SEE THE LATE MEDIEVAL NETHERLANDS

Famous monuments from this period are the Oude Kerk in Amsterdam (14th century, *see pp76–7)* and the Begijnhof, which has the city's oldest house (1420, *see p87)*; the Cathedral Tower (1382) and the Catharijne-convent (15th century) in Utrecht *(see p202)*; the Onze-Lieve-Vrouwebasiliek (11th–12th centuries) and the St-Servaasbasiliek (11th–15th centuries) in Maastricht *(see p377)*; the 13th-century Ridderzaal and the 14th-century Gevangenpoort in The Hague *(see p220)*; the Pieterskerk (15th century) and the town walls of the 12th-century castle in Leiden *(see p217)*; the Lange Jan (14th century, *see p249)* and the restored abbey (11th–15th centuries) in Middelburg *(see p250)*; the centre of Deventer around the Brink and Bergkerk, including the oldest stone house in Holland *(see p320)*; and the Martinitoren in Groningen (1469, *see p280)*.

Silver Chalice

As guilds prospered, they attached increasing importance to appearances. This chalice is decorated with a picture of St George defending a maiden against the dragon.

The Guild of St George *(1533)*
This painting by Cornelis Antonisz shows marksmen at a meal. Originally, each guild was responsible for protecting a part of the city walls; later, special guilds were set up.

Willem Beukelsz.

1296 Floris V is assassinated by the nobles	c.1380 Willem Beukelsz. invents the herring-gutter	1421 The Biesbosch is built as a result of the St Elizabeth Day flood	1477 Marriage of Maria of Burgundy and Habsburg Maximilian I brings together Holland and Zeeland under the House of Habsburg	1550 Charles V introduces the death penalty for all forms of heresy

1300	1350	1400	1450	1500	1550

1306 Amsterdam gains city status	1345 Dispute between the Hooks and the Cods begins. At first a disagreement over the successor to William IV, it develops into a struggle between the feudal barons and the cities	1428 Philip the Good of Burgundy forces Jacoba of Bavaria to withdraw from Holland, Zeeland and Hainaut	1517 Luther publishes the 95 theses

Luther

The Dutch Trading Empire

The early 17th century marked a period of expansion worldwide for northern Holland. Within a few decades, the Levant, the Gulf of Guinea, the Caribbean, North and South America, the East Indies, Persia, Arabia, Japan, India and China were all on the Dutch trading routes. The republic's merchant fleet became the world's largest. The powerful Dutch East India Company (VOC), established in 1602, dominated trade with Asia, with a monopoly on all profits from trade east of the Cape of Good Hope, while the Dutch West India Company, established in 1621, concentrated on the New World and the slave trade.

Brass compass

Dealers on the Stock Exchange
With its market traders and exchange, Amsterdam was the undisputed trading centre of Europe.

Purchase of Manhattan
Pieter Minnewit bought Manhattan Island in 1625 from the Delaware Indians for 60 guilders, 10 guns and a brass cauldron.

1625 The Dutch found New Amsterdam, later to become New York

1667 Abraham Crijnssen conquers Suriname

1627 Prince Maurits conquers Recife

1652 Jan van de Riebeeck founds Cape Town

The Dutch on Desjima
The Dutch trading office on the island of Desjima was in 1854 the main conduit between Japan and the world.

KEY

········	**1595–7**	De Houtman and Keyzer
--------	**1596–7**	Barents and Heemskerck
········	**1616**	le Maire and Schouten
--------	**1642–3**	Tasman

VOC Plaque
The Dutch East India Company (VOC) obtained sole rights to trade for the republic in Asia. It had the authority to make treaties with other powers and even to declare war.

The Silver Fleet
In 1628, Piet Hein captured the Silver Fleet of Spain off the north coast of Cuba.

Surviving the Winter in Novaya Zemlya (1596–97)
During an attempt to find a northern route to the Indies, an expedition led by W Barents and J van Heemskerck ended up on the coast of Novaya Zemlya. The group survived in the Behouden Huys, a hut built from pieces of ships.

THE 80 YEARS WAR

In the second half of the 16th century, Holland officially belonged to the Spanish branch of the House of Habsburg. In 1567, Philip II sent troops to put down Protestant unrest in Flanders and halt the Protestant Reformation sweeping through northern Europe; this led to a revolt against Spanish rule in northern Holland and resulted in years of civil war and religious strife. The 80 Years War ended in 1648 with the Peace of Münster.

Johan van Oldenbarnevelt

Prince Maurits

Statesman Johan van Oldenbarnevelt and the Count of Nassau, Prince Maurits, were the main Dutch figures in the conflict with Holland's Spanish rulers during the 17th century.

1596–1597 The winter camp in Novaya Zemlya

1641 The Dutch establish themselves on Desjima

1624 The Dutch establish themselves on Formosa

1658 The Dutch establish themselves in Ceylon

1619 JP Coen founds Batavia

1606 Willem Jansz discovers Australia

1642 Abel Tasman discovers Tasmania

Three-Master Ship
These top-of-the-line 17th-century Dutch merchant ships required only a small crew.

THE GREAT VOYAGES

While Willem Barents was exploring the Arctic seas, de Houtman and Keyzer set off on the "first voyages" to Java. In 1606, Willem Jansz discovered the north coast of Australia, and in 1616, Jacob le Maire and Willem Schouten were the first to sail around Cape Horn. Abel Tasman discovered Tasmania and New Zealand in 1642–3.

The Golden Age

The 17th century was for the north of Holland a time of unprecedented flowering in trade, art (*see pp26–7*) and science. While elsewhere in Europe economies were in stagnation, the republic's merchant fleet brought great prosperity, particularly to the towns of Amsterdam and Utrecht. The Amsterdam Exchange (Amsterdamse Wisselbank), which was founded in 1609, ensured that Amsterdam became the financial centre of the world. Trade was protected by a powerful navy, which enjoyed significant victories under Michiel de Ruyter.

Baruch de Spinoza

THE LOW COUNTRIES (1650)

- Republic
- Spanish possessions
- Germany

Johan de Witt

At the time known as the first stadholder-free period (1650–72), the political scene in the republic was dominated by the provincial governor Johan de Witt. This brilliant, impeccable statesman was murdered along with his brother Cornelis by Orange supporters in 1672.

Tapestries and exquisite gilded leather hangings decorated the living rooms.

View of the Weigh House in Haarlem
In the 17th century, Holland became Europe's main commodities market, with strategic logistic and financial advantages. Products from the Baltic Sea, southern Europe, the Levant and Asia were loaded into the holds of merchant ships which came from all over the world.

Oriental carpets were too valuable to put on the floor and so were draped over a table or bench.

Colourful cloths came into fashion in the second half of the 17th century and became a widespread object of study for portrait painters.

TIMELINE

	1559	1572	1574	1584	1585	Spanish stew-kettle recovered after the relief of Leiden	1602
	Philip II names Margaretha of Parma the governor of the Netherlands	The "Beggars of the Sea" take over Den Briel	The relief of Leiden	Assassination of William of Orange	Fall of Antwerp		Dutch East India Company founded

1550	1565	1580	1595	1610

Caricature painting of the Pope as a pontiff and devil	1566 Iconoclastic riots	1567 Duke of Alva arrives in Holland	1581 Northern Holland declares independence from Spain	1588 The States General proclaim the Republic of the Seven United Netherlands

Antonie van Leeuwenhoek

THE ENLIGHTENMENT

The Enlightenment, or the "Age of Reason", has its roots in the 16th century. In Holland, this emerged in the work of the natural scientists Swammerdam and Van Leeuwenhoek, and the thinker Spinoza. The jurist Hugo de Groot was the first to formulate a rational – as opposed to a theological – basis for what he called "natural law", that is, a universal law applicable to all humans everywhere, which was one of the great themes tackled by thinkers of the Enlightenment.

WHERE TO SEE THE NETHERLANDS' GOLDEN AGE

Good examples of 17th-century architecture are the Trippenhuis in Amsterdam *(see p78)*, the Lakenhal in Leiden *(see p216)* and the Mauritshuis in The Hague *(see pp222–3)*. Vlissingen has the Arsenaal *(see p251)*; Haarlem, the Grote Markt *(see p182)*. Outstanding merchant houses can be seen in the major trading towns of the time, such as Delft *(see pp226–9)* and Utrecht (for example, the Oudegracht, *see p200)*.

Wan-Li China Porcelain, also known as egg-shell porcelain, served as a model for blue Delft pottery.

Michiel de Ruyter

The admiral of the Dutch fleet during the Second and Third English-Dutch Naval Wars was a great tactician held in great esteem by his sailors. His nickname "Bestevaer" meant "Grand-father".

INTERIOR OF A PATRICIAN HOME

This painting by Pieter de Hooch, *Portrait of a Family Making Music* (1663), shows the wealth of a patrician residence in the second half of the 17th century. Around 1660, portrait painting shifted in style from sobriety to opulence, a reflection of the flourishing economic prosperity.

The Muider Circle
The artists and scholars who met at the home of the poet PC Hooft at Muiderslot Castle are now known as the members of the "Muiderkring" (Muider Circle).

Prince of Poets
Joost van den Vondel (1587–1679), depicted here by HG Pot as a shepherd, is widely regarded as the greatest Dutch poet and playwright of the 17th century.

17th-Century Microscope
Antonie van Leeuwenhoek made numerous important discoveries with his home-made microscope.

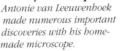

1625	1640	1655	1670	1685	1700

1642 Rembrandt completes *The Night Watch*

1650–1672 First stadholder-free period starts when the states fail to name a successor after the death of William II

1672–1702 Rule of stadholder William III

1698 Tsar Peter the Great visits Amsterdam and Zaandam

1625 Frederick-Henry becomes stadholder of Holland, Zeeland, Utrecht, Gelderland and Overijssel

1648 The Peace of Münster marks the end of the 80 Years War

1665–1667 The Second English-Dutch Naval War. Michiel Adriaansz. de Ruyter scores legendary victories (Four Days' Battle, The Battle of Chatham)

1689 William III becomes king of England

Calvinism

John Calvin

From the end of the 1500s, Calvinism took hold in the Netherlands as Protestant opposition to Spanish Catholic rule. Amsterdam, which had sided with Spain, switched loyalties in 1578 to become the fiercely Protestant capital of an infant Dutch Republic. Reformed Church doctrine was to have a profound influence on Dutch history. Strict living and industriousness became ingrained in the character of Calvinists as well as of Catholics and agnostics and was instrumental in the country's prosperity during the Golden Age.

Gold and paintings *decorated all churches.*

The iconoclasts use combined efforts to topple a huge religious image from the wall.

The Statenbijbel *was the translation of the Bible officially recognized by the Synod of Dordrecht (1618–19). The language used in it helped to standardize Dutch. The New Translation (Nieuwe Vertaling) did not appear until 1957.*

Traces of the damage *caused by the iconoclasts can still be seen today in some places, such as this retable in Utrecht.*

THE ICONOCLASTIC RIOTS

Underground Calvinist preachers goaded troublemakers into the Iconoclastic Riots of 1566, when the decorations of Catholic churches were destroyed with great violence. Invaluable works of religious art were lost in this way.

The interiors of Dutch churches were no longer given the Baroque ornamentation that characterizes churches in the rest of Europe. After all, according to the Ten Commandments in the Bible, "Thou shalt not make graven images" and "Thou shalt not worship nor serve them".

Pieter Saenredam (1597–1665) *painted unrivalled pictures of the plain Calvinist churches – this one is* Interior of the Sint-Odolphuskerk in Assendelft.

Priceless stained-glass windows are systematically smashed to pieces.

The leaders of the iconoclast riots came from all classes of the population. In addition to fervent Calvinists, there were also paid helpers and all kinds of hangers-on who used the opportunity to do some plundering.

WHERE TO SEE CALVINIST NETHERLANDS

Strict Calvinism can be found in the Netherlands' "Bible belt" which stretches from Zeeland and southeastern South Holland via the Veluwe to the cape of Overijssel and Drenthe. The strict Sunday worship, black clothes and head coverings when attending church, as well as abstinence from modern developments (such as television and vaccinations), are gradually disappearing. However, when visiting such areas, do remember that photography and driving are still not looked upon kindly in Reformed Church villages. These communities are closed, with strong social controls. Calvinist villages worth visiting are Goedereede *(see p241),* in South Holland, and Staphorst *(see p320),* in Overijssel, as well as the former Zuiderzee island of Urk *(see p326),* where older people continue to wear traditional dress.

Early to Church by A. Allebé

CLANDESTINE CHURCHES

Ons' Lieve Heer op Solder

When, in 1597, the Union of Utrecht proclaimed mandatory Calvinist services throughout the Netherlands and Zeeland, a blind eye – in return for payment – was turned to other confessions. Catholics, Remonstrants and Mennonites held their services in secret churches, which were unrecognizable as such from the outside. They were generally held in town houses, although later they were held in secret churches that were built for the purpose, particularly in Amsterdam, with De Zon and De Rode Hoed. The St Gertrudiskapel (1645) in Utrecht and Ons' Lieve Heer op Solder (1663, now the Amstelkring Museum) in Amsterdam are the finest surviving early examples of these institutions.

From Republic to Kingdom

After the death of the powerful stadholder William III, the republic no longer played an important role within Europe. Britain took over as most important maritime and trading power. At the end of the 18th century, a long dispute began between the House of Orange and democratically minded patriots, which was resolved in favour of the latter with the founding of the Batavian Republic (1795). After the Napoleonic era, the House of Orange returned to power, this time not as stadholder but as monarch. In 1839, the borders of the present-day Netherlands were finally established.

18th-century trader

THE LOW COUNTRIES IN 1800

Batavian Republic

French territory

WILLIAM I LANDING AT SCHEVENINGEN

In 1813, almost 20 years after the House of Orange had been ousted by the patriots, Prince William returned to the Netherlands. He landed on the shore at Scheveningen, the same place where his father had departed for England. Two days later, he was inaugurated as sovereign. In 1815, he also claimed possession of present-day Belgium and pronounced himself king of the Netherlands.

The British ensign flying on the English warship the *Warrior*, the boat which brought William I back to the Netherlands.

Goejanverwellesluis
In 1785, the patriots took power, and the stadholder William V and his wife Wilhelmina of Prussia fled from The Hague. Wilhelmina attempted to return in 1787 but was stopped at Goejanverwellesluis. It was at this point that the Prussian king decided to send troops to restore the power of the stadholder.

The prince is lowered from the ship in a rowboat, but a farmer's wagon from the beach picks him up to take him ashore through the surf.

TIMELINE

1702–1747 Second stadholder-free period	**1747** William IV "the Frisian" becomes hereditary stadholder of all provinces	**1756–1763** The great powers of Europe become embroiled in the Seven Years War. The republic remains neutral
		1791 Abolition of the Dutch West India Company

1700	**1720**	**1740**	**1760**	**1780**

| **1713** The Peace of Utrecht marks the end of the republic as a great power | | *The city hall of Utrecht, where the Peace of Utrecht was signed* | **1786** The patriots take hold of power in various towns. The rule of stadholder William V is restored in 1787 with the help of Prussia | **1795–1806** The Batavian Republic |

The Siege of Bergen op Zoom
During the War of Austrian Succession, the French occupied the Southern Netherlands, which had been a possession of Austria. In order to strengthen their hand at the peace negotiations vis-à-vis the republic, in 1747 they also annexed Zeeland Flanders and the fortified town of Bergen.

THE SCHOOLS CONTROVERSY

The 19th-century schools controversy between liberals and denominational supporters was over the inequality between independent education and public education. Under HJAM Schaepman and Abraham Kuyper, Catholics and Protestants joined forces and in 1889 laid the found-ations for government subsidies for independent education.

Dr Schaepman   **Dr Kuyper**

The church of the fishing village of Scheveningen is visible in the background.

Child Labour
The Industrial Revolution led to social deprivation in the towns. In 1875, Van Houten's child law was passed, prohibiting children under age 12 from working as paid labourers.

The people of The Hague were overjoyed at the return of the prince. Celebrations were held throughout the town. The times during which the House of Orange had been regarded as a "clique of tyrants" were definitely over.

1806
Louis Napoleon, brother of Napoleon I, becomes king of Holland

1830
The Belgian Revolution. Nine years later, the Netherlands and Belgium separate

1848
Revision of the consti-tution and introduction of parliamentary system

Domela Nieuwenhuis

1885
Van Gogh paints *The Potato Eaters*

1888
First socialist, Domela Nieuwenhuis elected to Parliament

1800   **1820**   **1840**   **1860**   **1880**   **1900**

1798
Abolition of the Dutch East India Company

1815
The Northern and Southern Netherlands are united under William I

1839
Haarlem-Amsterdam railway opens

Steam train

1863
Abolition of slavery

1870
Abolition of the death penalty

1886
Parliamentary enquiry reveals dire conditions in factories

Colonialism

Dutch colonial history started in the 17th century when trading settlements were established in Asia, Africa and America. Many colonies were lost during the course of time, but the Dutch Indies (Indonesia), Suriname and the Dutch Antilles remained under Dutch rule until far into the 20th century. In the Indonesian archipelago, Dutch power was for a long time limited to Java and the Moluccas. It was only in 1870 that a start was made on subjugating the remaining islands. Indonesia gained independence in 1949 and Suriname in 1975. The Antilles, Aruba and the Netherlands are now equal parts of the Kingdom of the Netherlands.

Tobacco trader

Tortured Slave
Rebellion was cruelly punished.

Jan Pieterszoon Coen
Appointed governor-general in 1618, Jan Pieterszoon Coen devastated the Javanese settlement of Jakarta in 1619, founding in its place the new administrative centre of Batavia. He bolstered the position of the Dutch East India Company on the spice islands (the Moluccas) and is considered one of the founding fathers of Dutch colonialism.

Selling female slaves half-naked at auctions was condemned by Holland.

Session of the *Landraad*
This landraad, or joint court, is presided over by the assistant resident. The landraad was the civil and criminal common-law court for native Indonesians and all non-European foreigners in the Dutch Indies. The court could, with government approval, inflict the death penalty.

SLAVE MARKET IN SURINAME

In total, over 300,000 slaves were shipped to the Dutch colony of Suriname to work the plantations. The slave trade was abolished in 1819, though slavery itself was not abolished until 1863, making Holland the last Western European power to do so.

Batavia During the 17th Century
This painting by Andries Beeckman shows the fish market with the "Kasteel" in the background, from which the Dutch ruled over the strategic Sunda Strait.

Multatuli
The writer Multatuli, in his novel from 1860 Max Havelaar, condemned colonial rule in the Dutch Indies. In the book's final chapter, the author directly addresses King William III, in whose name the people of the Indies were being exploited.

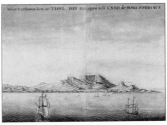

The Establishment of Cape Town
In 1652, Jan van Riebeeck set up a supply station for ships of the Dutch East India Company en route to the Indies. The settlement soon grew into a Dutch colony, which was settled by immigrants from the republic, and to a lesser extent from France (Huguenots) and Germany. Those who moved farther inland were later to become the Boers ("farmers") or Afrikaaners. In 1806, the Cape Colony was taken over by the British Empire.

Kris from Java
Many travellers to the Indies brought back characteristic items to Holland. The Javanese kris was a favourite souvenir.

The auctioneer sits taking notes at the table. The slaves whom he is selling were delivered by special traders. Until 1734, slaves were auctioned exclusively by the Dutch West India Company, which had the monopoly on the slave trade.

Colonial Wares
From the end of the 19th century, a number of Dutch grocers offered for sale "colonial wares" such as coffee, tea, rice, sugar and various exotic eastern herbs and spices, including the much-prized peppercorns, cloves, nutmeg, mace and cinnamon.

The Modern Netherlands

Neutrality during World War I meant that the
Netherlands survived the first decades of the 20th century
relatively unscathed. However, the economic crisis of
the 1930s and particularly World War II left deep wounds.
In 1957, as the country was rebuilding, it became one
of the six founding members of the European
Economic Community (EEC). The Dutch welfare state
flourished in the 1960s and 1970s, and Amsterdam's
tradition of tolerance made it a haven for the hippy
culture. In a survey carried out by the United Nations
in 2009, the Netherlands ranked seventh in the list
of best countries to live.

THE NETHERLANDS TODAY

1917
The magazine *De Stijl* is
set up by figures from the
movement of the same
name, such as Theo van
Doesburg, Piet Mondriaan
and JJP Oud

1930–1940
During the
economic crisis
of the 1930s,
hundreds of
thousands of
Dutch were on
the dole

1949
Holland recog-
nizes the inde-
pendence of its
former colony
Indonesia

1953
On 1 February, storms cause
severe flooding in Zeeland and
South Holland, drowning more
than 1,800 people

1910	1920	1930	1940	1950	1960

TIMELINE

1910	1920	1930	1940	1950	1960

1918
German
kaiser Wil-
helm II flees
to Holland,
where he is
given asylum

1926
Road tax
introduced.
Approxi-
mately
10,000 lor-
ries and
30,000 cars
are on the
roads of
Holland

1948
Willem Drees Sr
becomes prime
minister of four
successive Catholic
socialist Drees cabi-
nets and lays the
foundations of the
Dutch welfare state

1934
KLM's plane "Uiver", a
DC-2, wins the handicap section in
the London-Melbourne air race

1962
The release of Jan
Vrijman's film *De
werkelijkheid van
Karel Appel* brings
the postwar Dutch
painter to the atten-
tion of the general
public. Karel Appel
(b. 1921) caused a
sensation with his
statement: "I'll just
mess something up"

1940
On 10 May,
Nazi troops
enter Holland.
Rotterdam
capitulates on
14 May. Despite
this, the city
is bombed

2000
The Dutch team at the Sydney Olympics wins a record 25 medals, including 12 golds

1985
A government decision to deploy 48 NATO cruise missiles on Dutch territory causes a storm of opposition. The Komité Kruisraketten Nee (anti-cruise coalition) submits a petition of 3.5 million signatures to Prime Minister Lubbers in October

1995
Paul Crutzen is awarded the Nobel Prize for Chemistry for his ground-breaking investigations of the ozone layer

2002
On 2 February Crown Prince Wilem-Alexander marries Argentinian Máxima Zorreguieta in Amsterdam's Beurs van Berlage

1975
Holland recognizes the independence of its former colony Suriname

2010
Geert Wilders' PVV gains the most seats in the elections

1970	1980	1990	2000	2010	2020

1970	1980	1990	2000	2010	2020

1980
The KVP, ARP and CHU combine to form the CDA, the large Christian Democratic Party

1992
Under Dutch presidency, the European partners sign the draft Maastricht Treaty in 1991. In 1992, the treaty, under which the European Community becomes the European Union, is ratified

2004
On 2 November, controversial filmmaker Theo Van Gogh is murdered by a radical Islamist, spurring a national debate on immigration

2002
Right-wing politician Pym Fortuyn is assassinated on 6 May

1980
The coronation of Queen Beatrix on 30 April is accompanied by heavy battles between police and anti-monarchy demonstrators and squatters

1971
Ajax wins the First Division European Cup at Wembley Stadium in London with star player Johan Cruijff. The club continues as champion in 1972 and 1973

AMSTERDAM

Amsterdam's Best: Canals and Waterways

From the grace and elegance of the waterside mansions along the *Grachtengordel* (Canal Ring) to the rows of converted warehouses on Brouwersgracht and the charming houses on Reguliersgracht, the city's canals and waterways embody the very spirit of Amsterdam. They are spanned by many beautiful bridges, including the famous Magere Brug *(see pp114–15)*, a traditionally styled lift bridge. You can also relax at a canalside café or bar and watch an array of boats float by.

Brouwersgracht
The banks of this charming canal are lined with houseboats, cosy cafés and warehouses.

Bloemgracht
There is a great variety of architecture along this lovely, tree-lined canal in the Jordaan, including a row of houses with step gables.

Canal Ring

Prinsengracht
The best way to see all the beautiful buildings along Amsterdam's longest 17th-century canal is by bicycle.

Museum Quarter

Keizersgracht
A view of this canal can be had from any of its bridges. For an overview of the Canal Ring go to Metz & Co at Leidsestraat 34–36 (see p113).

Leidsegracht
Relax at a pavement café along the exclusive Leidsegracht.

◁ **17th-century houses along the waterside street of Zandhoek in Realeneiland**

Singel

The Poezenboot, *a boat for stray cats, is just one of the many sights to be found along the Singel, whose distinctive, curved shape established the horseshoe contours of the Canal Ring.*

Entrepotdok

The warehouses on the Entrepotdok (see p134) were redeveloped in the 1980s. The quayside is now lined in summer with lively café terraces that overlook an array of houseboats and pleasure craft.

| 0 metres | 500 |
| 0 yards | 500 |

Nieuwe Zijde

Oude Zijde

Plantage

Herengracht

Known as "the twin brothers", these matching neck-gabled houses at Nos. 409–411 are two of the prettiest houses on the city's grandest canal.

Reguliersgracht

Many crooked, brick buildings line this pretty canal, which was cut in 1664. The statue of a stork, located at No. 92, is symbolic of parental responsibility and commemorates a 1571 by-law protecting this bird.

Amstel

This river is still a busy thoroughfare, with barges and, above all, many sightseeing boats.

The Golden Age of Amsterdam

The 17th century was truly a Golden Age for Amsterdam. The population soared; three great canals, bordered by splendid houses, were built in a triple ring round the city; and scores of painters and architects were at work. Fortunes were made and lost, and this early capitalism produced many paupers, who were cared for by charitable institutions – a radical idea for the time. In 1648, an uneasy peace was formalized with Catholic Spain, causing tension between Amsterdam's Calvinist burgomasters and the less-religious House of Orange, which was dominant elsewhere in the country.

Spice Trade
In this old print, a VOC spice trader arrives in Bantam.

Self-Portrait as the Apostle Paul *(1661) Rembrandt (see p78) was one of many artists working in Amsterdam in the mid-17th century.*

The new Stadhuis (now the Koninklijk Paleis) was being constructed behind wooden scaffolding.

Nieuwe Kerk, 1395 *(see p86)*

Livestock and grain trading

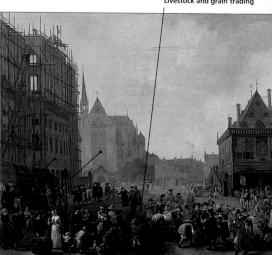

The Love Letter *(1666) Genre painting (see p123), such as this calm domestic interior by Jan Vermeer, became popular as society grew more sophisticated. Jan Steen, Honthorst and Terborch were other famous genre painters.*

DAM SQUARE IN 1656

Money poured into Amsterdam at this time of civic expansion. Holland was active overseas, colonizing Indonesia, and the spice trade brought enormous wealth. The Dutch East India Company (VOC), the principal trade organization in Holland, prospered – gold seemed almost as common as water. Dutch painter Jan Lingelbach (c.1624–74) depicted the city's Dam square as a busy, thriving and cosmopolitan market, brimming with traders and wealthy merchants.

Delft Tiles
Delicate flower paintings were popular themes on 17th-century Delft tiles (see pp28–9), used as decoration in wealthy households.

Flora's Bandwagon *(1636)*
Many allegories were painted during "tulip mania". This satirical oil by HG Pot symbolizes the idiocy of investors who paid for rare bulbs with their weight in gold, forcing prices up until the market collapsed.

Ships sailing up the Damrak

Commodities weighed at the Waag

WHERE TO SEE 17TH-CENTURY AMSTERDAM

Many public buildings, such as churches and palaces, sprang up as Amsterdam grew more wealthy. The Westerkerk *(see p110)* was designed by Hendrick de Keyser in 1620; the Lutherse Kerk *(see p90)* by Adriaan Dortsman in 1671. Elias Bouman built the Portugees-Israëlitische Synagoge *(see p80)* in 1675 for members of the city's immigrant Sephardic Jewish community.

Spices
A load of spices was worth a fortune in the 17th century. The VOC traded in a great variety of these costly spices, primarily pepper, nutmeg, cloves, mace and cinnamon. As early as 1611 the VOC was the largest importer of spices.

Cargo unloaded by cranes | Turkish traders | Pepper, nutmeg, cloves, mace, cinnamon

Apollo *(c.1648)* Artus Quellien's statue is in the South Gallery of the Koninklijk Paleis (see pp88–9). Construction of the place, a masterwork by Jacob van Capenwhich, began in 1648.

VOC
In the Scheepvaart Museum (see pp132–3), an entire room is dedicated to the Dutch East India Company.

Giving the Bread
This painting by Willem van Valckert shows the city's needy receiving alms. A rudimentary welfare system was introduced in the 1640s.

Museum het Rembrandthuis *(1606)*
Jacob van Campen added the pediment in 1633 (see p78).

Amsterdam's Best: Museums

For a fairly small city, Amsterdam has a surprisingly large number of museums and galleries. The quality and variety of the collections are impressive, covering everything from bibles and beer to shipbuilding and space travel. Many are housed in buildings of historical or architectural interest. The Rijksmuseum, with its Gothic façade, is a city landmark, and Rembrandt's work is exhibited in his original home.

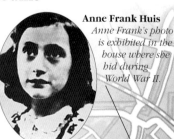

Anne Frank Huis
Anne Frank's photo is exhibited in the house where she hid during World War II.

Amsterdam Museum
A wealth of historical information is on display here. Once an orphanage for boys, it is depicted in Governesses at the Burgher Orphanage *(1683) by Adriaen Backer.*

Rijksmuseum
An extensive collection of paintings by Dutch masters can be seen in the country's largest national museum. Jan van Huysum's Still Life with Fruit and Flowers, *dating from about 1730, is a fine example (see pp122–5).*

Canal Ring

Museum Quarter

Van Gogh Museum
Van Gogh's Self-portrait with Straw Hat *(1870) hangs in this large, stark building, built in 1973 to house the bulk of his work.*

Stedelijk Museum
Gerrit Rietveld's simple Steltman chair (1963) is one of many exhibits at this modern art museum (see pp128–9).

Koninklijk Paleis
The royal palace on the Dam, a former town hall designed in 1648 by Jacob van Campen, is still regularly used today by the queen on official occasions (see pp88–9).

Science Center NEMO
This amazing building, designed in the form of a ship, overhangs the water by 30 m (99 ft) and houses an educational centre for science and technology (see pp136–7).

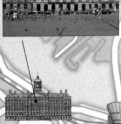

Nederlands Scheepvaart Museum
This maritime museum is decorated with reliefs relating to the city's maritime history. Moored alongside is a replica of the East Indiaman, Amsterdam, *which is open to the public.*

0 metres	500
0 yards	500

Nieuwe Zijde

Oude Zijde

Plantage

Joods Historisch Museum
Four adjoining synagogues are linked to form this museum.

Verzetsmuseum
Located in the Plantage, this museum documents and commemorates the activities of Dutch Resistance workers in World War II (see pg141).

Amsterdam's Best: Cafés

Amsterdam is a city of cafés and bars, about 1,500 in all. Each area has something to offer, from friendly and relaxed brown cafés – a traditional Dutch local pub characterized by dark wooden panelling and furniture, low ceilings, dim lighting and a fog of tobacco smoke – to lively and crowded designer bars. Each café and bar has some special attraction: a large range of beers, live music, canalside terraces, art exhibitions, board games and pool tables or simply a brand of *gezelligheid*, the unique Dutch concept of "cosiness".

Karpershoek
This lively café (the oldest café in Amsterdam) is close to the Centraal Station and is frequented by travellers looking for a cup of coffee.

Café Chris
This brown café in the Jordaan is patronized by regular customers (artists and students).

Odeon
This popular disco attracts a hip crowd. The basement café combines original 17th-century features with modern furnishings.

Canal Ring

Vertigo
The café terrace of the EYE Film centre in the Vondelpark is very busy on warm summer days.

Museum Quarter

Hoppe
The dark wooden interior and tang of cigar smoke in the air are the essence of this classic brown café, situated on the lively Spui.

De Drie Fleschjes
In one of the oldest pubs (1650) of Amsterdam, you can choose from a wide variety of gins.

Kapitein Zeppos
This café, frequented by trendy Amsterdammers, often hosts live concerts on Sunday afternoons.

Oude Zijde

euwe ijde

Plantage

De Jaren
Popular with students, this trendy two-storey café has a superb view of the Amstel and a wide selection of newspapers.

Grand Café Soccerworld
In the café of the arena you can admire the football shirts of the famous Ajax team.

0 metres	500
0 yards	500

OUDE ZIJDE

The eastern half of Amsterdam became known as the Oude Zijde (Old Side). Originally it occupied a narrow strip on the east bank of the Amstel river, running between Damrak and the Oudezijds Voorburgwal. At its heart was built the Oude Kerk, the oldest church in the city. In the early 15th century the Oude Zijde began an eastward expansion that continued into the 1600s. This growth was fuelled by an influx

Aäron from Mozes en Aäronkerk

of Jewish refugees from Portugal. The oldest of the four synagogues, now containing the Joods Historisch Museum, dates from this period. These were central to Jewish life in the city for centuries. During the Golden Age *(see pp50–51)*, the Oude Zijde was an important commercial centre. Boats could sail up the Geldersekade to Nieuwmarkt, where goods were weighed at the Waag before being sold at the market.

SIGHTS AT A GLANCE

Historic Buildings and Monuments

Agnietenkapel ❺
Montelbaanstoren ⓱
Oost-Indisch Huis ❼
Oudemanhuispoort ❻
Pintohuis ⓰
Scheepvaarthuis ⓲
Schreierstoren ⓳
Trippenhuis ❽
Waag ❷

Opera Houses

Stadhuis-Muziektheater ⓫

Museums

Hash Marihuana Hemp Museum ❹
Joods Historisch Museum ⓮
Museum het Rembrandthuis ❿

Churches and Synagogues

Mozes en Aäronkerk ⓭
Oude Kerk pp76–7 ㉑
Portugees-Israëlitische Synagoge ⓯
Zuiderkerk ❾

Streets and Markets

Nieuwmarkt ❸
Red Light District ❶
Waterlooplein ⓬
Zeedijk ⓴

GETTING THERE

The best way to reach the Oude Zijde is to get a tram to the Dam (trams 1, 2, 4, 5, 9, 13, 14, 16, 17, 24 and 25) and then walk along Damstraat. Alternatively, take tram 9 or 14 directly to Waterlooplein, or the metro to Nieuwmarkt.

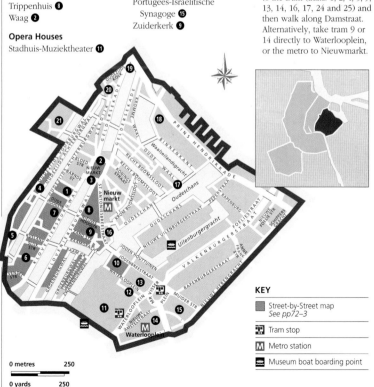

KEY

▨	Street-by-Street map *See pp72–3*
🚊	Tram stop
Ⓜ	Metro station
⛴	Museum boat boarding point

0 metres   250
0 yards   250

◁ **The enormous town hall/opera house, an unusual combination in the old part of town**

Street-by-Street: University District

The University of Amsterdam, founded in 1877, is predominantly located in the peaceful, southwestern part of the Oude Zijde. The university's roots lie in the former Athenaeum Illustre, which was founded in 1632 in the Agnietenkapel. Beyond Damstraat, the bustling Red Light District meets the Nieuwmarkt, where the 15th-century Waag evokes a medieval air. South of the Nieuwmarkt, Museum Het Rembrandthuis gives a fascinating insight into the life of the city's most famous artist.

★ **Red Light District**
The sex industry brings billions of euros to Amsterdam every year ❶

Hash Marihuana Hemp Museum
This museum showcases marijuana through the ages ❹

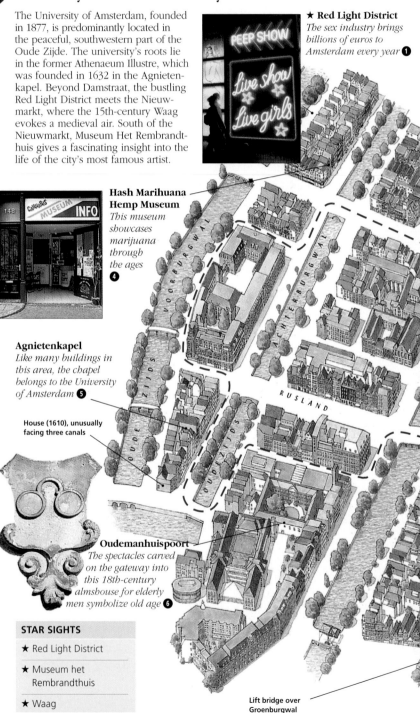

Agnietenkapel
Like many buildings in this area, the chapel belongs to the University of Amsterdam ❺

House (1610), unusually facing three canals

Oudemanhuispoort
The spectacles carved on the gateway into this 18th-century almshouse for elderly men symbolize old age ❻

Lift bridge over Groenburgwal

STAR SIGHTS

★ Red Light District

★ Museum het Rembrandthuis

★ Waag

For hotels and restaurants in this region see pp392–395 and pp410–414

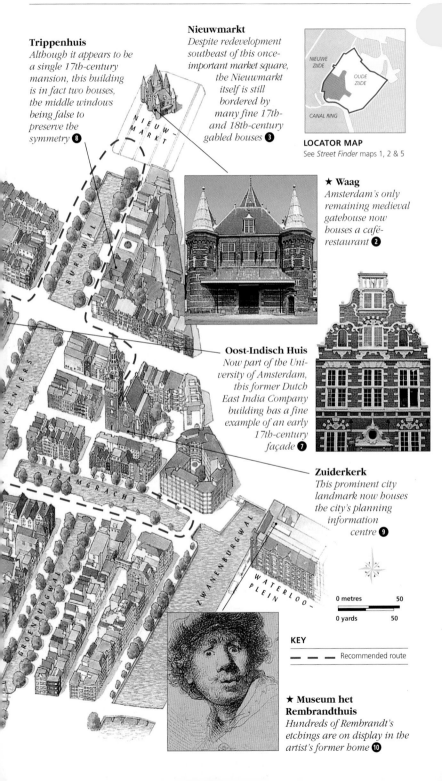

Trippenhuis
Although it appears to be a single 17th-century mansion, this building is in fact two houses, the middle windows being false to preserve the symmetry ❽

Nieuwmarkt
Despite redevelopment southeast of this once-important market square, the Nieuwmarkt itself is still bordered by many fine 17th- and 18th-century gabled houses ❸

LOCATOR MAP
See *Street Finder* maps 1, 2 & 5

★ **Waag**
Amsterdam's only remaining medieval gatehouse now houses a café-restaurant ❷

Oost-Indisch Huis
Now part of the University of Amsterdam, this former Dutch East India Company building has a fine example of an early 17th-century façade ❼

Zuiderkerk
This prominent city landmark now houses the city's planning information centre ❾

0 metres 50
0 yards 50

KEY
– – – Recommended route

★ **Museum het Rembrandthuis**
Hundreds of Rembrandt's etchings are on display in the artist's former home ❿

Red Light District ❶

Map 5 A1. 🚊 4, 9, 16, 24, 25.

Barely clad prostitutes bathed in a red neon glow and touting for business at their windows is one of the defining images of modern Amsterdam. The city's Red Light District, referred to locally as de Walletjes (the little walls), is concentrated on the Oude Kerk (see pp76–7), although it extends as far as Warmoesstraat to the west, the Zeedijk to the north, the Kloveniersburgwal to the east and then along the line of Damstraat to the south.

Prostitution in Amsterdam dates back to the city's emergence as a port in the 13th century. By 1478, prostitution had become so widespread that attempts were made to contain it. Prostitutes straying outside their designated area were marched back to the sound of pipe and drum.

A century later, following the Alteration, the Calvinists (see pp52–3) tried to outlaw prostitution altogether. Their attempts were half-hearted, and by the mid-17th century prostitution was openly tolerated. In 1850, Amsterdam had a population of 200,000, and more than 200 brothels.

Entrance to one of the clubs in the Red Light District

Today, the whole area is criss-crossed by a network of narrow lanes, dominated by garish sex shops, seedy clubs and unsavoury characters. At night, the little alleys assume a somewhat sinister aspect, and it is unwise to wander away from the main streets. But by day, hordes of visitors generate a festive buzz, and amid the sleaze there are interesting cafés, bars, restaurants and beautiful canalside houses to be discovered. The city council is trying to make the area more culturally attractive by cutting down on window-prostitutes, closing the seediest clubs and encouraging non-sex-industry businesses.

Waag ❷

Nieuwmarkt 4. **Map** 2 E5. 🚊 9, 14. Ⓜ Nieuwmarkt. 🚫 upper rooms closed to public.

The multi-turreted Waag is the city's oldest surviving gate-house. Built in 1488, it was then, and often still is, called St Antoniespoort. Public executions were held here, and condemned prisoners awaited their fate in the "little gallows room". In 1617, the building became the public weigh house (waaggebouw). Peasants had their produce weighed here and paid tax accordingly. Various guilds used the upper rooms of each tower. From 1619 the Guild of Surgeons had a meeting room and anatomy theatre here. They added the central octagonal tower in 1691. Rembrandt's Anatomy Lesson of Dr Nicholaes Tulp, now in the Mauritshuis (see pp222–3), and The Anatomy Lesson of Dr Jan Deijman, in the Amsterdam Museum (see pp92–3), were commissioned by guild members and then hung here.

The weigh house closed in the early 19th century and the Waag has since served as a fire station and two city museums. It is now home to the restaurant In de Waag.

The 15th-century Waag dominating the Nieuwmarkt, with an antique market on the right

Part of the commemorative photo display in Nieuwmarkt metro

Nieuwmarkt ❸

Map 2 E5. 🚊 9, 14. **M** *Nieuwmarkt.*
Antiques market ◯ *May–Sep:
9am–5pm Sun.* 🌾 *Organic farmers'
market 9am–5pm Sat.*

An open, paved square, the
Nieuwmarkt is flanked to
the west by the Red Light
District. With the top end of the
Geldersekade, it forms Amsterdam's Chinatown. The Waag
dominates the square, and
construction of this gateway led
to the site's development in the
15th century as a marketplace.
When the city expanded in
the 17th century *(see pp64–5)*,
the square took on its present
dimensions and was called the
Nieuwmarkt. It retains an array
of 17th- and 18th-century
gabled houses. True to tradition, an antiques market is held
on Sundays during the summer.
The old Jewish Quarter leads
off the square down St Antoniesbreestraat. In the 1970s,
many houses here were
demolished to make way for
the metro, sparking off clashes
between protesters and police.
The action of conservationists
persuaded the council to adopt
a policy of renovating rather
than redeveloping old buildings. Photographs of their
protests decorate the metro.

Hash Marihuana Hemp Museum ❹

Oudezijds Achterburgwal 148.
Map 2 D5. **Tel** *020-6248926.* 🚊 4,
9, 14, 16, 24, 25. **M** *Nieuwmarkt.*
◯ *10am–10pm.* 📷 🚫 📷

This museum is the only
one in Europe to chart the
history of hemp (marijuana).
Exhibits refer back 8,000 years
to early Asiatic civilizations,

which used the plant for
medicines and clothing. It was
first used in the Netherlands,
according to a herbal manual
of 1554, as a cure for earache.
Until the late 19th century,
however, hemp was the main
source of fibre for rope, and
was therefore important in the
Dutch shipping industry.
Other exhibits relate to the
psychoactive properties of
this plant. They include an
intriguing array of pipes
and bongs (smoking devices),
along with displays that
explain smuggling methods.
The museum also has a small
cultivation area where plants
are grown under artificial
light. Police sometimes raid
and take away exhibits, so
there may be occasional
gaps in displays.

Agnietenkapel ❺

Oudezijds Voorburgwal 231.
Map 2 D5. 🚊 4, 9, 14, 16, 24, 25.
🚫 *to the public.*

The Agnietenkapel was part
of the convent of St Agnes
until 1578 when it was closed
after the Alteration. In 1632,
the Athenaeum Illustre, the
precursor of the University
of Amsterdam, took over the
building and by the mid-17th
century it was a centre of
scientific learning. It also
housed the municipal library
until the 1830s. The Agnietenkapel itself dates from 1470,
and is one of the few Gothic
chapels to have survived the
Alteration. During restoration
from 1919 to 1921, elements
of the Amsterdam School
architecture were introduced
(see pp142–3). Despite
these changes and
long periods of
secular use,
the build-
ing still
has the
feel of a Franciscan
chapel. The large
auditorium on the
first floor is the old-
est in the city. It has a lovely
ceiling, painted with Renaissance motifs and a portrait of
Minerva, the Roman goddess
of wisdom and the arts. The
walls are hung with forty

portraits of European humanist scholars, including one of
Erasmus (1466–1536). The
Agnietenkapel once housed
the University of Amsterdam
Museum, but the museum's
collection can be seen
in Oude Turfmarkt 129
(next to the Allard Pierson
Museum). A conference
centre has taken its place.

Entrance to Agnietenkapel, now a university conference centre

Oudemanhuis-poort ❻

Between Oudezijds Achterburgwal
and Kloveniersburgwal. **Map** 2 D5.
🚊 4, 9, 14, 16, 24, 25. **Book
market** ◯ *10am–6pm Mon–Sat.*

The Oudemanhuispoort was
once the entrance to old
people's almshouses (Oude-
mannenhuis), built in 1754.
Today the building is part of
the University of Amsterdam.
The pediment over
the gateway in
the Oudezijds
Achterburgwal
features a
pair of
spectacles,
a symbol of
old age. Trading
inside this covered
walkway dates
from 1757 and today there
is a market for second-hand
books. Although the building
is closed to the public, visitors
may enter the 18th-century
courtyard via the arcade.

**Crest of Amsterdam,
Oudemanhuispoort**

Oude Kerk ㉑

The origins of the Oude Kerk date from the early 13th century, when a wooden church was built on a sand bank. The present Gothic structure is 14th century and has grown from a single-aisled church into a basilica. As it expanded, the building became a gathering place for traders and a refuge for the poor.

Carving on 15th-century choir misericord

Paintings and statuary were destroyed after the Alteration in 1578, but the gilded ceiling and stained-glass windows remain. The Great Organ was added in 1724, and there are two other fine organs. The floor is undergoing restoration, and part of the church will be screened off until 2012.

The spire of the bell tower was built by Joost Bilhamer in 1565. François Hemony added the 47-bell carillon in 1658.

Tomb of Saskia, wife of Rembrandt *(see p78)*

The Oude Kerk Today
The old church, surrounded by shops, cafés and houses, remains a calm and peaceful haven at the heart of the frenetic Red Light District.

Christening chapel

Tomb of Admiral Abraham van der Hulst (1619–66)

★ **Great Organ** *(1724)*
Vater-Müller's oak-encased organ has eight bellows and 4,000 pipes. The 54 pipes of the magnificent organ front are gilded.

TIMELINE

1412 North transept completed	**1462** First side chapel demolished to build south transept	**1552** Lady Chapel added	**1658** Carillon installed	**1724** Great Organ installed	**1979** Church re-opens to public	
1330 Church consecrated to St Nicholas					**1951** Church closes	

1300	1400	1500	1600	1700	1800	1900

	1500 Side chapels added	**1578** Calvinists triumph in the Alteration		**1912–14** Partial restoration of northwest corner		
1340 Church enlarged	**1566** Spire added to 13th-century tower	*Stained-glass coats of arms in Lady Chapel*				
1300 Small stone church built				**1955–99** Restoration of church		

★ **Gilded Ceiling**
The delicate 15th-century vault paintings have a gilded background. They were hidden with layers of blue paint in 1755 and not revealed until 1955.

VISITORS' CHECKLIST

Oudekerksplein. **Map** 2 D4. **Tel** 020-6258284. 4, 9, 16, 24, 25. **Church** 11am–5pm Mon–Sat, 1–5pm Sun. 11am Sun. **Tower** Apr–Sep: 1–5pm Thu–Sat; Oct–Mar: phone 020-6892565 to arrange a visit. www.oudekerk.nl

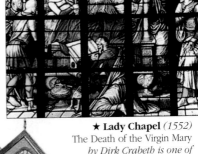

★ **Lady Chapel** (1552)
The Death of the Virgin Mary by Dirk Crabeth is one of three restored stained-glass windows in the Lady Chapel.

Tomb of Admiral Jacob van Heemskerk (1567–1607)

Brocaded Pillars
Decorative pillars originally formed niches holding a series of statues of the Apostles, all destroyed by the iconoclasts in 1578.

17th- and 18th-century houses

Former sacristy

The Red Door
The inscription on the lintel above the door into the former sacristy warns those about to enter: "Marry in haste, repent at leisure".

STAR FEATURES

★ Gilded Ceiling

★ Great Organ

★ Lady Chapel

Oost-Indisch Huis ❼

Oude Hoogstraat 24. **Map** 2 D5.
4, 9, 14, 16, 24, 25. **M** *Nieuwmarkt.*
⬜ *9am–5pm Wed.* ⬤ *during
graduation ceremonies.*

The austere Oost-Indisch
Huis, former headquarters of
the Dutch East India Company
(see pp48–9), is part of the
University of Amsterdam.
Built in 1605, it was expanded
several times to house spices,
silk and porcelain from the East
Indies. Little original interior
decoration remains,
but the meeting
room has been
restored to its
17th-century
grandeur.

**Ornate balustrade of
the Oost-Indisch Huis**

Trippenhuis ❽

Kloveniersburgwal 29. **Map** 2 E5.
🚋 *4, 9, 14, 16, 24, 25.*
M *Nieuwmarkt.* ⬤ *to the public.*

Justus Vingboons designed
this ornate Classical mansion,
completed in 1662. It appears
to be one house: it is in fact
two. The façade, outlined by
eight Corinthian columns, features false middle windows.
The house was designed for
arms merchants Lodewijk and
Hendrick Trip; the chimneys
look like cannons. The city's
art collection was housed here
1817–85, when it moved to the
Rijksmuseum *(see pp122–5)*.
Trippenhuis now houses the
Dutch Academy. Opposite at
No. 26 is the Kleine Trippenhuis (1698). Only 2.5 m (7 ft)
wide, it has detailed cornicing,
including two carved sphinxes.

Zuiderkerk ❾

Zuiderkerkhof 72. **Map** 2 E5.
Tel 020-5527987. 🚋 *9, 14.*
M *Nieuwmarkt.* ⬜ *9am–4pm
Mon–Fri, noon–4pm Sat.* 📷 ♿
Tower 📷 📋 *Apr–Sep: 1–3:30pm.*
www.zuiderkerk.amsterdam.nl

Designed by Hendrick de
Keyser in 1603 in the Renaissance style, the Zuiderkerk
was the first Calvinist church
to open in Amsterdam after
the Alteration. The spire has
columns, decorative clocks

The spire of the Zuiderkerk, a prominent city landmark

and an onion dome. The
Zuiderkerk ceased to function
as a church in 1929. Restored
in 1988, it is now a public
housing exhibition centre.
The surrounding community
housing includes the
"Pentagon" by Theo Bosch.

Museum het Rembrandthuis ❿

Jodenbreestraat 4-6. **Map** 2 E5.
Tel 020-5200400. 🚋 *9, 14.*
M *Nieuwmarkt.* ⬜ *10am–5pm
daily.* ⬤ *1 Jan.* 📷 📷 📋 📷 📷
www.rembrandthuis.nl

Rembrandt worked and
taught in this house from
1639 until 1660. He lived in
the ground-floor rooms with
his wife, Saskia, who died here
in 1642, leaving the artist with
their only surviving child, a
baby son, Titus.
Many of Rembrandt's most
famous paintings were created

in the first-floor studio. Lessons
were conducted in the attic. A
fine collection of Rembrandt's
etchings and drawings includes
various self-portraits. There
are also landscapes, nude
studies, religious and crowd
scenes, and sketches of the
artist with his wife. The house
has undergone historically
accurate restoration and a
further wing has been opened
to the public.

**Self-portrait by Rembrandt with his
wife, Saskia (1636)**

Stadhuis-Muziektheater ⓫

Waterlooplein 22. **Map** 5 B2. 🚃 4, 9, 14. Ⓜ *Waterlooplein*. **Stadhuis** *Tel* 020-6241111. ◯ *8:30am–4pm Mon–Fri (free concerts Sep–May: 12:30pm Tue)*. **Muziektheater** *Tel 020-6255455. See Entertainment pp146–7.* ♿ 🎟 www.hetmuziektheater.nl

Few buildings in Amsterdam caused as much controversy as the new Stadhuis (city hall) and Muziektheater (opera house). Nicknamed the "Stopera" by protesters, the plan required the destruction of dozens of medieval houses, which were virtually all that remained of the original Jewish quarter, and the temporary relocation of a popular market. This led to running battles between squatters and the police.

The building, completed in 1988, is a huge confection of red brick, marble and glass. A mural illustrating the Normaal Amsterdams Peil is shown on the arcade linking the two parts of the complex. The complex has the largest auditorium in the country, and it is home to the Netherlands' national opera and ballet companies.

Eclectic goods on offer at the Waterlooplein market

Waterlooplein ⓬

Map 5 B2. 🚃 9, 14. Ⓜ *Waterlooplein*. **Market** ◯ *9am–5pm Mon–Fri, 8:30am–5pm Sat.*

The Waterlooplein dates from 1882, when two canals were filled in to create a market square. The site was originally known as Vlooyenburg, an artificial island built in the 17th century to house Jewish settlers. The original market disappeared during World War II when most of the Jewish residents of Amsterdam were transported by the Nazis. After the war, a popular flea market grew up in its place, and today the northern end of the square still hosts a lively mix of stalls.

Mozes en Aäronkerk ⓭

Waterlooplein 205. **Map** 5 B2. *Tel 020-6221305.* 🚃 9, 14. Ⓜ *Waterlooplein*. 📷 *to the public except for exhibitions.*

Designed by Flemish architect T Suys the Elder in 1841, Mozes en Aäronkerk was built on the site of a hidden Catholic church. The later

church took its name from the Old Testament figures depicted on the gable stones of the original building. These are now set into the rear wall.

The church was restored in 1990, its twin wooden towers painted to look like sandstone. It is now used for exhibitions, public meetings and concerts.

The central hall in the Grote Synagoge, which opened in 1671

Joods Historisch Museum ⓮

Jonas Daniel Meijerplein 2–4. **Map** 5 B2. *Tel 020-5310310.* 🚃 9, 14. 🚋 *Muziektheater*. Ⓜ *Waterlooplein*. ◯ *11am–5pm daily.* 🔴 *Jewish New Year, Yom Kippur.* 🖼 📷 ♿ 🖥 🎟 *on request, incl. for the visually handicapped.* 🔊 📱 www.jhm.nl

This complex of four synagogues, built by Ashkenazi Jews in the 17th and 18th centuries, opened as a museum in 1987. The synagogues were central to Jewish life here, until the devastation of World War II left them empty. Restored in the 1980s, they are connected by internal walkways. Displays of art and religious artifacts depict Jewish culture and the history of Judaism in the Netherlands.

Highlights include the Grote Synagoge, its hall lined with galleries; and the Holy Ark (1791) from Enkhuizen (*see p178)* which dominates the Nieuwe Synagoge and holds two 18th-century silver Torah shields and three velvet mantles. Also not to be missed is the 1734 Haggadah containing the Passover order of service.

The buildings were renovated in 2006, when a basement print room was created, and one of the synagogues turned into a children's museum.

Portugees-Israëlitische Synagoge  🕒

Mr Visserplein 3. **Map** 5 B2. **Tel** 020-6245351. 🚋 9, 14. M Waterlooplein. ⏰ Apr–Oct: 10am–4pm Sun–Fri; Nov–Mar: 10am–4pm Sun–Thu, 10am–2pm Fri. ● Jewish hols, 30 Apr. 📷 📸 call 020 5310380 to book 📷 ♿ 🚻 www.esnoga.nl

Elias Bouman's design for the Portugees-Israëlitische Synagoge is said to be inspired by the Temple of Solomon in Jerusalem. Built for the wealthy Portuguese Sephardic community of Amsterdam and inaugurated in 1675, the huge brick building has a rectangular ground plan with the Holy Ark in the southeast corner facing towards Jerusalem, and the *tebah* (the podium from which the service is led) at the opposite end.

The wooden, barrel-vaulted ceiling is supported by four Ionic columns. The interior of the synagogue, with its pews made of mahogany, is illuminated by more than 1,000 candles and 72 windows.

Italianate façade of the 17th-century Pintohuis

Pintohuis 🕒

Sint Antoniesbreestraat 69. **Map** 2 E5. **Tel** 020-6243184. 🚋 9, 14. M Nieuwmarkt. ⏰ 2–8pm Mon, Wed, 2–5pm Fri, 11am–4pm Sat.

Isaac de Pinto, a wealthy Portuguese merchant, bought the Pintohuis in 1651 for the then enormous sum of 30,000 guilders. He had it

remodelled over the next decades to a design by Elias Bouman, and it is one of the few private residences in Amsterdam to follow an Italianate style. The exterior design was reworked from 1675 to 1680. Six imposing pilasters break up the severe, cream façade into five recessed sections, and the cornice is topped by a blind balustrade concealing the roof. Inside, the painted ceiling is decorated with birds and cherubs.

In the 1970s, the house was scheduled for demolition because it stood in the way of a newly planned main road. Concerted protest saved the building. It now houses a branch of the Amsterdam Public Library.

Montelbaanstoren 🕒

Oude Waal/Oudeschans 2. **Map** 5 B1. 🚋 9, 14. M Nieuwmarkt. ● to the public.

The lower portion of the Montelbaanstoren was built in 1512 and formed part of Amsterdam's medieval fortifications. It lay just beyond the city wall, protecting the city's wharves on the newly built St Antoniesdijk (now the Oudeschans) from the neighbouring Gelderlanders.

The octagonal structure and open-work timber steeple were both added by Hendrick de Keyser in 1606. His decorative addition bears a close resemblance to the spire of the Oude Kerk, designed by Joost Bilhamer, which was built 40 years earlier *(see pp76–7)*. In 1611, the tower began to list, prompting Amsterdammers to attach ropes to the top and pull it right again.

Sailors from the Dutch East India Company would gather at the Montelbaanstoren before being ferried in small boats down the IJ to the massive East Indies-bound sailing ships, anchored further out in deep water to the north.

The building appears in a number of etchings by Rembrandt, and is still a popular subject for artists. It now houses the offices of the Amsterdam water authority.

One of many stone carvings on the Scheepvaarthuis façade

Scheepvaarthuis 🕒

Prins Hendrikkade 108. **Map** 2 E4. 🚋 1, 2, 4, 5, 9, 13, 16, 17, 24, 25. M Centraal Station.

Built as an office complex in 1916, the Scheepvaarthuis (shipping house) is regarded as the first true example of Amsterdam School architecture *(see p142–3)*. It was designed by Piet Kramer (1881–1961), Johan van der May (1878–1949) and Michel de Klerk (1884–1923) for a group of shipping companies which no longer wanted to conduct business on the quay.

The imposing triangular building has a prow-like front and is crowned by a statue of Neptune, his wife and four female figures representing the four points of the compass.

The medieval Montelbaanstoren, with its decorative timber steeple

No expense was spared on the construction and internal decoration of the building, and local dock workers came to regard the building as a symbol of capitalism. The doors, stairs, window frames and interior walls are festooned with nautical images, such as sea horses, dolphins and anchors. Beautiful stained-glass skylights are also decorated with images of sailing ships, maps and compasses.

The Scheepvaarthuis is now a luxury hotel, the Grand Hôtel Amrâth *(see p392)*.

Schreierstoren ⑲

Prins Hendrikkade 94–95.
Map 2 E4. 🚊 *1, 2, 4, 5, 9, 11, 13, 16, 17, 24, 25.* Ⓜ *Centraal Station.*

The Schreierstoren (weepers' tower) was a defensive structure forming part of the medieval city walls, dating from 1480. It was one of the few fortifications not to be demolished as the city expanded beyond its medieval boundaries in the 17th century. The distinctive building now houses a basement café that offers tastings of genuine sailors' gin.

Popular legend states that the tower derived its name from the weeping (*schreien* in the original Dutch) of women who came here to wave their men off to sea. It is more likely, however, that the title has a less romantic origin and comes from the tower's position on a sharp (*screye* or *scherpe*), 90-degree bend in the old town walls. The earliest of four wall plaques, dated 1569, adds considerably to the confusion by depicting a weeping woman alongside the inscription *scrayer bovck*, which means sharp corner.

In 1609, Henry Hudson set sail from here in an attempt to discover a new and faster trading route to the East Indies. Instead, he unintentionally "discovered" the river in North America which still bears his name. A bronze plaque, laid in 1927, commemorates his voyage.

The Schreierstoren, part of the original city fortifications

Zeedijk ⑳

Map 2 E4. 🚊 *1, 2, 4, 5, 9, 13, 16, 17, 24, 25.* Ⓜ *Centraal Station.*

Along with the Nieuwendijk and the Haarlemmerdijk, the Zeedijk (sea dyke) formed part of Amsterdam's original fortifications. Built in the early 1300s, some 30 years after Amsterdam had been granted its city charter, these defences took the form of a canal moat with piled-earth ramparts reinforced by wooden palisades. As the city grew in prosperity and its boundaries expanded, canals were filled in and the dykes became obsolete. The paths that ran alongside them became the streets and alleys which bear their names today.

One of the two remaining wooden-fronted houses in the city is at No. 1. It was built in the mid-1500s as a hostel for sailors and is much restored. Opposite is St Olofskapel, built in 1445 and named after the first Christian king of Norway and Denmark. By the 1600s, the Zeedijk had become a slum. The area is on the edge of the city's Red Light District, and in the 1960s and 1970s it became notorious as a centre for drug-dealing and street crime. However, following an extensive clean-up campaign in the 1980s, the Zeedijk is much improved. Architect Fred Greves has built a Chinese Buddhist temple, Fo Kuang Shan.

Plaques on the gables of some of the street's cafés reveal their former use – the red boot at No. 17 indicates that it was once a cobbler's.

The Zeedijk, today a lively street with plenty of restaurants

NIEUWE ZIJDE

The western side of medieval Amsterdam was known as the Nieuwe Zijde (New Side). Together with the Oude Zijde it formed the heart of the early maritime settlement. Nieuwendijk, today a busy shopping street, was originally one of the earliest sea defences. As Amsterdam grew, it expanded eastwards, leaving large sections of the Nieuwe Zijde, to the west, neglected and in decline. With its many wooden houses, the city was prone to fires and in 1452 much of the area was burned down. During rebuilding, a broad moat, the Singel, was cut, along which warehouses, rich merchants' homes

"The calf" emblem on a house in the Begijnhof

and fine quays sprang up. The interesting Amsterdams Historisch Museum, which is now housed in a splendid former orphanage, has scores of maps and paintings charting the growth of the city from these times to the present day. One room is devoted to the Miracle of Amsterdam, which made the city a place of pilgrimage, and brought commerce to the Nieuwe Zijde. Nearby lies Kalverstraat, Amsterdam's main shopping street, and also the secluded Begijnhof. This pretty courtyard is mostly fringed by narrow 17th-century houses, but it also contains the city's oldest surviving wooden house.

SIGHTS AT A GLANCE

Historic Buildings, Monuments and Bridges
Beurs van Berlage ⑮
Centraal Station ⑫
Koninklijk Paleis pp88–9 ②
Magna Plaza ⑩
Nationaal Monument ④
Torensluis ⑨

Streets and Squares
Begijnhof ⑦
Nes ⑤

Churches
Lutherse Kerk ⑪
Nieuwe Kerk ①
St Nicolaaskerk ⑬

Museums
Allard Pierson Museum ⑧
Amsterdam Museum pp92–3 ⑥
Madame Tussauds Scenerama ③
Museum Ons' Lieve Heer op Solder ⑭

GETTING THERE
The Nieuwe Zijde is easily accessible by public transport. Most tram routes terminate at Centraal Station (1, 2, 4, 5, 9, 13, 16, 17, 24 and 25), as does the metro. Or take a tram (4, 9, 14, 16, 24 and 25) to the Dam. Or 1, 2, 5, 13 or 17 to Magna Plaza.

0 metres   250
0 yards   250

KEY

Street-by-Street map See pp84–5

Tram stop

M Metro station

Train station

Museum boat boarding point

◁ *The Fatal Fall of Icarus*, one of the many Classical sculptures in the Koninklijk Paleis

Street-by-Street: Nieuwe Zijde

Although much of the medieval Nieuwe Zijde has disappeared, the area is still rich in buildings that relate to the city's past. The Dam, dominated by the Koninklijk Paleis and Nieuwe Kerk, provides examples of architecture from the 15th to the 20th centuries. Around Kalverstraat, narrow streets and alleys follow the course of some of the earliest dykes and footpaths. Here, most of the traditional gabled houses have been turned into bustling shops and cafés. Streets such as Rokin and Nes are now home to financial institutions, attracted by the nearby stock and options exchanges. Nes is also well known for its venues which feature alternative theatre.

★ Amsterdam Museum
Wall plaques and maps showing the walled medieval city are on display in this converted orphanage that dates from the 16th century ❻

Kalverstraat
This busy tourist shopping area took its name from the livestock market which was regularly held here during the 15th century.

★ Begijnhof
Two churches and one of the few remaining wooden houses in the city nestle in this secluded, tree-filled courtyard ❼

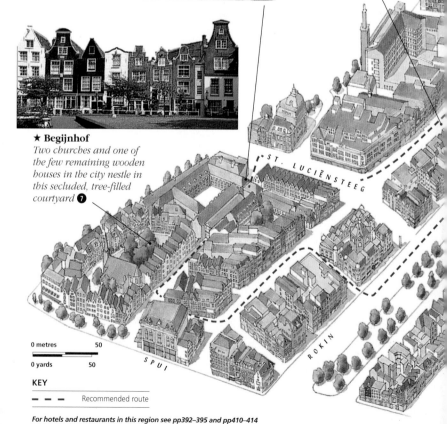

| 0 metres | 50 |
| 0 yards | 50 |

KEY

– – –   Recommended route

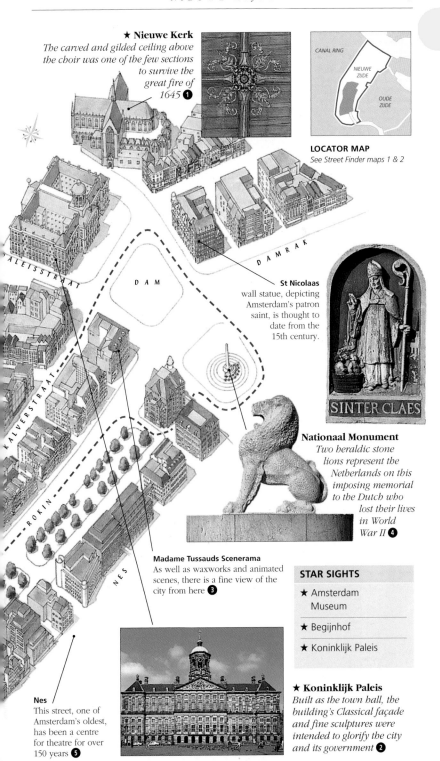

★ **Nieuwe Kerk**
The carved and gilded ceiling above the choir was one of the few sections to survive the great fire of 1645 ❶

LOCATOR MAP
See Street Finder maps 1 & 2

CANAL RING

NIEUWE ZIJDE

OUDE ZIJDE

PALEISSTRAAT

DAMRAK

D A M

KALVERSTRAAT

ROKIN

NES

St Nicolaas
wall statue, depicting Amsterdam's patron saint, is thought to date from the 15th century.

SINTER CLAES

Nationaal Monument
Two heraldic stone lions represent the Netherlands on this imposing memorial to the Dutch who lost their lives in World War II ❹

Madame Tussauds Scenerama
As well as waxworks and animated scenes, there is a fine view of the city from here ❸

STAR SIGHTS

★ Amsterdam Museum

★ Begijnhof

★ Koninklijk Paleis

Nes
This street, one of Amsterdam's oldest, has been a centre for theatre for over 150 years ❺

★ **Koninklijk Paleis**
Built as the town hall, the building's Classical façade and fine sculptures were intended to glorify the city and its government ❷

Nieuwe Kerk ❶

Dam. **Map** 1 C4. *Tel* 020-6386909.
📶 *1, 2, 4, 5, 9, 13, 14, 16, 17, 24,
25.* ⬜ *during exhibitions only (phone
to check).* 🌑 *30 Apr.* 📷 🅾 🅱 🖥
www.nieuwekerk.nl

Dating from the late 14th
century, Amsterdam's second
parish church was built
as the population outgrew
the Oude Kerk (*see pp76–7*).
During its turbulent history,
the church has been destroyed
several times by fire, rebuilt
and then stripped of its finery
after the Alteration. It reached
its present size in the 1650s.

The pulpit, not the altar, is
the focal point of the interior,
reflecting the Protestant belief
that the sermon is central to
worship. The carved central
pulpit, unusually flamboyant
for a Dutch Protestant church,
was finished in 1664 and took
Albert Vinckenbrink 15 years
to carve. Above the transept
crossing, grimacing gilded
cherubs struggle to support the
corners of the wooden barrel
vault. Magnificent three-tiered
brass candelabra were hung
from the ceilings of the nave
and transepts during restoration work following the fire
of 1645. The colourful arched
window in the south transept
was designed by Otto Mengel-
berg in 1898. It depicts Queen
Wilhelmina surrounded by
courtiers at her coronation. In
the apse is Rombout Verhulst's
memorial to Admiral De Ruyter
(1607–76), who died at sea in
battle against the French.

Stained-glass window, Nieuwe Kerk

Koninklijk Paleis ❷

See pp88–9.

Scene by Vermeer, in Madame Tussauds Scenerama

Madame Tussauds Scenerama ❸

Gebouw Peek & Cloppenburg, Dam 20.
Map 2 D5. *Tel* 020-5221010. 📶 *4,
9, 14, 16, 24, 25.* ⬜ *10am–5:30pm
daily (to 8:30pm Jul & Aug).*
🌑 *30 Apr.* 📷 🅾 🅱
www.madametussauds.com

Madame Tussauds offers an
audio-visual tour of Amsterdam's history, as well as pro-
jected future developments.
Some of the displays, such as
the animated 5-m (16-ft)
figure of "Amsterdam Man",
are bizarre, but the wax models of 17th-century people give
an insight into life in the city's
Golden Age. Current celebrities
and pop stars also feature.

Nationaal Monument ❹

Dam. **Map** 2 D5.
📶 *4, 9, 14, 16, 24, 25.*

Sculpted by John Raedecker
and designed by architect JJP
Oud, the 22-m (70-ft) obelisk

in the Dam commemorates
Dutch World War II casualties.
It was unveiled in 1956 and is
fronted by two lions, heraldic
symbols of the Netherlands.
Embedded in the wall behind
are urns containing earth
from all the Dutch provinces
as well as from the former
Dutch colonies of Indonesia,
the Antilles and Suriname.

Nes ❺

Map 2 D5. 📶 *4, 9, 14, 16, 24, 25.*

This quiet, narrow street is
home to several theatres.
In 1614, Amsterdam's first
pawnshop opened at Nes No.
57. A wall plaque marks the
site, and pawned goods
continue to clutter the shop
window. At night, Nes can
prove to be dangerous for
the unguarded visitor.

Amsterdam Museum ❻

See pp92–3.

Begijnhof ❼

Spui (but public entrance at Gedempte Begijnensloot).
Map 1 C5. 🚊 *1, 2, 5, 9, 14, 16, 24, 25.* ⬜ *9am–5pm daily.*

The Begijnhof was originally built in 1346 as a sanctuary for the Begijntjes, a lay Catholic sisterhood who lived like nuns, although they took no monastic vows. In return for lodgings, these women undertook to educate the poor and look after the sick. Nothing survives of the earliest dwellings, but the Begijnhof, cut off from traffic noise, retains a sanctified atmosphere. Among the houses that overlook its well-kept green is the city's oldest surviving house at No. 34. On the adjoining wall there is a fascinating collection of wall plaques taken from the houses. In keeping with the Begijntjes' religious outlook, the plaques have a biblical theme.

The southern fringe of the square is dominated by the Engelse Kerk (English Church), dating from the 15th century.

Directly west stands the Begijnhof Chapel, a clandestine church in which the Begijntjes and other Catholics worshipped in secret until religious tolerance was restored in 1795. Stained-glass windows and paintings depict scenes of the Miracle of Amsterdam. The occupants of the houses are trying to close public access to the Begijnhof, and public tours are not allowed.

Plaque on the Engelse Kerk

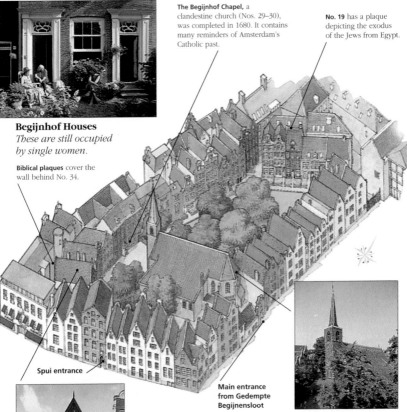

The Begijnhof Chapel, a clandestine church (Nos. 29–30), was completed in 1680. It contains many reminders of Amsterdam's Catholic past.

No. 19 has a plaque depicting the exodus of the Jews from Egypt.

Begijnhof Houses
These are still occupied by single women.

Biblical plaques cover the wall behind No. 34.

Spui entrance

Main entrance from Gedempte Begijnensloot

Houten House
No. 34 is Amsterdam's oldest house, dating from around 1420. It is one of the city's two wooden-fronted houses; timber houses were banned in 1521 after a series of catastrophic fires. Most of the Begijnhof houses were built after the 16th century.

Engelse Kerk
This church was built around 1419 for the Begijntjes. It was confiscated after the Alteration and rented to a group of English and Scottish Presbyterians in 1607. The Pilgrim Fathers may have worshipped here.

Koninklijk Paleis ❷

Formerly the town hall, the Koninklijk Paleis (Royal Palace) is still regularly used by the Dutch royal family on official occasions. Construction of the sandstone building began in 1648, at the end of the 80 Years War *(see p49)*. The Neo-Classical design of Jacob van Campen (1595–1657) reflected Amsterdam's new-found self-confidence after the victory against the Spanish. When not in use by members of the Royal House, the Paleis is open to the public.

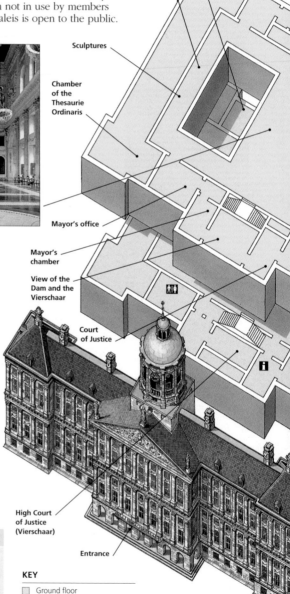

Chamber of the commissioners of small affairs

Courtyard

South gallery

Sculptures

Chamber of the Thesaurie Ordinaris

Mayor's office

Mayor's chamber

View of the Dam and the Vierschaar

Court of Justice

High Court of Justice (Vierschaar)

Entrance

★ **Burgerzaal**
The Burgerzaal (citizens' hall) has an inlaid marble floor depicting the two hemispheres (western and eastern).

★ **Sculptures**
The palace is decorated with a large number of sculptures of mainly allegorical figures.

STAR SIGHTS

★ Burgerzaal

★ Sculptures

★ Vroedschapszaal

KEY

☐ Ground floor

☐ First floor

Alderman's hall

Courtyard

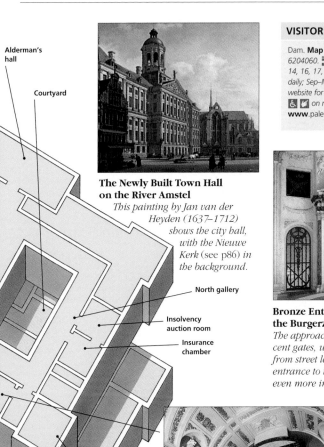

VISITORS' CHECKLIST

Dam. **Map** 1 C4. **Tel** 020-6204060. 🚉 1, 2, 4, 5, 9, 13, 14, 16, 17, 24, 25. ◯ Jul & Aug: daily; Sep–May: regularly, check website for details. 📷 🏠 📷 ♿ 📷 on request. 📷 www.paleisamsterdam.nl

The Newly Built Town Hall on the River Amstel
This painting by Jan van der Heyden (1637–1712) shows the city hall, with the Nieuwe Kerk (see p86) in the background.

North gallery

Insolvency auction room

Insurance chamber

Bronze Entrance Gates to the Burgerzaal
The approach to these magnificent gates, up a flight of stairs from street level, made the entrance to the Burgerzaal even more imposing.

Institution managing property of orphans

★ Vroedschapszaal
This hall, the Council Hall of the city fathers, has two fine fireplaces with mantelpieces by Govert Flinck and Han van Bronckhorst. The grisailles from 1738 are the work of Jacob de Wit.

TIMELINE

1648 Construction begins under Jacob van Campen	**1665** Building completed	**1720** Interior decoration completed	**1810** Complete refurbishment of the palace, with galleries divided up into rooms with wood partitions; the rooms are furnished in Empire style

1600	1700	1800	1900	2000
	1655 Ceremonial inauguration of the building	**1808** Louis Napoleon converts the town hall into a palace	**1960** Thorough restoration work throughout the 20th century undoes the building work of Louis Napoleon	**2002** Crown Prince Willem-Alexander kisses his bride, Maxima, on the palace balcony

Allard Pierson Museum **8**

Oude Turfmarkt 127. **Map** 5 A2.
Tel 020-5252556. 🚊 4, 9, 14,
16, 24, 25. ⏰ 10am–5pm
Tue–Fri, 1–5pm Sat, Sun & public
hols. 🚫 1 Jan, Easter Sun, 30 Apr,
Whitsun, 25 Dec. 🎫 📷 ♿ ✉
www.allardpiersonmuseum.nl

Amsterdam's only specialist
archaeological collection
is named after Allard Pierson
(1831–96), a humanist and
scholar. The collection was
moved into this handsome
Neo-Classical building in 1976.

The museum contains Cyp-
riot, Greek, Egyptian, Roman,
Etruscan and Coptic artifacts.

Torensluis **9**

Singel, between Torensteeg and Oude
Leliestraat. **Map** 1 C4. 🚊 1, 2, 5,
13, 14, 17.

The Torensluis is one of the
widest bridges in the city.
Built on the site of a 17th-
century sluice gate, it took its
name from a tower that stood
here until demolished in 1829.
Its outline is marked in the
pavement. A lock-up jail was
built in its foundations.

In summer, café tables on
the bridge offer pleasant
views down the Singel.

Allard Pierson Museum's Neo-Classical
façade of Bremer and Bentheimer stone

Magna Plaza **10**

Nieuwezijds Voorburgwal 182.
Map 1 C4. **Tel** 020-6269199. 🚊 1,
2, 5, 13, 14, 17. ⏰ noon–7pm Sun,
11am–7pm Mon, 10am–7pm Tue–
Sat. 🚫 public hols. See **Shopping**
p144. 📷 ♿ www.magnaplaza.nl

A post office building has
been sited here since 1748.
The present building was completed in 1899; CP Peters, the
architect, was ridiculed for the
extravagance of its Neo-Gothic
design. Redeveloped but well
preserved, in 1990 it opened as
the city's first shopping mall.

Lutherse Kerk **11**

Kattengat 2. **Map** 2 D3. **Tel** 020-
6212223. 🚊 1, 2, 5, 13, 17.

The Lutherse Kerk was
designed by Adriaan Dortsman
(1625–82) and opened in 1671.
It is the first Dutch Reformed
church to feature a circular
ground plan and two upper

galleries, giving the whole
congregation a clear view
of the pulpit.

In 1882 a fire destroyed
everything but the exterior
walls. When the interior
and entrance were rebuilt in
1883, they were made more
square and more ornate. A
vaulted copper dome replaced
the earlier ribbed version.
Falling attendance led to the
closure of the church in 1935.
The building is now used by
Renaissance Amsterdam Hotel
as a business centre. Concerts
are sometimes held here.

Centraal Station **12**

Stationsplein. **Map** 2 E3. **Tel** 0900-
9292. 🚊 1, 2, 4, 5, 9, 13, 16, 17,
24, 25. Ⓜ Centraal Station.
Information ℹ Inland and
international: 6:30am–9pm. 📷 ♿

When the Centraal Station
opened in 1889, it replaced
the old harbour as the
symbolic focal point of the
city and effectively curtained
Amsterdam off from the sea.
The Neo-Gothic red-brick
railway terminus was designed
by PJH Cuypers and AL van
Gendt. Three artificial islands
were created, 8,600 wooden
piles supporting the structure.
The twin towers and central
section have architectural

An outdoor café on the Torensluis bridge overlooking the Singel canal

For hotels and restaurants in this region see pp392–395 and pp410–414

echoes of a triumphal arch. The imposing façade's decorations show allegories of maritime trade, a tribute to the city's past. Although currently undergoing a major renovation until 2015, it still handles 250,000 train travellers daily.

Neo-Renaissance façade of the Sint-Nicolaaskerk

Sint-Nicolaaskerk ⑬

Prins Hendrikkade 73. **Map** 2 E4. *Tel* 020-6248749. 🚋 1, 2, 4, 5, 9, 13, 16, 17, 24, 25. Ⓜ *Centraal Station.* 🕐 *noon–3pm Mon & Sat, 11am–4pm Tue–Fri.* ✝ *12:30pm Mon–Sat, 10:30am & 1pm (Spanish) Sun.* 📷 www.nicolaasparochie.nl

Sint Nicolaas was the patron saint of seafarers, and so was an important icon in Amsterdam. Many Dutch churches are named after him, and the Netherlands' principal day for the giving of presents, 5 December, is known as Sinterklaasavond (*see p35*).

Completed in 1887, Sint-Nicolaaskerk was designed by AC Bleys (1842–1912). It replaced some clandestine Catholic churches set up in the city when Amsterdam was officially Protestant.

The exterior is forbidding, its twin towers dominating the skyline. The monumental interior has squared pillars and coffered ceiling arches.

Ons' Lieve Heer op Solder

Museum Ons' Lieve Heer op Solder ⑭

Oudezijds Voorburgwal 40. **Map** 2 E4. *Tel* 020-6246604. 🚋 4, 9, 16, 24, 25. 🕐 *10am–5pm Mon–Sat, 1–5pm Sun & public hols.* ⬤ *1 Jan, 30 Apr.* 📷📷📷📷

Tucked away on the edge of the Red Light District is a restored 17th-century canal house, with two smaller houses to the rear. The combined upper storeys conceal a secret Catholic church, known as Ons' Lieve Heer op Solder (Our Dear Lord in the Attic), built in 1663. Following the Alteration, when Amsterdam officially became Protestant,

many such hidden churches were built in the city.

The lower floors of the building became a museum in 1888 and today contain elegantly refurbished and decorated rooms, as well as a fine collection of church silver, religious artifacts and paintings.

Work due to be completed in 2012 will link the church to the house opposite, providing much-needed space for more exhibitions, a shop and a café. The museum will remain open during this work.

Beurs van Berlage ⑮

Damrak 243. **Map** 2 D4. *Tel (box office)* 020-5304141. 🚋 4, 9, 16, 24, 25. 🕐 *only during exhibitions.* ⬤ *1 Jan.* 📷📷📷📷 www.beursvanberlage.nl

The clean, functional appearance of Hendrik Berlage's 1903 stock exchange marked a departure from late 19th-century revivalist architecture. Many of its design features were adopted by the Amsterdam School. An impressive frieze shows the evolution of man from Adam to stockbroker. Now used for concerts and shows, it is home to the Nederlands Philharmonic Orchestra. The Beurs houses changing exhibitions.

Decorative brickwork on the façade of the Beurs van Berlage

Amsterdam Museum ❻

The convent of St Lucien was turned into a civic orphanage two years after the Alteration of 1578. The original red brick convent has been enlarged over the years; new wings were added in the 17th century by Hendrick de Keyser and Jacob van Campen. The present building is largely as it was in the 18th century. Since 1975 the complex has housed the city's historical museum, charting Amsterdam's development.

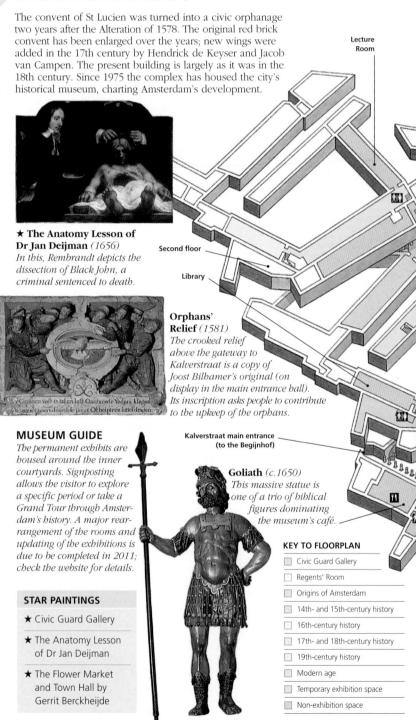

Lecture Room

★ **The Anatomy Lesson of Dr Jan Deijman** *(1656)*
In this, Rembrandt depicts the dissection of Black John, a criminal sentenced to death.

Second floor

Library

Orphans' Relief *(1581)*
The crooked relief above the gateway to Kalverstraat is a copy of Joost Bilhamer's original (on display in the main entrance hall). Its inscription asks people to contribute to the upkeep of the orphans.

MUSEUM GUIDE

The permanent exhibits are housed around the inner courtyards. Signposting allows the visitor to explore a specific period or take a Grand Tour through Amsterdam's history. A major rearrangement of the rooms and updating of the exhibitions is due to be completed in 2011; check the website for details.

Kalverstraat main entrance (to the Begijnhof)

Goliath *(c.1650)*
This massive statue is one of a trio of biblical figures dominating the museum's café.

STAR PAINTINGS

★ Civic Guard Gallery

★ The Anatomy Lesson of Dr Jan Deijman

★ The Flower Market and Town Hall by Gerrit Berckheijde

KEY TO FLOORPLAN

- ☐ Civic Guard Gallery
- ☐ Regents' Room
- ☐ Origins of Amsterdam
- ☐ 14th- and 15th-century history
- ☐ 16th-century history
- ☐ 17th- and 18th-century history
- ☐ 19th-century history
- ☐ Modern age
- ☐ Temporary exhibition space
- ☐ Non-exhibition space

For hotels and restaurants in this region see pp392–395 and pp410–414

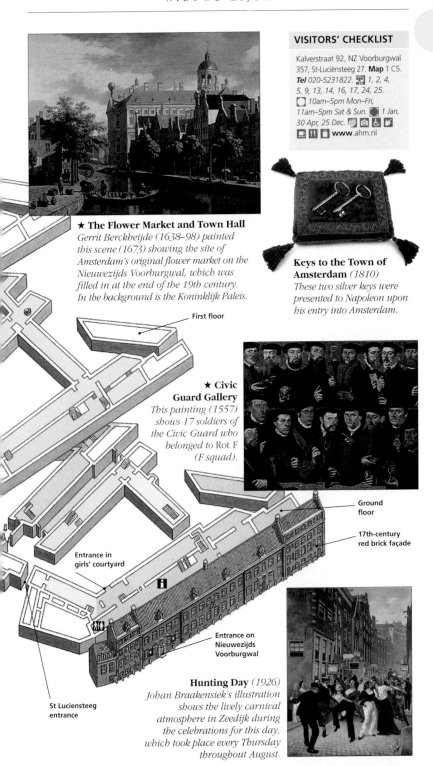

★ **The Flower Market and Town Hall**
*Gerrit Berckheijde (1638–98) painted
this scene (1673) showing the site of
Amsterdam's original flower market on the
Nieuwezijds Voorburgwal, which was
filled in at the end of the 19th century.
In the background is the Koninklijk Paleis.*

**Keys to the Town of
Amsterdam** *(1810)
These two silver keys were
presented to Napoleon upon
his entry into Amsterdam.*

First floor

★ **Civic
Guard Gallery**
*This painting (1557)
shows 17 soldiers of
the Civic Guard who
belonged to Rot F
(F squad).*

Ground
floor

17th-century
red brick façade

Entrance in
girls' courtyard

Entrance on
Nieuwezijds
Voorburgwal

St Luciensteeg
entrance

Hunting Day *(1926)
Johan Braakensiek's illustration
shows the lively carnival
atmosphere in Zeedijk during
the celebrations for this day,
which took place every Thursday
throughout August.*

GETTING THERE
It is a 15-minute walk from the Dam to Leidseplein, or take tram 1, 2 or 5; Nos. 7 and 10 also cross the square going east. It is a 5-minute walk from the Dam to the Jordaan. Trams 13, 14 and 17 go to Rozengracht; 3 and 10 to Haarlemmerpoort. Frederik-splein (Nos. 4, 7, 10) and Muntplein (Nos. 4, 9, 14, 16, 24, 25) are good starting points for exploring the eastern canal ring, a short walk from the Dam.

SIGHTS AT A GLANCE

◁ **Cyclist crossing a bridge on Leidsegracht**

CANAL RING

In the early 1600s, construction of the *Grachtengordel* (canal ring) began and the marshy area beyond these fashionable canals, later called Jordaan, was laid out for workers whose industries were prohibited in the centre. Immigrants fleeing religious persecution also settled here. Historically a poor area, it now has a bohemian air. As the major canals were extended, the merchant

Pillar decoration on the Felix Meritis Building

classes bought land along the Herengracht, Keizersgracht and Prinsengracht to escape the city's squalor. In the 1660s, the richest built houses on a stretch known today as the Golden Bend. The canal ring was also extended east to the Amstel. Houses here, like the Van Loon, convey a sense of life in the Golden Age. In 2010, the canal ring was declared a UNESCO World Heritage Site.

KEY

Street-by-Street map

Tram stop

Tourist information

Museum boat boarding point

0 metres 500

0 yards 500

A Guide to Canal House Architecture

Amsterdam has been called a city of "well-mannered" architecture because its charms lie in intimate details rather than in grand effects. From the 15th century on, planning laws, plot sizes and the instability of the topsoil dictated that façades were largely uniform in size and built of lightweight brick or sandstone, with large windows to reduce the weight. Canal house owners stamped their own individuality on the buildings, mainly through the use of decorative gables and cornices, ornate doorcases and varying window shapes.

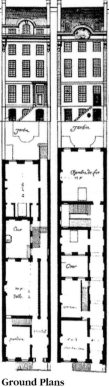

Ground Plans
Taxes were levied according to width of façade, so canal houses were often long and narrow, with an achterhuis (back annexe) used for offices and storage.

Broken pedi-ment and vase   "Broken handle" window surrounds

Bartolotti House *(1617)*
The contrasting brick and stone, flamboyant step gable, with its marble obelisk and scrolls, is typical of the Dutch Renaissance style of Hendrick de Keyser (see p110).

Pediment carvings symbolize

Felix Meritis Building *(1778)*
The Corinthian columns and triangular pediment are influenced by Classical architecture. This marks the building by Jacob Otten Husly as Dutch Classical in style.

CORNICES

Decorative top mouldings, called cornices, became popular from 1690 onwards when the fashion for gables declined. By the 19th century, they had become unadorned.

Louis XV-style with rococo balustrade (1739)

19th-century cornice with mansard roof

19th-century dentil (tooth-shaped) cornice

GABLES

The term "gable" refers to the front apex of a roof. It disguised the steepness of the roof under which goods were stored. In time, gables became decorated with scrolls, crests, and even with coats of arms.

Simple trian-gular gable

Warehouse-style spout gable

Dutch Renais-sance style

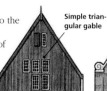

No. 34 Begijnhof (c.1420) is one of the few remaining timber houses.

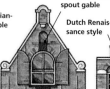

The style of gable on No. 213 Leliegracht (c.1620) was used for warehouses.

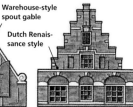

Step gables like the one on No. 2 Brouwervvsgracht were in vogue between 1600–65.

Leaning Façades
Canal houses were often built with a deliberate tilt, allowing goods to be winched up to the attic without crashing against the windows. A law dating from 1565 restricted this lean to 1:25, to limit the risk of buildings collapsing into the streets.

GOLDEN BEND

The stretch of the Herengracht between Leidenstraat and Vijzelstraat was first called the Golden Bend in the 17th century, because of the great wealth of the ship-builders, merchants and politicians who originally lived here. The majority of the buildings along this stretch are faced with imported sandstone, which was more expensive than brick. An excellent example is house No. 412, which was designed by Philips Vingboons in 1664. He was also responsible for the design of the Witte Huis at Herengracht No. 168 as well as Bijbels Museum at Herengracht 366. Building continued into the 18th century, with the Louis XIV style predominating. The house at No. 475, with its ornate window decoration, is typical of this trend. Built in 1730, it is often called the jewel of canal houses. Two sculpted female figures over the front door adorn its monumental sandstone façade.

Ground plan and façade of the building at Herengracht 168

Dutch *Hofjes*
Almshouses (hofjes) *were built throughout the Netherlands by rich benefactors in the 17th and 18th centuries. By providing accommodation for the elderly and infirm, the* hofjes *marked the beginning of the Dutch welfare system.*

Sign of a sailors' hostel

Noah's Ark – a refuge for the poor

Symbol of a dairy producer

WALL PLAQUES

Carved and painted stones were used to identify houses before street numbering was introduced in the 19th century. Many reflect the owner's occupation.

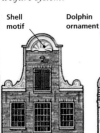

Shell motif

Dolphin ornament

Unadorned bell gable

Stonework with cornucopia decoration

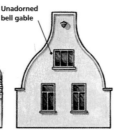

No. 419 Singel has a neck gable, a common feature from 1640 to around 1840.

No. 119 Oudezijds Voorburgwal has an ornate 17th-century neck gable.

No. 57 Leliegracht has a plain bell gable, popular from the late 17th century.

No. 298 Oudezijds Voorburgwal has a bell gable dating from the 18th century.

Dam Square to Herengracht 487

The walk along Amsterdam's finest canals begins in Dam square *(see pp84–5)*. Following the grey dots on the map, leave the square past the Koninklijk Paleis *(see pp88–9)*, cross Nieuwezijds Voorburgwal and Spuistraat down Paleisstraat, and turn left along the left bank of Singel, marked by purple dots. Further directions are incorporated into the route below.

LOCATOR MAP

SINGEL ●●●

No. 239 Singel
AL Van Gendt designed this massive stone office block for trader Julius Carle Bunge. Known as the Bungehuis, it was completed in 1934.

The double-fronted 17th-century canal house at No. 265 Singel has been rebuilt several times since it was first constructed.

The step gable at No. 279 Singel dates from the 19th century – most along this canal were built between 1600–65.

The three neck gables on Nos. 353–7 Keizersgracht date from the early 18th century.

Huidenstraat

No. 345a Keizersgracht is a narrow house sharing a cornice with its neighbour.

In 1708, No. 333 Keizersgracht was rebuilt for tax collector Jacob de Wilde. It has been converted into apartments.

The Sower at Arles *(1888)*
In March 1878, Vincent van Gogh (see pp126–7) visited his uncle, who ran a book-shop and art dealership at No. 453 Keizersgracht.

Nos. 289–293 Singel
These houses stand on an alley once called Schoorsteenvegersteeg (chimney sweeps' lane), home to immigrant chimney sweeps.

Yab Yum Brothel
This famous former brothel with its opulent interior was located at No. 295 Singel.

No. 365 Keizersgracht
The doorway was taken from an almshouse on Oudezijds Voorburgwal in the 19th century.

Jacob de Wit
The artist (see p115) bought Nos. 383 and 385 Keizersgracht, living in No. 385 until his death in 1754.

Metz & Co is an elegant department store located at No. 34–6 Leidsestraat on the corner with Keizersgracht.

Gerrit Rietveld
Rietveld designed the glass cupola on Metz & Co, and a line of plain, inexpensive furniture for the store.

De Vergulde Ster
(gilded star), at No. 387 Keizersgracht, was built in 1668 by the municipal stone-masons' yard. It has an elongated neck gable *(see pp96–7)* and narrow windows

DIRECTIONS TO HERENGRACHT

Turn left on to Leidse-straat, and walk to Koningsplein, then take the left bank of the Herengracht eastwards towards Thorbeckeplein.

HERENGRACHT

Keizersgracht

This photograph of the "emperor's canal" is taken at dusk, from the corner of Leidsegracht. The Westerkerk (see p110) is in the distance.

Behind the 18th-century façade at No. 319 Singel is a second-hand bookshop, which is well worth browsing through.

DIRECTIONS TO KEIZERSGRACHT

At Raamsteeg, cross the bridge, take the Oude Spiegelstraat, cross Herengracht and walk along Wolvenstraat to the left bank of Keizersgracht.

KEIZERSGRACHT

No. 399 Keizersgracht dates from 1665, but the façade was rebuilt in the 18th century. Its *achterhuis (see p96)* has been perfectly preserved.

No. 409 Keizersgracht
Built in 1671 on a triangular piece of land, this house contains a highly decorated wooden ceiling.

The wall plaque on No. 401 Keizersgracht shows a bird's-eye view of the port of Marseilles.

The plain, spout-gable building *(see pp96–7)* No. 403 Keizersgracht originally a warehouse rarity in this predomin residential area.

No. 469 Herengracht
The modern office block by KL Sijmons replaced the original 18th-century houses in 1971.

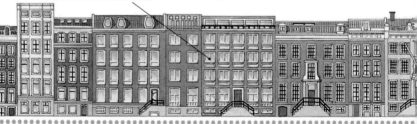

The unusual office block at No. 313 Keizersgracht was built in 1914 by CN van Goor.

No. 319 Keizersgracht
was built by the architect Philips Vingboons (1608–78) in 1639. It has a rare, highly decorated façade covered with scrolls, vases and garlands.

Peter the Great (1716)
The Russian tsar sailed up Keizersgracht to No. 317, the home of his friend Christoffel Brants. Legend says the tsar got drunk and kept the mayor waiting while at a civic reception.

The Louis XIV-style house at No. 323 Keizersgracht was built in 1728. It has a raised cornice embellished with two hoisting beams, one functional and the other to provide symmetry.

Leidsegracht
This canal marked the end of Daniel Stalpaert's city expansion plan of 1664. It has a mixture of fine 17th- and 18th-century canal houses.

No. 475 Herengracht
Art patron Jan Gildemester bought this house in 1792. Attributed to Jacob Otten Husly, it has a stuccoed entrance hall.

Jan Corver
Burgomaster of Amsterdam 19 times, Corver built No. 479 Herengracht in 1665.

Turn over to continue walk at top of page 102

Herengracht 489 to the Amstel

The second half of the walk takes you along Herengracht, winding past grand, wide-fronted mansions. It then follows Reguliersgracht and Prinsengracht down to the Amstel. Many of the fine houses have been converted into banks, offices and exclusive apartment blocks.

LOCATOR MAP

HERENGRACHT

The house at No. 491 Herengracht was built in 1671. The façade, rebuilt in the 18th century, is decorated with scrolls, vases and coats of arms.

No. 493 Herengracht
This 17th-century house was given a Louis XV-style façade in 1767 by Anthony van Hemert.

The Kattenkabinet at No. 497 Herengracht was created by financier B Meijer in 1984. It is devoted to exhibits featuring the cat in art.

DIRECTIONS TO REGULIERSGRACHT

At Thorbeckeplein, take the bridge to the right, which marks the beginning of Reguliersgracht. Follow the left bank.

REGULIERSGRACHT

Amstelveld in the 17th Century
This etching shows the construction of a wooden church at Amstelveld, with sheep grazing in front of it.

Restaurant Nel
The Amstelkerk (Amstel Church) now houses a restaurant and offices, while the square is a popular playground for children from the surrounding area.

DIRECTIONS TO PRINSENGRACHT

Turn left by the church, take the left bank of Prinsengracht and walk to the Amstel river.

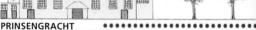

PRINSENGRACHT

Jan Six II

The façade of No. 495 Herengracht was rebuilt and a balcony added by Jean Coulon in 1739 for burgomaster and art expert Jan Six.

Riots in 1696

No. 507 Herengracht was the home of mayor Jacob Boreel. His house was looted in retaliation for the burial tax he introduced into the city.

Vijzelstraat

Three houses boasting typical neck gables, at Nos. 17, 19 and 21 Reguliersgracht, are now much sought after as prestigious addresses.

The Nieuwe Amsterdammer

A weekly magazine aimed at Amsterdam's Bolshevik intelligentsia was published at No. 19 Reguliersgracht from 1914–20.

The spout-gabled *(see pp96–7)* 16th-century warehouses at Nos. 11 and 13 Reguliersgracht are called the Sun and the Moon.

Café Marcella, at No. 1047a Prinsengracht, is a typical local bar which has seating outside in summer.

Houseboats on Prinsengracht

All registered houseboats have postal addresses and are connected to the electricity mains.

Utrechtsestraat

Tsar Peter (*see p101*) stayed at No. 527 Herengracht, home of the Russian ambassador, after a night of drunken revelry at No. 317 Keizersgracht in 1716.

Herengracht (*1790*)
A delicate watercolour by JPrins shows the "gentlemen's canal" from Koningsplein.

The asymmetrical building at Nos. 533–7 Herengracht was built in 1910 on the site of four former houses. From 1968–88 it was the Registry of Births, Marriages and Deaths.

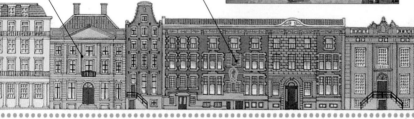

The façades of Nos. 37 and 39 Reguliersgracht lean towards the water, showing the danger caused by subsidence when building on marshland.

Reguliersgracht Bridges
Seven arched stone bridges cross the canal, which was originally designed to be a street.

Keizersgracht

Nos. 1059 and 1061 Prinsengracht have tiny basement entrances, rare amid the splendour of the Canal Ring, where the height of the steps was considered an indication of wealth.

The sober spout-gabled building at No. 1075 Prinsengracht was built as a warehouse in 1690.

My Domestic Companions
Society portraitist Thérèse van Duyl Schwartze painted this picture in 1916. She owned Nos. 1087, 1089 and 1091 Prinsengracht, a handsome row of houses where she lived with her extended family.

Herengracht *(c.1670)*
GA Berckheijde's etching shows one side of the canal bare of trees. Elms were later planted, binding the topsoil, to strengthen the buildings' foundations.

No. 543 Herengracht was built in 1743 under the supervision of owner Sibout Bollard. It has a double-fronted façade with an ornate balustrade and decorated balcony.

The small houses at the corner of Herengracht and Thorbeckeplein contrast with the grand neighbouring buildings.

Isaac Gosschalk
The architect designed Nos. 57, 59 and 63 Reguliers-gracht in 1879. They have ornate stone, brick and wood-work façades.

Reguliers Monastery
This engraving by J Wagenaar (1760) shows the monastery that once stood on the canal.

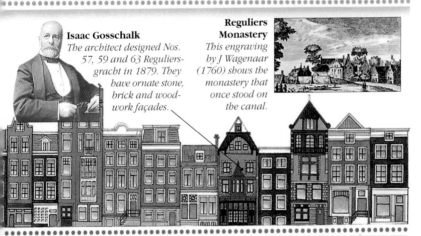

The Amstel
Turn left and follow the broad sweep of the Amstel river, up past the Magere Brug on up Rokin and back to the Dam, where the walk began.

Street-by-Street: Around the Jordaan

West of the *Grachtengordel*, the Jordaan still retains a network of narrow, characterful streets and delightful canals. Among the 17th-century workers' houses are dozens of quirky shops, which are well worth a browse, selling anything from designer clothes to old sinks, and lively brown cafés and bars, which spill onto the pavements in summer. A stroll along the *Grachtengordel* provides a glimpse into some of the city's grandest canal houses, including the Bartolotti House.

Egelantiersgracht is a charming tree-lined Jordaan canal overlooked by an interesting mixture of old and new architecture. Its numerous bridges provide pretty views.

The quiet Bloemgracht canal was once a centre for makers of paint and dye.

EGELANTIERSGRACHT

PRINSENGRACHT

BLOEMGRACHT

★ Westerkerk
Hendrick de Keyser's church is the site of Rembrandt's unmarked grave and was the setting for the wedding of Queen Beatrix and Prince Claus in 1966 ❸

★ Anne Frank Huis
For two years, the Frank family and four others lived in a small upstairs apartment that was hidden behind a revolving bookcase (see pp108–9) ❶

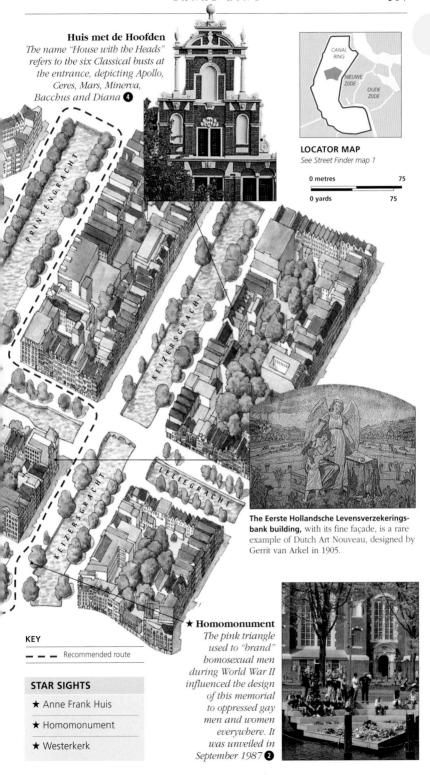

Huis met de Hoofden
*The name "House with the Heads"
refers to the six Classical busts at
the entrance, depicting Apollo,
Ceres, Mars, Minerva,
Bacchus and Diana* ❹

LOCATOR MAP
See Street Finder map 1

0 metres	75
0 yards	75

**The Eerste Hollandsche Levensverzekerings-
bank building,** with its fine façade, is a rare
example of Dutch Art Nouveau, designed by
Gerrit van Arkel in 1905.

★ Homomonument
*The pink triangle
used to "brand"
homosexual men
during World War II
influenced the design
of this memorial
to oppressed gay
men and women
everywhere. It
was unveiled in
September 1987* ❷

KEY

– – – Recommended route

STAR SIGHTS

★ Anne Frank Huis

★ Homomonument

★ Westerkerk

Anne Frank Huis ❶

Star of David

On 6 July 1942, to avoid their Nazi persecutors, the Jewish Frank family moved from Merwedeplein to the rear annexe of the house at Prinsengracht 263. Anne; her mother, Edith; her father, Otto; and her older sister, Margot, lived here, along with the Van Pels family and dentist Fritz Pfeffer. It was here that Anne wrote her famous diary. On 4 August 1944, the annexe was raided by the Gestapo. All those hiding here were arrested and taken to Nazi concentration camps.

The Secret Entrance
Behind the hinged bookcase was a small suite of rooms where the eight hideaways lived.

Anne in May 1942
This photograph was taken in 1942, when Anne started writing in the now-famous diary that she had been given on 12 June 1942, her 13th birthday. Less than one month later, the Frank family went into hiding.

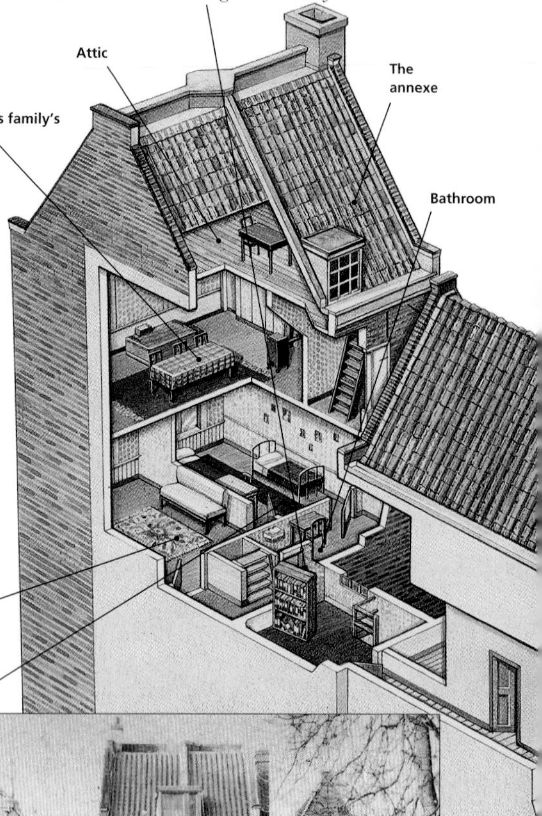

Attic

Van Pels family's room

The annexe

Bathroom

Frank family bedroom

Anne's bedroom

View of the Annexe
The rear annexe of the house adjoined the main building, which housed the offices of Otto Frank's herb and spice business.

Anne and Fritz Pfeffer's Bedroom
Anne and Fritz slept on the first floor of the annexe. On Anne's bedroom walls were photos of film stars, which she collected. Anne wrote most of her diary at the table here.

VISITORS' CHECKLIST

Prinsengracht 267. **Map** 1 B4. *Tel* 020-5567105. 13, 14, 17. 21. 15 Mar–14 Sep: 9am–9pm daily; 15 Sep–14 Mar: 9am–7pm daily. *Yom Kippur.* book ahead to avoid queues. www.annefrank.org

The Helpers
The people in hiding were wholly dependent on their helpers, all of whom were close colleagues of Anne's father, Otto Frank. From left to right: Miep Gies, Johannes Kleiman, Otto Frank, Victor Kugler and Bep Voskuijl.

Façade of Prinsengracht 263

Main building housing offices

MUSEUM GUIDE
The rear annexe is accessible via the reconstructed offices of Otto Frank. The building beside Anne Frank Huis holds various exhibitions. It also houses a café, shop and information desk.

THE DIARY OF ANNE FRANK

Otto Frank returned to Amsterdam in 1945 to discover that his entire family had perished: his wife, Edith, in Auschwitz and his daughters, Anne and Margot, in Bergen-Belsen. Miep Gies, one of the family's helpers while they were in hiding, had kept Anne's diary. First published in 1947, it has since been translated into 55 languages, with some 20 million copies sold. For many, Anne symbolizes the six million Jews murdered by the Nazis in World War II. The diary is a moving portrait of a little girl growing up in times of oppression.

School children visiting the Homomonument

Homomonument ➋

Westermarkt (between Westerkerk and Keizersgracht). **Map** 1 B4.
🚊 13, 14, 17. 🚤 Prinsengracht & Keizersgracht. **www**.
homomonument.nl

This monument to the homosexual men and women who lost their lives during World War II provides a quiet place of contemplation amid the bustle of the Westermarkt. The pink triangular badge that gay men were forced to wear in Nazi concentration camps later became a symbol of gay pride, and provided the inspiration for Karin Daan's 1987 design. The monument consists of three large pink granite triangles, one of which bears an engraving from a poem by Jacob Israël

de Haan (1881–1924). On Remembrance Day (4 May), hundreds of gay men and women from all over the Netherlands join delegates from the city council, police, the military and social organisations to lay wreaths and flowers.

Westerkerk ➌

Prinsengracht 281. **Map** 1 B4.
Tel 020-6247766. 🚊 13, 14, 17.
⬜ Apr–Sep: 11am–3pm Mon–Fri.
📷 **Tower** 🚫 🕐 Apr–Sep: hourly 10am–6pm Mon–Sat (to 8pm Jul & Aug); Oct–Nov: hourly 11am–4pm Mon–Sat. Phone 020-6892565 to book. ⬛ Dec–Mar.

Built as part of the development of the Canal Ring, this church has the tallest tower in the city at 85 m (279 ft), and

the largest nave of any Dutch Protestant church. It was designed by Hendrick de Keyser, who died in 1621, a year after work began. Rembrandt was buried here but his grave has never been found. The organ shutters (1686) were painted by Gerard de Lairesse, with lively scenes showing King David and the Queen of Sheba. The tower carries the crown bestowed on Amsterdam in 1489 by Maximilian, the Hapsburg emperor. The stunning views justify the climb.

Huis met de Hoofden ➍

Keizersgracht 123. **Map** 1 C4.
🚊 13, 14, 17. 🚫 to the public.

Built in 1622, the Huis met de Hoofden (house with the heads) is one of the largest double houses of the period. It has a fine step gable and takes its name from the six heads placed on pilasters along the façade. Legend has it that they commemorate a housemaid who, when alone in the house, surprised six burglars and cut off their heads. The sculptures are in fact portrayals of six Classical deities (from left to right):

The Westerkerk in the 18th century, a view by Jan Ekels

For hotels and restaurants in this region see pp392–395 and pp410–414

Apollo, Ceres, Mars, Minerva, Bacchus and Diana. The design of the building is sometimes attributed to Pieter de Keyser (1595–1676), son of Hendrick de Keyser. The Huis met de Hoofden has been bought by JR Ritman, owner of the Bibliotheca Philosophica Hermetica. This library of books on alchemy and mysticism will move during 2011.

Stone plaque on the *hofje* founded in 1616 by the merchant Anslo

Noorderkerk and Noordermarkt **5**

Noordermarkt 44–48. **Map** 1 C3. **Tel** *020-6266436.* 🚊 *3, 10, 13, 14, 17.* ⏰ *10:30am–12:30pm Mon, 11am–1pm Sat.* ⛪ *10am & 7pm Sun.* **General market** ⏰ *9am–1pm Mon;* **Boerenmarkt** ⏰ *9am–5pm Sat.*

Built for poor settlers in the Jordaan, the North Church was the first in Amsterdam to be constructed in the shape of a Greek cross. Its layout around a central pulpit allowed the congregation seated in the encircling pews to see and hear well.

The church, designed by Hendrick de Keyser, was completed in 1623, in time to hold its inaugural service at Easter. It is still well attended by a Calvinist congregation. By the entrance is a sculpture of three bound figures, inscribed: "Unity is Strength". It commemorates the Jordaan Riot of 1934. On the south façade, a plaque recalls the 1941 February Strike, protesting the Nazis' deportation of Jews.

Since 1627, the square that surrounds the Noorderkerk has been a market site. At that time, it sold pots and pans and *vodden* (old clothes), a tradition that continues today with a flea market. Since the 18th century, the area has been a centre for bed shops. Bedding, curtains and fabrics are still sold on Monday morning along the Westerstraat; you can buy anything from net curtain material to buttons. On Saturday mornings, the *vogeltjes* (small birds) market sells chickens, pigeons, small birds and rabbits. At 10am, the *boerenmarkt* takes over, selling health foods, ethnic crafts and candles.

Haarlemmer-poort **6**

Haarlemmerplein 50. **Map** 1 B1. 🚊 *3.* ⛔ *to the public.*

Originally a defended gateway into Amsterdam, the Haarlemmerpoort marked the beginning of the busy route to Haarlem. The present gateway, dating from 1840, was built for King William II's triumphal entry into the city and named Willemspoort. However, as the third gateway to be built on or close to this site, it is still called the Haarlemmerpoort by Amsterdammers.

Designed by Cornelis Alewijn (1788–1839), the Neo-Classical gatehouse was used as tax offices in the 19th century and was made into flats in 1986. Traffic no longer goes through the gate, since a bridge has been built over the adjoining Westerkanaal.

Brouwersgracht **7**

Map 1 B2. 🚊 *3.*

Brouwersgracht (brewers' canal) was named after the breweries established here in the 17th and 18th centuries. Leather, spices, coffee and sugar were also processed and stored here. Today, most of the warehouses, with their spout gables and shutters, are residences that look out on moored houseboats.

Western Islands **8**

Map 1 C1. 🚊 *3.*

This district comprises three islands built on the IJ in the early 1600s to quarter warehouses and shipyards. Some of these are still in use and many period houses have survived.

Merchant and developer Jan Bicker bought Bickerseiland in 1631. Today, the island is a mix of colourful apartment blocks and a jumble of houseboats.

Realeneiland has the pretty waterside street of Zandhoek. A row of 17th-century houses built by the island's founder, Jacobsz Reaal, overlooks the moored sailboats.

Prinseneiland is dominated by characterful warehouses, many now apartments.

DUTCH HOFJES

Before the Alteration, the Catholic Church often provided subsidized housing for the poor and elderly, particularly women. During the 17th and 18th centuries, rich merchants and Protestant organizations took on this charitable role and built hundreds of almshouse complexes, which were planned around courtyards and known as *hofjes*. Behind their street façades lie pretty houses and serene gardens. Visitors are admitted to some but asked to respect the residents' privacy. Many *hofjes* are found in the Jordaan and some still serve their original purpose.

The "house with the writing hand" (c.1630) in Claes Claeszhofje

De Melkweg's star-lit façade

Leidseplein ➒

Map 4 E2. 🚊 *1, 2, 5, 7, 10.*

Amsterdam's liveliest square, Leidseplein is also a busy tram intersection and centre of night-time transport.

The square developed in the 17th century as a wagon park on the outskirts of the city – farmers and peasants would leave their carts here before entering the centre. It takes its name from the Leidsepoort, the massive city gate demolished in 1862, which marked the beginning of the route out to Leiden.

During the day, the square is buzzing with fire-eaters, buskers and other street performers playing to café audiences. It is also popular with pickpockets. At night, it is the focal point for the city's youth, who hang out in the many bars, cafés, restaurants, nightclubs and cinemas in and around the square.

American Hotel ➓

Leidsekade 97. **Map** 4 E2.
Tel 020-5563000. 🚊 *1, 2, 5, 7, 10.*
🍴 🖥

Leidseplein was fast becoming a fashionable entertainment area when the American Hotel was built overlooking it in 1882. The hotel got its name because its architect, W Steinigeweg, studied hotel design in the United States, and adorned his Neo-Gothic creation with a bronze eagle, wooden figures of native Indians and murals of American landscapes. Within 20 years it was deemed *passé* and the hotel was demolished. The present building is by Willem Kromhout (1864–1940) and was completed in 1902.

His design marked a radical departure, interpreting the Art Nouveau style in an angular Dutch fashion. The building's turreted exterior and elaborate brickwork anticipated the progressive Amsterdam School *(see pp142–3).*

The Art Deco-style Café Americain is one of the most elegant in Amsterdam. It retains its period furnishings and stained-glass windows. The rest of the hotel was redecorated in the 1980s. Samples of the original furnishings are in the Rijksmuseum *(see pp122–5).*

Stadsschouwburg ⓫

Leidseplein 26. **Map** 4 E2. *Tel 020-6242311.* 🚊 *1, 2, 5, 6, 7, 10.* **Box office** ⏱ *10am–6pm Mon–Sat. See* **Entertainment** *p428.* 📷 🚫 ♿ **www.**stadsschouwburgamsterdam.nl

This Neo-Renaissance building is the most recent of the city's three successive municipal theatres, its predecessors having burned down. The theatre was designed by Jan Springer and AL van Gendt, who was responsible for the Concertgebouw *(see p120)* and for part of the Central Station *(see p90).* The planned ornamentation of the theatre's redbrick exterior was never carried out because of budget cuts. This, combined with a hostile public reaction to his theatre, forced a disillusioned Springer into virtual retirement. Public disgust was due, however, to the management's policy of restricting use of the front door to patrons who had bought expensive tickets.

The former home of the Dutch national ballet and opera companies, the theatre today stages plays by local drama groups such as the resident Toneelgroep, as well as international companies, including many English-language productions. A new auditorium opened in 2009.

The American Hotel seen from Singelgracht

De Krijtberg **⑫**

Singel 448. **Map** 4 F1. **Tel** 020-6231923. 🚊 1, 2, 5. ◯ 1:30–5pm Tue–Thu & Sun. ⬆ 12:30pm, 5:45pm Mon–Fri, 12:30pm, 5:15pm Sat, 9:30am, 11am, 12:30pm, 5:15pm Sun. ♿ www.krijtberg.nl

An impressive Neo-Gothic church, the Krijtberg (or chalk hill) replaced a clandestine Jesuit chapel in 1884. It is officially known as Franciscus Xaveriuskerk, after St Francis Xavier, one of the founding Jesuit monks.

Designed by Alfred Tepe, the church was built on the site of three houses; the presbytery beside the church is on the site of two other houses, one of which had belonged to a chalk merchant – hence the church's nickname. The back of the church is wider than the front, extending into the space once occupied by the original gardens. The narrowness of the façade is redeemed by its two magnificent, soaring, steepled towers.

The ornate interior of the building contains some good examples of Neo-Gothic design. The stained-glass windows, walls painted in bright colours and liberal use of gold are in striking contrast to the city's austere Protestant churches. A statue of St Francis Xavier stands in front and to the left of the high altar; one of St Ignatius, founder of the Jesuits, stands to the right.

Near the pulpit is an 18th-century wooden statue of the Immaculate Conception, which shows Mary trampling the serpent. It used to be housed in the original hidden chapel.

Bijbels Museum **⑬**

Herengracht 366–368. **Map** 4 E1. **Tel** 020-624-2436. 🚊 1, 2, 5. 🚊 Herengracht/Leidsegracht. ◯ 10am–5pm Mon–Sat, 11am–5pm Sun & public hols. ● 1 Jan, 30 Apr. 📷 📷 ♿ www.bijbelsmuseum.nl

Reverend Leendert Schouten founded the Bible museum in 1860, when he put his private artifact collection on public display. In 1975, the museum moved to its present site, two 17th-century houses designed by Philips Vingboons. Highlights are a copy of the Book of Isaiah from the Dead Sea Scrolls and the Delft Bible (1477).

Looier Kunst en Antiekcentrum **⑭**

Elandsgracht 109. **Map** 4 D1. **Tel** 020-6249038. 🚊 7, 10, 13, 14, 17. ◯ 11am–5pm Sat–Thu. ● public hols. 📷 ♿ www.looier.nl

The Looier antiques centre is a vast network of rooms in a block of houses near the canal. Its 100 stalls sell everything from glassware to dolls.

Grand façade of the Stadsarchief

Stadsarchief Amsterdam **⑮**

Vijzelstraat 32. **Map** 4 F2. **Tel** 020-572 0202. 🚊 16, 24, 25. ◯ 10am–5pm Tue–Fri, 11am–5pm Sat & Sun. ● Mon & public holidays. ♿ 📷 (with permission). **www.** stadsarchief.amsterdam.nl

The Stadsarchief, the city's municipal archives, moved from its former location in Amsteldijk to this monumental building. Designed by KPC de Bazel, one of the principal representatives of the Amsterdam school of architecture, the edifice was completed in 1926 for the Netherlands Trading Company. In spite of much renovation work at the end of World War II and in the 1970s, the building retains many attractive original features, such as colourful floor mosaics (designed by de Bazel himself). There is a permanent display of treasures from the archives in the monumental vaults.

ON THE CANALS

Though Amsterdam's canals were built for moving goods, today they provide a marvellous means of viewing the city's sights and its everyday life. There are many operators in the city offering canal tours with foreign-language commentaries; boats depart from an embarkation point, mainly from opposite Centraal Station, along Prins Hendrikkade, the Damrak and along the Rokin. Other canal-sightseeing options include the popular canalbus and the Museum Boat. The former runs along three routes, with 14 stops near the major museums, shopping areas and other attractions, while the Museum Boat takes in and stops near all the major city sights. If you feel energetic, try a canal bike, which is usually a two- or four-seater pedal-boat that can be picked up and left at any of the canal-bike moorings in the city centre.

Rembrandtplein ⓰

Map 5 A2. 🚊 4, 9, 14.

Formerly called the Botermarkt, after the butter market held here until the mid-19th century, this square acquired its present name when the statue of Rembrandt was erected in 1876.

Soon afterwards, Rembrandtplein developed into a centre for nightlife with the opening of various hotels and cafés. The Mast (renamed the Mille Colonnes Hotel) dates from 1889, and the Schiller Karena hotel and the Café Schiller both opened in 1892. De Kroon, which epitomizes a typical grand café, dates from 1898. The popularity of Rembrandtplein has endured, and the café terraces are packed during summer with people enjoying a pleasant drink and watching the world go by.

Museum Willet-Holthuysen ⓱

Herengracht 605. **Map** 5 A2. *Tel* 020-5231822. 🚊 4, 9, 14. 🕐 10am–5pm Mon–Fri, 11am–5pm Sat & Sun. ⬤ 1 Jan, 30 Apr, 25 Dec. ⬤ 📷
📱 📷 www.willetholthuysen.nl

Named after the building's last residents, the museum now housed here allows visitors a glimpse into the lives of the merchant class who lived in luxury along the Grachtengordel (Canal Ring). The house was built in 1685 and became the property of coal magnate Pieter Holthuysen (1788–1858) in 1855.

Two of the many outdoor cafés on Rembrandtplein

It passed to his daughter Louisa and her art-connoisseur husband, Abraham Willet – both fervent collectors of paintings, glass, silver and ceramics. When Louisa died childless in 1895, the house and its many treasures were left to the city. Room by room, the house is gradually being restored to appear as it did during the time when Abraham and Louisa lived here.

The Blue Room, hung with heavy blue damask and boasting a chimney piece by Jacob de Wit, was the exclusive preserve of the men of the house.

The wallpaper in the dining room today is a careful copy of the 18th-century silk original. The elaborate 275-piece Meissen dinner service provided up to 24 places.

The 18th-century kitchen has been restored using items salvaged from similar houses, including the sink and pump.

On the second floor is a full-length portrait of Willet.

Interior of Willet-Holthuysen

Magere Brug ⓲

Amstel. **Map** 5 B3. 🚊 4.

Of Amsterdam's 1,400 or so bridges, Magere Brug (skinny bridge) is the best-known. The original drawbridge was built in about 1670. According to legend, it was named after two sisters called Mager, who lived either side of the Amstel. It is more likely that the name comes from its narrow *(mager)* design.

Magere Brug, a traditional double-leaf Dutch drawbridge

The present drawbridge was put up in 1969 and, though wider than the original, it still conforms to the traditional double-leaf style. Constructed from African azobe wood, it was intended to last 50 years. Every 20 minutes, the bridge master has to let boats through. He then jumps on his bicycle and opens up the Amstelsluizen and Hoge Sluis.

Museum Van Loon ⑲

Keizersgracht 672. **Map** 5 A3. *Tel 020-6245255.* 🚆 *16, 24, 25.* ⬜ *11am–5pm Wed–Mon.* ⬤ *public hols.* 📷 🎦 www.museumvanloon.nl

The Van Loons were one of Amsterdam's most prestigious families in the 17th century. They did not move into this house on the Keizersgracht, however, until 1884. Designed by Adriaan Dortsman, No. 672 is one of a pair of symmetrical houses built in 1672 for Flemish merchant Jeremias van Raey. In 1752, Dr Abraham van Hagen and his wife, Catharina Elisabeth Trip, moved in.

In 1973, after many years of restoration, it opened as a museum, retaining the house's original character. Its collection of Van Loon family portraits stretches back to the early 1600s. The period rooms have fine pieces of furniture, porcelain and sculpture. Outside, the 18th-century coach house has been restored and houses the van Loon carriages and servants' livery.

Tuschinski Theater ⑳

Reguliersbreestraat 26–28. **Map** 5 A2. *Tel 0900-1458.* 🚆 *4, 9, 14.* **Box office** ⬜ *12:15pm–10pm.* 📷 🎦 🎦

Abraham Tuschinski's cinema and variety theatre caused a sensation when it opened in 1921. Until then, Amsterdam's cinemas had been sombre places; this was an exotic blend of Art Deco and Amsterdam School architecture *(see pp142–3)*. Built in a slum area known as Devil's Corner, it was designed by Heyman Louis de Jong and decorated by Chris Bartels, Jaap Gidding and Pieter de Besten. In its heyday, Marlene Dietrich and Judy Garland performed here.

Now a six-screen cinema, the building has been meticulously restored, inside and out. The best way to appreciate its opulence is to see a film. For a few extra euros, you can take a seat in one of the exotic boxes that make up the back row of the huge semi-circular auditorium.

View of the medieval Munttoren at the base of Muntplein

Munttoren ㉑

Muntplein. **Map** 4 F1. 🚆 *4, 9, 14, 16, 24, 25.* **Munttoren** ⬤ *to public.* **Gift shop** ⬜ *10am–6pm Mon–Sat.*

The polygonal base of the Munttoren (mint tower) formed part of the gate in Amsterdam's medieval wall. Fire destroyed the gate in 1618, but the base survived. In 1619, Hendrick de Keyser added the clock tower; François Hemony, the set of bells in 1699. During the 1673 French occupation, the city mint was housed here.

HOW THE MAGERE BRUG WORKS

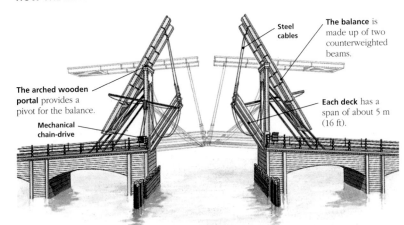

Steel cables

The balance is made up of two counterweighted beams.

The arched wooden portal provides a pivot for the balance.

Mechanical chain-drive

Each deck has a span of about 5 m (16 ft).

MUSEUM QUARTER

Until the late 1800s, the Museum Quarter was little more than an area of farms and small-holdings. At this time, the city council designated it an area of art and culture and plans were conceived for constructing Amsterdam's great cultural monuments: the Rijksmuseum, the Stedelijk Museum and the Concertgebouw. The Van Gogh Museum followed in 1973, its striking extension being added in 1999. The Museumplein has two memorials to the victims of World War II. The *plein* is still used today as a site for political demonstrations. To the north and south are late 19th-and early 20th-century houses, where the streets are named after artists and intellectuals, such as the 17th-century Dutch poet Roemer Visscher. To the west, the Vondelpark offers a pleasant, fresh-air break from all the museums.

"Russia" gablestone in Roemer Visscherstraat

SIGHTS AT A GLANCE

Museums and Workshops
Coster Diamonds ❷
EYE Film ❾
Rijksmuseum pp122–5 ❶
Stedelijk Museum pp128–9 ❹
Van Gogh Museum pp126–7 ❸

Concert Halls
Concertgebouw ❺

Historic Buildings
Hollandsche Manege ❼
Vondelkerk ❽

Parks
Vondelpark ❻

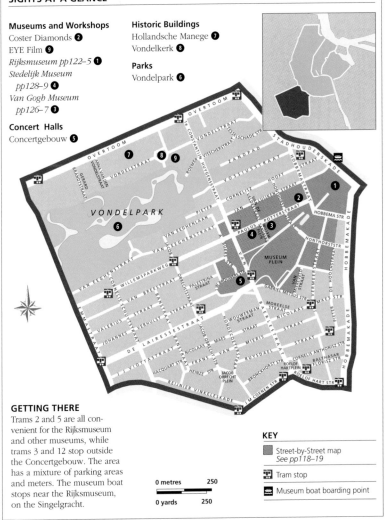

GETTING THERE
Trams 2 and 5 are all convenient for the Rijksmuseum and other museums, while trams 3 and 12 stop outside the Concertgebouw. The area has a mixture of parking areas and meters. The museum boat stops near the Rijksmuseum, on the Singelgracht.

0 metres   250

0 yards   250

KEY

▮ Street-by-Street map
See pp118–19

🚋 Tram stop

⛴ Museum boat boarding point

◁ **Statue of the sculptor Thomas de Keyser (1596–1667) on the façade of the Stedelijk Museum**

Street-by-Street: Museum Quarter

Statue on façade of Stedelijk

The green expanse of Museumplein was once bisected by a busy main road known locally as the "shortest motorway in Europe". But dramatic renovation between 1996 and 1999 has transformed it into a stately park, fringed by Amsterdam's major cultural centres. The district is one of the wealthiest in the city, with wide streets lined with grand houses. After the heady delights of the museums, it is possible to window-shop at the many up-market boutiques along the exclusive PC Hooftstraat and Van Baerlestraat, or watch the diamond polishers at work in Coster Diamonds.

★ **Van Gogh Museum**
The new wing of the museum, an elegant oval shape, was designed by Kisho Kurokawa and opened in 1999. It is dedicated to temporary exhibitions of 19th-century art ❸

Van Baerlestraat contains exclusive clothing shops *(see p144).*

★ **Stedelijk Museum**
Housing the civic collection of modern art, this museum also stages controversial contemporary art exhibitions. A sculpture garden is behind the building ❹

Concertgebouw
Designed by AL van Gendt, the building has a Classical façade and a concert hall with near-perfect acoustics ❺

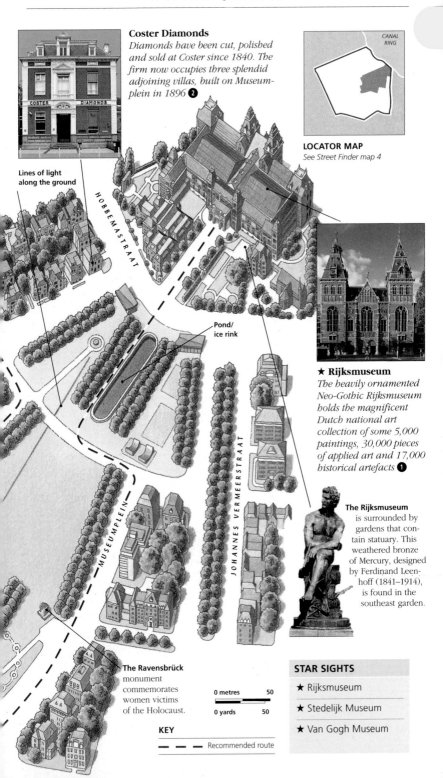

Coster Diamonds
Diamonds have been cut, polished and sold at Coster since 1840. The firm now occupies three splendid adjoining villas, built on Museumplein in 1896 ❷

CANAL RING

LOCATOR MAP
See Street Finder map 4

Lines of light along the ground

HOBBEMASTRAAT

Pond/ ice rink

★ **Rijksmuseum**
The heavily ornamented Neo-Gothic Rijksmuseum holds the magnificent Dutch national art collection of some 5,000 paintings, 30,000 pieces of applied art and 17,000 historical artefacts ❶

The Rijksmuseum is surrounded by gardens that contain statuary. This weathered bronze of Mercury, designed by Ferdinand Leenhoff (1841–1914), is found in the southeast garden.

JOHANNES VERMEERSTRAAT

MUSEUMPLEIN

The Ravensbrück monument commemorates women victims of the Holocaust.

| 0 metres | 50 |
| 0 yards | 50 |

KEY

– – – Recommended route

STAR SIGHTS

★ Rijksmuseum

★ Stedelijk Museum

★ Van Gogh Museum

Rijksmuseum ❶

See pp122–5.

Coster Diamonds ❷

Paulus Potterstraat 2–8. **Map** 4 E3.
Tel *020-3055555.* 🚋 *2, 5.* ⏰ *9am–5pm daily.* 🚫 *1 Jan, 25 Dec.* 📷 📹
💻 *www.*costerdiamonds.com

One of Amsterdam's oldest diamond factories, Coster was founded in 1840. Twelve years later, Queen Victoria's consort, Prince Albert, honoured the company by giving them the task of repolishing the enormous *Koh-i-Noor* (mountain of light) diamond. This blue-white stone is one of the treasures of the British crown jewels and weighs in at 108.8 carats. A replica of the coronation crown, which incorporates a copy of the fabulous stone, is found in Coster's spacious entrance hall.

More than 1,000 people visit the factory each day to witness the processes of grading, cutting and polishing the stones. The goldsmiths and diamond-cutters work together in the factory to produce customized items of jewellery, in a range of styles, which are available over the counter. In the Diamond Museum, the history of the diamond is traced, from its creation deep in the earth to the dazzling stones that are a girl's best friend.

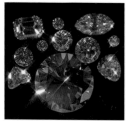

Glistening diamonds at Coster Diamonds

Van Gogh Museum ❸

See pp126–7.

Stedelijk Museum ❹

See pp128–9.

Façade of the award-winning Concertgebouw (1881) by AL van Gendt

Concertgebouw ❺

Concertgebouwplein 2–6. **Map** 4 D4.
Tel *0900-6718345.* 🚋 *2, 3, 5, 12, 16.* **Box office** ⏰ *1–7pm Mon–Fri, 10am–7pm Sat & Sun.* 🎵 🚫 ♿ *by arrangement.* 🎫 *5pm Mon, 12:15pm Sun.* **www.**concertgebouw.nl

Following an open architectural competition held in 1881, AL van Gendt (1835–1901) was chosen to design a vast new concert hall for Amsterdam. The resulting Neo-Renaissance building boasts an elaborate pediment and colonnaded façade, and houses two concert halls. Despite van Gendt's lack of musical knowledge, he managed to produce near-perfect acoustics in the Grote Zaal (main concert hall), which is renowned the world over.

The inaugural concert at the Concertgebouw was held on 11 April 1888, complete with an orchestra of 120 musicians and a choir of 600. A resident orchestra was established at the hall seven months later.

The building has been renovated several times over the years, most recently in 1983, when some serious subsidence threatened the building's entire foundation. To remedy this, the whole superstructure had to be lifted up off the ground while the original supporting piles, which rested on sand 13 m (43 ft) underground, were removed and replaced by concrete piles sunk into the ground to a depth of 18 m (59 ft). A glass extension and new entrance were added by Pi de Bruijn in 1988. The original entrance was relocated round to the side of the building. Though primarily designed to hold concerts, the Concertgebouw also hosts business meetings, exhibitions, conferences, political meetings and occasional boxing matches.

Bandstand in Vondelpark

Vondelpark ❻

Stadhouderskade. **Map** 4 E2. 🚋 *1, 2, 3, 5,12.* **Park** ⏰ *24hrs daily.*
Open-air theatre ⏰ *Jun–last week Aug: Wed–Sun.*

In 1864, a group consisting of prominent Amsterdammers formed a committee with the aim of founding a public park, and they raised enough money to buy 8 ha (20 acres) of land. JD and LP Zocher, a father-and-son team of landscape architects, were then commissioned to design the park in typical English landscape style. They used vistas, pathways and ponds to create the illusion of a large natural area, which was opened to the public on 15 June 1865, as the Nieuwe Park. The park's present name was adopted in 1867, when a statue of Dutch poet Joost van den Vondel

(1587–1679) was erected on the grounds. The committee soon began to raise money to enlarge the park, and by June 1877 it had reached its current dimensions of 47 ha (116 acres). The park now supports around 100 plant species and 127 types of tree. Squirrels, hedgehogs, ducks and garden birds mix with a huge colony of greedy, bright green para-keets, which gather in front of the pavilion every morning to be fed. Herds of cows, sheep, goats and even a lone llama graze in the pastures.

Vondelpark welcomes about 8 million visitors a year, and is popular with the locals for dog-walking, jogging, or just for the view. Free concerts are given at the *openluchttheater* (open-air theatre) or at the bandstand during summer.

Hollandsche Manege ❼

Vondelstraat 140. **Map** 3 C2.
Tel *020-6180942.* 📠 *1.*
⬜ *9am–11pm Mon–Fri,*
9:30am–6pm Sat & Sun. 📷 🔲

The Dutch riding school was originally situated on the Leidsegracht, but in 1882 a new building was opened, designed by AL van Gendt and based on the Spanish Riding School in Vienna. The riding school was threatened with demolition in the 1980s, but was saved after a public outcry. Reopened in 1986 by Prince Bernhard, it has been restored to its former glory. The Neo-Classical indoor arena

Façade of the Hollandse Manege, the Dutch riding school

boasts gilded mirrors and moulded horses' heads on its elaborate plasterwork walls. Some of the wrought-iron stalls remain and sound is muffled by sawdust. At the top of the staircase, one door leads to a balcony overlooking the arena, another to the café.

Vondelkerk ❽

Vondelstraat 120. **Map** 3 C2.
📠 *1, 3, 12.* ◐ *to the public.*

The Vondelkerk was the largest church designed by PJH Cuypers, architect of the Centraal Station. Work began in 1872, but funds ran out by the following year. Money gathered from public donations and lotteries allowed the building to be completed by 1880. When fire broke out in November 1904, firefighters saved the nave by forcing the burning tower to fall away into Vondelpark. A new tower was added later by the architect's son, JT Cuypers. The church was deconsecrated in 1979 and converted into offices in 1985.

EYE Film ❾

Vondelpark 3. **Map** 4 D2. ***Tel*** *020-58 91400.* 📠 *1, 3, 12.* **Library** ⬜ *1–5pm Mon–Fri.* ◐ *Jul & Aug.*
Box office ⬜ *9am–10:15pm Mon– Fri, 1 hr before screening Sat & Sun.*
Screenings: *from 5pm daily; plus 1:45pm Wed & Sun (children).* 🔲 *for cinema.* 🚫 🔲 🍴 *www.eyefilm.nl*

Vondelpark's pavilion was designed by the architects PJ Hamer (1812–87) and his son W Hamer (1843–1913), and opened on 4 May 1881 as a café and restaurant. After World War II, it reopened as a cultural centre. In 1991, the pavilion was renovated once more. The complete Art Deco interior of the Cinema Paris-ien, Amsterdam's first cinema, built in 1910, was moved into one of the rooms. It is now an important national film museum, showing more than 1,000 films a year. The muse-um also owns a film poster collection, runs a public film library at Nos. 69–71 Vondel-straat and holds free outdoor film screenings in summer.

At the end of 2011, EYE Film will move to a new building under construction on the Badhuisweg, across the IJ (behind Centraal Station); check the website for updates.

The terrace of Café Vertigo at EYE Film

Rijksmuseum ●

The Rijksmuseum, an Amsterdam landmark, possesses an unrivalled collection of Dutch art, begun in the early 19th century. The huge museum opened in 1885 to bitter criticism from Amsterdam's Protestant community for its Neo-Gothic style. The main building is closed until 2013 for a major renovation, but a selection of the best works from the Dutch Golden Age can be seen in the Philips Wing.

First floor

Winter Landscape with Skaters *(1608)*
Painter Hendrick Avercamp specialized in intricate icy winter scenes.

The Gothic façade
of Cuypers' building is red brick with elaborate decoration, including coloured tiles.

★ The Kitchen Maid *(1658)*
The light falling through the window and the stillness of this domestic scene are typical of Jan Vermeer.

Stair

Entrance

KEY TO FLOORPLAN

- Dutch history
- Foreign works
- 17th-century painting
- 18th- and 19th-century painting
- Hague School of Impressionism
- Sculpture and applied art
- Prints and drawings
- Asiatic art
- Non-exhibition space

STAR PAINTINGS

- ★ St Elizabeth's Day Flood
- ★ The Kitchen Maid by Vermeer
- ★ The Night Watch by Rembrandt

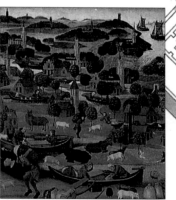

★ St Elizabeth's Day Flood *(1500)*
An unknown artist painted this altar-piece, showing a disastrous flood in 1421. The dykes protecting Dordrecht were breached, and 22 villages were swept away by the flood water.

Entrance

Study collections

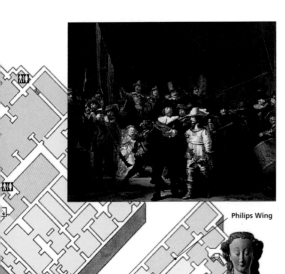

VISITORS' CHECKLIST

Jan Luykenstraat 1. **Map** 4 E3.
Tel 020-6747047. 🚋 2, 5, 7,
10. 🚌 Stadhouderskade.
🕐 9am–6pm daily. 🚫 1 Jan.
📷 🚫 ♿ 🎫 🏪 🚻
www.rijksmuseum.nl

Philips Wing

★ **The Night Watch** *(1642)*
*The showpiece of Dutch
17th-century art, this vast
canvas was commissioned
as a group portrait of an
Amsterdam militia company.*

GALLERY GUIDE

*The museum has been
undergoing renovation
since October 2003, and
all the highlights are on
show in the Philips Wing.*

**Ground
floor**

St Catherine *(c.1465)*
*This sculpture by the Master of
Koudewater shows the saint stamp-
ing on Emperor Maxentius, who
allegedly killed her with his sword.*

GENRE PAINTING

For the contemporaries of
Jan Steen (1625–79), this
cosy everyday scene was full
of symbols that are obscure
to the modern viewer. The
dog on the pillow may
represent fidelity, and the
red stockings, the woman's
sexuality; she is probably a
prostitute. Such genre paintings were often raunchy, but
most had a moral twist *(see
p223)* – domestic scenes by
artists such as Terborch and
Honthorst were symbolic of
brothels, while other works
illustrated proverbs. Symbols
such as candles or skulls
indicated mortality.

Jan Steen's *Woman at Her Toilet* **was
painted in about 1660**

Basement

Exploring the Rijksmuseum

The Rijksmuseum is almost too vast to be seen in a single visit. It is famous for owning probably the best collection of Dutch art in the world, from early religious works to the masterpieces of the Golden Age. However, the applied art and sculpture sections, and the Asiatic artefacts, are equally wonderful. Due to renovation, only a selection of works can be seen now in the Philips Wing. The selected pieces demonstrate the enormous prosperity of Holland's Golden Age in the 17th century. Rembrandt's *The Night Watch* is one of the masterpieces still on display.

Feeding the Hungry from a series of panels by the Master of Alkmaar

DUTCH HISTORY

The turbulent history of the Netherlands is encapsulated in this section. In the opening room is the medieval altar painting of *St Elizabeth's Day Flood (see p122)*. The central room has 17th-century ship models, artefacts salvaged from shipwrecks and paintings of factories and townscapes from the days of the Dutch Empire. Later displays recall battles in naval history; exhibits from the 18th century deal with the impact of revolutionary France on Amsterdam, ending in 1815 after the Napoleonic Wars.

EARLY PAINTING AND FOREIGN SCHOOLS

Alongside a small collection of Flemish and Italian art, including portraits by Piero di Cosimo (1462–1521), are the first specifically "Dutch" paintings. These works are mostly religious, such as *The Seven Works of Charity* (1504) by the Master of Alkmaar, Jan van Scorel's quasi-Mannerist *Mary Magdalene* (1528) and Lucas van Leyden's triptych, *Adoration of the Golden Calf* (1530). As the 16th century progressed, religious themes were superseded by pastoral subjects; by 1552, paintings like Pieter Aertsen's *The Egg Dance* were full of realism, by then the keystone of much Dutch art.

17TH-CENTURY PAINTING

By the alteration in 1578, Dutch art had moved away completely from religious to secular themes. Artists turned to realistic portraiture, landscapes, still lifes, seascapes, domestic interiors, including genre work *(see p123)*, and animal portraits. Rembrandt

(see p78) is the most famous of many artists who lived and worked around Amsterdam at this time. Examples of his work hanging in the Rijksmuseum include *Portrait of Titus in a Monk's Habit* (1660), *Self-Portrait as the Apostle Paul* (1661), *The Jewish Bride (see pp26–7)*, as well as *The Night Watch (see p123)*. Look out too for the work of his many pupils, who included, among others, Nicolaes Maes and Ferdinand Bol.

Don't miss Jan Vermeer's (1632–75) serenely light-filled interiors including *The Kitchen Maid (see p122)* and *The Woman Reading a Letter* (1662). Of several portraits by Frans Hals *(see pp186–7)*, the best known are *The Wedding Portrait* and *The Merry Drinker* (1630). *The Windmill at Wijk* by Jacob van Ruisdael (1628–82) is a great landscape by an artist at the very height of his power. Other artists whose works contribute to this unforgettable collection include Pieter Saenredam *(see p53)*, Jan van de Capelle, Jan Steen *(see p123)* and Gerard Terborch.

18TH- AND 19TH-CENTURY PAINTING

In many ways, 18th-century Dutch painting merely continued the themes and quality of 17th-century work. This is

The Wedding Portrait (c. 1622) by Frans Hals

For hotels and restaurants in this region see pp392–395 and pp410–414

particularly true of portraiture and still lifes, with the evocative *Still Life with Flowers and Fruit* by Jan van Huysum (1682–1749) standing out. A trend developed later for elegant "conversation pieces" by artists such as Adriaan van der Werff (1659–1722) and Cornelis Troost (1696–1750). Most had satirical undertones, like *The Art Gallery of Jan Gildemeester Jansz* (1794) by Adriaan de Lelie (1755–1820), showing an 18th-century salon whose walls are crowded with 17th-century masterpieces.

HAGUE SCHOOL AND THE IMPRESSIONISTS

The so-called Hague School was made up of a group of Dutch artists who came together around 1870 in The Hague. Their landscape work, which earned them the alternative title the "Grey School" for their overcast skies, captures the atmospheric quality of subdued Dutch sunlight. One of the prizes of the Rijksmuseum's 19th-century collection is *Morning Ride on the Beach* (1876) by Anton Mauve (1838–88), painted in soft pearly colours. Alongside hangs the beautiful polder landscape *View near the Geestbrug* by Hendrik Weissenbruch (1824–1903). In contrast, the Dutch Impressionists, closely linked to the French Impressionists, preferred active subjects such as *The Bridge over the Singel at Paleisstraat, Amsterdam* (1890) by George Hendrik Breitner (1857–1923).

SCULPTURE AND APPLIED ARTS

Beginning with religious medieval sculpture, this section moves on to the splendour of Renaissance furniture and decoration. Highlights that capture the wealth of the Golden Age include the exquisite collections of glassware and Delftware (*see pp28–9*), and diamond jewellery. A late 17th-century, 12-leaf Chinese screen incorporates European figures on one side, a phoenix on the other; and two dolls'

Still Life with Flowers and Fruit (c.1730) by artist Jan van Huysum (1682–1740), one of many still lifes exhibited in the Rijksmuseum

houses are modelled on contemporary town houses. Some outstanding 18th-century Meissen porcelain and Art Nouveau glass complete the collection.

PRINTS AND DRAWINGS

The Rijksmuseum owns about a million prints and drawings. Although the emphasis is on Dutch works (most of Rembrandt's etchings as well as rare works by Hercules Seghers (c.1589–1637) are here), there are prints by major European artists, including Dürer, Tiepolo, Goya, Watteau and Toulouse-Lautrec, as well as a set of coloured Japanese woodcuts. Small exhibitions are held on the ground floor of the museum, but particular prints can be viewed with special permission from the Study Collection in the basement.

ASIATIC ART

Rewards of the Dutch imperial trading past are on show in this department, which has a separate entrance at the rear of the museum. Some of the earliest artefacts are the most unusual: tiny bronze Tang dynasty figurines from 7th-century China and gritty, granite rock carvings from Java (c.8th century). Later exhibits include a lovely – and extremely explicit – Hindu statue entitled *Heavenly Beauty*, luscious Chinese parchment paintings of tigers, inlaid Korean boxes and Vietnamese dishes painted with curly-tailed fish. This is a veritable hoard of delights and, above all, a monument to the sophistication and skill of craftsmen and artists in early Eastern cultures.

Late 7th-century Cambodian *Head of Buddha*

Van Gogh Museum ❸

The Van Gogh Museum is based on a design by De Stijl architect Gerrit Rietveld *(see pp 204–5)* and opened in 1973. A new wing, designed by Kisho Kurokawa, was added in 1999. When Van Gogh died in 1890, he was on the verge of being acclaimed. His younger brother Theo, an art dealer, amassed a collection of 200 of his paintings and 500 drawings. These, combined with around 850 letters by Van Gogh to Theo, and selected works by his friends and contemporaries, form the core of the museum's outstanding collection.

KEY TO FLOORPLAN

- ☐ Works by Van Gogh
- ☐ Study collection and Print room
- ☐ Other 19th-century paintings
- ☐ Temporary exhibitions

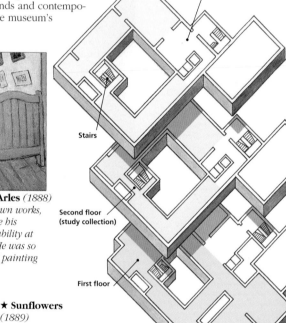

Third floor

Stairs

Second floor
(study collection)

First floor

19th-century art

Entrance

Ground floor

Shop

★ Vincent's Bedroom in Arles *(1888)*
One of Van Gogh's best-known works, this was painted to celebrate his achievement of domestic stability at the Yellow House in Arles. He was so delighted with the colourful painting that he did it twice.

★ Sunflowers
(1889)
The vivid yellows and greens in this version of Van Gogh's Sunflowers have been enriched by broad streaks of bright mauve and red.

STAR PAINTINGS

- ★ The Bedroom at Arles
- ★ Sunflowers
- ★ Wheatfield and Crows

MUSEUM GUIDE

Paintings from Van Gogh's Dutch period and from his time in Paris and Provence are on the first floor. The study collection, occasional exhibits of Van Gogh's drawings and other temporary exhibitions are on the second floor. Works by other 19th-century artists are on the third floor and the ground floor, where there is also a bookshop and café. The new wing houses temporary exhibitions.

AN ARTIST'S LIFE

Vincent van Gogh (1853–90), born in Zundert, began painting in 1880. He worked in the Netherlands for five years before moving to Paris, later settling in Arles. After a fierce argument with Gauguin, he cut off part of his own ear; his mental instability forced him into a psychiatric hospital in Saint-Rémy. He sought help in Auvers, where he shot himself, dying two days later.

Van Gogh in 1871

VISITORS' CHECKLIST

Paulus Potterstraat 7. **Map** 4 E3. *Tel* 020-5705200. 🚋 1, 2, 3, 5, 12. ☐ 10am–6pm daily, 10am–10pm Fri. ● 1 Jan. 🎨 🚫 🅿 ♿ 🎥 🏪 🍴 📷 www.vangoghmuseum.com

Pietà (after Delacroix) *(1889)*
Van Gogh painted this work while in the hospital at Saint-Rémy. The figure of Christ is thought to be a self-portrait.

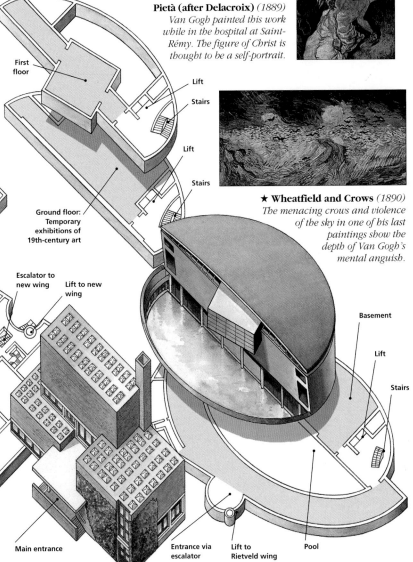

First floor

Lift

Stairs

Lift

Stairs

Ground floor: Temporary exhibitions of 19th-century art

★ **Wheatfield and Crows** *(1890)*
The menacing crows and violence of the sky in one of his last paintings show the depth of Van Gogh's mental anguish.

Escalator to new wing

Lift to new wing

Basement

Lift

Stairs

Main entrance

Entrance via escalator

Lift to Rietveld wing

Pool

Stedelijk Museum ❹

The Stedelijk Museum was built to house a personal collection bequeathed to the city in 1890 by art connoisseur Sophia de Bruyn. In 1938, the museum became the national museum of modern art, displaying works by artists such as Picasso, Matisse, Mondriaan, Cézanne and Monet. The museum is undergoing a thorough renovation and will reopen in 2011 with a larger exhibition space, a spectacular new wing (nicknamed "the bath tub") and a new café-restaurant.

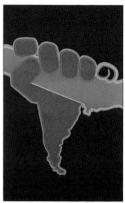

Portrait of the Artist with Seven Fingers (1912)
Marc Chagall's self-portrait is heavily autobiographical; the seven fingers of the title allude to the seven days of Creation and the artist's Jewish origins. Paris and Rome, the cities Chagall lived in, are inscribed in Hebrew above his head.

Solidaridad con America Latina (1970)
The Stedelijk's collection of rare posters comprises some 17,000 works, including this graphic image by the Cuban human rights campaigner Asela Perez.

THE MUSEUM BUILDING

The Neo-Renaissance building was designed by AW Weissman (1858–1923) in 1895. The façade is adorned with turrets and gables and with niches containing statues of artists and architects. Inside, it is ultra-modern. The museum is undergoing renovation.

Hendrick de Keyser (1565–1621)

Jacob Cornelisz van Oostzaanen (1470–1533)

Pieter Aertsen (1509–75)

Joost Jansz Bilhamer (1541–90)

DE STIJL MOVEMENT

The Dutch artistic movement known as De Stijl (The Style) produced startlingly simple designs which have become icons of 20th-century abstract art. These include Gerrit Rietveld's famous *Red Blue Chair* and Piet Mondriaan's *Composition in Red, Black, Blue, Yellow and Grey* (1920). The movement was formed in 1917 by a group of artists who espoused clarity in their work, which embraced the mediums of painting, architecture, sculpture, poetry and furniture design. Many De Stijl artists, like Theo van Doesburg, split from the founding group in the 1920s; their legacy can be seen in the work of the Bauhaus and Modernist schools which followed *(see pp204–5).*

Gerrit Rietveld's *Red Blue Chair* (1918)

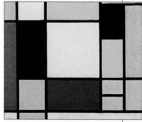

Composition in Red, Black, Blue, Yellow and Grey by Mondriaan

Dancing Woman *(1911)*
*Ernst Ludwig Kirchner (1880–1938) was
inspired by the primitive art of African
and Asian cultures, and by the natural
qualities of the materials he worked with.*

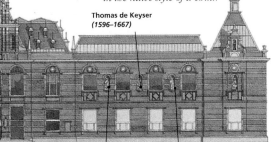

VISITORS' CHECKLIST

Museumplein 10. **Map** 4 D3.
Tel 020-5732911. 🚋 2, 3,
5, 12. ⬜ check website.
📷 🚫 ♿ 🍴 🛍 🚻
www.stedelijk.nl

Man and Animals *(1949)*
*Karel Appel (b. 1921) was a member of
the short-lived experimental Cobra movement (see p189). The human figure, dog
fish and mythical creature are painted
in the naive style of a child.*

Elaborate
bell tower

Thomas de Keyser
(1596–1667)

Jan van der Heyden
(1637–1712)

Jacob van Campen
(1595–1657)

**★ KAZIMIR MALEVICH
(1878–1935)**

The Russian visual artist
Kazimir Malevich can be
counted, along with Piet
Mondriaan, as one of the
founders of abstract art.
As well as paintings, Malevich created posters, sculptures, furniture, interior
decoration and costumes.

After studying Futurism
and Cubism in Moscow,
he formulated a new art
form called Suprematism,
an abstract movement
known for its experimen-
tation with colour. Suprematism's central element
is the theory of unlimited
pre-eminence of free
invention in the artistic
process. Up until his 20s,
Malevich painted abstract
geometric forms. The
square was his "supreme
element". The Stedelijk
Museum owns the largest
part of the paintings and
sketches from Malevich's
Suprematist period. One
of the most important
works, *Suprematisme
1920–1927*, was defaced
by a visitor to the
museum in 1997.

In 1999, a conflict arose
between the Malevich
estate and the Stedelijk
Museum over the owner-
ship of the dozens of
Suprematist works from
the Stedelijk's collection.

Self-portrait by Malevich

STAR COLLECTIONS

★ Cobra Collection

★ Works by Malevich

★ Works by Mondriaan

Untitled *(1965)*
*Jasper Johns (b. 1930)
believed viewers should
draw their own conclusions
from his work. This huge
canvas, with its bold rainbow (red, blue and yellow
streaks and slabs), invites
the viewer to think about
the symbolism of colour.*

OUTSIDE THE CENTRE

Sculpture on the fountain at Frankendael

Great architecture and good town planning are not confined to central Amsterdam. Parts of the Nieuw Zuid (New South) bear testament to the imagination of the innovative Amsterdam School architects *(see pp142–3)*. Many fine buildings can be found in De Dageraad Housing complex and the streets around the Olympic Quarter. The area known as the Plantation was once green parkland beyond the city wall, where 17th-century Amsterdammers spent their leisure time. From about 1848, it became one of Amsterdam's first suburbs. The tree-lined streets around Artis and Hortus Botanicus are still popular places to live. From the Werf 't Kromhout, once a thriving shipyard, there is a fine view of De Gooyer Windmill, one of the few in Amsterdam to survive. The national maritime collection is kept at Scheepvaart Museum, a former naval storehouse. NEMO, an educational science centre, is nearby. Fine parks are just a short tram ride from the city centre and offer a host of leisure activities.

SIGHTS AT A GLANCE

Historic Buildings and Structures
Amstelsluizen ❽
Amsterdam RAI ⓱
De Gooyer Windmill ❺
Entrepotdok ❷
Frankendael ⓫
Heineken Experience ⓮
Huizenblok de Dageraad ⓯
Java-eiland and KNSM-eiland ❸
Koninklijk Theater Carré ❼
Muiderpoort ❹

Markets
Albert Cuypmarkt ⓲

Museums and Zoos
Artis Amsterdam Zoo pp138–9 ❿
Hermitage Amsterdam ⓭
Nederlands Scheepvaart Museum pp132–3 ❶
Science Center NEMO pp136–7 ❾
Tropenmuseum ⓬
Verzetsmuseum ⓰
Werfmuseum 't Kromhout ❻

KEY

▦	Oude Zijde
▦	Nieuwe Zijde
▦	Canal Ring
▦	Museum Quarter
▦	Outside the Centre

0 km   2 km

0 yards   2000

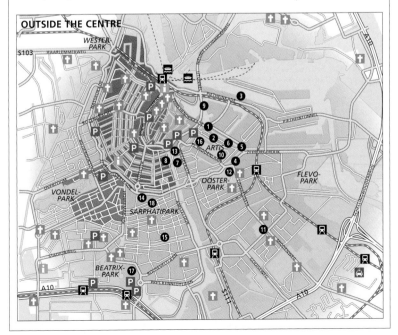

OUTSIDE THE CENTRE

WESTER-PARK
S103
VONDEL-PARK
OOSTER-PARK
FLEVO-PARK
SARPHATIPARK
BEATRIX-PARK
A10

◁ **Replica of the *Amsterdam*, an East Indiaman, moored alongside the Scheepvaart Museum**

Nederlands Scheepvaart Museum ❶

Once the arsenal of the Dutch Navy, this vast Dutch Classical building was designed by Daniël Stalpaert in 1655. Constructed around a massive courtyard, it was supported by thousands of piles driven into the bed of the Oosterdok. The navy occupied the building until the 20th century, and in 1973 it became the Netherlands Maritime Museum. After a major renovation it reopened in 2011; the courtyard, now covered by a vast glass roof, forms the heart of the new exhibition space.

Figure of a Dutch sea master, c.1750

First floor

★ Golden Age
Seven characters welcome you to this exhibition covering the golden era of Dutch exploration and trade in the 16th and 17th centuries.

Ajax
This figurehead is from a ship built in 1832. It portrays Ajax, a hero of the Trojan War, who killed himself in despair when Achilles' armour was given to Odysseus.

Classical sandstone façade

MUSEUM GUIDE
This museum's exhibits reveal Dutch maritime history. On a Virtual Sea Trip or aboard the East Indiaman Amsterdam *you can relive the past; other exhibits tell the stories of whaling, the Golden Age and the port of Amsterdam. Objects on Stage showcases the museum's superb collection of nautical paintings, navigation instruments and antique globes.*

STAR EXHIBITS

- ★ Virtual Sea Trip
- ★ Objects on Stage
- ★ Golden Age

Glass Canopy
The compass rose and navigational lines on old sea maps were the inspiration for architect Laurent Ney's criss-crossing steel armature supporting the glass roof.

Main entrance

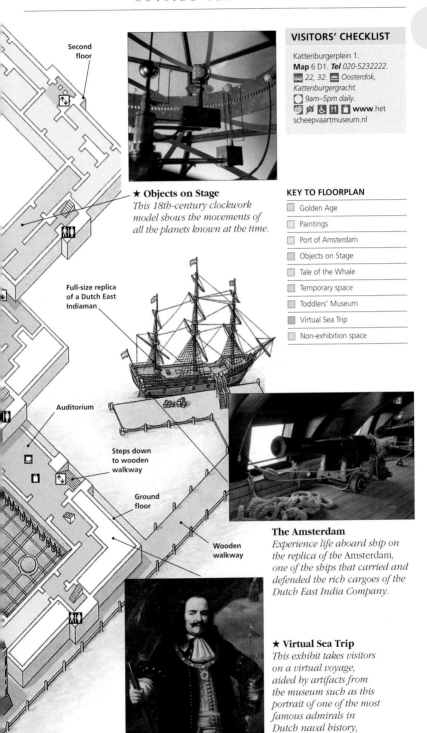

Second floor

★ Objects on Stage
This 18th-century clockwork model shows the movements of all the planets known at the time.

VISITORS' CHECKLIST

Kattenburgerplein 1.
Map 6 D1. *Tel 020-5232222.*
22, 32. Oosterdok, Kattenburgergracht.
9am–5pm daily.
www.het scheepvaartmuseum.nl

KEY TO FLOORPLAN

- Golden Age
- Paintings
- Port of Amsterdam
- Objects on Stage
- Tale of the Whale
- Temporary space
- Toddlers' Museum
- Virtual Sea Trip
- Non-exhibition space

Full-size replica of a Dutch East Indiaman

Auditorium

Steps down to wooden walkway

Ground floor

Wooden walkway

The Amsterdam
Experience life aboard ship on the replica of the Amsterdam, *one of the ships that carried and defended the rich cargoes of the Dutch East India Company.*

★ Virtual Sea Trip
This exhibit takes visitors on a virtual voyage, aided by artifacts from the museum such as this portrait of one of the most famous admirals in Dutch naval history, Michiel de Ruyter (1607–76).

Entrepotdok ❷

Map 6 D2. 🚊 9, 14, 32. 🚌 22, 43.

The redevelopment of the old VOC warehouses at Entrepotdok has revitalized this dockland area. During the mid-19th century, it was the greatest warehouse area in Europe, being a customs-free zone for goods in transit. The quayside buildings are now a lively complex of homes, offices and eating places. Some of the original façades of the warehouses have been preserved, unlike the interiors, which have been opened up to provide an attractive inner courtyard. Café tables are often set out alongside the canal. On the other side, brightly coloured houseboats are moored.

Java-eiland and KNSM-eiland ❸

Map 6 D2. *Java-eiland and KNSM-eiland* 🚌 41, 42. 🚊 10.

Situated side by side in the eastern docklands of the city are the islands of Java-eiland, which is long and narrow, and the broader KNSM-eiland. Java-eiland, designed by Sjoerd Soeters during the 1990s, demonstrates a wide variety of architectural styles. By combining these styles with a number of canals across the island, the architect succeeded in creating a very credible

The 18th-century De Gooyer windmill, with its renovated balcony

Amsterdam canal atmosphere. This is compounded by the many shops and small cafés. KNSM-eiland is slightly broader, giving architect Jo Coenen the space to create a central avenue flanked on either side by tower blocks.

Muiderpoort ❹

Alexanderplein. **Map** 6 E3. 🚊 7, 9, 10, 14. 🌙 *to the public.*

Formerly a city gate, the Muiderpoort was designed by Cornelis Rauws (1732–72) in about 1770. The central

archway of this Classical structure is topped with a dome and clock tower. Napoleon entered the city through this gate in 1811 and, according to legend, forced the citizens to feed and house his ragged troops.

De Gooyer Windmill ❺

Funenkade 5. **Map** 6 F2. 🚊 10, 14. 🌙 *to the public.*

Of the six remaining windmills within the city's boundaries, De Gooyer, also known as the Funenmolen, is the most central. Dominating the view down the Nieuwevaart, the mill, built around 1725, was the first corn mill in the Netherlands to use streamlined sails.

It first stood to the west of its present site, but the Oranje Nassau barracks, built in 1814, acted as a windbreak, and the mill was then moved piece by piece to the Funenkade. The octagonal wooden structure was rebuilt on the stone foot of an earlier water-pumping mill, demolished in 1812.

By 1925, De Gooyer was in a very poor state of repair and was bought by the city council, which fully restored it. Since then, the lower part of the mill, with its neat thatched roof and tiny windows, has been a private

Spout-gable façades of former warehouses along Entrepotdok

KNSM-eiland: a thriving modern city district

Koninklijk Theater Carré **7**

Amstel 115–125. **Map** 5 B3.
Tel 0900-2525255. 🚊 *4, 7, 9, 10, 14, 20.* Ⓜ *Weesperplein.*
Box office 🕐 *4–9pm daily.*
See **Entertainment** *p147.* 📷
📷 *11am Sat (phone in advance).*
♿ ⚞ 🖥 www.theatercarre.nl

During the 19th century, the annual visit of the Carré Circus was a popular event. In 1868, Oscar Carré built wooden premises for the circus on the banks of the Amstel river. The city council considered the structure a fire hazard, so Carré persuaded them to accept a permanent building modelled on his other circus in Cologne. Built in 1887, the new structure included both a circus ring and a stage. The Classical façade is richly decorated with sculpted heads of dancers, jesters and clowns.

The Christmas circus is still one of the annual highlights at the theatre, but for much of the year the stage is taken over by concerts and blockbuster musicals.

Pillar decoration on Theater Carré

Amstelsluizen **8**

Map 5 B3. 🚊 *4, 7, 9, 10, 14.*
Ⓜ *Weesperplein.*

The Amstelsluizen, a row of sturdy wooden sluice gates spanning the Amstel river, form part of a complex system of sluices and pumping stations that ensure Amsterdam's canals do not stagnate. Four times a week in summer and twice a week in winter, the sluices are closed while fresh water from large lakes north of the city is allowed to flow into Amsterdam's canals. Sluices to the west of the city are left open, allowing the old water to flow, or be pumped, into the sea.

The Amstelsluizen date from 1673, and were operated manually until 1994, when they were mechanized.

home, though its massive sails still creak into action sometimes. Next to the mill is the IJ brewery, with its own tasting room (www.brouwerijhetij.nl).

Werfmuseum 't Kromhout **6**

Hoogte Kadijk 147. **Map** 6 E2.
Tel 020-6276777. 🚊 *9, 10, 14.*
🚌 *22, 43.* 🚋 *Oosterdok or Artis.*
🕐 *10am–3pm Tue and by appointment.* ⚫ *public hol.* 📷 📷
♿ 🖥 www.machinekamer.nl

The Werfmuseum 't Kromhout is one of the oldest working shipyards in Amsterdam and is also a museum. Ships were being built here as early as 1757. In the second half of the 19th century, production changed from sailing ships to steamships. As ocean-going ships got bigger, the yard, due to its relatively small size, turned to building lighter craft for inland waterways. It is now used only for restoration and repair work.

In 1967, the Prince Bernhard Fund bought the site, saving it from demolition.

The Amsterdam Monuments Fund later became involved to safeguard the shipyard's future as a historical site and helped turn it into a museum.

The museum is largely dedicated to the history of marine engineering, concentrating on work carried out at the shipyard, with steam engines, maritime photographs and ephemera. Another point of interest is the shipyard's forge featuring a variety of interesting tools and equipment. Some impressive historical ships are moored at the quayside. The museum's eastern hall is sometimes used for receptions and dinners.

The Werfmuseum 't Kromhout

Science Center NEMO ❾

Science Center NEMO, an educational centre for science and technology, is housed in a striking modern building by the Italian architect Renzo Piano. Designed in the form of a ship, it overhangs the water by 30 m (99 ft): the view from the roof is breathtaking. There are five floors of constantly changing things to do and discover including interactive exhibitions, theatre shows, films, workshops and demonstrations.

Amazing Constructions
Discover why buildings and bridges are so strong and see a scale model of Rotterdam's Erasmus Bridge.

The motorway approach to the tunnel under the IJ is beneath the building.

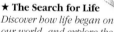

★ **The Search for Life**
Discover how life began on our world, and explore the possibilities of alien lifeforms.

★ **Chain Reaction**
This entertaining show demonstrates cause and effect and action and reaction, with plenty of audience participation.

Machine Park focuses on technology.

STAR SIGHTS

★ The Search for Life

★ Chain Reaction

★ View from the Roof

Bubble-blowing
Can you fit inside a giant bubble? Experiment with giant rings and vats of soapy water.

NEMO: THE PHILOSOPHY

The word "nemo" is Latin for "no one" and refers to a world between fantasy and reality. At NEMO visitors can become a scientist or technician for a day. The name has been used by a number of important writers over the centuries to describe events and people who find themselves on the thin line between reality and fantasy. For example, Nemo turns up in the Latin translation of Homer's *Odyssey*, when the protagonist Ulysses adopts the name to deceive the Cyclops. And Jules Verne, in his 1870 novel *20,000 Leagues Under the Sea*, enlists Nemo as the mystical captain of the underwater *Nautilus*, which journeys in the shadowy world between reality and fantasy. He crops up again in 1905, when American cartoonist Winsor McCay creates *Little Nemo*, a young boy whose dreamland adventures once again suggest a mingling of fact and fiction.

In Little NEMO's Bamboo House you can learn how a house is built.

★ **View from the Roof**
The view from the building's roof provides a stunning vista of the port and city. In summer, the roof terrace becomes a popular sunning and leisure area.

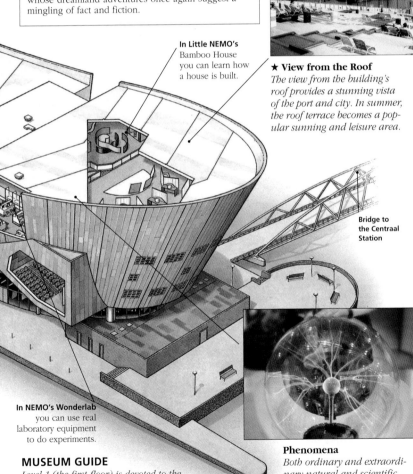

Bridge to the Centraal Station

In NEMO's Wonderlab you can use real laboratory equipment to do experiments.

Phenomena
Both ordinary and extraordinary natural and scientific phenomena can be experienced in this interactive exhibition.

MUSEUM GUIDE

Level 1 (the first floor) is devoted to the Zany World of Science, with sections dealing with gravity, light, sound and electricity. On Levels 2, 3 and 4 you will find areas such as The Search for Life, Machine Park, Water World and NEMO's Wonderlab.

Artis Royal Zoo ⑩

Elephant in Artis

Amsterdam's royal zoo is in Plantage, an elegant Amsterdam neighbourhood of broad tree-lined streets with elegant painted sandstone houses. Some 750 different animal species live in Artis Zoo. Visitors can see the historic nature of the zoo as soon as they pass through the entrance gates, which have been decorated since 1854 with two "golden" eagles. The Artis complex includes a planetarium, where you can learn about the heavens and stars, and the fine Neo-Classical aquarium, containing a wide variety of marine life, from tropical fish and sharks to huge moray eels.

The playground,
situated next to the Two Cheetahs restaurant, is popular with children.

★ **Planetarium**
The planetarium explores the relationship between humans and the stars. The night sky is recreated on the dome, and interactive exhibitions show the positions of the planets. Model spacecraft are on display in the hall around the auditorium. The interesting slide show is specially designed for youngsters.

Macaws
These birds are a highly endangered species which Artis helps preserve. The zoo is renowned for its breeding programmes.

Tiger Python
The female specimen in Artis has borne young simply by cloning herself.

STAR FEATURES

★ African Savannah

★ Aquarium

★ Planetarium

★ **African Savannah**
In the African Savannah, the animals roam in more natural surroundings. The zebras, gnus and gazelles feel at home here.

VISITORS' CHECKLIST

Plantage Kerklaan 38–40.
Tel 0900 2784796. 🚊 9, 10,
14. ⏱ summer: 9am–6pm daily
(open until sunset on Sat);
winter: 9am–5pm daily.
📷 ♿ 🖥 🍴 www.artis.nl

**The northern
side** of the zoo
is currently used
as a car park.

Gorillas
*Gorilla Binti's
son Bwana was
born as part of
the zoo's breed-
ing programme.*

Sea Lions
*Feeding time
for the sea
lions is a
popular daily
attraction at
the zoo.*

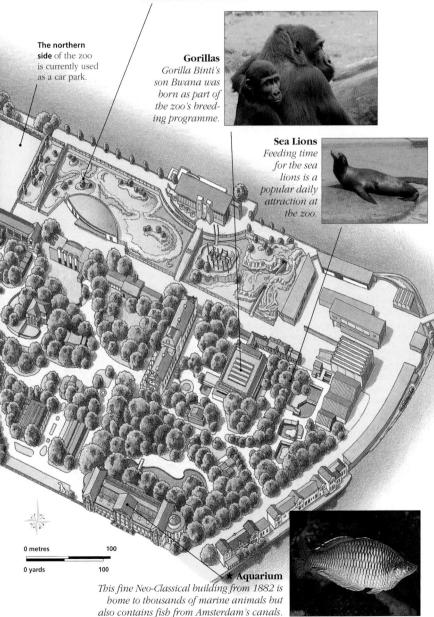

★ **Aquarium**
*This fine Neo-Classical building from 1882 is
home to thousands of marine animals but
also contains fish from Amsterdam's canals.*

0 metres   100

0 yards   100

Frankendael ⓫

Middenweg 72. **Map** 6 F5. 🚆 9.
🚌 41, 65, 101, 136, 152, 157.
🔘 dawn–dusk.

During the early part of the 18th century, many of Amsterdam's wealthier citizens built country retreats south of Plantage Middenlaan on reclaimed land called the Watergraafsmeer. The elegant Louis XIV-style Frankendael is the last survivor. The house is closed to the public; the best views of the ornamented façade are from Middenweg. This is also the best place to view the fountain made in 1714 by Ignatius van Logteren (1685–1732), a sculptor who, along with his son, played a central role in the development of Amsterdam's Louis XIV style.

The rear gardens have been restored and are open to the public. Behind the house is a small formal garden, and beyond lies a landscaped, English-style garden. There are also allotment gardens. The coach house is now home to café-restaurant Merkelbach.

The ornamental façade of Frankendael House

Ignatius van Logteren's fountain in the grounds of the Frankendael

Tropenmuseum ⓬

Linnaeusstraat 2. **Map** 6 E3. **Tropenmuseum** **Tel** 020-5688200. 🔘 10am–5pm daily, 10am–3pm 5 Dec, 24 Dec, 31 Dec. ● 1 Jan, 30 Apr, 5 May, 25 Dec. **www**.tropenmuseum.nl **Tropenmuseum Junior** **Tel** 020-5688233. 🔘 for special programmes in Dutch language only (phone or see website). ● As Tropenmuseum. 🚆 9, 14. 📷 ♿ ✏ 🍴 🛍 📷 **www**.kindermuseum.nl

Built to house the Dutch Colonial Institute, this vast complex was finished in 1926 by architects MA and J Nieuwkerken. The exterior is decorated with symbols of imperialism, such as stone friezes of peasants planting rice. Upon completion of the building's renovation in 1978, the Royal Tropical Institute opened a museum, with a huge central hall and three levels of galleries. The institute's aims are to study and to help improve the lives of the indigenous populations of the tropics. The displays focus on development issues regarding daily life, education and colonization.

Balinese tiger protector mask and model at the Tropenmuseum

The impressive mask collection includes feathered fertility masks from Zaire and carved wooden masks from Central America. Gerrit Schouten's 1819 diorama made of papier-mâché and painted wood depicts life in Suriname.

Hermitage Amsterdam ⓭

Amstel 51. **Map** 8 E5. **Tel** 0900 437 648243. 🚆 4, 9, 14. Ⓜ Waterlooplein. 🚉 Muziektheater. 🔘 10am–5pm daily (to 8pm Wed). 🆓 free for under 16s. ● 1 Jan, 30 Apr, 25 Dec. ♿ 🍴 📷 🛍 **www**.hermitage.nl

In the early 1990s the State Hermitage Museum in St Petersburg, Russia, chose Amsterdam as the ideal city in which to open a satellite museum displaying temporary exhibitions drawn from the Hermitage's rich collection. It opened in 2004 with a spectacular exhibition of fine Greek gold jewellery from the 6th to the 2nd century BC. Recently expanded, the museum now occupies the whole complex, with an auditorium and special children's wing.

Heineken Experience ⑭

Stadhouderskade 78. **Map** 4 F3. **Tel** 020-523 9222. 🚋 16, 25. ⬜ 11am–5:30pm daily. ⬤ 1 Jan, 25 Dec. 📷 ♿ ⬜ Under 18s with parents only. **www**.heinekenexperience.com

This historic 1867 building once housed the Heineken brewery. Now it offers an exhibition of how beer is made, culminating in a tasting room where you can have a drink.

Huizenblok De Dageraad ⑮

Pieter Lodewijk Takstraat. 🚋 4, 12, 25. ⬤ to the public.

One of the best examples of Amsterdam School architecture (*see pp142–3*), De Dageraad (the Dawn) housing project was developed for poorer families following the Housing Act of 1901, by which the city council condemned slums and rethought housing policy. Architect HP Berlage drew up plans for the suburbs, aiming to integrate rich and poor by juxtaposing their housing. After Berlage's death, Piet Kramer and Michel de Klerk adopted his ideas. From 1918–23, they designed this complex for the De Dageraad housing association.

Interior of Amsterdam RAI with a trade fair in progress

Verzetsmuseum ⑯

Plantage Kerklaan 61. **Map** 6 D2. **Tel** 020-6202535. 🚋 9, 14. ⬜ 10am–5pm Tue–Fri, 11am–5pm Mon & Sat. ⬤ 1 Jan, 30 Apr, 25 Dec. 📷 📷 ♿ 📷 ⬛ 🍴 **www**.verzetsmuseum.org

Previously based in a former synagogue in Nieuw Zuid (New South), now at a site in the Plantage, the Resistance Museum holds a fascinating collection of memorabilia recording the activities of Dutch Resistance workers in World War II. It was set up by former members of the Resistance and focuses on the courage of the 25,000 people actively involved in the movement. False documents, weaponry, film clips, photographs and equipment are on display.

By 1945 there were 300,000 people in hiding in the Netherlands, including Jews and anti-Nazi Dutch. Subsequent events organized by the Resistance, like the February Strike against the deportation of the Jews, are brought to life by exhibits showing where the refugees hid and how food for them was smuggled in.

Amsterdam RAI ⑰

Europaplein. **Tel** 0900-2678373. 🚋 4. Ⓜ 🚆 RAI. 🚌 62, 65. ⬜ depending on exhibition. **Enquiries**: 8:30am–5:30pm Mon–Fri. 📷 📷 ♿ with assistance. **www**.rai.nl

Amsterdam RAI is one of the largest exhibition and conference centres in the country. It hosts over 1,000 events annually, from cabaret to horse shows and trade fairs. The first Amsterdam trade fair was a bicycle exhibition in 1893. Subsequent shows included cars and became an annual event known as the "RAI" (Rijwiel Automobiel Industrie). The present complex opened in 1961. It has since undergone several extensions.

Albert Cuypmarkt ⑱

Albert Cuypstraat. **Map** 5 A5. 🚋 4, 16, 24, 25. ⬜ 9:30am–5pm Mon–Sat.

The Albert Cuypmarkt began trading in 1904. Described by the stallholders as "the best-known market in Europe", it attracts some 20,000 visitors on weekdays and often twice as many on Saturdays. Goods on sale at the 325 stalls range from fish, poultry, cheese, fruit and vegetables to clothes; prices are among the cheapest in the city.

Imposing corner block of De Dageraad public housing

The Amsterdam School

The industrial revolution at the end of the 19th century led to a boom in the growth of towns. New districts grew around Amsterdam to accommodate the growing number of factory workers. The architects of these districts, who sought new elements for decorating building façades, became known collectively as the Amsterdam School. Their designs were characterized by exotic rooflines, ornamental brickwork, cornices, window frames and corner formations which gave the façades "movement".

Curves and serpentines on façades are typical features of the Amsterdam School.

The **Scheepvaarthuis** was erected on the spot where in 1595 Cornelis Houtman set off on his first voyage to the East Indies.

The Betondorp (Concrete Village), officially known as Tuindorp Watergraafsmeer, was the first place where experimental concrete-work was used. It also features many brick buildings in the Amsterdam School style.

HP BERLAGE (1856–1934)

Berlage studied at the technical college of Zurich from 1875 to 1878, where he came into contact with architects such as Semper and Viollet-le-Duc. Inspired by their ideas, he developed his own style, which incorporated traditional Dutch materials. It later evolved into the Amsterdam School style of architecture. Berlage designed not only buildings but also interiors, furniture and graphics. In 1896, he was appointed to design the Beurs, the new stock exchange in Amsterdam *(see p91)*. Completed in 1903, it is an austere building whose structure is clearly visible. Berlage was also active as a town planner. His design of Amsterdam-Zuid ("Plan Zuid") consists of monumental residential blocks. At its centre stands JF Staal's *Wolkenkrabber* (skyscraper).

Detail of a set of windows on the Zaanstraat

Het Schip, *built by Michel de Klerk, is a former post office which now provides a home for the Museum voor de Volkshuisvesting (museum of public housing).*

Interiors and exteriors are characterized by an excess of expressionist glass ornamentation and details.

An astonishing variety of decoration *could be achieved with this kind of brickwork.*

Sculptures

Amsterdam School lettering

THE ARCHITECTURE OF THE AMSTERDAM SCHOOL

From 1911 to 1923, the members of the Amsterdam School built a large number of office and residential complexes. One of the greatest examples of this is the Scheepvaarthuis (1913–16 and 1926–8), which is today the head office of the Gemeente Vervoerbedrijf (municipal traffic directorate). It is the first building to be completed entirely in the Amsterdam School style. It was designed by the Van Gendt brothers and JM van der Meij. Michel de Klerk, who later designed Het Schip, was also involved in the project.

Michel de Klerk (1884–1923)

Street furniture *was among the repertoire of the Amsterdam School architects. In the Spaarndammerbuurt in particular, many examples can still be seen, including fire alarms, cable boxes and post boxes.*

SHOPPING IN AMSTERDAM

Traditional wooden clogs

Amsterdam has a huge range of shops and markets. Most of the large clothing and department stores are to be found in the Nieuwe Zijde, especially along Kalverstraat, but there are many other shopping areas to discover. The narrow streets crossing the Canal Ring, such as Herenstraat and Hartenstraat, contain a diverse array of specialist shops selling everything from ethnic fabrics and beads to unusual games and handmade dolls. The best luxury fashion is to be found on PC Hooftstraat and Van Baerlestraat. However, if you are looking for a bargain, take time to etxplore the street markets and numerous second-hand shops.

The northern end of the Waterlooplein, home to the famous flea market

OPENING HOURS

Shops are usually open from 9am to 6pm Tuesday to Saturday, from 1pm to 6pm Mondays. Many are open Sundays. In the city centre, shops stay open until 9pm on Thursdays.

HOW TO PAY

Cash is the most popular method of payment. If you intend to use a credit card, ask first if it is accepted. Cards are becoming more widely accepted, but department stores may require purchases to be paid for at a special till, and smaller shops may accept them only for non-sale items and goods costing more than 45 euros. Most shops accept travellers' cheques. Some tourist shops take foreign currency but usually offer a poor rate of exchange.

VAT EXEMPTION

Most Dutch goods are subject to value added tax (BTW) of 19 per cent for clothes and other goods, and 6 per cent for books. Non-EU residents may be entitled to a refund. Shops that stock the relevant customs forms post a "Tax free for tourists" sign.

SALES

Sales occur mainly in January and July but smaller shops and boutiques may offer discounts at any time. *Uitverkoop* describes anything from a closing-down sale to a clearance sale; *korting* merely indicates that discounts are offered. Towards the end of a sale, further discounts are often calculated at the till. Beware of clothes rails marked, for example, *VA 40* or *Vanaf 40,* as this sign means "From 40", not exactly 40 euros.

DEPARTMENT STORES AND MALLS

Amsterdam's best-known department store is **De Bijenkorf**. It has a huge perfumery and stocks a wide range of clothing. **Maison de Bonneterie** is more exclusive. Among the less expensive stores, **Hema** is popular for household goods, children's clothes and underwear. Also popular for basic items is **Vroom & Dreesmann**. The only shopping malls in central Amsterdam

A shop selling kitchen gadgets

are the Kalvertoren (Kalverstraat, near Singel) and **Magna Plaza** *(see p90)*, containing up-market boutiques and shops.

Trendy clothing for women and men in "De Negen Straatjes"

MARKETS

Amsterdammers' love of street trading is best illustrated on Koninginnedag *(see p32)*, when the city centre becomes the world's biggest flea market as locals sell off their unwanted junk.

Each district in Amsterdam has its own market. The best-known is the Albert Cuypmarkt *(see p141)*. There are also many specialist markets. Visitors and residents alike are drawn to the array of seasonal flowers at the Bloemenmarkt. Another market popular with tourists is Waterlooplein flea market *(see p79)*, where bargains can be found among the bric-à-brac; new and second-hand clothes are also for sale.

Browsers will be fascinated by the dozens of stalls at the **Looier Kunst en Antiekcentrum** *(see p113)*, selling anything from antique dolls to egg cups. On Wednesdays and Saturdays on Nieuwezijds Voorburgwal there is a stamp and coin market. Gourmets

Jenever of Amsterdam

should head for the **Noordermarkt** *(see p111)*, for the Saturday organic food market. The best prices, however, are to be found about 25 km (16 miles) northwest of Amsterdam at the weekend **Beverwijkse Bazaar**, one of Europe's largest indoor flea markets. Next door you will find Oriental merchandise.

SPECIALIST SHOPS

Specialist shops are dotted throughout the city. The unusual **Condomerie Het Gulden Vlies**, located in a former squat, sells condoms from all over the world. **Christmas Palace** sells festive adornments year round, and **Party House** has a vast collection of paper decorations. **Capsicum Natuurstoffen** has a huge selection of silks and linens, while **Coppenhagen 1001 Kralen** offers over 1,000 types of beads. It is also worth exploring **Joe's Vliegerwinkel** for kites, **Simon Levelt** for tea and coffee and **Jacob Hooy & Co.** for herbs.

BOOKS AND NEWSPAPERS

English-language books are easily available, particularly at **The American Book Center**, **Waterstone's** and **The English Bookshop**. They can also be picked up cheaply at second-hand shops, such as **De Slegte**. Comics collectors should not miss **Lambiek**. *Het Financieel Dagblad* has a daily business update in English and a weekly English-language edition, and there is the monthly *Time Out* listings magazine.

Organic foods for sale at the Noordermarkt

DIRECTORY

DEPARTMENT STORES AND MALLS

De Bijenkorf
Dam 1. **Map** 2 D5.
Tel 0900-0919.

Hema
Kalvertoren,
Kalverstraat. **Map** 4 F1.
Tel 020-4228988.
Nieuwendijk 174–176.
Map 2 D4.
Tel 020-6234176.

Magna Plaza
Nieuwezijds
Voorburgwal 182.
Map 2 D4.
Tel 020-6269199.

Maison de Bonneterie
Rokin 140–142.
Map 4 F1.
Tel 020-5313400.

Vroom & Dreesmann
Kalverstraat 201. **Map** 4 F1.
Tel 0900-2358363.

MARKETS

Boerenmarkt
☐ *summer: 9am–4pm Sat; winter: 9am–3pm Sat.*

De Beverwijkse Bazaar
Montageweg 35,
Beverwijk.
Tel 0251-262666.

Looier Kunst en Antiekcentrum
Elandsgracht 109.
Map 4 D1. 🚇 *7, 10, 17.*
☐ *11am–5pm Sat–Thu.*

Noordermarkt
Noordermarkt. **Map** 1 C3.
🚇 *3, 10, 13, 14, 17.*

SPECIALIST SHOPS

Capsicum Natuurstoffen
Oude Hoogstraat 1.
Map 2 D5.
Tel 020-6231016.

Christmas Palace
Singel 508.
Map 4 F1.
Tel 020-4210155.

Condomerie Het Gulden Vlies
Warmoesstraat 141.
Map 2 D5.
Tel 020-6274174.

Coppenhagen 1001 Kralen
Rozengracht 54.
Map 1 B4.
Tel 020-6243681.

Jacob Hooy & Co.
Kloveniersburgwal 12.
Map 2 E5.
Tel 020-6243041.

Joe's Vliegerwinkel
Nieuwe Hoogstraat 19.
Map 2 E5.
Tel 020-6250139.

Party House
Rozengracht 93a/b.
Map 1 B4.
Tel 020-6247851.

SPECIALIST SHOPS

Simon Levelt
Prinsengracht 180.
Map 1 B4.
Tel 020-6240823.

BOOKS AND NEWSPAPERS

The American Book Center
Spui 12. **Map** 4 F1.
Tel 020-6255537.

The English Bookshop
Lauriergracht 71. **Map** 1 B5. *Tel 020-6264230.*

Lambiek
Kerkstraat 132. **Map** 4 E1.
Tel 020-6267543.

De Slegte
Kalverstraat 48–52.
Map 2 D5.
Tel 020-6225933.

Waterstone's
Kalverstraat 152.
Map 4 F1.
Tel 020-6383821.

ENTERTAINMENT IN AMSTERDAM

Amsterdam offers a diverse array of world-class entertainment. A wide variety of performances are staged in hundreds of venues throughout the city, ranging from the century-old Concertgebouw *(see p120)* to the sleek modern Muziekgebouw on the IJ river. There is a huge choice of plays and films throughout the year, and plenty of free performances

Dutch National ballet

are given by a multitude of street performers and live bands in late-night bars and cafés. The city's hottest annual events include the Holland Festival and the Uitmarkt *(see pp33–4)*. Club-goers are in their element in the canal city, which offers club-nights to meet most tastes in music and skilled DJs, such as Tiësto, who are renowned around the globe.

The colonnaded façade of the Concertgebouw theatre

INFORMATION

Amsterdam's various tourist offices are a good starting point for what's going on in the city. They can usually provide copies of free listings magazines, including the *AUB/Uitburo* and the monthly *Uitkrant*, the definitive source of entertainment information. The monthly *Time Out Amsterdam* is an English-language magazine with entertainment listings, and the Amsterdam daily newspaper *Het Parool* publishes a supplement on Saturday with a cultural calendar and performance reviews.

The **AUB/Uitburo** has a last-minute window (open noon–7:30pm daily) selling tickets for same-day shows.

CLASSICAL MUSIC, OPERA AND DANCE

Amsterdam is the country's touchstone for classical music and opera, and the principal venues host some of the world's finest events. The open-air theatre in the

Vondelpark *(see pp120–21)* stages free concerts, and in summer, the Grachtenfestival features mainly classical music on floating canal stages.

The city's musical centre-piece is the **Concertgebouw** *(see p120)*, renowned for its acoustics and home to the celebrated Royal Concertgebouw Orchestra. International orchestras and soloists perform here regularly, and it hosts the Robeco Summer Concerts, a showcase of young talent. The **Beurs van Berlage** *(see p91)*, originally the city's stock exchange, is now a concert venue.

The Netherlands Opera stages performances in the 1,600-seat **Muziektheater** *(see p79)*, whose classical and modern repertoire is without parallel. The iconic **Muziekgebouw** is the place to go for anything from chamber music to the avant-garde.

The Netherlands is home to two world-class ballet companies. The Dutch National Ballet, based in the Muziektheater, puts on classical ballet

but also daring works by contemporary Dutch choreographers, while the Nederlands Dans Theater (NDT) specializes in works by its Czech artistic director, Jiri Kylian. Modern companies to look out for include Introdans, which combines jazz with flamenco and other ethnic dance, **Dansgroep Amsterdam**, which offers a platform for young choreographers and designers, and **De Meervaart** for experimental dance.

JAZZ, POP AND WORLD MUSIC

The Dutch are avid jazz fans, and big names such as Wayne Shorter, Branford Marsalis and Nicholas Payton show up regularly on local stages. The foremost jazz club is the **Bimhuis**, housed in a purpose-built hall of the Muziekgebouw. The Concertgebouw also hosts regular jazz concerts. Keep an eye out for local talent such as saxophonists

Bourbon Street, one of the city's jazz cafés

Disco in the Heineken Music Hall

and aircraft hangars. The musical dramas of Orkater appear mainly at the Stadsschouwburg and the **Bellevue Theater**. Summer outdoor theater can be seen in the Vondelpark *(see pp120–1)* and the Amsterdamse Bos *(see p189)*, a sprawling woodland park on the edge of town.

CINEMA

Film fanatics are well looked after, with more than 40 cinemas in town. Foreign-language films are shown in the original language with

The Art Deco Tuschinski Theatre, a luxurious cinema experience

Hans and Candy Dulfer. Good jazz cafés can be found along Zeedijk and around Leidseplein, namely **Jazzcafé Alto** and **Bourbon Street**.

For most Amsterdammers, rock and pop are synonymous with two venues. **Paradiso**, which has hosted the Rolling Stones, is housed in a converted church just off Leidseplein, while **Melkweg** occupies a former dairy nearby. Both offer a varied and entertaining diet of rock, pop, dance, rap and world music.

Mega-concerts are booked into the 50,000-seat **Amsterdam ArenA**, and headline acts sometimes play at the more intimate **Heineken Music Hall**.

As a multi-cultural society, the Netherlands is a natural breeding ground for world music. Traditions from West Africa and the West Indies, Indonesia, Surinam and Turkey come together in this fascinating melting pot. **Akhnaton** is a cultural centre with a potent cocktail of Caribbean, African and Arabic music. **De Badcuyp**, in the lively Pijp district, plays with salsa, tango, African music and other dance options. In bars like **Café Nol** and **De Twee Zwaantjes** you can hear traditional Dutch folk music.

THEATRE AND CABARET

The heart of the country's lively theatre scene is in Amsterdam. The premier venue is the **Stadsschouwburg** *(see p112)*, home to the Amsterdam Theatre Group and led by the imaginative

director Ivo van Hove. The annual highlight for opera, theatre and dance is the Holland Festival, held from late May to June. It overlaps with the International Theatre School Festival, whose experimental drama pops up at **De Brakke Grond** and **Frascati**.

The chief musical theatre is the **Koninklijk Theater Carré** *(see p135)*. It stages box-office hits such as Les Misérables and Miss Saigon. **De Kleine Komedie**, a magnificent 17th-century building on the Amstel river, is a favourite venue for cabaret groups. Stand-up comedy has gained in popularity, led by the hilarious English-language routines of **Boom Chicago**.

Experimental theatre can be found at a range of venues including **Westergasfabriek**, a converted former gas works in a lovely park setting. The company De Dogtroep stages offbeat street theatre, while Theatergroup Hollandia has won great acclaim with its performances in large halls

subtitles. The leading Dutch filmmaker is Amsterdam-born Paul Verhoeven (of *Basic Instinct* fame). He returned to his homeland to shoot *Black Book*, the highest-grossing Dutch film ever.

Cinema programmes change every Thursday, so check www.filmladder.nl or the Wednesday newspapers for listings. *De Filmkrant* is a free monthly film magazine

Musicians providing entertainment in the Vondelpark

with complete listings. The most stunning cinema in town is the **Tuschinski**, an Art Deco masterpiece with a luxurious foyer and stained-glass windows *(see p115)*. Some cinemas such as the mainstream **Pathé de Munt**, **City Theater** and the arthouse **Kriterion** show children's films at weekends. The **Uitkijk** is a cosy, 158-seat venue dating from 1913 that shows mainly classics.

CLUBS AND DISCOS

Amsterdam's nightclubs are famous for their variety and high energy. The scene throbs hardest in and around Leidseplein, Rembrandtplein and Reguliersdwarsstraat. Most clubs open at 11pm and are at their busiest from around 1am; closing time is 4am during the week and 5am on Friday and Saturday.

Jimmy Woo is famous for its tough door policy. Inside, it's Hong-Kong hip, with lots of black leather and a great sound system. **Escape** draws a young, trendy crowd to its huge split-level complex on Rembrandtplein, and another large, popular venue is **Club Roses**. On the opposite side of the square, **Rain** spins Latin and World beats.

The leading non-house club in town is **Sugar Factory**, with its diverse menu of soul, funk and jazz-dance. The other discos around Leidseplein are basically extended bars with small dance floors, catering to tourists. At **Odeon** near Spui Square, you can party your way up from the basement

The bright lights of Amsterdam ArenA, a premier sporting venue

brasserie to the dance palace on the third floor. Amsterdam's students have established their own club, **Dansen Bij Jansen**. The two sweaty dance floors are always packed at weekends, and you'll need a student card to get in. The college crowd also gravitates to the dancehall of **Hotel Arena**, located in a former orphanage.

Clubbing is also at the heart of Amsterdam's gay scene. Crowds are often mixed and most gay clubs will rarely turn away women or straight men. **Exit** is a slick bar with three levels and a balcony for viewing the dance scene below. Practically next door, **ARC** is a combination of bar and grand café, good for drinks during the day or for hooking up with the dance crowd later, and the nearby café **Reality** plays disco. A mixed lesbian/gay disco is **Club Roque**, while **Saarein II** is a friendly, relaxed bar tucked away in a small street in the Jordaan. Details of other venues are available from the Pink Point

kiosk next to the Westerkerk (www.pinkpoint.org).

SPECTATOR SPORTS

The Dutch are a sport-mad nation, and nothing makes their pulses race faster than

Two footballers clashing at an Ajax game

football. Three teams enjoy international standing: Ajax Amsterdam, Feyenoord Rotterdam and PSV Eindhoven *(see p362)*. They sometimes face off at the spectacular Amsterdam ArenA.

For something completely different, try watching a game of korfball, which was invented by Amsterdam teacher Nico Boekhuysen over 100 years ago. It mixes elements of basketball, netball and volleyball, and is the only unisex sport played professionally. Each team has four men and four women. Top-level matches are played on the indoor courts of the Olympic Stadium, built for the Games held in 1928.

Dancers at one of Amsterdam's many clubs

DIRECTORY

ENTERTAINMENT INFORMATION

AUB Ticketshop
Leidseplein 26. **Map** 4 E2.
Tel 0900 0191. **www.**
amsterdamsuitburo.nl

CLASSIC MUSIC, OPERA AND DANCE

Beurs van Berlage
Damrak 243. **Map** 2 D4.
Tel 020-5217575.
www.beursvanberlage.nl

Concertgebouw
Concertgebouwplein 2–6.
Map 4 D4.
Tel 0900 6718345.
www.concertgebouw.nl

Dansgroep Amsterdam
Luchtvaartstraat 2a.
Tel 020-6695755.
www.dansgroep
amsterdam.nl

De Meervaart
Meer en Vaart 300.
Tel 020-4107777.
www.meervaart.nl

Het Muziektheater
Amstel 3. **Map** 5 B2.
Tel 020-6255455.
www.muziektheater.nl

Muziekgebouw Aan 't IJ
Piet Heinkade 1. **Map** 2 F3.
Tel 020-7882000.
www.muziekgebouw.nl

Vondelpark
Stadhouderskade. **Map** 4
E2. *Tel 020-7882000.*
www.vondelpark.nl

JAZZ, POP AND WORLD MUSIC

Akhnaton
Nieuwezijds Kolk 25.
Map 2 D4. *Tel 020-624
3396.* www.akhnaton.nl

Amsterdam ArenA
ArenA Boulevard 1,
Zuidoost.
Tel 020-3111333.
www.amsterdamarena.nl

Bimhuis
Muziekgebouw aan 't IJ
Piet Heinkade 3. **Map** 2 F3.
Tel 020-7882188.
www.bimhuis.nl

Bourbon Street
Leidsekruisstraat 6–8.
Map 4 E2.
Tel 020-6233440.
www.bourbonstreet.nl

Café Nol
Westerstraat 109.
Map 1 B3.
Tel 020-6245380.

De Badcuyp
Sweelinckstraat 10.
Map 5 A5.
Tel 020-6759669.
www.badcuyp.nl

De Twee Zwaantjes
Prinsengracht 114.
Map 1 C3.
Tel 020-6752729.

Heineken Music Hall
Arena Boulevard 590.
Tel 0900 687 4242 55.
www.heineken-music-
hall.nl

Jazzcafé Alto
Korte Leidsedwarsstraat
115. **Map** 4 E2.
Tel 020-6263249.
www.jazz-cafe-alto.nl

Melkweg
Lijnbaansgracht 234a.
Map 4 E2.
Tel 020-5318181.
www.melkweg.nl

Paradiso
Weteringschans 6–8.
Map 4 E2.
Tel 020-6264521.
www.paradiso.nl

THEATRE AND CABARET

Bellevue Theater
Leidsekade 90. **Map** 4 D2.
Tel 020-5305301.
www.theaterbellevue.nl

Boom Chicago
Leidseplein 12.
Tel 020-4230101. **Map** 4
E2. www.boomchicago.nl

De Brakke Grond
Vlaams Cultureel
Centrum, Nes 45.
Map 2 D5.
Tel 020-6266866.
www.brakkegrond.nl

De Kleine Komedie
Amstel 56–58. **Map** 5 B3.
Tel 020-6240534.
www.dekleinekomedie.nl

Frascati
Nes 63. **Map** 2 D5.
Tel 020-6266866.
www.frascati.nl

Koninklijk Theater Carré
Amstel 115–125.
Map 5 B3.
Tel 0900 252 5255.
www.theatercarre.nl

Westergasfabriek
Haarlemmerweg 8–10.
Map 1 A1.
Tel 020-5860710.
www.westergasfabriek.
com

CINEMA

City Theater
Kleine Gartmanplantsoen
15-19. **Map** 5 C3.
Tel 0900 1458.

Kriterion
Roetersstraat 170.
Map 5 C3.
Tel 020-6231708.

Pathé de Munt
Vijzelstraat 15.
Map 4 F1.
Tel 0900 1458.

Tuschinski
Reguliersbreestraat 24–36.
Map 5 A2.
Tel 0900 1458.

Uitkijk
Prinsengracht 452.
Map 4 E2.
Tel 020-6237460.

CLUBS AND DISCOS

ARC
Reguliersdwarsstraat 44.
Map 4 F1.
Tel 020-6897070.

Club Roque
Amstel 178.
Map 5 A2.
www.clubroque.nl

Club Roses
Rozengracht 133.
Map 1 A5.
Tel 020-6242330.

Dansen Bij Jansen
Jansen
Handboogstraat 11.
Map 4 F1.
Tel 020-6201779.
www.dansenbijjansen.nl

Escape
Rembrandtplein 11.
Map 5 A2.
Tel 020-6221111.
www.escape.nl

Exit
Reguliersdwarsstraat 42.
Map 4 F1.
Tel 020-6258788.

Hotel Arena
's-Gravesandestraat 51.
Map 6 D4. *Tel 020-850
2400.* www.hotelarena.nl

Jimmy Woo
Korte Leidsedwarsstraat
18. **Map** 4 E2.
Tel 020-6263150.
www.jimmywoo.com

Odeon
Singel 460.
Map 4 F1.
Tel 020-5218555.
www.odeonamsterdam.nl

Rain
Rembrandtplein 44
Map 5 A2.
Tel 020-6267078.
www.rain-
amsterdam.com

Reality
Reguliersdwarsstraat 129.
Map 5 A2.
Tel 020-6393012.

Saarein II
Elandstraat 119.
Map 1 B5.
Tel 020-6234901.
www.saarein.nl

Sugar Factory
Lijnbaansgracht 238.
Map 4 E2.
Tel 020-6270008.
www.sugarfactory.nl

SPECTATOR SPORTS

Ajax Amsterdam Football team
http://english.ajax.nl

Olympic Stadium
Oud Zuid.
Tel 020-3054400.
www.olympischstadion.nl

STREET FINDER

The page grid superimposed on the *Area by Area* map below shows which parts of Amsterdam are covered in this *Street Finder*. Map references given for all sights, hotels, restaurants, shopping and entertainment venues described in this guide refer to the maps in this section (the *road map* is to be found on the book's inside back cover). An index of street names and places of interest marked on the maps is on pages 158–9. The key below indicates the maps' scale and other features marked on them, including transport terminals, emergency services and information centres. All major sights are clearly marked.

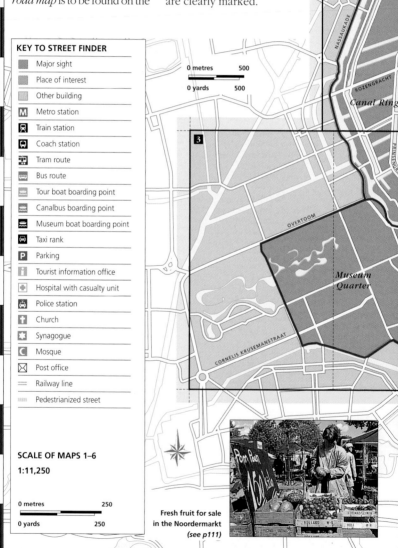

KEY TO STREET FINDER

	Major sight
	Place of interest
	Other building
M	Metro station
R	Train station
	Coach station
	Tram route
	Bus route
	Tour boat boarding point
	Canalbus boarding point
	Museum boat boarding point
	Taxi rank
P	Parking
i	Tourist information office
	Hospital with casualty unit
	Police station
	Church
	Synagogue
C	Mosque
⊠	Post office
=	Railway line
	Pedestrianized street

SCALE OF MAPS 1–6

1:11,250

| 0 metres | 250 |
| 0 yards | 250 |

| 0 metres | 500 |
| 0 yards | 500 |

Canal Ring

Museum Quarter

Fresh fruit for sale in the Noordermarkt
(see p111)

House with an elevated neck gable
(see p97) on the Geldersekade

HET IJ

UWERSGRACHT

EERLIGRACHT

DAMRAK

Oude
Zijde

Nieuwe
Zijde

VALKENBURGSTR

PLANTAGE MIDDENLAAN

AMSTEL

VIJZELSTRAAT

MAURITSKADE

LINNAEUSSTRAAT

ADHOUDERSKADE

Magere Brug, the
city's most famous
bridge *(see p114)*

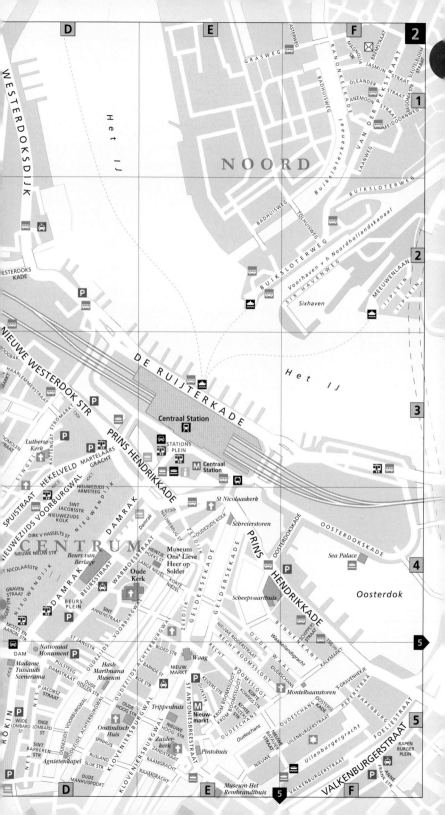

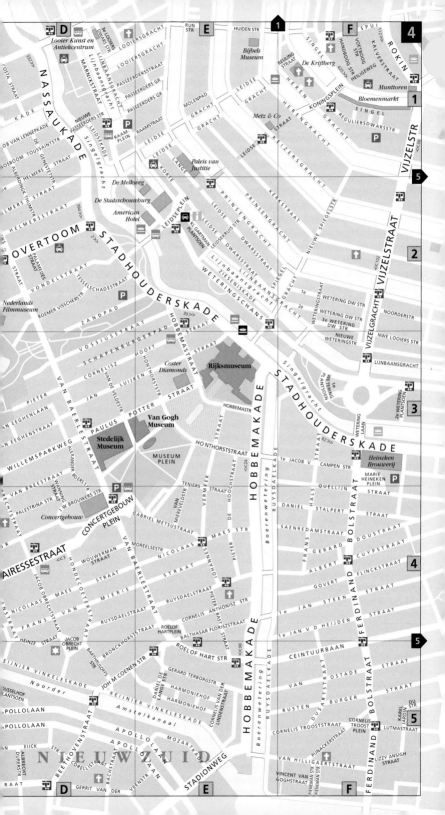

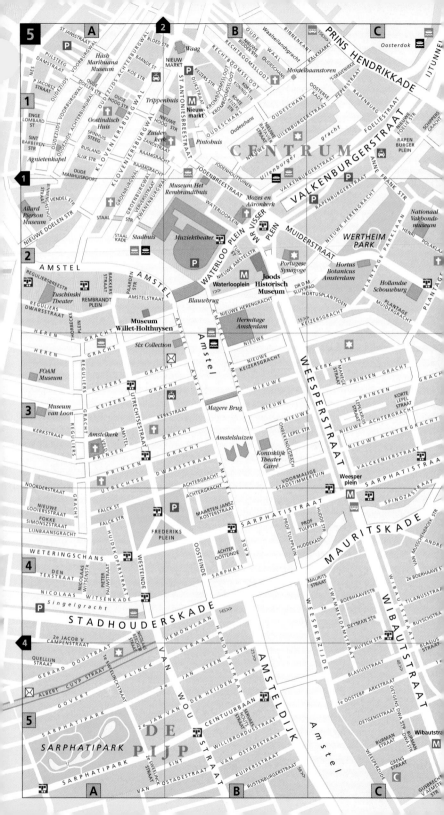

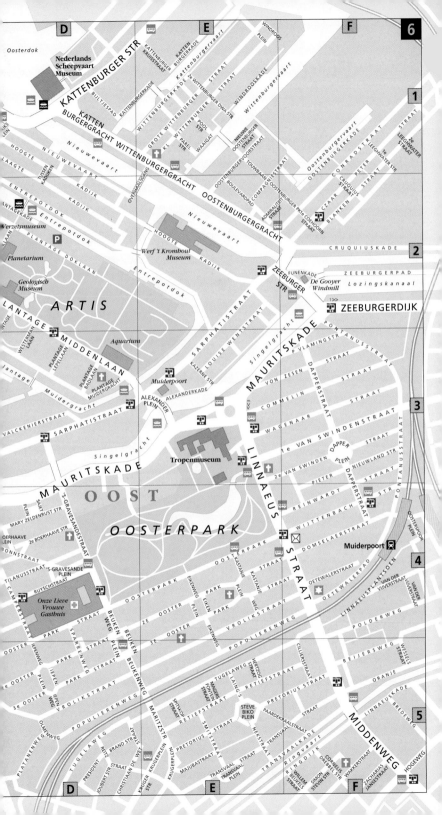

Street Finder Index

WESTERN NETHERLANDS

Exploring Western Netherlands

The landscape of the Western Netherlands is strongly influenced by the old ports and commercial towns, which claim a prosperous past. During the 20th century, the most important ones have grown together to form the Randstad *(see pp166–7)*. But you can still find plenty of quiet outside the cities – in Europe's biggest coastal dune area, boasting its distinct flora and fauna; along the Vecht, with its pretty country houses; and along rivers such as the Vlist and the Linge. Main watersports areas are Zeeland, on the IJsselmeer and the lakes in the peat region.

0 kilometres 20

0 miles

The gothic Sint Bavo Church
in Haarlem (see p184), known colloquially as the Grote Kerk, was built between 1400 and 1550. This gigantic building dominates the Grote Markt. Sint Bavo has one of the finest organs in Europe, built by Christiaan Müller.

The Hague

The Mauritshuis *at The Hague (see pp222–3) was built by Pieter Post in 1644 as instructed by Johan Maurits van Nassau, in the style of North Netherlands Neo-Classicism. Since 1821 it has been the home of the royal painting collection. This compact collection includes a number of first-rate works by old masters, including Rembrandt, Jan Steen and Johannes Vermeer.*

Middelburg

ZEELAND
(pp242–55)

Construction of the Oosterschelde Storm-vloedkering *(storm surge barrier) (see pp246–7) was prompted by the disastrous floods of 1953. To combat the water while preserving the unique mud-flat bed of the Oosterschelde, a half-open multiple but-tress dam with 62 sliding gates was built.*

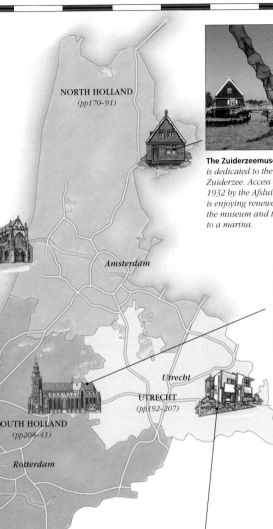

NORTH HOLLAND
(pp170–91)

Amsterdam

Utrecht

UTRECHT
(pp192–207)

OUTH HOLLAND
(pp208–41)

Rotterdam

The Zuiderzeemuseum *in Enkhuizen* (see pp176–7) *is dedicated to the history of the fishing ports of the Zuiderzee. Access to the North Sea was closed off in 1932 by the Afsluitdijk (barrier dam). Enkhuizen is enjoying renewed prosperity with the opening of the museum and the conversion of the fishing port to a marina.*

Gouda (see p238) *is one of the many commercial towns in the Western Netherlands that also has its prime position on the waterways to thank for its period of prosperity. The spirit of liberalism prevalent in Gouda during the 16th and 17th centuries protected the magnificent St Janskerk from the Iconoclasm, meaning that the Gouda stained glass is still here to be enjoyed today.*

The Rietveld Schröderhuis *in Utrecht* (see pp204–5) *is a famous example of "nieuwe bouwen" (new building). It was Rietveld's first complete architectural work and reveals his background as a furniture maker. At the time it was considered to be radically modern. Visitors nowadays are struck by the modesty and human proportions of the house.*

Reclaimed Land

The Netherlands is continually increasing in size. Various methods of reclaiming land have been employed as far back as the 11th century. One fairly simple method was to build a dyke around a marshy area. Later, deep lakes were drained with the help of windmills. The far-reaching IJsselmeer polders – fertile farmlands – were created after the Zuiderzee was closed off using ingenious reclamation methods. Even now, huge efforts are being made to extend areas of reclaimed land – hence the new Amsterdam residential area of IJburg, which has sprung up from the IJmeer.

To create a polder, *a ditch was first dredged. The dredgings were used to build up the dyke.*

GRADUAL DRAINAGE

To overcome the height difference between the polder and the ring canal, which is sometimes large, the water is continually raised metre by metre by three windmills placed in a row, known as a *driegang* or row of three.

Because a polder lies some metres below sea level, the ground water level is always very high and has to be continually drained.

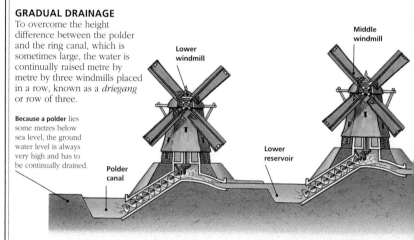

Lower windmill

Middle windmill

Lower reservoir

Polder canal

LAND RECLAMATION

About 3,000 years ago, houses were built on mounds so that they would not be flooded when the water rose. As far back as the 4th to 8th centuries, dykes were built around the houses and land. Land reclamation was carried out on a large scale from the 11th century, when the population increased sharply. In the 17th and 18th centuries, deeper lakes were drained with the help of rows of windmills. The steam engine meant a new phase of land reclamation: it was now finally possible to control the Haarlemmermeer. It is thought that, in Leeghwater's time *(see p165)*, at least 160 windmills were necessary for this. In 1891, the engineer C Lely put forward a plan to close off the treacherous Zuiderzee. This only actually happened in 1932, when the Afsluitdijk (barrier dam) was completed. Construction of the IJsselmeer polders then got underway.

Many dyke houses *are facing a threat to their continued existence because of the raising of the river dykes.*

An artificial island *in the North Sea is being considered for the site of a new airport, as Schiphol airport proves to be both inconvenient and with limited opportunities for expansion. Technical and financial problems, however, are delaying construction plans.*

The old port of Schokland *(see p326)* now lies firmly on the mainland

This view is of the oldest polder *in North Holland (anonymous, c. 1600). The West Friesland Omringdijk, which runs around Het Grootslag, is 126 km (78 miles) long and was completed as far back as 1250. North Holland ceased to exist to the north of the dyke.*

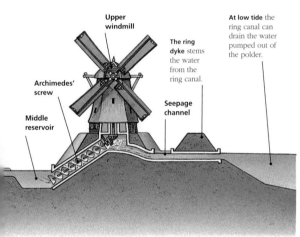

Upper windmill

The ring dyke stems the water from the ring canal.

At low tide the ring canal can drain the water pumped out of the polder.

Archimedes' screw

Middle reservoir

Seepage channel

In the 16th century, *Jan Adriaansz. Leeghwater invented a system that used windmills to drain a lake after a ring canal had been constructed around it. This meant that it became relatively easy to pump dry deeper and larger lakes, giving rise to the first pieces of reclaimed land.*

CONQUERING THE SEA

God created the earth – except Holland, for the Dutch did that. This statement by the French poet Voltaire comes close to the truth. This is because since the 14th century, the surface area of the Netherlands has increased by approximately 10 per cent, thanks to land reclamation. Land continues to be extended today, with the construction, for example, of IJburg, a new area of Amsterdam, which was built on an island in the IJmeer.

1860 Land could be drained only by using windmills. Limited areas were reclaimed.

1900 Thanks to the steam engine, increasingly lower-lying polders, such as the Zuidplaspolder, at -6.74 m (-22 ft), could be drained.

2000 The new Amsterdam district of IJburg is built in the IJmeer using the most modern methods available.

The Randstad

It appears that the term Randstad (literally, "rim city") was introduced by Albert Plesman, managing director of Dutch airline KLM, which was established in 1919. Apparently he pointed out to the passengers on one of his airplanes the horseshoe-shaped band of towns formed by Utrecht, Amsterdam, Haarlem, Leiden, The Hague, Rotterdam and Dordrecht. The relatively undeveloped area in the middle was quickly named the Groene Hart ("green heart").

Plan Linge III
75 vrije sector woningen

Inlichtingen en Verkoop:
01830 – 33933 | **03402-60606**
VAN GEFFEN MAKELAARDIJ B.V. | STICHTING WONINGBOUW CENTRAAL NEDERLAND

Opdrachgever:
Stichting Woningbouw Centraal Nederland
Nieuwegein

By 2015, *500,000 new houses are to be built in the Randstad.*

GROENE HART

The Groene Hart is a man-made landscape formed from an association with water that has lasted for centuries. It is characterized by elongated pieces of reclaimed land, peat lakes and river landscape with marshes and pools. The most important agrarian activity is dairy-cattle breeding; the cheese produced here is world-famous. Environmental organizations are dedicated to developing and protecting natural resources and historical landscapes. In de Venen, which surrounds the Nieuwkoopse and Vinkeveense lakes, a project is underway to combine extensive arable farming, natural development of the environment, and recreation facilities. It is hoped that this type of project will provide a balance to urbanization.

Hiking and cycling paths *have been erected throughout the Groene Hart. They pass dairy farms, windmills and old villages. Visit the local VVV (tourist board) for more information on recreational paths.*

Ring Rotterdam
Kralingen
Den Haag
Utrecht
Havens 200-1000
A 16
E19 8
afrit 25
Centrum
Capelle a/d IJssel
Havens 100-200
N 210

Congestion *is a major problem. During rush hour periods, the Randstad is clogged by traffic jams. The government is trying to reduce congestion on the roads by improving public transport and introducing other measures, such as road pricing. Up until now, this has not met with much success. The number of cars in the Randstad is constantly increasing.* Transferiums, *or park-and-rides, are meant to free up the town centres, which often still have old infrastructure and are not geared to a lot of traffic.*

P ↱ carpool

Car-pooling *is another way of reducing the number of cars. Over 750,000 people have car-pooled in the last few years.*

IJburg is a new district, built on the IJmeer to the east of Amsterdam. Another plan for municipal expansion into the water is Nieuw Holland, a long, narrow piece of land in front of the coast between Scheveningen and Hoek van Holland.

Schiphol *was, in the last decade, the fastest-growing airport in Europe. It benefits from a central location – close to many of Holland's major cities – and good rail and road connections. Expansion of the airport was halted by the objections of residents and environmental groups, but after considering other locations, such as an artificial island in the North Sea, Schiphol will indeed expand into adjacent areas.*

GROWTH OF THE RANDSTAD

As far back as the end of the 15th century, the Western Netherlands was one of the most urbanized regions of Europe. It was only during the 20th century that the borders between the towns became blurred and what is now known as the Randstad emerged. At present 6.5 million people live here.

Randstad around 1900

Randstad around 1950

Randstad around 2000

In contrast, the Groene Hart has only 600,000 inhabitants. Earnings in the Randstad account for half of the gross national product. The main product is provision of services, with Amsterdam as the financial centre, The Hague as the administrative centre, Hilversum as the focus of the audio-visual media and Rotterdam-Rijnmond and Schiphol as an important port and airport respectively.

Dunes

The Dutch coast is famous for its dunes. These natural sea walls, with a vegetation of their own, were used in earlier times as common ground for cattle grazing (the *oerol*, *see p274*) in the absence of sufficient grassland. They now play an important role in the purification of water. The dunes are also a particularly popular recreational area – many of the protected dune areas are open to ramblers and cyclists.

A catamaran on the beach

The sea supplies the sand from which the dunes are built.

On the beach, the dry, white sand drifts and piles up.

A sea inlet is formed when the sea breaks through the row of dune

Marram grass *is a sturdy plant whose root system holds new dunes together. It plays an important role in the formation and protection of Holland's dunes.*

Water collection *is done by way of the dunes, which retain the fresh water that falls inside them in the form of precipitation. Drinking water has been collected since the 19th century from the dunes of North and South Holland (such as at Meyendel, near Wassenaar, pictured above), helping to eliminate diseases like cholera from densely populated cities.*

NATURE RESERVES

The dunes are being used less and less as areas for water collection, meaning that the groundwater level is rising again and the damp dunes can once again be established. Protected against such environmentally damaging influences as industry and land development, they are becoming important nature reserves where there is a great deal for hikers and cyclists to enjoy. Vegetation includes gorse, spindle trees, creeping willow and hawthorn. Resident and migratory birds, such as curlews, tawny pipits and sometimes ospreys, inhabit the dunes. During World War II, anti-tank trenches with steep banks were built in the Midden-Heeren dunes (in Nationaal Park Zuid-Kennemerland). Today, even the rare kingfisher feels at home there.

The Dutch coast seriously damaged by storms

Rabbits *may look cute, but they have been known to seriously undermine the dunes with their intricate network of burrows.*

The first row of dunes, golden in colour because of the overgrowth, has higher summits.

The dune valleys have their own particular vegetation.

The sea inlet surface is home to many types of bird.

The dune overgrowth becomes richer as it moves inland, as limestone is replaced by humus.

ORIGINS

Dunes are created by a process which can be seen time and time again during a stormy day on the country's long, flat beaches. The sand carried by the sea dries on the surface of the beach and is then dragged by the wind like a white shroud over the beach. Held back by any obstacles in its way, the sand starts to accumulate. If the obstacle is a plant, a dune begins to form. Plants involved in forming dunes are called pioneer plants. They must be able to tolerate being buried by the sand and also be able to grow back through the sand. Sand couch grass (*Elymus farctus*) is renowned for being one such plant. After the initial dune formation, marram grass often begins to stabilize the new dune with its enormous root system. Dunes along the coast of the Netherlands can become as high as 10 m (33 ft). The dunes here – new dunes – were formed after 1200. When the sea breaks through dunes which have collapsed or have been cut through, it creates a sea inlet, or channel, around which an entire vegetation system develops, attracting all types of birds.

Sea holly and bee

Common sea buckthorn

Bulb fields *are evidence that the bulbs thrive in the sandy dune soil. The blooms' vivid colours are a pretty contrast to the yellowish-grey colour of the dunes.*

The beachcomber *gazes out to sea near the North Holland Camperduin, at the start of the Hondsbossche sea wall. The wall was constructed in the 19th century when the sea broke through the dunes. The lessons learned from this were used when building North Holland's Noorder-kwartier (north district).*

NORTH HOLLAND

*A*lthough North Holland's landscape is mainly flat, it is by no means featureless. Low-lying polders, with windmills and grazing cows, give way to market gardens and colourful bulb fields. Around Amsterdam the land is more built-up, with lively towns and picturesque villages almost cheek by jowl.

North Holland has always been one of the most important areas of the Netherlands economically, due to its industry, fishing and commerce. The Zuiderzee ports played a major part in the voyages of the Dutch East India Company *(see p48)* and their merchants became wealthy from the trade in exotic imports. They built splendid houses and filled them with expensive furniture and fine art, much of which has found its way into the province's leading museums.

This part of the country has learned to live with and profit from water. The province has it on three sides, with the unpredictable North Sea to the west and the vast IJsselmeer (formerly the Zuiderzee) to the east. The flat land in between is bisected by two major canals; one connects Zaandam to Den Helder in the north, while the other, the important North Sea Canal, gives Amsterdam's busy port access to the North Sea at IJmuiden. Land reclamation, in which the Dutch excel, has been going on since the 14th century, and many historical island communities are now surrounded by dry land.

Tourism is a major industry in North Holland, with Schiphol, the country's major airport, at its heart. The North Sea coast has a string of delightful resorts and sea-front hotels among the dunes, while in the communities on the IJsselmeer such as Edam, famous for its cheese, and picturesque Volendam, you can still find villagers wearing traditional costume and the famous Dutch wooden clogs.

Enkhuizen, a fine historical fishing town on the IJsselmeer

◁ The Afsluitdijk, a dyke which turned the Zuiderzee into the IJsselmeer

Exploring North Holland

The landscape of North Holland is varied and contains many old buildings and fine museums. The province can be easily explored on day trips from Amsterdam but areas such as West Friesland and Het Gooi, a woodland east of Amsterdam, are worth a longer visit. You can also alternate sightseeing with more relaxing activities such as walking in the beautiful nature reserve de Kennemerduinen (Kennemer dunes) near Zandfoort, sailing on the IJsselmeer or sun-bathing on one of the many beaches. Round trips through towns or on rivers are also good ways of exploring the province.

The working windmills on the Zaanse Schans

GETTING AROUND

During rush hour, roads around the large towns in the southern part of the province are fairly congested. Parking is also difficult to find in most of the larger towns and as bus and train connections in the area are good, it's often better to leave the car behind. The northern part of North Holland is also easily reached by public transport or by car on the A7 and A9 motorways. The natural landscape of North Holland lends itself to countless footpaths and cycle routes, each with different characteristics. Bicycles can be hired from most of the region's train stations.

SIGHTS AT A GLANCE

Aalsmeer **23**
Alkmaar **15**
Amstelveen **24**
Broek-in-Waterland **11**
Cruquius **21**
De Beemster **7**
Den Helder **13**
Edam **4**
Egmond **17**
Enkhuizen **9**
's-Graveland **27**
Haarlem **16**
Heemskerk **18**
Hilversum **28**
Hoorn **10**
Jisp **5**
Laren **30**

Marken **1**
Medemblik **12**
Monnickendam **2**
Muiden **25**
Naarden **26**
Naardermeer **29**
Ouderkerk aan de Amstel **22**
Velsen/IJmuiden **19**
Volendam **3**
Zaanse Schans **6**
Zandvoort **20**
Zuiderzee Museum
  pp176–7 **8**

Tour
West Friesland **14**

Julianadorp

Callantsoog

Noordhollan

N9

Schoorl

Heiloo

ALKMAAR
EGMOND **17**

A9

Uitgeest

HEEMSKERK **18**

VELSEN/ **19**
IJMUIDEN

Santpoort

Bloemendaal

HAARLEM **16** Zwanenbur

ZANDVOORT **20**

CRUQUIUS **21**

Hoofddorp

N201

N208

A4

A44

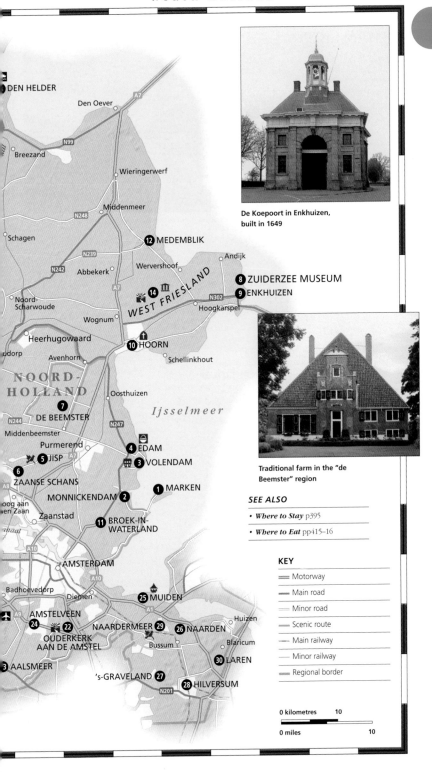

De Koepoort in Enkhuizen,
built in 1649

Traditional farm in the "de
Beemster" region

SEE ALSO

- *Where to Stay* p395

- *Where to Eat* pp415–16

KEY

===	Motorway
—	Main road
—	Minor road
—	Scenic route
—	Main railway
—	Minor railway
—	Regional border

0 kilometres   10

0 miles   10

Marken ❶

Road map C3. 🏘 *2,000.* 🚌
🚢 *from Volendam Apr–Oct.*
🛈 *Havenbuurt 19c (0900–4004040).*
www.vvv-waterland.nl

For almost eight centuries, Marken was a fishing community that saw little change. The construction of a causeway link to the mainland in 1957 put an end to its isolation. The island, however, has kept its original atmosphere, retaining its wooden houses built on mounds and piles to guard against flooding. Het Paard Lighthouse is a famous landmark. **Marker Museum**, located in six historic houses, gives a flavour of past and present life in Marken. There is also a cheese factory and clog-making workshop.

🏛 **Marker Museum**
Kerkbuurt 44–47. **Tel** 0299–601904.
◯ *Apr–Oct: daily.* 🏷 ♿

Monnickendam ❷

Road map C3. 🏘 *10,000.* 🚌
🚢 *Sat.*

This old town on the Gouwzee, founded by monks, has many buildings dating back to the 17th and 18th centuries, including the Stadhuis, or town hall, and the Waag, or weigh house. The **Museum de Speeltoren** explains the

Traditional dress, today worn as costume at Volendam's fishery

town's history. It is located in the Stadhuis clock tower, with its ornate 15th-century carillon: every hour, clockwork horsemen parade outside.

🏛 **Museum de Speeltoren**
Noordeinde 4. **Tel** 0299–652203.
◯ *due to reopen after restoration in late 2011; check website for updates.* 🏷 www.despeeltoren.nl

Volendam ❸

Road map C3. 🏘 *21,000.* 🚌
🛈 *Zeestraat 37 (0299–363747).*
🚢 *Sat.* www.vvv-volendam.nl

This old fishing village on the IJsselmeer is world-famous, attracting a huge number of tourists. The village is built along a dyke; at its small harbour, you can still buy all

sorts of fish. Traditional costume is one of this town's biggest attractions: the women wear tight bodices, lace caps and brightly striped skirts; the men, loose trousers and jackets. You too can dress up and have your photo taken. On the other side of the dyke is a different Volendam: an ancient, atmospheric maze of narrow streets, wooden houses and little canals.

Edam ❹

Road map C3. 🏘 *7,200.*
🛈 *Damplein 1 (0299–315125).*
🚢 *Wed.* www.vvv-edam.nl

Edam is known worldwide for the rounds of cheeses covered with red wax it exports. (Yellow wax is used if for local consumption.) Visit the **kaasmarkt** (cheese market) on Wednesday mornings in July and August to see how they are sold. Founded in the 12th century, the town has many historical buildings, including the brightly painted **Waag** (weigh house). The 17th-century stained-glass windows in the **Grote Kerk** are considered some of the finest in Holland.

The **Edams Museum** is located in a 16th-century merchant's house. Here you can see 17th-century portraits of famous Edammers, such as Trijntje Kever, who was supposedly 2.8 m (9 ft) tall.

🏛 **Edams Museum**
Damplein 8. **Tel** 0299–372644. ◯
Apr–Oct: Tue–Sun. ◯ *30 Apr.* 🏷

Distinctive 17th-century wooden houses at Marken

Typical Dutch windmill on the Zaanse Schans

Jisp ❺

Road map B3. 🏛 760. 🚌 👤 020-2018800. **www**.noord-holland.com

The old whaling village of Jisp, on one of the many former Zuiderzee islands, has a 17th-century feel. The *stadhuis* (town hall) and *dorpskerk* (village church) are worth a visit. The village lies in the middle of the **Jisperveld**, a nature reserve which is home to many different birds, such as lapwings, black-tailed godwits, redshanks, ruffs and spoonbills. This is a lovely spot to cycle, row, fish or, in the summer, visit on an excursion. The tourist office, VVV, has information about the various excursions offered.

Zaanse Schans ❻

Schansend 7, Zaandam. **Road map** C3. 🏛 50. 🚌 **Tel** 075–6810000. 🕐 daily, some buildings closed weekdays in winter. **www**.zaanseschans.nl

The Zaanse Schans is the tourist heart of the Zaan region. This open-air museum, created in 1960, has typical Zaan houses, windmills and buildings. When it's windy, you will be able to see the windmills working. The products (oil, paint, mustard) are for sale. All the houses are built from timber, as stone houses would sink at once into the soft peat earth. Also, at the time they were built, wood was readily available from local sawmills.

A visit to Zaanse Schans will also reveal **Albert Heijn's** first shop from 1887, a baking museum and cheese factory. The **Zaans Museum** showcases the history of the region. Pleasure boats offer trips on the Zaan.

🏛 **Zaans Museum**
Schansend 7, Zaandam. **Tel** 075–6810000. 🕐 daily. 🌑 1 Jan. 🎫 ♿

Environs
At the **Molenmuseum** (windmill museum) at Koog on the Zaan, you will learn everything you need to know about the windmills of the Zaan region. It is located in an 18th-century wooden house.

Haaldersbroek, opposite the Zaanse Schans, was once a boating village with narrow locks, brick paths and typical Zaan houses and farmhouses. Here, you'll feel as though you've gone back in time.

🏛 **Molenmuseum**
Museumlaan 18, Koog a/d Zaan. **Tel** 075–6288968. 🕐 Tue–Sun. 🌑 1 Jan, Easter Sun, Whitsun. 🎫

De Beemster ❼

Road map B3. 🚌 👤 Beemster (020-2018800).

The Beemster was once a lake that was drained in 1612 by **Jan Adriaans Leeghwater** (see p163). This unusual region has hardly changed since the 17th century, and in 1999 it was named a World Heritage Site by UNESCO. You can see historic objects and period rooms in the **Museum Betje Wolff**.

🏛 **Museum Betje Wolff**
Middenweg 178, Middenbeemster. **Tel** 0299–681968. 🕐 May–Sep: Tue–Sun; Oct–Apr: Sun. 🌑 1 Jan, 30 Apr, 25 Dec. 🎫

CZAAR-PETERHUISJE (TSAR PETER'S HOUSE)

In 1697, the Russian Peter the Great visited the shipyards of Zaandam in order to learn how the local people built ships. He lodged with Gerrit Kist, a tradesman whom he had

Peter the Great, who stayed in Zaandam twice

employed in St Petersburg. The tsar paid another visit to the town in 1717. The first mention of "Tsar Peter's house" in an official document was in 1780. This led to the tiny wooden house being supplied with a stone casing and foundations for protection. Every year, this humble house attracts a great number of tourists. (Krimp 23, Zaandam, tel. 075-6810000. Open 1–5pm Tue–Sun; closed 1 Jan, 25 Dec.)

Zuiderzeemuseum ❽

Enkhuizen was one of the towns whose economy was based on fishing and which was devastated when its access to the North Sea was blocked in 1932 by the construction of a barrier dam, the Afsluitdijk (*see p164*). Enkhuizen is today enjoying renewed prosperity with the opening of the Zuiderzeemuseum complex and the restructuring of the fishing port into a marina. The museum consists of an open-air section in the form of a museum-park, and an indoor area with a large number of exhibition spaces for permanent displays and temporary presentations.

★ Houses from Urk
Houses from the former island of Urk (see p326) have been rebuilt here. Actors portray life at the beginning of the 20th century.

Monnickendam smoke-houses

Entrance pavilion to Buitenmuseum

Reconstruction of Marken harbour

VIS Museum for Children

★ Schepenhal
The Schepenhal (marine hall) at the Binnen-museum (indoor museum) features an exhibition of 14 historic ships in full regalia. Children can listen to an exciting audio play while sitting in a boat.

Ferries take visitors from the station and entrance pavilion to the Buitenmuseum (open-air museum).

Entrance to Buitenmuseum

Sailmaker's Workshop
At the beginning of the 20th century, most ships and fishing boats had sails. The traditional craft of sailmaking is kept alive in this workshop.

Lime Kilns
Shells dredged from the sea bed were burned in bottle-shaped lime kilns. The resulting quicklime was then used as an ingredient in mortar for brickwork. These ovens come from Akersloot in North Holland.

★ Contemporary Delft Blue
Hugo Kaagman's paintings juxtapose traditional Delft motifs with present-day designs in refreshing combinations: windmills, tulips and fisherfolk sit beside portraits of popular singers.

VISITORS' CHECKLIST

Wierdijk 12–22, Enkhuizen.
***Tel** 0228–351111.* **Indoor and open-air museums** ☐ *Apr–Oct: 10am–5pm daily; indoor museum also open Nov–Mar: 10am–5pm daily.* ☐ *1 Jan, 25 Dec.* 🚋 *Enkhuizen.* 🚢 *from the station.* 📷 ◎ ♿ 🖥 🍴 📷
www.zuiderzeemuseum.nl

Fish Smoking
The Zuiderzee fishing industry relied mainly on herrings and anchovies, which were often salted or smoked. Here, herrings are smoked above smouldering wood chips.

Shipbuilding and repairs

A working windmill shows how polder drainage works *(see pp164–5).*

Houses from the Zuiderzee island of Urk

The houses in this area come from Zoutkamp, a fishing village on what was once the Lauwerszee.

0 metres	50
0 yards	50

The Church
The builders of this late-19th-century church, from the island of Wieringen, hid the organ in a cupboard to avoid the tax levied on church organs at that time.

STAR SIGHTS

★ Contemporary Delft Blue

★ Houses from Urk

★ Schepenhal

Hoorn harbour

Enkhuizen ❾

Road map C2. 🏠 *18,100*. 🚌 🚉
ℹ️ *Tussen twee havens 1 (0228-313164)*. 🏪 *Wed.*

Enkhuizen is still a major port. Its many fine buildings are evidence of the wealth of the Golden Age. The most famous building is the **Drommedaris**, dating back to 1540, used to keep watch over the old port. The city walls also date back to the 16th century. Enkhuizen has two splendid churches, the **Westerkerk** and the **Zuiderkerk**. Summer boat trips to Medemblik, Stavoren and Urk are especially pleasant.

Hoorn ❿

Road map C3. 🏠 *68,000*. 🚌 🚉
ℹ️ *Veemarkt 4 (072-5114284)*. 🏪
Sat; Jun–Aug: Wed. **www**.vvhoorn.nl

Hoorn's rich past, as the capital of the ancient province of West Friesland and one of the great seafaring towns of the Golden Age *(see pp50–51)*, has produced many beautiful

buildings. The late gothic **Oosterkerk** has a marvellous Renaissance façade, just like the St Jans Gashuis. Hoorn's historic past is set out in the **Westfries Museum**. A glimpse of the more recent past is found at the **Museum Hoorn**, which will move to a new site at some point in 2011–12; visit its website for updates.

🏛 **Westfries Museum**
Rode Steen 1. **Tel** *0229-280028.*
⏰ *Apr–Oct: daily; Nov–Mar: Tue–Sun.* 🔴 *1 Jan, 30 Apr, 3rd Mon in Aug, 25 Dec.* **www**.wfm.nl

🏛 **Museum Hoorn**
Bierkade 4. **Tel** *0229-214001.*
⏰ *Tue–Fri.* 🔴 *1 Jan, 30 Apr, 25 Dec.* **www**.museumhoorn.nl

Broek in Waterland ⓫

Road map C3. 🏠 *2350*. 🚌
ℹ️ *0299-363747.*

Broek in Waterland's status in the 17th century – as a retreat for sea captains of the East India Company – can still be seen everywhere in the village's crooked streets. The ornate clapboard villas are colour-coded: the captains lived in the pastel-tinted houses and non-seafarers in the ones painted grey. Along the **Havenrak**, the road winding along the lake, fine examples of *kralentuinen*, mosaics made from blue glass beads brought back by merchants from the East

Indies, can be seen in several of the gardens. To explore the village and surroundings from a different perspective, canoes and motorboats can be rented from **Kano & Electroboot Waterland** (Drs. J. van Disweg 4, 020-4033209).

Medemblik ⓬

Road map C2. 🏠 *8,000*. 🚌
ℹ️ *Kaasmarkt 1 (0227-542852)*.
🏪 *Mon.* **www**.vvvmedemblik.nl

Many pretty 17th-century houses can still be found in Medemblik. Also worth a look is **Kasteel Radboud**, built in 1288, and its museum. On the town's outskirts, an old pumping station is home to **Het Nederlands Stoommachinemuseum**, a hands-on collection of steam-driven industrial machinery.

Kasteel Radboud in Medemblik

🏛 **Het Nederlands Stoommachinemuseum**
Oosterdijk 4. **Tel** *0227-544732.*
⏰ *end Feb–early Nov: Tue–Sun.*
www.stoommachinemuseum.nl

Den Helder ⓭

Road map B2. 🏠 *57,000*. 🚌 🚉
ℹ️ *Bernhardplein 14 (0223–625544)*.
🏪 *Jul & Aug: Tue.* **www**.vvvkopvan noordholland.nl

This town, the base for the Dutch Royal Navy, has a **Marinemuseum** that displays marine history from 1488. At the North Sea Aquarium at Fort Kijkduin, a glass tunnel weaves among the fish.

🏛 **Marinemuseum**
Hoofdgracht 3. **Tel** *0223-657534.*
⏰ *May–Oct: daily; Nov–Apr: Tue–Sun.* 🔴 *1 Jan, 25–26 Dec.* 🖼 🅿️
www.marinemuseum.nl

Riverside setting of Broek in Waterland

For hotels and restaurants in this region see p395 and pp415–416

Windmills

Since the 13th century, windmills have been an inseparable part of the landscape of Holland. They have been used for a variety of purposes, including milling corn, extracting oil and sawing wood. One of their most important uses was to pump away excess water from the polders *(see pp164–5)*. Windmills consist of a fixed tower and a cap which carries the sails. The cap can be turned so that the sails face the wind. The sails can be very dangerous when they are turning – hence the Dutch saying, *"Een klap van de molenwiek hebben"* ("*To be struck by a windmill*"), that is, to have

Dutch miller

a screw loose. The Netherlands had thousands of windmills in earlier times, but since the arrival of modern machines, their number has dropped to just over 1,000. Many of these wind-mills are still working and are open for visits. See also *pp24–5.*

Watermill in the Schermer polder

Modern wind turbines *are common in Holland. They supply electricity without the pollution caused by burning oil or coal.*

Lattice and canvas sail

Polder mills *for draining became common during the 17th century. Standing in groups, they were each responsible for part of the pumping, through the use of an Archimedes' screw.*

Drive shaft

Archimedes' screw

Upper reservoir

The cogs *are turned by the sails. A rotating spindle makes a cog move, causing the water pump to start working.*

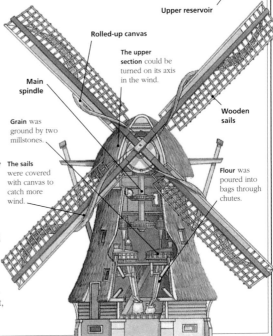

Rolled-up canvas

The upper section could be turned on its axis in the wind.

Main spindle

Grain was ground by two millstones.

The sails were covered with canvas to catch more wind.

Wooden sails

Flour was poured into bags through chutes.

FLOUR MILLS

Flour mills were covered with reeds and looked like enormous pepper mills. The millstones were linked to the sails by the spindle and gear-wheels and milled wheat, barley and oats.

West Friesland ⑭

During Holland's golden age, West Friesland played a major part in the Dutch economy as an important centre for trade and shipping. Nowadays the main inland activity is farming. Watersports bring in the most money on the IJsselmeer coast. If you take the route in spring, you will travel alongside blooming bulb fields and orchards. There is a pleasant bustle along the IJsselmeer in the summer, and part of the route is great for cycling.

't Regthuis, Abbekerk ④
This museum has collections of West Friesland clothing, curiosities and – most important for the children – toys.

Stoommachinemuseum (Steam Engine Museum) ③
The old steam pumping station "Vier Noorder Koggen" near Medemblik has a unique collection of steam-operated machinery.

Twisk ⑤
This long village has pretty farmhouses, many of which can often be reached only by little bridges.

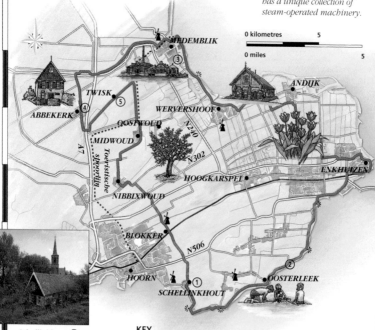

Schellinkhout ①
This attractive village just a stone's throw from Hoorn has been inhabited since prehistoric times. It once had an old sandy cove of the Zuiderzee.

KEY

▬▬	Suggested route
▬▬	Other road
—	Railway line
- - -	Tourist railway
⁂	Good viewing point
⚐	Windmill

West Friesland Omringdijk ②
In the 13th century, a ring dyke to protect against flooding was built around West Friesland. Through land reclamation, a large proportion of the dyke now lies inland. Two wiels, or pools, by the IJsselmeer are reminders of when water broke through the dyke.

Porters carrying cheese on sledges at Alkmaar's traditional cheese market

Alkmaar ⑮

Road map B3. 👥 94,000. 🚌 🚆
🛈 Waagplein 2 (072-5114284).
📅 Weekly market Sat; cheese
market Fri morning, Apr–Sep.
www.vvvalkmaar.nl

This old town has at least 400
monuments, and the street
layout has barely changed
over the centuries. Along the
canals, old merchants' houses
and small courtyards can still
be seen. The **Stedelijk Museum**
depicts the history of the town
through paintings, videos and
models. It also has a collection
of paintings from the Bergen
School of the 1920s and 1930s.

Alkmaar is famous for its
traditional **kaasmarkt** (cheese
market), which is held every
Friday morning from early
April to early September. The
large yellow wheels of cheese
arrive by barge. They are
tossed from the barges by
four groups of seven porters
from the 400-year-old cheese
porters' guild. The porters are
dressed in white and divided
into guild groups by the colour
of their hats. The cheese is
loaded onto sledges, which the
porters run with to the **waaggebouw** (public weigh house),
where the cheese is weighed.
Once tasting has taken place,
the cheese is auctioned off by
a system called *handjeklap*,
with sellers clapping each
other on the hands. The **Kaasmuseum** (cheese museum) at
the *waaggebouw* shows both

modern and traditional methods of dairy farming. A little
north of the cheese market is
the **Nationaal Biermuseum De
Boom**. Housed in an impressive 17th-century building,
in what had formerly been
the biggest brewery in
the town, the muse-
um explores a
millennium of
beer drinking in
the Netherlands.
The museum
illustrates, for
example, how in
the middle ages
Alkmaar lacked a
supply of safe drinking water,
so brewers would ship barrels
of clean water from the surrounding dunes and streams,
and then make it into beer.
The collection of equipment
shows the beer-making

process over the last 100
years, from copper vats,
kettles, barrels and bottles to
examples of the modern laboratory technology that breweries now use. There is also a
reconstruction of an old café
interior. Under the same roof
is a lovely waterside café and
"tasting house" where 86
different beers, many of them
Dutch, can be sampled.

South of the *kaasmarkt*,
on the corner where Mient
meets Verdronkenoord, is
the **vismarkt** or fish market,
which dates back to the 1500s
and was still in use until 1998.
The low, colonnaded stalls are
covered to protect traders and
their wares from the elements,
and contain brick and stone
benches where catches of fish
were displayed to customers.
The current buildings date
back to the mid-18th
century. Further along
Verdronkenoord is the Sint
Laurentiuskerk or **Grote
Kerk**. This 15th-century
church has one of
the most important
organs in Europe,
built from 1639–
46, and is note-
worthy for its
fresco depicting
the Miracle of
Alkmaar. In 1429,
a priest taking
mass knocked
wine onto the altar cloth; it
transformed into blood and,
although the priest cut out the
stained cloth and burned it,
the blood kept re-appearing in
the cloth. A relic containing
three red droplets is kept in
the church.

**The Renaissance façade
of the weigh house**

**The Biermuseum, where a variety
of beers can be sampled**

🏛 **Stedelijk Museum**
Canadaplein 1. **Tel** 072-5489789.
🕐 10am–5pm Tue–Fri, 1–5pm Sat
& Sun. ⬛ 1 Jan, 30 Apr, 25 Dec.
📷 ♿ **www**.stedelijkmuseum-
alkmaar.nl

🏛 **Waaggebouw** and
Kaasmuseum
Waagplein 2. **Tel** 072-5114284.
🕐 Easter–Oct: Mon–Sat. 📷 ♿

🏛 **Nationaal Biermuseum
De Boom**
Houttil 1. **Tel** 072-5113801.
🕐 Mon–Sat. ⬛ public hols. ♿
www.biermuseum.nl

🏛 **Grote Kerk**
Koorstraat 2. **Tel** 072-5140707. 🕐
Jun–Aug: Tue–Sun; during exhibitions.

Street-by-Street: Haarlem ⑯

Misericord in the Grote Kerk

Haarlem is the commercial capital of North Holland province and the eighth largest city in the Netherlands. It is the centre of the Dutch printing, pharmaceutical and bulb-growing industries, but there is little sign of this in the delightful pedestrianized streets of the historic heart of the city. Most of the sights of interest are within easy walking distance of the Grote Markt, a lively square packed with ancient buildings, cafés and restaurants. Old bookshops, antique dealers and traditional food shops are all to be discovered in nearby streets.

Statue of Laurens Coster
According to local legend, Haarlem-born Laurens Jansz Coster (1370–1440) invented printing in 1423, 16 years before Gutenberg. The 19th-century statue in the Grote Markt celebrates the claim.

The Hoofd-wacht is a 17th-century former guard house.

Stadhuis
Lieven de Key's allegorical figure of Justice (1622) stands above the main entrance. She carries a sword and the scales of justice.

★ **Vleeshal** *(1603)*
The old meat market is part of the Frans Hals Museum (see pp186–7).

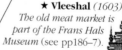

Grote Markt
The tree-lined market square is bordered with busy pavement restaurants and cafés. It has been the meeting point for the townspeople for centuries.

★ Grote Kerk
The huge church (see p184) is dominated by a decorative organ (1735) with soaring pipes, which drew many famous composers to Haarlem.

VISITORS' CHECKLIST

Road map B3. 147,000.
Stationsplein. Verwulft 11 (0900-6161600). Mon & Sat.
Haarlem Jazz Festival: end Aug; Bloemen Corso: end of Apr.
www.haarlem.nl

Shops and houses cling to the walls of the Grote Kerk.

★ Teylers Museum
Physical and astronomical instruments, like this brass electrostatic generator by Pieter van Marum (1784), form part of the collection in this museum of science, technology and art (see p185).

JANSSTRAAT

KLOKHUIS – LANGE BEGIJNESTRAAT PLEIN

WIJDEAPPELAARSTEEG

NAUWEAPPELAARSTEEG

BAKENESSERGRACHT

DONKERE SPAARNE

RIVER SPAARNE

Gravestenenbrug
This lift bridge crosses the river Spaarne. Located on the south bank is the embarkation point for boat trips along the river and canals.

STAR SIGHTS

★ Grote Kerk

★ Teylers Museum

★ Vleeshal

KEY

- - - Recommended route

0 metres   50
0 yards   50

Exploring Haarlem

Haarlem became a city in 1245, and had grown into a thriving clothmaking centre by the 15th century. But in the Spanish siege of 1572–3, the city was sacked, and a series of fires wreaked further destruction in 1576. The town's fortunes changed in the 17th century, when industrial expansion ushered in a period of prosperity lasting throughout the Golden Age. The centre was largely rebuilt by Lieven de Key (1560–1627) and still retains much of its character. The Grote Kerk continues to overlook the city's *hofjes* (almshouses), and the brick-paved lanes around the Grote Markt are little changed.

Grote Markt, Haarlem (c.1668) by Berckheijde, showing the Grote Kerk

� Frans Hals Museum
See pp186–7.

⚑ Grote Kerk
Oude Groenmarkt 23. **Tel** 023-5532040. ◯ Mon–Sat. ◉ Easter, Whitsun, 30 Apr, 5 May, 25 Dec–2 Jan. 🖼 & ✔ www.bavo.nl

The enormous Gothic edifice of Sint Bavo's great church, or Grote Kerk, was a favourite subject of the 17th-century Haarlem School artists Pieter Saenredam (1597–1665) and Gerrit Berckheijde (1639–98). Built between 1400 and 1550, the church and its ornate bell tower dominate the market square. Clinging on to the exterior of the south wall is a jumble of 17th-century shops and houses. The rents raised from these ramshackle, untidy buildings contributed to the maintenance of the church.

Today, the entrance to the Grote Kerk is through one of the surviving shops, a tiny antechamber that leads straight into the enormous nave. The church has a high, delicately patterned, vaulted cedarwood ceiling, white upper walls and 28 supporting columns painted in greens, reds and golds. The intricate choir screen, like the magnificent brass lectern in the shape of a preening eagle, was made by master metal worker Jan Fyerens in about 1510. The choirstalls (1575) are painted with coats of arms, and the armrests and misericords are carved with caricatures of animals and human heads. Not far away is the simple stone slab covering the grave of Haarlem's most famous artist, Frans Hals.

The Grote Kerk boasts one of Europe's finest and most flamboyant organs, built in 1735 by Christiaan Müller. In 1738 Handel tried the organ and pronounced it excellent. It also found favour with the infant prodigy Mozart, who shouted for joy when he gave a recital on it in 1766. The organ is still often used for concerts, recordings and teaching.

🏛 Stadhuis
Grote Markt 2. **Tel** 023-5115115. ◯ by appt only. &

Haarlem's Stadhuis (town hall) has grown rather haphazardly since 1250 and is an odd mixture of architectural styles. The oldest part of the building is the beamed medieval banqueting hall of the counts of Holland, originally known as the Gravenzaal. Much of this was destroyed in two great fires in 1347 and 1351, but the 15th-century panel portraits of the counts of Holland can still be seen.

The wing of the town hall bordering the Grote Markt was designed by Lieven de Key in 1622. It is typical of Dutch Renaissance architecture, combining elaborate gables, ornate painted detail and Classical features, such as pediments over the windows.

In a niche above the main entrance is a plump allegorical figure of Justice, bearing a sword in one hand and scales in the other as she smiles benignly upon the pavement cafés in the market below. To the left, in Koningstraat, an archway leads to the university buildings behind the Stadhuis, where there is a 13th-century cloister and library.

🏛 De Hallen
Grote Markt 16. **Tel** 023-5115775. ◯ daily. ◉ 1 Jan, 25 Dec. 🖼 www.dehallen.nl

The Verweyhal (museum for modern art) and the Vleeshal (exhibition space), both in the Grote Marskt, are part of the Frans Hals Museum (see pp186–7). The Verweyhal accommodates exhibitions of Dutch Expressionism, the Cobra School (see p189), Impressionism and contemporary works. It is named after the painter Kees Verwey, whose Impressionist still lifes are an important feature of the collection. The heavily ornamented Vleeshal (meat market), just to the west of the church, houses temporary

Detail on Vleeshal façade by Lieven de Key

The west gate of the Amsterdamse Poort (1355)

exhibitions of modern art. It was built in 1602 by the city surveyor, Lieven de Key, and has a steep step gable which disguises the roof line. The extravagantly over-decorated miniature gables above each dormer window bristle with pinnacles. A giant painted ox's head on the façade signifies an earlier function of the building.

⊞ Amsterdamse Poort
Amsterdamsevaart. 🚊 to public.
The imposing medieval gateway that once helped protect Haarlem lies close to the west bank of the river Spaarne. The Amsterdamse Poort was one of a complex of 12 gates guarding strategic transport routes into and out of Haarlem. The gate was built in 1355, though much of the elaborate brickwork and tiled gables date from the late 15th century.

The city defences were severely tested in 1573, when the Spanish, led by Frederick of Toledo, besieged Haarlem for seven months during the Dutch Revolt. The city fathers agreed to surrender the town on terms that included a general amnesty for all its citizens. The Spanish appeared to accept the terms, but once the city gates were opened, they marched in and treacherously slaughtered nearly 2,000 people – almost the entire population of the city.

🏛 Teylers Museum
Spaarne 16. *Tel* 023-5319010.
🕐 Tue–Sun. 🔴 1 Jan, 25 Dec. 🎫 ♿
📷 🖐 www.teylersmuseum.nl
This was the first major public museum to be founded in the Netherlands. It was established in 1778 by the silk merchant Pieter Teyler van der Hulst to encourage the study of science and art. The museum's eccentric collection of fossils, drawings and scientific paraphernalia is displayed in Neo-Classical splendour in a series of 18th-century rooms.

Tiles in Haarlem Station

The two-storey Oval Hall was added in 1779 and contains bizarre glass cabinets full of minerals and cases of intimidating medical instruments. A significant collection of sketches by Dutch and Italian masters, including Rembrandt and Michelangelo, is shown a few at a time.

🏛 Historisch Museum Haarlem
Groot Heiligland 47. *Tel* 023-5422427.
🕐 Tue–Sun. 🔴 1 Jan, Easter, Whitsun, 25 Dec.
www.historischmuseumhaarlem.nl
Haarlem is well known for its *hofjes* (almshouses), set up to minister to the poor and sick *(see p111)*. They first appeared in the 16th century and were run by rich guild members, who took over the role traditionally filled by the monasteries until the 1578 Alteration.

St Elisabeth's Gasthuis was built in 1610 around a courtyard opposite what is now the Frans Hals Museum. A 1612 plaque above the main doorway depicts an invalid being carried off to hospital. After restoration, the almshouse was opened in 1995 as Haarlem's principal historical museum.

🚉 Haarlem Station
Stationsplein.
The first railway line in the Netherlands opened in 1839 and ran between Haarlem and Amsterdam. The original station, built in 1842, was refurbished in Art Nouveau style between 1905 and 1908. It is a grandiose brick building with an arched façade and rectangular towers. The interior is decorated with brightly coloured tiles depicting various modes of transport. Other highlights are the woodwork of the ticket offices and the highly decorative wrought ironwork, particularly on the staircases.

17th- and 18th-century gabled houses along the river Spaarne in Haarlem

Frans Hals Museum

Celebrated as the first "modern" artist, Frans Hals (c.1582–1666) introduced a new realism into painting. Although his contemporaries strove for perfect likenesses, Hals knew how to capture his models' characters by using an impressionistic technique. Even at the age of 80, he still painted impressive portraits, such as *De regentessen van het Oude Mannenhuis in Haarlem* (Regentesses of the Old Men's Home in Haarlem) (1664). The Oude Mannenhuis (old men's home) became the Frans Hals Museum in 1913. It also has on show many paintings by other artists from the Dutch Golden Age.

★ **Stilleven (Still Life)** *(1613)*
Floris Claeszoon van Dyck (1574–1651)
was famous for his minute attention to detail and texture.

KEY TO FLOORPLAN

☐ Works by Frans Hals
☐ Renaissance Gallery
☐ Old Masters
☐ History of 17th-century Haarlem
☐ Non-exhibition space

Militia paintings by Hals

★ **Banket van de Officieren van de St-Jorisdoelen (Banquet of the Officers of the Civic Guard of St George)** *(1616) The features of each of the archers and the luxury of their banquet room are beautifully portrayed in this group portrait by Frans Hals.*

Courtyard

STAR PAINTINGS

★ Mercurius

★ Banket van de Officieren van de St-Jorisdoelen

★ Stilleven

Moeder en Kind (Mother and Child)
After the Reformation (see pp52–3), artists such as Pieter de Grebber (1600–53) painted secular versions of religious themes. This work of a mother feeding her child (1622) is reminiscent of Mary with Jesus.

★ **Mercurius** *(1611)*
*Hendrick Goltzius
(1558–1617) is particularly
well known for his studies
of classical nudes. One of a
three-part set, this canvas
was donated to the museum
by a rich Haarlem mayor.*

VISITORS' CHECKLIST

Groot Heiligland 62, Haarlem.
Tel 023-5115775. ☐ 11am–
5pm Tue–Sat, noon–5pm Sun &
public hols. ● 1 Jan, 25 Dec.
📷 🅿 ♿ 🎁 ☐ 📷
www.franshalsmuseum.nl

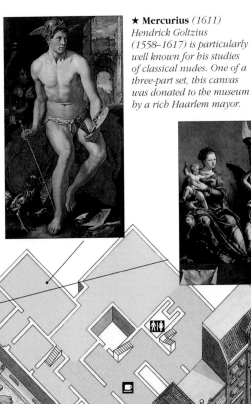

**St Luke Painting the
Virgin and Child**
*(1532), Maerten Jacobsz
van Heemskerck.
St Luke was the patron
saint of artists' professional
associations, the Guilds of
St Luke. This was painted
for the Haarlem Guild.*

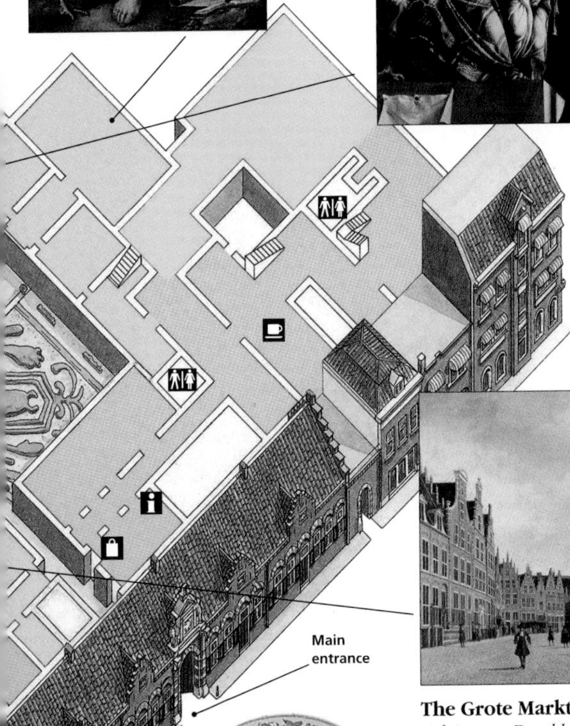

Main
entrance

The Grote Markt in Haarlem, *(1696), Gerrit
Adriaensz Berckheijde. The Grote Kerk or St
Bavokerk, seen here from the west, is built in
the Gothic style and is Haarlem's largest church.*

**Delft
Plate** *(1662)
The Grote
Markt and Grote
Kerk in Haarlem (see
p182) are depicted on this
earthenware plate by M Eems.*

MUSEUM GUIDE
*The best direction to take through the
museum is counter-clockwise, as exhibitions
of the works of Frans Hals, other portraits,
still lifes and pieces of genre paintings are
displayed in roughly chronological order.
In the Verweyhal and the Vleeshal (see
p184) temporary exhibitions are held of
modern and contemporary art.*

Egmond lighthouse, a welcoming beacon for ships at sea

Egmond ⑰

Road map B3. 🏠 *11,600.* 🚌
🛈 *Voorstraat 82a, Egmond aan Zee (072-5813100).* 🏛 *Thu.*
www.vvvegmond.nl

Egmond is divided into three parts: Egmond aan de Hoef, Egmond-Binnen and the seaside resort of Egmond aan Zee. The counts of Egmond once lived in Egmond aan de Hoef. Only the foundations remain of the **kasteel** (castle), which is open to visitors.

Egmond abbey, in Egmond-Binnen, is the oldest abbey in Holland and Zeeland. This 10th-century structure was destroyed, however, by Sonoy, chief of the Beggars of the Sea *(see p241)*. It was not until 1934 that a new abbey was built; Benedictine monks still live here today. The small **Abdijmuseum** (abbey museum) and **candle factory** can be visited (tel. 072-5062786).

Heemskerk ⑱

Road map B3. 🏠 *36,200.* 🚌
Tel 0251-374253. 🏛 *Fri.*
www.vvvijmondnoord.nl

An obelisk honouring Dutch artist Maarten van Heemskerck stands in the cemetery of the 17th-century **Hervormde Kerk** (Reformed church). **Slot Assumburg** (Assumburg castle), dating from the 15th century, was built on the site of a 13th-century fortified house. **Slot Marquette** is just as old but acquired its present form only two centuries ago. **Fort Veldhuis** is part of the **Stelling van Amsterdam**, a 135-km (84-mile) defensive line that encircles Amsterdam. It is now a small war museum, dedicated to the sacrifices made by pilots during World War II.

🏛 **Fort Veldhuis**
Genieweg 1. *Tel 0251-230670.*
⭕ *May–Oct: Sun.* 🎫 ♿

Velsen/IJmuiden ⑲

Road map B3. 🏠 *67,600.* 🚆 🚌
🚢 🛈 *Dudokplein 16, IJmuiden (0255-525353).* 🏛 *Thu.*

Holland's largest fishing port is IJmuiden. This can easily be guessed from the penetrating smell of fish and the many wonderful restaurants in the port. The **Noordersluis** (north lock), which forms part of the North Sea canal lock system, is one of the biggest locks in the world. As you come across you will pass by the Hoogovens (blast-furnaces), where you can take

a round trip on a steam train. The area around Velsen was already inhabited in Roman times; archaeological findings are exhibited in the **Ruïne van Brederode**, a 13th-century fortress. You will also feel you are going back in time in the Romanesque **Engelmundus-kerk. Slot Beeckestijn** is one of the many houses built on the coast in the 17th and 18th centuries by rich Amsterdammers. Only its gardens are open to the public at present.

🏰 **Ruïne van Brederode**
Velserenderlaan 2, Santpoort. *Tel 023-5378763.* ⭕ *Mar–Oct: Wed–Sun.* 🎫

⛲ **Slot Beeckestijn**
Rijksweg 136. *Tel 0255-512091.*

Zandvoort ⑳

Road map B3. 🏠 *15,500.* 🚆 🚌
🛈 *Bakkerstraat 2b (023-5717947).* 🏛 *Wed.* **www**.vvvzandvoort.nl

Once a fishing village, Zandvoort is now a modern seaside resort where in the summer half the population of Amsterdam relaxes on the beach or saunters down the busy main street. The village centre still has old fishermen's houses. Zandvoort is famous for its motor racing circuit, where Formula 1 races were once held. It has since been restored and is now attempting to achieve its former status. To escape the crowds, ramble through the **Amsterdamse Waterleidingduinen**.

🏎 **Circuit Park Zandvoort**
Burg. van Alphenstraat 108.
Tel 023-5740740. ⭕ *daily.*
🎫 *during meets.* **www**.cpz.nl

Stoomgemaal De Cruquius ㉑

Cruquiusdijk 27. **Road map** B3. 🚌
Tel 023-5285704. ⭕ *Mar–Oct: daily; Nov–Feb: Sat & Sun.* 🎫 ♿
www.museumdecruquius.nl

The Stoomgemaal (steam-driven pumping station) at De Cruquius is one of the three steam-driven pumping stations used to drain the **Haarlemmermeer**. It has not been

Slot Assumburg in Heemskerk, a youth hostel since 1933

The Cruquius steam pump

in use since 1933 and is now a museum. The original steam engine is in the machine hall, which has eight pumps moved by beams. An exhibition gives a comprehensive overview of water management in the Netherlands.

Ouderkerk aan de Amstel ㉒

Road map B3. 🏛 8,200.
🚌 Amstelveen.

This pretty village at the junction of the Amstel and the Bullewijk rivers has been a favourite with Amsterdammers since the Middle Ages. They had no church of their own until 1330, and worshippers had to travel to the 11th-century Ouderkerk that gave the village its name. The Old Church was destroyed in a tremendous storm in 1674, and a fine

18th-century church now stands on its site. Today Ouderkerk aan de Amstel is popular with cyclists who come to enjoy its waterfront cafés and restaurants.

Aalsmeer ㉓

Road map B3. 🏛 22,900. 🚌 🚋 Tue.

Aalsmeer is famous as the centre for floriculture in the Netherlands (see pp30–31). It also holds the biggest **bloemenveiling** (flower auction) in the world; you can take part in the auction from a special gallery.

Many greenhouses are to be seen around Aalsmeer. One important activity here is the development of new varieties and colours of flower. Many modern heroes have a "new" flower named after them.

🏛 **Bloemenveiling Flora Holland**
Legmeerdijk 313. **Tel** 0297-392185.
🕖 7–11am Mon–Fri. 🚫 📷 www. floraholland.nl

Amstelveen ㉔

Road map B3. 🏛 78,800.
🚌 🚋 Fri.

Electric tram

Amstelveen is home to many interesting modern art museums, such as **Museum van der Togt**, with its unique collection of glass objects. The **Electrische Museumtramlijn** (electric museum tramline) (tel. 020-6737538) keeps the past alive. On Sundays from April to October (and Wednesdays from July to August) you can take a return trip from Amsterdam to Amstelveen on a historic tram. The **Amsterdamse Bos** (Amsterdam forest) is lovely for rambling, picnicking or playing sport. The **Bosmuseum** is dedicated to the origins of the forest.

The **Cobra Museum voor Moderne Kunst** (Cobra museum of modern art) concentrates on the work of the Cobra group, established in 1948 by Danish, Belgian and Dutch artists. During its brief existence, Cobra abandoned dreary postwar art and introduced modern art definitively to the Netherlands.

🏛 **Museum Van der Togt**
Dorpsstraat 50. **Tel** 020-6415754.
🕖 Wed–Sun. 🔴 1 Jan, 30 Apr, 25 Dec. 🚫 www.vdtogt.nl

🏛 **Cobra Museum voor Moderne Kunst**
Sandbergplein 1–3. **Tel** 020-5475050.
🕖 Tue–Sun. 🔴 1 Jan, 30 Apr, 25 Dec. 🚫 🚻 www.cobra-museum.nl

Women, Children, Animals (1951) by Karel Appel in the Cobra Museum

The Muiderslot, built in 1280, a site of many legends

Muiden 25

Road map C3. 🕍 6,700. 🚌

In the Middle Ages, the pretty town of Muiden was an outpost for Utrecht but later became part of the defence system of the **Stelling van Amsterdam** *(see p188)*, together with **forteiland Pampus**. The town is mainly known for its castle, the **Muiderslot**, which is more than 700 years old and was built by Floris V. After his death it was demolished and rebuilt. The most famous inhabitant was the 17th-century poet PC Hooft, who formed the *Muiderkring* (Muiden circle), a circle of friends occupied with literature and music. Most of the castle rooms are furnished in 17th- and 18th-century style. The garden and orchard also retain their former glory. Boats once left from the castle jetty for the fortified island of Pampus.

Knight in armour

rebuilt around 1350. In the 15th and 16th centuries, it was occupied in turn by the Spanish and the French. The first thing you notice on arrival is the tower of the 14th-century **Grote Kerk**. The church's wooden vaulted ceiling has been beautifully decorated with pictures from the Old and New Testament. Around 400 years ago, Czech priest Comenius fled to the Netherlands, and now lies buried in the 15th-century **Waalse kapel** (Walloon chapel). The Spaanse Huis (Spanish house), which was converted into the Waag (weigh house), is now home to the **Comeniusmuseum**, which explores the life and ideas of the Czech scholar Jan Amos Comenius (1592–1670), who is buried here. The **Nederlands Vestingmuseum** (fortress museum) is in one of the six bastions of the fortress and has an exhibition of the Hollandse Waterlinie, a

⚓ **Muiderslot**
Herengracht 1. *Tel* 0294-256262.
🕐 Apr–Oct: daily; Nov–Mar: Sat & Sun. 🎫 🏷 www.muiderslot.nl

Naarden 26

Road map C3. 🕍 17,000. 🚌 🚊 🚌 Sat.

The fortified town of Naarden lies behind a double ring of canals and walls. The original town is thought to have been founded in the 10th century, then later destroyed and

strip of land flooded as a defence line in Holland, and of Naarden's eventful past. Costumed gunners regularly demonstrate the ancient artillery. There is a nice walk around the town along the footpaths on the walls.

🏛 **Comeniusmuseum**
Kloosterstraat 33. *Tel* 035-6943045. 🕐 Tue–Sun. 🔴 1 Jan, 30 Apr, 25 Dec, 31 Dec. 🎫 🏷
www.comeniusmuseum.nl

🏛 **Nederlands Vestingmuseum**
Westwalstraat 6. *Tel* 035-6945459. 🕐 Mar–Oct: Tue–Sun; Nov–Feb: Sun. 🔴 1 Jan, 25 Dec, 31 Dec. 🎫 ♿ 🏷 www.vestingmuseum.nl

's-Graveland 27

Road map C3. 🕍 9,200. 🚌

's-Graveland is a special place in Het Gooi *(see p172)*. In the 17th century, nine country estates were built here for rich Amsterdammers. Just across from these lie the modest houses that belonged to the labourers. Businesses now use the country houses, as the upkeep is too expensive for individuals. Five parks are owned by the Vereniging Natuurmonumenten and are open to visitors. You can learn more at the **Bezoekerscentrum** (visitors' centre).

🏢 **Bezoekerscentrum Gooi-en Vechtstreek**
Noordereinde 54b. *Tel* 035-6563080. 🕐 Wed–Sun.
www.natuurmonumenten.nl

Aerial view of the fortress of Naarden's star formation

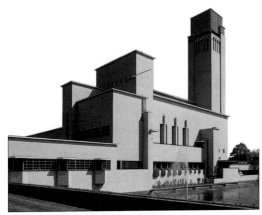

Hilversum town hall, finished in yellow brick

Hilversum 28

Road map C3. 84,500. Wed & Sat. **www**.vvhilversum.nl

This dynamic centre in Het Gooi (*see p172*) is known as the media centre of the Netherlands, because of the large number of broadcasting companies that have been established here.

Hilversum boasts a busy shopping centre and attractive residential areas with a lot of greenery. Here and there you will see houses and buildings designed by architect Willem Dudok (1884–1974), a representative of the Nieuwe Bouwen. One of his most famous creations is the 1931 **Raadhuis** (town hall), with its towers and beautiful interior (tours are given on Sundays). Its basement holds an exhibition on Dudok and temporary architectural exhibitions. The **Museum Hilversum** combines the Goois Museum and the Dudok Centrum, illuminates the past of Het Gooi and features an archaeological collection. The Neo-Gothic **Sint-Vituskerk**, designed by PJH Cuypers (*see p90*), with its 98-m (322-ft) tower, dates from 1892 and is worth a visit.

THE ERFGOOIERS

During the Middle Ages, the farmers of Het Gooi (*see p172*) joined together in a group to regulate the use of the heathland and meadows. Since 1404, their rights were held in plough share notes. Members of the group were known as *erfgooiers*, men living in Het Gooi who were descendants of these medieval farmers. The right of use was later converted into common property. The *erfgooiers* had to constantly fight for their rights. From the 19th century onwards, the government strived to disband the group. In 1932, the heathland was sold, as were the meadows after 1965. The Association of *Erfgooiers* was disbanded in 1971.

De Erfgooiers (1907) by F Hart Nibbrig

🏛 **Museum Hilversum**
Kerkbrink 6.
Tel 035-6292826. ⬜ Tue–Sun.
⬤ 1 Jan, 30 Apr, 25 Dec.

Naardermeer 29

Road map C3. 🛈 Natuurmonumenten (035-6559955). **www**.natuurmonumenten.nl

The Naardermeer is an area of lakes and marshland renowned for its breeding colonies of cormorants and purple herons. Several other birds, such as the marsh harrier, the bittern, the reed warbler and the spoonbill, can also be observed here. Unusual orchids, rare mosses and fungi grow here. The Naardermeer is the oldest protected nature reserve in the Netherlands. Its creation was the start of the Vereniging Natuurmonumenten (nature reserve association). The association has set out several walking tours around the area, which are accessible to everyone. From April to November there are guided boat tours on the lakes. Book on 035-6559955. No dogs.

Laren 30

Road map C3. 🛝 11,100. 🚌 🅿 Fri.

Alongside pretty villas and country houses, Laren has many converted old farmhouses, a reminder of the time when it was a farming village. In the 19th and early 20th century, Laren and its surroundings was the inspiration for many landscape and interior painters, such as Mauve, Israëls and the American W Singer. The **Singer Museum** has been set up in his old house. Here you can see his work and that of other 19th- and 20th-century artists. There is also a sculpture garden. **Sint-Jansbasiliek** (1925) towers above the Brink and its charming restaurants.

🏛 **Singer Museum**
Oude Drift 1. *Tel* 035-5393939.
⬜ Tue–Sun. ⬤ 1 Jan, 25 Dec.
www.singerlaren.nl

UTRECHT

The province of Utrecht, with the lively university city of the same name at its heart, has a vast range of attractions for visitors, including farmhouses, mansions, museums and castles, all set in a varied and attractive wooded landscape, and with a fascinating history dating back to Roman times.

The city of Utrecht has its origins in AD 47, when the Romans built a camp by a ford *(trecht)* at the river Rhine, which followed a different course in those days. In 695, Bishop Willibrord established himself here to promote the spread of Christianity. From the 11th century, the church authorities enjoyed not only spiritual but also secular power in this region, which has seen much conflict: over the centuries the counts of Holland, the dukes of Burgundy, the Spaniards, the French and the Germans have all tried to make their mark here.

The region's proximity to Amsterdam has meant that it has been able to share in the capital's prosperity as wealthy merchants and landowners built their mansions and estates along the river Vecht *(see p198)*.

In more recent times, the University of Utrecht has been a great source of economic and artistic development, and the city is home to a modern manufacturing industry and major Dutch corporations.

Visitors will enjoy the pretty countryside – ideal for car or cycle touring – the country houses and historic buildings, the street markets and a great variety of attractions ranging from eclectic furniture and old steam locomotives to barrel-organs and Australian Aboriginal art. But in this eco-conscious country, with its awareness of the need for conservation, it may be the outdoors, with its sparkling lakes and possibilities for leisurely country walks, that will appeal the most.

De Haar castle in Haarzuilens, a Neo-Gothic construction (1892) built by Pierre Cuypers

◁ IJsselstein flour mill, still worked in the traditional manner

Exploring Utrecht

The city of Utrecht is the central point of the province and is therefore the ideal base for sight-seeing in the surrounding area. The Vinkeveense Plassen (Vinkeveense Lakes) are popular for water-sports, and nature lovers will appreciate the woodland area of the Utrecht Heuvelrug. There are castles in Amerongen and Wijk bij Duurstede and numerous imposing country houses along the Vecht. Windmills and working farms can be spotted here and there in the countryside. Many defence points, such as in Woerden, serve as reminders of the turbulent past of this province, which has been at stake during fierce battles more than once.

The Vinkeveense Plassen, formed by excavations

The *heksenwaag* (witches' scales) in Oudewater

GETTING THERE

Larger towns have railway stations; smaller ones can be reached easily by bus. Utrecht, the capital of the province, is the biggest railway junction in the Netherlands and so train connections from this town are excellent. There is also a regional bus station. Utrecht has a highly developed road network and is served by important main roads such as the A2 (north-south) and the A12 (east-west), but there is also a large number of minor roads, tourist routes and cycle paths in the area.

VINKEVEENSE PLASSEN ①

LOENEN ②

COUNTRY ESTATES ON THE VECHT ⑦

Loosdrechtse Plassen

Abcoude

Mijdrecht

Vinkeveen

Breukelen

Maarssen

SLOT ZUYLEN ③

Groenekan

Vleuten

⑥

WOERDEN ④

Harmelen

De Meern

UTRECHT ⑫

Nieuwegein

Montfoort

OUDEWATER ⑤

IJsselstein

Tull en 't Waal

Lopik

Vianen

N201 · N212 · N228 · N210

KEY

▬	Motorway
▬	Main road
▬	Minor road
▬	Scenic route
▬	Main railway
▬	Minor railway
▬	National border

View of Rhenen, with its characteristic Cuneratoren

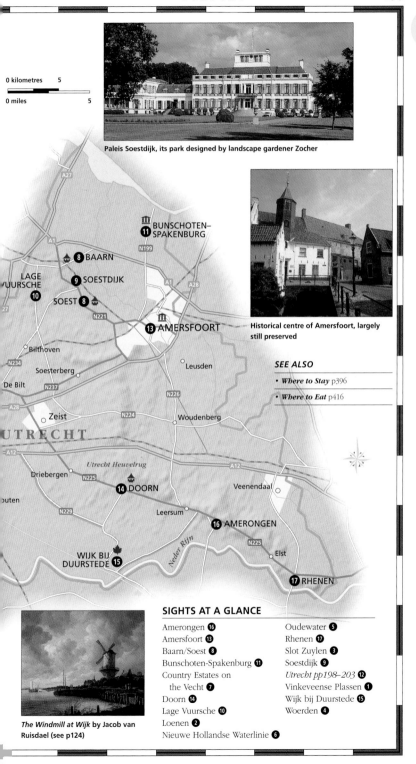

Paleis Soestdijk, its park designed by landscape gardener Zocher

Historical centre of Amersfoort, largely still preserved

BUNSCHOTEN–SPAKENBURG 11

BAARN 8

SOESTDIJK 9

LAGE VUURSCHE 10

SOEST 8

AMERSFOORT 13

Bilthoven

Soesterberg

De Bilt

Leusden

Zeist

UTRECHT

Woudenberg

Utrecht Heuvelrug

Driebergen

DOORN 14

Veenendaal

Leersum

AMERONGEN 16

WIJK BIJ DUURSTEDE 15

Nieder Rijn

Elst

RHENEN 17

SEE ALSO

• *Where to Stay* p396

• *Where to Eat* p416

The Windmill at Wijk by Jacob van Ruisdael (see p124)

SIGHTS AT A GLANCE

Amerongen 16
Amersfoort 13
Baarn/Soest 8
Bunschoten-Spakenburg 11
Country Estates on the Vecht 7
Doorn 14
Lage Vuursche 10
Loenen 2
Nieuwe Hollandse Waterlinie 6

Oudewater 5
Rhenen 17
Slot Zuylen 3
Soestdijk 9
Utrecht pp198–203 12
Vinkeveense Plassen 1
Wijk bij Duurstede 15
Woerden 4

Vinkeveense Plassen ❶

Road map C3. 🚌 🛥️

De Vinkeveense Plassen (Vinkeveense Lakes) came about through human intervention – this site was once marsh. The thick peat layers have been excavated over the centuries. The large towns in the surrounding area needed peat; sales of this fuel meant that the people here started to earn a decent living. The peat was therefore dug up more and more extensively, eventually leading to a large area of lakes.

Today, the Vinkeveense Lakes attract many watersports lovers, as well as cyclists and walkers. When it's not the breeding season, you can take a rowing boat through the nature reserve of **Botshol**, which is home to marsh and grassland birds.

Loenen ❷

Road map C3. 🏠 8,350. 🚌 🚤 Tue am.

In the 10th century, this place was called Lona, meaning "water" or "mud". Loenen fell under two different jurisdictions and has, therefore, two courts dating from the beginning of the 18th century.

Stately Slot Zuylen, where Belle van Zuylen lived in the 18th century

Loenen on the Vecht is famous for its rural atmosphere as well as for its castles and country estates complete with coach houses, summerhouses and boathouses, built over the centuries by wealthy citizens. It is now a protected village.

Kasteel Loenersloot, built on the bank of the Angstel, is one of the oldest country estates. The building dates back to the 13th century, though only the round defence tower remains; the rest dates from the 17th and 18th centuries. The castle is not open to the public.

Slot Zuylen ❸

Road map C3. 🚌 36,120. **Castle** Tournooiveld 1, Oud-Zuilen. **Tel** 030-2440255. ⬤ 15 Mar–15 May & 15 Sep–15 Nov: Sat & Sun; groups by appointment; 15 May–15 Sep: Tue–Thu, Sat & Sun. ⬤ 15 Nov–15 Mar. 🎥 🛈 www.slotzuylen.nl

The original U-shaped castle was built around 1520 on the remains of a medieval residential tower. At the beginning of the 16th century, a new castle was built on the foundations of the old house and the gateway was added. Up to the 18th century, extensive rebuilding brought the castle into line with contemporary architectural style.

The author Belle van Zuylen (1740–1805) was one of the castle's most famous inhabitants. She was famous for her correspondence at home and abroad, which she cleverly used to show her modern attitude. Several rooms are furnished as they were when she resided here.

The serpentine wall that runs alongside the castle is interesting because its unique shape provides so much protection that even in this cool sea climate, subtropical fruits such as peaches and grapes can flourish here.

Loenen on the Vecht still has an aristocratic appearance

For hotels and restaurants in this region see p396 and p416

Woerden ❹

Road map C4. 🏘 34,800. 🚈 🚌
ℹ️ Molenstraat 40 (0348-414474).
📧 Sat am. **www**.vvvwoerden.nl

Woerden came into being on the dykes along the Rhine and Lange Linschoten. Granted its town charter in 1372, it has been besieged many times but always managed to hold out. Between 1575 and 1576, during the 30 Years War, the Spaniards tried to conquer Woerden, as did the French in 1672, but neither invader succeeded in capturing the town. Impenetrable **kasteel van Woerden** (Woerden castle), built between 1405 and 1415, was extensively restored around 1990.

In the 18th century, the **Oude Hollandse Waterlinie** (old Holland waterline) – a strip of land flooded as a defence line – was extended, thereby strengthening Woerden.

Oudewater ❺

Road map C4. 🏘 10,000. 🚌
ℹ️ Leeuweringerstraat 10 (0900-468 3288). 📧 Wed. **www**.vvoudewater.nl

This little town, thanks to its favourable position on the IJssel and the Linschoten, became a prosperous town early on and, by 1265, had been granted its city charter.

Nesting storks in Oudewater

The counts of Holland and the bishops of Utrecht fought fiercely for Oudewater, which was converted into a border stronghold by Floris V. In 1349, Oudewater was captured by Jan van Arkel, the Bishop of Utrecht. In 1572, Oudewater sided with the Prince of Orange and, as a result, the town was seized in 1575 by the Spanish. They exacted a bloody revenge by burning the town to the ground. Oudewater flourished again during Holland's Golden Age.

The town's most famous attraction is the scales, dating from the 16th century, better known as the *heksenwaag* (witches' scales). Women who were suspected of witchcraft came here to be weighed. If their weight and their outward appearance tallied, they were given a certificate as proof of

their innocence. Oudewater was the only place where "witches" could be legally weighed in public.

🏛 Heksenwaag
Leeuweringerstraat 2. **Tel** 0348-563400. 🕐 11am–5pm Tue–Sun. ⓘ Nov–Mar. 📷 ♿ ground floor.
www.heksenwaag.nl

Nieuwe Hollandse Waterlinie ❻

Road map C3–C4.
www.hollandsewaterlinie.nl

The Nieuwe Hollandse Waterlinie (New Dutch Inundation Line), laid out from 1815 to 1940, is comprised of 68 forts and public works, from Muiden and Naarden in North Holland to Werkendam in North Brabant. Utrecht has 27 installations, more than any other province. The Waterlinie was intended as a defence against invading armies; a wide strip of land would simply be flooded. Utrecht's installations are now being protected, and have been put forward for UNESCO's World Heritage Site register. The original reconnaissance positions and unimpeded lines of fire will hopefully be preserved. The best installations are at Rijnauwen, Groenekan en Tull and 't Waal.

"Bombproof" barracks of the Nieuwe Hollandse Waterlinie (Fort Rijnauwen, Bunnik)

Country Estates along the Vecht ❼

Country estate houses, with their summerhouses, magnificent railings and extensive gardens, can be seen threaded along the Vecht, especially between Maarssen and Loenen. They were built in the 17th and 18th centuries by wealthy Amsterdam inhabitants who wanted to escape the noise and stench of the city in the summer. The estates were status symbols, places where city-dwellers could devote themselves to hobbies such as tree cultivation, hunting and still-life painting.

Plaque with coat of arms

GOUDESTEIN IN MAARSSEN

One of the first country estates in the Vecht, Goudestein was built in 1628 by Joan Huijdecoper. The present building, which dates from 1775, is now used as government offices. The coach house is now a fascinating pharmacy museum.

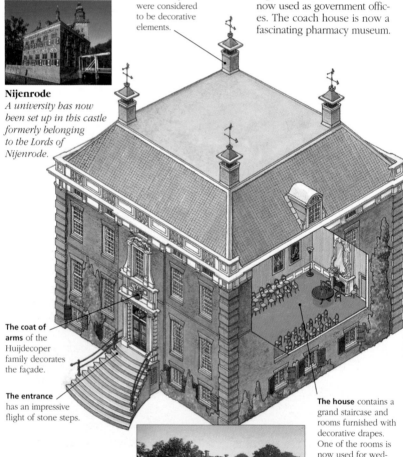

The chimneys were considered to be decorative elements.

Nijenrode
A university has now been set up in this castle formerly belonging to the Lords of Nijenrode.

The coat of arms of the Huijdecoper family decorates the façade.

The entrance has an impressive flight of stone steps.

The house contains a grand staircase and rooms furnished with decorative drapes. One of the rooms is now used for wedding ceremonies.

Between Breukelen and Loenen *the Vecht resembles an architectural museum. The country estates (Vechtvliet is shown here) are surrounded by established parks and ornamental outbuildings.*

Baarn/Soest 8

Roadmap C4. *70,000.*
Brinkstraat 12, Baarn (035-5413226). Baarn Tue, Soest Thu.

During the Netherlands' Golden Age, regents and wealthy merchants had splendid summer residences built in Baarn and its environs. This place has retained its leafy, elegant appearance. The **Kasteel Groeneveld** (1710) lies in the middle of a magnificent park. Soest's past is pre-9th century, and the old centre remains largely in its original state. The church dates from 1400. The surrounding area is beautiful and offers a wealth of leisure activities.

Kasteel Groeneveld
Groeneveld 2. ***Tel** 035-5420446.*
11am–5pm Tue–Sun.
Mon.

Soestdijk 9

Roadmap C3. *Steenhoffstraat 9b (035-6012075).*

Just outside Baarn lies **Paleis Soestdijk**. It was built in 1674 as a place for Viceroy William III to hunt. In 1815, it came into the hands of the crown prince, who later became King William II. The two wings of the palace were added in 1816 and the park was designed by landscape gardener Zocher. The **Naald van Waterloo** (Waterloo needle) stands opposite, erected in honour of William Frederick, Prince of Orange, for his services during the Battle of Waterloo. The estate closes for renovation in 2012.

Lage Vuursche 10

Roadmap C3. *250.*
Brinkstraat 12, Baarn (035-5413226).

The name "Furs" for Lage Vuursche has been around since 1200, though the village itself has existed only since the 17th century. The village, surrounded by woodland, is very popular with ramblers. Before her accession to the throne in 1980, the former Crown Princess Beatrice lived in the small octagonal castle **Drakenstein**, which dates back to 1640–43.

Bunschoten-Spakenburg, once home to an important fishing industry

Bunschoten-Spakenburg 11

Roadmap C3. *19,500.*
Oude Schans 90 (033-2982156).
Sat.

Over the years, the towns of Bunschoten and Spakenburg have merged into one another. Livestock farming was the traditional livelihood in Bunschoten, and there are still some pretty farms to see here. Bunschoten, granted its town charter in 1383, is older than Spakenburg, which came into being in the 15th century. It was once an important fishing town; its smokehouses, fishermen's houses and shipbuilding yard are reminders of this time. When the Zuiderzee was closed in 1932 because of partial land reclamation, the inhabitants had to look for other work.

Some of the women in the town still wear traditional dress. **Museum Spakenburg** brings the fishing activities of the past back to life.

Museum Spakenburg
Oude Schans 47–63. ***Tel** 033-2983319. Apr–Oct: 1:30–5pm Mon, 10am–5pm Tue–Sat; Nov–Mar: 1–4pm Wed–Sat.*
www.museumspakenburg.nl

Outdoor cafés in Lage Vuursche offering respite after a walk in the woods

Street-by-Street: Utrecht **⓬**

Museum van Speelklok tot Pierement

The area to the south of the centre gives one a good idea of how people once lived in Utrecht. Rich citizens lived in the stately houses on the Nieuwegracht, with its typical Utrecht wharves, and built almshouses for their less fortunate neighbours. No doubt because of the great number of museums in this area, it came to be called Museumkwartier (museum district). The old city walls gave way to a magnificent park which was designed by landscape gardener Zocher.

★ Oudegracht

The Oudegracht represented a vital transport route for the economy of Utrecht in the 13th century. When the water level fell, cellars were built along the wharves. These were used as warehouses or workshops. Today, some of them house cafés and restaurants.

```
0 metres          100
0 yards           100
```

STAR SIGHTS

★ Catharijneconvent

★ Centraal Museum

★ Oudegracht

★ Centraal Museum

The rich and varied contents include works by the 16th-century artist Jan van Scorel, as well as the largest collection of Rietveld furniture in the world.

Almshouses

The Pallaeskameren (Pallaes rooms) are 12 little almshouses built on the instructions of Maria van Pallaes in 1651. The inhabitants had free accommodation and a certain amount of food and drink annually.

Cathedral

BRIGITTENSTRAAT

TRAAT

NIEUWEGRACHT

BRUNTENHO

SERVAASBOLWERK

NIEUWEGRACHT

RAAT

KEY

– – – Recommended route

★ **Catharijneconvent**
*Museum Catharijneconvent
(Lange Nieuwstraat 38) is devoted
to religious art. It is located in the
former St Catherine's convent,
dating back to 1468. Part of the
convent church dates from 1529.*

**Nederlands
Spoorwegmuseum
(Dutch railway museum)**
*Old carriages and steam
locomotives can be seen
in the former Maliebaan
Station, dating back to the
19th century. The exhibi-
tion room features the history of the Dutch railways.*

Sonnenborgh
*The 19th-century
observatory, now
home to the Royal
Dutch Meteorological
Institute, was estab-
lished on one of the
four bulwarks along
the Singel.*

Exploring Utrecht

A euro coin from the Mint

Utrecht, founded by the Romans in AD 47, has been a bishopric and university town for centuries. It has grown into a lively city, thanks to its central position. Utrecht was very prosperous during the 16th and 17th centuries, when many of the magnificent canalside houses were built. These houses are a characteristic feature of the town centre, as are the medieval churches and monasteries. The city centre is compact so is very suitable for exploring on foot.

The 112-m (367-ft) Domtoren

🏰 Domtoren
Domplein. 📞 **Tel** 030-2360010.
⭕ 📷 obligatory. Apr–Sep: hourly 11am–4pm Tue–Sat, noon–4pm Sun & Mon; Oct–Mar: 2pm & 4pm Sun–Fri, hourly 11am–4pm Sat. 🌑 1 Jan, 25 Dec. 🎫 📷

The first thing you will see from the distance is the Domtoren (cathedral tower) rising above the town. The Dom (cathedral) has become the symbol of the town. Utrecht came into being on the Domplein (cathedral square), where the Romans had a settlement in the 1st century AD. In 695, Bishop Willibrord established himself here. In 1040, Bishop Bernold ordered a "cross of churches" to be built, which meant four churches with the later Domkerk in the centre. Work began on building the Domkerk in 1254 and in 1321 on the tower. The Gothic tower was finally finished in 1382.

Collegiate churches usually have two towers, but the

Domkerk has only one. The nave of the church was connected to the tower by an arch, allowing the bishop to move safely to and from the church. In 1674, the nave was destroyed by a hurricane. The tower has stood on its own since then. The interior of the church, with its stained-glass windows, Neo-Gothic organ (1831) and magnificent chancel, is worth a visit.

🏛 Aboriginal Art Museum
Oudegracht 176. 📞 **Tel** 030-2380100.
⭕ 10am–5pm Tue–Fri, 11am–5pm Sat & Sun. 🌑 1 Jan, 30 Apr, 25 Dec.
🎫 ♿ 📧 🌐 www.aamu.nl

This museum, the only one of its kind in Europe, is devoted to the many different styles of Aboriginal art, including painting and sculpture. The focus is on traditional art produced in Australian co-operatives.

🏛 Museum Catharijneconvent
Lange Nieuwstraat 38. 📞 **Tel** 030-2313835. ⭕ 10am–5pm Tue–Fri, 11am–5pm Sat, Sun & hols. 🌑 1 Jan, 30 Apr. 🎫 ♿ 📷 📧 📷
www.catharijneconvent.nl

The museum is split between a canalside house and a 15th-century former convent. Its fascinating collection provides a good overview of the troubled history of Christianity in the Netherlands. It includes paintings by, among others, Rembrandt van Rijn, ancient manuscripts and richly decorated books. The museum also houses numerous visiting exhibitions. From the museum you can enter into the Catharijnekerk (1551).

🏛 Centraal Museum
Nicolaaskerkhof 10. 📞 **Tel** 030-2362362. ⭕ 11am–5pm Tue–Sun.
🌑 1 Jan, 30 Apr, 25 Dec. 🎫 ♿ 📷
🌐 www.centraalmuseum.nl

Centraal Museum, the oldest municipal museum in the Netherlands, has a large and extremely varied collection, the oldest pieces of which date from the Middle Ages. Extensive rebuilding and renovations were carried out in 1999, giving rise to an interesting combination of old and new. The museum has the largest collection of Gerrit Rietveld furniture in the world. Works by Utrecht artists such as Van Scorel and Bloemaert, as well as 20th-century artists such as Pyke Koch and Dick Bruna – creator of the children's character Nijntje (Miffy) – are also showcased. Bruna's works are shown in the Brunahuis across the road. The varied exhibitions range from traditional art to fashion and historical costumes, to modern art and applied art and design, to the local history of Utrecht.

The Matchmaker by Gerard van Honthorst in the Centraal Museum

The Domkerk quadrangle

🏛 Nederlands Spoorwegmuseum

Maliebaanstation. 🚃 *Tel 030-2306206.* ⏲ *10am–5pm Tue–Sun & public hols (also Mon in school hols).* ● *1 Jan, 30 Apr.* 🎨 ♿ 🎫 🛍 www.spoorwegmuseum.nl
The superb Dutch railway museum is very appropriately situated in a former railway station dating from 1874 which was used as such until 1939.

Magnificent old locomotives, carriages and trains line the platforms. Children can ride over the museum grounds on a miniature railway. Adults and children alike will enjoy the exhibition inside, which includes old advertising posters and model trains.

🏛 Nationaal Museum van Speelklok tot Pierement

Buurkerkhof 10. 🚃 *Tel 030-2312789.* ⏲ *10am–5pm Tue–Sun & hols.* ● *1 Jan, 30 Apr, 25 Dec.* 🎨 ♿ 🎫 🛍 www.museumspeelklok.nl
This museum is inside the 13th-century Buurkerk – Utrecht's oldest church. The museum's collection displays the history of mechanical musical instruments. The showpiece is a rare 15th-century musical clock. You will also see – and hear – *pierementen*, the large organs pushed by organ grinders, music boxes, fairground organs and chiming clocks, as well as many smaller instruments with chiming mechanisms. Many of the instruments are demonstrated on the guided tour.

🏛 Universiteitsmuseum

Lange Nieuwstraat 106. 🚃 *Tel 030-2538008.* ⏲ *11am–5pm daily.* ● *1 Jan, 30 Apr, 25 Dec.* 🎨 ♿ 🎫 🛍 📷 www.uu.nl
The Universiteitsmuseum is in a purpose-built building close to the Centraal Museum. The collection here covers education since the university was established in 1636 and includes weighing and measuring instruments and a "collection of curiosities". Behind the museum is the University of Utrecht's lovely Old Botanical Garden (1723), which is open to the public.

🛍 Markets

The Vredenburg holds a general market on Wednesdays and Saturdays. On Fridays it holds a market for ecologically genuine agricultural produce. On Saturdays, the Janskerkhof hosts a large flower and plant market. On the same day, magnificent bouquets are sold along the Oudegracht, the old canal. The Breedstraat market, also held on Saturdays, is the venue of the cloth market.

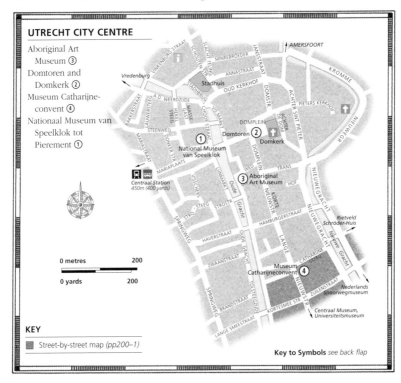

UTRECHT CITY CENTRE

Aboriginal Art Museum ③
Domtoren and Domkerk ②
Museum Catharijne-convent ④
Nationaal Museum van Speelklok tot Pierement ①

0 metres   200
0 yards   200

KEY

▨ Street-by-street map *(pp200–1)*

Key to Symbols *see back flap*

Rietveld Schröderhuis

Gerrit Rietveld and his employees

When designing this house, architect Gerrit Rietveld worked closely with his client, Mrs Schröder, who lived here from 1924 until her death in 1985. The house was to epitomize all that was "modern" and broke with many of the architectural standards of the time. This can be seen in the design of the top floor, which may be divided in different ways by sliding partitions, according to the requirements of the inhabitants. The house was declared a World Heritage Site by UNESCO in 2001.

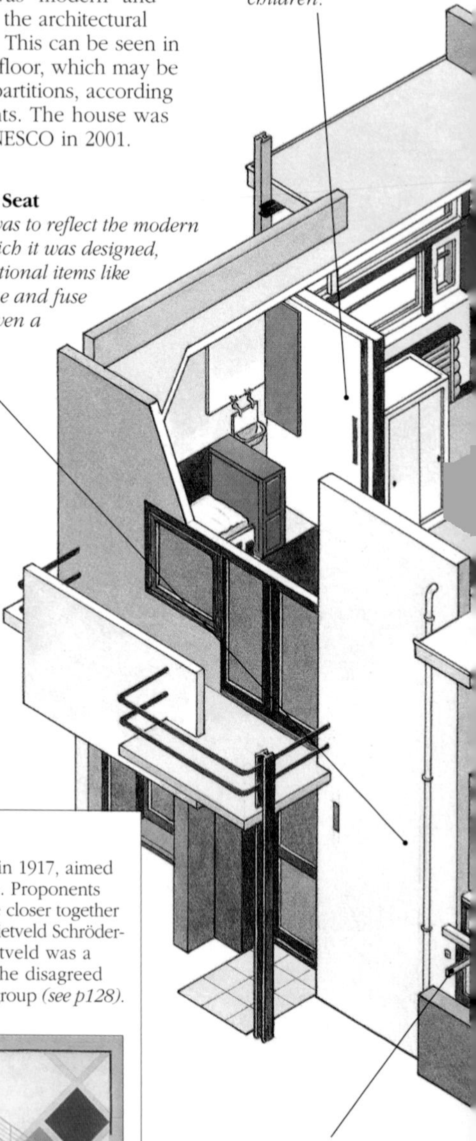

★ **Sliding Partitions**
Using sliding partitions, the top floor could be divided into separate rooms for Mrs Schröder's children.

Telephone Seat
The house was to reflect the modern times in which it was designed, and so functional items like the telephone and fuse box were given a prominent location.

STAR SIGHTS

★ Disappearing Corner

★ Rietveld Furniture

★ Sliding Partitions

DE STIJL

This Dutch artistic movement, founded in 1917, aimed to integrate art further into everyday life. Proponents wanted to bring painting and architecture closer together in a new way. The use of colour in the Rietveld Schröderhuis is one expression of this idea. Rietveld was a member of De Stijl from 1919, though he disagreed with certain ideas held by others in the group *(see p128)*.

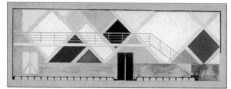

De Stijl member Theo van Doesburg was mainly interested in straight lines and primary colours. The geometric surfaces of this painting do not depict reality but offer a glimpse of universality.

BOODSCHAPPEN
EERST BELLEN BIJ GEEN GEHOOR SPREEKBUIS

Intercom
The Schröder's intercom sign instructed visitors to "First ring. If no answer use mouthpiece".

The Hanging Lamp
Rietveld designed this unusual lamp in around 1922.

Gerrit Rietveld
The architect always used scale models when designing houses but could also draw excellent floor plans, contrary to what was often said.

The skylight in the roof above the stairs allows additional light to reach the top floor.

★ Rietveld Furniture
In 1918, Rietveld designed what we now know as the red-blue chair. It was originally finished in clear varnish; only in 1923 did Rietveld paint it in what would become classic De Stijl colours.

★ Disappearing Corner
The dining corner has a spectacular feature: when the windows are opened, the corner disappears. Formerly the view from here was panoramic but in 1939, much to Rietveld's consternation, a road was built just next to the house.

Amersfoort ⓭

Road map C4. 👥 *144,800.* 🚉
🚌 ℹ️ *Stationsplein 9–11 (0900-
1122364).* 🛍️ *Thu, Fri & Sat.*
www.vvvamersfoort.nl

The old town centre of
Amersfoort contrasts sharply
with the districts that surround
it, which reflect a contemporary architectural style. The
centre is defined by small
streets with old houses and
gardens. The **Muurhuizen**
(wall houses) were built on
the site of the old defence
ring. The **Onze Lieve
Vrouwetoren** (Tower of Our
Lady) is difficult to miss. The
contours of this old chapel can
still be seen in the stones of the
pavement. In 1787, the chapel,
which was used to store gunpowder, was blown up.

The **Amersfoortse kei** boulder appeared in the town in
1661, when a nobleman bet
he could drag the stone from
the Leusderheide. Ever since,
Amersfoort has held the annual Keistadfeest (Keistad festival)
in celebration of the event.

The **Museum Flehite** gives
an overview of the history of
Amersfoort from the Middle
Ages. The town was the birthplace of the abstract painter
Mondriaan, the leading light of
the De Stijl and Neo-Plasticist
movements. The house where
he was born is now home to
the **Mondriaanhuis voor
Constructieve en Concrete
Kunst**, a study centre and
archive of the artist's life and
work, including several of his
paintings. Another artist
who lived in the town was

The 15th-century Koppelpoort, one of Amersfoort's three surviving gates

Armando (b. 1929). The
Armando Museum showcases
the work of this versatile
Amsterdam-born artist, whose
disciplines include painting,
sculpture, film, and poetry.
The church housing the collection burned down in 2007,
and the surviving works are
currently displayed in the Riet-
veldpaviljoen De Zonnehof.

Environs
Some 4 km (2 miles) away, in
the village of Leusden, **Kamp
Amersfoort** is a grim reminder
of the area's history. A Dutch
army barracks was transformed
in 1941 into a work camp for
more than 35,000 people,
including Jewish prisoners
and Jehovah's Witnesses.
Many were later transported
to concentration camps. The
camp also held American and
Russian prisoners of war. The
site is now a national monument. Several commemorative
ceremonies are held each year.

🏛️ **Museum Flehite**
Westsingel 50. *Tel 033-2471100.*
⏰ *11am–5pm Tue–Fri, noon–5pm
Sat & Sun.* 🚫 *Mon & public hols.*
🖥️ *www.museumflehite.nl*

🏛️ **Mondriaanhuis voor Con-
structieve en Concrete Kunst**
Kortegracht 11. *Tel 033-4600170.*
⏰ *Tue–Sun.*

🏛️ **Armando Museum**
Zonnehof 8, Amersfoort. *Tel 033-
4614088.* ⏰ *11am–5pm Tue–Fri,
noon–5pm Sat, Sun & hols.* 🚫 *1
Jan, Easter Sun, 30 Apr, 25 Dec.* 🖥️
www.armandomuseum.nl

🏛️ **Kamp Amersfoort**
Loes van Overeemlaan 13, Leusden.
Tel 033-4613129. ⏰ *Tue–Sun.*
www.kampamersfoort.nl

Doorn ⓮

Road map C4. 👥 *10,000.* 🚌
ℹ️ *Kerkplein 6 (0343-412015).*
🛍️ *Thu am.* **www.vvvheuvelrug.nl**

Doorn, originally called
Thorheim (home of Thor,
god of thunder), is a pretty village in wooded surroundings.
The greatest tourist attraction
here is **Huis Doorn**, where
between 1920 and 1941 the
German Kaiser, Wilhelm II,
lived with his retinue. (He fled
his country after World War I.)
The kaiser lies buried in a
mausoleum in the castle gardens. Deer and birds of prey
live in the **Kaapse Bossen**,
woods situated east of Doorn.

The **Von Gimborn Arboretum**
is a 27-hectare botanical garden begun in 1924. Part of
the University of Utrecht, it
was originally the private garden of Max von Gimborn, an
ink manufacturer who was a
tree expert and plant collector

Die Leiter by Armando (1990)

Von Gimborn Arboretum, one of the
Netherlands' largest gardens

in his spare time. One of the country's largest gardens, it is home to ten huge sequoia trees and an impressive collection of rhododendrons. Although best visited in spring and summer to see (and smell) the flowers in bloom, the gardens contain plants for all seasons.

🔹 **Huis Doorn**
Langbroekerweg 10. *Tel* 0343-421020. ⬜ 10am–5pm Tue–Sat, 1–5pm Sun (1 Nov–Mar: 1–5pm Wed, Sat & Sun). 🎦 mandatory. 📷 ♿ 🅿 www.huisdoorn.nl

🔹 **Von Gimborn Arboretum**
Velperengh 13. *Tel* 0343-412144 ⬜ daily. www.gimbornarboretum.nl

Wijk bij Duurstede ⓫

Road map C4. 🏘 23,000. 🚍
ℹ️ Markt 24 (0343-575995). 🔼 Wed.

Dorestad was an important trade centre in Carolingian times. Plundering Vikings and a shift in the river basin of the Rhine led to its decline. Then soon after, in the 13th century, Wijk (near Dorestad) emerged and became the home of the Utrecht bishops around 1450. They brought prosperity and influence to the town until, in 1528, the bishop lost his secular power. The impressive **Kasteel Duurstede** dates from the 13th century, when it was originally built as a donjon, the castle's fortified inner tower. This was extended in 1500, and bishops lived here until 1580. The castle's park was laid out in 1850 by Jan David Zocher.

🔹 **Kasteelpark Duurstede**
Langs de Wal 7. *Tel* 088-0001510. ⬜ 10am–5pm Tue–Sun (castle by appt).

Amerongen ⓬

Road map C4. 🏘 7,000. 🚍
ℹ️ Burg. Jhr van den Boschstraat 46 (0343-456500). 🔼 Thu.

Situated on the bank of the lower Rhine, which can be crossed by ferry, Amerongen lies in the ridge of hills known as the Utrechse Heuvelrug, a national park.

Castle tower in Wijk bij Duurstede

The Amerongense Berg marks the highest point in the ridge and has earned the name "mountain", despite being just 69 m (225 ft) high. The town lay originally on the Via Regia, the "royal route" from Utrecht to Cologne. From the 17th to 19th centuries, tobacco was grown in this area, as is evident by the drying sheds which are still standing. You can have a proper look at an old drying shed in the **Tabakteelt Museum**. In 1672, the town's castle, **Kasteel Amerongen**, was destroyed by the French. It was rebuilt in the Dutch Classical style.

🏛 **Tabakteelt Museum**
Burg. Jhr van den Boschstraat 46. *Tel* 0343-456500. ⬜ Tue–Sun pm. ♿ 📷

🔹 **Kasteel Amerongen**
Drostestraat 20. *Tel* 0343-454212. ⬜ check website. 📷 🎦 mandatory. www.kasteelamerongen.nl

Rhenen ⓭

Road map C4. 🏘 17,700. 🚉 🚍
ℹ️ Markt 20 (0317-612333). 🔼 Thu.

Rhenen lies on the north bank of the Rhine, at the border between the flat Betuwe and the Utrecht Heuvelrug. This area was inhabited as far back as the Iron Age. Many of the town's historic buildings were destroyed during World War II, but the Late Gothic **Cuneratoren** (Cunera tower), built between 1492 and 1531, escaped the bombs. The **Raadhuis** (town hall) dates from the Middle Ages. May 1940 saw a fierce battle on the 53-m (174-ft) **Grebbeberg**, a long-time strategic point in the surrounding area. The victims lie buried in the military cemetery.

East of the town, on the road to Wageningen, is the **Ouwehands Dierenpark**. This zoo contains all the favourites, like tigers, monkeys and elephants. There is also a large "bear wood", the *berenbos*, 20,000 sq m (66,000 sq ft) of forest-like landscape, where brown bears and wolves wander free. Other attractions include a tropical aquarium and plenty of children's activities, from a huge, jungle-themed adventure playground called RavotAapia, to special weekends dedicated to particular animals, and educational programmes.

🔹 **Ouwehands Dierenpark**
Grebbeweg 111. *Tel* 0317-650200. ⬜ daily. www.ouwehand.nl

A country house set in one of the large parks surrounding Wijk bij Duurstede

SOUTH HOLLAND

F or tourists, South Holland is pure delight. Although densely populated, the province still has plenty of open space and offers a remarkable range of attractions for visitors of all kinds. The landscape is typically Dutch, with large areas of reclaimed land dotted with windmills and grazing cattle.

From Roman times on, South Holland was principally a low-lying swampy delta as the various courses of the river Rhine reached the sea. The influence of the counts of Holland (9th–13th centuries), who took up residence in The Hague, attracted trade with Flanders, Germany and England, and settlements became towns. Leiden's university, the oldest in the country, was founded as long ago as 1565. Peat extraction for fuel created lakes, reclaimed land *(see pp22–3)* was turned into productive farmland, and the Dutch dairy industry flourished. Other products in international demand included beer and textiles and, in more recent times, year-round flowers and the famous Dutch bulbs. Overseeing all this activity is the port of Rotterdam, one of the largest in the world, and The Hague, home of the Dutch government, the royal family, and the International Court of Justice. Delft is famous for its exquisite hand-painted porcelain and china, while Gouda is renowned for its cheese. The North Sea coast has charming resorts, from busy Scheveningen, with its attractive pier, to the smaller seaside towns of Katwijk and Noordwijk, with long sandy beaches. It is an ideal region for family holidays and for children of all ages.

Visitors in spring are in for a treat when they tour the north of the province. Bulb fields erupt in a riot of colour, and the Keukenhof's flower gardens are simply unforgettable.

Servants waiting for the queen next to her Golden Coach on the third Tuesday of September (Prinsjesdag)

◁ One of numerous windmills that once drained the land in the Alblasserwaard

Exploring South Holland

In the north of the province of South Holland are the colourful bulb fields and the Keukenhof, while to the south in a semi-circle lie the old university town of Leiden, bustling The Hague, cosy Delft and the modern port city of Rotterdam. The islands of South Holland bear witness to the country's military history in Hellevoetsluis and Brielle. Ramblers will find all they wish for in the dunes by Wassenaar or in the river countryside at Leerdam, which is best known for its glass-blowing industry. From Gorinchem you can take a passenger ferry to the 14th-century castle of Slot Loevestein, which played a key role in the history of Holland.

The 14th-century Huis Dever by Lisse

The Panorama Mesdag in The Hague

SEE ALSO

- *Where to Stay* pp397–8
- *Where to Eat* pp417–18

Greenhouses in the Westland

Noordwijk aan Ze

Katwijk aan Zee

Wassenaar

SCHEVENINGEN **6**

THE HAGUE **5**

Rijswijk

Monster   Wateringen

Hoek van Holland

DELFT **7**

Europoort

Oostvoorne

MAASSLUIS **8**   SCHIEDAM **9**

BRIELLE **18**   Vlaardingen

Goeree

GOEDEREEDE **21**

Spijkenisse   Hoogv

19 HELLEVOETSLUIS

Oud-Beijerland

Oude Maas

Haringvliet

20 MIDDELHARNIS

Overflakkee

Oude-Tonge

GETTING AROUND

South Holland has a comprehensive system of roads, and both big cities and small towns can be reached equally quickly. However, during the morning and afternoon rush hours you should watch out for traffic jams. In the centres of the big cities it is best to leave your car in a car park, as finding an on-street parking space can often be a problem. Trains are a fast way of getting from A to B. As a rule you will find a train for your particular destination departing every quarter or half hour. Lisse and the bulbfields, Nieuwpoort and the towns on South Holland's islands can be reached only by local bus. VVV and ANWB tourist information offices provide information on cycling routes.

Knotwilgen in the Groene Hart

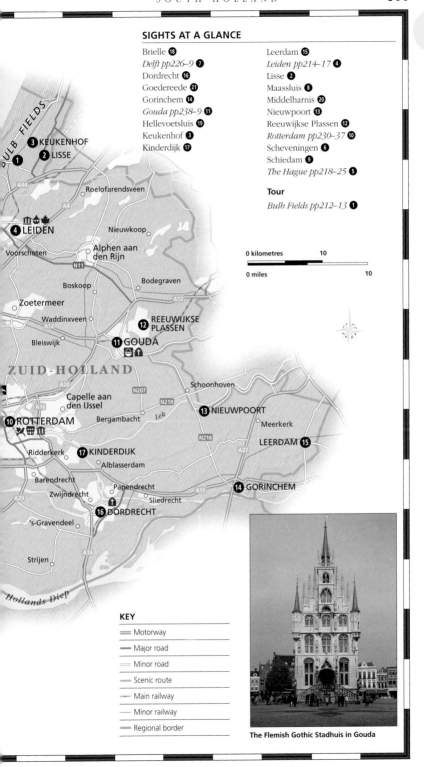

SIGHTS AT A GLANCE

Brielle **18**

Delft pp226–9 **7**

Dordrecht **16**

Goedereede **21**

Gorinchem **14**

Gouda pp238–9 **11**

Hellevoetsluis **19**

Keukenhof **3**

Kinderdijk **17**

Leerdam **15**

Leiden pp214–17 **4**

Lisse **2**

Maassluis **8**

Middelharnis **20**

Nieuwpoort **13**

Reeuwijkse Plassen **12**

Rotterdam pp230–37 **10**

Scheveningen **6**

Schiedam **9**

The Hague pp218–25 **5**

Tour

Bulb Fields pp212–13 **1**

---

0 kilometres   10

0 miles   10

KEY

═══ Motorway

━━━ Major road

═══ Minor road

━━━ Scenic route

━━━ Main railway

──── Minor railway

═══ Regional border

The Flemish Gothic Stadhuis in Gouda

Bulb Fields ❶

The Bollenstreek, a 30-km (19-mile) stretch between Haarlem and Leiden, is Holland's primary bulb-growing area. From March, the polders are aglow with glorious colours – the crocuses are the first to flower and the season culminates around mid-April with the majestic tulips. The lilies then follow at the end of May. Visitors without cars can obtain information about cycle routes from the tourist information office, the VVV, at Lisse (see p213). Bikes can be hired at railway stations in Haarlem and Heemstede-Aerdenhout.

TIPS FOR DRIVERS

Starting point: Haarlem.
Distance: approximately 30 km (19 miles).
Stopping-off points: along with the places discussed below, where various cafés and restaurants are to be found, Noordwijk aan Zee is worth a short detour. This lively coastal town, with its wonderful beach and dunes, makes an ideal place for a stopover.

The dunes of North Holland

Cruquiusmuseum ①
In this former steam-driven pumping station, you can see how the people of Holland managed to keep the water in check (see pp188–9).

Keukenhof ③
Visitors are greeted by the intoxicating aroma and vivid colours of millions of flowering bulbs.

Sassenheim ⑤
To the west of the town lie the ruins of Burcht Teylingen, the 11th-century castle where Jacoba of Bavaria, countess of Holland, died in 1436.

Linnaeushof ②
This huge park, named after the famous 18th-century botanist, has one of the biggest playgrounds in Europe.

Lisse ④
Lisse's museum showcases the bulb-growing industry; you can also take a boat trip on the lakes.

0 kilometres   4
0 miles   4

KEY
- ▬ Route
- ═ Roads
- ❀ Good viewing point

Katwijk ⑦
An unusual early 17th-century lighthouse stands to the north of this coastal town, which lies on the estuary of the Oude Rijn.

Voorhout ⑥
Panorama Tulip Land is a panoramic painting of the Bollenstreek. Its dimensions are enormous: 63 m (207 ft) wide and 4 m (13 ft) tall.

A tulip field in the Bollenstreek

FLOWERING BULBS

Flowers such as gladioli, lilies, narcissi, hyacinths, irises, crocuses and dahlias are mainly grown in the Bollenstreek. By far the most important, though, is the tulip, which originally came from Turkey and was cultivated by Carolus Clusius in 1593 for the first time in the Netherlands.

"Aladdin" tulips

"China Pink" tulips

"Tahiti" narcissi

"Minnow" narcissi

"Blue Jacket" hyacinths

Colourful flowering bulbs in the shady Keukenhof

Lisse ❷

Map B3. 🏘 20,000. 🚌 50 & 51 *(from Leiden & Haarlem)* & 59 *(from Noordwijk).* 🛈 *Grachtweg 53 (0252-414262).*

The best time to see Lisse is at the end of April, when the colourful **Bloemen Corso** (flower parade) takes place *(see p32)*. A vibrant procession of floats passes from Noordwijk to Haarlem, where they are brightly illuminated at night and can still be seen the next day. On the two days before the parade, you can see close-up how the floats are decorated in the *Hobaho* halls in Lisse.

The **Museum De Zwarte Tulp** (black tulip museum) covers the history of bulb growing and illustrates the life cycle of bulbs. It also touches upon the "tulipomania" from 1620–37 *(see pp30–31)*, when investors pushed up the demand for rare tulip bulbs to such an extent that they were worth their weight in gold.

🎪 Bloemen Corso
Tel 0252-428237 *(Stichting Bloemencorso Bollenstreek).*

🏛 Museum De Zwarte Tulp
Grachtweg 2a. *Tel* 0252-417900.
🕐 *1–5pm Tue–Sun.* ● *public hols.*
📷 ♿ 🖵

Environs

Just outside Lisse is **Huys Dever**, a fortified residential tower which dates from the second half of the 14th century. The permanent exhibition at the tower illustrates the lives of the families who lived here.

🏰 Huys Dever
Heereweg 349a. *Tel* 0252-411430.
🕐 *2–5pm Tue–Sun.* ● *public hols.*
📷 *by arrangement.*

Keukenhof ❸

Map B3. 🚌 *54 (from Leiden), 58 (from Schiphol airport). Tel 0252-465555.* 🕐 *daily late Mar–mid-May, 8am–6pm (ticket office).* 📷 ♿ 🍴
www.keukenhof.nl

Lying in a wooded park of 32 ha (79 acres) close to Lisse, the Keukenhof is one of the most spectacular public gardens in the world. It was set up in 1949 as a showcase for bulb-growers and currently has around 6 million bulbs planted in it. Fields are full of dazzling narcissi, hyacinths and tulips in bloom from the end of March to the end of May. You can also see the white blossom of the Japanese cherry tree in the park early in the season and, later, the bright flowers of the azaleas and rhododendrons.

Street-by-Street: Leiden ⊙

Leiden is a thriving university town which dates from Roman times. The town developed because of its position on a branch of the Rhine and is still an important trade centre. Some excellent museums chart Leiden's eventful past, including the Golden Age, when the town was a centre for world trade *(see pp48–9)*. Rembrandt van Rijn *(see pp26–7)* was born here in June 1606 – a plaque on the façade of a Weddesteeg house marks his birthplace. During term time, the streets of Leiden are busy with students cycling between lectures or frequenting the cafés and bookshops.

Statue of Justice on Stadhuis wall

★ **Rijksmuseum van Oudheden**
This squat statue of a kneeling treasury scribe is just one of the many impressive Egyptian artefacts on display in this fascinating museum of antiquities.

★ **Hortus Botanicus**
The botanical gardens belonging to the University of Leiden (see p216) were started in 1590 "for the teaching of every body who studies in the medicinal sciences".

Façades
Aristocrats, professors and textile families all contributed to the face of the Leiden canals.

Dutch Classicism can be seen in the university buildings on Rapenburg.

Het Gravensteen
Part of the law faculty is now accommodated in this former count's prison, built between the 13th and 17th centuries.

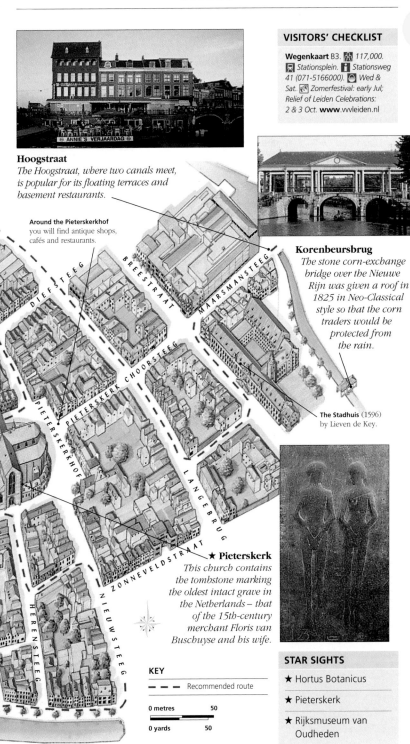

Hoogstraat
The Hoogstraat, where two canals meet, is popular for its floating terraces and basement restaurants.

Around the Pieterskerkhof
you will find antique shops, cafés and restaurants.

Korenbeursbrug
The stone corn-exchange bridge over the Nieuwe Rijn was given a roof in 1825 in Neo-Classical style so that the corn traders would be protected from the rain.

The Stadhuis (1596) by Lieven de Key.

★ **Pieterskerk**
This church contains the tombstone marking the oldest intact grave in the Netherlands – that of the 15th-century merchant Floris van Buschuyse and his wife.

VISITORS' CHECKLIST

Wegenkaart B3. 🚉 117,000.
🚊 *Stationsplein.* 🏠 *Stationsweg 41 (071-5166000).* 🛒 *Wed & Sat.* 🎭 *Zomerfestival: early Jul; Relief of Leiden Celebrations: 2 & 3 Oct.* **www**.vvvleiden.nl

KEY

- - - Recommended route

0 metres   50
0 yards   50

STAR SIGHTS

★ Hortus Botanicus

★ Pieterskerk

★ Rijksmuseum van Oudheden

Exploring Leiden

Leiden is famous for its university, which is the oldest in the country. It was founded in 1575, one year after the Beggars of the Sea *(see p241)* freed the town from a protracted siege by the Spanish *(see p49)*. As a reward for their endurance, William of Orange offered the people of Leiden the choice between a university and the abolition of taxes. The people made a shrewd choice and the town went on to become a centre of intellectual progress and religious freedom. English Puritan dissidents, victims of persecution in their homeland, were able to settle here in the 17th century before undertaking their journey to the New World.

One of the 35 almshouses in Leiden

🏛 Stedelijk Museum de Lakenhal

Oude Singel 28–32. **Tel** 071-5165360.
◯ 10am–5pm Tue–Fri, noon–5pm Sat & Sun (3 Oct: 10am–noon).
● 1 Jan, 25 Dec. 🖼 🕭 🎟 ▢
www.lakenhal.nl

In the 17th century, the *lakenhal* (cloth merchants' hall) was the centre of the Leiden textile industry. Arent van 's Gravesande designed the building in 1640 in Dutch Classical style. The municipal museum has been here since 1874. The showpiece of the collection, which was rescued from the Pieterskerk (St Peter's Church) during the religious disputes of 1566 *(see pp52–3)* is *The Last Judgment* (1526–7), a triptych in Renaissance style by Lucas van Leyden. Other Leiden artists, from Rembrandt to Theo van Doesburg, are also featured. The museum has

displays of silver, glass, tin and tiles and explores the history of Leiden. Not to be missed is the large bronze cooking pot said to have been left by the Spaniards during the relief of Leiden in 1574. The spicy casserole it contained is recreated as a stew cooked every year on 3 October to commemorate Dutch victory over the Spanish.

🌿 Hortus Botanicus Leiden

Rapenburg 73. **Tel** 071-5277249.
◯ summer: 10am–6pm daily; winter: 10am–4pm Tue–Sun. ● 3 Oct, 23 Dec–1 Jan. 🎟 🖼 🕭 (partial).

The botanical garden of Leiden was founded in 1590 as part of the university. A number of its trees and shrubs are

particularly old, such as a laburnum dating from 1601. In 1593, Carolus Clusius, who introduced the tulip to Holland *(see pp30–31)*, became the first professor of botany at the University of Leiden. The Hortus Botanicus features a reconstruction of his walled garden. Also worth a look are the tropical greenhouses, the rose garden and the Von Siebold Japanese memorial garden.

🏛 Museum Boerhaave

Lange St Agnietenstraat 10. **Tel** 071-5214224. ◯ 10am–5pm Tue–Sat (Mon on school hols), noon–5pm Sun & public hols. ● 1 Jan. 🎟 🖼 🕭 🎟 ▢
www.museumboerhaave.nl

Located in the former Caecilia Hospital in the centre of Leiden, this is the Netherlands' National Museum of the History of Science and Medicine. It is named after the great Dutch

Lucas van Leyden's triptych of *The Last Judgment*, in the Stedelijk Museum de Lakenhal

professor of medicine Herman Boerhaave (1668–1738). The collection reflects the development of mathematics, astronomy, physics, chemistry and medicine. Exhibits range from a magnificent 15th-century astrolabe and pendulum clocks by Christiaan Huygens (1629–95) to surgeons' equipment of yesteryear and early electron microscopes.

🏛 Museum Volkenkunde

Steenstraat 1. *Tel* 071-5168800.
⬜ 10am–5pm Tue–Sun & public hols. 🌑 1 Jan, 30 Apr, 3 & 4 Oct, 25 Dec. 🏷 ♿ 🖥 📷
www.volkenkunde.nl

This excellent ethnological museum, founded in 1837, has collections which feature non-Western cultures, such as ethnographic items brought by the German explorer Philipp von Siebold from Japan in the 19th century. The vast collection focuses on the interaction between various cultures and their links with the Netherlands; hence Indonesia has a considerable amount of floor space. The museum covers practically the whole world, from the Arctic to Oceania.

🏛 Naturalis

Darwinweg 2. *Tel* 071-5687600.
⬜ 10am–5pm daily. 🌑 1 Jan, 30 Apr, 4 Oct, 25 Dec. 🏷 ♿ 🖥 📷 www.naturalis.nl

As soon as it opened in 1998, the national natural history museum attracted a record number of visitors. It provides a truly fascinating insight into the evolution of the earth and its inhabitants with displays of fossils more than a million years old, and lifelike replicas of animals, stones and minerals. Special exhibitions for children are also held.

⛪ Pieterskerk

Pieterskerkhof 1a. *Tel* 071-5124319.
⬜ check website. 🌑 3 Oct & when church is hired out. ♿ 📷 2pm Sun.
www.pieterskerk.com

This impressive Gothic cruciform church, built mainly in

THE PILGRIM FATHERS

In the 17th century, the Netherlands was a refuge for English Puritans. Minister John Robinson (1575–1625) founded a church in Leiden in 1609, where he inspired his congregation with his dream of the New World. The Pilgrim Fathers set out in 1620 from Delfshaven aboard the *Speedwell*, but the ship proved to be unseaworthy. They then crossed the Atlantic from Plymouth, England, on the *Mayflower*, but Robinson stayed behind, too ill to travel. He died in Leiden in 1625.

The *Mayflower* crossing the Atlantic Ocean

---

the 15th century, stands in the middle of a shady square that seems to be from a different age. It is worth a visit for its austere interior and the carefully restored Van Hagerbeer organ (1639–43), one of the few meantone-tuned organs. The floor of the nave is covered with worn stones which mark the graves of famous 17th-century intellectuals such as Puritan leader John Robinson, physician Hermanus Boerhaave and Golden Age artist Jan Steen.

Heraldic lion at De Burcht

♣ De Burcht

Burgsteeg. ⬜ *daily.*

The Burcht is a 12th-century fortress which features a still-intact circular wall and crenellated battlements. At the foot of the 12-m (39-ft) artificial mound is a wrought-iron gate

---

covered in heraldic symbols. There is a marvellous view of Leiden's historic centre from the gallery.

🏛 Rijksmuseum van Oudheden

Rapenburg 28. *Tel* 0900-6600600.
⬜ 10am–5pm Tue–Sun & public hols. 🌑 1 Jan, 30 Apr, 3 Oct, 25 Dec. 🏷 ♿ 📷 🖥 📷 www.rmo.nl

This museum has one of the top seven Egyptian collections in the world, the centrepiece of which is the 2,000-year-old Taffeh Temple. Other civilizations from the Near East and from Classical Antiquity are also represented. The section on archaeology of the Netherlands gives visitors an idea of what the Low Countries were like from prehistoric times to the Middle Ages. Mummies, textiles and shoes, musical instruments and fragments of Roman mosaics and frescoes form just part of the museum's impressive holdings.

A drawbridge across the Oude Rijn in Leiden

Street-by-Street: The Hague ❺

The village of Die Haghe ("the hedge") grew around the Binnenhof (inner courtyard), which has been an important political centre since the 13th century. The princes of Orange, the upper classes and an extensive diplomatic corps gave instructions for palaces and mansion houses to be built, and a stroll across the Voorhout or along the Hofvijver will still evoke its aristocratic charm.

The Hague today is represented by the new Spuikwartier (Spui district), with the city hall by Richard Meier and the Lucent Danstheater by Rem Koolhaas. To the west, the dunes and many parks and woods are still reminiscent of the country estate it once was.

Jantje

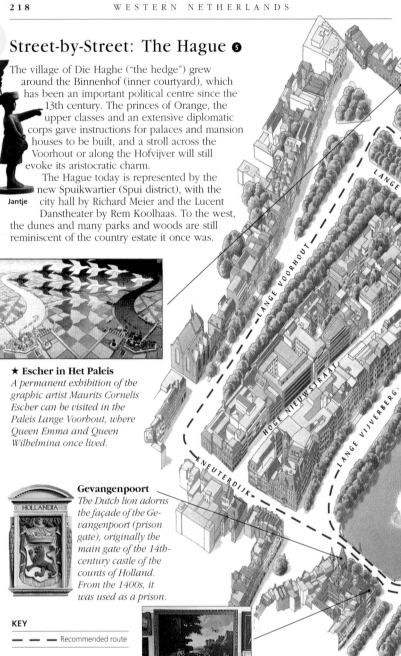

★ Escher in Het Paleis
A permanent exhibition of the graphic artist Maurits Cornelis Escher can be visited in the Paleis Lange Voorhout, where Queen Emma and Queen Wilhelmina once lived.

Gevangenpoort
The Dutch lion adorns the façade of the Gevangenpoort (prison gate), originally the main gate of the 14th-century castle of the counts of Holland. From the 1400s, it was used as a prison.

HOLLANDIA

KEY

– – – Recommended route

STAR SIGHTS

★ Binnenhof

★ Escher in Het Paleis

★ Mauritshuis

0 metres   50

0 yards   50

Prince William V's Picture Gallery
This was the first public art gallery in the Netherlands.

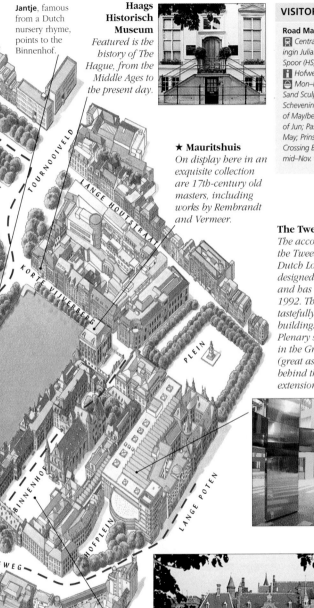

Jantje, famous from a Dutch nursery rhyme, points to the Binnenhof.

Haags Historisch Museum
Featured is the history of The Hague, from the Middle Ages to the present day.

★ **Mauritshuis**
On display here in an exquisite collection are 17th-century old masters, including works by Rembrandt and Vermeer.

VISITORS' CHECKLIST

Road Map B4. 446,000. Centraal Station (CS); Koningin Julianaplein 10; Hollands Spoor (HS); Stationsplein 25. Hofweg 1 (0900-3403505). Mon–Fri. Scheveningen Sand Sculpture Festival: May; Scheveningen Vlaggetjesdag: end of May/beg of Jun; Parkpop: end of Jun; Pasar Malam Besar: mid–May; Prinsjesdag: 3rd Tue in Sep; Crossing Borders Festival: mid–Nov. www.denhaag.com

The Tweede Kamer
The accommodation for the Tweede Kamer, the Dutch Lower House, was designed by Pi de Bruijn and has been in use since 1992. The building blends tastefully with the older buildings surrounding it. Plenary sessions are held in the Grote Vergaderzaal (great assembly hall) behind the circular extension.

"The Hague, you tap it and it sings" wrote Dutch poet Gerrit Achterberg in "Passage". The elegant covered arcade of shops in Neo-Renaissance style on the Hofweg is a famous feature of the town centre.

★ **Binnenhof**
This ancient structure comprises the parliament and government buildings and was originally the 13th-century hunting lodge of the counts of Holland.

Exploring The Hague

Cartoon character Haagse Harry

The Hague has numerous attractions and museums, of which the Mauritshuis *(see pp222–3)* and the Gemeentemuseum (municipal museum) *(see p224)* are the most famous. There are many bookshops, antique shops and cafés on and around the Denneweg, which comes out onto the Lange Voorhout, as well as luxury boutiques on the promenade beginning at Paleis Noordeinde *(see p221)*. Behind the Mauritskade lies the stately late 19th-century Willemspark, which is still almost completely intact, with the Panorama Mesdag *(see p224)*. You can admire the peaceful Japanese garden in Park Clingendael *(see p224)*. The old fishing village of Scheveningen has expanded to become a lively seaside resort but the dunes all around still offer peace and quiet.

🏛 Binnenhof met Ridderzaal

Binnenhof. **Tel** 070-3646144.
🔲 🖥 ⭕ *10am–4pm Mon–Sat.*
⭘ *Sun, public hols, 3rd Tue in Sep.*
📷 ☑ *Booking recommended.*
www.binnenhofbezoek.nl
The historic Binnenhof is a series of buildings erected around the hunting lodge of the counts of Holland. In 1247, William II was proclaimed Holy Roman Emperor; he later had the gothic Ridderzaal (Hall of the Knights) built as a banqueting hall. The Binnenhof has since then been the residence of stadholders, princes and governments. The court of Holland has administered justice since 1511 in the Rolzaal (roll court). The northern provinces of the Netherlands broke free from Spanish rule in 1581 with the *Plakkaat van*

Verlatinge ("Decree of Abandonment"); they held a huge feast for William of Orange in the Ridderzaal. The Binnenhof was one of the most important European centres of diplomacy in the Golden Age. The magnificently ornate meeting hall dates from this period and is where the Upper House currently sits. The Lower House met in William V's old ballroom until 1992, when it was moved to a new location. Tours of the building begin in the medieval cellars and pass through the Ridderzaal and debating chambers of the Upper or Lower House.

Porcelain from the Museum Bredius collection

Landscape by Fading Light **by Albert Cuyp (Museum Bredius)**

🏛 Museum De Gevangenpoort

Buitenhof 33. **Tel** 070-3460861. 🖥
🔲 ⭕ *check website.* ⭘ *1 Jan, 25 Dec.* 📷 ☑ *obligatory; last guided tour 4pm.* **www.**gevangenpoort.nl
The prison gate museum, in a 14th-century gatehouse, contains an old prison still largely in its original state. Cornelis de Witt was kept here on suspicion of conspiracy against Prince Maurice. In 1672, as he and his brother Johan left the prison, they were murdered by a provoked mob. The museum has a unique collection of horrific torture instruments. It shares an entrance with Galerij Prins Willem V.

🏛 Galerij Prins Willem V

Buitenhof 33. **Tel** 070-3023456.
🖥 🔲 ⭕ *check website.* 📷
www.mauritshuis.nl
Prince William V was an enthusiastic collector of 17th-century art. In 1774, his private collection was put on show for the public in this former inn, which the prince had converted into his office. The treasures in this gallery include paintings by Rembrandt, Jan Steen and Paulus Potter (1625–54).

🏛 Museum Bredius

Lange Vijverberg 14.
Tel 070-362 0729.
🖥 🔲 ⭕ *11am–5pm Tue–Sun.*
⭘ *1 Jan, 25 Dec.*
📷 **www.**museumbredius.nl
Art historian and art collector Abraham Bredius was also director of the Mauritshuis *(see pp222–3)* from 1895 to 1922. On his death in 1946 he bequeathed his collection of 17th- and 18th-century art, including paintings by Rembrandt and Jan Steen, to the city of The Hague. The elegant 18th-century mansion on the north side of the Hofvijver which houses the museum also has fine antique furniture and porcelain and beautifully engraved silver.

🏛 Escher in Het Paleis

Lange Voorhout 74. **Tel** 070-427 7730. 🖥 🔲 ⭕ *11am–5pm Tue–Sun.* ⭘ *1 Jan, 3rd Tue in Sep, 25 Dec.* 📷 **www.**escherinhetpaleis.nl

The Classical-style Paleis Noordeinde, where Queen Beatrix has her offices

A large proportion of MC Escher's (1898–1972) work is displayed in the Paleis Lange Voorhout, including well-known works such as *Day and Night*, *Rising and Falling* and *Belvédère*. In addition to graphic works, there are sketches, personal documents and photographs. The museum also features the Escher Experience, a virtual journey through his world.

🏛 Paleis Noordeinde
Noordeinde. ⬜ only the Paleistuin (palace garden) is open to the public.
In 1640, Stadholder Frederik Hendrik had his mother's house converted into a palace in the classical style. The property of the Princes of Orange since William V (1748–1806), this is where Queen Beatrix has her offices and also where she leaves from for the state opening of parliament.

🏛 Vredespaleis
Carnegieplein 2. 🚌 4 and 13. 🚊 1. **Tel** 070-3024137. ⬜ Mon–Fri, a few guided tours daily. 🎫 obligatory. ⬤ public hols and when court is in session. 📷 ♿ 🚫
In 1899, The Hague hosted the first international peace conference. Contributions from the court's members decorate the interior of the mock-Gothic Vredespaleis (peace palace), designed by the French architect Louis Cordonnier and completed in 1913. The International Court of the United Nations, formed in 1946, is based here.

🏛 Passage
Between the Spuistraat, Hofweg and Buitenhof. 🚌 🚊
A visit to The Hague would not be complete without a stroll along the elegant Passage, the only covered arcade remaining from the 19th century in the Netherlands. Unusual specialist shops can be found here, such as the umbrella and fountain pen shop. The arcade wing that leads to the Hofweg was added in 1928–9.

DEN HAAG CITY CENTRE

Galerij Prins Willem V ③
Het Paleis ①
Passage ⑥
Mauritshuis ⑦
Museum Bredius ④
Museum De Gevangenpoort ②
Ridderzaal ⑤

Madurodam
SCHEVENINGEN

① Het Paleis
KORTE VOORHOUT Park Clingendael
LANGE VOORHOUT
SCHOUW BURGSTRAAT
CASUARISTRAAT

Paleis Noordeinde & Panorama Mesdag
HOGE NIEUWSTRAAT
Museum ④ Bredius
LANGE VIJVERBERG
KORTE VIJVERBERG
KNEUTERDIJK

Mauritshuis ⑦
HEERENSTR
KORTE POTEN

Centraal Station
500m (550 yards)

Vredespaleis
Gemeentemuseum
Omniversum
MOLENSTRAAT
OUDE MOLSTRAAT
PLAATS Hofvijver
PLEIN
Museum De ② Gevangenpoort ③
⑤ Ridderzaal
Binnenhof
Parliament
LANGE POTEN

PRINSESSTRAAT
TORENSTRAAT
HOOGSTRAAT
Galerij Prins Willem V
GRAVENSTR
HOFWEG
⑥ Passage
SPUI
KALVERMARKT

KERKPLEIN
Rotunda
RIVIERVISMARKT
Oude Stadhuis
Grote Kerk
VENESTRAAT
VLAMINGSTR
SPUISTRAAT
GROTE MARKTSTRAAT
DELFT, ROTTERDAM

JAN HENDRIKSTRAAT
LAAN
GROTE MARKT

0 metres 250
0 yards 250

KEY
🟦 Street-by-street map (pp218–19)

Key to Symbols see back flap

Mauritshuis

After he was recalled as captain general of Brazil, Johan Maurits of Nassau commissioned this house. It was completed in 1644 by Pieter Post in the North Dutch Classical style with influences from the Italian Renaissance and has a marvellous view of the Hofvijver. After the death of Maurits in 1679, the house passed into state hands and, in 1822, became the home of the royal painting collection. Though the collection is not large, it contains almost exclusively superior works by old masters. The Mauritshuis closes mid-2012–14 for renovation, during which time some works will tour while others will be housed elsewhere in The Hague – check the website for details.

★ **The Anatomy Lesson of Dr Nicolaes Tulp** (1632)
Rembrandt's painting of doctors examining a corpse reflects the burgeoning contemporary interest in anatomy and science.

MUSEUM GUIDE

The three floors of this little museum are hung with paintings from top to bottom. To feature all aspects of the collection, the exhibited artwork is constantly changing. The masterpieces are always on view, although not always hanging in the same location. Presentation is pleasantly haphazard, but all the paintings are labelled with the artist, title and year. If you have any questions, you can ask for help at the information desk located in the museum's golden room.

Bordello Scene
(1658) This typical 17th-century genre painting of a brothel scene by Frans van Mieris de Oude (1635–81) has an unmistakable erotic undertone.

Ground floor

Offices and secretariat

Vase with Flowers (1618)
Ambrosius Bosschaert captured the beauty of summer flowers but added the flies to remind us of our mortality.

Basement

Main staircase

The Goldfinch *(1654)*
This small, elegant painting is by Carel Fabritius (1622–54), a pupil of Rembrandt.

First floor

VISITORS' CHECKLIST

Korte Vijverberg 8, The Hague.
🚌 4, 10. 🚎 8, 16, 17. **Tel** 070-3023456. ⏰ 10am–5pm Tue–Sat, 11am–5pm Sun (also Mon 1 Apr–1 Sep). ⬤ 1 Jan, 25 Dec. ♿ 📷 www.mauritshuis.nl

KEY TO FLOORPLAN

☐ Portrait gallery

☐ 15th- and early 16th-century works

☐ Late 16th- and 17th-century works

☐ Golden room

☐ 17th-century art

☐ 17th-century Flemish artists

☐ Early 17th-century collection

☐ Non-exhibition space

The Way You Hear It Is the Way You Sing It *(1663)*
This moralistic genre painting by Jan Steen (see p123) probably shows what is meant by a "huishouden van Jan Steen" – keeping one's house like a pigsty.

★ **The Louse Hunt** *(1653)*
Gerard ter Borch's painting depicts a domestic tableau and reflects the Dutch preoccupation with order and cleanliness during the 17th century.

Main entrance

★ **Girl with a Pearl Earring** *(1665)*
At the mid-point of his career, Johannes Vermeer painted this haunting portrait of a girl wearing a pearl earring. Stories about the true origins of the girl abound.

STAR PAINTINGS

★ Girl with a Pearl Earring

★ The Anatomy Lesson of Dr Nicolaes Tulp

★ The Louse Hunt

The Hague's municipal museum, one of HP Berlage's most handsome designs

🏛 Panorama Mesdag

Zeestraat 65. 🚌 5, 22, 24. 🚊 1.
Tel 070-3644544. ⏲ 10am–5pm
Mon–Sat, noon–5pm Sun & public
hols. 🚫 1 Jan, 25 Dec. 🎫 📷 By request. **www.**panorama-mesdag.com

Panorama Mesdag is one of
the best remaining panoramic
paintings of the 19th century.
The circular canvas, with an
impressive circumference of
120 m (395 ft), depicts the old
fishing village of Scheveningen.
It is a breathtaking moment
when, after climbing the
creaking stairs leading up to
the panorama, you sud-
denly emerge into
daylight, to be sur-
rounded by the
dunes and the
sea. The illusion is
strengthened by gen-
uine sand and pieces of
wreckage laid at the
foot of the painting.
The painting was done
in 1881 by members
of the Haag School, led by
HW Mesdag (1831–1915) and
his wife Sientje (1834–1909).
George Hendrik Breitner
(1857–1923) painted the
cavalrymen on the sand.

🏛 Gemeentemuseum
Den Haag en Fotomuseum

Stadhouderslaan 41. 🚌 24. 🚊 17.
Tel 070-3381111. ⏲ 11am–5pm Tue–
Sun. 🚫 1 Jan, 25 Dec. 🎫 📷 ♿
🖥 🍴 **www.**gemeentemuseum.nl

The Gemeentemuseum (muni-
cipal museum) was the last
piece of work to be carried
out by HP Berlage, founder of
the Amsterdam School. The
museum was completed in

1935, one year after his death,
and now contains the largest
collection of paintings by
Mondriaan in the world, with
works from all his various
periods. One of the high points
of the collection is *Victory
Boogie Woogie* (1943). Other
works exhibited here include
paintings by JH Weissenbruch
and brothers Maris and Josef
Israëls, all of whom were
representatives of the Haag
School, which was profoundly
inspired by the coastal landscape. The main feature of
the applied art section is
the antique Delftware
and oriental porce-
lain. An exhibit
of clothing from
the 18th century
onwards is displayed in
an annex. Another major
attraction is the stunning
collection of musical
instruments from the
15th to the 19th centu-
ries. Part of the Gemeentemuseum, with its entrance
next door, is the **Fotomuseum**,
which stages temporary
exhibitions of Dutch and
international photography.

*Victory Boogie
Woogie*

The picturesque Japanese garden in Park Clingendael

🎬 Omniversum

President Kennedylaan 5. 🚌 24.
🚊 17. **Tel** 0900-6664837.
⏲ hours depends on programme,
phone or check website. 🎫 ♿ 🖥
www.omniversum.nl

The Omniversum (next to the
Gemeentemuseum) is a cross
between a planetarium and a
high-tech cinema. It puts on a
great programme of exciting
films of space flights, volcanic
eruptions and ocean life.

🌳 Park Clingendael

Entrance from Alkemadelaan or
the Ruychrocklaan. 🚌 18. 🖥
Japanese Gardens
Park Clingendael. ⏲ end of Apr–
mid-Jun: from sunrise to sunset daily.

This country estate already
existed in the 16th century,
when it had a large, formal
French-style garden. In 1830
it was converted into a pretty
landscaped park. It contains
a Dutch garden, a rose garden, grazing land for animals,
rhododendron woods and
an ancient beech tree.

Overgrown bunkers in the
wood are a sombre reminder
of World War II, when the
Netherlands was occupied

and the most senior German authorities took up quarters in Huis Clingendael. At the centre of the park lies the famous Japanese garden, which was laid out in 1903 on the instructions of Baroness Marguérite Mary after a trip to Japan. The tea house and all the stones and ornaments in the garden were brought over from Japan by boat at the time.

Madurodam

George Maduroplein 1. 22.
1. *Tel* 070-4162400.
Sep–Mar: 9am–6pm; Apr–Jun: 9am–8pm; Jul & Aug: 9am–11pm.
www.madurodam.nl

Madurodam depicts the Netherlands in miniature – it consists of replicas of historically significant buildings like the Binnenhof in The Hague *(see p220)*, canalside houses in Amsterdam and the Euromast tower in Rotterdam *(see p232)*, built to a scale of 1:25. Other models here include Schiphol Airport, windmills, polders, bulb fields and some intriguing examples of the country's modern architecture. At night time the streets and buildings are illuminated by 50,000 tiny lamps.

Madurodam was opened in 1952 by Queen Juliana. JML Maduro designed the town in memory of his son George, who died at Dachau concentration camp in 1945. Profits go to children's charities.

The model city of Madurodam

Scheveningen ❻

Road map B4. 18,000. 14, 22, 23. 1, 9, 11. Gevers Deynoot-weg 1134 (0900-3403505). Thu.

This pleasant seaside resort is just 15 minutes by tram from the centre of The Hague. Like so many of the North Sea beach resorts, Scheveningen had its heyday in the 19th century. Nowadays it is a mixture of faded charm and modern garishness, though it remains a popular holiday resort because of its long sandy beach and the **Pier**. There are many places to eat, including good seafood restaurants.

The impressive **Kurhaus**, designed in the Empire style and now a luxurious hotel, was built in 1885, when Scheveningen was still a major spa town. Not far from the Kurhaus is **Sea Life**

Scheveningen, where you can look through transparent tunnels at stingrays, sharks and many other fascinating sea creatures. **Muzee Scheveningen** is devoted to the history of the fishing village and the spa. Tours of Scheveningen lighthouse can also be booked.

Designed by Wim Quist, **Museum Beelden aan Zee** (seaside sculpture museum) can be found on the boulevard, half-hidden by a sand dune. Contemporary sculptures on the theme of the human figure are shown in the light, airy rooms, on the terraces and in the garden.

Although the seaside resort has all but swallowed up the original fishing village, there is still a harbour and a large fish market. Fishing boat trips can be booked on the southern side of the harbour – a fun outing for the afternoon.

Sea Life Scheveningen
Strandweg 13. *Tel* 070-3542100.
10am–6pm Dec & Jan; to 7pm Feb–Jun, Sep–Nov; to 8pm Jul & Aug. 25 Dec.
www.sealife.nl

Muzee Scheveningen
Neptunusstraat 92. *Tel* 070-3500830.
10am–5pm Tue–Sat, noon–5pm Sun. 1 Jan, 31 Dec.
www.muzee.nl

Museum Beelden aan Zee
Harteveltstraat 1. *Tel* 070-3585857.
11am–5pm Tue–Sun.
www.beeldenaanzee.nl

Thsuki-no-hikari (Light of the Moon) by Igor Mitoraj in the dunes of the Museum Beelden aan Zee

Street-by-Street: Delft ⑦

19th-century Delftware

Delft dates back to 1075, its prosperity based on the weaving and brewing industries. In October 1654, however, an enormous explosion at the national arsenal destroyed much of the medieval town. The centre was rebuilt at the end of the 17th century and has remained relatively unchanged since then – houses in Gothic and Renaissance styles still stand along the tree-lined canals. Town life is concentrated on the Markt, which has the town hall at one end and the Nieuwe Kerk at the other. Visitors can dip into the scores of shops selling expensive, hand-painted Delftware or take a tour of local factories, the shops of which are often reasonably priced.

★ Stedelijk Museum Het Prinsenhof
William of Orange was killed on this staircase in 1584, the bullet holes still visible.

0 metres 50
0 yards 50

SCHOOLSTRAAT

ST AGATHAPLEIN

HIPPOLYTUSBUURT

OUDE DELFT

★ Oude Kerk
The 13th-century Oude Kerk contains the graves of prominent citizens such as that of the inventor of the microscope, Antonie van Leeuwenhoek.

NIEUWSTRAAT

The Oude Delft
is lined with canalside houses in Renaissance style.

BOTERBRUG

WINHA

OUDE DELFT

STAR SIGHTS

- ★ Nieuwe Kerk
- ★ Oude Kerk
- ★ Stedelijk Museum Het Prinsenhof

Sint-Hippolytuskapel
This austere red-brick chapel (1396) was used as an arsenal during the Reformation (see pp52–3).

PEPERSTRAA

KEY

– – – Recommended route

VISITORS' CHECKLIST

Road map B4. 🚊 95,000. 🚉
Stationsplein. 📞 0900-5151555.
🚢 Tue, Thu, Sat. 🎭 Mooi Weer
Spelen (street theatre): mid-Jun;
Delft Chamber Music Festival:
early Aug. **www**.delft.nl

View of Delft (c.1660)
*Johannes Vermeer's painting captures Delft on a
cloudy summer afternoon. The original tower of
the Nieuwe Kerk can be seen in the distance.*

Stadhuis (1618)
*The Renaissance-style town
hall was designed by
Hendrick de Keyser.
The building is
erected around a
13th-century
Gothic tower.*

★ Nieuwe Kerk
*The church was built in
several phases spread over
many years. This statue of
William of Orange stands
in the middle of his opulent
mausoleum.*

Koornbeurs (1650)
*The façade of the old meat
hall is decorated with animal
heads. After 1871, the building
was used as a corn exchange.*

Exploring Delft

Attractive Delft is world-famous for its blue-and-white pottery and is renowned in Holland as being the resting place of William of Orange (1533–84), the "father of the Netherlands". William led the resistance against Spanish rule in the 80 Years War *(see p49)* from his Delft headquarters; his victory meant religious freedom and independence for the Dutch. Delft was the Republic's main arsenal in the 17th century; an explosion of gunpowder destroyed a large part of the town in 1654. Artist Johannes Vermeer (1632–75) was born and lived in Delft.

The impressive Renaissance-style pulpit (1548) in the Oude Kerk

🔒 Oude Kerk

Heilige Geestkerkhof 25. *Tel 015-2123015.* ☐ *Apr–Oct: 9am–6pm Mon–Sat; Nov–Jan: 11am–4pm Mon–Fri, 10am–5pm Sat; Feb & Mar: 10am–5pm Mon–Fri.* 📷 ♿ **www.**oudekerk-delft.nl

The original 13th-century church on this site has been extended many times. The beautifully carved clock tower, with its eye-catching steeple, dates from the 14th century. The Gothic north transept was added in the early 16th century by architect Anthonis Keldermans. Inside, the most striking feature is the wooden pulpit with canopy. The floor is studded with 17th-century gravestones, many beautifully decorated, including those for Johannes Vermeer and admiral Piet Hein (1577–1629).

🔒 Nieuwe Kerk

Markt 80. *Tel 015-2123025.* ☐ *Apr–Oct: 9am–6pm Mon–Sat; Nov–Jan: 11am–4pm Mon–Fri, 10am–5pm Sat; Feb & Mar: 10am–5pm Mon–Fri.* 📷 ♿ **www.**nieuwekerk-delft.nl

The Nieuwe Kerk was built between 1383 and 1510 but needed large-scale restoration after the fire of 1536 and the massive explosion of 1654 in the arsenal. In 1872, PJH Cuypers *(see p371)* added the 100-m (328-ft) tower to the Gothic façade. Inside, the most noticeable feature is William of Orange's imposing mausoleum, designed in 1614 by Hendrick de Keyser. In the middle stands a statue of William, impressive in his battledress. Not far from him is the lonely figure of his dog, which died a few days after his master. The tombs of the royal family lie in the crypt.

🏛 Stedelijk Museum Het Prinsenhof

St-Agathaplein 1. *Tel 015-2602358.* ☐ *11am–5pm Tue–Sun & hols.* 🚫 *1 Jan, 30 Apr, 25 Dec.* 📷 📷 **www.**prinsenhof-delft.nl

This peaceful former convent was the scene of William of Orange's assassination. It now houses Delft's history museum, with pottery, tapestries and portraits of royalty. In 1572, during the uprising against the Spanish, William commandeered the convent as his headquarters. In 1584, a fanatical Catholic, Balthasar Geraerts, shot and killed him on the instructions of Philip II of Spain.

The Nieuwe Kerk overlooking Delft market

For hotels and restaurants in this region see pp397–398 and pp417–418

DELFTWARE

Delftware *(see pp28–9)* stems from majolica, introduced to the Netherlands in the 16th century by Italian immigrants who had settled around Delft and Haarlem and begun producing wall tiles with Dutch designs, such as birds and flowers. By the next century, however, Dutch traders had started to deal in delicate Chinese porcelain; this eventually led to the collapse of the market for the less refined Dutch earthenware. Towards 1650, though, the Chinese example was adopted in the Netherlands and craftsmen designed plates, vases and bowls with pictures of Dutch landscapes, biblical tableaux and scenes from everyday life. De Porceleyne Fles factory, which dates from 1652, is one of the several Delftware potteries open to the public for tours.

17th-century hand-painted Delft tiles

🏛 Legermuseum Delft

Korte Geer 1. **Tel** 015-2150500.
🕐 10am–5pm Tue–Fri, noon–5pm Sat & Sun. 🕐 1 Jan, 25 Dec. 📷
www.legermuseum.nl

The Legermuseum (army museum) is located in the former arsenal for the old provinces of Western Friesland and Holland. A large number of weapons are on display alongside uniforms, scale models of battlefields and army vehicles.

Coat of arms on the façade of the Legermuseum

The exhibition shows the history of the Dutch army from the Middle Ages to the present day. The museum moves to Soesterberg, near Utrecht, in late 2012.

Maassluis 🔞

Road map B4. 🏘 31,600. 🚉
ℹ️ Dr Kuyperkade 25 (010-5923469). 🛍 Tue, Fri.

The settlement of Maassluis grew up around the locks, which date from 1367; the herring trade brought prosperity to the town. The historic town centre is adorned with 17th-century buildings, such as the **Grote Kerk**, with its famous organ, and the **Stadhuis**, from 1650. The town's fine steam tug still goes out to sea. Many of Maarten 't Hart's novels are set in the Maassluis of his youth.

Schiedam 🔟

Road map B4. 🏘 75,000.
🚉 ℹ️ Buitenhavenweg 9 (010-4733000). 🛍 Tue am, Fri.

Schiedam was granted its city charter in 1275 and soon afterwards expanded into a centre for trade and fishing. It became the centre of the genever (Dutch gin) industry. The production of genever is still important to the town, as evidenced by the **five tallest windmills in the world** and the old warehouses and distilleries. In the bar of the **Jenever Museum** (national genever museum), you can familiarize yourself with the enormous range of Dutch genevers and liqueurs.

The **Stedelijk Museum** (municipal museum), with exhibits of contemporary art and on modern history, is in the former St-Jacobs Gasthuis. Its main attraction is the collection of artwork by the group known as COBRA (consisting of painters from COpenhagen, BRussels and Amsterdam).

🏛 Jenever Museum

Lange Haven 74. **Tel** 010-2469676.
🕐 noon–5pm Tue–Fri, 1–6pm Sat, Sun & public hols. 🕐 1 Jan, Easter Mon, 30 Apr, Pentecost, 25 Dec. ♿
www.jenevermuseum.nl

🏛 Stedelijk Museum

Hoogstraat 112. **Tel** 010-2463666.
🕐 10am–5pm Tue–Sun. 🕐 1 Jan, 25 Dec. ♿ 📷 📱
www.stedelijkmuseumschiedam.nl

Genever and corn brandy, products of the Genever capital of Schiedam

Street-by-Street: Rotterdam ❿

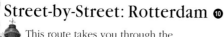

Museumhaven
lighthouse

This route takes you through the area to the south of the town centre, which was devastated by heavy bombing in May 1940. On your way you will see the Witte Huis (white house), one of the few buildings spared by the bombs. Further on you will pass by some unusual modern architecture, such as the cube-shaped apartments, "Het Potlood" ("the pencil"), and the maritime museum, devoted to the history of shipping. In front of this museum is a monument by Ossip Zadkine, which is one of the symbols of Rotterdam. The undeveloped area around Station Blaak was completely built up before the bombing.

★ **Schielandhuis,**
Rotterdam's history museum, holds exhib- tions of paintings and textiles and serves as a solemn reminder of th World War II bombin

BLAAK

★ **De Verwoeste Stad**
The statue De Verwoeste Stad (The Devastated City) *by Ossip Zadkine, located in front of the maritime museum, commemorates the bombing of May 1940. It is considered one of the most famous statues in the country.*

GLASHAVEN

De Buffel
The old armoured vessel De Buffel, *now open for visitors, was for many years a training ship.*

BOOMPJES

STAR SIGHTS

★ De Verwoeste Stad

★ Kubus-Paalwoningen

★ Schielandhuis

| 0 metres | 150 |
| 0 yards | 150 |

KEY

‒ ‒ ‒ Recommended route

**Erasmusbrug
(Erasmus Bridge)**
*The glittering
Erasmusbrug is
now one of the
symbols of
Rotterdam.*

VISITORS' CHECKLIST

Road map B4. 🏠 598,500. 🚊
Stationsplein. 🚌 *Stationsplein.*
ℹ️ *Coolsingel 195–7 (0900-403
4065).* 🛒 *Tue–Sun.* 🎬 *Film
festival: Jan; Dunya festival: May;
Metropolis (pop concerts): Jul;
Zomercarnaval: Jul; Wereldhaven-
dagen: Sep.* **www**.rotterdam.info

Station Blaak is
an unusual metro
and railway station,
designed by
architect HCH
Reijnders.

Het Potlood (the pencil), an
unusually shaped apartment
block near Station Blaak, was
designed by P Blom.

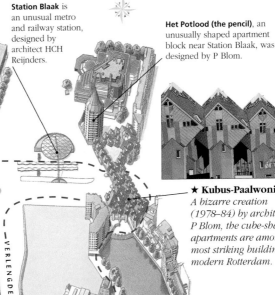

★ **Kubus-Paalwoningen**
*A bizarre creation
(1978–84) by architect
P Blom, the cube-shaped
apartments are among the
most striking buildings of
modern Rotterdam.*

VERLENGDE WILLEMSBRUG

**Witte Huis (White
House)**
*This is one of the few
buildings to survive the
World War II bombing
raids. For a long time,
the 45-m (148-ft) build-
ing was one of the tallest
office blocks in Europe.*

Willemswerf
*Willemswerf is one of
Rotterdam's highest
and most impressive
office blocks. The build-
ing, which is completely
white, was completed in
1989 and is a design by
architect WG Quist.*

Exploring Rotterdam

Bram Ladage sculpture

Rotterdam is not only a symbol of post-war economic recovery – it has more to offer than endless stretches of thriving docklands and industrial areas. Rotterdam has increasingly become one of the most important cultural centres of the Netherlands. Although the city was a wasteland immediately after World War II, it quickly recovered and now boasts one of the country's largest universities, a park containing a number of interesting museums and a large zoo.

Canalside houses in a peaceful corner of Delfshaven

Gorilla and her young at Blijdorp

🦍 Blijdorp

Blijdorplaan 8. 🚋 3, 11. 🚌 33, 40, 44. **Tel** 010-4431495. ◯ winter: 9am–5pm daily; summer & school hols: 9am–6pm daily. 🅿 www.rotterdamzoo.nl

Rotterdam Zoo, often called *Diergaarde Blijdorp*, is in many ways a unique zoo. Its predecessor, De Rotterdamsche Diergaarde (Rotterdam zoo), was built in 1857 in the town centre. In 1937, the zoo was moved to Blijdorp polder, outside the centre. The architect Van Ravesteyn designed the new zoo and Blijdorp became one of the first zoos to be designed by one architect.

Blijdorp is also one of the few European zoos to have its own research department. It plays an important part in breeding programmes for rare and endangered species, such as the black-footed penguin.

For the last few years, attempts have been made to convert Blijdorp to the type of zoo which tries to present the animals in the most natural habitat possible. Another addition at the zoo is the gorilla island. The huge,

extremely popular, Oceanium is a theme park showcasing sea creatures, including sharks.

🏛 Delfshaven

Informatiecentrum Historisch Delfshaven, Voorhaven 3. 🚋 4.

Delfshaven, which is outside the town centre and is mainly famous for being the birthplace of naval hero Piet Hein, looks very different from the rest of Rotterdam. This oasis of both history and culture within the modern city consists of a few streets with historic buildings and a harbour with old sailing boats. The former warehouses are now shops selling antiques, paintings and antiquarian books. There are also museums and restaurants.

It was from Delfshaven that the Dutch Pilgrim Fathers left for America in 1620.

🌊 Euromast

Parkhaven 20. 🚋 8. Ⓜ Dijkzicht. **Tel** 010-4364811. ◯ Apr–Sep: 9:30am–11pm daily; Oct–Mar: 10am–11pm daily. 🅿 www.euromast.nl

One of the most famous symbols of Rotterdam, Euromast is the tallest building in the town. Before its construction began, in 1960, the mayor at the time, Van Walsum, complained that there was only enough money to build a 50 m (165 ft) tower. This caused an uproar, because the mast was meant to be higher than the Utrecht Domtoren (cathedral tower), which was, at 112 m (367 ft), the highest building in the country. That same evening, the mayor was called by rich Rotterdam port barons wanting to contribute money to the construction of the building. These donations in part enabled the tower to reach 110 m (361 ft). A space tower was later added to the top of the building for the Communicatie-'70 show in 1970, bringing the tower to a total height of 185 m (607 ft).

The Rotterdam Beurstraverse, or "Koopgoot", a bustling shopping mall

Peter Struycken's masterpiece of light effects under the NAI

🏛 Kunsthal

Westzeedijk 341, Museumpark. 🚋 8, 20. **Tel** 010-4400301. ⬤ Tue–Sun. ⬤ Mon, 1 Jan, 30 Apr, 25 Dec. 🏖 🅿 🚻 www.kunsthal.nl

The Kunsthal, with its very austere style, is used for temporary exhibitions. It offers museums the opportunity to show those parts of their collections which would normally be in storage due to lack of exhibition space. This gives refreshing insight into the possessions of Dutch museums and gives the Kunsthal a unique and respected position in the art-life of the country.

Designed by the avant-garde architects OMA, the building has ramps instead of stairs.

🏛 Kinderkunsthal Villa Zebra

Stieltjesstraat 21. **Tel** 010-2411717. 🚋 20, 23, 25. 🚌 48. 🅼 D. ⬤ 11am–5pm Tue–Sun; from 10am daily summer hols. ⬤ 1 Jan, 30 Apr, 25 Dec. 🏖 🅿 🚻 www.villazebra.nl

This is an arts centre specifically for children, where they can become familiar with art and express themselves via poetry, theatre and visual arts.

🏛 NAI

Museumpark 25. **Tel** 010-4401200. 🚋 4, 5. 🚌 32. 🅼 Eendrachtsplein. ⬤ 10am–5pm Tue–Sat, 11am–5pm Sun & public hols. ⬤ 1 Jan, Easter, 30 Apr, 25 Dec. 🏖 🚻 📷 www.nai.nl

After being bombed in 1940 and then ravaged by fire, the old city centre was a wasteland. Because of large-scale rebuilding after the war, Rotterdam now has more modern architecture than any other town in the Netherlands. This includes famous structures such as the *paalwoningen* (cube-shaped apartments). It is appropriate that Nederlands Architectuur Instituut (the Netherlands Architectural Institute), housing the country's architectural archives, should be in Rotterdam, in a building that is itself an architectural phenomenon. Temporary exhibits are held here.

ROTTERDAM CITY CENTRE

Euromast ②
Kunsthal ①
Museum Boijmans Van
   Beuningen *(see pp234-5)* ④
Nederlands Architectuur
   Instituut ③

0 metres   250
0 yards   250

Key to Symbols *see back flap*

KEY

▮ Street-by-street map *(pp230–31)*

Museum Boijmans Van Beuningen

The museum is named after two art experts, FJO Boijmans and DG van Beuningen, who presented their own private collections to the town. The museum thus ended up with one of the finest collections in the Netherlands. Although it is particularly renowned for its unique collection of old masters, the museum also represents all aspects of art and design, from medieval works by Jan van Eyck to imaginative exhibitions of contemporary artists' work. The museum's layout is currently being re-worked.

Three Marys at the Open Sepulchre *(1430) Brothers Jan and Hubert Van Eyck collaborated on this colourful work depicting the tomb of the resurrected Christ.*

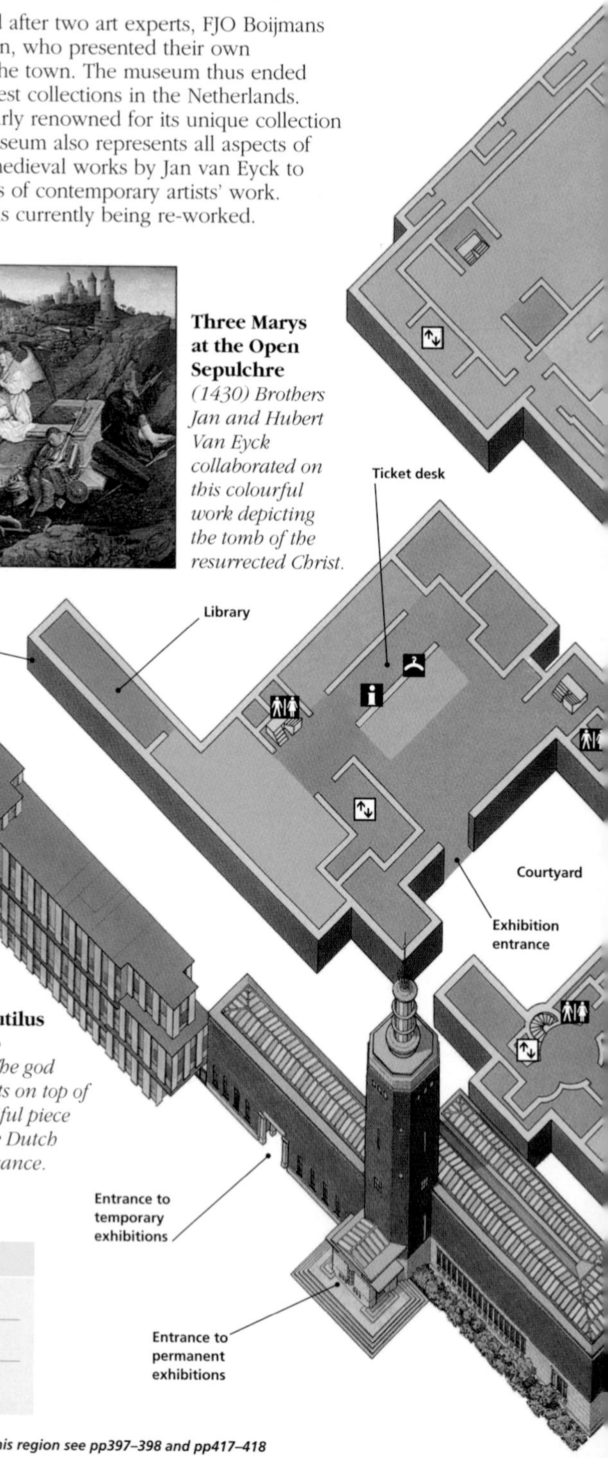

Ticket desk

Ground floor

Library

Courtyard

Exhibition entrance

Nautilus Cup *(1590) The god Neptune sits on top of this beautiful piece from the Dutch Renaissance.*

Entrance to temporary exhibitions

Entrance to permanent exhibitions

STAR PAINTINGS

★ The Pedlar

★ Titus at his Desk

★ The Tower of Babel

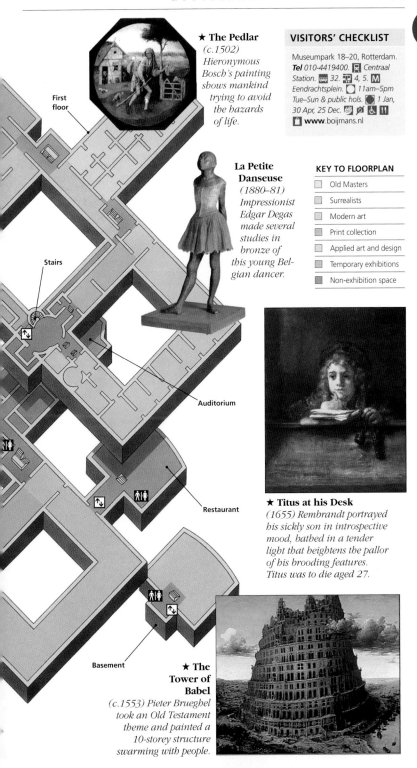

★ **The Pedlar**
(c.1502)
*Hieronymous
Bosch's painting
shows mankind
trying to avoid
the hazards
of life.*

First floor

VISITORS' CHECKLIST

Museumpark 18–20, Rotterdam.
Tel 010-4419400. ☐ Centraal
Station. ⬛ 32. ⬛ 4, 5. Ⓜ
Eendrachtsplein. ☐ 11am–5pm
Tue–Sun & public hols. ☐ 1 Jan,
30 Apr, 25 Dec. ⬛ ⬛ ⬛ ⬛
☐ www.boijmans.nl

**La Petite
Danseuse**
*(1880–81)
Impressionist
Edgar Degas
made several
studies in
bronze of
this young Bel-
gian dancer.*

KEY TO FLOORPLAN

☐	Old Masters
☐	Surrealists
☐	Modern art
☐	Print collection
☐	Applied art and design
☐	Temporary exhibitions
☐	Non-exhibition space

Stairs

Auditorium

★ **Titus at his Desk**
*(1655) Rembrandt portrayed
his sickly son in introspective
mood, bathed in a tender
light that heightens the pallor
of his brooding features.
Titus was to die aged 27.*

Restaurant

Basement

★ **The
Tower of
Babel**
*(c.1553) Pieter Brueghel
took an Old Testament
theme and painted a
10-storey structure
swarming with people.*

Rotterdam, City of Water

Sailor

One of Rotterdam's biggest and busiest attractions is its port, one of the largest ports in the world. Various operators organize daily tours around the port area, where you will see container ports, shipyards and dry docks. The sheer scale of the port and related industrial areas, which have a turnover of billions of euros, is quite staggering. Europe's largest container port, the Europoort alone stretches for 40 km (25 miles) along the river banks.

Rotterdam
The port sees approximately 30,000 vessels docking each year. Germany's Ruhr district is the main destination for the transported goods.

THE PORT OF ROTTERDAM

The port of Rotterdam, of which only a fraction is shown by this map, stretches from the town centre to the North Sea coast and is divided into nine areas. These are, from east to west, the Stadhavens, the Vierhavens, Merwehaven, Waalhaven, Eemhaven, Vondelingenplat, Botlek, Europoort and the Maasvlakte. The port is still expanding and will soon run out of available space. Land reclamation from the North Sea is considered the most appropriate solution.

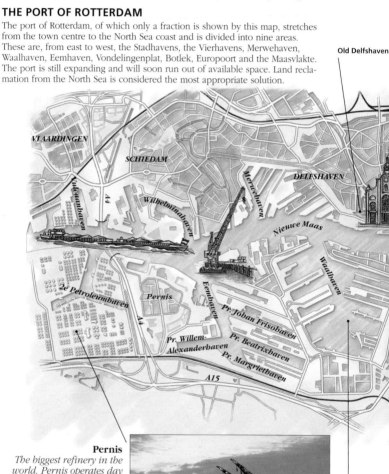

Old Delfshaven

VLAARDINGEN

SCHIEDAM

Kalandhaven

A4

Wilhelminahaven

Merwehaven

DELFSHAVEN

Nieuwe Maas

Waalhaven

2e Petroleumhaven

Pernis

Eemhaven

Pr. Johan Frisohaven

A4

Pr. Willem-Alexanderhaven

Pr. Beatrixhaven

Pr. Margriethaven

A15

Pernis
The biggest refinery in the world, Pernis operates day and night refining crude oil, which is used to make hundreds of products. Lit up at night, it looks like something out of a science fiction story.

Dry docks

Spido Tour
Various tours around the port of Rotterdam are available. Those lasting an hour and a half visit the town centre ports (see map below), whereas the day-long tours travel as far as the Maasvlakte.

World Port Days
There are many types of ships to be admired on the World Port Days, which are held in early September and attract thousands of visitors.

Euromast

Maasbaven

Zuiderpark

Maastunnel
filtration plant

0 kilometres   3

0 miles   3

KEY

Road

Railway

Hotel New York
This hotel has been set up in the early 20th-century head office of the former Holland-America Line. The nearby arrival halls are also of architectural significance.

EUROPOORT

A total of 33,252 ocean-going vessels and 110,000 inland vessels put in at Rotterdam Port during 2008. This makes it the busiest port in Europe. The name "Europoort" says it all – Rotterdam is Europe's port. Rotterdam Port is one of the major employers of the Netherlands, with more than 300,000 people working for it either directly or indirectly. Total added value of the port is more than €28 billion, approximately 10 per cent of the country's gross domestic product.

Bustling Rotterdam port, loading and unloading many millions of containers every year

St Janskerk, Gouda

This former Catholic church dating from 1485 was rebuilt in the Gothic style after it was struck by fire in 1552. The church received a number of unusual stained-glass windows from rich Catholic benefactors, such as Philip II of Spain, between 1555 and 1571. After the Reformation (*see pp52–3*), the church became Protestant, but even the fanatical Iconoclasts did not have the heart to destroy the windows. Prominent Protestants, including Rotterdam aldermen, donated stained-glass windows to the church up to 1604. The stained-glass windows are heavily symbolic of the politics of the time – Bible stories had to be covered after the conflict between the Catholics and Protestants, which led to the 30 Years War between Spain and the Netherlands.

Benefactor's coat of arms (1601)

The Nave
At 123 m (404 ft), this nave is the longest in Holland. The floor is inset with memorial stones.

The Adulteress *(1601)*
Dressed as a Franciscan monk, Jesus appeals to the people in the temple to forgive the adulteress, who is being guarded by Spanish soldiers.

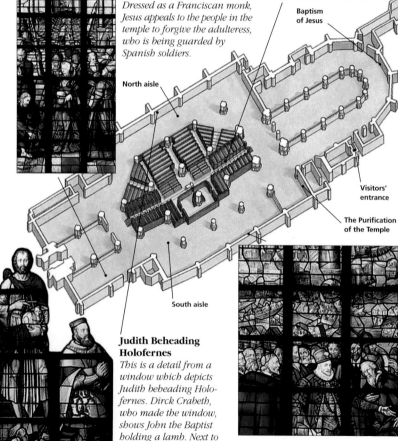

Baptism of Jesus

North aisle

Visitors' entrance

The Purification of the Temple

South aisle

Judith Beheading Holofernes
This is a detail from a window which depicts Judith beheading Holofernes. Dirck Crabeth, who made the window, shows John the Baptist holding a lamb. Next to him kneels Jan de Ligne, the count of Arenberg, who commissioned the window.

The Relief of Leiden *(1603)*
William of Orange as leader of the resistance of the people of Leiden against the Spanish siege of 1574.

**The Purification
of the Temple**
*William of Orange donated
this window, symbolizing
the Netherlands' longing to
drive out the Spaniards, in
1567. Traders watch angrily
as Jesus drives moneylenders
from the temple.*

Baptism of Jesus *(1555)
John the Baptist baptizes
Jesus in the Jordan River.
The window was a gift
from the Bishop of Utrecht.*

Nieuwpoort town hall, built over the canal in 1696

Gouda ⑪

Road map B4. 🏠 *72,000.* 🚆
ℹ *Lange Tiendeweg 29–31 (0900-
4683288).* 🛒 *Thu am & Sat; phone
tourist office for information on
cheese markets.* **www**.vvvgouda.nl

In 1272, Floris V granted
Gouda its city charter. Thanks
to its strategic position on
the Hollandse IJssel and the
Gouwe, the town developed
into a flourishing centre for
beer brewing and the textile
industry in the 15th century.
However, Gouda became
economically and politically
isolated during the 30 Years
War. The town recovered in
the 17th and beginning of the
18th century due to its trade
in cheese, candles and pipes.
　Gouda is still famous today
for its **cheese** and **cheese
markets**. The markets are
held on an enormous three-
sided square around the
Stadhuis, which dates from
1450 and is one of the oldest
in the Netherlands. With its
many pinnacles and turrets,
the building gives the
impression of being in the
Flemish Gothic style.
　The **Gouda Museum**
(municipal museum) is in the
former **Catharina Gasthuis**
(St Catherine's hospital), which
dates from the 14th century
and later. The museum
features paintings from the
Hague School and unusual
16th-century altar pieces.

🏛 Stadhuis
Markt 1. **Tel** 0182-588211.
☐ 9am–5pm Mon–Fri, 11am–3pm
Sat. 🔒 public hols. 🖼 🅰 by appt.

🏛 Gouda Museum
Achter de Kerk 14. **Tel** 0182-
331000. ☐ 10am–5pm Wed–Fri,
noon–5pm Sat & Sun. 🔒 1 Jan,
25 Dec. 🖼 over 18s.

Reeuwijkse
Plassen ⑫

Road map B4. ℹ *VVV by Gouda.*

The Reeuwijk lake district was
formed through peat excava-
tion. Narrow roads pass
through the rectangular lakes,
which owe their shape to former parcels of land. The small
village of **Sluipwijk** seems
almost to fade away into the
water. The best way to explore
this area is by bicycle or on
foot. In the summer months
you can also take a boat trip
through this typically Dutch
lakeland scenery.

Nieuwpoort ⑬

Road map C4. 🏠 *1,600.*
🚌 *90 from Utrecht or Rotterdam.*

The whole of this magnificent fortified town, which
obtained its city charter in
1283, has been declared a
listed area. The 17th-century
street layout is practically
intact. The city walls, which
are also intact, were originally
built to ward off attacks from
the French but served mainly
to protect the town against
flooding. The town hall, built
over the inundation lock, dates
from 1696, while the arsenal
dates from 1781. Restoration
work was carried out in 1998.

Gorinchem

Road map C4. 🏘 35,000. 🚊
🚉 *Grote Markt 17 (0183-631525).*
🏛 *Mon am.* **www.**vvvgorinchem.nl

Gorinchem, situated on the Linge and the Waal, was the property of the Lords van Arkel in the 13th century. They were driven out by Count William VI and the town was then absorbed into Holland. Fortifications built at the end of the 16th century are still partially intact and offer marvellous views over the water meadows and the Waal. Of the four town gateways, only the **Dalempoort** remains. The Linge harbour, in the heart of the town, is still mostly authentic, especially the narrow part.

Environs
On the other side of the Waal is the 14th-century **Slot Loevestein**. It has a very eventful history as a toll castle, a defence point along the Hollandse Waterlinie (a strip of land flooded as a defence line) and a state prison in the 17th century. A ferry for foot passengers runs between Gorinchem and the castle between May and September.

🏰 **Slot Loevestein**
Poederoijen. **Tel** 0183-447171.
🕐 *May–Sep: 11am–5pm Tue–Fri, 1–5pm Sat & Sun; Oct–Apr: 1–5pm Sat & Sun.* 🈲 *1 Jan, 25–31 Dec.* 📷
📷 📱 🎧 **www.**slotloevestein.nl

Glass blower in Leerdam

Leerdam

Road map C4. 🏘 20,000. 🚊 🚉
Dr Reilinghplein 3 (0345-613057). 🏛
Thu am, Sat pm. **www.**vvleerdam.nl

Leerdam is renowned for its glass industry. Royal Dutch Glass Factory designs by Berlage, Copier and other artists can be admired in the **Nationaal Glasmuseum** (national glass museum), and traditional crystal production can be observed at Royal Leerdam Kristal. **Fort Asperen**, on the Linge, is one of the best-preserved defence points remaining along the Nieuwe Hollandse Waterlinie.

🏛 **Nationaal Glasmuseum**
Lingedijk 28. **Tel** 0345-614960.
🕐 *10am–5pm Tue–Sat, noon–5pm Sun.* 📷 🅿 **www.**nationaalglas museum.nl

Dordrecht

Road map B4. 🏘 118,600. 🚊
🚉 *Spuiboulevard 99 (0900-4636888).* 🏛 *Tue am, Fri & Sat.*
www.vvvdordrecht.nl

The oldest town in Holland, Dordrecht received its city charter in 1220 and was the most important harbour and commercial town of the region until the 1500s. Even after being outstripped by Rotterdam, Dordrecht remained an important inland port. In the old port area, mansions, warehouses and almshouses are reminders of the past. The **Grote Kerk** (13th to 17th century), in the Brabant Gothic style, has an ornate interior. **Museum Simon van Gijn**, in the period rooms of an 18th-century house, has a collection of old prints, clothes and toys. The shady **Hof** (court of justice) (1512) contains the **Statenzaal** (state room), where the States of Holland met. The Hof complex will be closed 2012–14 for restoration.

🔔 **Grote Kerk**
Lange Geldersekade 2. **Tel** 078-614 4660. 🕐 *Apr–Oct: 10:30am–4:30pm Tue–Sat, noon–4pm Sun; Nov & Dec: 2–4pm Tue, Thu & Sat.* 🎵 *2:15pm Thu & Sat.* 📱 **www.**grotekerk-dordrecht.nl

🏰 **Hof and Statenzaal**
Hof 12. **Tel** 078-6492311.
🕐 *11am–5pm Tue–Sat, 1–5pm Sun.*
www.erfgoedcentrumdiep.nl

A group of windmills at Kinderdijk, for centuries draining water from the Alblasserwaard

Kinderdijk ⑰

Road map B4. 🚌 *90 from Rotterdam Akkeroord.* 🍴

The famous **19 windmills** which were used to drain the Alblasserwaard in the past are situated where the Noord and the Lek converge. New *boezems* (drainage pools) and windmills, however, were needed time and time again in order to span the height differences as the land settled. The group of windmills is a UNESCO World Heritage Site.

Brielle ⑱

Road map B4. 👥 *16,000.* 🚌 *metro Rotterdam CS to Spijkenisse, then 103.* 🛈 *Turfkade 18 (0181-472662).* 🛶 *Mon; Jul & Aug: Wed.*

The magnificent port of Brielle is a protected town. The 18th-century fortifications are still mostly intact. The town, birthplace of Admiral van Tromp, held a strategic position until the 1872 opening of the *Nieuwe Waterweg* (new waterway). The **Historisch Museum Den Briel** (historic museum of Brielle) depicts this and the famous Beggars of the Sea invasion in 1572 *(see box)*. The 15th-century **St.-Catharijnekerk**, in Brabant Gothic style, rises from the surrounding monuments.

🏛 **Historisch Museum Den Briel**
Markt 1. **Tel** *0181-475477.*
⏰ *Tue–Sun.* ⬤ *Mon, public hols, Nov–Mar: Sun.* 📷 ♿ **www.** historischmuseumdenbriel.nl

Hellevoetsluis ⑲

Road map B4. 👥 *40,000.* 🚌 *metro Rotterdam CS to Spijkenisse, then 101.* 🛈 *Oostzand-dijk 3 (0181-312318).* 🛶 *Sat.*

At the end of the 16th century, this was the naval port for the States of Holland. Fleets led by van Tromp, de Ruyter and Piet Hein left from Hellevoetsluis for their naval battles in the 1600s. Within the old fortifications, visitors are reminded of the town's

Middelharnis Lane (c.1689) by Meindert Hobbema

naval past by the **Prinsehuis**, the 17th-century lodgings of the Admiralty of the Maze, the dry dock and **Fort Haerlem** from the 19th century.

You can learn all about fire and fire-fighting in the local **National Brandweermuseum** (fire service museum).

🏛 **Nationaal Brandweermuseum**
Industriehaven 8. **Tel** *0181-314479.*
⏰ *Apr–Oct: 10am–4pm (from noon Sun).* ♿ 📷

Middelharnis ⑳

Road map B4. 👥 *17,900.* 🚌 *136, 396 from Rotterdam Zuidplein.* 🛈 *Vingerling 3 (0187-484870).* 🛶 *Wed.*

During the 16th century, Middelharnis became the regional port, outstripping Goedereede. Until the end of

the 19th century, fishing remained the most important source of income.

The Late Gothic cruciform church (15th century) stands at the heart of the village. Outside the town hall (1639) hang the wooden blocks that women branded as gossips had to carry through the town.

Goedereede ㉑

Road map A4. 👥 *1,900.* 🚌 *metro R'dam CS to Spijkenisse, then 101 to Hellevoetsluis, then 104.* 🛈 *Bosweg 2, Ouddorp (0187-681789).* 🛶 *Tue.*

Goedereede was an important port in the 14th and 15th centuries. This town, where Pope Adrianus VI was born, began to decline when it began to silt up. The early harbour houses are reminiscent of the livelier days of old.

THE BEGGARS OF THE SEA

The Beggars of the Sea were a pirate fleet which consisted of minor Dutch and Flemish nobles who had fled at the beginning of the Inquisition and sailed across the North Sea. They plundered other ships and caused trouble in English and

Van Lumey

German ports. They were forced to leave England, where some of their ships were berthed, in spring 1572. Without any clear plan, they entered Den Briel on 1 April under the command of van Lumey, which they then held "for the Prince". Other towns joined the Beggars of the Sea or were forcibly occupied by them. Their pursuits represented the first steps towards Dutch independence from Spain and the creation of Dutch sea power.

ZEELAND

The tiny province of Zeeland, as its name implies, is inextricably linked with water and the sea. From earliest times, the power of the North Sea and the flooding deltas of the Maas and Schelde rivers have shaped the landscape, encouraging resilience in the inhabitants and the desire to control the elements.

From earliest times, storms and floods have taken their toll here. In the last century, the devastation of two world wars was followed by the disastrous floods and storm surges of 1953. Although there are a number of fine churches and public buildings dating as far back as the 14th century, in places near the coast there are very few houses more than 50 years old. As a result, determination to keep the waters at bay has spawned massive construction and canal building, with giant dams and land reclamation schemes offering a level of security that has changed the landscape forever.

The storms were not all bad news. Traces of Roman settlements were uncovered, and lakes and inland waterways have become a haven for wildlife and a playground for lovers of watersports. Towns such as Middelburg, Zierikzee and Veere and villages such as Nisse, St Anna-ter-Muiden and Dreischor have lots of old buildings, some of which have been restored to their 17th-century grandeur, with attractive features such as bell towers and frescoes.

The close relationship with water and the sea is well documented in a variety of small museums. The tangible benefits are perhaps twofold: an abundance of seafood for the province's restaurants, and marvellous opportunities for watersports. Few regions in Europe offer as much scope for sailing, windsurfing, water skiing and diving as does little Zeeland.

The 15th-century Stadhuis (town hall) dominating the historic town of Veere

◁ Groynes covered with cockles, a characteristic feature of the beaches along the Zeeland coast

Exploring Zeeland

Memorial plaque

Touring around Zeeland, you cannot ignore the sea. The journey becomes a small adventure as you encounter bridges, dams and ferry docks. Sometimes you will travel along a straight ribbon of a road, sometimes a windy lane. The ever-present and often turbulent water is never the same colour for long: it can quickly change from a grey green reflecting the vivid blue sky to the white of wave crests beneath leaden skies. Passing over one of the many dams, you will reach the next island, with its own special character. Tholen, for example, is quiet – almost morose – whereas Walcheren is full of surprises and has a wonderful atmosphere. Travelling through Zeeland is a journey of discovery.

GETTING AROUND

The best way to visit all the islands of Zeeland is by car. The roads here are excellent – the A58 or the N57 will quickly bring you to the centre of the province, where you can choose one of the smaller roads to take you to your destination. The through train will take you from Amsterdam to Middelburg and Vlissingen in just two and a half hours. If you want to explore other islands, you will need to continue on a regional bus – though this can be quite time-consuming. There are many cycle paths and it is great fun cycling over the dykes.

SIGHTS AT A GLANCE

Brouwershaven **9**
Bruinisse **10**
Cadzand **20**
Domburg **4**
Goes **14**
Haamstede **8**
Hulst **17**
Middelburg pp248–9 **2**
Nisse **16**
*Oosterschelde Stormvloed-
   kering pp246–7* **1**
St Annaland **11**
St Maartensdijk **12**
Sluis **19**
Terneuzen **18**
Tholen **13**
Veere **3**
Vlissingen **5**
Westkapelle **6**
Yerseke **15**
Zierikzee **7**

Tilting at the ring – a Zeeland sport

KEY

═══ Motorway

──── Main road

──── Minor road

──── Scenic route

──── Minor railway

▬▬▬ National border

▬▬▬ Regional border

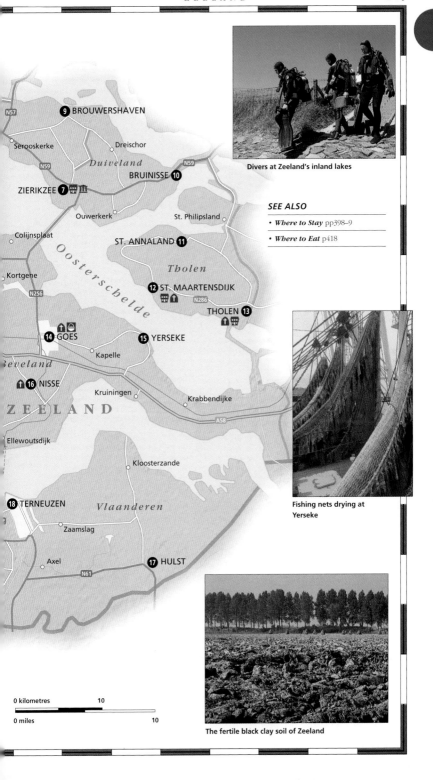

9 BROUWERSHAVEN

Serooskerke

Dreischor

Duiveland

BRUINISSE **10**

ZIERIKZEE **7**

Ouwerkerk

St. Philipsland

Colijnsplaat

ST. ANNALAND **11**

Kortgene

Oosterschelde

Tholen

12 ST. MAARTENSDIJK

THOLEN **13**

14 GOES

15 YERSEKE

Kapelle

Beveland

16 NISSE

Kruiningen

Krabbendijke

Z E E L A N D

Ellewoutsdijk

Kloosterzande

18 TERNEUZEN

Vlaanderen

Zaamslag

Axel

17 HULST

Divers at Zeeland's inland lakes

SEE ALSO

• *Where to Stay* pp398–9

• *Where to Eat* p418

Fishing nets drying at
Yerseke

0 kilometres 10

0 miles 10

The fertile black clay soil of Zeeland

Oosterschelde Stormvloedkering ❶

Throughout the centuries, the history of the Netherlands has been dominated by its people's struggle against the sea. After the disastrous floods of 1953, which hit Zeeland heavily, the battle to remove the danger of the sea once and for all was undertaken in earnest. Now the Dutch seem to have minimized the threat of flooding by building dykes and dams and closing off tidal inlets, all of which has had a major impact on the landscape.

The Windsock
When the windsock is full, a warning is sounded, and people are advised to avoid driving over the dams and bridges between the islands. Vigilance saves lives.

A road has been built over the dam.

Storms
Storms are a part of every-day life in Zeeland: storms on the beach or over the flat polders, storms which blow the cobwebs away and storms which make you fear for your life.

The sliding gates are closed only when the water is high.

Concrete piers bear the sea wall.

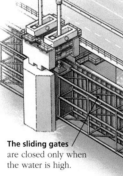

The Fateful Night of 1953
On the night of 31 January 1953, an event considered impossible in modern times occurred. A combination of spring tides and storms breached the dykes and washed them away as loose sand. A total of 1,835 people lost their lives.

DELTAPARK NEELTJE JANS

This attraction has been built on an artificial island, Neeltje Jans, on which the piers for the Oosterschelde Stormvloedkering (storm surge barrier) were assembled, then taken by special barges to their positions. Now that task is finished, the island is being used mainly for recreational and informative purposes. At the Deltapark you can find out about the Delta projects and about how the barrier works. You can see the barrier from the inside, and then take a boat trip to view it from the outside. There is an aquarium here, as well as a seal show; you can also experience a simulated hurricane in the "hurricane machine".

Neeltje Jans, educating about the sea

Luctor et Emergo
This Latin motto meaning "I struggle and emerge victorious" is on Zeeland's coat of arms, which depicts the Netherlands lion half in the water. This was wholly appropriate for 1953.

Concrete Piers
The piers were made on the artificial island of Neeltje Jans and then transported by special barges to their destination. This mighty task attracted a great deal of attention.

VISITORS' CHECKLIST

Road map A4–5. Deltapark Neeltje Jans, Faelweg 5, Vrouwen-polder. **Tel** 0111-652702. 133. ☐ Apr–Oct: 10am–5:30pm daily; Nov–Mar: 10am–5pm Wed, Sat & Sun.

The Delta Works
The Delta Works have had far-reaching consequences for the landscape and environment. The Zeeland islands, having been joined to the mainland, are no longer isolated.

HALF-OPEN BUTTRESS DAM

It took 13 years and €3.6 billion (two-thirds of the cost of the Delta Works) to build the Oosterschelde-kering. After much deliberation, the decision was made to keep open the estuary and to preserve the salty estuary habitat. A half-open multiple buttress dam was built, with 62 sliding gates, which are closed on average once a year during heavy storms. This keeps the water salty and has preserved the unique salt marshes and mud flats of the Oosterschelde.

Ground protection
prevents the earth from being washed away.

The Terps
Man-made mounds, such as these near Borssele, were built in the 11th and 12th centuries to protect farms and villages from the water.

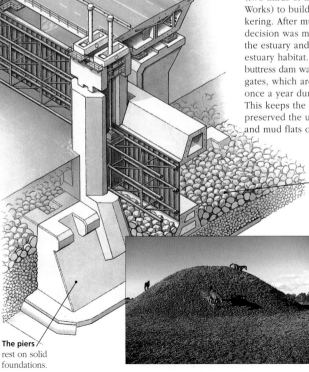

The piers rest on solid foundations.

Street-by-Street: Middelburg

Detail from Middelburg's Stadhuis

Middelburg suffered heavy Nazi bombing in 1940. A lot of what is to be seen in the town today has been rebuilt, including the Stadhuis (town hall) and the abbey. The town is still redolent with the atmosphere of the Golden Age, an era during which the Dutch East India Company thrived in the port area along the quay. Middelburg is a pretty town and there is plenty to be seen on a walk around the centre. Children will be kept busy by Miniatuur-Walcheren.

★ St-Jorisdoelen
This doelen, the guardsmen's guild building, was built in 1582 and destroyed in 1940; the façade was rebuilt in 1969.

Zeeuws Archief, the archives of the province, are now housed in a historic monument, the van de Perre House on the Hofplein, which has been given a spectacular new wing.

KEY

--- — Recommended route

★ Stadhuis
The 15th-century town hall was completely destroyed by fire in 1940 and has been partially rebuilt. A 20th-century extension can be seen on the northern side.

0 metres 50
0 yards 50

The fish market
already existed in 1559. The passageway, with its Tuscan pillars, dates from 1830.

STAR SIGHTS

★ Abbey
★ St-Jorisdoelen
★ Stadhuis

Mini Mundi
This miniature town started in 1954 now contains more than 350 buildings, and forms part of the Mini Mundi amusement park.

VISITORS' CHECKLIST

Road map A5. Markt 51. **Tel** 0118–674300. **www**.tour istshop.nl 47,500. Thu, Sat. **Stadhuis** Markt. **Abbey** (see p250). **Mini Mundi** Podium 35, Zep Middelburg. **Tel** 0118-415400. check website. **www**.minimundi.nl

★ Abbey
Many years of restoration work on the abbey have finally paid off.

Lange Jan
The 91-m (300-ft) tower called the tall Jan belongs to the Nieuwe Kerk in the abbey complex. It has an octagonal plan and dates from the 14th century.

London Quay
The names of the quays reflect the goods that were being exported from and imported to the Netherlands during the Golden Age (see pp50–51).

Zeeuws Museum

Bronze armband from 50 BC

Middelburg Abbey dates back to 1100, when it was inhabited by Norbertine monks from the monastery of St Michiel of Antwerp. These very powerful monks were driven away in 1574 by William of Orange, after which the abbey was secularized. The renovated Zeeuws Museum is situated in the wing of the building that was once the monks' quarters. The completely redesigned interior presents the museum's fine collections of china, silver, paintings and its famous tapestries in a completely new light.

VISITORS' CHECKLIST

Zeeuws Museum. **Road map** A5.
Tel 0118-653000. ☐ 11am–
5pm Tue–Sun. ● 1 Jan, 25 Dec.
🌐 www.zeeuwsmuseum.nl

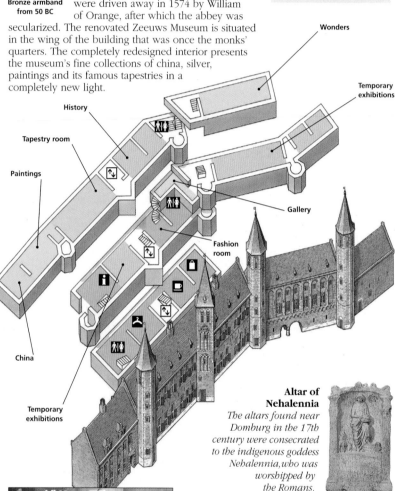

Wonders

Temporary exhibitions

History

Tapestry room

Paintings

Gallery

Fashion room

China

Temporary exhibitions

Altar of Nehalennia
The altars found near Domburg in the 17th century were consecrated to the indigenous goddess Nehalennia, who was worshipped by the Romans.

Costume Collection
The museum has a collection of jewellery, accessories and costumes, here displayed with video made for the museum by contemporary artists.

MUSEUM GUIDE

The Zeeuws Museum is accommodated in one of the oldest wings of the abbey. It is a provincial museum with various different sections, including History, Fashion, Wonders and the famous Tapestry Room. There are also temporary exhibitions that cover a wide variety of subjects.

Veere ❸

Road map A5. 👥 *1,500.* 🚌
ℹ️ *Oudestraat 28 (0118-581342).*
www.vvvzeeland.nl

Past and present merge in
Veere. Modern pleasure boats
moor along the quay opposite
the Gothic façades of **Het
Lammetje** (the lamb) (1539)
and **De Struijs** (the ostrich)
(1561). These **Schotse Huizen**
(Scottish houses) serve as a
reminder of the time that the
port was important for its
trade in precious Scottish
wool. Other monuments to
Veere's illustrious past are the
stadhuis (1474), the **Camp-
veerse Toren,** a tower dating
to around 1500, and the
OL-Vrouwekerk (Church of
Our Lady), dating from the
15th–16th centuries. This
enormous church, once
almost demolished, is
now used as a venue for
contemporary music concerts.

Domburg ❹

Road map A5. 👥 *1,600.* 🚌 ℹ️
Schuitvlotstraat 32 (0118-581342).

Domburg was one of the
first seaside resorts in the
Netherlands. In the 19th
century, this little town on
Walcheren was popular
among prominent Euro-
peans, who came here to
relax and recuperate in
the chic seaside hotels on
the dunes. It has now
given way to mass tourism.

Environs
An inland lake lies hidden
between dunes, woods and
the Oostkapelle polder. The
pretty nature reserve **De
Manteling** is worth visiting,
as is **Westhove** castle, which
was the Abbot of Middelburg's
country house until the
16th century. **Terra Maris**,
Zeeland's natural scenery
museum, is in the castle's
former orangery.

🏛 **Terra Maris**
Duinvlietweg 6. **Tel** 0118-582620.
🕐 May–Oct: 10am–5pm daily;
Nov–Apr: noon–5pm Wed–Fri,
noon–4pm Sat & Sun. 🚻 🅿
www.terramaris.nl

Pleasure boats moored at the marina in Vlissingen

Vlissingen ❺

Road map A5. 👥 *43,200.* 🚌 🚉
ℹ️ *Spuistraat 46 (0118-715320).*
🗓 Fri.

Vlissingen is a bustling town.
The main thrust behind the
economy of this, the largest
town in Zeeland, are the
ports in Vlissingen itself, as
well as those of the industrial
area Vlissingen-Oost and the
famous **scheepswerf De
Schelde** (De Schelde shipyard). Vlissingen has
always been of great
military significance.
The wartime activity this
attracted meant that the
town could not escape
the consequences. One
of the few remaining
buildings from the time
of Michiel de Ruyter to
have withstood the rav-
ages of time is the **Arsenaal**,
dating from 1649. A second
arsenal dating from 1823 is
now the **Amusement Park Het
Arsenaal** *(see p434),* which is

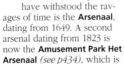
**Michiel
de Ruyter**

especially interesting for children. The reptiles and insects
showcased at **Reptielenzoo
Iguana**, which is housed in
two adjoining 18th-century
mansions, offer a completely
different type of attraction.

🏛 **Amusement Park Het
Arsenaal**
Arsenaalplein 7. **Tel** 0118-415400.
🕐 check website for opening
times. 🚫 1 Jan, 25 Dec, 31 Dec.
🚻 ♿ www.arsenaal.com
🏛 **Reptielenzoo Iguana**
Bellamypark 35. **Tel** 0118-417219.
🕐 Jun–Sep: 10am–5:30pm
Tue–Sat, 1–5:30pm Sun & Mon;
Oct–May: 1–5:30pm daily.
🚫 1 Jan, 25 Dec. 🚻

Westkapelle ❻

Road map A5. 👥 *2,800.* 🚌 ℹ️
Zuidstraat 134 (0900-2020280). 🗓 Fri.

The most impressive sight in
Westkapelle is its sea wall, the
history of which is fascinating.
In former times, this town lay
securely behind the dunes, but
these were washed away in
the 15th century. This meant
that the access route to the
island shifted. A dyke was
built, which was completed in
1458. The lighthouse also dates
from this time; it was once a
church tower, until the demolition of the church in 1831. In
1944, the dyke was bombed
by the Allies in order to flood
Walcheren so it could be liberated. In 1987 the dyke was
built to the height of the delta.

The chic Badhôtel in Domburg

For hotels and restaurants in this region see pp398–399 and p418

The medieval Zuidhavenpoort in Zierikzee

Zierikzee **❼**

Road map A4. 🎭 *9,900.* 🚌
🛈 *Nieuw Haven 7 (0900-2020233).*
🚢 *Thu.*

With 558 listed houses, Zierikzee ranks eighth in the list of Dutch historic towns. The impressive city gateways can be seen from afar. The many terraces on the Havenplein offer a marvellous view of the two harbour entrances and ornate mansion houses on Oude Haven (old harbour), and the trickle of the **Gouwe**, the creek that brought trading prosperity to Zierikzee. The Gothic **Gravensteen** (1524–6), once the home of the Count of Holland, is now the **Maritiem Museum** (maritime museum).

The Zierikzee skyline shows the still unfinished **Dikke Toren** (great tower), construction of which began in 1454. At 130 m (425 ft), it must have been the highest point of the colossal 12th-century **St-Lievenskerk**, which burnt to the ground in 1832.

Strolling through the narrow streets along the new and old harbours, you will chance upon passageways that offer glimpses of old façades, such as of the 14th-century De Haene house, or the former Stadhuis (1550–54), now the **Stadhuismuseum**.

One of the most famous historic events in Holland, the revolt of Zierikzee in 1472 against Charles the Stout, is re-enacted each summer.

🏛 **Maritiem Museum**
Mol 25. *Tel* 0111-454464.
⬤ *closed 2011 for renovation: the collection is temporarily displayed at the Stadhuismuseum.*

🏛 **Stadhuismuseum**
Meelstraat 6. *Tel* 0111-454464. ⬤ *reopens 2011 following renovation: phone or check website for details.*
www.museaschouwenduiveland.nl

Environs
A museum in Ouwerkerk is devoted to the floods of 1953.

🏛 **Museum Watersnood 1953**
Weg van de buitenlandse pers 5.
Tel 0111-644382. ⬤ *Apr–Oct: 11am–5pm Tue–Sun; Nov–Mar: 1–5pm Tue–Sun.* 📷
www.watersnoodmuseum.nl

Haamstede **❽**

Road map A4. 🎭 *3,800.* 🚌 🛈 *Noordstraat 45a (0900-2020233).* 🚢 *Thu.*

Slot Haamstede, painstakingly restored in the 1960s

Haamstede is a peaceful town built around a church. The nearby **Slot Haamstede**, a castle dating from the 13th century, is surrounded by a park with pleasant walks.

♠ **Slot Haamstede**
Haamstede, near church. ⬤ *grounds only; castle closed to public.*

Environs
Westerschouwen, 5 km (3 miles) southwest of Haamstede, has an impressive landscape and illustrious past. The dunes lie on the western edge, sometimes barren with a scattering of gorse, sometimes covered with coniferous forest.

You can climb to the top of **Plompetoren**, the tower of the now-submerged Koudekerke, which rises from the salt marshes. On the edge of the dunes is **Slot Moermond**.

🏛 **Plompe Toren**
Corner of Plompetorenweg & Koudekerkseweg.
⬤ *10am–4:30pm daily.*

Isolated Plompe Toren of the now-submerged Koudekerke

Brouwershaven **❾**

Road map A4. 🎭 *1,400.* 🚌
🚢 *Mon.*

Quiet Brouwershaven combines a historic centre with a modern port. The Havenkanaal to the marina and the Stadhuis date from 1599. The 14th-century **St-Nicolaaskerk** (Church of St Nicholas) is a monument to past glory. The town prospered again as an outport to Rotterdam until the Nieuwer Waterweg (new waterway) was built in 1870.

🏛 **Brouws Museum**
Haven Zuidzijde 14–15. *Tel* 0111-691342. ⬤ *9am–5pm Mon–Fri.* 📷

Brouwershaven, now a focus for water recreation

Bruinisse ⑩

Road map B4. 🚶 3,000. 🚌
ℹ️ *Brusea Visserijmuseum, Oude-straat 23 (0111-481412)*. 🚢 *Wed*.

Bruinisse is now mainly a centre for watersports. The modern bungalow park **Aqua Delta** is situated outside the old village next to the marina.

Environs
To get an idea of what this countryside looked like in earlier times, visit the *ringdorp* (circle-shaped village) **Dreischor**, 10 km (6 miles) west of Bruinisse. It has a typical village church and town hall. On the edge of the village is **Goemanszorg**, an agricultural museum devoted to farming past and present.

🏛 **Goemanszorg**
Molenweg 3, Dreischor.
Tel 0111-402303. 🕐 Easter–Oct:
10am–5pm Tue–Fri, noon–5pm
Sat–Mon & public hols. 📷 ♿ 📷
www.goemanszorg.nl

St.Annaland ⑪

Road map B5. 🚶 3,000. 🚌
ℹ️ *see St Maartensdijk*.

Tholen is the least well-known island of Zeeland. Here there is a constantly changing scenery of poplars and pollard willows, fields and quiet towns, such as St Annaland, with its picturesque harbour on the Krabbenkreek. **Streekmuseum De Meestoof** (regional madder museum) is an interesting reminder of Zeeland's industrial past. The cultivation of the madder plant and processing of its root into a red dye was, until the 19th century, one of the main livelihoods of the region. It was brought to an end in 1868 by the invention of artificial dyes.

🏛 **Streekmuseum De Meestoof**
Bierensstraat 6–8. **Tel** 0166-652901.
🕐 Apr–Oct: 2–5pm Tue–Sat. 📷
www.demeestoof.nl

St Maartensdijk ⑫

Road map B5. 🚶 3,300. 🚌
ℹ️ *Haven 10 (0166-663771)*.

St Maartensdijk has been the "capital" of Tholen since 1971. This town has much to remind us of its patrons, the powerful Lords van Borssele. The remains of the tomb of Floris van Borssele (who died in 1422) and his wife are still to be seen in a burial chapel of the slender 14th- to 15th-century church. Much of the original carving and fragments of the old painting have been preserved. The foundations and moat of the van Borssele castle, which was demolished in 1820, can still be found outside the town.

The most impressive part of the town itself is the Markt, with its 16th-century houses and elegant Stadhuis.

Tholen ⑬

Road map B5. 🚶 6,100. 🚌
ℹ️ *see St Maartensdijk*.

Tholen is a Zeeland town with a Brabant flavour. Two buildings dominate the town – the marvellous Stadhuis (1452) with its robust battlements and the ornate **OL-Vrouwekerk** (Church of Our Lady), dating from the 14th to 16th centuries. The **kapel van het St-Laurensgasthuis** (St Laurensgasthuis chapel), which has been rebuilt into a residential home, stands opposite the church. Even though Tholen became a fortified town in the 16th century, it has retained its old character. Gothic façades are everywhere to remind us of its former prosperity.

Pumping station in a rural setting in the neighbourhood of Tholen

Goes

Road map A5. 👥 *24,000.* 🚌 🚉
ℹ️ *Singelstraat 13 (0113-235990).*
📅 *Tue, Sat.*

Some of the historical towns
of Zeeland are charming but
sleepy, but Goes is wide-
awake. Every Tuesday there
is an old-fashioned market
featuring fabrics and groceries
which takes place on a square
full of Brabant atmosphere,
the Grote Markt. The Raadhuis
(town hall), dating from 1463
(rebuilt between 1771 and
1775), stands at the front of
the square, representing the
magistrates' power with all its
bulk and loftiness. The rococo
interior with its grisailles and
stucco ceiling is particularly
attractive. The majestic St-
Maria-Magdalenakerk (Church
of Mary Magdalen) (15th to
16th century) rises up behind
the town hall. The cruciform
basilica has been restored.

Imposing heraldic ornament on Goes Raadhuis

Yerseke

Road map A5. 👥 *6,100.* 🚌 🚉
ℹ️ *Kerkplein 1 (0113-571864).*
📅 *Fri.*

As they say in Zuid-Beveland,
*"De een zijn dood de ander
zijn brood"* ("One man's meat
is another man's poison").
Yerseke came to be situated
on the Oosterschelde following the St-Felixstormvloed

(St Felix storm flood) of 1530.
So began a tradition of oyster
farming and mussel fishing
that has continued until the
present day.

The nature reserve Yerseke
Moer to the west of the village
shows how the island used to
look: a desolate patchwork of
inlets, hamlets, rough pasture

A fishing boat in Yerseke bringing
home the catch

lands, coves, castles, peat
moors and water holes. To
the east of Yerseke lies the
submerged land of Zuid-
Beveland, lost in 1530 along
with Reimerswaal, at the time
the third largest Zeeland town.

Nisse

Road map A5. 👥 *580.* 🚌
ℹ️ *see Goes.*

Nisse is a typical Beveland
village with square, ford and
church. The church is worth a
visit; though it does not look
like much from the outside,
inside you will be surprised by
unique, 15th-century frescoes
depicting the saints, scenes
from the life of Mary and the
coats of arms of the Lords van
Borssele. Carvings on the
choir vault and stalls are also
from the 15th century.

🏛️ **Hervormde kerk**
*Key available from church secretary
(0113-649650/649780).*

Environs
The **Zak van Zuid-Beveland**,
south of the railway line to
Middelburg, is characteristic
for its balance between nature
and culture. The landscape
is a succession of polders,
divided by dykes covered with
flowers or sheep grazing.

Hulst

Road map B5. 👥 *10,800.* 🚌 ℹ️
Steenstraat 37 (0114-315221). 📅 *Mon.*

Cross over the Westerschelde
and you are at the same time
in Flanders and in the Netherlands. **St-Willibrordus-basiliek**
(St Willibrordus basilica)
towers above the town from

OYSTER FARMING

Oysters apparently have all sorts of beneficial side effects,
improved virility being the most well known. Whether this
is true or not, this slippery delicacy makes any meal seem
festive. Oyster farming began in 1870 when suitable parts
of the river bed were no longer available for free fishing and
were transferred to private use. Oyster farming flourished
along the Oosterschelde, particularly in Yerseke, but the oysters were vulnerable to disease and harsh winters. Concern

that oyster farming
would be impossible
when the Grevelingen
was changed from an
open estuary to a lake
after the completion
of the Delta Works *(see
pp246–7)* has so far
proved unfounded –
the oysters already are
less prone to disease.

Oysters, a tasty delicacy

the distance. Generations of Keldermans, a Mechelen building family, have worked on this church. One unusual feature in Hulst is the trio of hostels, once safe houses for the monks from the Flemish abbeys Ten Duinen, Baudelo and Cambron.

Nearby is the former village of Hulsterloo, famous from the medieval epic Reynard the fox.

Terneuzen ⑱

Road map A5. 24,500.
Markt 11–13 (0115-617960).
Wed, Fri.

Terneuzen has an important port. The mighty sea locks in the **Kanaal van Gent naar Terneuzen** (Gent-Terneuzen canal), built between 1825 and 1827, are also impressive. The town has industrial areas to the north and nature reserves to the west (de Braakman) and the east (Otheense Kreek).

Sluis ⑲

Road map A5. 2,100. St Annastraat 15 (0117-461700). Fri.

The Zeeland-Flanders landscape is scarred by the effects of floods and the dykes built to deal with them. Both polders and inner dykes bear witness to the constant struggle with the sea. The liberation of Zeeland-Flanders in 1944 was also hard-fought, devastating towns and villages such as Sluis. The 14th-century **Stadhuis**, with its belfry, the only one existing in the Netherlands, was restored in its former style after 1945, including the bell tower with the statue which has the nickname Jantje van Sluis.

Environs
St-Anna-ter-Muiden, 2 km (1.5 miles) to the west of Sluis is a village beloved by artists. Once prosperous, the town now has just a few houses around the square, with a village pump and the stump of a tower. To the south is the oldest town in Zeeland: **Aardenburg**. The Romans built a fort here in the 2nd century to ward off Saxon

Gentse Poort, the gateway to the Flemish-tinged town of Hulst

pirates. Aardenburg later became one of the most powerful towns in Flanders. This can still be seen from **St-Baafskerk**, a flawless 13th-century example of the Scheldt Gothic style famous for its painted sarcophagi. The **Gemeentelijk Archeologisch Museum Aardenburg** (Aardenburg municipal archaeological museum) deals solely with the Romans.

> 🏛 **Gemeentelijk Archeologisch Museum Aardenburg**
> Marktstraat 18. **Tel** 0117-492888.
> Apr–Oct: 10am–noon, 1:30–5pm Tue–Fri, 1–5pm Sat & Sun.
> www.museumaardenburg.nl

Cadzand ⑳

Road map A5. 800. Boulevard de Wielingen 44d (0117-391298). Jul & Aug: Mon pm.

Modern seaside resort Cadzand is particularly popular for its wide stretch of sand. A popular pursuit here is to search for fossilized sharks' teeth. Along the dunes are dignified seaside hotels reminiscent of those of Domburg. A little way past Cadzand is the nature reserve the Zwin, which extends as far as Knokke in Belgium. The resort Nieuwvliet lies to the east of Cadzand.

The broad sandy beaches of Cadzand, always popular in summer

NORTHERN AND EASTERN NETHERLANDS

Exploring the Northern and Eastern Netherlands

The Northern and Eastern Netherlands are comparatively sparsely populated. They encompass the West Frisian Islands (Waddeneilanden) and the provinces of Groningen, Friesland, Drenthe, Overijssel, Flevoland and Gelderland. Agriculture has always played a predominant role here. This part of Holland has many natural and recreation areas, such as the Waddenzee mud flats, Frisian coast, coastal Lauwersmeergebied, Hondsrug, Nationaal Park De Hoge Veluwe, Sallandse Heuvelrug and the Oostvaardersplassen.

WADDEN ISLANDS
(see pp264–275)

Leeuward

FRIESLAND
(see pp290–301)

De Elfstedentocht (see pp294–5) *has been held 15 times during the last century. Over 16,000 skaters have skated the Tocht der Tochten, a 200-km (124-mile) stretch.*

The waddengebied (see pp268–9) *provides a habitat for many species of birds. It is an important area for annual and migrating birds. The worms, molluscs and crustaceans are an ideal source of food for ducks, seagulls and wading birds.*

Lelystad

FLEVOLAND
(see pp322–329)

The Batavia (see p327) *was owned by the Dutch East India Company. This three-master was 45 m (148 ft) long and had room for 350 men. A replica of the* Batavia *was built between 1985 and 1995 at the Batavia-Werf (Batavia wharf) in Lelystad, which is now working on a replica of Michiel de Ruyter's 17th-century flagship, De Zeven Provinciën.*

0 kilometres   20

0 miles   20

◁ **Punting in one of the many canals in the region of Giethoorn, Overijssel**

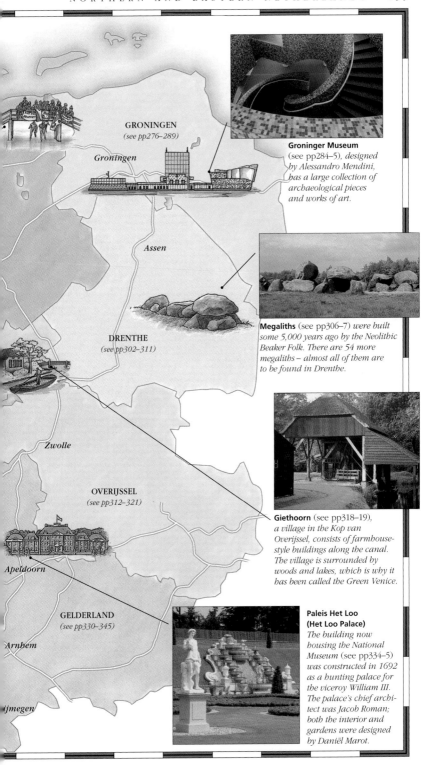

GRONINGEN
(see pp276–289)

Groningen

Groninger Museum
(see pp284–5), *designed
by Alessandro Mendini,
has a large collection of
archaeological pieces
and works of art.*

Assen

DRENTHE
(see pp302–311)

Megaliths (see pp306–7) *were built
some 5,000 years ago by the Neolithic
Beaker Folk. There are 54 more
megaliths – almost all of them are
to be found in Drenthe.*

Zwolle

OVERIJSSEL
(see pp312–321)

Giethoorn (see pp318–19),
*a village in the Kop van
Overijssel, consists of farmhouse-
style buildings along the canal.
The village is surrounded by
woods and lakes, which is why it
has been called the Green Venice.*

Apeldoorn

GELDERLAND
(see pp330–345)

Arnhem

ijmegen

**Paleis Het Loo
(Het Loo Palace)**
*The building now
housing the National
Museum (see pp334–5)
was constructed in 1692
as a hunting palace for
the viceroy William III.
The palace's chief archi-
tect was Jacob Roman;
both the interior and
gardens were designed
by Daniël Marot.*

Environmental Policy

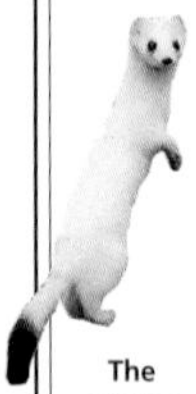

In the 1990s, the Dutch government drew up the Natuurbeleidsplan, a programme designed to make nature reserves accessible to the public. This is of great importance to the northern and eastern Netherlands, with their many lakes, woods and polders. The region's ecosystem has been divided into core areas, development areas and connecting zones in an attempt to give permanence to the natural environment. The connecting zones join the areas together. When the policy is fully implemented, it will aid in the survival of many plant and animal species.

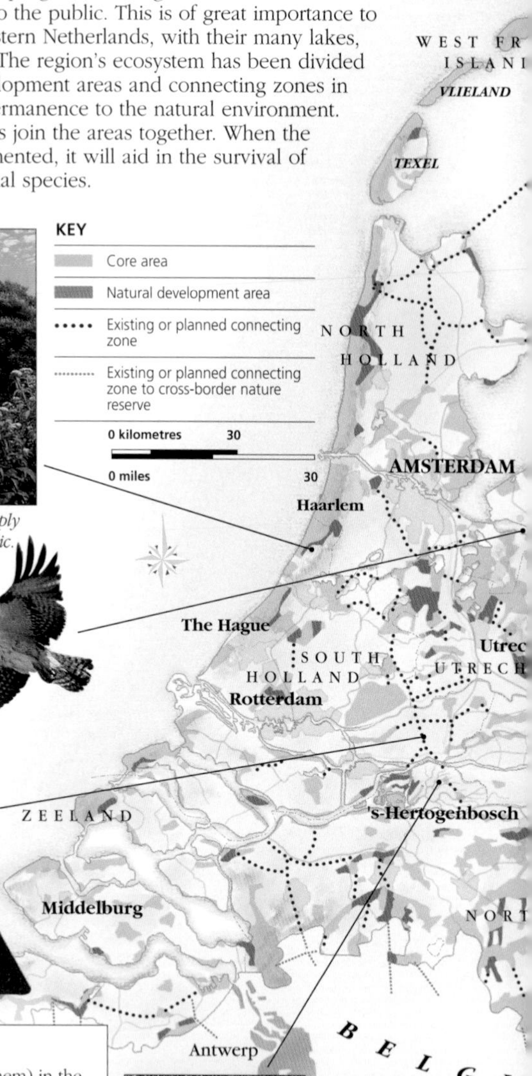

The ermine

KEY

Core area

Natural development area

•••• Existing or planned connecting zone

·········· Existing or planned connecting zone to cross-border nature reserve

0 kilometres   30

0 miles   30

WEST FR
ISLAN
VLIELAND

TEXEL

N O R T H
H O L L A N D

AMSTERDAM

Haarlem

The Hague

SOUTH
HOLLAND

Rotterdam

Utrec
U T R E C H

ZEELAND

's-Hertogenbosch

Middelburg

N O R

BELGI

Antwerp

The Waterleidingduinen *(water supply dunes) are only partly open to the public.*

The osprey *was a rare sight in Holland for many years. Thanks to the Natuurbeleidsplan, sightings of this bird of prey have become more frequent in recent years.*

Special road signs *have been designed to warn motorists of migrating toads during that animal's mating season. Usually shy, toads come out en masse when mating.*

READ THE SIGNS!

Most natural areas (or parts of them) in the northern and eastern Netherlands are freely accessible. However, some parts are open only from sunrise *(zonsopkomst)* to sunset *(zonsondergang)*, and it is therefore important to read the signs. It goes without saying that you should not make excessive noise, cause damage or leave litter in the area. Further information is available at VVV offices, the ANWB and the Vereniging Natuurmonumenten (tel. 035-6559933).

The adder *is the only venomous snake in Holland and is very rare here. However, this small, distinctive snake can still be found in sandy regions and peat moors. In order to feed properly, adders require an extensive habitat.*

The otter *can no longer be found in Holland, but there are plans to re-establish it in the provinces of Flevoland, Friesland and Overijssel, although the areas required for this must meet quality requirements, since otters are very sensitive to pollution.*

The golden plover, *a rare wading bird which has been put under pressure by the reclamation of peat bogs and heathland, is the object of a special plan that will enable it to recover its numbers in the Netherlands.*

Connecting zones *in Flevoland linking various natural areas are now being set up for, among others, the common and edible frog, the polecat, the European water shrew, the pond bat, the grass snake and the beaver. Specific corridors are being developed for butterflies.*

The common hamster *and other protected animals cause headaches for developers. The Nature Protection Act prevents building on or the use of areas they inhabit.*

Connections *between core areas and development areas in some cases consist of "ecoducts". The vegetated passages atop the tunnels are designed to allow wildlife access to either side of the road, thereby linking two areas of great importance for flora and fauna without exposing them to road hazards.*

Distinctive Landscapes

The northeast of the Netherlands has a number of distinctive landscape types, such as the unique mud flats, or Waddenzee, where the sand and clay is exposed at low tide; the peat moors in southeast Groningen; the enchanting heathland of Drenthe; the endless polder landscape of Flevoland; the splendid forests of Gelderland (Hoge Veluwe and Posbank) and the magnificent riverscapes and seascapes in the northeast of Overijssel.

Heath spotted-orchid

The Oostvaardersplassen (lakes), *between Lelystad and Almere, make up a unique natural landscape. It is a breeding ground and feeding area for hundreds of species of birds.*

Glasswort *is a wild plant which grows in mud flats and on silt deposits. It is a prized culinary delicacy.*

Water crowfoot *occurs in both flowing and standing water.*

WEST FRISIAN ISLANDS
The Waddenzee *(see pp270–1)* is an area of mud flats which is largely dry at low tide. It attracts many species of birds that come here to forage and to feed. The island of Texel features the peat walls of the Hoge Berg.

Rapeseed plantations *are used for land improvements in new polders. The yellow fields seem to stretch endlessly to the horizon.*

Bulrushes *were once common in the region. The "cigars" grow only by fresh water and are now protected.*

POLDER LANDSCAPE
Forests (het Knarbos), lakes (the Oostvaardersplassen) and coastal lakes (the Veluwemeer) distinguish the flat polder landscape of the "new" province of Flevoland *(see pp322–9).*

Boletus edulis *is a delicious edible mushroom. Picking it, however, is no longer allowed.*

Bracken fern *grows in sparse woodland on lime and nutrient-poor sand and loamy ground, and on dried peat moors.*

Common polypody *occurs in juniper brush and in woodlands on poor sandy soil.*

Mosses *thrive in humid environments such as forest floors. Shady areas with acidic soil are ideal for sphagnum moss.*

The cran-berry *grows in sphagnum moss on peat moors and in fens.*

FORESTS

One of the best-known and largest forest areas in the Netherlands is at Hoge Veluwe in the province of Gelderland *(see pp330–45)*, where a variety of animals, such as wild boar and red deer, are to be found.

Common sundew, *an insect-eating plant, grows on heathland and in the fenland of Groningen and Drenthe.*

Cross-leaved heath *thrives on nutrient-poor, dry, sandy soil and in the troughs of dunes.*

Heather *occurs mainly in sand and peat bogs, typically poor in nutrients.*

HEATHLAND

The northeastern Netherlands abounds with delightful heathland. Some of the most picturesque heathland can be found at Drenthe *(see pp302–11)*; herds of sheep still graze in the region of Ellertsveld.

THE WEST FRISIAN ISLANDS

Perhaps the least known part of the Netherlands despite their natural beauty, the West Frisian Islands form a barrier protecting the north of the country from the worst of the North Sea. Comprising five main islands and a few sandbanks, they are among Europe's last areas of wilderness.

The West Frisian Islands are the remaining fragments of an ancient sandbank that once stretched from Cap Gris Nez in France to Esbjerg in Denmark, a remnant of the last Ice Age. Since Roman times the sea has been eroding this sandbank, creating the shallow Waddenzee behind and washing away much of the peat soil that lay beyond the dunes. The islands of Griend and Rottumeroog were threatened to such an extent that they were abandoned. Rottumerplatt, too, is uninhabited.

Monks established the first settlements as far back as the 8th century; islanders made a living from farming, fishing and collecting shellfish. On Texel and Terschelling, the two largest islands, churches dating from the 15th century still stand. Later, the islands prospered from links with the Dutch East India Company and, in the 19th century, from whaling. Vlieland and Ameland are quieter islands, good for bird-watching. Schiermonnikoog is the most isolated, with rare plant life.

Nowadays the islands, reached by ferries from the mainland, have much to offer the visitor in search of peace and quiet, with nature rambles over dunes and salt marsh, and seal- and bird-watching, especially in summer. The islands' quaint museums are strong on ecology and conservation. The best way to get around is by bicycle and visitors will find a wide range of hotels and guesthouses, excellent seafood restaurants, and some of the best sunsets anywhere.

Former captain's house *(commandeurhuisje)* on Ameland

◁ **Aerial view of the head of Texel island, with its lighthouse**

Exploring the West Frisian Islands

The history of the West Frisian Islands (Waddeneilanden) has been shaped by the wind and the sea. It was not until the 17th century that the larger islands were stabilized by dykes. Den Burg on Texel, the largest village on the islands, is a historic fortification with a pleasant old centre. Nearby is Hoge Berg, with its characteristic peat walls; in the west, the distinctive tower of Den Hoorn can be seen. To the north is the unique natural area of De Slufter. The crown of the Frisian Islands, Vlieland, has the prettiest village of the islands. Terschelling, Ameland and Schiermonnikoog are typical Frisian islands, with wide beaches, partly forested dunes, villages and polders or mud flats on the Waddenzee side.

Cranberry liqueur

Shrimp fishermen sorting their catch

SIGHTS AT A GLANCE

Ameland **9**
De Koog **3**
Den Burg **2**
Den Hoorn **5**
De Slufter **4**
Griend **7**
Noorderhaaks **1**

Rottumeroog **12**
Rottumerplaat **11**
Schiermonnikoog **10**
Terschelling **8**
Vlieland **6**

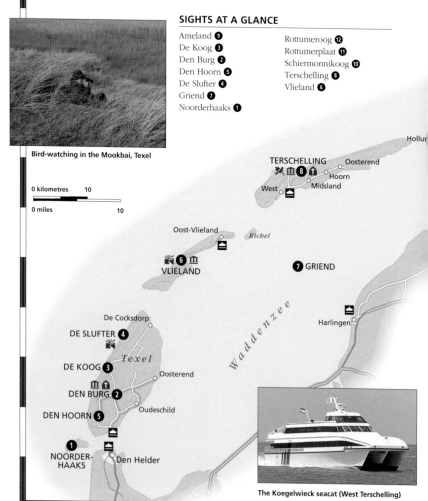

Bird-watching in the Mookbai, Texel

0 kilometres 10
0 miles 10

Hollum

TERSCHELLING **8** Oosterend
West Hoorn
Midsland

Oost-Vlieland *Richel*

6 🏛
VLIELAND

7 GRIEND

De Cocksdorp

DE SLUFTER 4

Texel

Harlingen

DE KOOG 3
Oosterend

DEN BURG 2
Oudeschild

DEN HOORN 5

W a d d e n z e e

1
NOORDER-HAAKS Den Helder

The Koegelwieck seacat (West Terschelling)

For additional map symbols see back flap

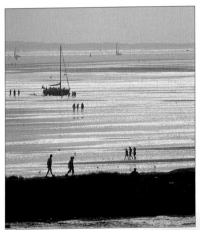
De Wadden – the mud flats are ideal for beach walks

GETTING AROUND

The West Frisian Islands are reached by ferries from the mainland. **Texel** is served by TESO (tel. 0222-369600); no cars allowed, no reservations. Foot passengers can take a bus to De Koog or De Cocksdorp via Den Burg, or order a taxi-bus when buying their ticket. **Vlieland** is served by Rederij Doeksen (tel. 0900-3635736); cars not permitted. On arrival, a bus takes passengers to Posthuis, where there are taxis. **Terschelling** is served by Rederij Doeksen (0900-3635736); reservations recommended for cars. There is a bus service on the island, and taxis are available on arrival. **Ameland** is served by Rederij Wagenborg (tel. 0519-546111); reservations recommended. There are bus services to all villages. **Schiermonnikoog** is served by Rederij Wagenborg (tel. 0519-349050); foot passengers only. Bus service and taxi-buses connect the dock and village. Bicycles can be hired easily.

ROTTUMERPLAAT **11**

12
ROTTUMEROOG

SCHIERMONNIKOOG
10

AMELAND
9
○Buren
Nes

Schiermonnikoog

Lauwersoog

W a d d e n z e e

Holwerd

SEE ALSO

• *Where to Stay* p399
• *Where to Eat* pp 418–19

Rescued seals being returned to the wild by members of EcoMare, Texel *(see p435)*

KEY

═══ Motorway

━━━ Main road

═══ Minor road

━━━ Scenic route

─── Minor railway

The splendid coastline of Vlieland

Birds of the Waddenzee

The extensive wetlands of the Waddenzee are an important area for breeding and migratory birds. The North Sea coasts of the islands are sandy, with little animal life; the Waddenzee coasts of the islands, however, consist of fine sand and clay which are rich in minerals and nutrients. The innumerable worms, molluscs and crustaceans that live here are an ideal source of food for a huge variety of ducks, seagulls and wading birds. At the peak of the migratory season (August), the number of birds here runs into millions.

Black-headed gull

Curlew
This is the largest European wading bird and is easily recognizable by its long, curved beak.

Bird-watching Hide
There are many hides for bird-watchers on the mud flats of the Waddenzee, allowing the birds to be observed without disturbance.

BIRD CATCHERS
Bird catchers, whose interests in The Netherlands have gone far beyond mere hunting, have become an important pressure group for the protection of birds and the natural environment. Their organization is Vogelbescherming Nederland, based in Zeist.

BEAK SHAPES
People are often surprised at the many varieties of birds that feed on the mud flats. The different species, however, have managed to avoid competing with one another. The various shapes and lengths of their beaks are suitable for the assorted types of food that can be found in the water and in the sand. Ducks get their food from the surface or dive for it, whereas wading birds get their food from underground – what prey at which depth underground depends on the shape of the beak. Other birds catch fish (spoonbills, cormorants or terns), shellfish (eider ducks) or even other seabirds (the white-tailed eagle), or steal their food from other birds.

The ringed plover feeds from the surface.

The lapwing feeds on small crabs in the mud.

The silver plover catches small sea-worms.

The oyster-catcher pulls shellfish out of the sand.

The black-tailed godwit feeds on worms living underground.

The curlew, with its curved sharp beak, can reach invertebrates living deep in the sand.

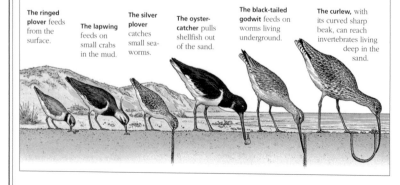

Arctic Tern
This extremely rare bird, which breeds in the West Frisian Islands, spends the winter in the Antarctic. This gives it the longest migratory path of all birds.

Sandwich Tern
This bird has its largest breeding colony in Holland on Griend. Its dwindling numbers mean it requires careful protection.

Oystercatcher
The oystercatcher is characteristic of the Waddenzee. It forages for cockles and mussels.

BIRD SPECIES

The wealth of bird species – including diving birds, petrels, cormorants, spoonbills, ducks, birds of prey, waders, scavengers, seagulls, terns, razorbills and songbirds – that occur in the Waddenzee is a good reason to ensure that the area is carefully protected. For many of the birds, these are the only breeding grounds in the Netherlands, as they are the only wetlands remaining in the Netherlands. Various parts are closed to visitors, and it is important to observe the regulations in order to help preserve the bird population.

Avocet
This magnificent wading bird has an upward-curving bill and black and white plumage.

Black-Tailed Godwit
This wading bird, with fiery red-brown plumage, is a bird of passage but spends the winters and summers in the Waddenzee.

Large numbers of oyster-catchers can be seen both in winter and in summer.

Ringed Plover
This is an active bird that rarely breeds here but passes through in large numbers.

Eider Duck
The eider duck has breeding colonies on Texel, Vlieland and Terschelling. The male is far more impressive in appearance than the brown-coloured female.

Herring Gull
The herring gull is just one of the many varieties of gull that occur here. At more than half a metre (1.5 ft) long, it is an impressive bird.

Red Knot
This bird of passage stops over sometimes in summer and sometimes in winter. It is a robust bird, one that is always on the move.

The Waddenzee

The Waddenzee is a tidal area whose sand or mud flats *(wadden)* are mainly exposed at low tide and disappear at high tide. Together with the West Frisian Islands, the Waddenzee forms the last extensive wild part of Holland. The entire area has an extremely rich ecosystem because of the large sources of nourishment. It is a feeding and breeding ground for many species of birds. Two species of seal, 30 species of fish, shrimps and crabs live in the Waddenzee or come here to breed.

Cockle

Cockles (Cardium edule), *which form the diet for many bird species, are intensively harvested using mechanical methods. The catch is exported.*

The VVVs *(tourist offices) on the West Frisian Islands offer all kinds of sailing trips around the islands, including romantic luxury cruises on a three-master. Rederij Vooruit (tel. 0515-531485) arranges sailing trips on local boats.*

Sea Lavender (Limonium vulgare), *along with sea purslane and sea aster, grows in the higher parts of the salt marshes. Fields of blue-violet sea laven-der flowers make a very pretty sight.*

Exposed Sections of the Mud Flats
Much of the Waddenzee mud flats is exposed during low tide. This leaves places like the marina pictured below high and dry. Mooring places that are inaccessible at low tide are increasingly being dredged as marinas.

Low tide

High tide

FLORA IN THE WADDENZEE

Because of the diversity of the Waddenzee landscape, with its changing environment (salt water and fresh water, lime-rich soil and lime-poor soil, wet land and dry land, clay ground and sandy ground), almost 900 plant species grow here. Many of them grow on the island-side of the old dunes in the dune valleys. Amongst the flowers to be found here are autumn gentian and creeping willow, as well as grasses and weeds such as black bog-rush, fragrant orchid and grass of Parnassus. Lavender is among the plants which grow on the higher ground.

Lavender (Salicornia europaea) *is one of the first plants to colonize the mud flats and the low-lying parts of the salt marshes. When the land has silted up completely, the salt marsh grass establishes itself.*

Cracks *in the dried silt provide a good foothold for lavender, as well as for other plants.*

THREATS TO THE WADDENZEE

According to the Dutch oil company NAM, there are between 70 and 170 billion cubic metres (2,500 and 6,000 billion cubic feet) of natural gas beneath the Waddenzee. The value of this gas runs into many billions of euros. The Waddenzee Society is completely opposed to any gas drilling in the Waddenzee on several grounds: first, because there is no social need for it and second, because the environmental effects of drilling – in particular, the consequences the falling ground level would have on life in the Waddenzee – have not been properly investigated. For the time being, therefore, drilling on the Waddenzee is banned, pending further environmental impact studies. But the Waddenzee is also threatened by the harvesting of mussels and cockles. Since 1992, the Dutch government has scaled this back, and is considering closing the area to the shellfish industry.

WADLOPEN (WALKING THE MUD FLATS)

A walk on the Waddenzee takes you through salt marshes and past the *wantij*, a place below an island where two tidal flows meet. Since the mid-1970s, walking on the mud flats has been a popular hobby. There are now six major mud-flat walking societies: De Fryske Waedrinners (Leeuwarden, tel. 06-53359622; Dijkstra's Wadlooptochten (Pieterburen, tel. 0595-528345); Lammert Kwant (Ezinge, tel. 0594-622029); Stichting Uithuizer Wad (only for Rottumeroog; tel. 0511-522271), Stichting Wadloopcentrum Friesland (Holwerd, tel. 0519-242100) and Stichting Wadloopcentrum Pieterburen (tel. 0595-528300).

Cockle harvesting

Noorderhaaks, above sea level at high tide for some decades now

Noorderhaaks ❶

Road map B2. 🚶 *none.* 🛈 *district Den Helder (0223-671333).*

Noorderhaaks, also known as Razende Bol (raging ball), is a fairly bleak sandbank west of Den Helder, 2.5 km (1.5 miles) offshore. The sea currents cause the island to shift eastwards towards Texel, after which another "raging ball" appears at the same point off Den Helder. The Dutch air force occasionally uses the island for target practice, but it is not off-limits for visitors. Rowing and swimming here are risky because of the powerful currents. Adventure-seekers regularly visit Noorderhaaks by boat or by helicopter, unable to resist this piece of total wilderness, where mirages are common.

Den Burg ❷

Road map B2. 🚶 *6,000.* 🚢 🚌 🛈 *Emmalaan 66 (0222-314741).* 🏛 *Mon am.*

Den Burg is the main town of Texel and situated right in its centre. Around 1300, the village was fortified by a circular rampart with a moat, which are now marked by the Burgwal and Parkstraat Streets. A sheep market was once held in April and May at the Groeneplats, Den Burg's main square with the present-day town hall. Today, a sheep day is held on the first Monday of September. Further on, by the Binnenburg, or inner castle, stands the 15th-century

Late Gothic **Hervormde kerk** (Protestant church). The Kogerstraat runs the length of the Binnenburg. Located here is the **Oudheidkamer**, an antiquities museum set up in a picturesque 16th-century building, which used to be a doss-house. Today it contains period rooms, a display of artefacts and works of art in the attic, and a herb garden.

Along and around the town wall are several interesting shopping streets, such as the Weverstraat. A number of excellent restaurants are to be found on the Warmoesstraat.

🏛 **Oudheidkamer**
Kogerstraat 1, Den Burg. *Tel* 0222-313135. 🕐 *2 Apr–1 Nov: 10am–12:30pm & 1:30–3:30pm Mon–Fri.* 🚫 *1 Jan, Easter, Whitsun, 25, 26 & 31 Dec.* 📷

Environs
South of Den Burg is a sloping landscape with the 15 m (50 ft) **Hoge Berg** (high

mountain), which offers a great view of the island. For a good walk, follow the Skille-paadje from the tomb of the Georgiers (resistance fighters who died fighting the Germans in 1945) to the fishing village of Oudeschild, past the peat walls and sheep pens.

Beachcomber on Texel

De Koog ❸

Road map B2. 🚶 *825.* 🚢 🚌 🛈 *Emmalaan 66, Den Burg (0222-314741).* 🚢 *Tue.*

In 1900, the former fishing settlement of De Koog consisted of a church (built in 1415) and a few houses and farms. The first tourist facility was the Badhotel, later the Hotel Prinses Juliana, with a garden overlooking the sea. Today, Den Koog has accommodation for 20,000 visitors in hotels, pensions and camp sites. The centre of De Koog is the Dorpsstraat, which has cafés, snack bars and discos. De Koog's attractions for visitors are the Calluna waterpark and Eco Mare, an information centre for the Waddenzee and the North Sea *(see p449).*

The Nederlands-Hervormde church in Den Burg (1481)

De Slufter ❹

Road map B2. 🚶 none. 🚌 🚐
⭕ all year, northern part closed
1 Mar–1 Sep. ℹ️ Emmalaan 66,
Den Burg (0222-314741).

The unique natural area of
De Slufter, consisting of salt
marshes covering 450 ha
(1,100 acres), is covered with
salt-loving plants such as sea
thrift and sea lavender, and is
an important breeding and
feeding ground for many different bird species. De Slufter,
and the neighbouring **De Muy**,
where spoonbills breed, are
magnificent rambling areas.

Den Hoorn ❺

Road map B2. 🚶 450. 🚌 🚐
ℹ️ Emmalaan 66, Den Burg (0222-
314741). 🛒 Thu.

Like Den Burg, Den Hoorn
stands on boulder clay. It has
a distinctive **Hervormde kerk**
(Protestant church) with a
pointed steeple and churchyard dating from 1425. This
exquisitely restored village has
been given protected status.

Vlieland ❻

Road map C1. 🚶 1,150. 🚌
ℹ️ Havenweg 10 (0562-451111).

Vlieland is the smallest of the
Waddenzee Islands. In some
places, less than one kilome-
tre (half a mile) separates the
Waddenzee and the North Sea.
Unlike the other islands,

Salt-loving plants thriving at the water's edge, De Slufter

Vlieland consists only of
dunes, covered with a purple
haze of heather, marram grass
and sea buckthorn. In the
east, the woods planted just
after 1900 provide a bit of
variety in the landscape.

In the south is the only village, **Oost-Vlieland**, where
the boat from Harlingen
docks. Many old buildings
line the main street. One of
them, the **Tromp's Huys**
(1576), used to belong to the
Amsterdam Admiralty. Today
it houses a museum with

19th-century paintings. The
houses are separated by alleys
known as "gloppen". There is
no room for cars here, not
even for those of the islanders.

The best way to explore
Vlieland is by bicycle; the
island can be covered in one
day. From Oost-Vlieland, you
can cycle westwards along
tracks through the dunes or
along the Waddenzee shore-
line to the **Posthuys** (post
house), where in the 17th
century the overseas mail was
brought from Amsterdam to
be loaded onto ships waiting
to sail. Further westwards is
de Vliehors, an area of natural
interest which can be
explored if no military exer-
cises are taking place here.
Beware, though: you run the
risk of getting stuck in the
soft drifting sand. This is also
where the wealthy village of
West-Vlieland once stood. It
was consumed by the waves
after it was abandoned in 1736.

🏛 **Tromp's Huys**
Dorpsstraat 99, Vlieland. **Tel** 0562-
451600. ⭕ May–Sep: 10am–noon
& 2–5pm Mon–Sat; Nov–Mar:
2–5pm Wed & Sat. ⬤ 1 Jan,
Easter, Pentecost. 📷

The village hall in Oost-Vlieland

The Oerol Festival on Terschelling

Griend ❼

Road map C1. 🚶 *none.* 🚢 *very limited.* ℹ️ *Vereniging Natuur-monumenten (035-6559933).*

Half-way through the boat trip from Harlingen to Terschelling or Vlieland, one will come across Griend. The island was abandoned by its inhabitants after the St Lucia Flood of 1287. For centuries it seemed about to disappear beneath the waves. In 1988, the Natuurmonu-menten trust, which has leased Griend since 1916, had a dam built to prevent further erosion. At high tide, the highest part of the island is just 1 m (3 ft) above the water. Access to Griend is forbidden, save for a handful of bird wardens and biology students. This is Holland's largest breeding ground for great tern.

Tombstone from Striep

Terschelling ❽

Road map C1. 🚶 *5,000.* 🚢 🚍 ℹ️ *Willem Barentszkade 19a, West-Terschelling (0562-443000).*

Terschelling is the second largest of the West Frisian Islands. The north of the island consists of dunes, where in the olden days cattle were let out to graze everywhere ("oerol"). This is where the Oerol Festival, held each year in June, gets its name.

In Formerum, West, and Hoorn, the dunes have been planted with conifer-ous and deciduous woods. In the south are polders, and beyond the dykes are the salt marshes. There is a nature reserve at either end of the island: the Noordvaarder in the west, and the Boschplaat in the east. If you happen to be sailing over from Harlingen at low tide on a sunny day, you may see seals basking in the sun on the de Richel and Jacobs Ruggen sandbanks.

West is a real mud-flat village, with old houses and a famous lighthouse, the **Brandaris**, dating from 1594. It is closed to visitors, but the same view can be enjoyed from the high dune known as the Seinpaalduin behind the village. **Het Behouden Huys** is a local history museum dedicated to famous islanders such as Willem Barentsz; there is also the educational **Centrum voor Natuur en Landschap**, where you can learn about the ecology of the mud flats.

The two largest villages in the west are Midsland and Hoorn. Midsland is surrounded by small hamlets with intriguing names such as Hee, Horp and Kaart, which date back to when the Frisians settled on the islands. The hamlet with the **kerkhof van Striep** cemetery is where the first church on the island was built, in the 10th century. Its outline is still visible. Further eastwards is Hoorn, with 13th-century Gothic-Romanesque St Janskerk standing on the site of the original church.

Ameland ❾

Road map C/D1. 🚶 *3,200.* 🚢 🚍 ℹ️ *Bureweg 2, Nes (0519-546546).* **www**.vvvameland.nl

The dunes in the north of this island are dry, with the exception of **Het Oerd**, a wet valley in the east which is a bird reserve. The region is best explored by bicycle; there is a cycle track to a scenic spot on a 24-m (79-ft) dune. In the mud flats in the south there are four villages. The largest of these is **Nes**, where the boat from Holwerd calls. **Commandeurshuizen** (commodores' houses) in the old centre recall the days when many islanders made their living from whaling.

Het Oerd – the edge of the mud flats on Ameland

A horse-drawn lifeboat, the pride of Ameland

If you want to see the real Ameland, you must visit Hollum. The Zuiderlaan and Oosterlaan are steeped in the atmosphere of past times. At the southern end of the village is the church, surrounded by an oval cemetery with tombstones where the deeply pious inscriptions are overgrown with lichen.

Beyond Hollum lies the **Reddingsmuseum Abraham Fock**, a museum dedicated to life-saving, where the pride of Ameland, a lifeboat launched by horses, is kept operational.

🏛 **Reddingsmuseum Abraham Fock**
Oranjeweg 18, Hollum. *Tel* 0519 554243. ◯ Apr–Nov: 10am–noon & 1:30–5pm daily.

Schiermonnikoog ⑩

Road map D1. 🏠 1,000. 🚤 🚌
🛈 Reeweg 5, Schiermonnikoog (0519-531233/531900).

Schiermonnikoog, or Lytje Pole (small land), was a farm belonging to Cistercian monks during the Middle Ages. The village of Schiermonnikoog, which is named after them, has many exquisitely restored houses. The island as a whole is a national park and under the protection of Natuurmonumenten. The beach of Schier is one of the widest in Europe. The eastern side of the island (Het Balg, Kobbeduinen and the salt marshes) in particular make

for wonderful walking areas, with their varied flora (including many orchids) and bird life. No cars at all are allowed on the island.

Rottumerplaat ⑪

Road map D1. 🏠 none.
🛈 Staatsbosbeheer (050-5207247).

Nature has been left to her own devices with the 900 ha (2,225 acre) uninhabited island of Rottumerplaat. This protected nature reserve is jointly managed by the Ministry of Agriculture, Waterways and Planning, and the Friends of Rottumeroog and Rottumerplaat Society (SVRR). Outsiders are rarely admitted to the island. This has had a good effect on Rottumeroog as well as on Rottumerplaat, which has been expanding quickly. Dunes many metres in height

and an impressive salt marsh are its characteristic features. The island also belongs to the seals and birds.

Rottumeroog ⑫

Road map D1. 🏠 none. 🚤 very limited. 🛈 Staatsbosbeheer (050-5207247).

This most eastern of the West Frisian Islands is due to disappear into the mouth of the Ems soon. Since 1991 it has been left in the hands of nature. Attempts over many years to prevent it from drifting eastwards were unsuccessful. In 1998, the northern dunes collapsed, after which the last traces of human settlement were removed by the state forestry commission. The island is now less than 300 ha (740 acres) in size and shrinks with each storm. Walkers are prohibited in the area.

The uninhabited island of Rottumerplaat, with its high dunes

GRONINGEN

The Netherland's northernmost province is distinguished by its rich cultural history and unusual landscape, where you often see terps or small areas of elevated land. To the north and west it is bounded by the shallow Waddenzee and to the east by the Ems river estuary and the border with Germany.

The *terps* originated centuries ago, when the inhabitants of this region needed to protect themselves from high water levels. The elevated land is sometimes crowned by a solitary Romanesque church, visible for miles across the fens. Elsewhere in the province you will see straight roads and canals, often evidence of reclaimed land. The region grew rich during the Middle Ages from agriculture and peat extraction, and the medieval port of Appingedam, nowadays a little town inland from the port of Delfzijl, was once a member of the powerful Hanseatic League.

Groningen province is also noted for its windmills, castles and moated manor houses and, in the east, for its restored fortified towns, such as picturesque Bourtange, which is right on the border with Germany. Conservation areas abound. Close to Lauwersoog, where you can catch a ferry to Schiermonnikoog, one of the West Frisian Islands *(see p275)*, a vast nature reserve has been established. Nearby Pieterburen has a seal sanctuary.

Groningen, the provincial capital, is proud of its glorious past and boasts a wealth of world-class museums, historic buildings and other attractions. A number of Dutch corporations have their headquarters in this thriving university city, and a further boost to the economy arrived in the 1960s after the discovery in nearby Slochteren of some of the world's largest natural gas deposits.

Hay bales in Westerwolde near the old fortified town of Bourtange

◁ Monumental spiral staircase in the Groninger Museum designed by Alessandro Mendini

Exploring Groningen

Some of the most attractive and historically interesting castles, or *borgs*, are in the Groningen region: the medieval Fraeylemaborg in Slochteren, Menkemaborg in Uithuizen and the charming Verhildersum in Leens. The natural area around the Lauwersmeer is particularly suitable for rambling. Not far from here, in Pieterburen, is a famous refuge for seals. Ter Apel, which is on the province's eastern boundary, is a magnificent medieval monastery. Groningen itself *(see pp280–85)* has much to offer, including the peaceful Prinsenhof, with its beautiful gardens, and the ultra-modern Groninger Museum *(see pp284–5)*, which houses collections that range from archaeology to oriental porcelain to modern art.

Wensum, one of the prettiest villages in Groningen

The Lauwersmeer nature reserve, created through the draining of the Lauwerszee

GETTING AROUND

Groningen can be reached from the south along the A28 motorway; the A7 crosses the province from Friesland in the west to Germany in the east. The best way to see the town of Groningen is on foot. From Groningen there are rail links to Roodeschool in the north, Delfzijl in the northeast and to Nieuweschans in the east. Most of the countryside is accessible by regional *(interlokal)* or local *(buurt)* buses. The Groningen region is well suited for cycling and rambling, especially the area around the Lauwersmeer, the mud-flat region *(waddengebied)* and Westerwolde, in the south.

SEE ALSO

- *Where to Stay* pp399–400
- *Where to Eat* p419

SIGHTS AT A GLANCE

Recreation possibilities on the Paterswoldse Meer, south of Groningen

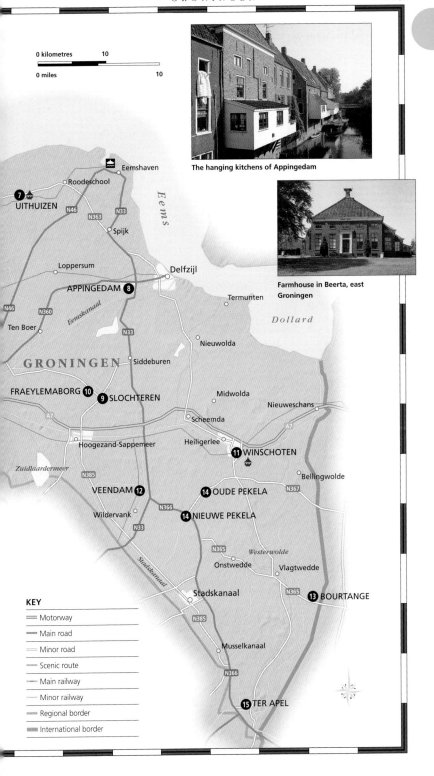

0 kilometres 10

0 miles 10

The hanging kitchens of Appingedam

Farmhouse in Beerta, east Groningen

Eemshaven
Roodeschool
7 UITHUIZEN
N46
N363
N33
Spijk

Eems

Loppersum
Delfzijl
APPINGEDAM **8**

Termunten

N46
N360
Eemskanaal
Ten Boer
N33

Dollard

GRONINGEN
Siddeburen
Nieuwolda

FRAEYLEMABORG **10**
9 SLOCHTEREN
Midwolda
Nieuweschans
A7
Scheemda
Hoogezand-Sappemeer
Heiligerlee
11 WINSCHOTEN
Zuidlaardermeer
N385
Bellingwolde
VEENDAM **12**
14 OUDE PEKELA
N367
Wildervank
N366
14 NIEUWE PEKELA
N33

Westerwolde
N365
Onstwedde
Vlagtwedde

Stadskanaal
Stadskanaal
N365
13 BOURTANGE

KEY

━━ Motorway
━━ Main road
━━ Minor road
━━ Scenic route
━━ Main railway
━━ Minor railway
━━ Regional border
━━ International border

N385
Musselkanaal
N366

15 TER APEL

Street-by-Street: Groningen ❶

The town of Groningen has for centuries been the
cultural and historical capital of the province. Its
glory was at its height in the 15th century, when the
town was freed from the jurisdiction of the Bishop
of Utrecht and was able to extend its influence into
the present-day province of Friesland. In 1614, the
Groninger Academie was founded, which was the
precursor of the Rijksuniversiteit. Thus, in addition
to being a centre of trade and government, the
town also became an academic centre.

★ Prinsenhof
*In the gardens of the
Prinsenhof, where in
1568 the first Bishop of
Groningen, and later the
stadholder, resided,
stands a magnificent
sundial from 1730. The
garden is laid out as it
was in the 18th century.*

★ Martinitoren
*The 97-m (318-ft) Martinitoren
(St Martin tower) dating from 1496 is
called The Old Grey by the locals because
of the colour of the Bentheim sandstone.*

The Martinikerk
(St Martin's Church) dates
back to the 13th century,
though only parts of that
basilica are preserved. The
Romanesque church which
followed was refurbished
in Gothic style in the 1400s.

Stadhuis
*The Stadhuis on the Grote
Markt is a monumental
Neo-Classical building,
completed in 1810.*

Goudkantoor
*This 1635 Renaissance
building on the Waagplein
was known as the "Goud-
kantoor" (gold depository)
in the 19th century, when it
functioned as a treasury. It
now houses an inn.*

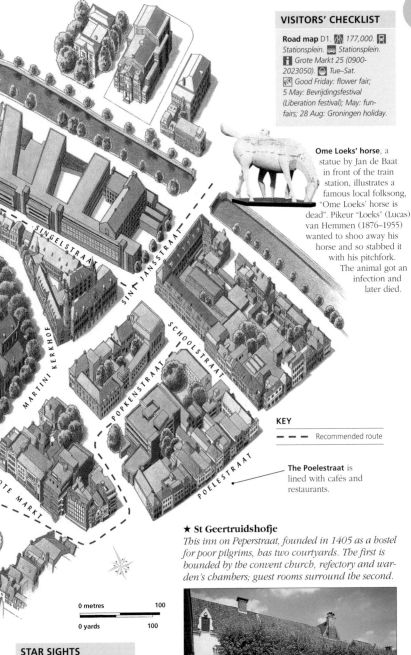

VISITORS' CHECKLIST

Road map D1. *177,000.*
Stationsplein. Stationsplein.
*Grote Markt 25 (0900-
2023050). Tue–Sat.*
*Good Friday: flower fair;
5 May: Bevrijdingsfestival
(Liberation festival); May: fun-
fairs; 28 Aug: Groningen holiday.*

Ome Loeks' horse, a
statue by Jan de Baat
in front of the train
station, illustrates a
famous local folksong,
"Ome Loeks' horse is
dead". Pikeur "Loeks" (Lucas)
van Hemmen (1876–1955)
wanted to shoo away his
horse and so stabbed it
with his pitchfork.
The animal got an
infection and
later died.

KEY

- - - Recommended route

The Poelestraat is
lined with cafés and
restaurants.

★ St Geertruidshofje
*This inn on Peperstraat, founded in 1405 as a hostel
for poor pilgrims, has two courtyards. The first is
bounded by the convent church, refectory and warden's chambers; guest rooms surround the second.*

0 metres   100
0 yards   100

STAR SIGHTS

★ Martinitoren

★ Prinsenhof

★ St Geertruidshofje

Exploring Groningen

The city of Groningen has a number of interesting buildings and museums, among them the Noordelijk Scheepvaartmuseum (northern maritime museum) which illustrates the history of navigation. The Groninger Museum *(see pp284–5)* possesses an art collection of international stature. A visit to one of the gardens of Groningen will provide peace in the middle of the bustling university city.

The distinctive Gasunie building, known locally as the "monkey cliff"

🏰 Martinikerk and Martinitoren

Martinikerkhof 3. *Tel* 050-3111277.
☐ *Easter–11 Nov: noon–5pm Sat; Jun–Aug & two Sats in Sep: noon–5pm Tue–Sat.* 🗓 *1:30pm.*
Martinitoren *Grote Markt. Tel 050-3135713.* ☐ *1 Apr–31 Oct: 11am–5pm Mon–Sat; 1 Nov–31 Mar: noon–4pm Mon–Sat; Jul & Aug: 11am–4pm Sun.* 🌙 *1 Jan, 25 Dec.* 📷

The Grote Markt is the old city centre. Many of the buildings standing on the square were badly damaged by air raids near the end of World War II. When it was rebuilt, the market was enlarged on the northern and eastern sides, and new buildings of a modern character were added.

The famous Martinitoren (St Martin tower) was also damaged but still standing, and it was possible to rebuild it. The carillon of d'Olle Grieze ("The Old Grey"), whose bells were cast by the Hemony brothers, has since been enlarged and now has four octaves and 49 bells. The

Martinikerk (St Martin's Church), dating from the 13th century, still retains traces of the original building: both the northern and southern façades of the transept and the ornamental brickwork of the windows and window niches of the northern side are recognizably 13th century. During the 15th century, when the city was at the height of its development, the church was extended in Gothic style. The choir, which features sumptuous murals from 1530 illustrating the life of Christ, had been completed before 1425. The central part of the church became a hall-type church. East of the Grote Markt is the Poelestraat, which on fine days comes to life with outdoor cafés and restaurants.

🚌 Gebouw van de Gasunie

Concourslaan 17. *Tel* 050-5219111.
🔒 *to the public.*

The main office of the Dutch Gasunie (gas board) was designed by the Alberts and Van Huur architects on the principles of "organic" architecture, the inspiration of which lies with natural forms. The "organic" nature of the building can be seen at every turn, even in the specially designed furniture. The locals' nickname for the building is the "apenrots" (monkey cliff).

🌷 St Geertruidshofje

Peperstraat 22. *Tel* 050-3124082.
Groningen has a number of pretty *hofjes*, or gardens, often belonging to inns. They were once charitable institutions whose aim was to help the poor. The finest of these is the garden of the 13th-century Heilige Geest-gasthuis, or Pelstergasthuis (in the Pelsterstraat), and St Geertruidshofje *(see p281),* whose Pepergasthuis inn was established in 1405. It later became a senior citizens' home. The pump in the courtyard dates from 1829.

The Poelestraat: a favourite haunt for the students of Groningen

🏛 Noordelijk Scheepvaart en Tabaksmuseum

Brugstraat 24–26. **Tel** 050-3122202.
🕐 10am–5pm Tue–Sat, 1–5pm Sun
& hols. ⬤ public holidays. 📷
This maritime museum, arranged over two restored medieval houses, deals with the history of navigation in the northern provinces from 1650 to the present. Exhibits are arranged in chronological order, from the Utrecht ships, Hanseatic cogs, West Indies merchantmen, peat barges and Baltic merchant ships to Groningen coasters from the 20th century. A number of historical workshops, such as a carpenter's shop and a smithy, are held in the attic of the museum. In the same building, the Tobacco Museum covers the use of the weed in western Europe from 1500 up to today.

🍀 Prinsenhof and Prinsenhoftuin

Martinikerkhof 23.
Tel 050-3183688.
🕐 Apr–15 Oct.
Theeschenkerij
(tea room) ⬤ Mon & Tue.
The Prinsenhof originally housed the monastic order of the Broeders des Gemenen Levens. It later became the seat of the first Bishop of Groningen, Johann Knijff, who had the entire complex converted into a magnificent bishop's palace. Until late into the 18th century, the building served as the residence of the stadholder. The Prinsenhoftuin (Prinsenhof Gardens) is truly an oasis in the midst of the busy city.

Decorative element from the Provinciehuis of Groningen

The magnificent Prinsenhof, formerly the stadholder's residence

Its highlights include a herb garden and a rose garden. There is also a flowerbed that is arranged into two coats of arms, one with the letter W (for William Frederick, the stadholder of Friesland), the other with a letter A (for Albertine Agnes, William's wife). At the side of the entrance is a fine sundial *(see p280)* which dates back to 1730. The course of the old city walls of Groningen is still clearly discernible in the Prinsenhoftuin.

🏛 Hortus Haren

Kerklaan 34, Haren. **Tel** 050-5370053.
🕐 9:30am–5pm daily. ⬤ 1 Jan, 25 Dec. 📷 ♿ 🖥 🏛
Immediately south of the city is the fashionable town of Haren, where an extensive park, Hortus Haren, is situated. The park was set up in 1642 by Henricus Munting. Its 20 ha (50 acres) include a large hothouse complex comprising several different greenhouses dedicated to a wide array of climatic zones. There is a tropical rainforest with a great variety of exotic flowers. A sub-tropical hothouse numbers orange trees among its plants. The various climatic areas continue with a desert section. Here, gigantic cacti are showcased. Another greenhouse featuring a monsoon climate contains unusual carnivorous plants. In the tropical culture greenhouse, you can admire a traditional Indonesian *sawah* (ricefield).

The Chinese garden ("Het verborgen rijk van Ming", or "The hidden Ming Empire") is well worth a visit. It is a faithful reconstruction of a real garden owned by a 16th-century high Chinese official of the Ming Dynasty (1368–1644). It features original Chinese pagodas, which have been painstakingly restored by Chinese craftsmen into fine pavilions and then beautifully decorated with carvings of lions and dragons. Het verborgen rijk van Ming also has a waterfall and a tea house where visitors can enjoy Chinese refreshments.

Another interesting theme garden is the Ogham Gardens, a Celtic garden whose main attractions is the Horoscope of Trees, consisting of an earth-and-stone circular wall, which is a replica of the enclosures the ancient Celts built to live within. Inside the circle is a labyrinth representing life; at its centre is a small garden and the Well of Wisdom.

In summer, a variety of exhibitions and events are held on the grounds, attracting locals and tourists alike.

The fascinating Hortus Haren, with its innumerable attractions

Groninger Museum

Mirror by Jeff Koons

Between the central station and the inner city lies the Groninger Museum, standing on an island in the 19th-century Verbindingskanaal. Designed by internationally renowned Italian architect Alessandro Mendini and opened in 1994, the museum showcases archaeology and history, applied arts (including a remarkable collection of Chinese and Japanese porcelain), early art and cutting-edge modern art.

★ **Spiral Staircase**
The spiral staircase which visitors have to descend to see the exhibits is the museum's main meeting point and a work of art in itself.

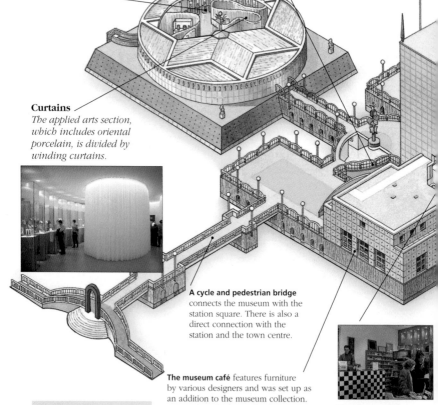

Temporary exhibitions

Curtains
The applied arts section, which includes oriental porcelain, is divided by winding curtains.

A cycle and pedestrian bridge connects the museum with the station square. There is also a direct connection with the station and the town centre.

The museum café features furniture by various designers and was set up as an addition to the museum collection.

The museum shop sells reproductions of the exhibits and books about the artists who are represented in the museum.

STAR SIGHTS

★ De Ploeg

★ Chinese and Japanese Porcelain

★ Spiral Staircase

Rembrandt
This ink drawing of Saskia in Bed *by Rembrandt can sometimes be seen in the Mendini Pavilion.*

★ De Ploeg
The Groningen art collective De Ploeg has its own pavilion. In addition to works by the group, the section also displays works by other expressionists from northern Europe. The picture Rotating Door of the Post Office *is by De Ploeg painter HN Werkman.*

The Mendini Pavilion is easily distinguished by its apparent haphazardness and chaos, and is a good example of deconstructivism.

MUSEUM GUIDE
Groninger Museum was designed by Alessandro Mendini (1931). He based the design around the collections of the museum, which consisted of archaeology, applied arts and early and modern pictorial arts. The focus of the building is the 30-m (98-ft) tower in the middle.

Bridge in the Coop Himmelb(l)au Pavilion

A large concrete staircase in the spectacular Mendini Pavilion leads to the upper pavilion, where some of the collection of art is on display.

This wing of the museum was designed by Wolfgang Prix and Helmut Swiczinsky.

Grootegast ❷

Road map D1. ⚇ *11,500.* 🚌 *33, 38, 39, 98, 101, 133.* ℹ️ *Tolberterstraat 39, Leek (0594-512100).* 🛒 *Fri.*

The little town of Lutjegast, close to Grootegast, is the birthplace of the 17th-century explorer Abel Tasman *(see box)*. The **Abel Tasman-kabinet** houses an interesting exhibition about his life. The fascinating collection includes old sea charts and books.

🏛 **Abel Tasmankabinet**
Kompasstraat 1. **Tel** *0594-613576.*
◯ *1:30–4:30pm Tue–Sat.*

Leek ❸

Road map D2. ⚇ *18,000.* 🚌 *81, 85, 88, 98, 306, 316.* ℹ️ *Tolberterstraat 39 (0594-512100).* 🛒 *Thu.*

In the small town of Leek stands the castle of Nienoord, built in approximately 1524 by Wigbold van Ewsum. During the 19th century, things at the castle

Landgoed Nienoord

seemed to be taking a turn for the worse. In 1846, the then owner, Ferdinand Folef Kniphausen, nicknamed "the mad squire", burned all the family portraits in a drunken fit. Later, the orangery and part of the upper floor were destroyed by fire. In 1950, the municipality bought the castle. Eight years later, the **Nationaal Rijtuigmuseum**, featuring horse-drawn vehicles, was established here. It contains a unique collection of royal coaches, gigs, mail coaches and hackney carriages.

🏛 **Nationaal Rijtuigmuseum**
Nienoord 1. **Tel** *0594-512260.*
◯ *Apr–Oct: 10am–5pm Tue–Fri, 1–5pm Sat, Sun & public hols.*
🔴 *Mon.* 📷 ♿

ABEL TASMAN (1603–59)

Abel Janszoon Tasman was born in Lutjegast in 1603 but lived in Amsterdam from an early age. In 1633, as a navigating officer for the Dutch East India Company *(see pp48–9)*, he travelled to Asia. In 1642, he sailed on the yacht *De Heemskerck* and then with the cargo ship *Zeehaen* in search of the legendary southern continent. Tasman charted some of the coast and later reached New Zealand's South Island. On 13 June 1643, he arrived in Batavia (now Jakarta), which he called home until his death 16 years later. From 1644 to 1648, he sat on the Batavian council of justice; during this time he also joined trading missions to Sumatra (1646) and Siam (1647). Tasman died on 10 October 1659, having bequeathed his money to the poor of Lutjegast.

The harbour of the delightful fishing village of Zoutkamp

Zoutkamp ❹

Road map D1. ⚇ *1,200.* 🚌 *63, 65, 69, 136, 163, 165.* ℹ️ *Reitdiepskade 11 (0595-401957).*

The small fishing village of Zoutkamp changed its character dramatically after the damming of the Lauwerszee in 1969. By the waterside (Reitdiepskade) there are still a number of fisherman's cottages retaining the erstwhile charm of the village.

Lauwersoog ❺

Road map D1. ⚇ *350.* 🚌 *50, 63, 163.* ℹ️ *Het Bozewift, Strandweg 1 (0519-349133).*

At Lauwersoog, from where the ferry leaves for Schiermonnikoog *(see p275)*, is the Lauwersmeer, a 2,000-ha (4,940-acre) nature reserve. When the Lauwerszee was drained, the land was designated for four purposes: agriculture, recreation, a nature reserve and an army training area.

Environs

Lauwersoog is a good base from which to explore the tuff churches that, in the middle ages, were built in villages such as Doezum, Bedum and Zuidwolde. They can be recognized by their grey or green porous stone.

Pieterburen ❻

Road map D1. 🏠 500. 🚌 65, 67, 68. ℹ️ *Waddencentrum, Hoofdstraat 83 (0595-528522).*

One of the best-known places in Groningen is Pieterburen, home to the **Zeehonden-crèche**. This seal nursery was founded by Lenie 't Hart and others as a reception centre for sick and disabled seals from the nearby Waddenzee, where some 1,750 seals live. Half of these owe their lives to care they received here.

The **Waddencentrum**, also located here, is an exhibition centre dedicated to the mud flats of the Waddenzee. It also provides useful information for people wishing to walk there.

🦭 Zeehondencrèche Pieterburen
Hoofdstraat 94a. **Tel** *0595-526526.* ⬜ *9am–6pm daily.*

🦆 Het Waddencentrum
Hoofdstraat 83. **Tel** *0595-528522.* ⬜ *9am–6pm daily.* 📷

Environs
In Leens, 10 km (6 miles) to the southwest of Pieterburen is the stunning 14th-century *borg* (moated manor house) Verhildersum, which contains 19th-century furnishings. The castle is surrounded by a wide moat. Its gardens

Recovering seal in one of the ponds at Pieterburen

include an arbour and sculptures. The castle's coach house is regularly used as a venue for exhibitions, while the Schathuis (treasury) is now a lively café and restaurant.

🏰 Borg Verhildersum
Wierde 40, Leens. **Tel** *0595-571430.* ⬜ *Apr–Oct: 10:30am–5pm Tue–Sun.* 📷

Uithuizen ❼

Road map E1. 🏠 5,300. 🚌 41, 61, 62, 641, 662. ℹ️ *Mennonietenkerk-straat 13 (0595-434051).* 🛍️ *Sat.*

The exceptionally pretty castle of Menkemaborg in Uithuizen dates back to the

14th century. It acquired its present-day form around 1700. The bedroom features a ceremonial bedstead dating from the early 18th century, when King William III stayed here. The kitchen in the cellar has all the old fittings. The gardens were laid out during restoration work in the 18th century. The Schathuis (treasury), formerly used to store the food brought by the townspeople to the castle, currently houses a café and restaurant.

🏰 Menkemaborg
Menkemaweg 2. 🚌 61. **Tel** *0595-431970.* ⬜ *Mar–Apr & Oct–early Jun: 10am–noon, 1–4pm Tue–Sun; May–Sep: 10am–5pm daily.* ⬛ *Jan–Feb.* 📷

Wedding in traditional dress in the gardens of the 14th-century Menkemaborg in Uithuizen

Appingedam ⑧

Road map E1. 🏘 *12,400*. 🚌 *40, 45, 78, 140, 178*. ℹ *Dijkstraat 26 (0596-620300)*. 🗓 *Sat.*

This town, a member of the Hanseatic League in the Middle Ages, was granted its charter in 1327. Standing at a junction of waterways as it once did and with a seaport, it quickly grew into a major international trading city. The medieval layout of the city has remained largely unchanged. The **hanging kitchens**, visible from the Vlinterbrug bridge, were built this way to create more space in the houses. Directly over the water are doors from which people drew water for their household needs.

In the 18th century, the town again prospered, as the **Ebenhaëzerhuis** well illustrates. Appingedam, with over 65 listed buildings, has a preservation order as a town of historical interest.

Slochteren ⑨

Road map E1. 🏘 *2,600*. 🚌 *78, 178*. ℹ *Noorderweg 1 (0598-422970)*. 🗓 *Thu.*

When a natural gas field was discovered here in 1959, Slochteren gained overnight national renown. The "Slochteren Dome" appeared to be the largest in the world when it was first discovered, and the revenue it brought in made Holland rich.

The past of this historic town is closely associated with the lords of the Fraeylemaborg. The Reformed Church in Slochteren consists of the remnants of a 13th-century

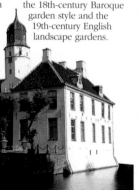

The historical castle of Fraeylemaborg at Slochteren

Steam pumping station (1878) at the Winschoten polder, now a museum

Romanesque-Gothic cross-naved church. The environs are excellent for walking or cycling, particularly around places like nearby Schildmeer.

Fraeylemaborg ⑩

Road map E1. ℹ *Noorderweg 1, Slochteren (0598-422907)*.

Fraeylemaborg is one of the most imposing castles of Groningen. It dates back to the Middle Ages. Three embrasures in the kitchen and the hall above it bear silent witness to the defensive functions the castle once had. In the 17th century, two side wings were added, and in the 18th century it was given its present form with the addition of the monumental main wing. The castle is surrounded by a double moat.

The extensive wooded park just beyond the castle is an interesting combination of the 18th-century Baroque garden style and the 19th-century English landscape gardens.

🏰 **Fraeylemaborg**
Hoofdweg 30–32, Slochteren.
Tel 0598-421568. ⬚ 1 Mar–31 Dec: 10am–5pm Tue–Fri, 1–5pm Sat, Sun & public hols. 🈺

Winschoten ⑪

Road map E2. 🏘 *18,500*. 🚌 *10, 12, 13, 14, 17, 29*. ℹ *Israëlplein 6 (0597-412255)*. 🗓 *Sat.*

This little town in Oost-Groningen is known primarily for its three mills: Berg, a corn and hulling mill from 1854; Dijkstra, which is 25 m (82 ft) in height and dates from 1862; and Edens, a corn and hulling mill from 1761. The interesting **Museum Stoomgemaal** contains a steam-powered pump from 1878 which was used to drain the flooded polderland.

🏛 **Museum Stoomgemaal**
Oostereinde 4. **Tel** 0597-425070.
⬚ Jun–Sep: 1–5pm Mon–Fri; Jul & Aug also 11am–5pm Sun. 🈺

Environs
In Heiligerlee stands a monument to the Battle of Heiligerlee in 1568. This battle is famous for being over in just two hours and for the death of Count Adolf of Nassau. The **Museum "Slag bij Heiligerlee"** has an exhibition dedicated to the bloody battle.

🏛 **Museum "Slag bij Heiligerlee"**
Provincialeweg 55. **Tel** 0597-418199. ⬚ Apr: 1–5pm Tue–Sun; May–mid-Sep:10am–5pm Tue–Sat, 1–5pm Sun; mid-Sep–Oct: 1–5pm Tue–Fri & Sun. ⬤ public hols. 🈺

Veendam 🅬

Road map E2. 🏠 28,500. 🚍 71, 73. 🛈 Museumplein 5b (0598-626255). 🚢 Mon am, Thu pm.

Parkstad Veendam (Veendam Garden City) is so called for the lush greenery in the town, which for centuries was the industrial heart of the peat colonies. However, at the end of the 19th century, peat-cutting fell into decline. Although shipping grew in importance – Veendam even had its own maritime school – the town retained its character as a peat-cutting town.

The **Veenkoloniaal Museum** (peat colony museum) offers a permanent exhibition illustrating the history of peat-cutting, navigation, agriculture and industry in the Groningen peatlands.

The most renowned inhabitant of Veendam was Anthony Winkler Prins (1817–1908), who wrote the famous encyclopaedia which is still associated with his name.

🏛 **Veenkoloniaal Museum**
Museumplein 5.
Tel 0598-364224. ◻ 11am–5pm Tue–Thu, 1–5pm Fri–Sun. ◉ public hols. 📷

Bourtange 🅭

Road map E2. 🏠 600. 🚍 70, 72. 🛈 Willem Lodewijkstraat 33 (0599-354600).
www.bourtange.nl

Right at the German border is the magnificent fortified town of Bourtange, whose history dates back to 1580, when William of Orange ordered that a fortress with five bastions be built in the swampland at the German border. The defence works were continuously upgraded, until the fort gradually lost its defensive functions. It has now been painstakingly restored to its 18th-century appearance. **Museum "De Baracquen"** exhibits artifacts excavated in the fort.

The charming town itself lies within a star-shaped labyrinth of moats.

Aerial view of the impressive fortress of Bourtange

🏛 **Museum "De Baracquen"**
Willem Lodewijkstraat 33. **Tel** 0599-354600. ◻ Apr–Oct: 10am–5pm Mon–Fri, 12:30–5pm Sat & Sun; Nov–Mar: 1:30–5pm Sat & Sun. ◉ 25 & 26 Dec. 📷

Oude en Nieuwe Pekela 🅮

Road map E2. 🏠 13,500. 🚍 75. 🛈 Restaurant Het Turfschip/Flessings – terrein 3, Oude Pekela (0597-618833). 🚢 Wed pm, Thu pm.

The "old" and "new" villages of Pekela are typical ribbon developments with a marked rural, peatland character. In the 18th century, potato flour and straw-board manufacture grew in importance in the region. There are pleasant footpaths along the main canal.

Ter Apel 🅯

Road map E2. 🏠 7,800. 🚍 26, 70, 73. 🛈 Hoofdstraat 49a (0599-581277). 🚢 Thu.

In Ter Apel, situated in the Westerwolde region between Drenthe and Germany, is a 1465 **monastery** of the same name. In 1933, the monastery was thoroughly restored and now functions as a museum devoted to ecclesiastic art and religious history. The fragrant herb garden located in the cloisters contains a collection of nutrient-rich herbs such as birthwort and common rue.

🏛 **Museum-klooster Ter Apel**
Boslaan 3. **Tel** 0599-581370. ◻ 10am–5pm Tue–Sat, 1–5pm Sun & public hols. ◉ 1 Jan, Mon (Nov–Mar). 📷 ♿ ◻ ◻

The beautifully restored cloisters at the Ter Apel monastery

FRIESLAND

F riesland, or Fryslân as it is officially called, is a remarkable province perhaps best known outside the Netherlands for its distinctive Frisian cows. Parts of it are below sea level, and its size has increased since historic times as a result of land reclamation schemes on the former Zuiderzee.

Much of the province is fenland, a feature which no doubt helped the freedom-loving Frisians fight off invaders. The 1345 battle of Warns, when the Frisians beat the Dutch army, is still commemorated every year. In the 7th century, the Frisians under their king Radboud inhabited an independent territory that stretched all the way to Flanders and Cologne *(see pp44–5)*, and they have preserved their distinctive language to this day. Other features peculiar to this province are unique sports and recreations like sailing and racing in *skûtjes* (traditional Frisian boats), hunting for plovers' eggs, *fierljeppen* (pole-vaulting), *keatsen* (a ball game), and the famous *Elfstedentocht*, a winter ice-skating marathon around 11 Frisian towns.

The provincial capital of Leeuwarden has some interesting and unique museums, while elsewhere in the province visitors can enjoy collections consisting of items as diverse as historic costumes and hats, ceramics, letters, ice skates and sledges, vernacular paintings, bells, model boats and human mummies. Outside the towns, the landscape is interesting too, from the mud flats on the Waddenzee to the forests and heathland of the Drents-Friese Woud National Park, away to the east. Tourism is becoming increasingly important in Friesland nowadays and its inhabitants less insular. Visitors are greeted with open arms and *Jo binne tige welcom* – "You are heartily welcome."

Bartlehiem, the junction of the *Elfsteden* (11 towns) – a favourite summer destination for day-trippers

◁ The famous Waterpoort van Sneek (Sneek Gateway), dating from 1613

Exploring Friesland

Frisian flag

Friesland is famous for its vast meadows and its distinctive farmhouses of the *kop-hals-romp* and *stelp* types. It also boasts a varied landscape. In the south-west are the popular *Friese meren* (Frisian lakes), while the north is typified by undulating dykes, *terp* villages and church steeples with pitched roofs. Gaasterland in the south has rolling woodlands and cliffs, whereas the *Friese wouden* (Frisian woods) in the province's southeastern corner, with their forests, heathland and drifting sands, are more reminiscent of Drenthe.

The sea dyke at Wierum

SIGHTS AT A GLANCE

Appelscha ⑭
Beetsterzwaag ⑬
Bolsward ⑤
Dokkum ②
Franeker ③
Gaasterland ⑧
Harlingen ④
Hindeloopen ⑦
Leeuwarden ①
Oude Venen ⑫
Sloten ⑨
Sneek ⑩
Thialfstadion ⑪
Workum ⑥

The Noorderhaven in Harlingen

GETTING AROUND

Friesland is convenient and easy to get to. It is crossed by the A7 (east-west) and the A32 (north-south) motorways. Rail and bus links are unproblematic. Most of the larger villages and towns have a railway station; those which don't can be reached by bus. From Harlingen, Holwerd or Lauwersoog, the islands are only a short boat ride away. The province also has a good network of minor roads, walking routes and cycle tracks.

Gabled houses along Het Diep in Sloten

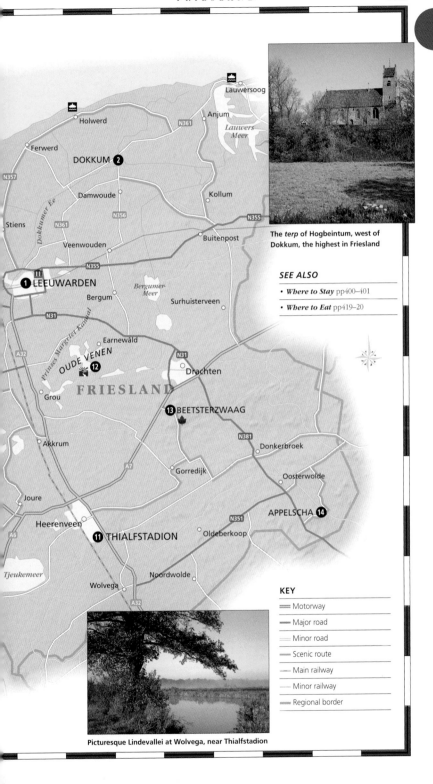

The *terp* of Hogbeintum, west of
Dokkum, the highest in Friesland

SEE ALSO

- *Where to Stay* pp400–401
- *Where to Eat* pp419–20

Lauwersoog

Holwerd

Anjum

*Lauwers
Meer*

Ferwerd

N361

DOKKUM 2

N357

Damwoude

Kollum

Stiens

N361

N356

Veenwouden

Buitenpost

N355

N355

1 LEEUWARDEN

Bergum

*Bergumer
Meer*

Surhuisterveen

N31

A32

Prinses Margriet Kanaal

Earnewâld

OUDE VENEN 12

N31

Drachten

FRIESLAND

Grou

13 BEETSTERZWAAG

Akkrum

N381

Donkerbroek

A7

Gorredijk

Oosterwolde

Joure

APPELSCHA 14

Heerenveen

N351

11 THIALFSTADION

Oldeberkoop

A6

Tjeukemeer

Noordwolde

Wolvega

A32

KEY

═══ Motorway

─── Major road

─── Minor road

─── Scenic route

─── Main railway

─── Minor railway

═══ Regional border

Picturesque Lindevallei at Wolvega, near Thialfstadion

The Elfstedentocht

1909: the first official *tocht*

The Elfstedentocht, or 11-town race, is a 200-km (124-mile) ice-skating marathon which passes through Leeuwarden, Skeen, IJlst, Sloten, Stavoren, Hindeloopen, Workum, Bolsward, Harlingen, Franeker, Dokkum and back to Leeuwarden. Participants are awarded the famous Elfstedenkruisje only when they have collected all the stamps on their starter's card and provided they get back to Leeuwarden before midnight. The winner of the race is guaranteed eternal fame.

The **"Elfstedenkruisje"** (Elfsteden cross) is in the shape of a Maltese cross. In the middle is an enamel coat of arms of Friesland and the inscription "De Friesche Elf Steden" – "The 11 Frisian towns".

THE TOCHT DER TOCHTEN

The Tocht der Tochten (literally, "Race of Races"), as the Elfstedentocht is known, is a combination of race and touring marathon and has acquired almost mythical status in the Netherlands. The race is a real media event, keeping millions glued to their television screens. Although the marathon has been held only 15 times in the last century, the entire country falls under the spell of the event as soon as the mercury falls even slightly below zero. If there is a lasting frost, the area supervisors measure daily the thickness of the ice, as it has to be at least 15 cm (6 in) thick for the race to be held. When the magic words *It sil heve* (It shall happen) are uttered by the supervisors, Friesland is transformed, overflowing with excited

Franeker in a festive mood

crowds. Trains are packed, the roads are jammed with cars and entire villages are mobilized to provide hot tea and oranges for the skaters. Wandering musicians whip the crowd into a frenzy of enthusiasm. The Dutch language has been enriched with the Frisian word *klûnen*, which means to walk overland on skates past places where the ice is impassable.

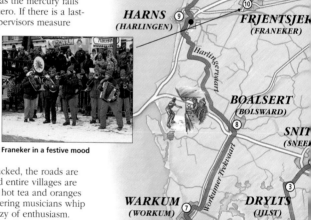

STARUM ⑤
(STAVOREN)

HARNS ⑨
(HARLINGEN)

FRJENTSJE
(FRANEKER) ⑩

BOALSERT ⑧
(BOLSWARD)

SNIT
(SNEE

③

WARKUM ⑦
(WORKUM)

DRYLTS
(IJLST)

HYLPEN ⑥
(HINDELOOPEN)

④

SLEAT
(SLOTEN)

Harlingervaart

Workumer Trekvaart

Dropping out is a common occurrence during the race. Despite being affected by snow blindness and symptoms of frostbite, many participants in the race attempt to complete the course. Some break down in tears when they realize that they will be unable to collect the much-coveted Elfstedenkruisje (Elfsteden cross).

0 kilometres   10

0 miles   10

The hamlet of Bartlehiem *is famous for its foot-bridge over the Finkumervaart. Bartlehiem is the best-known skating area in all of Holland and is a psychological milestone for the skaters. Those who still must get to Dokkum may pass skaters travelling in the opposite direction, having already won their stamp from the northernmost point on the route. Many skaters have to take the Bartlehiem-Dokkum section in the dark. The Northern Lights seen at this time of year also attract thousands of spectators.*

DOKKUM ⑪

Two-time winner
Evert van Benthem

BARTLEHIEM

FINISH

START ①
LJOUWERT
(LEEUWARDEN)

A32

All winners of the Elfstedentocht *are national heroes, but Evert van Benthem even more so. A farmer from Sint-Jansklooster, he managed to cross the finishing line at the Bonkevaart in Leeuwarden in first place twice in a row (1985 and 1986). Van Benthem's double victory gave him a legendary status throughout the Netherlands. The prize itself is a laurel wreath, both for men and for women. The names of the winners are engraved on the Elfstedenrijder monument in Leeuwarden.*

Long before sunrise, tens of thousands of skaters start off from the FEC (Frisian Exhibition Centre) in Leeuwarden.

THE EERSTE FRIESE SCHAATSMUSEUM

The Eerste Friese Schaatsmuseum (first Frisian skating museum) in Hindeloopen *(see p298)* has among its exhibits such items as antique skates, original workshops, sleds and historical documents covering the 90 or so years that the Elfstedentocht has been held. Displays on innumerable winners, including Reinier Paping, Jeen van den Berg and Henk Angenet, are also featured here. Among the highlights of the museum's collection are the skating packs of various heroes of the event, the skates of two-time winner Evert van Benthem and the starter's card of WA van Buren. One of the most moving exhibits in the collection is the right big toe of Tinus Udding, which he lost to frostbite during the harsh race in the cold winter of 1963.

Willem-Alexander, alias WA van Buren, in the arms of his mother, Queen Beatrix, after the 1985 race

KEY

 Route of the Elfstedentocht

═ Road

Leeuwarden ❶

Road map D1. 🏚 89,000. 🚉 🚗
ℹ *Achmeatoren, Sophialaan 4
(0900-2024060).* 🛒 *Fri & Sat.*

Frisian capital and home to
Mata Hari, Peter Jelles Troelstra
and Jan Jacob Slauerhoff,
Leeuwarden was also the residence of the Frisian Nassaus
(1584–1747). The town park
and gardens of the Prinsentuin
and Stadhouderlijk Hof date
back to this period.
  Characteristic of Leeuwarden
is the statue of **Us Mem** (our
mother), honouring the
famous Frisian cattle. The
Fries Museum, situated in an
18th-century patrician house,
has a large collection of items
excavated from *terps*, as well
as collections of clothes,
art and applied arts.
The same building
also houses the
**Verzetsmuseum
Friesland**, a collection
and educational
facility dedicated to
the resistance move-
ment in the province,
where more than 600
Jewish people were
killed, and nearly 300
members of the resistance
also lost their lives. There is a
chronological exhibition on the
Second World War and its
aftermath, explorations of
contemporary wars and
racism, and documents and
artifacts from the time.
  On Oldehoofsterkerkhof,
the leaning tower of the
Oldehove dominates the skyline. When building began in
1529, the church tower was
going to be the tallest in the
Netherlands. Unfortunately,
the foundations began to
sink, and so the work
stopped just three years later.
The tower has remained
incomplete ever since. The
top of the tower offers an
excellent view over
Leeuwarden and its environs,
reaching as far as the coast.
  The museum **Het Princessehof**, housed in a palace
which was formerly the residence of Maria Louise van
Hessen-Kassel (also known as
Marijke Meu), contains a
unique collection of ceramics

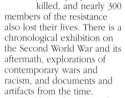

**Frisian coat of
arms**

of international importance.
The holdings include Asian,
European and contemporary
ceramics and tiles.
  The old municipal orphanage is now home to the
Natuurmuseum Fryslân
(natural history museum),
whose exhibition of
"Friesland underwater" is well
worth a visit.

🏛 **Fries Museum**
Turfmarkt 11. **Tel** 058-2555501.
⏰ *11am–5pm Tue–Sun.* 🎟 ♿ 🐾

🏛 **Verzetsmuseum
Friesland**
Turfmarkt 1. **Tel** 058-2120111.
⏰ *Tue–Sun.* ⚫ *1 Jan, 25 Dec.*

🏛 **Het Princessehof**
Grote Kerkstraat 11. **Tel** 058-2948958.
⏰ *11am–5pm Tue–Sun.* ⚫ *1 Jan,
30 Apr, 25 Dec.* 🎟 ⬜ ⬜

🏛 **Natuurmuseum Fryslân**
Schoenmakersperk 2. **Tel** 058-
2332244. ⏰ *11am–5pm Tue–Sun.*
🎟 ♿

**The leaning tower of the Oldehove
(1529), still incomplete**

Atmospheric Dokkum, a major port in the 8th century

Dokkum ❷

Road map D1. 🏚 13,000. 🚉
ℹ *Op de Fetze 13 (0519-293800).*
🛒 *Wed.*

The trading and garrison
town of Dokkum was the
headquarters of the Frisian
Admiralty between 1596 and
1645, though it owes its fame
above all to the killing here of
St Boniface by pagan Frisians
in AD 754 *(see pp44–5).* The
local history museum, the
Admiraliteitshuis, has an
exhibition on the life of the
saint. Other exhibits include
artifacts excavated from *terps*,
costumes, silverware, handicrafts and folk art. In addition
to the **Bonifatiuskerk**,
Dokkum has a park for
religious processions with the
stations of the cross and a
chapel. Water drawn from the
well of **Bonifatiusbron** is
believed to have therapeutic
qualities. Near the well is a
statue of the saint after whom
it is named. Saint Boniface
was actually an Englishman,
born in 675, who came to the
region on a mission to convert
the Frisians. Heathens attacked
Boniface and his companions.
Despite holding a bible in
front of his face, Boniface
was killed by a sword.
  In the centre, **Natuurmuseum
Dokkum** explores all aspects of
the natural world in Friesland,
both living and inanimate.
There are cabinets of rocks,
stones, shells and insects, and
there is a "sound cabinet" that
plays the songs of various
birds from the area.

On the former **town walls**, now a park, are two 19th-century **stellingmolen**-type mills known as *De Hoop* and *Zeldenrust (see p25).*

🏛 **Admiraliteitshuis**
Diepswal 27. **Tel** 0519–293134.
⬜ Apr–Oct: 1–5pm Tue–Sat. 📷
www.museumdokkum.nl

🏛 **Natuurmuseum Dokkum**
Kleine Oosterstraat 12. **Tel** 0519-297318. ⬜ Oct–May: Mon–Fri; Jun–Oct: Mon–Sat. ⬛ public hols.

Franeker ❸

Road map C1. 🏘 13,000. 🚌 🚊
🛈 Voorstraat 35 (0517-392192).
🛥 Wed & Sat.

Franeker was a university town from 1585 to 1811. Today, it is the centre of skating in Friesland. In and around the Voorstraat are several monumental buildings, including the 15th-century Martenahuis. The Cammingahuis, which dates from the 14th century, now houses the **Kaatsmuseum** (skating museum). The **Museum Martena**, in a fine 18th-century building, has a collection about the former university. The Renaissance **Stadhuis** (town hall) has an ornate façade. Opposite is the **Planetarium Friesland** (1781), built by wool industrialist Eise Eisinga. For two centuries, the planets have rotated around its ceiling. Beside the Sjûkelân, a sacred place for Frisian skating, is the Bogt fen Guné (16th century), Holland's oldest student residence.

Eise Eisinga Planetarium

🏛 **Kaatsmuseum**
Voorstraat 2. **Tel** 0517-393910.
⬜ 15 May–Sep: 1–5pm Tue–Sat. 📷

🏛 **Museum Martena**
Voorstraat 35. **Tel** 0517-392192.
⬜ 10am–5pm Tue–Sat; Apr–Sep: also 1–5pm Sun. 📷

🏛 **Planetarium Friesland**
Eise Eisingastraat 3. **Tel** 0517-393070.
⬜ 10am–5pm Tue–Sat; May–mid Sep: also 1–5pm Sun & Mon. 📷 📷

Harlingen ❹

Road map C2. 🏘 14,500. 🚌 🚊
🛈 Grote Bredeplaats 17b (0517-430207). 🛥 Wed am, Sat.

The port town of Harlingen retains much of its old charm. The **Zoutsloot** and **Noorderhaven** have been painstakingly restored. A statue of **Hans Brinker** *(see p23)* stands at the ferry port. South of Harlingen is **Pingjum**. Menno Simons (1496–1561), the evangelical preacher after whom many of the Dutch Anabaptists named themselves, started his religious life here. Mennonites from all over the world now visit.

Bolsward ❺

Road map C2. 🏘 10,000. 🚌 🛈
Wipstraat 6 (0515-572701). 🛥 Thu.

Modest Bolsward first arose in the 11th century as a trading post, enjoying the height of its development in the 15th century. **Martinikerk**, a pseudo-basilica whose tower features a saddleback roof, was built during this period. The **Stadhuis** (town hall), with its local history museum, the **Oudheidkamer**, is the town's centrepiece.

Bolsward town hall

Local brews can be sampled at the **Us Heit Bierbrouwerij**, the smallest brewery in the country. A museum has displays of beer-making equipment while a guided tour shows how the beer is made. Attached to the brewery is a bar selling the house ales, with plenty available by the bottle to take away as souvenirs.

🏛 **Oudheidkamer**
Jongemastraat 2. **Tel** 0515-578787.
⬜ 2–4pm Mon, 9am–noon, 2–4pm Tue–Fri. 📷

🏛 **Us Heit Bierbrouwerij**
Snekerstraat 43. **Tel** 0515-577449.
⬜ Mon, Tue, Thu–Sat.

MATA HARI

Margaretha Geertruida Zelle (1876–1917), who became known to all the world as Mata Hari (Malaysian for "eye of the day"), grew up in Leeuwarden. Her life came to a tragic end in Vincennes outside Paris, where she was executed by firing squad after a French tribunal found her guilty of spying for the Germans. The Fries Museum tells you more about this legendary woman, who had gained international notoriety through films and books about her life. The house where she lived with her parents from 1883 to 1890 on Grote Kerkstraat 212 now houses the Frysk Letterkundig Museum (Frisian museum of letters).

Workum ●

Road map C2. ⚑ *4,000.* 🚌 🚉
ℹ *Merk 4 (0515-541045).*

The elongated Zuiderzee town of Workum flourished around 1300. Workum is known for the fine façades of its houses and its unfinished 16th-century church, the **Grote of Gertrudiskerk**. Beside the lock is the centuries-old wharf of **de Hoop**, where traditional boats are still built. The most popular attraction in Workum is **Jopie Huisman Museum**, which is the most-visited

The Football Boots of Abe Lenstra by Jopie Huisman

museum in Friesland. It features the autodidactic art of painter and scrap metal merchant Jopie Huisman (1922–2000). His drawings and paintings tell the stories of the daily grind and poverty, the drudgery and toil of the tradesman, the housewife and the ordinary person.

The picturesque 17th-century weigh house contains the **Museum Warkums Erfskip**. This museum delves into the history of Workum, and, principally, that of its shipping and pottery industries.

🏛 **Jopie Huisman Museum**
Noard 6. **Tel** *0515-543131.* ◯ *Apr–Oct: 10am–5pm Mon–Sat, 1–5pm Sun; Mar & Nov: 1–5pm daily.* 🖼 ♿

🏛 **Museum Warkums Erfskip**
Merk 4. **Tel** *0515-543155.*
◯ *Apr–Oct: 10am–5pm Tue–Sat, 1:30–5pm Sun & Mon; Nov–Mar: 1:30–5pm Thu–Sun.* 🖼

Hindeloopen ●

Road map C2. ⚑ *850.* 🚌 🚉
ℹ *Nieuwstad 26 (0514-851223).*

Hindeloopen plays a special role in Friesland. This picturesque old town of seafarers and fishermen has its

A sea rescue centre with its inviting bench, in Hindeloopen

own dialect, its own costume and its own style of painting. The town is full of little canals with wooden bridges and a variety of pretty captains' houses, with their characteristic façades. One of the most distinctive spots is the picturesque 17th-century lockkeeper's house by the port, with its wooden bell-tower.

In the **Museum Hidde Nijland Stichting** (museum of the Hidde Nijland foundation), the life of the wealthy citizens of Hindeloopen during the 18th century is showcased. Well-appointed period rooms show the colourful clothes and the now-famous painted furniture of the time. A substantial exhibition of paintings vividly illustrates the development of painting in Hindeloopen.

The **Eerste Friese Schaatsmuseum** (first Frisian skating museum) *(see p295)* offers a unique collection of old skates. It also has a fine exhibition dedicated to the Elfstedentocht and various traditional workshops (such as a smithy and a carpenter's), as well as a comprehensive collection of sledges and historical material such as old tiles and prints.

🏛 **Museum Hidde Nijland Stichting**
Dijkweg 1. **Tel** *0514-521420.*
◯ *Mar–Oct: 10am–5pm Mon–Sat, 1:30–5pm Sun & public hols.* 🖼

🏛 **Eerste Friese Schaatsmuseum**
Kleine Weide 1–3.
Tel *0514-521683.* ◯ *10am–6pm Mon–Sat, 1–5pm Sun.* 🖼

Gaasterland ●

Road map C2. 🚌 ℹ *De Brink 4, Oudemirdum (0514-571777).*

This area of fine, rolling woodlands in the southwestern corner of Friesland offers many opportunities for walking and cycling. The region's name comes from the word "gaast", which refers to the sandy heights formed during the last two Ice Ages.

At the edge of Gaasterland are a number of steep cliffs, such as the **Rode Klif** and the **Oudemirdumerklif**, formed when the Zuiderzee eroded the coastline. On the Rode Klif at Laaxum is an enormous boulder bearing the inscription *Leaver dea as slaef,* or, *Rather dead than a slave,* a memento of the 1345 Frisian victory over the Dutch.

A cyclist in Gaasterland

The **Rijsterbos** wood, with its abundant bracken, dates from the 17th century and once consisted mainly of oak. The little river of Luts, which is now known because of the Elfstedentocht, was used for the transport of oak logs and oak bark for tanneries. In the village of **Oudemirdum** is a hostel, shops and an old pump. **Informatiecentrum Mar en Klif** (Sea and Cliff Information Centre) has information about how the landscape was formed and about local flora and fauna. Special attention is paid to badgers, and in the wild garden, a bat tower has been built.

The Luts river in **Balk**, flanked by linden trees, inspired the poem *Mei* by Herman Gorter (1864–1927).

🏛 Informatiecentrum Mar en Klif
De Brink 4. **Tel** 0514-571777.
🕐 Apr–Oct: 10am–5pm Mon–Sat.

Sloten ❾

Road map C2. 🏠 650. 🚌 🛈
Museum Stedhûs Sleat, Heerenwal 48 (0900-540001).

The smallest town in Friesland, replete with pretty canals, embankments and water-gates, was designed by famous Frisian fortifications engineer Menno van Coehoorn. Built at a junction of roads and waterways, it was at the height of its development in the 17th and 18th centuries.

Typical stepped gables in Sloten

On either side of the town are old cannons. The old fortress mill at the Lemsterpoort is an octagonal *bovenkruier*-type mill from 1755. The **Museum Stedhûs Sleat** houses the **Laterna Magica**, a museum of magic lanterns, an antique museum and a collection of costumes, hats, fans and bells.

🏛 Museum Stedhûs Sleat
Heerenwal 48. **Tel** 0514-531541.
🕐 10am–noon & 2–5pm Tue–Fri. 📷

Sneek ❿

Road map C2. 🏠 31,600. 🚌 🚉
🛈 Marktstraat18 (0515-414096).
🍲 Tue am, Sat.

Sneek's centrepiece is the Waterpoort (water-gate) dating from 1613. Sneekweek is the name of a popular sailing event that in early August brings together amateur sailors and partygoers from all over

Mummy in Wieuwerd

the country. **Fries Scheepvaart Museum** focuses on the history of navigation and shipbuilding. Its exhibits include a *skûtje* deckhouse, the cabin of a *boeier* yacht and approximately 200 model ships. The *zilverzaal* (silver room) houses one of the richest collections of Frisian silver.

🏛 Fries Scheepvaart Museum
Kleinzand 14. **Tel** 0515-414057.
🕐 10am–5pm Mon–Sat, noon–5pm Sun. ● public hols. 📷 ♿ partly.

Environs
The village of **Wieuwerd**, north of Sneek, is known for the human mummies in its 13th-century St Nicholas church (open in summer). They were discovered by chance in 1765 and the reason for their mummification is not known.

SCHUITJE SAILING

Schuitje sailing, *or skûtsjesilen,* is a sport which has gained great popularity in the lakes of Friesland, *skûtje* being the name of the typical local spritsail barges. Originally used for the carriage of goods and as ferries, these boats are raced by representatives of various towns and villages. The result is a series of spectacular events held in July and August in various places, each time on a different lake and from a different base. Every day certain prizes are won, and on the last day, in Sneek, the champion of the year is announced and fêted. The races are held over the course of 11 racing days and three rest days.

The Thialfstadion ⓫

The Thialfstadion in Heerenveen, completely
renovated in 2001, is regarded as the temple of
Dutch ice-skating and has international renown.
The exuberant crowds that converge on the stadium
for international events create a unique atmosphere.
Skating heroes such as Marianne Timmer, Gunda
Niemann and Rintje Ritsma have all experienced
emotional highlights in their sporting careers here.

VISITORS' CHECKLIST

Pim Mulierlaan 1, Heerenveen.
🚉 *Heerenveen.* **Tel** *0513-
637700/0900-2020026.*
⬜ *variable opening hours so
visitors should phone ahead or
check website for exact opening
hours.* 🗓 *Apr–Sep.* 📷 ⬜
www.thialf.nl

THE ART OF ICE-MAKING

Making a good ice surface is an art. The
Thialf ice-makers strive to strike a balance
between deformation – the extent to which
the ice breaks down under the pressure of
the skate – and the smoothness of the ice.

Thialf Spectators
*The fans here are
famous for their
colourful garb and
their imaginative
banners.*

**Underneath the
ice** are 70 km
(43 miles)
of cooling
elements.

The great hall covers
an area of 15,000 m²
(17,950 sq yd) and
can accommodate
13,000 spectators.

The ice hockey
hall is 1,800 m²
(2,150 sq yd) and
has room for 4,000
spectators.

Hinged Skates
*Skates which have a hinge between the
shoe and the blade give significantly better results. All new world records have
been achieved with the help of* klap-
schaatsen *(hinged
skates).*

Triumph
*The climax of every major skating event
in the Thialfstadion is the procession of
winners through the stadium on a special
sleigh drawn by a Frisian horse.*

Stately Lauswolt, now a luxury hotel with a restaurant

Oude Venen ⑫

Road map D2. 🚏 ℹ️ *P Miedema-weg 9, Earnewâld (0511-539500).*

This region, whose name literally means "the old fens", is a fine area of peat-marshes with reedlands, swampy woodlands and sunken polders between

The Oude Venen

Earnewâld and Grou. The lakes were formed in the 17th and 18th centuries by peat-cutting and now offer a home to over 100 species of birds and approximately 400 plant species. There is a large colony of great cormorants and various rare birds such as the spotted crake, the purple heron, the white-fronted goose, the barnacle goose, the Eurasian wigeon and the ruff, all of which are best watched in spring.

In and around the water are water lilies, yellow water lily, marsh lousewort and cotton-grass. The area's hayfields are yellow with marsh marigold in spring.

Reidplûm visitors' centre of *It Fryske Gea* at Earnewâld provides information on the surrounding area and is a good starting point for hiking and sailing expeditions. Beside the centre is the Eibertshiem, a breeding centre for storks.

A great deal of attention has been paid to water cleanliness in the region, and now otters have returned to breed. In winter, the area hosts many skating tours.

🏛 Bezoekerscentrum De Reidplûm
Ds v.d. Veenweg 7, Earnewald.
Tel 0511-539410. 🕐 *mid-Apr–Sep: 1–5pm daily.*

Beetsterzwaag ⑬

Road map D2. 🚏 *3,700.* 🚏 ℹ️ *Hoofdstraat 67, (0512-381955).*

This village was once one of the seats of the Frisian landed gentry and so has a number of stately homes and gardens. Fine examples of these are **Lauswolt**, the **Lycklamahuis** and the

Harinxmastate. Beetsterzwaag is surrounded by a varied countryside, with coniferous and deciduous forests, heath and fens offering ample opportunities for a leisurely afternoon of rambling and cycling.

Appelscha ⑭

Road map D2. 🚏 *4,500.* 🚏 ℹ️ *Boerestreek 23 (0516-431760).*

The vast coniferous forests, drifting sands and colourful heath and fen areas around Appelscha form stunning surroundings. The village was created in the 19th century when the main industry was peat-cutting and is now on the edge of the **Nationaal Park Drents-Friese Woud**.

A favourite place with visitors is the **Kale Duinen** area of drifting sands. On the Bosberg – at 26 m (85 ft) above sea level, the highest spot in the area – is a viewing tower and information centre.

A distinctive phenomenon in southeast Friesland is the **Klokkenstoel** (bell stool). This "poor men's church tower" was a provisional church tower built when funds were low; it was usually situated in the churchyard. In Appelscha you will find a *klokkenstoel* dating from 1453. Langedijke is home to what is presumed to be the oldest bell in the Netherlands, dating from 1300.

Environs

At Ravenswoud, 5 km (3 miles) northeast of Appelsche, an 18-m (59-ft) observation tower provides outstanding views.

Drifting sand dune near the small town of Appelscha

For hotels and restaurants in this region see pp400–401 and pp419–420

DRENTHE

*D*renthe was once a free republic of farmers, and its inhabitants have always lived close to the land. Although the region has no cities and few towns, the rural poverty that once prevailed is no more, and tourists, especially those interested in archaeology and nature, are arriving in increasing numbers.

Drenthe, whose landscape is a product of the last Ice Age, has managed to keep time at bay by holding on to its character, reputed by the rest of the country to have been born of peat, gin and suspicion. Moraines and megaliths dot the countryside. The extensive woodland, heathland and peat bogs have a primeval atmosphere, although this does not mean that there has been no human intervention. The top level of peat has been largely removed, while the traditional *esdorps*, the local hamlets, have modern outskirts. However, peat moors and forests, ancient burial mounds, canals, flocks of sheep and green fields are the principal features here.

There are more than 50 megaliths in Drenthe, the remains of tombs dating from the Neolithic era; information about this period, with archaeological finds, is displayed in the museum at Borger. Other museums in the region feature glass blowing, artworks, natural history and paper-cutting. Orvelte boasts a fine open-air museum with Saxon farmhouses and traditional crafts, while Dwingeloo looks to the future at the Planetron observatory and planetarium.

Visitors come to Drenthe for peace and quiet after the rigours of city life. But this does not mean there are no facilities – local centres such as Assen, Emmen and Hoogeveen are urbanized areas that grew out of villages, and there is a variety of hotels, guesthouses and restaurants throughout the region.

The largest horse market in western Europe, at Zuidlaren

◁ Keystone in the 13th-century Romanesque church near the village of Norg

Exploring Drenthe

The finest natural areas of Drenthe are the
Hondsrug ridge, between Zuidlaren and
Emmen, and the Ellertsveld region between
Assen and Emmen. The areas around Diever,
Dwingeloo and Norg are a resplendent green
(or purple, when the heather is in bloom).
The eastern part of the region, with its endless
excavated peatlands and the wilderness of the
Amsterdamsche Veld, is relatively unknown.
The provincial capital of Assen is also a regional
centre, as is Emmen, where Noorder Dierenpark
Zoo, in the middle of the town, has become
one of the most-visited attractions in Holland.
The megaliths are concentrated around
Emmen, along the Hondsrug and at Havelte.

SIGHTS AT A GLANCE

Assen ❷
Borger ❽
Coevorden ⓭
Diever ⓬
Dwingeloo ⓫
Eelde-Paterswolde ❹
Emmen ⓮
Hondsrug ❻
Norg ❸
Orvelte ❾
Rolde ❼
Westerbork ❿
Zuidlaren ❺

Tour
The Megalith
Route pp306–7 ❶

The 14th-century Siepelkerk at
Dwingeloo

The broad and silent heath

KEY

═══ Motorway
──── Major road
═══ Minor road
──── Scenic route
─·─· Major railway
──── Minor railway
═══ Regional border
═══ International border

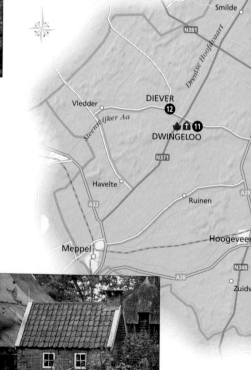

Thatcher at work in Havelte

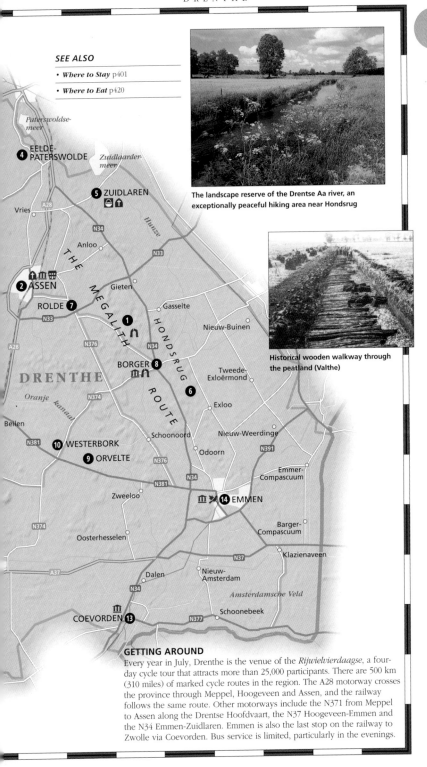

The landscape reserve of the Drentse Aa river, an exceptionally peaceful hiking area near Hondsrug

Historical wooden walkway through the peatland (Valthe)

SEE ALSO

• *Where to Stay* p401

• *Where to Eat* p420

GETTING AROUND

Every year in July, Drenthe is the venue of the *Rijwielvierdaagse*, a four-day cycle tour that attracts more than 25,000 participants. There are 500 km (310 miles) of marked cycle routes in the region. The A28 motorway crosses the province through Meppel, Hoogeveen and Assen, and the railway follows the same route. Other motorways include the N371 from Meppel to Assen along the Drentse Hoofdvaart, the N37 Hoogeveen-Emmen and the N34 Emmen-Zuidlaren. Emmen is also the last stop on the railway to Zwolle via Coevorden. Bus service is limited, particularly in the evenings.

The Megalith Route ●

Of the 54 Megaliths in Holland, 52 are in Drenthe and the remaining two are in Groningen. These megaliths, or *hunebedden*, are the remains of ancient tombs built of boulders some 5,000 years ago by the Neolithic Beaker Folk. What can be seen today are only the frameworks of the tombs, which were all hidden underneath sandhills. It is still not known whether these were common graves or the tombs of prominent individuals.

At Diever and Havelte *are three megaliths which are not on the route described here. The largest consists of 23 upright stones, 9 top stones, 2 keystones and a gate of 4 uprights and 2 top stones. At least 665 ancient pots have been found here. In World War II, the megalith was demolished to make way for an airfield. It was reconstructed in 1950.*

Witte Wieven ① are ghosts that inhabit the tumuli, such as the Negen Bergen at Norg. They come out at midnight – particularly when it is misty – to dance.

The Great Megalith ⑧ of Balloo is at the end of a sandy path in the Tumulibos woods, an area which abounds with tumuli.

0 kilometres   5

0 miles   5

KEY

- 🟫 Tour route
- ═ Other road
- ▬ Railway
- 🪨 Megalith
- 🏛 Museum

Megalith at Loon ⑨ *One of the best-preserved megaliths in Holland is at Loon, northeast of Assen. Before 1870 it was in even better condition, when the original top stone was still in place.*

De Zeven Marken ⑦, the open-air museum of Schoonoord, tells you about such things as the legend of the giants Ellert and Brammert.

BUILDING THE MEGALITHS

Until the 19th century, it was believed that the megaliths were built by the *buynen*, giants of great strength and after whom the *hunebedden* are named. Modern historians believe that the boulders were placed with their flat edges on rollers, which thus allowed them to be moved to the site of the tomb. The upright stones were placed in pits dug beforehand. A gentle slope of earth was then made to allow the top stones to be dragged up. There is, however, no explanation of how the people of the Stone Age managed to organize such large-scale projects.

17th-century depiction of megalith builders

Typical beakers *after which the Beaker Folk are named. Pottery shards of these containers are the most common finds in the megaliths.*

Beaker

Pitcher

Anloo ② is one of the most picturesque Drenthe villages.

Collared flask

The largest megalith in Holland ③ *measures 22.5 m (74 ft), has 9 top stones and 26 upright stones. Excavations were carried out in Borger in 1685, but none of the finds has been preserved.*

Het Flint'n Hoes, the Nationaal Hunebedden Informatiecentrum ④, *(National Megalith Information Centre), has been set up beside Holland's largest megalith.*

The Exloo Necklace ⑤ *was found in the peat in 1881. It is made of beads of tin, faience, bronze and amber, which is evidence of trading links between prehistoric Drenthe and the Baltic countries, Cornwall and even Egypt.*

Flint *was the main material used by the hunter-gatherers of prehistoric Drenthe to make such items as knives, axes, scrapers and arrowheads.*

MEGALITHS (HUNEBEDDEN)

There are no longer any complete megaliths. Until 1734, when trading in boulders was forbidden, thousands of megaliths were hacked up to be used as building material. There are definite traces of 88 megaliths, 82 of them in Drenthe. The 54 surviving megaliths are all restorations. The most common finds from excavations are pottery shards. Scrapers, axes, arrowheads, and amber and copper jewellery – all extremely valuable trading goods in Drenthe in 3000 BC – are much rarer finds.

De Papeloze Kerk *(the Popeless Church)* ⑥ *This megalith is so called because of the Calvinist sermons that were held here in the 16th century against the "popish" (Catholic) faith. In 1959, the megalith was restored to its original state, to the extent of covering half of the tomb with sand.*

Map labels:
Annen · Anloo · BALLOOËRVELD · Eext · Balloöerkuil · Gieten · Balloo · N33 · N34 · DROUWENERZAND · Drouwen · HONDSRUG · N857 · N376 · N374 · Borger · Buinen · Schoonloo · Uitzichttoren · Exloo · ELLERTSVELD · Schoonoord · Open-air museum · Odoorn · Valthe · N376 · N381 · 't Haantje · SLEENERZAND

Assen ❷

Road map D2. 👥 61,500. 🚉
ℹ️ *Marktstraat 8 (0900-2022393).*
🗓️ *Wed, Sat.*

Assen is the capital of Drenthe, although it was only upgraded from a village to a town in 1809. The **cloister** of the abbey church of Maria in Campis (1258–1600) now forms part of the Rijksarchief (national archive) of the Brink. Also on the Brink is the **Drents Museum** of local history, which is housed in the abbey church, the Ontvangershuis (1698), the Drostenhuis (1778) and Provinciehuis (1885). The museum contains a wealth of exhibits on prehistoric times and the town's history as well as collections of local art and a "discovery room" for children. There are also collections of local art, including works by Bernard Von Dülmen-Krumpelmann (1897–1987).

The controversial finds of Tjerk Vermaning (1929–87), who in the 1960s single-handedly extended the history of human habitation in Holland by tens of thousands of years, are in a separate display case: disputes on the genuineness of the flint tools he found have not yet been resolved.

Outside the formal gardens of the Drostenhuis is the town's trademark **Bartje**, a statue of the little peasant boy from Dutch author Anne de Vries' book (1935) who

did not want to pray before his daily meals of brown beans.

The Vaart and the Markt have the characteristic stately white houses of Assen, which were built in the late 18th to the early 19th century.

Bartje

Between Markt and Brink is the commercial centre with its pedestrian precinct and excellent facilities. Modern-day Assen comes to life when the **circuit van Assen** TT motorcycle racing event is held here each year on the last Saturday in June. Around 100,000 spectators descend on the town, which is home to the only remaining circuit from the championship's inaugural season in 1949. Younger children who have gained a taste for speed and bikes at the TT circuit will enjoy a visit to **Verkeerspark Assen** *(see p435).* This is a "traffic park" for children, where they can learn the

The 13th-century Romanesque church on the Brink of Norg

rules of the road while driving miniature cars and scooters around an artificial town, complete with traffic lights, road signs and traffic police. Older children can use quad bikes and go-karts. Other attractions include a boating lake, mini-golf and a climbing tower.

🏛️ **Drents Museum**
Brink 1–5. **Tel** 0592-37773.
🕐 Tue–Sun (Mon during hols).
🚫 1 Jan, 25 Dec. 🎫 ♿ 🛍️ 📷

🎢 **Verkeerspark Assen**
De Haar 1–1a. **Tel** 0592-350005.
🕐 Apr: days vary; May–Aug: daily; Sep & Oct: days vary. 🚫 29 Nov–Mar. **www**.verkeersparkassen.nl

Norg ❸

Road map D2. 👥 3,500. 🚌
ℹ️ *Brink 1 (0592-613128).* 🗓️ *Wed.*

The Romanesque church on the Brink dates from the 13th century. The unique frescoes in the choir have barely survived through the centuries and are in very poor condition.

Environs
The area around Norg is steeped in prehistory. Three megalithic tombs are to be found there, while in the Noorderveld are Bronze Age tumuli (the **Negen Bergen**). Norgerholt is the name given to the oak woods where the local people used to assemble during the Middle Ages.

Children Bathing in a Stream (c.1935) by Von Dülmen-Krumpelmann

Eelde-Paterswolde ❹

Road map D2. 🏠 10,500.
🚌 52. ℹ️ B Boermalaan 4
(050-3092136). 🗓️ Wed.

Two villages merge together at Eelde-Paterswolde and are squeezed between the **Paterswoldse Meer** lake and **Groningen Airport**, which despite its name is in Drenthe not Groningen. The lake is popular among water sports enthusiasts. The airport serves mainly domestic flights (it is a half-hour flight to Schiphol) and flying enthusiasts.

The distinctive modern brick building housing the **Museum voor figuratieve kunst De Buitenplaats** (De Buitenplaats museum of figurative art) was designed by the architects Alberts and Van Huut. It is a fine example of their organic architecture. In addition to hosting changing exhibitions, the museum is used as a concert hall. There are also formal and landscape gardens, the former fronting the 17th-century curator's residence, the **Nijsinghuis**. Since 1983 the house has been painted by figurative artists and is periodically opened to visitors by arrangement.

The Eelde part of town is home to the **Klompenmuseum Gebroeders Wietzes**. Named in honour of the last two clog-makers to live in the village, the museum gives an overview of the development of the clog. It displays examples of clogs from around the world. Most visitors, however, come to see the world's largest clog, which is 6.5 m (21 ft) long.

Dense woodland in the Hondsrug area

🏛 **Museum voor figuratieve kunst De Buitenplaats**
Hoofdweg 76. **Tel** 050-3095818. 🕐
11am–5pm Tue–Sun, Easter Sun &
Easter Mon. ● 1 Jan, 25 Dec. 🎫 📷

🏛 **Klompenmuseum Gebroeders Wietzes**
Wolfhorn 1a. **Tel** 050-3091181.
🕐 1 Apr–1 Oct: Tue–Sun.

Zuidlaren ❺

Road map E2. 🏠 10,000. 🚌 ℹ️
Stationsweg 69 (050-4092333). 🗓️ Fri.

The colourful Zuidlaren **horse market**, now the largest in Western Europe, predates even the 13th-century church which stands on the Brink. The market is held in April and October. The 17th-century **Havezathe Laarwoud** was built on the remnants of the fortified residence of the counts of Heiden, who ruled the region in the 14th century. Today it is the town hall. The **Zuidlaardermeer** lake offers everything that watersports enthusiasts may require. Children will especially enjoy

the subtropical swimming complex of Aqualaren as well as De Sprookjeshof recreation centre with playpark; they can be combined on a round tour.

Hondsrug ❻

Road map E2. 🚌 ℹ️ VVVs in Zuid-
laren, Rolde, Gieten (0900-2022393),
Exloo (0591-549182), Borger,
SchoonoOrd (0591-381242) or Emmen.

Between the Drentse sand plateau in the west and the Drents-Groningen peat moors in the east lies the Hondsrug ridge. Prehistoric people found it a safe place to settle, and it is the area where the megaliths now stand (see pp306–7).

The Drentse Aa river basin, the old villages of Gieten, Gasselte, Exloo and Odoorn, the drifting sand areas of the Drouwenerzand and the heathland of Ellertsveld are particularly attractive hiking areas, with plenty of streams in which to cool off.

In the centre of Eexloo, the **Bebinghehoes** is a cultural museum in a beautiful 18th-century, thatched farmhouse. The house itself gives an impression of farming life 200 years ago, while the coach house presents a display of carriages from the age of horse-drawn transport. There is also a children's farm, with goats, sheep, chickens and ducks, and a petting area.

🏛 **Bebinghehoes**
Zuiderhoofdstraat 6. **Tel** 0591-
549242. 🕐 1 Apr–1 May: Wed–Sat;
May, Jun & Sep: Tue–Sat; Jul & Aug:
daily.

Colourfully decorated Klompenmuseum Gebroeders Wietzes

Rolde ❼

Road map E2. 🏠 *6,200.* 🚌
ℹ️ *Onder de Molen, Grote Brink 22
(0900-2022393).*

Rolde was important for a considerable time. There are prehistoric tumuli (in the **Tumulibos** woods), and three megaliths, two of which are on the mound directly behind the church. During the Middle Ages, people were tried at the **Ballooërkuil**; if guilty they were held prisoner in the 15th-century church, a magnificent Gothic edifice. Forests, peatland and drifting sands surround the village. Sheep graze on the Ballooërveld.

Borger ❽

Road map E2. 🏠 *4,700.* 🚌 *59.* ℹ️
Grote Brink 2a (0599-234855). 🚃 *Tue.*

Borger is the capital of the *hunebeddengebeid,* or megalith region. There are eight megaliths in and around the town, including the largest in Holland. Nearby is the **Nationaal Hunebedden Informatiecentrum** ('t Flint'n Hoes), with a fine exhibition about the Beaker Folk and a stone casket from the most recently excavated megalith, which was discovered in 1982 in Groningen.

🏛 **Nationaal Hunebedden Informatiecentrum**
Bronnegerstraat 12. *Tel 0599-236374.*
⬜ *daily.* 🌑 *1 Jan, 25 Dec.* 📷 ♿ 🖥

Environs
Drents Boomkroonpad (tree-top walk), 2 km (1 mile) down the "Staatsbossen" turn-off on the Rolde-Borger road,

Boomkroonpad's tree-top walkway

is an interesting attraction. The walk starts at the roots, with a 23-m (75-ft) tunnel. This leads into a 125-m (410-ft) ascent to a height of 22.5 m (74 ft), affording a fascinating view of the forest.

🏕 **Drents Boomkroonpad**
Bezoekerscentrum, Drents Boomkroonpad, Steenhopenweg 4, Drouwen. *Tel 0592-377305.*
⬜ *daily.* 🌑 *1 Jan.* 📷 🖥

Orvelte ❾

Road map E2. 🏠 *90.* 🚌 *22, 23.*
ℹ️ *Dorpsstraat 1a (0593-322335).*

The whole of Orvelte is in effect an open-air museum. In the restored Saxon farm-houses from the early 19th century, there are exhibits on agriculture and displays of traditional crafts. Cars are banned from the area, but tours in horse-drawn trams or covered waggons are offered. The more interesting attractions of the town include a tinsmith's shop.

🏛 **Bezoekerscentrum**
Dorpsstraat 3. *Tel 0593-322335.*
⬜ *Apr–Oct daily.* 📷 ✅ ♿ 🍴 🖥

Westerbork ❿

Road map E2. 🏠 *8,000.* 🚌 *22.* ℹ️
BG van Wezelplein 10 (0593-331381).

The Hoofdstraat (main street) features a Late Gothic 14th-century church, which now houses the **Museum voor Papierknipkunst** (paper-cutting museum) and Saxon farmhouses which bear witness to a prosperous past. However, Westerbork is visited primarily for its more recent history. In World War II, the Westerbork Transit Camp stood here. It was from this camp that 107,000 Jews, Gypsies and resistance fighters were held before deportation to the Nazi extermination camps. Anne Frank *(see pp108–9)* was one of its inmates.

🕍 **Herinneringscentrum Kamp Westerbork**
Oosthalen 8, Hooghalen. *Tel 0593-592600.* ⬜ *daily.* 📷 ♿

Dwingeloo ⓫

Road map D2. 🏠 *1,800.* 🚌 *20.*
ℹ️ *Brink (0521-591331).* 🚃 *Tue.*

The first thing that strikes visitors about Dwingeloo is the deformed dome of the 14th-century church tower (the **Siepelkerk**). You can read about the legend behind this oddity on the information board located nearby.

There is some impressive countryside around the town. The **Dwingelderveld** is a national park and the **krentenbossen** (currant planta-tions) which flower in April and May – the fruit ripening in July or August – are delight-ful in every respect: they are pleasant to the eye and to the taste buds. At the edge of the Dwingelose Heide heath is a radio-telescope.

The interesting and child-friendly **Planetron** nearby is an observatory where there is a planetarium as well as an electronic games area.

🔭 **Planetron**
Drift 11b. *Tel 0521-593535.* ⬜ *daily during school hols.* 🌑 *1 Jan, Mon outside school hols.* 📷 🍴 🖥

Farmers at work in the Orvelte open-air museum

Diever ⑫

Road map D2. 🚶 *3,700.* 🚌 *20.*
ℹ️ *Bosweg 2a (0521-591748).*

Diever was an important
centre from prehistoric times
to the Middle Ages. Tumuli,
megaliths and remains of the
9th-century wooden foundations of the village church
lend it historical importance.
The church features a 12th-
century Romanesque tower of
tufa stone. Diever is in the
middle of the **Nationaal Park
Het Drents-Friese Woud**: the
town is now synonymous
with cycling and rambling.
In summer, the **Shakespeare-
markten** (Shakespeare fair) is
held during performances of
the playwright's works in the
open-air theatre.

Environs
In **Vledder**, 10 km (6 miles)
west of Diever, is a **museum**
of graphic art and glass-
blowing and art forgery.

Lime kilns at Diever

🏛️ **Museum voor
Valse Kunst/Museum
voor Hedendaagse Grafiek/
Museum voor Glaskunst**
Brink 1, Vledder. **Tel** *0521-383352.*
⭘ *Apr–beg Jan: Wed–Mon.* 📷 📷

Coevorden ⑬

Road map E3. 🚶 *34,000.* 🚌 🚉
ℹ️ *Kerkstraat 2 (0524-525150).*
🅿️ *Mon.*

The castle here dates
from around 1200. The star-
shaped moat and surviving
bastions and town walls
define the look of the town,
while the façades of the
Friesestraat and Weeshuis-
straat are telling of past
centuries. **Stedelijk Museum**

Brown bears in the popular Noorder Dierenpark in Emmen

Drenthe's Veste highlights the
town's history.

🏛️ **Stedelijk Museum
Drenthe's Veste**
Haven 6. **Tel** *0524-516225.* ⭘ *10am–
5pm Tue–Fri, 10am–3pm Sat.* 📷 📷

Emmen ⑭

Road map E2. 🚶 *105,000.* 🚌 🚉
ℹ️ *Hoofdstraat 22 (0900-2022393).*
🅿️ *Fri am.*

Drenthe's largest district
has grown only since World
War II. Eleven megaliths,
including **Langgraf op de
Schimmer Es** or long
barrow on the Schimmer
Es, the urn-fields *(see p43)*
and prehistoric farmland
(the **Celtic Fields**) in the
vicinity and the 12th-century
tower on the Hoofdstraat
reflect the district's history.
At **Noorder Dierenpark**,
animals roam freely. The
Biochron museum and
Vlindertuin butterfly gardens
are also here.

🐾 **Noorder Dierenpark**
Hoofdstraat 18. **Tel** *0591-850850.*
⭘ *daily.* 📷 📷 📷 📷
www.noorderdierenpark.nl

Environs
Roughly 10 km (6 miles) east
of Emmen are the **Amsterdamsche Veld** upland peat
marshes, perhaps the loneliest
place in Holland. In Barger-
Compascuum, **Veenpark**
re-creates the times when
the people of Drenthe lived
in poverty, cutting peat. In
1883, Vincent van Gogh
stayed at the Scholte ferry-
house in Veenoord (Nieuw-
Amsterdam). At the **Van Gogh
House**, his room on the first
floor has been restored to the
way it was in 1883, as has
the café-restaurant below.

🏛️ **Veenpark**
Berkenrode 4, Barger-Compascuum.
Tel *0591-324444.* ⭘ *Apr–Nov:
10am–5pm daily.* 📷 📷 📷
🏛️ **Van Gogh Huis**
Van Goghstraat 1, Nieuw-
Amsterdam. **Tel** *0591-555600.*
⭘ *1–5pm Tue–Sun.* 📷 📷 📷

Van Gogh's *Peat Boat with Two Figures* (1883) in Drents Museum, Assen

OVERIJSSEL

*O*verijssel, a province in the east of Holland, has many areas of natural beauty and lovely old towns. In a sense it is a province of two halves, divided by the heathland and woods of the Sallandse Heuvelrug near Nijverdal, which separate the eastern district of Twente from the rest of the province.

This division is noticeable in many ways. The two halves differ in their spoken dialect, and they each have their own cultural traditions. There are also religious differences, with Twente being mainly Catholic while the rest of the province is strictly Protestant. Twente, with its larger towns, has a more modern appearance, and Enschede, for example, is livelier than western towns like Zwolle and Deventer.

Zwolle, however, is the capital of the province, a charming town dating back to the 13th century, when its port at a busy river junction led it to join the powerful Hanseatic League, growing rich from trade with England and the Baltic. Kampen and Deventer, on the IJssel river, were later members of the same league.

Overijssel's numerous unique museums and attractions highlight local history and printing, tobacco, salt and farmhouses, as well as traditional costumes, tin soldiers, Dutch painting and modern art. For children, the Hellendoorn adventure park *(see p434)*, the Los Hoes open-air museum and Ecodrome Park are always popular.

Apart from these activities, however, the principal attraction in Overijssel is the countryside, which is ideal for walking, hiking and touring by bicycle. In places like Giethoorn you can tour the rivers, lakes and canals by boat, while the Weerribben wetlands in the northwest offer opportunities for nature rambles and watersports.

Cigar-maker at work at the Tabaksmuseum (tobacco museum) in Kampen

◁ Weerribben wetlands nature reserve in the northwest of Overijssel

Exploring Overijssel

The impressive historical monuments of Deventer and Kampen recall their prosperous pasts as Hanseatic cities. However, Overijssel has plenty to offer those who are interested in more than splendid old buildings. Those who enjoy peace and natural surroundings will find some of the finest spots in Holland. The peaceful countryside of the Sallandse Heuvelrug is ideal for rambling walks, while De Weerribben is suitable for yachting. There are many picturesque spots, such as Ootmarsum, Delden and Giethoorn, and children will love the amusement part at Hellendoorn *(see p434)*. In addition to this, Overijssel also has many interesting museums, such as the national tin figure museum in Ommen.

The quiet port of Blokzijl near Vollenhove

OVERIJSSEL AT A GLANCE

Delden ⑩
Deventer ⑧
De Weerribben ④
Enschede ⑪
Giethoorn
  pp318–19 ⑤
Kampen ②
Nijverdal ⑨
Ommen ⑦
Ootmarsum ⑫
Staphorst ⑥
Vollenhove ③
Zwolle ①

The IJssel north of the old Hanseatic city of Deventer

GETTING AROUND

Overijssel can be explored easily by car, bicycle or on foot. Large parts of the region are also well connected by public transport. Note, however, that bus timetables are different on weekends than on weekdays. Areas of natural beauty such as De Weerribben, for example, are not easy to reach by public transport on weekends. In some places, too, buses operate only during the daytime.

KEY

═══ Motorway

── Major road

── Minor road

── Scenic route

┄┄ Major railway

── Minor railway

▬▬ Regional border

▬▬ International border

0 kilometres 10

0 miles 10

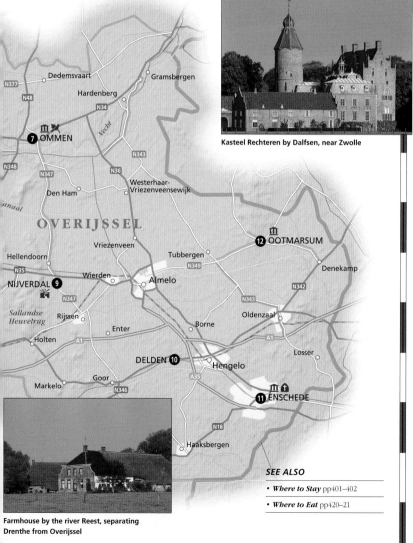

Kasteel Rechteren by Dalfsen, near Zwolle

Dedemsvaart
N377
N48
Gramsbergen
Hardenberg
N34
Vecht
🏛 ✕
7 OMMEN
N343
N348
N347
N36
Westerhaar-
Vriezenveensewijk
Den Ham
OVERIJSSEL
Vriezenveen
Tubbergen
🏛
12 OOTMARSUM
Hellendoorn
N349
Denekamp
N35
Wierden
Almelo
N342
NIJVERDAL 9
N347
N343
Oldenzaal
Sallandse
Heuvelrug
Rijssen
Enter
Borne
Holten
A1
DELDEN **10**
Hengelo
Losser
Markelo
Goor
A35
N346
🏛 ℹ
11 ENSCHEDE
N18
Haaksbergen

anaal

**Farmhouse by the river Reest, separating
Drenthe from Overijssel**

SEE ALSO

• *Where to Stay* pp401–402

• *Where to Eat* pp420–21

Zwolle ❶

Road map D3. 🏛 *107,000.* 🚉
ℹ️ *Grote Kerkplein 15 (0900-1122375).* 🐄 *Fri (cattle market), Sat.*

In the middle ages, Zwolle, capital of the province of Overijssel, was, along with towns such as Deventer, Kampen and Zutphen, a city of the Hanseatic League, a network of trading cities. Its past is evident in the relatively large historical centre. The finest buildings in Zwolle, which was granted its city charter in 1230, are largely to be found in the area that used to fall within the city fortifications, which can still be seen in the form of a moat. However, only a few dozen metres of these ancient fortifications are left standing, along with the fine Sassenpoort gate, dating from 1406, and the Late Gothic 15th-century Pelsertoren tower.

On one side of the Grote Kerkplein is a sculpture by Rodin entitled *Adam*, while on the Grote Markt stands the magnificent building of the Hoofdwacht (guard house), which dates from 1614. Today it houses a police station.

The **Grote Kerk**, also known as **St Michaelskerk**, is worth a visit as well. The original Romanesque church, built in 1040, was enlarged in 1370 and again in 1452 to become the present-day three-naved Gothic church.

The most recent addition to Zwolle's cultural landscape is the **Paleis aan de Blijmarkt**, a contemporary art museum that opened in 2005. Housed in a grand Neo-Classical building dating from 1838, the

View of Zwolle during the Hanseatic Period (anonymous, c.14th century)

renovated light-filled galleries hold works by the likes of Van Gogh, Picasso and Mondrian.

The **Stedelijk Museum Zwolle** (Zwolle local history museum) features, among its other interesting exhibits on local history, an 18th-century kitchen and a Renaissance room from Blokzijl. The fine façade of the old part of the building, which dates from 1741, is impressive.

The town is also home to the **Ecodrome Park**, which is dedicated to the natural environment in the past, present and future.

🏛 **Stedelijk Museum Zwolle**
Melkmarkt 41. **Tel** *038-4214650.*
🕐 *10am–5pm Tue–Sat, 1–5pm Sun.*
🌐 *public hols.* 🖼 🎞 ♿ 🔲 🔲

🦋 **Ecodrome Park**
Willemsvaart 19. **Tel** *038-4215050.*
🕐 *Nov–Mar: 10am–5pm Wed, Sat & Sun; Apr–Oct: 10am–5pm daily.* 🔲

🏛 **Paleis aan de Blijmarkt**
Blijmarkt 20. **Tel** *0572-388188.*
🕐 *Tue–Sun.*

The grand Neo-Classical façade of the Paleis aan de Blijmarkt

Environs

The Kunstwegen (Art Paths) are outdoor sculpture installations on the country estate of **Landgoed Anningahof**. The five-hectare open-air sculpture park was the brainchild of art collector Hib Anninga and contains dozens of works, from bright blue ceramic dogs to giant iron hoops, by around 80 contemporary Dutch sculptors. The work is spread throughout meadows and landscaped gardens, and exploring them makes for a pleasant afternoon's stroll.

🏛 **Landgoed Anningahof**
Hessenweg 9. **Tel** *038-4534412.*
🕐 *May–Oct: Wed–Sun.*

Kampen ❷

Road map D3. 🏛 *48,000.* 🚉
ℹ️ *Oudestraat 151 (0900-112375).*
🐄 *Mon am.*

Kampen, known for its theological university where Protestant theologians are educated, is a pleasant and lively town containing 500 monuments. The beauty of this former Hanseatic city is immediately apparent from the IJssel riverfront. The fact that the town used to be well fortified is evident from the three remaining town gates: the Koornmanspoort, the Broederpoort and the Cellebroederspoort. The area inside the old fortifications features the magnificent Dutch Reformed church

The waterfront of the magnificent, well-preserved Hanseatic city of Kampen on the river IJssel

St Nicolaaskerk, and the Gotische Huis, which now houses the **Stedelijk Museum Kampen**, the town's local history museum. Particularly noteworthy is the old town hall, or Oude Raadhuis, with a façade decorated with fine sculptures.

Kampen, which is first mentioned in documents in 1227, is also famed for its cigars, which explains why the **Kamper Tabaks-museum** (Kampen tobacco museum) is located here. A rather more surprising find is the **Ikonenmuseum**, a collection of religious icons and the only museum of its kind in the Netherlands. The museum is housed in a former cloister, and is home to 150 mainly Russian and Greek Orthodox painted icons, spanning the 16th to 19th centuries. It also hosts temporary exhibitions.

Kampen was at the height of its development between 1330 and 1450. It revived its fortunes only when the Flevoland and Noordoostpolder regions were reclaimed and it acquired the function of regional centre. However, Kampen was never a mighty city because it did not have any powerful ruler. Kampen did not apply to join the Hanseatic League until relatively late – 1440. At that time, the Netherlands was involved in a war with the Hanseatic League, and Kampen joined the powerful league for the sake of security.

🏛 **Stedelijk Museum Kampen**
Oude Straat 158. *Tel* 038-3317361.
⬜ 11am–5pm Tue–Sat.

🏛 **Kamper Tabaksmuseum**
Botermarkt 3. *Tel* 038-3315868.
⬜ by appointment only.

🏛 **Ikonenmuseum**
Buitennieuwstraat 2. *Tel* 0527-246644. ⬜ 1 Apr–1 Nov: Tue–Sun;
1 Jun–1 Sep: daily.

Religious image at the Ikonenmuseum

Environs
Five km (3 miles) south of the town, in Kamperveen, is the **Herten-houderij Edelveen**, a working deer farm that welcomes visitors. The owners give guided tours of their farmland, explaining their jobs and allowing visitors to see their herds close up. The farmers also sell venison, paté and sausages.

🏛 **Hertenhouderij Edelveen** Leidijk 10a. *Tel* 0525-621564. ⬜ by appointment only.

Vollenhove ❸

Road map D2. 🚌 71, 171. ℹ *Aan Zee 2–4 (0900-5674637).* 🅿 *Tue.*

Vollenhove is a picturesque place which was once known as the town of palaces due to the many nobles who lived here. The aristocratic residences are known as *baveza-ten*, or manors. The large 15th-century church is known variously as the **Grote Kerk, St Nicolaaskerk** or **Bovenkerk**.

De Weerribben ❹

Road map D3.

De Weerribben is an unspoiled area of wetlands at the northwestern end of Overijssel. There is plenty for cyclists, walkers and also canoeists to do in this beautiful nature reserve.

🚣 **Natuuractiviteitencentrum De Weerribben**
Hoogeweg 27, Ossenzijl. *Tel* 0561-477272. ⬜ *Apr–Oct: daily,
Nov–Mar: Tue–Fri & Sun.* 🍴 🖥

Water lilies in the nature reserve of De Weerribben

For hotels and restaurants in this region see pp401–402 and pp420–421

Street-by-Street: Giethoorn ❺

If any village were to be given the title "prettiest village in Holland", quaint Giethoorn would be the one. This well-deserved accolade is due to the village's picturesque canals which are flanked by numerous farmhouse-style buildings. Many of these buildings now contain interesting, if small, museums. The village of Giethoorn can be easily explored both by boat and by bicycle. Founded in 1230 by religious refugees, the village's distinctive form came about from peat-cutting, eventually resulting in the formation of ponds and lakes. The small canals were used for transporting peat.

Giethoorn is also known as the Green Venice because of its abundant natural beauty. Several ponds and lakes surround this charming town. The best way to enjoy the area is by hiring a small boat.

★ **Tjaskermolen**
This windmill, which turns an Archimedes' screw, is located in Giethoorn-Noord. Another one can be seen in the Olde Maat Uus museum.

★ **Olde Maat Uus**
This pleasant farmhouse which has been converted into a museum should definitely not be missed. It illustrates life in Giethoorn as it used to be.

BINNENPAD

STAR SIGHTS

★ Olde Maat Uus

★ Punts

★ Tjaskermolen

The delightful houses of Giethoorn contain numerous and varied tourist attractions, giving visitors plenty to do on each visit.

| 0 metres | 50 |
| 0 yards | 50 |

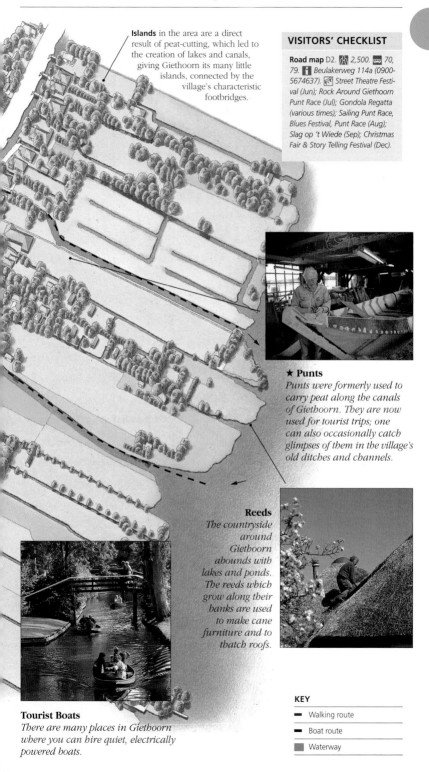

Islands in the area are a direct result of peat-cutting, which led to the creation of lakes and canals, giving Giethoorn its many little islands, connected by the village's characteristic footbridges.

VISITORS' CHECKLIST

Road map D2. 🚶 2,500. 🚌 70, 79. 🛈 Beulakerweg 114a (0900-5674637). 🎭 Street Theatre Festival (Jun); Rock Around Giethoorn Punt Race (Jul); Gondola Regatta (various times); Sailing Punt Race, Blues Festival, Punt Race (Aug); Slag op 't Wiede (Sep); Christmas Fair & Story Telling Festival (Dec).

★ Punts

Punts were formerly used to carry peat along the canals of Giethoorn. They are now used for tourist trips; one can also occasionally catch glimpses of them in the village's old ditches and channels.

Reeds

The countryside around Giethoorn abounds with lakes and ponds. The reeds which grow along their banks are used to make cane furniture and to thatch roofs.

Tourist Boats
There are many places in Giethoorn where you can hire quiet, electrically powered boats.

KEY

━ Walking route

━ Boat route

⬛ Waterway

Deventer, larger than Amsterdam in its heyday

Staphorst **❻**

Road map D3. 🏠 *15,000.* 🚌 *40.*
ℹ️ *Gemeenteweg 44 (0900-1122375).* 🛍️ *Sun.* 🏠 *Wed am.*

Staphorst is known throughout Holland as a stronghold of strict Christian beliefs. It was where the Gereformeerde Bond (reformed union), one of the strictest embodiments of Protestantism, ruled within the Dutch Reformed Church. The lovely old farmhouses, painted in a characteristic green and blue, are often monumental buildings. To get an idea of what they once looked like, visit the **Museumboerderij** (farmhouse museum).

The townspeople continue to wear traditional dress, a custom which has practically vanished elsewhere in the country. Throughout Staphorst you will see women, especially elderly women, wearing the blue and black outfits.

🏛️ **Museumboerderij**
Gemeenteweg 67. **Tel** *0522-462526.* ☐ *1 Apr–31 Oct: 10am–5pm Mon–Sat.* ⭕ *Sun & hols.* 📷

Ommen **❼**

Road map D3. 🏠 *17,000.* 🚉
ℹ️ *Kruisstraat 6 (0900-1122375).* 🏠 *Tue am.*

The district of Ommen lies in stunningly beautiful countryside extending from the town to nearby villages and hamlets. One-third of its total area of 18,000 ha (44,500 acres) is covered by nature reserves and forests. A former Hanseatic city, Ommen itself is home to a few interesting museums, including the **Nationaal Tinnen Figuren Museum** (national tin models museum).

🏛️ **Nationaal Tinnen Figuren Museum**
Markt 1. **Tel** *0529-454500.* ☐ *Apr–Oct: 10am–5pm Tue–Sat, 1–5pm Sun & hols; Nov–Mar: 11am–5pm Sat, 1–5pm Sun & hols.* ⭕ *1 Jan, 25 Dec.* 📷

A tin soldier

Environs
To find out more about the nature reserves in Ommen, visit the **Natuurinformatiecentrum Ommen**, which houses a permanent exhibition illustrating the cultural history of the surrounding countryside. Particularly worth seeing are the typical Saxon farmhouses at Beerze, Junne, Stegeren, Besthem and Giethmen.

🌿 **Natuurinformatie-centrum Ommen**
Hammerweg 59a. **Tel** *0529-450702.* ☐ *May–Oct: 1–5pm Wed–Sun; Nov–Apr: 1:30–4pm Wed, Sat & Sun.*

Deventer **❽**

Road map D3. 🏠 *86,000.* 🚉
ℹ️ *Keizerstraat 22 (0900-3535355).* 🏠 *Fri am & Sat.*

The lively centre of the old Hanseatic city of Deventer features numerous medieval houses, including the oldest stone house in Holland today. Buildings worth seeing in particular are those situated on the pleasant Brink (green) and the Bergkerk. In the middle of the Brink stands the impressive Waag (weigh house) from 1528, which now contains the renovated **Historisch Museum de Waag,** with interesting exhibits that illustrate the town's history. On the first Sunday of August, the town holds the **Deventer Boeken-markt** (book fair), the largest in Europe. It is preceded by a poetry festival.

🏛️ **Historisch Museum de Waag**
Brink 56. **Tel** *0570-693780.* ☐ *10am–5pm Tue–Sat, 1–5pm Sun.* ⭕ *public hols.* 📷

Nijverdal **❾**

Road map D3. 🏠 *23,500.* 🚉
ℹ️ *Willem Alexander Straat 7c (0540-612729).* 🏠 *Sat.*

The impressive beauty of the Sallandse Heuvelrug, with its fine heathland and woodland, is especially apparent at Nijverdaal. This is the last remaining breeding ground in the Netherlands for black grouse. An interesting

Flock of sheep in the Bezoekerscentrum Sallandse Heuvelrug

exhibition on the Heuvelrug region can be seen at the **Bezoekerscentrum Sallandse Heuvelrug** (Sallandse Heuvelrug visitors' centre), with its clever and unusual "Forester's Corner".

Bezoekerscentrum Sallandse Heuvelrug
Grotestraat 281. *Tel* 0548-612711.
☐ Mar–Oct, Dec & spring hols: 10am–5pm Tue–Sun; Nov, Jan & Feb: 10am–4pm Sat & Sun. ● Mon, 1 Jan, 25 & 31 Dec.

Environs
Avonturenpark Hellendoorn (Hellendoorn adventure park) *(see p434)* is great for children.

Delden ❿

Road map E3. 🏠 7,000. 🚉
🛈 Langestraat 29 (074-3761363).
🚢 Fri afternoon.

Delden is a pretty residential village, ideal for rambling walks. This Twente hamlet has a number of attractions, including the **Zoutmuseum** (salt museum) and the 12th-century **Oude Blasiuskerk**.

🏛 Zoutmuseum
Langestraat 30. *Tel* 074-3764546.
☐ May–Sep: 11am–5pm Mon–Fri, 2–5pm Sat & Sun; Oct–Apr: 2–5pm Tue–Fri & Sun. 🎨

Environs
Some 2 km (1.2 miles) north-east of Delden are the lovely gardens of **Kasteel Twickel**.

🏛 Tuinen Kasteel Twickel (Kasteel Twickel Gardens)
Twickelerlaan 1a, Ambt Delden. ☐ May–Oct: 11am–4:30pm Mon–Fri. 🎨

Enschede ⓫

Road map E3. 🏠 150,000. 🚉
🛈 Stationsplein 1a (053-4323200).
🚢 Tue, Sat.

Enschede is regarded as the capital of Twente, as it is the largest town in Overijssel. It was devastated in 1862 by a fire – little of the old town survived. One of the few historical buildings that can still be seen in the otherwise pleasant centre is the **Grote Kerk** on the Oude Markt.

In addition to this centre, with its theatres, concert halls and cinemas, Enschede has a number of museums, of which the **Rijksmuseum Twenthe** should not be missed. The exhibits here range from manuscripts and paintings to modern, primarily Dutch, art.

Miracle Planet Boulevard, just outside town, offers non-stop entertainment in three mega-complexes.

🏛 Rijksmuseum Twenthe
Lasondersingel 129–131.
Tel 053-4358675. ☐ 11am–5pm Tue–Sun & hols. ● 1 Jan, 25 Dec.
🎨 🍴 🏠

Ootmarsum ⓬

Road map E3. 🏠 4,000. 🚌 64 from Almelo. 🛈 Markt 9 (0541-291214).
🚢 Thu am.

The village of Ootmarsum is one of the prettiest places in all of Holland. On the map since 900, Ootmarsum was granted its town charter in 1300. It has grown little since then; indeed, not much has changed here at all, making it

Stained glass in the 13th-century Catholic church at Ootmarsum

quite suitable for an open-air museum. Places of interest not to be missed are the Roman Catholic church, the only Westphalian hall-type church in Holland, built between 1200 and 1300. Here you can see the burial vaults and some impressive works of art. The rococo former town hall dates from 1778 and is now the VVV (tourist) office. There are also some interesting old draw-wells.

The **Openluchtmuseum Los Hoes** (Los Hoes open-air museum) showing what life was once like in Twente is also worth a visit.

🏛 Openluchtmuseum Los Hoes
Smithuisstraat 2. *Tel* 0541-293099.
☐ 10am–5pm daily (Dec–Jan: weekends only & Christmas hols). 🎨

Environs
Nature lovers will find plenty to do in the countryside surrounding Ootmarsum, which is located in one of the finest parts of Twente. The landscape offers an ever-changing scenery, with its rushing brooks, old watermills, woodland paths, prehistoric tumuli and Saxon farmhouses.

The viewing point on the Kuiperberg affords a stunning vista over the entire Twente region and provides the place names of the various sights.

The half-timbered Stiepelhoes in Ootmarsum, dating from 1658

FLEVOLAND

*F*levoland is Holland's youngest province, created by the Dutch entirely out of water, sandbanks and mud flats, thanks to massive reclamation schemes which created dykes and polders (reclaimed land, sometimes below sea level) from the turbulent Zuiderzee following an Act of Parliament in 1918.

This act provided funds for damming the northeastern part of the Zuiderzee and reclaiming the land behind the dykes. When the Afsluitdijk was completed in 1932, drainage works on the Noordoostpolder began and, with the seawater pumped out, the islands of Urk and Schokland and the town of Emmeloord became by 1942 a part of the mainland. Further schemes to the south and southwest were completed in 1957 and 1968 respectively, and since 1986 these three new polders have officially constituted the Netherlands' newest province, named Flevoland after "Flevo Lacus", the original name given to the Zuiderzee by the Roman historian Pliny nearly 2,000 years ago.

Initially, the idea had been to use the polders as farmland only, with the occasional village here and there.

However, as the built-up areas around Amsterdam and Utrecht became increasingly congested, new towns have grown up. The conurbation around Almere, with its highly impressive modern architecture, is among these. Other towns include Lelystad, with its several modern museums, and Dronten, where the Walibi World amusement park proves an irresistible magnet for younger visitors. Lelystad, whose name honours Cornelius Lely, the genius behind the massive land creation project (see p326), is the provincial capital. There are many other attractions for visitors to this compact and attractive region, including a number of fascinating museums featuring subjects as varied as archaeology and World War II.

The exotic spoonbill, an icon of the new wildlife in Flevoland

◁ Beekeepers at work in the rape fields of Flevoland, which are gradually disappearing

Exploring Flevoland

Urk
villager

The Noordoostpolder, which is the northern-most part of Flevoland, is distinguished by its polder landscape and its rich farmland, fruit orchards and bulb fields. There are also many young forests, which are good for walking in. Apart from the main town of Emmeloord, there are a number of small new villages, as well as the old fishing village of Urk. Oostelijk (eastern) and Zuidelijk (southern) Flevoland are relatively sparsely populated and have a lot of greenery. Between Almere, the largest town of Flevoland, characterized by modern architecture, and Lelystad, the provincial capital, there stretches a fine nature reserve known as the Oostvaardersplassen, or Oostvaarder lakes. The coastal lakes have inviting sand beaches and marinas.

The picturesque harbour of the fishing village of Urk

SIGHTS AT A GLANCE

Almere **12**
Bataviawerf **8**
Dronten **6**
Emmeloord **1**
Knardijk **10**
Lelystad **7**
Nagele **3**

Oostvaardersplassen **9**
Schokland **4**
Swifterbant **5**
Urk **2**
Zeewolde **11**

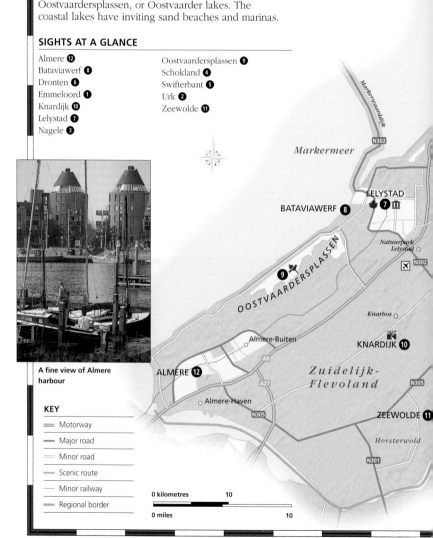

Markermeer

BATAVIAWERF **8**

LELYSTAD **7**

Natuurpark Lelystad

OOSTVAARDERSPLASSEN **9**

Knarbos

KNARDIJK **10**

Almere-Buiten

ALMERE **12**

Zuidelijk-Flevoland

A fine view of Almere harbour

Almere-Haven

ZEEWOLDE **11**

Horsterwold

KEY

═══ Motorway

─── Major road

═══ Minor road

─── Scenic route

─── Minor railway

═══ Regional border

0 kilometres   10

0 miles   10

The replica of the *Batavia* at Lelystad

The Poldertoren in the small town of Emmeloord

The Ketelbrug bridge over the Ketelmeer

SEE ALSO

• *Where to Stay* pp402–403

• *Where to Eat* p421

GETTING AROUND

Flevoland has an efficient road network. All the municipalities in the region are easily accessible by car or bus. Interliner coaches cover both the Lelystad-Emmeloord and Lelystad-Dronten routes. Almere and Lelystad can also be reached by train, and a ferry links Urk and Enkhuizen during July and August. The flat expansive landscape of Flevoland also makes exploration by bicycle ideal. Numerous excellent cycling and hiking routes have been laid out throughout the province.

Flat farmland of Flevoland

Emmeloord ❶

Road map D2. Noordoostpolder.
🏠 24,800. 🚌 ℹ️ De Deel 25a
(0527-612000). 🛒 Thu am.

When the oldest polder in
Flevoland was drained,
Emmeloord sprang up like a
pioneer settlement. Over the
years it has developed into a
pleasant town. It is the main
town of the municipality of
Noordoostpolder, encompass-
ing *groendorps* (green villages).
Emmeloord is known mainly
for its octagonal **Poldertoren**
built in 1959, a 65-m (214-ft)
water tower topped by a 5-m
(16-ft) wind vane in the shape
of an old merchant ship. The
carillon, one of Holland's biggest, has 48 chimes. The viewing platform (open in summer)
offers a view of the polder.

Urk ❷

Road map C3. 🏠 16,500. ⛴ from
Enkhuizen, summer only. 🚌 ℹ️ Wijk
2–3 (0527-684040). 🛒 Sat am.

The fishing village of Urk
attracts many tourists with its
sloping alleys and charming
fishermen's cottages. Until its
land was reclaimed, Urk was
an island. Some 1,000 years
ago, the island was much larger
and had five villages; flooding
gradually reduced its size. The
townspeople moved to the
highest point on the island,

a hill of boulder clay. Even
after the polder was drained,
Urk managed to retain its
character in the middle of the
new land surrounding it. Some
of the older residents wear
the traditional dress, though
this is increasingly rare.

Beside the old village centre
the fishing quay, the lighthouse (1844) and the little
church (1786) are worth a
look. In the **Museum Het
Oude Raadhuis**, situated in
the old town hall, you can
find out about the history of
Urk and the fishing industry.

🏛 **Museum Het Oude
Raadhuis**
Wijk 2–3. **Tel** 0527-683262.
🕙 Apr–Sep: 10am–5pm Mon–Sat;
spring & autumn hols: 2–5pm.
🖼 ♿ 🎁 📷 by appointment.

Nagele ❸

Road map D3. 🏠 1,900. 🚌
ℹ️ Emmeloord, (0527-612000).

This village was built in
the 1950s to designs by the
De Acht en de Opbouw, a
group of architects which
included the famous Rietveld,
Van Eyck and van Eesteren,
who represented the Nieuwe
Bouwen movement. The
flat-roofed residential buildings surround a park-like
centre with shops, schools
and churches. The village
is surrounded by a belt of

Schokland before land reclamation

Schokland after reclamation

woodland. **Museum Nagele**
provides information about
the village's architecture.

🏛 **Museum Nagele**
Ring 23. **Tel** 0527-653077.
🕙 1–5pm Thu–Sun. 🌑 1 Jan,
25, 26 & 31 Dec. 🖼 ♿ 🎁 🍴

Schokland ❹

Road map C3. 🚌 ℹ️ see museum.

Like Urk, Schokland was
once an island. Archaeological
finds show that the site was
inhabited in prehistoric times.
In 1859, the population had
to abandon the island
because it was disappearing
into the sea. Today the "island"
is a hill on the landscape.
Museum Schokland, consisting of the restored church and
reconstructions of fishermen's
cottages, is dedicated to
geology and local history
from the Ice Age up until the
land was reclaimed. At the
south end of the village are
the ruins of a medieval
church. In the Schokkerbos
forest to the west is the
Gesteentetuin, gardens
featuring Ice Age boulders.

🏛 **Museum Schokland**
Middelbuurt 3, Ens. **Tel** 0527-251396.
🕙 Apr–Oct: 11am–5pm Tue–Sun; Jul
& Aug: daily; Nov–Mar: Fri–Sun.
🌑 1 Jan, 25 Dec. 🖼 ♿ 🍴

CORNELIS LELY (1854–1929)

Flevoland has come into existence thanks largely to the
plans and ambitions of civil engineer Cornelis Lely. From
1885 to 1891, as a member of the Zuiderzee-
vereniging (Zuiderzee Society), he was
responsible for studying the possibility of
closing off and draining the Zuiderzee.
His appointment as minister for trade and
industry in 1891 gave him the chance to
convince the government and parliament
how necessary it was to tame the unpredictable Zuiderzee, though it was not
until his third term in office (1913–18) that
the law for retaining and draining the
Zuiderzee was finally passed. Apart from
the Zuiderzee projects, Lely worked to
improve the Noorzeekanaal. From 1902 to
1905 he was governor of Suriname. He
died in 1929, but his name lives on in
that of Flevoland's capital, Lelystad.

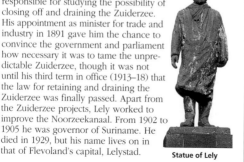

Statue of Lely

Swifterbant ❺

Road map C3. 🏘 6,500. 🚌 ⓘ
Dronten (0321-318687). 🛒 Tue pm.

This young village is known
primarily to archaeologists
for the flint tools and earthenware of the **Swifterbant
culture** that were unearthed
here. The Swifterbant culture
inhabited the region in the
4th millennium BC.
   In spring, flower enthusiasts
can enjoy the riot of vivid
colour in the nearby bulbfields.

Environs
The Swifterbos forest nearby
is an excellent spot for recreation. The Ketelbos is a resting
place for migrant bird species.

Dronten ❻

Road map D3. 🏘 22,500. 🚌
ⓘ De Rede 80–82 (0321-318687).
🛒 Wed.

Dronten is well-endowed
with greenery and recreation
facilities. The Meerpaal Complex here combines a theatre,
cinema and events venue.
Outside the town hall stands
the Airgunnersmonument,
honouring airmen who lost
their lives in World War II.

Environs
Around Dronten are many
pretty woods and
recreation areas that offer
opportunities for walking
and cycling.

Lelystad ❼

Road map C3. 🏘 67,000. 🚌 🚉
ⓘ Stadhuisplein 2 (0320-278222).
🛒 Sat (Gordiaan), Tue (Lelycentre).

Lelystad, a provincial capital,
has a modern centre with a
number of outstanding buildings. The cylindrical **Nieuw
Land Erfgoedcentrum** has
models and audio-visual materials illustrating the history of
the fight against the sea, of
the land reclamation and of
the culture of the Zuiderzee.
   On the Airship Plaza is the
Zepallon museum of balloon
and airship flight. East of the
town is **Natuurpark Lelystad**,
where there are animals such
as bison and Przewalski horses.
As well as cycling and pedestrian paths, the park boasts a
shipwreck and a reconstructed
prehistoric village. The
**Nationaal Luchtvaart Thema-
park Aviodrome**, at Lelystad
airport, has historic aircraft, a
cinema and a reconstruction
of Schiphol Station from 1928.

🏛 **Nieuw Land
Erfgoedcentrum**
Oostvaardersdijk 01–13. **Tel** 0320-
260799. ⦿ 10am–5pm Tue–Fri
(Mon in Jul & Aug); 11:30am–5pm
Sat & Sun. ⦿ 1 Jan, 25 Dec. 📷
🅿 🛒 🍴 ♿

🍂 **Natuurpark Lelystad**
Vlotgrasweg 11. **Tel** 0320-286111. ⦿
sunrise–sunset daily. 🎫 by appt. 🍴 🅿

🍂 **Nationaal Luchtvaart
Themapark Aviodrome**
Pelikaanweg 50, Luchthaven Lelystad.
Tel 0900-2846376. ⦿ 10am–5pm
Tue–Sun (Mon in Jul, Aug & school
hols). ⦿ 25 Dec. 📷 🍴 🅿 ♿

Bataviawerf ❽

Road map C3. Oostvaardersdijk 01–09,
Lelystad. **Tel** 0320-261409.
⦿ 10am–5pm daily. ⦿ 1 Jan,
25 Dec. 📷 🎫 🛒 🏢
www.bataviawerf.nl

From 1985 to 1995, a replica
of the Dutch East India
Company ship Batavia (see
p258) was built at the Batavia-
werf on the Oostvaardersdiep.
The shipyard's current project
is a replica of the 17th-century
De Zeven Provinciën. Visit the
sailmaking and woodcarving
workshops. The entry ticket is
also valid for **NISA**, the Netherlands Institute for Submarine
Archaeology, with its fascinating display on shipwrecks.

The *Batavia*, which went down off the Australian coast in 1629 with 341 people on board

Observation huts on the Oostvaardersplassen lakes, situated amidst abundant bird populations

Oostvaarders-plassen ❾

Road map C3. ⓘ *Staatsbosbeheer, Bezoekerscentrum, Kitsweg 1, Lelystad (0320-2545.85).*

Between Lelystad and Almere is internationally renowned marshland covering 6,000 ha (14,825 acres). The land was originally earmarked as an industrial area. When Zuidelijk Flevoland was drained, the low-lying area beyond the Oostvaardersdijk remained a wetland. Plans to drain this area were put forward but were ultimately dismissed because the place had by this time become an area of unique natural interest.

The nature reserve includes lakes, mud flats, marshes, willow thickets and grasslands and serves as a port of call for hundreds of species of birds that come here to forage and feed. Indeed, some birds which have been unable to settle elsewhere have found their place here, including the hen harrier (the symbol of Flevoland) and the great cormorant. Other birds seen here include the great bittern, the Eurasian spoonbill, heron, rail and, more recently, the sacred ibis. The many grey geese that forage here, along with the wild cattle, wild horses and red deer that occur here, have helped the region's vegetation to proliferate.

The marshland is largely off-limits to visitors, but some fine views are to be had from the edge of the swamp, the Oost-vaardersdijk and the Knardijk.

Additionally, the region of **De Driehoek** has a 5-km (3-mile) walking route, open sunrise to sunset. The route starts at the information centre and passes by natural woodland, lakes and observation huts.

Knardijk ❿

Road map C3. ⓘ *Staatsbosbeheer (0320-254585).*

The Knardijk marks the border between Oostelijk and Zuidelijk Flevoland (eastern and southern Flevoland). It was built in the 1950s between the island of Lelystad-Haven and Harderwijk to enable the entire area to be placed within a polder at one time. After Oostelijk Flevoland had been dried out, it formed the southwestern ring dyke of this

Hen harrier

polder. The Knardijk is of great interest to nature lovers, as it offers a fine view of the Oostvaardersplassen lakes. A great many birds live at the foot of the dyke, including hen harriers and marsh harriers. Two bird-watching huts can also be reached along the dyke. The dyke leads in a southeasterly direction along the nature reserve known as the **Wilgenreservaat**, which has evolved naturally into a mixture of woodland and clearings. Many songbirds, woodland birds, and birds of prey are to be found here, as are deer, foxes, polecats and ermines. Part of the reserve can be seen via a circular path. Nearby is the Knarbos forest, also boasting a variety of flora and fauna. A 6-km (4-mile) hiking route has been marked out.

The Knardijk, looking out over a variegated natural landscape

Zeewolde ⓫

Road map C3. 🏘 19,400. 🚌
🛈 Raadhuisstraat 15 (036-
5221405). 🛒 Fri.

With its picturesque marina,
this village on the Wolderwijd
coastal lake is a popular
recreational spot. Zeewolde is
the youngest village in Flevoland, having officially become
a municipality in 1984. Its
youth is evident from the
imaginative architecture, particularly that of the town hall,
library and church. An enjoyable 7-km (4-mile) walking
route has been laid out in and
around Zeewolde, with
landscape art along the way
(for information, call De
Verbeelding, 036-5227037).

Environs
South of Zeewolde is the
Horsterwold, which is the
largest deciduous forest in
Western Europe.

Almere ⓬

Road map C3. 🏘 176,000. 🚌 🚆
🛈 Stadhuispromenade 1 (036-
5485041). 🛒 Wed & Sat (Almere-
Stad), Thu (Almere-Buiten), Fri
(Almere-Haven).

Almere is Holland's fastest-
growing town. Its name
recalls the 8th-century name

Almere, a laboratory for modern architects

for the Zuiderzee. The earliest
signs of habitation date from
65 centuries earlier. Almere
today consists of three centres: Almere-Stad, which is
undergoing major renovation
and is where all the facilities
are; Almere-Buiten, which is a
green suburb; and Almere-
Haven, with its lovely marina.
If you are interested in modern and unusual architecture,
the districts to visit are
Muziewijk, Filmwijk and
Stedenwijk in Almere-Stad,
and the colourful Regenboog-
buurt (rainbow neighbour-
hood) in Almere-Buiten. Also
worth a visit are the town
hall, and the Almeers Centrum Hedendaagse Kunst
ACHK – De Paviljoens (Almere

centre for modern art), with
works by late 20th-century
Dutch and foreign artists.

Environs
Near Almere are many recreation areas and nature reserves:
the Weerwater; the Leegwater-
plas lake; the Beginbos forest,
with walking, cycling and
bridleways; the Buitenhout;
the Kromslootpark, with its
polder vegetation; the
lakes of Noorderplassen;
Lepelaarsplassen, where rare
wading birds occur; and the
Oostvaardersplassen.

ACHK – De Paviljoens
Odeonstraat 3–5. **Tel** 036-5450400.
🕐 noon–5pm Wed–Sun (to 9pm
Thu & Fri). 🔴 1 Jan, 25 Dec. 🈺 🖼

LANDSCAPE ART
In the countryside around Flevoland
you will come across the odd works of
"landscape art". These are associated
with various features of the landscape.
East of Almere-Haven, for instance, is
the *Groene Kathedraal (Green Cathedral)*
(top photo), designed by Marinus Boezem
and consisting of 178 Lombardy poplars
planted to re-create the outline and pillars
of Reims Cathedral. The *Observatorium
Robert Morris* (bottom photo) consists of
two round earth embankments, with
three notches in them from which the
sunrise can be observed when the
seasons change. On the Ketelmeerdijk,
you will find Cyriel Lixenberg's *Wachters
op de Dijk (Watchmen on the Dike)*,
consisting of a circle, a triangle and a
square. Piet Slegers' *Aardzee (Earth Sea)*,
situated between Zeewolde and Lelystad,
consists of a series of elongated artificial
ridges resembling waves.

GELDERLAND

*G*elderland is The Netherland's largest province. Its name derives from the 11th-century county of Gelre, which was linked with the town of Geldern, just over the border in Germany. The town was the fiefdom of Gerard de Rossige, whose grandson Gerard II of Wassenberg pronounced himself Count of Gelre in 1104.

Succeeding counts skilfully expanded their territory to include the Veluwe region to the north, the Betuwe in the southwest and the county of Zutphen *(see p341)*. When in 1248 the imperial town of Nijmegen was annexed, Gelre became a power to be reckoned with. A number of its towns joined the Hanseatic League, and in 1339 the county was promoted to a duchy by the German emperor. The increasing power of the Burgundians threatened the independence of the Gelders, eventually leading to the duke having to cede the territory in 1543 to Charles V. Gelderland thus became part of the Netherlands.

This colourful history is manifest today in the number of medieval buildings, churches, castles and fortified towns that welcome visitors throughout the province. In more recent times, the region, and especially the strategically located towns of Arnhem and Nijmegen, saw heavy fighting towards the end of World War II. The heroic action at Arnhem is remembered in the town's Airborne Museum, while the museum in Nijmegen recalls this town's long history from pre-Roman times to the tyranny of the Holy Roman Empire.

While visitors can enjoy many modern attractions, perhaps Gelderland's greatest asset is its contrasting natural scenery, which ranges from heaths and woodlands in the north to the beautiful Betuwe river valley and the pretty agricultural region of the Achterhoek.

A 17th-century granary near Winterswijk

◁ The mighty Waal, one of Holland's primary waterways

Exploring Gelderland

Gelderland is made up of three distinct regions. In the north is the Veluwe, an extensive natural area of woodland, heaths and large tracts of drifting sand, where those looking for peaceful natural surroundings can find exactly that. To the east is the Achterhoek. This region, too, is rich in natural beauty but has a completely different character: it consists of small fields with wooden fences, old farms, stately homes and castles. In the southwest of the province, between the Rhine, the Maas and the Waal rivers, is the river-valley region with the Betuwe. This area is distinguished by its many small dykes and river banks, which offer ample opportunities for cycling and walking.

The dolphinarium in Harderwijk

SIGHTS AT A GLANCE

Apeldoorn **2**
Arnhem **12**
Barneveld **8**
Bronkhorst **14**
Buren **26**
Culemborg **25**
Doesburg **20**
Elburg **4**
Gelderse Poort **22**
Groesbeek **23**
Harderwijk **6**
Hattem **3**
's-Heerenberg **18**
Kröller-Müller Museum pp338–9 **10**

Lochem **16**
Montferland **19**
Nationaal Park De Hoge Veluwe **11**
Nijkerk **7**
Nijmegen pp342–3 **21**
Nunspeet **5**
Paleis Het Loo pp334–5 **1**
Tiel **24**
Vorden **15**
Wageningen **9**
Winterswijk **17**
Zaltbommel **27**
Zutphen **13**

ELBURG **4**

Veluwemeer

NUNSPEET **5**

HARDERWIJK **6**

Ermelo   N310

N302   Elspeet

A28   Putten

7 NIJKERK   N303   N344

Voorthuizen

Hoevelaken

BARNEVELD **8**   N312

KRÖLLER-MÜLLER MUSEUM
Lunteren   Otterlo   **10**   **11**

Scherpenzeel   A30   NATIONAAL PARK DE HOGE VELUWE
          Ede   N224

Bennekom   Renkum

WAGENINGEN **9**

Lek   Maurik   Neder Rijn   A50

CULEMBORG **25**   N320   N320   Kesteren   Zetten   Elst

          A2   BUREN **26**   A15

Asperen   Geldermalsen   **24** TIEL   Druten   Waal

Brakel   Waal   Beneden-Leeuwen   Beuningen   A32

ZALTBOMMEL **27**   Bergse Maas   NIJMEGEN **21**

          A2   Megen   Wijchen

Ammerzoden   Kerkdriel   A50   Malden

          Grave

0 kilometres   10

0 miles   10

The majestic red deer – king of the Veluwe

GETTING AROUND

Gelderland has an excellent road network. A number of major motorways pass through the province, including the A2 and the A50. Public transport is also good. Many towns have rail links, and the bus will even take you deep into the Nationaal Park De Hoge Veluwe. The numerous bicycle tracks and footpaths allow the province to be conveniently explored either on foot or by bicycle. Cycling routes of varying lengths are well marked, and there are several walking routes across the province, including the very scenic Maarten van Rossum route.

SEE ALSO

- **Where to Stay** p403
- **Where to Eat** pp421–2

The Veluwe, characterized by large sandy areas

HATTEM ❸
Wezep
A28
A50
Heerde
Epe
Vaassen

🏛 PALEIS HET LOO ❶
❷ 🏛 ✈
APELDOORN
A1
Gorssel
Laren
N345
N348
Voorst
ZUTPHEN ❶❸
❶❻ LOCHEM
Neede
N346
N315
Eerbeek
Borculo
Eibergen
N348
ℹ🏠
❶❺ VORDEN
Ruurlo
N18
❶❹ BRONKHORST
GELDERLAND
N316
N319
Groenlo
Dieren
N314
Hengelo
Rheden
Zelhem
Lievelde
N319
Velp
❷⓪ DOESBURG
N330
Lichtenvoorde
WINTERSWIJK
⓬ ARNHEM
IJssel
N317
❶❼
✈🌳🏛
Doetinchem
Duiven
A12
Didam
A18
Varsseveld
N318
Zevenaar
MONTFERLAND
Aalten
Beek ❶❾
Terborg
Zeddam
N317
⓶⓶ GELDERSE
POORT
❶❽ 's-HEERENBERG
Dinxperlo
Millingen
aan den Rijn
Neder Rijn

⓶❸ GROESBEEK

Bronkhorst, the Netherlands' smallest town

KEY

━━━ Motorway
━━━ Major road
═══ Minor road
━━━ Scenic route
╍╍╍ Main railway
──── Minor railway
━━━ Regional border
▬▬▬ International border

Paleis Het Loo ●

The Stadholder William III built the elegant palace of Het Loo in 1692 as a hunting lodge. For generations, the Orange family used it as a summer residence. Its pomp and splendour have led to its being dubbed the "Versailles of the Netherlands". Its main architect was Jacob Roman (1640–1716); the interior and the gardens were designed by Daniel Marot (1661–1752). The severe Classical façade belies the ornate interior. After intensive restoration work was carried out, the palace is now open as a museum.

Coat of Arms *(1690) of William and Mary, future king and queen of England.*

★ Bedroom of the Stadholder William III *(1713)*
The wall coverings and draperies in this bedroom are of rich orange damask and purple silk.

William III's bedroom

King's Garden

Closet of the Stadholder William III
(1690)
The walls of William's private chamber are covered in scarlet damask. His paintings and Delftware are on display here.

Vintage Cars
This 1925 Bentley, nicknamed Minerva, was owned by Prince Hendrik, husband of Queen Wilhelmina. It is one of the royal family's many old cars and carriages on display in the stables.

STAR FEATURES

★ Dining Hall

★ The Formal Gardens

★ William III's Bedroom

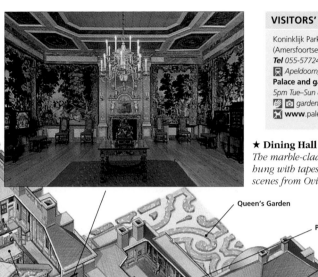

VISITORS' CHECKLIST

Koninklijk Park 1
(Amersfoortseweg), Apeldoorn.
Tel 055-5772400.
Apeldoorn, then bus.
Palace and gardens ☐ 10am–
5pm Tue–Sun & hols. ● 1 Jan.
🖼 📷 gardens only. 🎫 ⏸ ♿
✖ www.paleishetloo.nl

★ **Dining Hall** (1686)
*The marble-clad walls are
hung with tapestries depicting
scenes from Ovid's poems.*

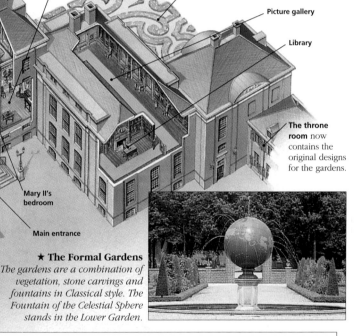

Queen's Garden

Picture gallery

Library

**The throne
room** now
contains the
original designs
for the gardens.

Mary II's
bedroom

Main entrance

★ **The Formal Gardens**
*The gardens are a combination of
vegetation, stone carvings and
fountains in Classical style. The
Fountain of the Celestial Sphere
stands in the Lower Garden.*

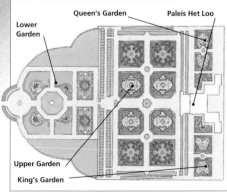

Queen's Garden   Paleis Het Loo

Lower
Garden

Upper Garden

King's Garden

Plan of the formal gardens

THE FORMAL GARDENS

When the formal gardens on the land
behind the palace were reconstructed, garden designers based their
designs on old illustrations, prints,
documents and plans. In the 18th
century, the original ornamental
gardens had been grassed over. In
1983, the intricate patterns of the
original gardens were restored and
planting began. The Het Loo gardens
are typical of a formal garden in the
17th century in which the ideal was
the harmonization of art and nature.

Stroking monkeys in Apenheul

Apeldoorn ❷

Road map D3. 🏛 152,000. 🚊 🚌
ℹ️ Deventerstraat 18 (055-5360200).

Apeldoorn is first mentioned as Appoldro in 793, and for centuries it was a small rural town in the Veluwe. This was changed by William III in 1692 when he built his hunting lodge Het Loo *(see pp334–5)* here. Many wealthy burghers followed William's example and set themselves up in Apeldoorn. The engaging **Historisch Museum Apeldoorn** gives a good overview of the area's history.

The **Apenheul** is a special zoo situated in the Berg en Bos nature park, where more than 30 species of monkeys run free among the visitors.

🏛 **Historisch Museum Apeldoorn**
Raadhuisplein 8. **Tel** 055-5788429.
⏰ 10am–5pm Tue–Sat, 1–5pm Sun & Tue. 🔵 public hols. 🈂️ ♿

🐾 **Apenheul**
JC Wilslaan 31. **Tel** 055-3575757.
⏰ Apr–Oct: 9:30am–5pm; Jun–Aug: 9:30am–6pm. 🈂️ ♿ ✖️

Hattem ❸

Road map D3. 🏛 12,000. 🚌
🔵 Wed pm.

The picturesque town of Hattem (first mentioned in 891) was granted its town charter as early as 1299, joining the Hanseatic League in the 15th century. Its monumental buildings, such as the house of Herman Willem Daendals, later the governor-general of the Dutch Indies,

bear witness to Hattem's eventful and prosperous past. St Andreaskerk (St Andrew's Church) is particularly remarkable, its oldest part dating from 1176. The **Anton Pieck Museum** is dedicated to the Dutch painter and graphic artist Anton Pieck (1895–1987); it has been merged with the **Voerman Museum**, which showcases the IJssel painter Jan Voerman and his son, who illustrated the famous Verkade card albums.

🏛 **Anton Pieck Museum/ Voerman Museum**
Achterstraat 46–48. **Tel** 038-4442192 & 038-4442897. ⏰ 10am–5pm Mon–Sat (Jul & Aug also open 1–5pm Sun). 🔵 1 Jan, 9–31 Jan, 30 Apr, 25 Dec; Nov–Apr: Mon. 🈂️ ♿

Elburg ❹

Road map D3. 🏛 21,500. 🚌
ℹ️ Jufferenstraat 8 (0525-681520).
🔵 Tue.

Elburg is the best-preserved fortified town on the former Zuiderzee. The prosperity of this old town is illustrated in the 14th-century St Nicolaaskerk, with its imposing Quellhorst organ. From the 38-m (125-ft) tower you can clearly make out the medieval rectangular street pattern.

Beside the **Vischpoort** (fish gate), a former defence tower, is the oldest ropemaker's workshop in Holland. Elburg was once much nearer to the coast, but in the late 14th century the flood-plagued town was moved well away from the sea. The interesting local history museum, the **Gemeentemuseum**, is in a 15th-century monastery. Also well worth a visit is the herb garden designed by Alfred Vogel.

🏛 **Gemeentemuseum Elburg**
Jufferenstraat 6–8. **Tel** 0525-681341.
⏰ 10am–5pm Tue–Fri, 2–5pm Mon. 🔵 Oct–Mar: Mon. 🈂️ 📷

Nunspeet ❺

Road map D3. 🏛 26,000. 🚊 🚌
ℹ️ Stationsplein 1 (0341-274747).
🔵 Thu am.

The Oudheidkamer at Nunspeet

Nunspeet is a good starting point from which to explore the nearby wooded countryside. Nunspeet's history comes to life in the **Oudheidkamer**. The nearby **Veluwemeer** lake is a popular watersports centre.

Environs
Some 15 km (9 miles) south of Nonspeet is the idyllic **Uddelermeer** lake, a remnant from the last ice age.

The pleasant market square of Hattem, with its 17th-century town hall

Harderwijk ❻

Road map C3. 🏠 38,500. 🚉 🚌
ℹ️ *Bleek 102 (0341-426666).*
📅 *Sat am.*

The eel-smoking frames may have disappeared from the streets, but the Zuiderzee town of Harderwijk is still a pleasant place to wander around. The town has an interesting history. In the 13th century it had become so important through fishing and the trade in dyes that in 1221 Count Otto II of Gelre granted it a town charter and ordered fortifications to be built. Remnants of the old fortifications are still intact in places, including the **Vischpoort** gate. Between 1647 and 1811 Harderwijk even had a university, from which the Swedish scholar Linnaeus graduated in 1735. Harderwijk's main attraction is the **Dolfinarium** *(see p434),* Europe's largest zoo for marine animals. Here visitors can stroke a ray or even a hound fish. The **Veluws Museum** of local history in the Donkerstraat is also worth visiting.

One of the favourite inhabitants of Harderwijk's Dolfinarium

Ray

Nijkerk ❼

Road map C3. 🏠 27,000. 🚉 🚌
ℹ️ *Barneveld (0342-420555).*
📅 *Fri pm.*

Nijkerk is a pleasant old town with many shops, restaurants and open-air cafés. The tobacco industry made the town rich in the 18th century. The Grote Kerk features the tomb of Kiliaen van Renselaer, one of the founders of New York. Just outside Nijkerk, on the Arkemheem polder, is the **Hertog Reijnout** *stoomgemaal,* a paddlewheeled steam pumpingstation, the last functioning one of its kind in Europe. Even today it is used to pump water out at times of flooding.

Environs
On the road to Putten is the **Oldenaller** estate with a castle from 1655. The cycling and walking area is open to the public. In **Putten** itself you can visit **De Gedachenisruimte** (hall of remembrance) in honour of the 600 men who in October 1944 were taken from the village to the Neuengamme concentration camp, from where only 50 returned alive.

🏭 **Stoomgemaal Hertog Reijnout**
Zeedijk 6. **Tel** 033-2457757. 🕐 *13 Apr–1 Oct: 10am–4pm Tue–Fri, 10am–1pm Sat.* 🔴 *Sun & Mon.* 📷 🎫

Barneveld ❽

Road map D4. 🏠 47,000. 🚉 🚌
ℹ️ *Langestraat 85a (0342-420555).*
📅 *Thu, Sat am.*

Barneveld owes its place in history books to one individual: **Jan van Schaffelaar**, commander-in-chief of the armed forces who on 16 July 1482 chose suicide rather than surrender and leapt from the tower of today's Nederlands Hervormde kerk (Reformed church). The **Nairac** museum of local history devotes considerable attention to this event. Today Barneveld is known as a poultry centre. The local **Pluimveemuseum** (poultry museum) shows how this industry has developed here.

🏛 **Pluimveemuseum**
Hessenweg 2a. **Tel** 0342-400073. 🕐 *Apr–Oct: 10am–5pm Tue–Sat.* 📷 🎫

Wageningen ❾

Road map C4. 🏠 33,000. 🚌
📅 *Wed am, Sat.*

Wageningen, at the southwestern edge of the Veluwe, is a pleasant town that is home to the local Landbouw Universiteit (agricultural university). The university's botanical gardens are open to the public. The town played an important role at the end of World War II; the Germans signed the official surrender in the **Hotel de Wereld**.

🏭 **Hotel De Wereld**
5 mei Plein. **Tel** 0317-482030. 🕐 *5 May–20 Aug & telephone bookings.*

The leap of Jan van Schaffelaar

Kröller-Müller Museum ⑩

This museum owes its existence above all to one person: Helene Kröller-Müller (1869–1939). In 1908, with the support of her industrialist husband Anton Kröller, Helene Kröller-Müller started to collect modern art. In 1935, she donated her entire collection to the state, and a special museum was built to house it. As well as its large collection of modern art, which includes 278 works by Vincent van Gogh, the museum is renowned for its unique sculpture garden, the Beeldentuin.

★ Beeldentuin
Jardin d'Email *by Jean Dubuffet is one of the most distinctive sculptures in the 25-ha (62-acre) sculpture garden. The garden provides a natural backdrop for works by sculptors such as Auguste Rodin, Henry Moore, Barbara Hepworth and Richard Serra.*

Mondriaan
In addition to old Flemish masters, the Kröller-Müller also has a major collection of 19th- and 20th-century French paintings and a dozen abstract paintings by Piet Mondriaan.

Entrance to the Beeldentuin

STAR FEATURES

★ Beeldentuin

★ Van Gogh Collection

Shop

Main entrance

Jachthuis St Hubertus
This hunting lodge, from 1914 to 1920 by the architect HP Berlage, was commissioned by the Kröller-Müller family.

The Studio Boat
Claude Monet's 1874 painting is in the 19th- and 20th-century French collection.

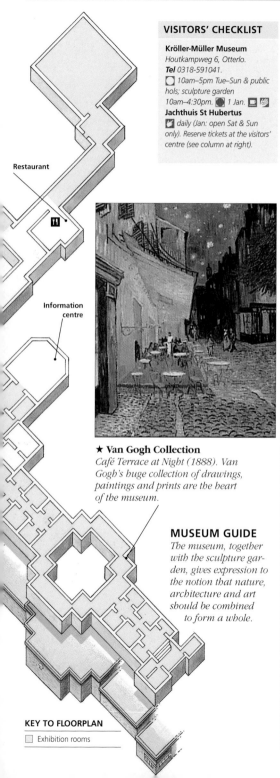

Restaurant

Information centre

★ **Van Gogh Collection**
Café Terrace at Night (1888). Van Gogh's huge collection of drawings, paintings and prints are the heart of the museum.

MUSEUM GUIDE
The museum, together with the sculpture garden, gives expression to the notion that nature, architecture and art should be combined to form a whole.

KEY TO FLOORPLAN

⬜ Exhibition rooms

Nationaal Park De Hoge Veluwe ⑪

Houtkampweg, Otterlo. **Tel** *0900-4643835.* 🚌 *Ede, Apeldoorn.* ⬜ *daily.*

Like the Kröller-Müller Museum, De Hoge Veluwe is also the result of a collector's ambition. The Kröller-Müllers collected plots of unused land in the Veluwe until they possessed one single tract of natural land. They even bought, in 1914, the public road between Otterlo and Hoenderlo. The 5,500 ha (13,600 acres) of woodland, marshland, heath and drifting sand now make up the largest nature reserve in Holland. The park is a treasure trove for all kinds of wildlife: rare birds, butterflies, plants and fungi. Red deer, roe deer and mouflon sheep still live freely here. If you are lucky, you may be able to catch a glimpse of a wild boar or a stag (they are very shy animals). Bicycle and pedestrian paths have been laid out everywhere, and at the visitors' centre you can borrow a white bicycle free of charge.

Underneath the visitors' centre is the world's first underground museum, the **Museonder**, giving visitors an idea of what life is like below the earth's surface. You can see the roots of a 140-year-old beech tree, experience a re-created earthquake and drink ancient Veluwe groundwater. The park has two restaurants: the Rijzenburg at the Schaarsbergen entrance and the De Koperen Kop café-restaurant located in the visitors' centre.

Underground museum

Arnhem ⑫

Road map D3. 🏙 136,500. 🚉 🚌
ℹ️ *Stationsplein 13 (0900-1122344).*
🏠 *Fri, Sat (Kerkplein).*

Arnhem, the capital of the province of Gelderland, was declared the centre of the regional government back in 1544 by Charles V. In September 1944, the town suffered serious damage in the Battle of Arnhem, one of the most notorious battles of World War II. All the townspeople were forced to abandon their homes and were not able to return until 1945, when the peace treaty was signed. Arnhem rose again from the ashes and is now sprucing itself up rapidly. The monuments that have been restored include the

Traditional houses in the Openluchtmuseum

Allied troops landing in Arnhem on 17 September 1944

Eusebiuskerk from 1560, which was almost totally destroyed during the war. The tower, at 93 m (305 ft), is now taller than it ever was and has a glass lift which affords visitors a stunning view of the Rhine valley. The **Duivelshuis**, built in 1545 by Maarten van Rossum *(see p345)*, is an outstanding example of Dutch Renaissance architecture. Arnhem is also known for its monumental parks, such as the **Sonsbeek**, a romantic landscape park, and **Zypendaal**. In **Bronbeek**, a home for ex-servicemen, there is an exhibition dedicated to the former

Dutch Indies. It is also worth allowing time for a visit to the **Burgers' Zoo** *(see p434)* and **Openluchtmuseum** (open-air museum), where the staff, dressed up in traditional costume, illustrate the rural way of life, handicrafts and industry in the Netherlands of the 19th century.

🏛 **Openluchtmuseum**
Schelmseweg 89. **Tel** 026-3576100.
⏰ *Apr–Oct: 10am–5pm daily.* 📷

Environs
The **Posbank** at Rheden is an example of the lateral moraine landscape of Veluwe.

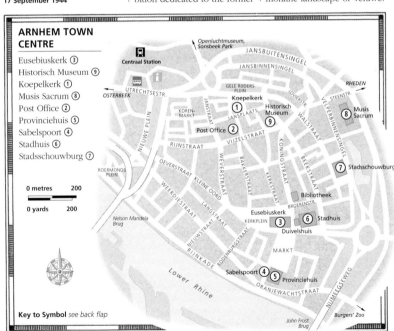

ARNHEM TOWN CENTRE

Eusebiuskerk ③
Historisch Museum ⑨
Koepelkerk ①
Musis Sacrum ⑧
Post Office ②
Provinciehuis ⑤
Sabelspoort ④
Stadhuis ⑥
Stadsschouwburg ⑦

0 metres   200
0 yards   200

Key to Symbol *see back flap*

Old book at St Walburgskerk library

Zutphen ⑬

Road map D4. 🏠 *36,000.* 🚉
ℹ️ *Stationsplein 39 (0575-519355).*
🛍️ *Thu morning, Sat.*

The hanseatic town of Zutphen is one of the Netherlands' first historical towns. One of the most distinctive features of the town, which is first mentioned in 1030, is the preserved medieval street layout. The main sights of Zutphen are the **St Walburgskerk**, the church square and the remains of the fortifications. They include the **Drogenapstoren** tower, which dates from 1444.

Zutphen has a number of interesting museums, including the informative **Stedelijk Museum** (local history museum) and the **Grafisch Museum** (graphic art museum), which is highly recommended.

Definitely worth visiting is the reading room of the unique **Librije** (library) of the St Walburgskerk. All of the 750 books in it date from before 1750 and include 80 incunabula printed before 1500. The books in the library, which was built in 1564, are chained to the desks. This is because it was a public library which

was unsupervised at the time. There are only four other libraries of this kind in the world: two are in England and two are in northern Italy.

> 🏛️ **St Walburgskerk and Librije**
> Kerkhof 3. **Tel** *0575-514178.*
> 🕐 *usually 1:30–4:30pm in spring and summer, but call first.* 🖼️

Bronkhorst ⑭

Road map D4. 🏠 *160.* 🚌 *52 from Zutphen train station.*

Bronkhorst's 160 inhabitants make it the smallest town in the Netherlands. The lords of Bronkhorst were granted a town charter in 1482. This very rural town, which once stood in the shadow of a castle (the castle no longer exists), never really flourished and has remained a village of farmsteads. It has many restored farmhouses, has no new buildings and prohibits motor vehicles, which means cars must be left in a car park outside the town. All that remains of the once-mighty castle of the Lords of Bronkhorst, which had fallen into disrepair by the 17th century, is the *kasteelheuvel* (castle hill).

The Lords of Bronkhorst, together with the noble Bergh, Baer and Wisch families, belonged to the *Baanderheren*. They were nobles who were allowed to wage war under their own flag, which was an old hereditary right.

Vorden ⑮

Road map D4. 🏠 *8,400.* 🚉
ℹ️ *Kerkstraat 1b (0575-553222).*
🛍️ *Fri morning.*

There is mention of a Huis Vorden (Vorden house) as early as 1208; the first record of the family dates from 1315. The **Nederlands-herformde kerk**, which dates from around 1300, is well worth a visit. The best-known figure to come from Vorden is the poet of Achterhoek **ACW Staring** (1767–1840), who lived in De Wildenborch castle from 1791 until his death.

Environs
Around Vorden are eight castles in very picturesque surroundings. A bicycle trip of the area, passing farms and country estates, is definitely worth the effort.

A water mill at Vorden

Lochem ⑯

Road map D3. 🏠 *19,000.* 🚉
ℹ️ *Tramstraat 4 (0573-251898).*
🛍️ *Wed morning.*

Lochem, one of the oldest villages in the Achterhoek to have its own parish church, was granted its town charter in 1233. During the 80 Years War, the town was often besieged. It was razed to the ground in 1615. Only the **Grote kerk**, also known as **St Gudulakerk**, with its 56-m (185-ft) steeple, was spared. This 14th-century hall-type church has fine murals from Catholic times (it is now a Reformed Church). The **Stadhuis** (town hall) across from the church dates from 1615.

Bronkhorst, a tiny picturesque village of farmsteads

For hotels and restaurants in this region see p403 and pp421–422

A charming old farmhouse near Winterswijk

Winterswijk ⑰

Road map E4. 🏠 28,000. 🚉
ℹ️ *Markt 17a (0543-512302).*
🅿️ *Wed morning, Sat.*
www.winterswijk.nl

The 20th century was not kind to the town of Winterswijk and the grand railway station bears witness to better times. There is now only a single railway track, although it is evident that in the past the rail traffic was much heavier. The **Museum Freriks** is pleasant with its exhibits relating to the textile industry that flourished here after World War II. The museum also has prints by Pieter Mondriaan Sr, whose famous painter son Piet spent his childhood in Winterswijk.

On the outskirts of the town lies a pleasant sculpture park, **De Beeldtuin**. Set out in the shady mature orchards of an old farm, there are also meadows and wooded areas. The works of art, by contemporary, mainly Dutch sculptors, are dotted all over the grounds, and represent just about every genre, from Pop Art to traditional to highly abstract. The park also hosts changing temporary exhibitions of 3D art.

🏛 **Museum Freriks**
Groenloseweg 86. *Tel 0543-533533.* 🕙 *10am–5pm Tue–Fri, 2–5pm Sat & Sun.* 📷

🏛 **De Beeldtuin**
Steggemansweg 1. 🕙 *phone ahead.*

's-Heerenberg ⑱

Road map D4. 🏠 18,000. 🚌 24.
ℹ️ *Hof van Bergh 8 (0314 632822).*
🅿️ *Thu.*

The old castle town of 's-Heerenberg and its surroundings are among the prettiest corners of Achterhoek. The little town, which was granted its charter in 1379, retains its historical centre, with buildings from the 15th and 16th centuries. **Huis Bergh** is one of Holland's finest castles and houses the art collection of the textile magnate JH van Heek.

🏛 **Huis Bergh**
ℹ️ *Hof Van Bergh 8 (0314-661281).*
🕙 *May–Dec: 12:30–4:30pm Tue–Sun.* ● *1 Jan, 24, 25 & 31 Dec.* 📷

Montferland ⑲

Road map D4. ℹ️ *Hof van Bergh 8, 's-Heerenberg (0314-632822).*

Montferland, one of the few hilly areas in the Netherlands, is exceptionally attractive. Apart from **'s-Heerenberg** *(see above)*, there is a number of other attractions, such as Zeddam, Beek and nature reserves where you can walk, cycle, swim or even dive. The natural spring in Beek, "het Peeske", and the historic farmhouses along the Langeboomseweg in Velthuizen are worth seeing.

Doesburg ⑳

Road map D4. 🏠 11,000.
🚌 27/29 Arnhem & 26/28 Dieren.
ℹ️ *Kerkstraat 6 (0313-479088).*
🅿️ *Wed am, Sat.*

Doesburg is a snug Hanseatic town on the IJssel. Granted its town charter in 1237, this small town's well-preserved old town centre has had listed status since 1974. Doesburg contains at least 150 national monuments, including a Late Gothic town hall, one of the earliest in Holland. The **Grote or Martinuskerk**, a Late Gothic basilica with a 97-m (320-ft) tower, is another of the town's noteworthy buildings, along with the local museum **De Roode Toren**.

🏛 **De Roode Toren**
Roggestraat 9–11–13.
Tel 0313-474265. 🕙 *10am–noon, 1:30–4:30pm Tue–Fri, 1:30–4:30pm Sat (Nov–Mar: pm only).*

Nijmegen ㉑

Road map D4. 🏠 152,000.
🚉 ℹ️ *Keizer Karelplein 32h (0900-1122344).* 🅿️ *Mon, Sat.*

Nijmegen is one of the oldest towns in Holland. Archaeological remains show

Huis Bergh, one of Holland's finest castles

that the Batavians were settled here even before the first millennium, while the Romans had a fort here from 12 BC. In AD 104, the emperor Trajan granted trading rights to a new settlement west of present-day Valkhof. The town's ancient name of Ulpia Noviomagus Batavorum is presumably also from this time.

Nijmegen owes its existence to its strategic position on the river Waal. A fort has stood here since early times, and even in World War II, the town was an important battle scene. The most important sights include the **Valkhof**, with its new **museum**, which stands on the spot where the fort of the Batavians, Roman engineering works and, later, one of Charlemagne's palaces stood. All that remains of the palace which was rebuilt by Frederick Barbarossa is the **St Maartenskapel** from 1155 and the **St Nicolaaskapel**, one of the earliest stone buildings in all of Holland. This chapel (part of which dates back to 1030) is a rare example of Byzantine architecture in northern Europe. Other noteworthy buildings include the St Stevenskerk, the construction of which began in 1254, the **Waag** (weigh house) and the **Kronenburgerpark**, with the remnants of fortifications (the Kruittoren tower).

A fascinating insight into the Dutch national obsession with all things two-wheeled can be found at **Velorama**, the bike museum. Spread over two floors, there are examples

Nijmegen's Waag, dating from 1612

from the entire history of cycling, from the earliest "hobby horse"-type bikes that date back to 1817. The upstairs room is devoted to the bicycle's modern incarnation, with beautifully shiny examples of racers, recumbants and everyday bikes. Star of the show, however, is the bicycle that belonged to Queen Wilhelmina in the 1940s and 1950s.

Nijmegen is perhaps best known for its annual four-day rambling meet, the Wandelvierdaagse, in which tens of thousands of ramblers take part. With its many cafés, the town also has a vibrant nightlife.

Each July, **de-Affaire**, a week-long festival of music, accompanies the **Vierdaagse** long-distance marches (*see box*). Events take place all over town, but many are focused around the Waalpark.

Featuring around 100 acts, international cutting-edge rock and pop bands play alongside DJs and world musicians. There are also workshops on such activities as Latin music and dancing.

🏛 **Museum Het Valkhof**
Kelfkensbos 59, Nijmegen.
Tel 024-3608805. ⬚ 10am–5pm Tue–Fri, noon–5pm Sat, Sun & public hols. ● 25 Dec. 🗺 ⬚ ⬚
🏛 **Velorama National Bicycle Museum**
Waalkade 107. *Tel* 024-3225851.
⬚ 10am–5pm Mon–Sat, 11am–5pm Sun. ● 1 Jan, 25 Dec.

Environs
Close to Nijmegen is the Ooypolder, a beautiful, relaxing oasis for nature lovers. Here you can cycle and walk.

Ruins of the Valkhof in Nijmegen

NIJMEGEN'S FOUR DAYS MARCHES

In mid-July thousands of people from all around the Netherlands (and beyond) descend on the city to take part in the annual De Vierdaagse, the Four Days Marches. This is a series of hikes in and around Nijmegen, divided into daily legs of 30 km (20 miles) to 50 km (30 miles). The walks began in 1909 as a military exercise for soldiers, who marched from Nijmegen's garrison to Breda's, where they participated in a sports tournament. In that year, 309 soldiers completed the 150 km route. After a few years, civilians began to join in, until the march became a highlight of the national sporting calendar. In recent years, the number of participants has topped 45,000. Those who complete the walk receive a commemorative medal.

Walkers tackling the Four Days Marches

Beavers introduced to the Gelderse Poort now thrive

Gelderse Poort ㉒

Road map D4. ⓘ *Arnhem (0900 1122344).*

At the point where the Rhine enters the Waal, the IJssel and the Neder-Rijn (Lower Rhine) is the Gelderse Poort. This is a protected area where the flora and fauna have been allowed to grow freely. At the heart of it is the Millingerwaard, where the currents are particularly strong and where, at high water, the surrounding area regularly floods. The river banks, woodlands and marshes provide ideal breeding grounds for endangered species of birds such as the corncrake and the penduline tit.

Gelderse Poort Visitors' Centre
Molenhoek 2, Herwen. **Tel** 0316-246 505. ⓘ Apr–Oct: 9am–5pm daily.

Groesbeek ㉓

Road map D4. 19,000. ⓘ Dorpsplein 1a (024-3977118).

Its hilly woodland surroundings make Groesbeek an attractive place for cyclists and hikers. The route of the four-day annual hike *(Wandelvierdaagse)* follows the Zevenheuvelenweg from Groesbeek to Berg and Dal, past the Canadian war cemetery. Groesbeek was subjected to heavy bombardment at the

end of World War II. The **Bevrijdingsmuseum** (liberation museum) illustrates the development of Operation Market Garden (1944) and Operation Veritable (1945), which brought about the final liberation of Holland. Groesbeek has two other popular museums: the **Bijbels Openluchtmuseum** and the **Afrika Museum**.

🏛 **Bevrijdingsmuseum 1944**
Wylerbaan 4. **Tel** 024-3974404. ⓘ 10am–5pm Mon–Sat, noon–5pm Sun & hols. ⓘ 25 Dec, 1 Jan. ⓘ ⓘ

Tiel ㉔

Road map C4. 36,500. ⓘ ⓘ De Zaak van de Staat Tolhuisstraat 30 (0900-63363888). ⓘ Mon pm, Sat.

Tiel, situated on the Waal, is an ancient town that flourished during the Middle Ages because of its strategic location on the trading routes to and from Cologne. One of the best-preserved monuments from this time is the **Ambtmanshuis**, dating back to 1525. The town also has the oldest elm tree in the country. The local history museum, **De Groote Sociëteit** on the Plein, is worth a visit. Tiel is the centre of fruit farming in the Betuwe region. On the second Saturday in September of each

THE GREAT RIVERS
The three great rivers – the Rhine, the Maas and the Waal – have made an important mark on the history and landscape of Gelderland. The fortified trading towns that grew on the banks of the rivers brought prosperity to the region; dykes were built to protect the land from flooding.

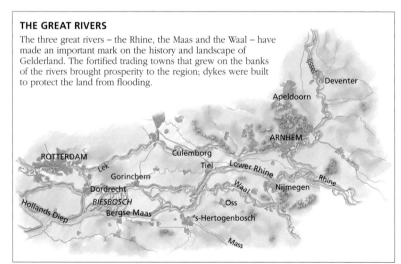

Dyke house on the Linge

year, it also becomes the centre of the **Fruitcorso** *(see p34)*, as a procession of floats decorated with fruit winds through the streets of the town. Tiel is also renowned for its tinsmith industry.

Environs
Asperen is a peaceful little town on the River Linge. On the Lingedijk is **Fort Asperen**, which is part of the Nieuwe Hollandse Waterlinie. Farther upstream is the little town of **Acquoy**, with its crooked 15th-century tower. A Lady Pisa is buried in the churchyard, but there is no connection to the Leaning Tower in Italy.

Culemborg ㉕

Road map C4. 👥 24,000. 🚃 🚌
🛈 Camping de Hogekuil, Achterweg 4 (0900-63363888). 🛒 Tue.

The old "Driestadje" (triple town) of Culemborg, formerly consisting of three walled towns, is picturesquely situated on the River Lek. It is a great place to wander around. If you enter the former fortress through the old Binnenpoort gate, you'll reach the Markt. Here is the Late Gothic Stadhuis (town hall), built by Flemish masterbuilder Rombout Keldermans for Vrouwe Elisabeth van Culemborg (1475–1555). Her estate was sufficient to finance the Elisabeth Weeshuis (1560), which is now operated as a historical museum.

Other well-preserved buildings in Culemborg are the Huize de Fonteyn in the Achterstraat and the house where Jan van Riebeeck, who founded Cape Town,

South Africa, was born. The large clock in the Grote Kerk was a gift from South Africa. Even today, the "papklok" bell, which is used to announce the closing of the town gates, is tolled each and every evening at 10 o'clock.

🏛 **Museum Elisabeth Weeshuis**
Herenstraat 29. **Tel** 0345-513912.
🕐 1–5pm Tue–Fri, 2–5pm Sat & Sun. 📷

Buren ㉖

Road map C4. 👥 1,800. 🚌
🛈 Markt 1 (0344-571922). 🛒 Fri.

On the main road between Tiel and Culemborg is Buren. This little town is known for its historic links with the House of Orange, and the entire town has been listed. One of the most beautiful houses is the **Koninklijk Weeshuis** (Royal Orphanage), which was built in 1613 by Maria of Orange. The late Gothic **Lambertuskerk** is also worth seeing.

Zaltbommel ㉗

Road map C4. 👥 11,000. 🚗 🚌 🛈
Markt 15 (0418-518177). 🛒 Tue, Sat.

Bommel, as its inhabitants say, is more than 1,000 years old. During the 80 Years War *(see p49)*, it was an important mainstay of the Republiek der Zeven Verenigde Nederlanden (Republic of the Seven United Netherlands). The town is surrounded by two well-preserved sets of walls, which have now been laid out as a park. Within the town walls, the first building worth mentioning is the 15th-century **St Maartenskerk**, whose low towers give the town its distinctive skyline. The interior of the church is worth a look.

Another worthwhile stop is at the house of the Gelderland commander-in-chief **Maarten van Rossum** (1478–1555), who is known for plundering The Hague in 1528. The house is now an intimate museum with a large collection of drawings and prints from the region; it also hosts visiting exhibitions.

🏛 **Maarten van Rossummuseum**
Nonnenstraat 5. **Tel** 0418-512617.
🕐 10am–12:30pm, 1:30–4:30pm Tue–Fri, 2–4:30pm Sat (Apr–Oct). 📷

The house of Maarten van Rossum in Nonnenstraat, Zaltbommel

SOUTHERN NETHERLANDS

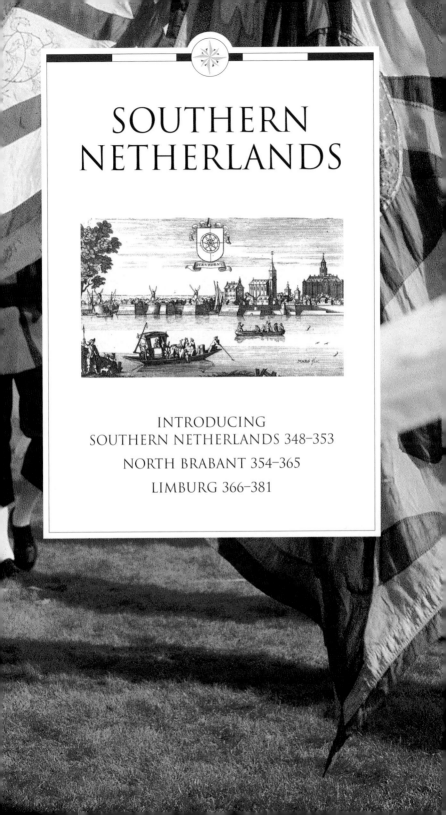

Exploring the Southern Netherlands

South of the great rivers lie the provinces of North Brabant and Limburg, whose ambience is quite different from that of the northern provinces. The atmosphere here is more easygoing, more sociable. Both eating and drinking well are held in high regard here. Visitors to the Southern Netherlands will also find cities with historical centres, such as Den Bosch, Breda, Thorn and Maastricht; the beautiful countryside of Kempen, Peel and the hills of Zuid Limburg; thriving modern towns; and peaceful rural villages.

The Gothic Church of Sint Jan (see pp360–61) *in Den Bosch was started in the late 14th century and completed in the 1500s.*

's-Hertogenbosch

Eindhoven

The construction of the Grote or Onze Lieve Vrouwe-kerk *(Church of Our Lady)* (see p362–3) *in Breda began in 1410. The church, which is finished in the Brabant Gothic style, has a 97-m (318-ft) tower, offering a stunning view over the town and the surrounding countryside.*

0 kilometres   20

0 miles   20

The Van Abbemuseum (see p364) *in Eindhoven has undergone extensive renovation. Architect Abel Cahen has preserved the old building while creating light-filled spaces in the angular, slanting new wing. A large collection of modern art, including video and other installations, is on display.*

The Kasteeltuinen, *the gardens of the 17th-century Castle Arcen (see p370), in the town of the same name on the river Maas, have a lovely rose garden, as well as subtropical gardens, a forest of Scots pines and a golf course.*

NORTH BRABANT *(pp354–365)*

The Bonnefantenmuseum (see pp374–5) *in Maastricht is housed in a striking building designed by the Italian architect Aldo Rossi. The collections of old works of art and contemporary international art are impressive.*

LIMBURG *(pp366–381)*

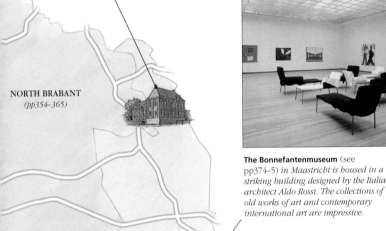

Maastricht

The route through the Heuvelland (see pp380–81) *passes among hills and dales and by meandering rivers, their banks dotted with old castles. Outstanding examples of these are the 17th-century Kasteel Eijsden and Kasteel Schaloen in Valkenburg.*

Catholicism and Devotion

One of the main reasons for the differences between Holland's southern and northern provinces is the marked presence of Catholicism in the south, even in these secular times. Religious imagery is a common sight here. The churches in the Brabant Gothic or Neo-Gothic style are decorated flamboyantly and many hold traditional processions throughout the year.

Crucifix

Religious images, *usually of the Madonna and Child, are a common roadside sight in Limburg. This one is set into the façade of a house in Mechelen.*

The Maria Magdalena Chapel *(1695) in Gemert is also known as the Spijkerkapelleke ("nail chapel") because people made offerings of nails here in the hopes of having their skin disorders cured. Every 22 July, which is the day of Mary Magdalene, an open-air mass is held here.*

Decorative carving

Candles abound around images of St Mary.

Detail from the retable *of the Holy Family in the Basilica of the Holy Sacrament in Meerssen, Limburg. It depicts Mary, Joseph and the infant Jesus fleeing from Egypt. This fine altar is richly decorated with scenes from the life of the Holy Family. The Holy Sacrament is honoured in the church. The hosts are kept in the Unique Sacramentstoren (sacrament tower) in the choir. The church itself is an example of Maasland Gothic and part of it (the nave and the choir) dates from as far back as the 14th century.*

This tomb *in the Late Romanesque/Early Gothic Onze-Lieve-Vrouwemunsterkerk (Minster Church of Our Lady) in Roermond dates from the 13th century. Inside the tomb lies Count Gerard van Gelre and his wife Margaretha van Brabant. At the time, Roermond was part of the duchy of Gelre.*

St Anna-te-Drieën *– the trinity of Anna, her daughter Mary and the infant Jesus – is a familiar image in religious art. This statue from Mechelen incorporates the town's coat of arms.*

Statue of St Mary in the Onder de Linden Chapel in Thorn (Limburg).

The Basiliek van de HH Agatha en Barbara *(Basilica of SS Agatha and Barbara) in Oudenbosch is a copy of St Peter and St John of the Laterans in Rome. The picture on the right shows the façade, based on St John of the Laterans. The church is richly decorated in the interior, though appearances are deceiving: what appears to be marble is actually painted wood.*

ONDER DE LINDEN CHAPEL IN THORN

The Onder de Linden Chapel, located just outside the town of Thorn in Limburg, was founded in 1673 by Clara Elisabeth van Manderscheidt-Blankenheim, who lies buried in the parish church of Thorn. This chapel, dedicated to St Mary, is opulently decorated with carvings and Baroque paintings depicting scenes of the life of the Mother of God. Shown in the picture on the left is the Onze-Lieve-Vrouwebeeld (statue of Our Lady). St Mary's Chapel is also called the Loretokapel, after the Holy House of Nazareth in the Italian town of Loreto, on which the earlier 17th-century part of the chapel is based.

The 15th-century tower *of the Michielskerk is all that remains of the North Brabant Sint-Michielsgestel. The medieval church was built in honour of the archangel Michael. The village, also named after the saint, grew up around the church. Neglect and the elements have meant that the church building itself has been levelled to the ground, but the solid tower has withstood the ages.*

The church of Rolduc, *a former canon's abbey at Kerkrade which today houses a Catholic middle school and a training school for priests, has a fine altar depicting the Lamb of God. The Lamb of God represents Christ, who was sacrificed in the same way as a lamb, in order to take away the sins of the world.*

Carnival

Carnival-goers

Every year in February, in the week before Ash Wednesday, carnival breaks out along the great rivers. While life goes on as usual in the north of the country, people in the south celebrate this old tradition, which is also honoured in other parts of the Catholic world. A festive mood abounds everywhere, with the best-known celebrations being held in Den Bosch, Bergen op Zoom and Maastricht. For days on end, there is drinking, singing and dancing all over Brabant and Limburg.

Carnavalsstokken (carnival rods) are brightly decorated. They are carried by the Prince of the Carnival when he passes through the streets on his float.

Music plays an important role at carnival time. Every year, the associations choose the official carnival anthem that will be played over and over again. The Zaate Herremienekes of Maastricht (pictured left) are among the better-known bands. Dozens of its members march through the streets blaring out enthusiastically; what their music may lack in elegance is made up for by their verve. On Shrove Tuesday they compete in the Herremienekes competition.

Although in high spirits, his question is profound (the sign on the pram reads "where are we going?")

CARNIVAL – PUTTING YOUR WORRIES ASIDE

The carnival season officially starts on 11 November – the eleventh of the eleventh – or "day of fools", when the Council of Eleven names the Prince of the Carnival. From then on, the municipalities are busy with preparations, and on the Sunday (in many places now on the Friday) before Ash Wednesday, the festivities begin. Wild celebrations are held throughout North Brabant and Limburg, and most public institutions are closed. Long processions with floats parade through the towns. People dress up festively: the more colourful and exuberant the costume, the better. "Dansmarietjes" (dancing girls) accompany the floats in their colourful costumes, and the mood everywhere is upbeat. All the merriment comes to an end after Shrove Tuesday, the climax of the carnival.

Refreshments both indoors and outdoors at carnival time

CARNIVAL FLOATS

At carnival time, long processions with extravagantly decorated floats wind their way through the main streets of towns and villages. Months of preparation often go into creating the floats, and secrecy prevails during their preparation. The decoration of the float is usually on an upbeat and amusing theme, but current events are sometimes illustrated in imaginative ways. When leading politicians are featured, they are more often than not caricatured mercilessly, and social ills are exposed, often using costumed participants in *tableaux vivants*.

A festive float

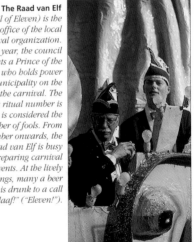

The Raad van Elf *(Council of Eleven) is the central office of the local carnival organization. Every year, the council appoints a Prince of the Carnival, who holds power in a municipality on the days of the carnival. The council's ritual number is 11, which is considered the number of fools. From 11 November onwards, the Raad van Elf is busy preparing carnival events. At the lively meetings, many a beer is drunk to a call of "Alaaf!" ("Eleven!").*

Prince Carnival's adjutant

Characteristic carnival cap with feather

Prince Carnival

Colourful fool

Silly clothes *are mandatory at carnival time. In earlier times it was customary to put on masks, whereas today the trend is to dress up in as unusual a way as possible. The northerners' belief that it is enough to put on a peasant's smock to be properly dressed is a misconception.*

NORTH BRABANT

The Netherland's second largest province is distinguished primarily by its natural beauty. In the south and southeast are the relatively high elevations of Kempen and the Peel; in the northwest, the watery Biesbosch. Here, arms of the Waal and Maas rivers converge through a wilderness of sandbanks.

North Brabant has been inhabited by humans since the earliest times. The Celts settled here in the 7th century BC and stayed for many centuries. They were defeated by Julius Caesar (see p43), who describes them as the "Belgae" in his writings. The Rhine became the northern frontier of the Roman Empire and Roman remains have been found in the area. When the Romans left, the Franks took charge of Toxandria, as the region was known in those days. Under Charlemagne (see p45), this region grew in importance as new towns expanded at points along trade routes, and in the 12th century became part of the Duchy of Brabant. The Dukes of Brabant, among them Godfried III and Henry I, expanded their territory and founded towns such as Breda and 's-Hertogenbosch. The Duchy flourished until the 16th century, when the 80 Years War left the south of Brabant under Spanish rule and the north under the rule of the Netherlands.

Although North Brabant has its fair share of commerce and industry, and Eindhoven is a major manufacturing centre, tourism has become increasingly important. The region's colourful history is evident from the medieval buildings and bastions in many of the towns, and the castles dotted around the countryside, with a range of fine exhibits in churches and museums. For younger visitors the highlight is the fairytale theme park De Efteling at Kaatsheuvel, northeast of Breda.

Het Grote Peel, an area of outstanding natural beauty in North Brabant

◁ The Binnen-Dieze in 's-Hertogenbosch, now fully restored and here straddled by houses

Exploring North Brabant

North Brabant's rich historic past and unspoiled countryside have given the province its unique character. The centres of 's-Hertogenbosch and Breda and the picturesque fortified towns of Heusden and Willemstad are of great historical interest. The beautiful natural areas of the Loonse and Drunense dunes, Peel, Kempen and Biesbosch areas provide opportunities for various tours. Van Abbemuseum in Eindhoven, De Wieber in Deurne and the many other museums in the region offer a great deal of cultural interest. De Efteling is one of Europe's best-known theme parks.

Shipping locks at the historical fortress town of Willemstad

SIGHTS AT A GLANCE

Bergen op Zoom ❼
Breda ❹
Deurne ⓬
Eindhoven ❽
Gemert ⓭
Heeze ❾
Helmond ⓫
's-Hertogenbosch
pp358–62 ❶

Heusden ❷
Nuenen ❿
Oudenbosch ❺
Tilburg ❸
Willemstad ❻

The Markiezenhof in Bergen op Zoom, dating from 1511

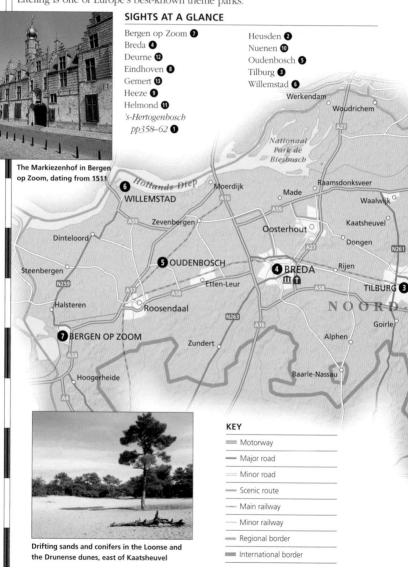

KEY

═══	Motorway
▬▬	Major road
═══	Minor road
▬▬	Scenic route
╼╼	Main railway
───	Minor railway
▬▬	Regional border
▬▬	International border

Drifting sands and conifers in the Loonse and the Drunense dunes, east of Kaatsheuvel

GETTING AROUND

North Brabant has an excellent transport infrastructure. All the larger towns, as well as many
smaller towns and villages, can be reached
easily by train. There is an extensive network
of long-distance coaches which will take you
to even the smallest village. The province can
be explored by car with great ease thanks to
its dense motorway network, which includes
the A2, and the A58, as well as to its many
good major roads. Areas of natural beauty such
as the Peel and Kempen are ideal countryside
for cycling.

The 14th-century Kasteel Heeswijk, rebuilt
numerous times during its lifetime

0 kilometres   10

0 miles   10

SEE ALSO

• *Where to Stay* p404

• *Where to Eat* p422

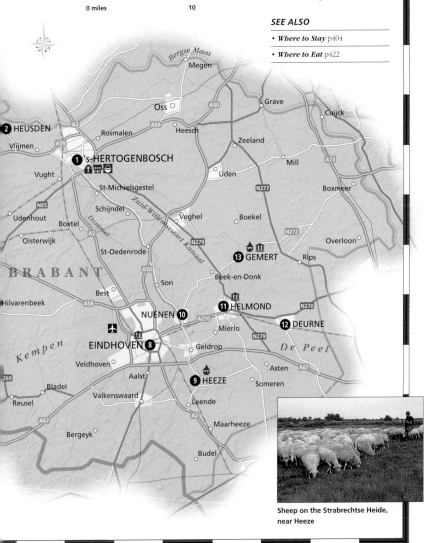

Sheep on the Strabrechtse Heide,
near Heeze

Street-by-Street: 's-Hertogenbosch ❶

In 1185, Henry I of Brabant founded the town of 's-Hertogenbosch. The strategically positioned town – usually called Den Bosch – grew rapidly. From the 16th century its prosperity waned, when the States General *(see p50)* ignored Brabant and chose to favour other regions. Its prestige rose again after 1815, when it became the capital of North Brabant. Today, it is a vibrant, lively town.

Carved figure of St Lucia

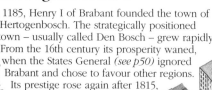

Stone Plaque with Swan
Such plaques are a common sight in the city centre.

Moriaan
The medieval building known as De Moriaan, with its stepped gable, is the town's oldest building. It now houses the town's tourist office.

★ Binnen-Dieze
The Binnen-Dieze, the city's inner canal, runs partly underground. It is possible to make a spectacular round trip along the restored town walls.

STAR SIGHTS

★ Binnen-Dieze

★ Noordbrabants Museum

★ Sint Jan

★ Sint Jan
The flying buttresses of the Sint Jan Church (see pp360–1) are decorated with a variety of figures.

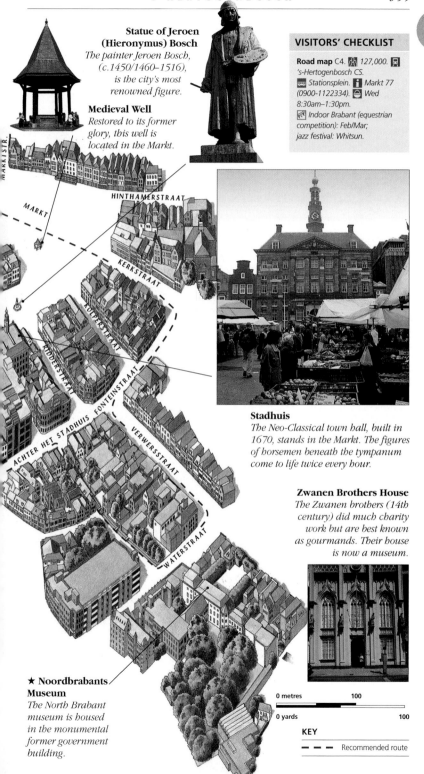

Statue of Jeroen (Hieronymus) Bosch
The painter Jeroen Bosch, (c.1450/1460–1516), is the city's most renowned figure.

Medieval Well
Restored to its former glory, this well is located in the Markt.

VISITORS' CHECKLIST

Road map C4. 🏠 127,000. 🚆
's-Hertogenbosch CS. 🚌
Stationsplein. 🛈 Markt 77
(0900-1122334). 🗓 Wed
8:30am–1:30pm.
🎠 Indoor Brabant (equestrian
competition): Feb/Mar;
jazz festival: Whitsun.

MARKT STR

MARKT

HINTHAMERSTRAAT

KERKSTRAAT

KOPPERSTRAAT

RIDDERSTRAAT

ACHTER HET STADHUIS FONTEINSTRAAT

VERWERSSTRAAT

WATERSTRAAT

Stadhuis
The Neo-Classical town hall, built in 1670, stands in the Markt. The figures of horsemen beneath the tympanum come to life twice every hour.

Zwanen Brothers House
The Zwanen brothers (14th century) did much charity work but are best known as gourmands. Their house is now a museum.

★ Noordbrabants Museum
The North Brabant museum is housed in the monumental former government building.

0 metres   100

0 yards   100

KEY

– – – Recommended route

Sint Jan

There was a church of Sint Jan (St John) in Den Bosch as early as the beginning of the 13th century, although nothing of the original Romanesque church exists today. The present-day Gothic church was built from the late 14th to the 16th century. The majestic cathedral survived the iconoclastic riots of 1566 *(see p52)* and a devastating fire in 1584. The damaged building is undergoing continuous restoration.

Statue of St Mary
The 13th-century miracle-working figure of the Zoete Lieve Vrouw of Den Bosch (Our Good Lady of Den Bosch) was for centuries kept in Brussels but was returned to Sint Jan in 1853.

★ Organ
The great organ (1617) was fully refurbished in 1985 and restored to its original state.

Gargoyles
The gargoyles are designed to channel rainwater pouring off the roof. Here, the drain pipes are encased by the head of mythical animals.

Flying buttresses are designed to strengthen the structure of the building. They are richly ornamented with saints, angels and other figures.

Baptistery
The baptismal font in the baptistery dates from 1492. The figures on the cover depict the baptism of Jesus by St John.

The ornamental south portal is dedicated to Saint John the Evangelist.

STAR SIGHTS

★ Organ

★ Sanctuary

★ Stained-Glass Windows

Antoniuskapel
*The Chapel of St Anthony
contains a spectacular Passion
altar made by a studio in
Antwerp. The Church of Sint
Jan managed to buy the retable
in 1901 for one guilder.*

VISITORS' CHECKLIST

Choorstraat 1. **Tel** 073-6130314.
🕐 8am–5pm daily. ✝ 9am &
12:30pm Mon–Fri, 9am & noon
Sat, 10:15am & noon Sun.
📷 book at Kringvrienden van
's-Hertogenbosch, Verweestraat
19a (073-6135098)
www.sint-jan.nl

Baldachin
*The revolving baldachin
in the middle of the
cathedral is ascribed to
Alart Duhameel. The
all-seeing eye looks
down from the vaults.*

**The stained-glass
window frame**
depicts the woman
and the dragon from
The Book of Revelation.

★ **Stained-Glass Windows**
*The Church of Sint Jan was
restored in Neo-Gothic style during
the 19th century. A great deal was
changed, including the lively and
colourful stained-glass windows.*

★ **Sanctuary**
*The sanctuary was built
from 1380 to 1425 by
Willem van Kessel. The
vaults are painted with
a variety of biblical
scenes, among them the
coronation of St Mary.*

The seven radiating chapels around
the choir form an elegant crown.

Exploring 's-Hertogenbosch

Along with a large number of historical buildings and interesting museums, the town of 's-Hertogenbosch offers a wide choice of fine restaurants. The excellent Noordbrabants Museum has an excellent exhibition of art from the Southern Netherlands from 1500 to the present. The most striking building in 's-Hertogenbosch is the majestic Gothic church of Sint Jan. The historic district of Uilenburg offers ample opportunities to while away the time with a drink or a bite to eat in a café.

Four putti (1731) by Walter Pompe, Noordbrabants Museum

The splendid church of Sint Jan *(see pp360–1)* is Den Bosch's crowning glory. In the Markt stand historical buildings such as **De Moriaan** (parts of which date back to the 12th century) and the town hall, dating from 1670. A statue of the great painter Hieronymus Bosch (c.1453–1516) stands between the two grand buildings. Born in 's-Hertogenbosch, Bosch spent most of his life here. In the town's historical district of Uilenburg, beyond the Markt, are plenty of good cafés and restaurants. The **Binnen-Dieze**, the city's inner canal, surfaces at this point; houses here stand directly in its water. Right by Sint Jan is the majestic **Zwanenbroedershuis** *(see p359)*, as well as the Museum Slager, which showcases paintings by the Slager family.

🏛 **Noordbrabants Museum**
Verwersstraat 41. **Tel** 073-6877877.
🕙 10am–5pm Tue–Fri, noon–5pm Sat, Sun & public hols. 🖼 🚻 ▯
The excellent Noordbrabants Museum displays art by renowned artists such as Pieter Brueghel and Teniers, as well as modern artists such as van Gogh, Mondriaan and Sluyters. The museum also features exhibits on the history of the province of North Brabant, from prehistoric times to the present.

Heusden ❷

Road map C4. 🏠 *42,000*. 🚌 ▯
Pelsestraat 17 (0416-662100). 🛒 *Thu.*

After a thorough refurbishment that started in 1968 and lasted for decades, the picturesque ancient fortified town of Heusden on the river Maas has been restored to its former glory. That Heusden fell victim to the redevelopment craze of the 1960s matters little. Walls, houses, moats, the **Veerpoort** (ferry gate) and the **Waterpoort** have all been restored in the old style. As advertising is banned in Heusden, it is easy to imagine that time has stood still here, save for the fact that motor vehicles are allowed into the fortress.

Tilburg ❸

Road map C5. 🏠 *190,000*. 🚇
🚌 ▯ *Nieuwlandstraat 34 (0900-2020815).* 🛒 *Tue–Sat.*

Tilburg, the sixth largest town in Holland, once had a flourishing textile industry. The interesting **Nederlands Textielmuseum**, which is housed in a former textile mill, illustrates the history of the country's textile industry and explains how textiles were produced.

The **kermis van Tilburg** (Tilburg fair), held each year at the end of July, is the biggest fair in Holland. The entire town puts all its energy into the event, and people come from far and near to attend.

🏛 **Nederlands Textielmuseum**
Goirkestraat 96. **Tel** 013-5494564.
🕙 10am–5pm Tue–Fri, noon–5pm Sat & Sun. 🌑 1 Jan, Carnival, 25 Dec.
🖼 🚻 🎥 by appointment. ▯ 🍴 ▮

Environs
Kaatsheuvel is home to **De Efteling**, the famous theme park where all kinds of fairytale personalities come to life *(see p435)*.

Breda ❹

Road map B5. 🏠 *157,000*. 🚇 🚌
▯ *Willemstraat 17–19 (0900-5222444).* 🛒 *Tue & Sat.*

The Old Bastion of Breda was built at the confluence of the rivers Aa and Mark around the **Kasteel van Breda**, where the Koninklijke Militaire Academie (royal military academy) is now established. Breda was granted its town charter in 1252.
    A walk through the old centre will take you to the **Grote kerk**, also known as the

Mills on the bastion of the old fortified town of Heusden

Onze Lieve Vrouwe Kerk (Church of Our Lady). It is prominent on the Grote Markt and cannot be missed. Construction of this magnificent Brabant Gothic-style church began in 1410; in 1995–8 it underwent restoration.

At the Spanjaardsgat watergate, near the castle, legend has it that in the 16th century, during the 80 Years War of independence from Spain, Adriaen van Bergen tricked his way past the Spanish with a peat barge full of soldiers and liberated the town.

Breda's Museum is housed in the old barracks of the Chassékazerne. The museum displays interesting exhibits that illustrate local history.

🏛 **Breda's Museum**
Parade 12–14. **Tel** 076-5299300.
⭕ 10am–5pm Tue–Sun. 📷 ♿ 🖥

Oudenbosch ❺

Road map B5. 🏘 29,400 (municipality of Halderberge). 🚉 🚌 ℹ
Parklaan 15 (0165-390555). 🚌 Tue.

Between 1860 and 1870, Oudenbosch was the point from which the Zouaves set out on their journey to Rome to defend the pope against Garibaldi. Upon their return, they had the architect PJH Cuypers *(see p371)* build a replica of St Peter's basilica in Rome, the **Basiliek van de HH Agatha en Barbara** (Basilica of SS Agatha and Barbara).

Willemstad ❻

Road map B4. 🏘 36,500 (municipality of Zevenbergen). 🚌 ℹ Hofstraat 1 (0168-476055). 🚌 Mon.

The Bastions of Willemstad, were built in 1583 by William of Orange. The Mauritshuis (1623), the former hunting lodge of Maurice, Prince of Orange, is today a museum. The influence of the Oranges can also been seen in the white Oranjemolen mill (1734). There is a pleasant harbour and a tree-lined "Wedding Walk", which leads to a domed church, the Koepeikerk.

The basilica of Oudenbosch, a miniature copy of St Peter's in Rome

Bergen op Zoom ❼

Road map B5. 🏘 64,000. 🚉 🚌
ℹ Korte Meesstraat 19 (0164-277482). 🚌 Thu.

The old town of Bergen op Zoom grew around a chapel that was dedicated to St Gertrude. In 1260, Bergen op Zoom was granted its town charter, after which it enjoyed a period of prosperity. The 15th-century **St Geertruidskerk**, with its striking tower, stands on the site of the original chapel. The lords of Bergen op Zoom built the **Markiezenhof**, which was finally completed in 1511. The castle is today a museum, with period rooms and an unusual collection of fairground items. There are also changing exhibitions, which vary from cultural history to modern art.

🏛 **Markiezenhof**
Steenbergsestraat 8. **Tel** 0164-27707.
⭕ Oct–Mar: 2–5pm Tue–Sun; Apr–Sep: 11am–5pm Tue–Sun. 📷 ♿ 🖥

THE SURRENDER OF BREDA

During the 80 Years War, Breda was kept under siege by Spain for ten months, before finally surrendering to Ambrosio Spinola's troops on 5th June 1625. The moment of capitulation is captured in Velazquez's painting, known as both *The Surrender of Breda* and *Las Lanzas* – the lances – after the line of weapons that dominate the background. Velazquez, the great court painter of King Philip IV, is said to have painted the scene from memory. His picture shows the moment when the commander of the Dutch troops, on the left of the picture in a supplicating position, hands the key of the Dutch fortress to a straight-backed Spinola. The painting is famous for its composition, with the canvas divided into two balanced parts: left and right contain a group of soldiers and a horse, while the fore- and background are split into human activity and the smouldering city behind. The work is also noted for the lively way it portrays the men, several of whom look the viewer directly in the eye. The painting now hangs in Madrid's Museo del Prado.

The Surrender of Breda by Velázquez

Woman in Green (1909) by Picasso, Van Abbemuseum (Eindhoven)

Eindhoven ❽

Road map C5. 198,000.
Stationsplein 17 (0900-1122363). Mon–Sat.

The old market town of Eindhoven was merged with the villages of Strijp, Woensel, Tongelre, Stratum and Gestel in the 19th century. The municipality of Eindhoven grew enormously in the last century when Philips, the electronics company, sited its factory there. Philips's best-known building, the distinctive **Witte Dame** (White Lady) was built in 1922 by architect Dirk Rozenberg; it has now been sold and converted into a design college, library and centre for artists. The former Philips area in Strijp is also being developed into a residential area with shops, restaurants and theatres.

On an industrial estate on the fringes of the city (easily reachable by bus 401 or 402),

the **Philipsmuseum** holds a fascinating collection of electrical objects dating back to the earliest days of the company. On display are dozens of examples of the very first light bulbs dating from the 19th century, beautiful bakelite radios and hulking television cabinets from the birth of broadcasting.

In the city centre, the Philips light bulb even has a museum all to itself, at the **Philips Gloeilampenfabriekje**. Visitors can learn about the history of light-bulb making, from hand-made to mass-produced, and how the light bulb transformed Eindhoven from a small town into an industrial giant.

A rather more surprising find in the centre of the industrial city is the **Historisch Openlucht Museum Eindhoven**. This open-air museum in the middle of the Genneper Park contains reconstructions of an iron-age village, a Viking settlement and a medieval town. Actors in costume people the scene, and are on hand to answer questions. There's also a restaurant where visitors can eat meals based on ancient recipes, like grain stew and lentil paté.

Looming over the railway station is the space-age **Philips Stadion**, home of the PSV Eindhoven football team. The stadium, although ultra-modern these days, still stands in the spot where the first pitch was laid out for the team in 1913. Guided tours allow visitors to enter the players' changing rooms and to walk down the tunnel onto the pitch.

Eindhoven's most important sight, however, is the **Van Abbemuseum**, which is devoted to modern art. The original building was designed in 1936 by AJ Kropholler and has been described as a "brick castle". In the 1990s, architect Abel Cahen was

Eindhoven's fascinating Historische Openlucht Museum

commissioned to expand the museum. Cleverly integrating the existing building into a large new wing, he quadrupled the exhibition space and added a restaurant and multimedia centre. Queen Beatrix opened the museum in January 2003. The collection contains works by Chagall, Lissitzky and Beuys, and is particularly known for Picasso's *Woman in Green* (1909).

🏛 **Philipsmuseum Eindhoven**
Looyenbeemd 14. *Tel* 040-2723308.
☐ Mon, Tue & Wed. ● public hols.

🏛 **Philips Gloeilampenfabriekje**
Emmasingel 31. *Tel* 040-2755183.
☐ Tue–Sun.

🏛 **Historisch Openlucht Museum Eindhoven**
Boutenslaan 161b. *Tel* 040-2522281.
☐ Apr–Oct: daily; Nov–Mar: Sun.

🏛 **Philips Stadion**
Frederiklaan 10a. *Tel* 040-2505505.
✍ booking essential.

🏛 **Van Abbemuseum**
Bilderdijklaan 10. *Tel* 040-2381000.
☐ 11am–5pm Tue–Sun, 11am–9pm Thu.
www.vanabbemuseum.nl

Philips Stadion, home to the football team PSV Eindhoven

Heeze ❾

Road map C5. 🚶 *15,300.*
🚊 🚌 ℹ️ *Schoolstraat 2
(040-2260644).* 🛒 *Thu am.*

The 17th-century castle of
Kasteel Heeze is the centrepiece of this small Brabant
town just outside Eindhoven.
Designed by Pieter Post, it
stands amidst lovely streams,
woods and meadows. Among
the many exhibits set out
in the castle's 30 halls are
valuable Gobelin tapestries.

♠ **Kasteel Heeze**
Kapelstraat 25. **Tel** 040-2264435. ⏲
Mar–Oct. 🎫 🎬 Mar–Oct: 2pm Wed,
2 & 3pm Sun (Jul & Aug: also 2pm Wed).

The vast Strabrechtse Heide at Heeze and Geldrop

Nuenen ❿

Road map C5. 🚶 *23,000.* 🚌
ℹ️ *Berg 29 (040-2839615).*
🛒 *Mon pm.*

Nuenen, northeast of Eindhoven, is the village where
van Gogh lived from 1883 to
1885. **Van Gogh Documentatiecentrum** deals comprehen-
sively with his time in Nuenen.

The magnificent Kasteel Heeze

🏛 **Van Gogh
Documentatiecentrum**
Papenvoort 15. **Tel** 040-2631668.
⏲ 11am–4pm Tue–Sun.

Helmond ⓫

Road map C5. 🚶 *77,600.* 🚊 🚌
ℹ️ *Watermolenwal 11 (0492-
522220).* 🛒 *Wed am, Sat am.*

The most outstanding feature
of Helmond is the **castle**
dating from 1402, today the
Gemeentemuseum (local
history museum). The
museum has many historical
artifacts as well as a fine
collection of modern art
including works by Breitner
and Charley Toorop.

🏛 **Gemeentemuseum**
Kasteelplein 1. **Tel** 0492-587716.
⏲ 10am–5pm Tue–Fri, 2–5pm Sat
& Sun. 🎫 ♿ 🎬 ▫️

Deurne ⓬

Road map D5. 🚶 *32,000.* 🚊 🚌
ℹ️ *Markt 14 (0493-323655).*
🛒 *Fri pm.*

The relaxing town of Deurne
is an artistic centre. The
house (1922) of the extravagant doctor and painter Henrik
Wiedersma, who used to make
house calls on his motorcycle,
is now a **museum** of expressionist works by the doctor
and his avant-garde friends,
including Ossip Zadkine, who
often stayed with him. Poets
such as Roland Holst, Nijhoff
and Bloem were also regular
visitors to the house.

🏛 **Museum De Wieger**
Oude Liesselseweg 29. **Tel** 0493-
322930. ⏲ noon–5pm Tue–Sun.
🗓 Mon & public hols. 🎫 ▫️

Gemert ⓭

Road map C5. 🚶 *27,300 (community of Gemert-Bakel).* 🚌 ℹ️ *Ridderplein 49 (0492-366606).* 🛒 *Mon pm.*

Gemert is a town of historical
importance; its nickname
was once "Heerlijkheid
Gemert" ("glorious Gemert").
Until 1794 it was ruled by the
Knights of the Teutonic Order;
their **castle** still stands and is
now used as a monastery.
The **Boerenbondmuseum**
(agricultural museum) is in a
farmhouse dating from the
beginning of the 20th century;
the displays portray what rural
life was like at that time.

VAN GOGH IN BRABANT

Vincent van Gogh was born in 1853
in Zundert, south of Breda. There, in
the Cultureel Centrum, you can learn
about his childhood. In 1883, he
moved to Nuenen, where his father
was rector. He stayed there until 1885,
when he moved on to Antwerp. The
Nuenen period was very prolific for
van Gogh. Rural life in Brabant
inspired him, and he painted farms,
labourers and weavers in the
blue and brown tones that are so
characteristic of his Nuenen work.
A famous painting dating from this
period is *The Potato Eaters* (1885).

Statue of van Gogh in Nuenen

LIMBURG

Limburg is The Netherland's southernmost province, squeezed by the course of history into its present unusual shape bounded partly by Belgium to the west and to the south and by Germany on the eastern flank. Yet its outline is not the only remarkable thing about this delightful multilingual province.

From a geological point of view, Limburg is much older than the rest of Holland, sitting on coal deposits that are around 270 million years old. In the mining museum at Kerkrade, east of Maastricht, you can see how coal used to be mined in this region. The caves that can be seen in many places in South Limburg are also mines, albeit for the local limestone laid down between 60 and 70 million years ago. The best-known cave systems, parts of which date from the Roman era, are at Valkenburg and at St Pietersberg near Maastricht.

The Maas river valley has been attractive to settlers since the last Ice Age. There is evidence of early nomads, followed by sedentary society like the "Bandkeramikers" and the Beaker Folk (see p42). The Romans were here for around 400 years and Maastricht, which they founded, has much evidence of their impressive buildings. Heerlen was also an important Roman crossroads and the bathhouse museum here makes an excellent and informative visit. In the Middle Ages, Limburg was split up and fought over at various times by the German Empire, Gelder, Liège, Brabant and the Spanish. It acquired its present borders in the 19th century. Nowadays it has plenty to offer visitors, from historic towns with fine architecture, shops and nightlife to countryside dotted with half-timbered houses, farms, water mills in the rivers, and countless castles and country houses.

Half-timbered houses in the South Limburg town of Cottessen

◁ The countryside of Limburg with its rolling hills, unique in Holland

Exploring Limburg

Noord Limburg is made up of the Peel and the
Maas regions. Between the river Maas and the
German border are nature reserves with fens,
woodland, heathland and river dunes. The former
wilderness known as the Peelgebied is on the
border with North Brabant. Middle Limburg is
the section from the Maasplassen lakes, which
were created by the digging of gravel pits. It
is now one of the most important watersports
areas in the country. Zuid Limburg consists of
Maastricht, the Mijnstreek (mining country) and
the pretty chalk-hill landscape to the south.

Picking asparagus in Noord Limburg

National park of De Grote Peel

SEE ALSO

- **Where to Stay** p405
- **Where to Eat** p423

GETTING AROUND

Limburg is easily reached by rail and by road,
which are also the best ways to explore it.
The motorways and railways invariably follow
the same routes, that is to say: Nijmegen-
Venlo-Roermond-Geleen-Maastricht, Weert-
(Roermond)-Geleen-Maastricht and, finally, the
triangle Maastricht-Geleen-Heerlen. For cyclists
there are long sections of cycle paths along the
Julianakanaal and the Zuid-Willemsvaart. The
south of Zuid Limburg in particular is simply
ideal for cycling (including racing) and rambling. The tourist railway or "environmental
line" from Schin near Geul to Kerkrade via
Wijlre, Eys and Simpelveld operates from
April to October on Sundays and Wednesdays,
with two steam-trains and a "rail-bus".

The St.-Martinuskerk in Weert

Limestone quarry with old passageways

MOOK ❶

Meijel
*Nationaal
Park de
Grote Peel*

Nederweert

WEERT ❺ L I M

Stramproy

THORN ❾

Maasbracht

Ech

Susteren

SITTARD ❿

Stein Geleen

ELSLOO ❶❺ Beek

Nuth

Meerssen

VALKENBURG ❶❸

MAASTRICHT ❽

Wijlre

GULPEN ❶❹

HEUVELLAND

EIJSDEN ❶❻ ❶❽

SIGHTS AT A GLANCE

Arcen ❸
De Meinweg ❼
Eijsden ⓰
Elsloo ⓯
Gulpen ⓮
Heerlen ⓬
Hoensbroek ⓫
Maastricht
pp372–7 ❽
Mook ❶
Roermond ❻
Sittard ❿
Thorn ❾
Vaals ⓱
Valkenburg ⓭
Venlo ❹
Venray ❷
Weert ❺

Tour
Heuvelland
pp380–81 ⓲

Field chapel in Heuvelland

KEY

═══ Motorway
─── Major road
═══ Minor road
─── Scenic route
─── Major railway
─── Minor railway
─── Regional border
═══ International border

0 kilometres   10

0 miles   10

Mining, once the mainstay of Limburg's industry

Kasteel Schaloen at Valkenburg (13th century), rebuilt in the 17th century

Mook ❶

Road map D4. 🏠 825. 🚌 83.
ℹ️ *Henseniusplein 13, Venray
(0900-0400216).*

The village of Mook is
on the river Maas in the
very north of Limburg. On
14 April 1574, the Prince of
Orange's army was routed
on the nearby **Mookerhei**
by the Spanish. The star-
shaped fortifications of the
Heumense Schans from the
80 Years War stand atop a
43-m (141-ft) ridge from the
Saalian Ice Age. It offers a
fantastic vantage point from
which to view the Maas valley.
   South of Mook is the recreation area of the Mookerplas
lake and the fine estate of **Sint
Jansberg**, where the Bovenste
Plasmolen, an ancient watermill, has been restored.

Venray ❷

Road map D5. 🏠 37,000. 🚗 27,
29, 30, 39. 🚌 ℹ️ *Henseniusplein 13
(0900-0400216).* 🚗 *Mon pm.*

The magnificent 16th-century Venlo town hall in the Markt

During World War II, Noord
Limburg was the scene of
heavy fighting. An English
and a German (at Ysselsteyn)
military cemetery lies near the
town. Nearby Overloon is
home to the Oorlogs-en Verzetsmuseum (war museum).
In 1944, Venray was largely
destroyed. The 15th-century
basilica of **St Petrus Banden**,
with its magnificent interior,
was given a new 80-m (262-ft)
tower in restoration works. The
Geijsteren estate on the Maas,
where old Maas terraces are
visible in the terrain, is an
outstanding rambling area.

Arcen ❸

Road map D5. 🏠 9,000. 🚌 83.
ℹ️ *Nieuwstraat 40–42, Venlo (0900-
0400216).*

The main attraction of Arcen,
picturesquely located on the
Maas, is the finely restored
17th-century Arcen castle with
its **Kasteeltuinen** (castle gardens). They incorporate a rose
garden, subtropical gardens,
Eastern gardens, a pine forest

and a golf course. You can also
take the waters at the **Ther-
maalbad Arcen** spa; its miner-
al-rich water is extracted from
900 m (2,955 ft) underground.
Other local delights include
special Arcen beer, asparagus
(with an asparagus market on
Ascension Day), and the drink
distilled by the Branderij De
IJsvogel, housed in the 17th-
century **Wijmarsche water mill**.
Outside Arcen is the **Nationaal Park Landgoed de Hamert**.

🌷 **Kasteeltuinen**
Lingsforterweg 26. **Tel** 077-4736020.
◻️ *Apr: 10am–5pm; May–Sep:
10am–6pm; Oct & Nov: 10am–5pm.*
🚫 *23 Dec–7 Jan.* 📷 🔲 🔳

The exquisite gardens of Arcen

Venlo ❹

Road map D5. 🏠 60,000. 🚗
ℹ️ *Nieuwstraat 40–42 (0900-
0400216).* 🚗 *Fri pm, Sat.*

The combined city of Venlo/
Blerick began as a Roman
settlement. In the Middle Ages
it grew rich on trade. The
15th-century St Martinuskerk,
a Gothic hall-type church, and
Ald Weishoes, a Latin school
dating from 1611 built in the
Gelderland Renaissance style,
are among the few historical
buildings to survive World War
II. The town hall was designed
between 1597 and 1600 by
Willem van Bommel. The local
**Museum Van Bommel-Van
Dam** features modern art; the
Limburgs Museum, archaeological finds.

🏛 **Museum Van Bommel-
Van Dam**
Deken van Oppensingel 6. **Tel** 077-
3513457. ◻️ *11am–5pm Tue–Sun.*
🚫 *Mon, 1 Jan, Carnival, 25 Dec.*

🏛 **Limburgs Museum**
Keulsepoort 5. **Tel** 077-3522112.
◻️ *11am–5pm Tue–Sun.* 🚫 *1 Jan,
Carnival, 25 Dec.*
www.limburgsmuseum.nl

Weert ❺

Road map C5. 🏘 47,700. 🚇
ℹ️ *Maasstraat 18 (0495-536800).*
🚌 *Sat.*

The jewel of Weert is the
St Martinuskerk, one of the
few Late Gothic hall-type
churches in Holland (in hall-
type churches, the side aisles
are equal in height and width
to the nave). When restoration
works were carried out
around 1975, paintings from
the 15th and 16th centuries
were discovered beneath the
layers of whitewash on the
vaulted ceilings. Before the
high altar (1790) by Italians
Moretti and Spinetti lies the
tomb of the lord of Weert,
beheaded in 1568 on the order
of Alva in Brussels. Not far
from the church is the
Ursulinenhof, an
example of a new
building successfully
integrated into a
historical centre.
　Surrounding areas such
as Weerterbos forest and
the **Nationaal Park De
Grote Peel** are remnants
of a region of peat moors.

Limburg asparagus

Roermond ❻

Road map D5. 🏘 43,000. 🚇
ℹ️ *Markt 17 (0475-335847).*
🚌 *Wed pm, Sat.*

The oldest church in the
see of Roermond is the 13th-
century Late Romanesque,
Early Gothic **Onze-Lieve-**

Interior of the Onze-Lieve-Vrouwemunsterkerk in Roermond

Vrouwemunsterkerk (minster
church of Our Lady), which
was originally the church of a
Cistercian abbey. The interior
of the church is worth a
visit. The **St Christoffel-
kathedraal**, a Gothic
cruciform basilica
with a gilded statue of
St Christopher on the
tower, dates from the early
15th century. The
church's stained-glass
windows are by the
local glazier Joep Nicolas.
　Roermond is by the
Maasplassen lakes, one of
the country's largest areas for
watersports. The lakes cover
more than 300 ha (740 acres)
and have a length of approximately 25 km (15 miles). The
Maasplassen were created
through large-scale gravel
quarrying in the Maas valley,
which went on as far as
Maaseik in Belgium.

De Meinweg ❼

Road map D6. 🏘 none. 🚌 78, 79.
ℹ️ *Bezoekerscentrum, Meinweg 2,
Herkenbosch (0475-528500).*

The expansive national park
of De Meinweg in the east
of the province possesses a
unique natural beauty. Six
hiking routes have been laid
out here. You can also tour
the park by horse-drawn cart,
accompanied by expert guides.

DR PJH CUYPERS

Architect Pierre Cuypers
was born in Roermond in
1827. He lived and worked
both in his hometown and
in Amsterdam. One of
Cuypers' sons and one of
his nephews also became
renowned architects.
Considered one of the
prime representatives of
the Netherlands Neo-
Gothic, Cuypers designed
the Central Station and the
Rijksmuseum in Amster-
dam, and De Haar castle in
Haarzuilens. He was also
the architect and restorer of
countless churches, including the *munsterkerk* (minster church) in Roermond.

Munsterkerk in Roermond

The 1,600-ha (3,955-acre) De Meinweg national park

Street-by-Street: Maastricht ❽

Gevelsteen

Maastricht emerged in Roman times at a point along the river Maas which could be crossed on foot (Mosae Traiectum), on the Roman road that led from Colonia Agrippina (Cologne) to Bononia (Boulogne). The founder of Christian Maastricht was St Serviatus, bishop of Tongeren, who died in AD 384 in Maastricht and was buried in the cemetery then located outside the town walls. The magnificent basilica of St Servaas was built over his tomb. In addition to the basilica, another fine church is the Romanesque Onze-Lieve-Vrouwebasiliek.

Sculpture of Pieke
This sculpture in Stokstraat is of Pieke and his dog, from a book by Ber Hollewijn.

KEY

- – – – Recommended route

The Generaalshuis
Now the Theater aan het Vrijthof, this Neo-Classical palace was built in 1809. General Dibbets, who succeeded in keeping Maastricht part of the Netherlands, lived here around 1830.

STAR SIGHTS

★ Cemetery

★ Onze-Lieve-
  Vrouwebasiliek

★ Stadhuis

★ Cemetery
Now one of the city's main squares, the cemetery was located outside the town walls when the construction of St Servaas began.

In den Ouden Vogelstruys
One of the many street cafés flanking the Vrijthof, this lively, popular spot serves a small selection of meals.

★ **Stadhuis**
The town hall on the Markt was built from 1559–1664 and is a masterpiece by Pieter Post of the Northern Netherlands. The lobby is open to visitors.

St Servaasbrug
This bridge is a solid yet elegant structure of seven semicircular arches dating from 1280. Ships can reach the Wyck side through a modern section.

GROTE STAAT

KLEINE STAAT

M BRUGSTRAAT

LELIESTRAAT

M SMEDEN STRAAT

WOLFSTRAAT

PLATIELSTRAAT

MINCKELERSTRAAT

MAASBOULEVARD

PLANKSTRAAT

STOKSTRAAT

0 metres 100

0 yards 100

★ **Onze-Lieve-Vrouwebasiliek**
In one of the chapels of this Romanesque cruciform basilica is the votive statue of Our Lady "Sterre der Zee".

The Wall Lizard
This animal can be seen in parts of Maastricht, the only Dutch town it occurs in.

Bonnefantenmuseum

The Bonnefantenmuseum is one of Maastricht's most prominent landmarks, situated on the right bank of the Maas in a distinctive building designed by the Italian architect Aldo Rossi. The museum's exhibits include old masters, painting and sculpture from the medieval period to 1650, and a celebrated international collection of modern art.

Bounds of Sense

★ Cupola by Aldo Rossi
The tower houses a restaurant and an exhibition hall.

Domed hall

Terrace

La Natura è l'Arte del Numero
This installation designed by Mario Merz consists of tables covered with glass, branches, stones, vegetables and numbers fashioned out of fluorescent tubes.

Cimon and Pero
Peter Paul Rubens (1577–1640) depicted Pero feeding her starving father Cimon while he awaited execution in prison.

★ Wood Carvings
The fine collection of medieval wood carvings includes St Anna-te-Drieën, a walnut sculpture by Jan van Steffeswert (1470–1525).

STAR FEATURES

★ Staircase

★ Cupola by Aldo Rossi

★ Wood Carvings

Plattegronden
by René Daniels (b. 1950) is a simplified re-creation of a museum hall. Daniels painted yellow rectangles over the red flat paintings, which are out of sync with the perspective of the hall, thus creating a disorienting effect.

Bonnefantopia
The Rotterdam group of artists Atelier van Lieshout created this large installation in 2002. It features stylized polyester bodies hanging, squatting and lying down throughout the structure.

View on a City from a River
by Jan Brueghel the Elder (1568–1625).

Entrance

Inner tower

★ Staircase
The monumental staircase runs through the middle of the museum and leads into the different wings and floors of the museum.

MUSEUM GUIDE
The Bonnefantenmuseum was designed by Aldo Rossi. It has a permanent collection of early and contemporary art; in addition, a range of temporary exhibitions are organized. The highlight of the museum is its magnificent collection of medieval wood carvings.

St Stephen
Giovanni del Biondo (1356–99) painted this work, thought to be part of a triptych, as the panel has signs of being cut with a saw.

Exploring Maastricht

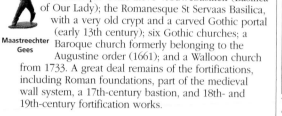

Maastreechter Gees

Maastricht is considered to be one of the oldest towns in Holland. It was the country's first bishopric and an impressive fortress. It has some outstanding historical monuments, including the Romanesque Onze-Lieve-Vrouwebasiliek (Basilica of Our Lady); the Romanesque St Servaas Basilica, with a very old crypt and a carved Gothic portal (early 13th century); six Gothic churches; a Baroque church formerly belonging to the Augustine order (1661); and a Walloon church from 1733. A great deal remains of the fortifications, including Roman foundations, part of the medieval wall system, a 17th-century bastion, and 18th- and 19th-century fortification works.

The medieval Helpoort gate, the oldest city gate in the country

🏛 Natuurhistorisch Museum

De Bosquetplein 7. **Tel** 043-3505490. 🕐 10am–5pm Mon–Fri, 2–5pm Sat & Sun. 🌑 public hols. 🖼

This attractive natural history museum showcases the natural history of the south of Limburg through the ages. High lights of the museum include the remains of the enormous mosasaur and giant tortoises found in the limestone strata of St Pietersberg.

🏰 Roman Foundations of the Tower

OL Vrouweplein. **Tel** 043-3251851. 🕐 Easter Day–autumn hols: 11am–5pm Mon–Sat, 1–5pm Sun.

In the courtyard of the Onze-Lieve-Vrouwebasiliek you can see the foundations of a Roman tower which was once part of the Roman *castellum*. The *castellum* stood on the banks of the river Maas, just south of the St Servaasbrug

bridge, where the Romans settled in 50 BC and where the district of Stokstraat, with its medieval and Golden Age buildings, now lies. The pavement of Op de Thermen, a small and peaceful square in this district where the original Roman fort once was, has been marked with the outlines of the old Roman baths. The first medieval wall around Maastricht dates from around 1229. Of these, the Onze-Lieve-Vrouwewal – which has cannons standing in front of it – and the Jekertoren tower can still be seen.

🏰 Helpoort

St Bernardusstraat 24b. **Tel** 043-3212586. 🕐 Easter Day–Oct, 1:30–4:30pm daily. 🖼 voluntary donation.

Mosasaurus hofmanni in the natural history museum, known locally as the terrible Maas lizard

The Helpoort gate, dating from the early 13th century, also forms part of the early medieval town fortifications. It stood at the southern end of the town and is the oldest surviving town gate in Holland, and the only one still standing in Maastricht.

Other structures from this period can be seen across the river Maas in Wyck: the Waterpoortje gate, the Stenen Wal (wall) along the river, and the Maaspunttoren. The second medieval fortifications, made necessary by the rapid growth of the city, were built around 1350. Of these, the Pater Vinktoren near the Helpoort gate, and the romantic embankment wall and the semicircular towers known as De Vijf Koppen and Haet ende Nijt continue to survive to this day.

The impressive Pater Vink tower

For hotels and restaurants in this region see p405 and p423

⌂ Museum Spaans Gouvernement

Vrijthof 18. **Tel** 043-3217878. ☐ 1:30–5pm Tue–Sun. ⬤ public hols. ♿
This museum, housed in a 16th-century chapterhouse, features period rooms from the 17th and 18th centuries, and Dutch paintings from that era.

⌂ Centre Céramique

Avenue Céramique 50. **Tel** 043-350 5600. ☐ call ahead. ⬤ public hols. ♿ ☐ www.centreceramique.nl
This information centre has a library, archive, cafés and the European Journalism Centre.

⌂ Grotten St-Pietersberg

Luikerweg. ✏ phone for details (043-3252121). ♿ ☐ ⛏
The famous St Peter's caves were created when limestone was quarried through the centuries. Eventually a maze of over 20,000 passageways came into being. Some of the inscriptions on the walls are very old indeed, and some of the miners reveal considerable artistic skills.

The Gothic Bergportaal (15th century) of the St Servaasbasiliek

⌂ St-Servaasbasiliek

Keizer Karelplein. **Treasury Tel** 043-3210490. ☐ 10am–5pm daily (Jul & Aug: 10am–6pm, Nov–Apr: 12:30–5pm on Sun). ⬤ 1 Jan, Carnival, 25 Dec.
Construction on St Servatius Basilica began around the year 1000 on the spot where the saint was buried (upon which stood an earlier church). The nave, the crypt, the transept and the chancel are the oldest parts of the basilica, dating back to the 11th century. The apse and the two chancel towers were built in the following century. The western end also dates from the 12th century. The southern Bergportaal gate dates from the early 13th century, and is one of the earliest Gothic buildings in the Maasland

Crypt in the eastern part of the Onze-Lieve-Vrouwebasiliek

region. This portal is dedicated to St Mary, with representations of her life, death and Assumption in the arch. The side chapels and the Gothic transept date from approximately 1475.

Highlights of the basilica's treasury are the 12th-century reliquary containing the relics of St Servatius and St Martin of Tongeren, and the golden bust of St Servatius. The latter was donated to the town by the Duke of Parma when Maastricht was taken over by the Spaniards in 1579.

During the 19th century, thorough restoration works were undertaken by Pierre Cuypers. He restored the western end to its original Romanesque splendour, as well as commissioning new murals and ceiling paintings. These were repainted during a subsequent restoration which was completed in 1990.

⌂ Onze-Lieve-Vrouwebasiliek

O-L-Vrouweplein. **Treasury Tel** 043-3251851. ☐ Easter Day–autumn hols: 11am–5pm Mon–Sat, 1–5pm Sun. **Church** ⬤ during services.
Construction of Onze-Lieve-Vrouwebasiliek began around 1000. The oldest part of the basilica is the imposing west façade. Once this was completed, work began on the nave and transept. The chancel followed in the 12th century, built over an 11th-century crypt. The apse pillars, made from limestone, are crowned with lavishly sculpted capitals, such as the renowned Heimokapiteel.

THE RELIQUARY OF ST SERVATIUS

The magnificent restored reliquary is a monumental shrine containing the relics of St Servatius and St Martin of Tongeren. It is made of wood covered with embossed gilded copper plate in the shape of a house. It dates from about 1160 and was built by artists from the Maasland region. The front of the reliquary depicts Christ, with the 12 apostles along the sides, and St Servatius surrounded by angels on the back. The "roof" of the "house" is decorated with scenes from the Last Judgement.

The 12th-century reliquary

The impressive medieval Kasteel Hoensbroek

Thorn ❾

Road map D5. 🏘 2,600. 🚌 72, 73, 76. ℹ Wijngaard 14 (0475-561085).

Southeast of Weert on the A2 is the little town of Thorn, which with its picturesque narrow streets and houses, historical farm buildings and monumental **Abbey Church** looks like an open-air museum. For some 800 years, until 1794, Thorn was the capital of an autonomous secular foundation headed by an abbess. The Wijngaard, the village square, is surrounded by whitewashed houses where the noble ladies of the foundation once lived. The 14th-century abbey church with its 18th-century interior

A whitewashed house of Thorn

was thoroughly restored at the end of the 19th century by renowned architect Pierre Cuypers, who also added a splendid Gothic tower. Clara Elisabeth van Manderscheidt-Blankenheim, a canoness of the foundation, founded the **Kapel van O-L-Vrouwe onder de Linden** (Chapel of Our Lady under the Linden) north of the town in 1673.

Sittard ❿

Road map D6. 🏘 46,500. 🚉 ℹ Kitzraedhuis, Rosmolenstraat 2 (0900-5559798). 🛒 Thu am, Sat.

In the 13th century, Sittard was granted its town charter and built its defensive walls, of which considerable sections remain intact, including **Fort Sanderbout**. The Grote Kerk, or St Petruskerk, built around 1300, is worth a visit. The 80-m (262-ft) tower is built of layers of alternating brick and limestone blocks, or "speklagen" (bacon layers). In the Markt is the 17th-century Baroque **St Michielskerk**; Our Lady of the Sacred Heart basilica stands in the Oude Markt. The oldest house in Sittard is the half-timber house built in 1530 on the corner of the Markt and the Gats and containing the De Gats coffee house. The Jacob Kritszraedthuis, a patrician house, was built in 1620 in Maasland Renaissance style.

Hoensbroek ⓫

Road map D6. 🏘 25,500. 🚉 ℹ Hoofstraat 26 (0900-5559798). 🛒 Fri am.

Before the state-run Emma mine was opened here in 1908, Hoensbroek was a sleepy farming town. It subsequently grew into the centre of the Dutch coal mining industry. Its industrial importance waned with the closing of the mines. **Kasteel Hoensbroek** was built in the Middle Ages. All that remains of the original castle is the round corner-tower. The wings and towers around the rectangular inner courtyard date from the 17th and 18th centuries. The castle is moated and today functions as a cultural centre.

Thermae at the Thermenmuseum

Heerlen ⓬

Road map D6. 🏘 95,000. 🚉 ℹ Orange Nassaustraat 16 (0900-5559798). 🛒 Tue, Thu am & Fri.

The Roman town of Coriovallum has been discovered beneath Heerlen. **Thermenmuseum** contains the foundations of the ancient *thermae* and many everyday items from Roman times. Romanesque **St Pancratiuskerk** dates back to the 12th century. In the 20th century, until 1974, Heerlen was the centre of coal mining in Limburg. FPJ Peutz built the town hall and Schunck department store (known as the *Glaspaleis*, or crystal palace) in the 1930s.

🏛 **Thermenmuseum**
Coriovallumstraat 9. **Tel** 045-5605100. ⏰ 10am–5pm Tue–Fri, noon–5pm Sat, Sun & public hols. 1 Jan, Carnival, 24 & 25 Dec.

Valkenburg ⑬

Road map D6. 🏠 5,500. 🚉 🚌
36, 47, 63. ℹ️ Th. Dorrenplein 5
(0900-5559798). 🛒 Mon am, Tue am.

The old fortified town of
Valkenburg, situated in an
area dotted with castles, is
popular with visitors. In
addition to sights such as the
old gates of Berkelpoort and
Grendelpoort, a 13th-century
Romanesque church and the
ruins of a 12th-century castle,
there are many new attractions, such as a casino, catacombs, the Fluweelen cave,
Gemeentegrot (a Roman quarry), a cable car, the Prehistor-
ische Monstergrot and the
Steenkolenmijn (coal mine).

> 🏠 **Gemeentegrot**
> Cauberg 4. **Tel** 043-6012271. ⏺
> Palm Sun–31 Oct: 9am–5pm Mon–
> Sat, 10am–5pm Sun; 31 Oct–Palm
> Sun: 10am–4pm Sat & Sun. ⏺ 1
> Jan, Carnival, 25 Dec. 📷 📹 📷 🏠

Gulpen ⑭

Road map D6. 🏠 7,500.
ℹ️ Dorpsstraat 27 (0900-5559798).
🛒 Thu morning.

Gulpen lies on the confluence
of the Geul and Gulp streams.
The town's surrounding countryside, with its half-timbered
houses, water mills and
orchards, is probably the
prettiest in Limburg. Hiking

The picturesque sloping streets of the Maasland village of Elsloo

routes are marked. The 17th-
century Kastell Neubourg, built
on the site of a Roman temple
from 2,000 years ago, is now a
hotel and restaurant. Beside the
castle is the Neubourgermolen
mill with a fish ladder for trout.
The Gulpen brewery is worth a
visit. The common kingfisher,
a rare bird, can be seen here.

Elsloo ⑮

Road map D6. 🏠 8,650. 🚉 🚌 31
ℹ️ Rosmolenstraat 2, Sittard (0900-
5559798).

Artifacts from the banded
pottery culture found at
Elsloo are on display in the
Maasland local history muse-
um, De Schippersbeurs. In the
Waterstaatskerk, dating from

1848, is the 16th-century **St-
Anna-te-Drieën** by the Master
of Elsloo. Remnants of Elsloo's
earliest castle can be seen in
the middle of the river at low
water. Of the
later Kasteel
Elsloo, only one
tower survives.

Eijsden ⑯

Road map C6. 🏠 4,800.
🚉 🚌 58, 59. ℹ️ Breuster-
straat 41, Epen (0900-
5559798). 🛒 Thu pm.

Kingfisher

Eijsden, the southernmost
municipality in the Netherlands, is a protected rural area.
There is a pleasant walk to be
had along the Maas quay. Kasteel Eijsden was built in 1636
in the Maasland Renaissance
style on the foundations of an
earlier stronghold. The castle
is not open to the public, but
the park makes for a nice stroll.

Vaals ⑰

Road map D6. 🏠 5,500. ℹ️ Landal
HoogVaals Randweg 21 (0900-
5559798). 🛒 Tue am.

Vaals' wooded countryside
is known for the Drielan-
denpunt, from which three
countries are visible. At 322 m
(1,058 ft), it is also the highest
point in Holland. Worth visiting
are Kasteel Vaalsbroek and
the Von Clermonthuis; both
date from the 18th century.
De Kopermolen, once a
church, is now a museum.

Limburg's picturesque countryside, with the meandering Jeker river

Heuvelland ⑱

In the Zuid Limburg region of Heuvelland, the hills, and the valleys cut through them by the river, are covered with fertile loess soil, which occurs nowhere else in Holland. In the peaceful rolling countryside, with its stunning views, is a region of wooded banks, orchards and fields, dotted with picturesque villages and castles, and criss-crossed by narrow roads passing through cuttings with roadside shrines and field chapels. Heuvelland just may be one of the prettiest parts of Holland.

The orchid garden ③ *in the traffic-free Gerendal, a dry valley between Schin op Geul and Scheulder, is the pride of the region. The garden was laid out by the national forestry commission and is situated behind the forester's lodge. Twenty varieties of wild orchid grow here.*

The Basilica of the Holy Sacrament ② *in Meerssen, built in the late 14th century of limestone in Maasland Gothic style, is one of the most elegant churches in all of Holland. The chancel features a lavishly decorated tabernacle.*

Kasteel Eijsden ⑧ *was built in the Maasland Renaissance style in 1636. This style is easily distinguished by its combined use of brick and stone masonry, with stone being used to frame doors and windows.*

TIPS FOR DRIVERS

Length: 80 km (50 miles). Part of the route passes through hilly areas with narrow roads.
Stopping-off points: especially good viewing points are to be found at Noorbeek, Slenaken and Epen.

GRAPE-GROWING IN ZUID LIMBURG ①

In the past, grape-growing and wine-making was more widely practised in Zuid Limburg than it is today. For example, in the 18th century, there were at least 200 ha (495 acres) of vineyards on and around St-Pietersberg. Today, a few small professional vineyards can still be found in the region, the most famous being the Apostelhoeve. On this vine-growing estate situated to the south of Maastricht on the Louwberg above the de Jeker valley, white wine is made from Müller-Thürgau, Riesling, Auxerrois and Pinot Gris grapes.

Grapes from Limburg

The American War Cemetery ④ *at Margraten contains the graves of 8,300 American soldiers who died in World War II, marked by plain white crosses.*

KEY

▬▬ Tour route

═══ Other road

━ Railway

☼ Viewpoint

0 kilometres 2

0 miles 2

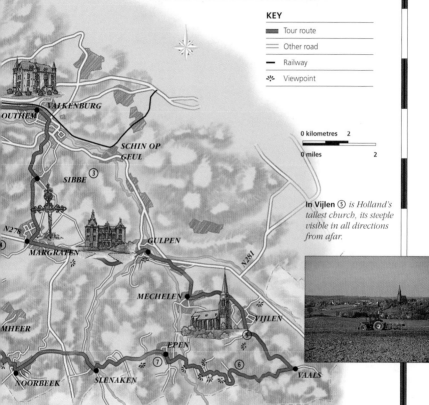

VALKENBURG

OUTHEM

SCHIN OP GEUL

SIBBE ③

N278

MARGRATEN

GULPEN

N281

MECHELEN

MHEER

VIJLEN

EPEN ⑤

NOORBEEK

SLENAKEN ⑦

⑥

VAALS

In Vijlen ⑤ *is Holland's tallest church, its steeple visible in all directions from afar.*

Large stretches of forest ⑥ *are rare in Zuid Limburg, which is otherwise very densely wooded. Exceptions are the Boswachterij Vaals with the Vijlenerbos forest, and the forests by the Brunsummerheide (Brunsummer heath). The wooded slopes of Zuid Limburg with their many springs are well known.*

Rambling in the Geuldal ⑦

At Epen, turn off towards Plaat and take the road to the fulling mill in Geul. Carry on after the bridge. A path on the opposite side follows the river upstream into Belgium. Along the Geul are poplars with mistletoe growing in the branches, which can be seen particularly well in winter. The path leads past the Heimansgroeve, a quarry for rock from the Carboniferous period.

TRAVELLERS'
NEEDS

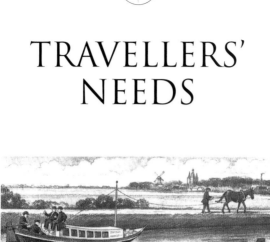

WHERE TO STAY

The Netherlands offers a variety of accommodation to suit every traveller's taste and needs, ranging from cheap budget accommodation to expensive luxury. You can stay in one of the luxury hotels of international chains, although there is also good accommodation to be had in old castles, farms, historical buildings and houses that have been converted into hotels, *pensions,* youth hostels or B&Bs. Campers, too, will be spoiled for choice in the Netherlands, with numerous

Hotel porter

campsites and caravan parks, which are often situated in stunning locations. Camping is an especially economical way to stay in a particular area over a longer period of time. If you need more spacious or convenient accommodation over a longer period, you can book into one of the 350-odd bungalow parks in the country, or rent an apartment in one of the many coastal towns. The hotels listed on pages 392–405 vary in both class and price, and are considered either the best or the most pleasant hotels in that particular area or town.

HOTEL TYPES

There is a huge difference in the price, quality and facilities offered by different hotels. The choice is greatest in Amsterdam and the larger cities, where there is something to suit every traveller's pocket. But even further afield there is also plenty of choice. After hotels, bed-and-breakfast (B&B) accommodation is becoming increasingly plentiful in the Netherlands. This type of accommodation varies greatly, as these lodgings are provided by individuals rather than by chains. One night you might be staying in an ordinary family home, and the next you might be staying in an old historical building. **Bed & Breakfast Nederland** can help with reservations at specific B&Bs.

Traditional *pensions* are now fewer in Holland than they were some decades ago. The main difference between a *pension* and a bed-and-breakfast is that in a *pension* everybody eats the same meal and guests tend to stay slightly longer. You will find *pensions* mainly in the south of the country. You can also stay in a farmhouse. Farmhouses offering accommodation are usually members of **Hoeve-Logies Nederland**, and they often provide stabling for horses, or you can help with the farm work. For slightly more upmarket farm accommodation, you can visit the **Hotel de Boerenkamer** in

The hotel Groot Warnsborn in Arnhem, a country manor until 1950

North Holland. The least expensive form of overnight accommodation is the youth hostel *(jeugdherberg)*. **Stayokay** runs no fewer than 30 youth hostels throughout the country. They are no longer exclusively reserved for young people. Accommodation is usually in dormitories of four to six people, and you have to bring your own bed linen, or you can rent it for the night.

HOTEL CHAINS

Just about all major hotel chains are represented in the Netherlands. You will find most of them, such as the **Hilton, Mercure, Golden Tulip**, Marriott, Best Western, **Holiday Inn** and Ramada in the big cities, although some like the **Bilderberg** are situated in country areas. The hotels range from good to luxury, both for tourists

Château Hotel De Havixhorst in Schiphorst

◁ **The restaurant d'Vijff Vlieghen in Amsterdam dating back to 1627**

The hotel Het Schimmelpenninck Huys in Groningen

and for business travellers.

The scale of these hotels and the often internationally recognized style means that they are less personal than small hotels, but when you spend the night in one of them you get what you pay for and are assured of excellent service and a high level of comfort.

CATEGORIES

Hotels are classed by a variety of systems. Some hotels, for instance, are recognized by the ANWB. ANWB sets store by the management of the hotel and the quality of the facilities. Regular checks are carried out on these hotels. You can recognize them by the blue ANWB sign, and they are listed in a guide which is available from the ANWB office and bookshops. After ANWB-recommended hotels, there are those listed by Holland Hotels Hartverwarmend which are characterized by the personal atmosphere they offer. Lists of these hotels are available for a small charge from places such as the VVV offices. All hotels in the Netherlands have to be categorized under the Benelux Hotel Classification system, which awards each hotel with between one and five stars. The number of stars given depends on the minimum facilities on offer.

The more stars a hotel has, the more luxurious it is. A one-star hotel is simple and may or may not offer breakfast. In two-star hotels, at least 25 per cent of the rooms will have their own bathroom or shower and WC. These hotels will also have a guest lounge, and it will have a lift if it is more than three storeys high. A three-star hotel is considered middle of the range. Their rooms have central heating and at least half have their own bathrooms. Four-star hotels will have a night bar, 80 per cent of the rooms will have en-suite bathrooms, and all of them will have telephones. A five-star hotel will be of deluxe category, having 24-hour service, large rooms with ensuite facilities, a restaurant and so on. One slight drawback of this classification, which looks mainly at the facilities provided and ignores both the hotel's location and atmosphere,

is that many simple but pleasant little hotels do not score well.

The hotel's star rating is displayed on a blue and white sign by its main entrance.

APARTMENTS

The number of self-catering apartments in the cities is limited, and you will usually have to pay a considerable deposit. VVV will inform you of organizations which rent out apartments, or you can look in the Visitors' Guide section of the Yellow Pages (*Gouden Gids*). If you hire an apartment through an agency, you will generally be required to stay for at least one week. It is also possible to hire apartments through some hotels, for example, the Renaissance Amsterdam Hotel.

Along the Dutch coast, in Zeeland and on the West Frisian Islands, there are many "apartment-hotels", which are apartment buildings with hotel facilities, such as bars, swimming pools and reception areas.

PRICES

Room prices generally include the *toeristenbelasting* (tourist tax) as well as breakfast. In the larger and more expensive hotels, breakfast is usually charged separately. Obviously, a hotel which provides more than the average facilities will be pricier than a basic hotel. Hotels in larger cities, particularly in Amsterdam, are relatively more pricey than those further afield, although in large towns it is easier to find hotels in wider-ranging price categories.

People travelling alone usually end up paying only 20 per cent less than the same accommodation would cost two people sharing. People travelling in larger groups can stay more cheaply by sharing a *meerpersoonskamer* (multiple room).

The hotel Oortjeshekken, situated in Ooij

The bar of the Hotel Van der Werff on Schiermonnikoog

BOOKING ACCOMMODATION

The springtime, when the tulips are in bloom, is the busiest time for tourists in the Netherlands. If you wish to book a hotel room at this time, you should do so several weeks ahead, particularly if booking in the major cities and along the coastline. For popular hotels along Amsterdam's canals, book well in advance all year round.

Bookings can be made by telephoning the hotel directly. It is a good idea to ask for written confirmation of your booking in order to avoid problems upon your arrival.

You can also select and book hotels online over the Internet. There is a wide range of hotel booking websites both in Dutch and in English. As well as general websites featuring a variety of hotels, many hotels and hotel chains also have their own websites where you can find information about them and online booking forms. Some useful websites are www.hotels-holland.com, www.hotelnet.nl, www.booking.com, **www.anwb.nl** (hotels listed by ANWB) and ase.net (a search engine which allows you to search for hotels all over the world). The best way of searching for individual hotels or major hotel chains is by name. Stayokay hostels can be found through www.stayokay.com. Another way of booking hotel rooms anywhere in Holland is through the **Amsterdam Tourist Board Offices (VVV)**, which also arranges bed and breakfast in private homes, for which it charges a small commission. You will have to pay the VVV for the first night's accommodation, the hotel for the remaining nights. The **Netherlands Reservations Centre** will help you book just about any form of accommodation by phone or via the Internet, at **www.hotelres.nl**. At Schiphol airport KLM runs a counter where travellers can book hotels; of course, most agents can also help you to book hotel accommodation.

PAYMENT

Major credit cards are accepted at most hotels. When you give your credit card number when booking a hotel, payment is often required in advance. Smaller hotels, *pensions*, B&Bs and youth hostels do not generally accept credit cards, and usually require cash payment.

DISCOUNTS

Discounts are often available with many hotels for accommodation booked well in advance. This applies particularly to the major US hotel chains. Many hotels which cater to business travellers during the week often offer reductions at the weekends in order to attract more customers. Conversely, hotels which are usually full with tourists at the weekends may offer reductions on weekdays.

Children under the age of 12 can usually stay free of charge if they share their parents' room (sometimes this means sharing a bed with their parents) or can in any case stay at a greatly reduced rate. Parents who are members of the Stayokay usually get a free membership card for children under the age of 15.

PACKAGES

In addition to overnight accommodation, many of the hotels in the Netherlands, including the major chains, offer special packages of one or two nights, with breakfast and dinner included. These packages are often based on a particular theme; for example, a cycling or rambling package may include cycle hire, or a beauty package may include treatment by beauty experts. More detailed information is available from the hotels themselves or from the VVV.

Amstel Hotel (right) in Amsterdam, with its picturesque riverside location

TRAVELLERS WITH DISABILITIES

The hotel listings in this book state whether a hotel has wheelchair access, has other facilities for disabled travellers and whether it has a lift. This information is based on the information provided by the hotels themselves. Some hotels which have wheelchair access but no lifts will have some bedrooms on the ground floor. It is best to check when making your reservation.

Some hotels post the international disabled access symbol (a pictogram of a person in a wheelchair), which is recognized by the provincial disabled department. These hotels provide independent disabled access.

ANWB has many publications specifically for disabled travellers, and the VVV's hotels folder also shows which hotels have access and facilities for people with disabilities. International hotel booking websites like www.booking.com and www.laterooms.com have search features to select hotels that have rooms suitable for disabled travellers, including a growing selection in The Netherlands.

Holland's smallest hotel, De Kromme Raake in Eenrum, featuring an authentic "bedstede" or traditional in-built bed

GAY HOTELS

Most gay-oriented hotels are in Amsterdam; indeed, a gay couple is unlikely to produce a raised eyebrow in this tolerant city. One advantage of gay-oriented hotels, which include the **Black Tulip** and **The Golden Bear**, is that they provide a great deal of information on gay hangouts and events. Then there are hotels which are not specifically gay-oriented but make special provision for gay clients, or are gay-friendly. One of these is the **Quentin**, which is popular with women, and the Waterfront which attracts mainly male guests. The Pulitzer and the Grand, among others, have been classed as "gay-friendly" by the International Gay and Lesbian Travel Association. This organization can provide information on gay-friendly accommodation over the Internet (www.iglta.com). The **Gay & Lesbian Switchboard** (also accessible over the Internet) provides further information about hotels.

English-language publications offering comprehensive listings are available and can be found in some bookshops.

DIRECTORY

TYPES OF HOTEL

Bed & Breakfast Nederland
Hallenstraat 12a
5531 AB Bladel.
www.bedandbreakfast.nl

Hoeve-Logies Nederland
Guide with addresses can be ordered on the Internet:
www.dutch-farm holidays.com

Hotel de Boerenkamer
Tel 0299-655726.
(9am–5pm daily). **www**.hotel-boerenkamer.nl

Stayokay
Tel 020-5513155.
www.stayokay.com

HOTEL CHAINS

Bilderberg
Tel 0900-2402400.
www.bilderberg.nl

Golden Tulip
Tel 033-2544800.
www.goldentulip.nl

Hilton
Tel 0800-44466677.
www.hilton.nl

Holiday Inn
Tel 0800-5565565.
www.ichotelsgroup.com

Mercure
Tel 020-6545727.
www.mercure.com

RESERVATIONS

Amsterdam Tourist Board (VVV) Offices *See p441.*
www.vvv.nl

ANWB
ww.anwb.nl/hotels/index.jsp

Netherlands Reservations Centre
Plantsoengracht 2, 144IDE Purmerend. *Tel* 0299-689 144. **www**.hotelres.nl

GAY HOTELS AND INFORMATION

Black Tulip
Geldersekade 16
1012 BH Amsterdam.
Tel 020-4270933.
Fax 020-6244281.

Gay & Lesbian Switchboard
Tel 020-6236565
(2–10pm daily).
www.switchboard.nl

The Golden Bear
Kerkstraat 37
1017 GB Amsterdam.
Tel 020-6244785.
Fax 020-6270164.

Quentin
Leidsekade 89
1017 PN Amsterdam.
Tel 020-6262187.
Fax 020-6220121.

Bungalow Parks

The Netherlands has at least 350 "bungalow parks", which is not surprising considering that they provide an excellent way of enjoying the country in all types of weather. These parks are holiday villages with dozens to hundreds of bungalows or cabins, many designed for four to eight persons, together with numerous facilities such as supermarkets and restaurants. They also provide many recreation facilities, some open-air and others indoors for days when the weather is not at its best. Rental is usually by the week. The parks are often situated in areas of natural beauty and offer plenty to do in the surrounding area. A selection of the best parks in the country is given here.

KEY AND BOOKING NUMBERS

- Euroase-parken (0900-8810)
- Zilverberk (0900-8810)
- CenterParcs (0900-6606600)
- Landal GreenParks (0900-8842)
- Overheemparken (0572-3392798)
- RCN-recreatiecentra (0343-513547)
- Hogenboom Vakantieparken (0297-389180)
- Other parks

TERSCHELLING
WEST FRISIAN ISLANDS
VLIELAND
SLUFTERVALLEI
KRIM
PARC TEXEL TEXEL
CALIFORNIË CREATIEF BEACH PARK TEXEL

NORTH HOLLAND

AMSTERDAM
ZANDVOORT
Haarlem

SOLLASI

'T EEKHOORNNEST
UTRECHT
Den Haag
KIJKDUINPARK
Utrecht
SOUTH HOLLAND
Rotterdam
TOPPERSHOEDJE
PORT ZÉLANDE
DUINOORD PARK PORT GREVE
PARC BURGH-HAAMSTEDE
EFTELING DROOMRIJK
NOORD
DE SCHOTSMAN
DE ROSEP
DE FLAASBLOEM
Middelburg
BRABANTS BOERDERIJDORP ZWARTVEN
HOF VAN ZEELAND
ZEEBAD PANNENSCHUUR ZEELAND
HET VENNENBOS
BELGIU

Port Zélande
The CenterParcs Park in a south-of-France style at Lake Grevelingenmeer features numerous recreation facilities and comfortable bungalows.

Fun for the Children
All recreation parks pay special attention to giving children plenty to do. Illustrated here is RCN's De Flaasbloem Park in Chaam.

0 kilometres 20
0 miles 20

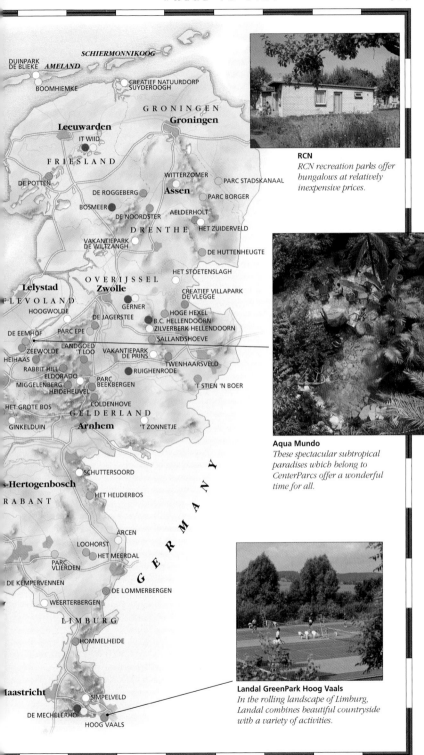

RCN
RCN recreation parks offer bungalows at relatively inexpensive prices.

Aqua Mundo
These spectacular subtropical paradises which belong to CenterParcs offer a wonderful time for all.

Landal GreenPark Hoog Vaals
In the rolling landscape of Limburg, Landal combines beautiful countryside with a variety of activities.

Camping

Many people regard camping as the ideal way to take a holiday. It's cheap, you are in the open air and generally in beautiful natural locations. Camping can take many different forms: moving from one location to another, or settling on one site for the whole holiday; you can camp in a tent, a caravan, a tent-trailer or a camper van; you can camp in natural surroundings, on a farm or on a campsite. The Netherlands, with its many different types of campsites, has something for everyone.

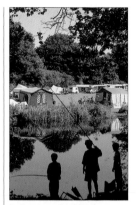

De Roos campsite at Beerze, located on the river Vecht

TYPES OF CAMPSITE

Campsites in the Netherlands fall into two main categories. There are *natuurterreinen,* (nature sites), which are small or medium-sized campsites with basic facilities, often situated in the most spectacular

Camping at one of Holland's many nature sites

countryside that the Netherlands has to offer. The other group consists of larger campsites with a good range of facilities, often near recreation areas or other attractions. Both types of campsite are to be found throughout the Netherlands. On both types of campsite you can either set up your own tent

or caravan or you can rent accommodation. The advantage of renting, of course, is that you can travel lighter.

NATURE CAMPING

Camping off designated campsites is prohibited by law. However, there are plenty of campsites which give you the feeling that you are camping in nature. These campsites are known as *natuur-kampeerterreinen.* They are situated in breathtaking locations with plenty of countryside around for exploring on foot or by bicycle. You can pitch a tent or park your caravan, tent-trailer, camper or motorhome here. There are no fixed pitches. Sanitary arrangements are fairly basic but good. The campsites are usually equipped with children's playgrounds. Using these facilities requires having a Natuurkampeerkaart membership card, which is

available from the **Stichting Natuurkampeerterreinen**. This organization will also provide you with a booklet containing the addresses of more than 100 campsites.

The campsites of the Vereniging Gastvrije Nederlandse Landgoederen en Kastelen (**LKC**) combine the attraction of natural surroundings with that of cultural history. These sites are privately owned and are situated on private estates, usually by forests or a castle or stately home. The association's 16 sites are distinguished by their peace, atmosphere and wide spaces. Camping on a farm means you will be assured of a tranquil rural atmosphere. LKC campsites are almost invariably near areas of natural beauty which provide abundant opportunities for rambling,

Camping in Zeeland, popular among Dutch and foreign holidaymakers alike

cycling or horse-riding. Farms offer a variety of experiences. For example, you will often be able to help the farmers feed the animals or harvest the crops.

Another excellent way of experiencing the countryside is by using *trekkershutten*, or hikers' huts. These huts are designed for use by walkers on hiking-trips. They offer very basic accommodation for up to four people at a time. They are often situated at campsites whose facilities are available to the hikers. It is necessary to bring your own bedding.

LARGE FAMILY CAMPSITES

Large *Gezinscampings* (family campsites) are popular among Dutch holidaymakers taking a break in their own country. The most important aspect of these camping sites is the social life. The management of the sites, be they individually owned or part of a chain of sites, organizes various events, such as barbecue evenings, karaoke, games and competitions, and sports events. In this way people quickly get to know their fellow campers.

Hanging the laundry to dry among the fragrant blossoming trees

This form of camping is also ideal for the children, as they can meet others of their age and there is plenty of room for running around and playing. The largest campsites have extensive sanitary facilities and hot water. They also provide electrical hook-ups for caravans, as well as running water and sewage connections. Campsite shops mean that you can do most of your shopping on-site, and if you don't feel like cooking your own food, there is frequently a restaurant or snackbar where you can get something to eat. Launderettes and dry-cleaning services are also often available. Many have a swimming pool and other recreation facilities such as tennis courts, mini-golf and so on.

The ANWB has classed the best campsites in Europe as "Eurotopcampings". These offer excellent sanitary facilities and have large pitches. Their other facilities are also top of the range. Thirteen of these campsites are located in the Netherlands. You will find these in the organization's camping guides or on the Internet at www.anwb.nl/verblijven/campings/home.jsf.

DIRECTORY

NATURE CAMPING

Kleine Groene Campings
Sparrenbergstraat 37,
Tollem Gaanderen.
www.kgc.nl

LKC
Tel & Fax 0318-578555.
www.gasturijeland
goederen.nl

NIVON
Hilversumsestraat 332
1024 MB Amsterdam.
Tel 020-4350700.
Fax 020-6376533.
www.nivon.nl

Stichting Natuur-kampeerterreinen
Postbus 413
3430 AK Nieuwegein.
Tel 030-6033701.
www.natuur
kampeerterreinen.nl

Stichting Trekkershutten Nederland
Ruigeweg 49
1752 HC St-Maartensbrug.
Tel 0224-563345.
Fax 0224-563318.
www.trekkershutten.nl

SVR (Stichting Vrije Recreatie)
Broekseweg 75-77
4231 VD Meerkerk (ZH).
Tel 0183-352741.
Fax 0183-351234.
www.svr.nl

VeKaBo (Vereniging van Kampeerboeren)
Havenstraat 14
9591 AK Onstwedde.
Tel 0900-3336668.
www.vekabo.nl

LARGE FAMILY CAMPSITES

Euroase
Main reservation and information line:
Tel 0900-8810.
www.euroase.nl

Zilverberk
Postbus 12
4493 ZG Kamperland.
Tel 0900-8810.
www.zilverberk.nl

GUIDES

ANWB Camping-gids Nederland
Lists over 750 campsites inspected by the ANWB.

ANWB-gids Kleine Campings
Lists over 1,500 small campsites in 13 countries.

www.campinggids.nl

www.kamperen.nl

Choosing a Hotel

Hotels have been selected across a wide price range for facilities, good value and location. Additonal symbols help you choose a hotel that best meets your needs. Hotels within the same category are listed alphabetically. For Amsterdam street map references, see pp150–7 and for Road Map references, see the back inside cover.

> **PRICE CATEGORIES**
> The following prices are for a standard double room per night, including breakfast, tax and service.
>
> €   Under €120
> €€   €120–€170
> €€€   €170–€220
> €€€€   €220–€270
> €€€€€   Over €270

AMSTERDAM

OUDE ZIJDE Stayokay Stadsdoelen   €

Kloveniersburgwal 97, 1011 KB **Tel** *(020) 624 6832* **Fax** *639 1035* **Rooms** *8*   **Map** *5 A2*

Aimed at the backpack brigade, Stayokay Stadsdoelen offers packages themed around nature or architecture. In a townhouse near Nieuwmarkt, spartan rooms accommodate 8 to 20 people. There is a courtyard garden and a simple bar where evening meals are served. **www.stayokay.com**

OUDE ZIJDE Residence Le Coin   €€

Nieuwe Doelenstraat 5, 1012 CP **Tel** *(020) 524 6800* **Fax** *524 6801* **Rooms** *42*   **Map** *5 A2*

On a pleasant café-lined street near the university, this residence offers spacious apartment-style rooms. Furnished in a bright, modern style with big windows and equipped with kitchenettes, Le Coin is a good bet for families and visitors on longer stays (there are special monthly rates). **www.lecoin.nl**

OUDE ZIJDE Misc   €€€

Kloveniersburgwal 20, 1012 CV **Tel** *(020) 330 6241* **Fax** *330 6242* **Rooms** *6*   **Map** *5 A1*

This funky, small hotel nestled among the cafés and bars of Nieuwmarkt is ideally situated for carousing and culture. The bright rooms are decorated individually by theme, such as "Afrika". The owners are very helpful and will organize everything from a walking tour to a boat trip. **www.hotelmisc.nl**

OUDE ZIJDE Grand Hôtel Amrâth Amsterdam   €€€€

Prins Hendrikkade 108–114, 1011 AK **Tel** *(020) 552 0000* **Fax** *552 0900* **Rooms** *165*   **Map** *2 E4*

Overlooking the old harbour, this luxury hotel occupies the 1913 Scheepvaarthuis, one of the landmark Amsterdam School buildings. The hotel offers spacious rooms equipped with every comfort. The Seven Seas restaurant serves fine French/international cuisine. **www.amrathamsterdam.com**

NIEUWE ZIJDE Avenue   €€

Nieuwezijds Voorburgwal 33, 1012 RD **Tel** *(020) 530 9530* **Fax** *530 9599* **Rooms** *80*   **Map** *5 D4*

Great for exploring Nieuwe Zijde nightlife, Avenue consists of nine canal houses, one a former East India Company spice warehouse. The rooms are good, but some residents complain of lack of attention to detail (such as running out of breakfast foods). The two lifts are useful for those with mobility problems. **www.embhotels.nl/avenue**

NIEUWE ZIJDE Rho Hotel   €€

Nes 5–23, 1012 KC **Tel** *(020) 620 7371* **Fax** *620 7826* **Rooms** *170*   **Map** *2 D5*

Just metres from bustling Dam Square, though tucked down a backstreet bristling with interesting bars, restaurants and theatres, this hotel is well placed and good value. The beautiful Art Nouveau lobby was once part of a theatre built in 1908. Though plain, the rooms are neat and tidy. **www.rhohotel.nl**

NIEUWE ZIJDE Singel Hotel   €€

Singel 13–17, 1012 VC **Tel** *(020) 626 3108* **Fax** *620 3777* **Rooms** *32*   **Map** *2 D3*

One of the few budget choices in the city, the Singel is good for its proximity to the station and its accessibility to canal walks. Once inside the attractive, 17th-century house, things are pretty basic. Rooms are all ensuite with showers and are mainly clean and tidy. Those at the front, however, can get a little noisy. **www.singelhotel.nl**

NIEUWE ZIJDE Citadel   €€€

Nieuwezijds Voorburgwal 98–100, 1012 SG **Tel** *(020) 627 3882* **Fax** *627 4684* **Rooms** *38*   **Map** *2 D4*

A reliable town-centre hotel halfway between the Jordaan and the old quarter, the Citadel is ideal for urban explorers. It has been refurbished but though rooms are clean, they are on the plain side. Public spaces like the reception area and bar, however, are decorated in warm wood tones. Staff are helpful. **www.centrehotels.nl**

NIEUWE ZIJDE Die Port van Cleve   €€€

Nieuwezijds Voorburgwal 176–180, 1012 SJ **Tel** *(020) 718 9013* **Fax** *421 0310* **Rooms** *120*   **Map** *2 D4*

Beer fans will be delighted to stay here, in the very building where Heineken began brewing in the 1870s. Non-drinkers will be equally satisfied with the hotel's big, luxurious rooms and suites. Gourmets will enjoy the renowned on-site steak restaurant, as well as the city's restaurant scene on the doorstep. **www.dieportvancleve.com**

Key to Symbols *see back cover flap*

NIEUWE ZIJDE Estherea

Singel 305, 1012 WJ **Tel** *(020) 624 5146* **Fax** *623 9001* **Rooms** *92*
Map *1 C5*

An elegant, family-run hotel that has been in the same careful hands for more than 60 years. There are 71 rooms spread across six canal houses, all with an emphasis on opulent fabrics and luxury, from DVD players to marble bathrooms. Facilities include an intimate library and a lounge with watery views. **www.estherea.nl**

NIEUWE ZIJDE Hotel Sint Nicolaas

Spuistraat 1A, 1012 SP **Tel** *(020) 626 1384* **Fax** *623 0979* **Rooms** *27*
Map *1 C5*

Located near Centraal Station, this hotel (owned by the same company as the Citadel, *see p392*) has quirky touches (an outsized lift and odd-shaped rooms) that reflect its former life as a mattress factory. Although fairly basic, all rooms are neat and have ensuite facilities – some with baths. Free Wi-Fi in every room. **www.centrehotels.nl**

NIEUWE ZIJDE NH Barbizon Palace

Prins Hendrikkade 59–72, 1012 AD **Tel** *(020) 556 4564* **Fax** *624 3353* **Rooms** *274*
Map *2 E4*

The jewel in the NH crown, this hotel's public area has sleek black-and-white decor. Rooms, by contrast, are all dowdy beiges and browns, and seem a little tired. Facilities are outstanding: excellent breakfasts, the Michelin-starred Restaurant Vermeer and a 14th-century chapel serving as one of the eight conference rooms. **www.nh-hotels.com**

NIEUWE ZIJDE Grand Hotel Krasnapolsky

Dam 9, 1012 JS **Tel** *(020) 554 9111* **Fax** *622 8607* **Rooms** *468*
Map *2 D5*

The location of this hotel – on Dam Square, overlooking the Koninklijk Paleis – is great. Accommodation ranges from utter luxury in the Tower Suite to compact rooms at the back. Facilities are top-notch and include restaurants, a café and a cocktail bar. The Winter Garden is where weekend brunches are enjoyed. **www.nh-hotels.com**

WESTERN CANAL RING Hotel van Onna

Bloemgracht 102–108, 1015 TN **Tel** *(020) 626 5801* **Rooms** *41*
Map *1 A4*

On the most scenic canal in Amsterdam, this hotel spread over three canal houses dating from the 17th to 20th centuries is a few minutes' walk from the Westerkerk and Anne Frank's house. Rooms are basically furnished and equipped, with reasonable rates for single travellers. **www.hotelvanonna.nl**

WESTERN CANAL RING 't Hotel

Leliegracht 18, 1015 DE **Tel** *(020) 422 2741* **Fax** *626 7873* **Rooms** *8*
Map *1 C4*

A plain name for a lovely hotel nesting on a beautiful Jordaan canal. Rooms are not full of luxuries, but they are very stylish, painted in neutral tones with 1920s-influenced furniture. They are also spacious and have enormous windows. Room number 8, at the very top, is on a split level and sleeps five. **www.thotel.nl**

WESTERN CANAL RING Truelove Antiek and Guesthouse

Prinsenstraat 4, 1015 DC **Tel** *(020) 320 2500* **Fax** *0847 114950* **Rooms** *2*
Map *1 C3*

A small, two-roomed, romantic bolt hole in the heart of Amsterdam's most interesting shopping area. It is simple and stylish; although there is no breakfast (you are spoiled for choice nearby), there are considerate touches like wine, water and fresh flowers in the rooms. **www.truelove.be**

WESTERN CANAL RING Hotel de Looier

3e Looiersdwarsstraat 75, 1016 VD **Tel** *(020) 625 1855* **Fax** *627 5320* **Rooms** *27*
Map *4 D1*

The building was once a diamond factory; now it is a comfortable hotel that is a good base for exploring the Jordaan's markets. The De Looier antiques market is directly opposite, and the Noordermarkt a short stroll away. Although fairly characterless, rooms are ensuite, spotless and have in-house movies. **www.hoteldelooier.com**

WESTERN CANAL RING Hotel The Toren

Keizersgracht 164, 1015 CZ **Tel** *(020) 622 6352* **Fax** *626 9705* **Rooms** *96*
Map *1 C4*

A stylish place decorated in tasteful pastel hues and stripes, Hotel Toren boasts a fascinating history: it has been a merchant's house and a university, and it was also used to hide Jews during World War II. On the downside, standard rooms are small, so spend a little extra on a superior: you get extra legroom and a spa bath. **www.hotelthetoren.nl**

CENTRAL CANAL RING Best Western Eden

Amstel 144, 1017 AE **Tel** *(020) 530 7878* **Fax** *623 3267* **Rooms** *218*
Map *5 B2*

A chain hotel situated on the Amstel, close to Rembrandtplein and the sights. It is handy for travellers with mobility problems: most rooms are wheelchair accessible, and one has full disabled facilities. For individuality, pay extra for an "art room" designed by students from the Rietveld art school. **www.edenhotelgroup.com**

CENTRAL CANAL RING Hotel Brouwer

Singel 83, 1012 VE **Tel** *(020) 624 6358* **Fax** *520 6264* **Rooms** *8*
Map *1 C4*

This hotel has been in the same family's hands since 1917. The eight rooms, all named after Dutch artists, are individually decorated and well maintained, and the canal views are lovely. All rooms are ensuite and there is even a lift, making the Brouwer all-round great value. **www.hotelbrouwer.nl**

CENTRAL CANAL RING Amsterdam Wiechmann

Prinsengracht 328–332, 1016 HX **Tel** *(020) 626 3321* **Fax** *626 8962* **Rooms** *40*
Map *4 D1*

A cosy place ideal for exploring the Jordaan, Wiechmann combines its old-fashioned charm with modern touches like free Wi-Fi Internet access. The comfortable rooms have chintzy decor, and eccentric knick-knacks abound. The teapot-lined breakfast room has huge windows looking onto the canal. **www.hotelwiechmann.nl**

CENTRAL CANAL RING Dikker & Thijs Fenice Hotel

Prinsengracht 444, 1017 KE **Tel** *(020) 620 1212* **Fax** *625 8986* **Rooms** *42*   **Map 4 E1**

Owned by a publisher, this hotel is proud of its literary connections and the authors who stay here. The 18th-century warehouse building is magnificent, and the decor is smart. Although just moments from Leidseplein, the atmosphere here is resolutely upmarket. All the sights are within walking distance. **www.dtfh.nl**

CENTRAL CANAL RING Mercure Hotel Arthur Frommer

Noorderstraat 46, 1017 TV **Tel** *(020) 622 0328* **Fax** *620 3208* **Rooms** *93*   **Map 4 F2**

Within walking distance of the sights, Rembrandtplein and restaurant-lined Utrechtsestraat, this is one of the best placed hotels in Amsterdam. It is pleasantly arranged around a courtyard, and rooms look out onto quiet residential streets. Rooms are comfortable, smart and fairly spacious. **www.mercure.com**

CENTRAL CANAL RING Ambassade Hotel

Herengracht 341, 1016 AZ **Tel** *(020) 555 0222* **Fax** *555 0277* **Rooms** *59*   **Map 1 C5**

With its long literary associations, this is the bookworm's choice of lodgings: the library is lined with signed copies from the numerous authors who have stayed here. Arranged across ten buildings, rooms are furnished in an unfussy, classic way, and bathrooms, though small, are marbled. Staff are discreet and attentive. **www.ambassade-hotel.nl**

EASTERN CANAL RING Armada

Keizersgracht 713–715, 1017 DX **Tel** *(020) 623 2980* **Fax** *623 5829* **Rooms** *26*   **Map 5 A3**

On a quiet part of Keizersgracht, near Utrechtsestraat's great shops and restaurants and close to the bright lights of Rembrandtplein, this hotel has one major selling point: location. Rooms have been renovated and have ensuite facilities. A good budget bet if you want to save your euros for shopping or clubbing. **www.armada-hotel.com**

EASTERN CANAL RING NH Schiller

Rembrandtplein 26–36, 1017 CV **Tel** *(020) 554 0700* **Fax** *624 0098* **Rooms** *92*   **Map 5 A2**

Fun-seekers should look no further than this hotel, with its commanding view over Rembrandtplein. The rooms at the back are not so noisy, and all are decorated with smart furnishings. Brasserie Schiller is very cosy, while the eponymous next-door bar has Art Deco fittings and attracts a media crowd. **www.nh-hotels.com**

EASTERN CANAL RING Albus Grand

Vijzelstraat 49, 1017 HE **Tel** *(020) 530 6200* **Fax** *530 6299* **Rooms** *74*   **Map 4 F1**

The former breakfast room here has been transformed into a hip little café. Standard rooms are bright, though rather cramped; pay extra for superior or deluxe ones, which have slick fitted furnishings and chocolate hues. There are three apartments for long stays. **www.albusgrandhotel.com**

MUSEUM QUARTER Hestia

Roemer Visscherstraat 7, 1054 EV **Tel** *(020) 618 0801* **Fax** *685 1382* **Rooms** *18*   **Map 4 D2**

On an architecturally fascinating street between Leidseplein and the museums, this small, private hotel is aimed at families and small groups. Rooms, sleeping up to five, offer nothing fancy but are spotlessly clean and have comfortable beds. There is a small garden for guest use; room 15 has a balcony overlooking it. **www.hotel-hestia.nl**

MUSEUM QUARTER Stayokay City Hostel Vondelpark

Zandpad 5, 1054 GA **Tel** *(020) 589 8996* **Fax** *589 8955* **Rooms** *105*   **Map 4 D2**

The second Amsterdam outpost of a worthy organization, this hostel on the edge of the Vondelpark is ideal for families and nature lovers. Accommodation ranges from double rooms to 20-bed dorms. There is a TV room, and Brasserie Backpackers has a lovely terrace looking onto the park. **www.stayokay.com**

MUSEUM QUARTER Owl

Roemer Visscherstraat 1, 1054 EV **Tel** *(020) 618 9484* **Fax** *618 9441* **Rooms** *34*   **Map 4 D2**

Close to Leidseplein, but on a quiet street ensuring a restful sleep, this enduring, family-run favourite is housed in an attractive villa. There is a bar and a relaxing conservatory overlooking a garden. Rooms are not spacious or particularly stylish, but they are well-looked after, as are guests, many of whom come back. **www.owl-hotel.nl**

MUSEUM QUARTER Piet Hein

Vossiusstraat 52–53, 1071 AK **Tel** *(020) 662 7205* **Fax** *662 1526* **Rooms** *36*   **Map 4 D3**

A stylish hotel that has been refurbished in soothing caramel and cream tones. The rooms are pleasing on the eye and gentle on the wallet, and rather spacious for Amsterdam. The most popular ones overlook Vondelpark. There is a late-opening bar and relaxing lounge area, and the staff are helpful. **www.hotelpiethein.nl**

MUSEUM QUARTER Sandton Hotel De Filosoof

Anna van der Vondelstraat 6, 1054 GZ **Tel** *(020) 683 3013* **Fax** *685 3750* **Rooms** *38*   **Map 3 C2**

A much-loved hotel on a street off the Vondelpark. Every room here is individually decorated according to a different philosopher or treatise. There is Passion, Wittgenstein or local boy Spinoza, for example. It is a favourite of brooding intellectuals, who make use of the lovely garden and, of course, the library. **www.sandton.eu/amsterdam**

PLANTAGE Bridge Hotel

Amstel 107–111, 1018 EM **Tel** *(020) 623 7068* **Fax** *624 1565* **Rooms** *43*   **Map 5 B3**

In a former stonemason's workshop, this hotel stands in splendid isolation right on the river bank, looking towards Rembrandtplein. All of the rooms are simple and bright, but those looking onto the water cost extra. There are apartments with kitchenettes for stays of three nights or longer. **www.thebridgehotel.nl**

Key to Price Guide *see p392* **Key to Symbols** *see back cover flap*

PLANTAGE Rembrandt 🕴 €

Plantage Middenlaan 17, 1018 DA **Tel** *(020) 627 2714* **Fax** *638 0293* **Rooms** *17* **Map** *5 C2*

One of the few cheaper options in this area, this hotel is good for families intent on visiting nearby Artis zoo. Public spaces are covered in flamboyant murals that recall the hotel's namesake, and have dark, wooden furniture. The bedrooms, meanwhile, are brighter and more modern, and all are ensuite. **www.hotelrembrandt.nl**

PLANTAGE Ibis Stopera €€

Valkenburgerstraat 68, 1011 LZ **Tel** *(020) 531 9135* **Fax** *531 9145* **Rooms** *207* **Map** *5 C1*

One of two central branches of this useful chain, the Stopera lies on a busy road just behind the opera house. Nevertheless, it is ideally placed for the old Jewish quarter and the Eastern Docklands. The air-conditioned rooms, with Wi-Fi Internet acccess, deliver no surprises, but are none the worse for it. Pets are welcome. **www.ibishotel.com**

NORTH HOLLAND

BROEK IN WATERLAND De Schaapskooi €

Molengouw 34, 1151 CJ **Tel** *(020) 403 8317* **Fax** *403 8318* **Rooms** *4* **Road map** *C3*

On the edge of the beautiful Golden age village in the middle of the wildlife-filled Waterland landscape, this friendly hotel is part of a working sheep farm. Rooms are functional and plainly decorated, but come fitted with kitchenettes, fridges and spa baths – ideal for relaxing after a long day's exploring. **www.hoteldeschaapskooi.nl**

EGMOND AAN ZEE Hotel de Vassy €

Boulevard Ir. de Vassy 3, 1931 CN **Tel** *(072) 506 1573* **Rooms** *28* **Road map** *B3*

This attractive white, wooden hotel with balconies overlooks the long expanse of beach and the town's landmark lighthouse. It's a good base for exploring the North Sea dunes and coast. Inside, rooms are spacious, decorated in plaids and pastels. Free coffee, tea and hot chocolate is available in the guests' lounge. **www.vassy.nl**

HAARLEM Haarlem Hotelsuites €€

Kleine Houtstraat 13, 2011 DD **Tel** *(023) 540 7146* **Fax** *551 8923* **Rooms** *3* **Road map** *B3*

On a restaurant-lined street at the heart of the city, the apartments here are spacious and stylish. They have large living rooms with squashy sofas, and bedrooms have comfy big beds; some apartments have private roof terraces. Breakfast is served in the nearby Boulangerie café, or delivered to the apartment. **www.haarlem-hotelsuites.nl**

HEEMSKERK Stayokay Heemskerk €

Tolweg 9, 1967 NG **Tel** *(0251) 232 288* **Fax** *251 024* **Rooms** *32* **Road map** *B3*

This branch of the reliable hostel chain is within an atmospheric, 13th-century castle, Slot Assumburg. Renovated rooms and dormitories are minimally furnished, but the moated surroundings and facilities retain many old features: the restaurant and public spaces are in beamed-ceilinged rooms. Closed Nov–Mar. **www.stayokay.com**

HUIZEN Hotel Newport €€€€

Labradorstroom 75, 1271 DE **Tel** *(035) 528 9600* **Fax** *528 9611* **Rooms** *61* **Road map** *C3*

Overlooking the yacht harbour and Gooimeer lake, this upmarket hotel offers deluxe rooms and suites, all decorated in inviting neutral shades, with the latest designer furniture and technology (flatscreen televisions), and large bathrooms (most have showers) with Aveda products. The 8th-floor penthouse has a roof terrace. **www.hotelnewport.nl**

SANTPOORT Hotel Duin en Kruidberg €€€€

Duin en Kruidbergerweg 60, 2071 LE **Tel** *(023) 512 1800* **Fax** *512 1888* **Rooms** *75* **Road map** *B3*

A country retreat, in the middle of a national park, that's ideal for hiking and cycling through dunes and woods. The estate was built between 1907 and 1909. Reception rooms and bedrooms show an eclectic mix of styles; public spaces look particularly opulent. As well as a gym, there's a Finnish sauna. **www.duin-kruidberg.nl**

VOLENDAM Hotel Restaurant Van den Hogen €

Haven 106, 1131 EV **Tel** *(0299) 363 775* **Fax** *369 498* **Rooms** *5* **Road map** *C3*

This small hotel is right on the waterfront, close to all the fishing boats, and near the bars and restaurants. Most rooms have views over the IJsselmeer, and are clean and tidy, though decorated in plain, functional style, and all are ensuite. There's a cosy, traditional fish restaurant downstairs. **www.hogen.nl**

WEESP Boerenhofstede de Overhorn €

s-Gravelandseweg 50–51, 1381 HK **Tel** *(0294) 455 888* **Fax** *430 830* **Rooms** *2* **Road map** *C3*

Accommodation here, in a beautiful 19th-century farmhouse, is in either a large room under wooden beams overlooking the Vecht river, or a smaller room at the back of the farmhouse. Both rooms share bathroom facilities. **www.overhorn.nl**

ZANDVOORT AAN ZEE Pension Zandvoort aan Zee €

Brederodestraat 56, 2042 BH **Tel** *(06) 2697 9645* **Rooms** *8* **Road map** *B3*

This pension offers rooms, apartments and studios. Bedrooms are functional but stylish, with bright bed linen. They are equipped with kettles and fridges. The larger studios are similar, but with kitchenettes, and apartments are equipped for a longer stay. **www.zandvoortpension.nl**

UTRECHT

AMERSFOORT Logies de Tabaksplant €

Coninckstraat 15, 3811 WD **Tel** *(033) 472 9797* **Fax** *0842 151030* **Rooms** *25*   **Road map** *C4*

This town-centre hotel occupies a row of 17th-century houses, one of which was built by the owner of a tobacco plantation. The façade maintains many original features, while the rooms are furnished in contemporary style. Larger rooms come with kitchenettes, luxury ones with saunas, and there are also big apartments. **www.tabaksplant.nl**

BREUKELEN Hotel Breukelen A2 €€

Stationsweg 91, 3621 LK **Tel** *(0346) 265 888* **Fax** *262 894* **Rooms** *141*   **Road map** *C3*

Although in an uninspired location near a main road, this hotel is rather surprising: it's a copy of the Imperial Palace in Beijing. The interior is less extravagant, but the quiet rooms are decorated in bright colours and swathes of fabric. The restaurant and breakfast are good, and staff are courteous. **www.hotelbreukelen.nl**

BUNNIK Stayokay Utrecht €

Rhijnauwenselaan 14, 3981 HH **Tel** *(030) 656 1277* **Fax** *657 1065* **Rooms** *23*   **Road map** *C4*

This branch of the family-friendly hostel chain is beautifully situated in a 19th-century house, next to a little river in woodland. Accommodation is Stayokay standard: dorms and private rooms, all clean and well-maintained. The bar and restaurant are pleasant, and there's a lovely terrace. Closed Nov–Feb. **www.stayokay.com**

DRIEBERGEN De Bergse Bossen €

Traaij 299, 3971GM **Tel** *(0343) 528 150* **Fax** *521 973* **Rooms** *65*   **Road map** *C4*

At the heart of the rolling Heuvelrug, this hotel and conference centre is a good base after a day's exploring. The quiet rooms are decorated in appropriate woodland shades, with wicker furniture and hung with modern prints, though some can be dark. More expensive rooms have baths. Staff are pleasant. **www.debergebossen.nl**

LAAGE VUURSCHE De Kastanjehof €€

Kloosterlaan 1, 3749 AJ **Tel** *(035) 666 8248* **Fax** *666 8444* **Rooms** *11*   **Road map** *C3*

In a lovely little village in the middle of a forest, this hotel makes an ideal romantic hideaway. Rooms are decorated in a homely, relaxed style with sofas, paintings and ornaments; many have balconies and some pricier ones are two storey. Bathrooms, however, can be cramped. The staff are helpful. **www.dekastanjehof.nl**

UTRECHT B&B Utrecht €

Lucas Bolwerk 4, 3512 EG **Tel** *(06) 504 34884* **Rooms** *8*   **Road map** *C4*

Popular with the international backpacking crowd for its cheap rates, friendly atmosphere and free breakfast, lunch and (self-cooked) dinner, there are private rooms here as well as dorms. The kitchen and public spaces are bright and clean. The rooms are basic with decorative flourishes, though they can be a bit careworn. **www.hostelutrecht.nl**

UTRECHT Hotel Oorsprongpark €

F.C. Dondersstraat 12, 3572 JH **Tel** *(030) 271 6303* **Fax** *271 4619* **Rooms** *38*   **Road map** *C4*

In a nice old house, on a quiet street of a residential district away from the centre, this hotel's secret is the lovely waterside garden at the back (open to guests). Rooms, though small and simple, are clean and neat, the breakfast room is cosy, and breakfast itself is tasty and filling. **www.oorsprongpark.nl**

UTRECHT NH Utrecht €€

Jaarbeursplein 24, 3521 AR **Tel** *(030) 297 7977* **Fax** *297 7999* **Rooms** *276*   **Road map** *C4*

Handy for the railway station and centre, this hotel is part of a reliable Dutch chain. Rooms are spacious and pleasantly turned out, and bathrooms have high-powered showers. The breakfast buffet is particularly good, with a wide choice of food. There are also two restaurants and a bar. **www.nh-hotels.com**

UTRECHT Grand Hotel Karel V €€€

Geertebolwerk 1, 3511 XA **Tel** *(030) 233 7555* **Fax** *233 7500* **Rooms** *121*   **Road map** *C4*

The best hotel in the city is housed in a former military building filled with historical detail. The luxurious rooms and suites have great bathrooms, and are arranged across different wings. Amenities are tip-top: a Michelin-starred restaurant, a brasserie, a wine bar and huge gardens. Breakfasts are excellent. **www.karelv.nl**

VINKEVEEN Motel Café Restaurant De Plashoeve €

Baambrugse Zuwe 167, 3645 AG **Tel** *(0294) 291 381* **Fax** *293 556* **Rooms** *14*   **Road map** *C3*

This hotel is part of a busy café and restaurant, and so sometimes gets noisy. However, it's wonderfully situated right on a lake, with a large terrace on the water (there's even a hotel boat for hire). Rooms are plain but well cared for, quite large and have comfortable beds. **www.plashoeve.nl**

ZEIST Bilderberg Kasteel 't Kerckebosch €€€

Arnhemse Bovenweg 31, 3708 AA **Tel** *(030) 692 6666* **Fax** *692 6600* **Rooms** *30*   **Road map** *C4*

This atmospheric hotel is located a 15-minute walk out of the town centre, in a Gothic castle, one of the oldest in the country. Public areas reflect the building's history, with stained-glass windows, candelabra and heavy wooden furniture. Rooms, meanwhile, are bright, modern and stylish, in neutral and pastel shades. **www.bilderberg.nl**

Key to Price Guide *see p392* **Key to Symbols** *see back cover flap*

SOUTH HOLLAND

DELFT Hotel de Koophandel €
Beestenmarkt 30, 2611 GC **Tel** *(015) 214 2302* **Fax** *212 0674* **Rooms** *25*   **Road map** *B4*

On a charming old square near all the tourist sights, this attractive 16th-century townhouse was the birthplace of Vermeer's father. Rooms, decorated in muted colours with huge prints of paintings by famous Dutch artists, have big windows and thoughtful touches like tea/coffee-makers. Breakfasts are ample and tasty. **www.hoteldekoophandel.nl**

DELFT Hotel de Ark €€
Koornmarkt 65, 2611 EC **Tel** *(015) 215 7999* **Fax** *214 4997* **Rooms** *38*   **Road map** *B4*

Arranged across four houses beside a bustling canal, De Ark is convenient for the station and city centre. Rooms, in bright, fresh colours are well-sized (as are bathrooms), with lovely touches like Delft-tiled fireplaces. The bridal suites boast two-person whirlpool baths and saunas, and there are also apartments for longer stays. **www.deark.nl**

DORDRECHT Aan de Haven Bed and Bread €
Achterhakkers 71, 3311 JA **Tel** *(078) 648 3332* **Fax** *648 3331* **Rooms** *4*   **Road map** *B4*

Near the railway station, overlooking a lively working harbour, this cheerful B&B offers friendly, value-for-money accommodation. There are just four rooms, two with garden views. One has a carved fireplace and an ornate ceiling, another a large terrace, a third water views; all come with fridge and microwave. **www.bedandbread.nl**

GORINCHEM Bed & Breakfast Gorinchem €
Vissersdijk 45, 4201 ZB **Tel** *(06) 3058 6184* **Rooms** *3*   **Road map** *C4*

In an atmospheric town house in the centre of the pretty harbour town, accommodation here is made up of two rooms and a studio. The latter is nicely decorated in scrubbed wood, with DVD player and kitchenette. The rooms, in chocolates and beiges, are spacious and comfortable, with big bathrooms. **www.slapeningorinchem.nl**

GOUDA Hotel de Keizerskroon €
Keizerstraat 11–13, 2801 NJ **Tel** *(0182) 528 096* **Fax** *511 777* **Rooms** *10*   **Road map** *B4*

In this compact hotel, convenient for all of Gouda's sights, accommodation is divided into luxury and budget. All rooms are clean, tidy and simply furnished; cheaper ones share bathrooms, pricier ones have private bathrooms, though these are rather small. The filling breakfast offers extensive choice. Staff are helpful. **www.hotelkeizerskroon.nl**

LEIDEN Hotel Mayflower €
Beestenmarkt 3, 2312 CC **Tel** *(071) 514 2641* **Fax** *512 8516* **Rooms** *27*   **Road map** *B3*

A short walk from the railway station, this clean, central hotel is on a large, café-lined square near several canals. A good unpretentious family-orientated place, rooms are large, if a little dated; those at the front get a bit noisy. There are also separate apartments for long stays. **www.hotelmayflower.nl**

LEIDEN Pension De Witte Singel €
Witte Singel 80, 2311 BP **Tel** *(071) 512 4592* **Rooms** *6*   **Road map** *B3*

This simple, unpretentious little guesthouse occupies a lovely townhouse overlooking a canal. There are just six rooms; the ones at the back have views over the chestnut trees in the garden, while the front-facing ones overlook the water. Accommodation is clean and tidy, with either private or shared facilities. **www.pension-ws.demon.nl**

RIJSWIJK The Grand Winston €
Generaal Eisenhowerplein 1, 2288 AE **Tel** *(070) 414 1500* **Fax** *414 1510* **Rooms** *252*   **Road map** *B4*

In a quiet residential suburb south of The Hague, this designer hotel is decorated with huge prints of Winston Churchill. Although thoroughly modern, with acres of plate glass and inventive lighting, leather armchairs and high ceilings give a gentleman's club feel. There are two restaurants, a bar and a wine-cellar. **www.grandwinston.nl**

ROTTERDAM Hotel Bazar €
Witte de Withstraat 16, 1073 BL **Tel** *(010) 206 5151* **Fax** *206 5159* **Rooms** *27*   **Road map** *B4*

Cheap, cheerful and exotic sums up this souk-style hotel in Rotterdam's fashionable bar and gallery district. It's not intimidatingly trendy, however, and children will have great fun in the no-frills, North Africa- and South America-themed rooms painted in sizzling shades. The attached Middle Eastern restaurant is pleasant. **www.bazarrotterdam.nl**

ROTTERDAM Hotel New York €€€
Koninginnenhoofd 1, 3072 AD **Tel** *(010) 439 0500* **Fax** *484 2701* **Rooms** *72*   **Road map** *B4*

This monumental hotel in a former shipping-line HQ feels gloriously isolated, though it's near the centre. Most rooms are decorated in bold modern designs with lovely bathrooms; the more expensive ones, in the directors' boardrooms, remain untouched, with wood-panelling and chandeliers. The grand restaurant is unreliable. **www.hotelnewyork.nl**

ROTTERDAM Stroom €€€
Lloydstraat 1, 3024 EA **Tel** *(010) 221 4060* **Fax** *221 4061* **Rooms** *5*   **Road map** *B4*

This funky hotel gives guests a slice of decadent loft-style living. Flatscreen TVs, surround-sound, designer bathrooms (pricier rooms with two-person showers) and the latest in interior design are standard here. Healthy breakfasts are eaten in the trendy café or on the roof terrace. There's also a restaurant and bar. **www.stroomrotterdam.nl**

THE HAGUE Hotel Petit
Groothertoginnelaan 42, 2517 EH **Tel** *(070) 346 5500* **Fax** *346 3257* **Rooms** *20*   **Road map** *B4*

For those who want a quiet place away from the centre, and a personal touch, this small, private hotel in the embassy district is ideal. There is nothing fashionable about the large bedrooms, but they are bright and furnished with comfortable beds and armchairs or sofas. Staff are kind. **www.hotelpetit.nl**

THE HAGUE Ibis Den Haag City Centre
Jan Hendrikstraat 10, 2512 GL **Tel** *(070) 318 4318* **Fax** *318 4319* **Rooms** *197*   **Road map** *B4*

This branch of the reliable chain is well-situated in the city centre, and close to an atmospheric church and square. Staff are helpful and courteous; rooms are spotless, comfortable and reasonably sized, and come with the Ibis guarantee: if a problem isn't solved within 15 minutes, the stay is free. **www.ibishotel.com**

THE HAGUE Le Meridien Hotel des Indes
Lange Voorhout 54-56, 2514 EG **Tel** *(070) 361 2345* **Fax** *361 2350* **Rooms** *92*   **Road map** *B4*

One of the most famous – and best – in the whole country, this monumental hotel is a luxurious base for exploring the city. Decor references the colonial period with dark heavy wood, swathes of marble and potted palms. Rooms are spacious and well equipped. One minus point: staff could be more gracious. **www.hoteldesindes.nl**

ZEELAND

DOMBURG Hotel de Burg
Ooststraat 5, 4357 BE **Tel** *(0118) 581 337* **Fax** *582 072* **Rooms** *22*   **Road map** *A5*

It's just a moment's stroll to the beach from this hotel on Domburg's pleasant main thoroughfare. It's geared to guests on seaside visits, with safe storage for bikes and surfing equipment. Decor in public spaces and rooms is plain but comfortable, and there's an informal restaurant downstairs, serving hearty food. **www.hoteldeburg.nl**

DOMBURG Badhotel Domburg
Domburgseweg 1a, 4357 BA **Tel** *(0118) 588 888* **Fax** *588 899* **Rooms** *116*   **Road map** *A5*

A large, rather old-fashioned – though not staid – hotel near the main road into town, boasting a pleasant indoor pool. Staff are courteous and attentive, and rooms are large and well equipped. With tables and chairs, coffee-makers and fridges, they are ideal for longer stays. There's a range of good children's facilities. **www.badhotel.com**

GOES Grand Café Hotel Jersey
Grote Markt 28, 4461 AJ **Tel** *(0113) 232 323* **Fax** *251 755* **Rooms** *12*   **Road map** *A5*

This hotel is on the main market square at the heart of the historic harbour town, and makes a good base for exploring the Zuid-Beveland region. There are just 12 rooms, neat, very clean and plainly furnished; all are situated at the back of the building, away from the busy square. There is a pleasant café-restaurant. **www.grandcafejersey.nl**

KRUININGEN Manoir Restaurant Inter Scaldes
Zandweg 2, 4416 NA **Tel** *(0113) 381 753* **Fax** *381 763* **Rooms** *12*   **Road map** *A5*

This big manor house with a two-star Michelin restaurant is ideal for luxury sojourns: it is isolated on a spit of land between the Ooster- and Westerschelde estuaries. Rooms are large with restrained tasteful decor; some have private terraces, some are split-level and others have whirlpool baths. **www.interscaldes.nl**

MIDDELBURG Hotel het Princenjagt
Nederstraat 2, 4332 AZ **Tel** *(0118) 613 416* **Rooms** *8*   **Road map** *A5*

This small family hotel is nicely situated on the edge of the yacht harbour, just a few minutes' walk from the centre of town. Rooms have plain but pleasant furnishings; the most characterful ones are up in the eaves. Geared towards families, all rooms come with a microwave, fridge and coffee-maker. **www.hotelhetprincenjagt.nl**

OUDDORP Pension Ouddorp
Dorpsweg 26, 3253 AH **Tel** *(0187) 681 724* **Fax** *687 335* **Rooms** *15*   **Road map** *A5*

Within walking distance of the centre of the seaside village, this small, family-run pension is located above a cosy café-restaurant. The rooms are minimally furnished in a homely style, and are clean, neat and tidy. Some rooms have private bathrooms, others share toilet and washing facilities in the hall. **www.pensionouddorp.nl**

RENESSE Landgoed Moermond
Stoofwekken 5, 4325 BC **Tel** *(0111) 461 788* **Fax** *461 754* **Rooms** *43*   **Road map** *A5*

This dramatic, 13th-century castle on a large country estate is the setting for a pleasant hotel and restaurant. Standard and luxury rooms are large with lovely views, though they are rather business-like in style. The bridal suite is draped in fabrics and has a large whirlpool bath. Public areas are atmospheric. **www.slot-moermond.nl**

RILLAND-BATH t Klooster van Rilland
Hoofdweg 60, 4411 NA **Tel** *(0113) 551 177* **Fax** *551 021* **Rooms** *45*   **Road map** *B5*

Housed in an attractive former abbey, accommodation here varies between value-for-money apartments and family-sized rooms – which are rather institutional and uninspiring – to a dramatic, scarlet bridal suite with luxurious bathroom. The public spaces are charming and hint at the building's former use. **www.kloostervanrilland.nl**

Key to Price Guide *see p392* **Key to Symbols** *see back cover flap*

SLUIS D' Ouwe Schuure
🏠 €

St. Annastraat 191, 4524 JH Tel (0117) 462 232 Rooms 8 **Road map** *A5*

Right next to the Belgian border, this traditional, family-run hotel is situated in an old farmhouse in a historic village. The eight rooms are spacious, and are decorated in a rustic, homely style; ceilings are beamed and some rooms have brick fireplaces. Breakfast is eaten in the cosy, ground-floor restaurant. **www.ouweschuure.nl**

ZIERIKZEE Hotel Zierikzee
P 🏠 €

Driekoningenlaan 7, 4301 HK Tel (0111) 412 323 Fax 413 243 Rooms 15 **Road map** *A4*

Staff at this hotel in a handsome white, 18th-century townhouse offer a warm welcome. It's a good bet for families, with some rooms sleeping up to four people. Accommodation itself is spotlessly clean and, although plain, thought has been put into colour schemes and decoration. The breakfasts are very good. **www.hotelzierikzee.nl**

WEST FRISIAN ISLANDS

AMELAND/HOLLUM Dit Eiland
P €€

Burenlaan 1, 9161 AJ Tel (0519) 554 405 Rooms 4 **Road map** *C1*

This small hotel is ideal for those who want intimacy and the personal touch. In the home of an artist couple, the atmosphere is cultured, with paintings, music and books everywhere. The rooms are white and minimalist, with luxurious handmade mattresses and a free minibar. French doors open to the garden. **www.diteiland.nl**

AMELAND/NES Hotel Zeewinde
P 🏠 €

Torenstraat 22, 9163 HE Tel (051) 954 6500 Fax 954 6509 Rooms 34 **Road map** *D1*

This hotel, just over a kilometre from the beach, is geared to active seaside stays, with patio terraces, tennis courts and children's facilities. Rooms are smart, large and comfortable in bright blues and whites, and come with microwaves and coffee-makers. There's a pleasant onsite bar. **www.hotelzeewinde.nl**

SCHIERMONNIKOOG Hotel Van der Werff
🛏 🏠 🔳 €€

Reeweg 2, 9166 PX Tel (0519) 531 203 Fax 531 748 Rooms 57 **Road map** *D1*

A vintage bus whisks guests from the ferry to this hotel in an imposing white building on a bustling street. Old-fashioned stylishness prevails throughout: public areas evoke the 1940s, with velvet chairs and wood-panelling, while rooms and apartments, though modern, have dark wood pieces, wicker chairs and squashy sofas. **www.hotelvanderwerff.nl**

TERSCHELLING/WEST AAN ZEE Paal 8 Hotel aan Zee
P 🏠 🔳 €€

Badweg 4, 8881 HB Tel (0562) 449 090 Rooms 58 **Road map** *C1*

This dramatic, modern hotel is built right over a wide expanse of beach. It's luxurious and very stylish throughout, with pool and saunas. Rooms have either dune or (pricier) sea views, and have designer furniture in soothing sandy shades. For longer stays, there are apartments. The hotel rents out bikes. **www.paal8.nl**

TERSCHELLING/WEST-TERSCHELLING Hotel Pension Buren
🔳 €

Burg. Mentzstraat 20, 8881 AL Tel (0562) 442 226 Rooms 13 **Road map** *C1*

A 19th-century house is home to this unpretentious but rather stylish little guesthouse. Rooms, arranged over two floors, are painted in bright colours; others are cosy and in the eaves; some share bathrooms. The wood-panelled breakfast room is beautiful. **www.hotel-buren.nl**

TEXEL/DE KOOG Hotel Restaurant Cooghen
🛏 P 🏠 €€

Dorpsstraat 10, 1796 BB Tel (0222) 367 020 Fax 367 021 Rooms 27 **Road map** *B2*

At the heart of the lively village in the north of the island, this modern hotel is a stylish bolt-hole. Rooms are bright, airy and painted sea-sidey blues and whites, with fashionable designer furniture, and the comfortable beds are extra long. Breakfast is in the restaurant or on the terrace. Rooms above the café can get noisy. **www.cooghen.nl**

TEXEL/OUDESCHILD Texel Suites
P 🏠 🔳 €€€€

Haven 8, 1792 AE Tel (0222) 367 021 Fax 310 404 Rooms 3 **Road map** *B2*

This old fisherman's warehouse on the dock has been converted into large, ultra-stylish apartments. Old beams contrast with state-of-the-art furniture, and box-spring beds, rain-showers, a mini wine-cellar, espresso machines and LCD TVs come as standard. The biggest apartment has a stainless-steel kitchen. **www.texelsuites.com**

GRONINGEN

ADUARD Herberg Onder de Linden
P 🏠 🔳 €€

Burg. van Barneveldweg 3, 9831 RD Tel (050) 403 1406 Fax 403 1814 Rooms 5 **Road map** *D1*

A beautiful, compact little country house is the setting for this lovely restaurant with rooms. Stays are taken in conjunction with dining, and there are value-for-money dinner, bed and breakfast arrangements. Rooms, up in the attic, have character, with low, beamed ceilings, dark leather sofas and vases of fresh flowers. **www.slenema.nl**

DELFZIJL Het Eemshotel
Zeebadweg 2, 9933 AV **Tel** *(0596) 612 636* **Fax** *619 654* **Rooms** *20*   **Road map** *E1*

Perched on stilts over the sea, this hotel is an architectural feat, and provides a dramatic backdrop for overnight stays. Inside the modern building, there are 20 rooms, all pleasantly fitted out with comfortable beds and armchairs, and all the bathrooms have baths. Twelve of the rooms have unsurpassed sea views. **www.eemshotel.nl**

DEN HAM Piloersemaborg
Sietse Veldstraweg 25, 9833 TA **Tel** *(050) 403 1362* **Fax** *403 0755* **Rooms** *5*   **Road map** *D1*

This lovely country house dating from the 16th century is now a conference centre and meeting place, and has just five rooms and apartments, with sober, tasteful decor. Bikes can be rented for exploring the attached farmland and environs. Breakfast, with home-made jams, breads and organic meat, is a treat. **www.piloersema.nl**

EENRUM De Kromme Raake
Molenstraat 5, 9967 SL **Tel** *(0595) 491 600* **Rooms** *1*   **Road map** *D1*

Officially the smallest hotel in the world, this one-roomed place, though small in stature, is big on atmosphere. The ideal romantic retreat, painted motifs cover every surface and the bed is tucked away in a cupboard. Nightshirts are supplied! The bathroom, with sunken bath, is thoroughly modern. **www.hoteldekrommeraake.nl**

GRONINGEN Pension Café Tivoli
Gedempte Zuiderdiep 67, 9711 HC **Tel** *(050) 318 0999* **Rooms** *16*   **Road map** *D1*

Reasonably priced, basic accommodation is the order of the day at this guesthouse that's convenient for the railway station, city centre and university. Rooms have bright bed linen and colour schemes. Some have shared bathroom facilities, but all come with sinks and microwave ovens. Breakfast is served in the café. **www.pensioncafetivoli.nl**

GRONINGEN Hotel Het Schimmelpenninck Huys
Oosterstraat 53, 9711 NR **Tel** *(050) 318 9502* **Fax** *318 3164* **Rooms** *54*   **Road map** *D1*

A grand and stylish hotel-restaurant, in the heart of the city centre, housed in a gentleman's town house. Bedrooms have tall windows, high ceilings and tiled fireplaces. Luxury rooms have Jacuzzis and marble bathrooms; the penthouse has a private roof terrace. The lounge has carved ceilings and a piano. **www.schimmelpenninckhuys.nl**

SELLINGEN Herberg Sellingen
Dorpstraat 37 **Tel** *(0599) 322 285* **Fax** *322 026* **Rooms** *5*   **Road map** *E2*

The rooms in this lovely village guesthouse and restaurant have been decorated with loving care. All have baths, extra-long beds and CD players. The English-themed room is floral with chaises longues; the Scandinavian room is sleek, with infrared sauna and Jacuzzi; the biggest offers a romantic canopied bed. **www.herbergsellingen.nl**

TER APEL Hotel Bosch Huis
Boslaan 6, 9561 LH **Tel** *(0599) 581 208* **Fax** *581 906* **Rooms** *10*   **Road map** *E2*

The building that houses this smart hotel was originally a brewery run by monks. Still hospitable, the ten rooms here are well cared for, if a little plainly decorated. They offer good value for money and are a base for exploring the surrounding woodland. Public areas are cosy, with roaring fires. **www.hotelboschhuis.nl**

FRIESLAND

DOKKUM Hotel Café Restaurant 't Raedhûs
Koningstraat 1, 9101 LP **Tel** *(0519) 294 082* **Rooms** *6*   **Road map** *D1*

An atmospheric little town-centre hotel above a café, which sometimes leads to noisy rooms – ask for those to the rear. Staff are friendly, and the accommodation offers good value. The rooms are simply furnished but comfortable; some share facilities, others have private bathrooms. Breakfast is eaten in the café. **www.raedhus.nl**

FRANEKER De Stadsherberg
Oude Kaatsveld 8, 8801 AB **Tel** *(0517) 392 686* **Fax** *398 095* **Rooms** *10*   **Road map** *C1*

This little inn with rooms on the water's edge provides cosy, reasonably priced accommodation near the town centre. The ten rooms are comfortably and simply furnished – one has a whirlpool bath. Nice touches, such as the loan of video recorders and access to a roof terrace, make this place special. **www.stadsherbergfraneker.nl**

HARLINGEN Vuurtoren van Harlingen
Dromen aan Zee, Postbus 89, 8860 AB **Tel** *(0517) 414 410* **Rooms** *1*   **Road map** *C2*

Book well ahead for this lighthouse, now offering state-of-the-art accommodation. Arranged over several narrow floors, the furnishings are stylish and the views over Harlingen unsurpassed – especially from the living room in the top-floor dome. A luxury converted lifeboat and vertiginous crane are also available to rent. **www.vuurtoren-harlingen.nl**

OUDKERK Landgoed de Klinze
Postbus 71, 9062 ZJ Oenekerk **Tel** *(058) 256 1050* **Fax** *256 1060* **Rooms** *27*   **Road map** *D1*

This beautiful old 17th-century manor house set in acres of parkland makes for an indulgent stay. As well as a pool and a restaurant, there's a Guerlain beauty salon, and trips on the hotel's own boat. Room decor is baronial, with restrained florals, carved wooden beds and armchairs, and bathrooms are marble. **www.klinze.nl**

Key to Price Guide *see p392* **Key to Symbols** *see back cover flap*

STAVOREN Hotel De Vrouwe van Stavoren

🅿 🍴 €

Havenweg 1, 8715 EM **Tel** *(0514) 681 202* **Fax** *681 205* **Rooms** *21*   **Road map** *C2*

Those looking for an out-of-the-ordinary night's rest will love this hotel, where some rooms are converted wine vats! Dark wood, curved walls and old-fashioned decor create a cosy atmosphere. Standard vats are compact, with showers, pricier ones have baths and living rooms. There's a pleasant conservatory café. **www.hotel-vrouwevanstavoren.nl**

TERNAARD Herberg de Waard van Ternaard

🛏 🅿 🍴 🛁 €€

De Groedse 3, 9145 RG **Tel** *(0519) 571 846* **Fax** *572 218* **Rooms** *5*   **Road map** *D1*

There are just five rooms in this squat little 19th-century villa, transformed into a very modern boutique hotel. Stark, boxy oak furniture figures large, along with spotlights, softened with fluffy bright rugs. The big buffet breakfast with home-baked bread is indulgent. Mid-week and longer stays see drops in nightly rates. **www.herbergdewaard.nl**

DRENTHE

DWINGELOO Landhotel De Börken

🅿 🍴 ♿ 📺 €

Lhee 76, 7991 PJ **Tel** *(0521) 597 200* **Fax** *597 287* **Rooms** *42*   **Road map** *D2*

This hotel in the middle of an outdoor activity centre is great for families. Behind the attractive old façade are modern rooms, which are spacious and tidy, though frill-free. Facilities are outstanding: horse-riding, golf, swimming, even a shop selling wine and local produce. **www.deborken.nl**

EEXT Herberg de Hondsrug

🅿 🛁 €

Annerweg 4A, 9463 TA **Tel** *(0592) 272 739* **Fax** *273 684* **Rooms** *5*   **Road map** *E2*

This unassuming guesthouse is well-priced and welcoming. The rooms are smart and unfussy, with big beds fitted with comfortable mattresses. In the middle of the rolling Hondsrug landscape, it's a good base for exploring the countryside, and the hotel rents out bicycles and Nordic walking poles. **www.herbergdehondsrug.nl**

NIEUW-AMSTERDAM Hotel Emmen

♿ 🅿 🍴 🏃 🛁 €

Verlengde Herendijk 50, 7833 JD **Tel** *(0591) 571 800* **Fax** *571 805* **Rooms** *78*   **Road map** *E2*

On the outskirts of town, this hotel is part of the reliable national Van Der Valk chain. A rather unattractive façade hides a smart interior, in chocolatey shades. All rooms have Jacuzzis; standard ones are neat and business-like, family rooms are spacious. Flamboyant Afrika and Hollywood suites have Turkish steam rooms. **www.hotelemmen.nl**

ROLDE Camping de Weyert

🛏 🅿 🍴 🏃 €

Balloërstraat 2, 9451 AK **Tel** *(0592) 241 520* **Fax** *241 043* **Rooms** *5*   **Road map** *E2*

In the middle of this family-friendly campsite are five unusual haylofts that have been transformed into bright, fun holiday apartments. The cute, one-storey structures look like stylish homes inside, with high ceilings, long sofas and wicker furniture. Each has a kitchenette, with picnic table outside, and sleeps up to four. **www.deweyert.nl**

WESTERBORK Abdij de Westerburcht

♿ 🅿 🍴 🏃 🛁 €

Hoofdstraat 7, 9431 AB **Tel** *(0593)331 238* **Fax** *331 710* **Rooms** *37*   **Road map** *E2*

This large hotel is rather plain from the outside, but inside there is plenty of atmosphere. Rooms are decorated in abbey-themed style, with gothic mirrors, wooden beams and torch-like wall lamps. Luxury rooms have spa baths. The public areas and grand café are attractive. **www.westerburcht.nl**

WITTEVEEN Hotel Het Witte Veen

🅿 🍴 €

K Brokweg 16, 9439 TC **Tel** *(0593) 552 429* **Fax** *552 570* **Rooms** *25*   **Road map** *E2*

Situated in the triangle formed by Emmen, Hoogeveen and Assen, this affordable hotel in a former farm is ideally placed for exploring the surrounding countryside or visiting nearby attraction parks. Rooms are basic but comfortable and some are suitable for disabled guests. Golf can be arranged, as can bicycle rental. **www.hotelwitteveen.eu**

OVERIJSSEL

DE LUTTE Landgoed de Wilmersberg

♿ 🅿 🍴 ♿ 🏃 📺 🛁 €€

Rhododendronlaan 7, 7587 NL **Tel** *(0541) 585 555* **Fax** *585 565* **Rooms** *64*   **Road map** *E3*

A former country estate that belonged to a local industrial family is nowadays an indulgent bolt-hole in the Bilderberg luxury hotel chain. Accommodation is divided between standard and "English" rooms: all have big beds, but the latter have private terraces or balconies. There's a wellness centre and pool. **www.bilderberg.nl**

ENSCHEDE Hotel Restaurant Rodenbach

🅿 🍴 🛁 €

Parkweg 35–39, 7513 AR **Tel** *(053) 480 0200* **Fax** *480 0299* **Rooms** *25*   **Road map** *E3*

Convenient for both the city centre and the railway station, this imposing hotel is situated next to a large park. Rooms, in cream and brown colours, are straightforward and attractive, and brightened with potted plants and art prints. One penthouse apartment suits longer stays. There's a rather formal on-site restaurant. **www.rodenbach.nl**

GIETHOORN Hotel De Harmonie
Beulakerweg 55, 8355 AB **Tel** *(0521) 361 372* **Fax** *361 082* **Rooms** *16*   **Road map** *D3*

A charming hotel sitting right on the water in the famous boating village. Standard rooms are clean, neat and tidy with unfussy decor; the one luxury room has French windows that open directly onto a delightful waterside terrace. All have lovely views. The hotel rents out boats, canoes and bicycles. **www.harmonie-giethoorn.nl**

LATTROP Erfgoed Bossem
Dorpsstraat 7, 7635 NA **Tel** *(0541) 221 392* **Fax** *221 946* **Rooms** *5*   **Road map** *D3*

This country estate houses a hotel in the main farmhouse. Decor is rustic yet modern: there is lots of blonde wood, bold contemporary wallpaper and lamps; furniture is designer, beds are large, and there are lots of fresh flowers. Breakfast is in the farm's kitchen; the lounge has a roaring fire. **www.bossem.nl**

LATTROP Landgoed de Holtweijde
Spiekweg 7, 7635 LP **Tel** *(0541) 229 234* **Fax** *229 445* **Rooms** *76*   **Road map** *D3*

Accommodation at this country house estate comes in various forms, all good. There are suites: junior, royal and country house are incrementally luxurious; the panorama suite has sweeping views. There are also six family-sized cottages. As well as a pool, there's an on-site beauty treatment centre. Price includes dinner. **www.holtweide.nl**

OOTMARSUM Hotel Restaurant Van der Maas
Grotestraat 7, 7631 BT **Tel** *(0541) 291 281* **Fax** *293 462* **Rooms** *20*   **Road map** *E3*

This welcoming family hotel with a restaurant beneath is in a pretty village in the middle of the Twente countryside. Rooms are plain, with decorative flourishes here and there, and are comfortable. All double rooms have baths and singles have showers. Helpful staff will advise on hiking and cycling routes. **www.vandermaas.nl**

TUBBERGEN Droste's
Uelserweg 95, 7651 KV **Tel** *(0546) 621 264* **Rooms** *20* **Fax** *622 828*   **Road map** *E3*

Rooms in this modern boutique hotel are individually styled, but each follows the same designer theme of bright, airy colours and sleek lines. Standard rooms open onto a patio, and there are three types of "loft" accommodation from small to large. Breakfast is eaten in the enclosed glass winter garden. **www.drostes.nl**

WETERING An't Waeter
Wetering West 77, 8363 TN **Tel** *(0521) 371 311* **Fax** *371 100* **Rooms** *5*   **Road map** *D3*

The name translates as "on the water", and you can't get much closer than this well-priced little guesthouse and café, situated on the edge of a lake. The ten rooms are basic but tidy and well cared for. A couple have shared bathrooms, while some have private terraces. **www.antwaeter.nl**

ZWOLLE Hotel Fidder
Kon. Wilhelminastraat 6, 8019 AM **Tel** *(038) 421 8395* **Fax** *423 0298* **Rooms** *22*   **Road map** *D3*

An old-fashioned elegance pervades this Art Deco hotel in Zwolle's city centre. Rooms are dark, atmospheric and authentically furnished with wood and heavy fabrics; some are Victorian-themed. All come with baths and coffeemakers. Breakfast, in a beautiful dining room, is delicious, with pancakes and a champagne option. **www.hotelfidder.nl**

FLEVOLAND

BIDDINGHUIZEN Dorhout Mees
Strandgaperweg 30, 8256 PZ **Tel** *(0321) 331 138* **Fax** *331 057* **Rooms** *42*   **Road map** *C3*

This big, farmhouse hotel should appeal to active holidaymakers, as it offers all kinds of activities: shooting, abseiling, quad-biking and golfing. The hotel's interior is relaxing in a rustic way, with fireplaces and chintzy chaises longues in the lounges, and stylish muted shades in the rooms. Hearty breakfasts fuel the day ahead. **www.dorhoutmees.nl**

EMMELOORD Hotel Emmeloord
Het Hooiveld 9, 8302 AE **Tel** *(0527) 612 345* **Fax** *612 845* **Rooms** *109*   **Road map** *D2*

A little uninspiring and barn-like from the outside, this hotel on the edge of town certainly boasts plenty of excellent facilities. Apart from good conference and business facilities, there is a gym, sauna and steam bath for pampering. Rooms and suites are all spacious and decorated in country house style. **www.hotelemmeloord.nl**

KRAGGENBURG Van Saaze
Dam 16, 8317 AV **Tel** *(0527) 252 353* **Fax** *252 559* **Rooms** *27*   **Road map** *D3*

A large 1950s building is home to this hotel, lively café and cosy restaurant. Accommodation is good value for money: rooms are quiet and spacious, all with ensuite facilities and even minibars. More expensive rooms come with whirlpool baths and sleep up to four, making them economical for families. **www.hotelvansaaze.nl**

LELYSTAD Apollo Hotel Lelystad City Centre
Agoraweg 11, 8224 BZ **Tel** *(0320) 242 444* **Fax** *227 569* **Rooms** *86*   **Road map** *C3*

A large, business-oriented hotel and conference centre with excellent facilities for work-related travel. Rooms are smart and upmarket, with modern aspects like exposed brick walls; wheelchair access and good room service, too. There's a tapas bar and two restaurants, one Oriental and one serving steak. **www.apollohotelresorts.nl**

Key to Price Guide *see p392* **Key to Symbols** *see back cover flap*

URK Pension de Kroon   €

Wijk 7-54, 8321 TA **Tel** *(0527) 681 216* **Fax** *681 216* **Rooms** *5*   **Road map** *C3*

At the heart of the ancient village, this pleasant guesthouse makes a good base for exploring the region. Rooms have views to the IJsselmeer, and are simply furnished, with nice flourishes: ornate lamps, original artworks. Some share bathrooms, all come with tea and coffee-making facilities. Two rooms are balconied. **www.pensiondekroon.nl**

ZEEWOLDE Hotel Restaurant Hardersluis   €

Harderhaven 32, 3898 LN **Tel** *(0320) 288 093* **Fax** *268 064* **Rooms** *6*   **Road map** *C3*

This bright yellow hotel is perched on the edge of a working harbour. The modern rooms are well-sized and decorated in florals, with pine furniture, plants and framed pictures adding to the homely atmosphere. All rooms have comfortable beds and great views. There's large waterside terrace and restaurant. **www.hardersluis.nl**

GELDERLAND

APELDOORN Bilderberg Hotel De Keizerskroon   €€

Koningstraat 7, 7315 HR **Tel** *(055) 521 7744* **Fax** *521 4737* **Rooms** *93*   **Road map** *D3*

A large, popular hotel with good facilities, pleasingly situated on the edge of a park near the Royal Palace. Rooms are big, and decorated in trendy citrus and brown shades, with big comfortable beds; the largest rooms have sofas. There's a smart restaurant, a snug bar and a small swimming pool. **www.bilderberg.nl**

ARNHEM Hotel Groot Warnsborn   €€

Bakenbergseweg 277, 6816 VP **Tel** *(026) 445 5751* **Fax** *443 1010* **Rooms** *40*   **Road map** *D4*

This old aristocratic country pile has been converted into an upmarket hotel, in lots of lush countryside. Rooms are divided between the main house and coach house. All are individually decorated in a style to please the landed gentry, whether rustic or modern. There's a good formal restaurant. **www.grootwarnsborn.nl**

BRUMMEN Kasteel Engelenburg   €€€

Eerbeekseweg 6, 6971 LB **Tel** *(0575) 569 999* **Fax** *569 992* **Rooms** *41*   **Road map** *D4*

This beautiful white château, dating back to the 16th-century, is a listed monument, as well as a top of the range hotel. There's a gentleman's residence feel throughout: rococo mirrors, leather furnishings and regency stripes abound. Standard rooms are decorated colonial-style; luxury ones and the suite are furnished in antiques. **www.engelenburg.com**

DEVENTER Gilde Hotel   €€

Nieuwstraat 41, 7411 LG **Tel** *(0570) 641 846* **Fax** *641 819* **Rooms** *29*   **Road map** *D3*

A very atmospheric hotel, right in the city centre, occupying an unusual 18th-century brick building. The lobby has a sweeping wooden staircase and the bar exudes old-fashioned warmth. Standard rooms are pleasantly decorated, pricier ones have balconies overlooking the courtyard garden. There are also larger studios. **www.sandton.eu**

HARDERWIJK Hotel Marktzicht   €

Markt 6–10, 3841 CE **Tel** *(0341) 413 032* **Fax** *413 230* **Rooms** *34*   **Road map** *C3*

A charming hotel in a sweet red-brick building overlooking a market square, right in the town centre. Rooms here are pleasantly decorated and spotlessly tidy, with nice views over the bustling square below, but also peaceful. Staff are helpful and friendly, check-in and out is efficient, and the breakfast comes highly rated. **www.hotelmarktzicht.nl**

HOENDERLOO Golden Tulip Victoria   €€

Woeste Hoefweg 80, 7351 TP **Tel** *(055) 506 2828* **Fax** *506 1605* **Rooms** *110*   **Road map** *D3*

This hotel in the middle of the Hoge Veluwe makes a good base for exploring the forests. Rooms are arranged throughout the grounds in small units; some come with private terraces. Suites face onto a courtyard. All are smartly furnished. Facilities are good: tennis courts, swimming pool, restaurant and pub. **www.goldentulipvictoria.nl**

NIJMEGEN Hotel Courage Sionshof   €

Nijmeegsebaan 53, 6564 CC **Tel** *(024) 322 7727* **Fax** *322 6223* **Rooms** *17*   **Road map** *D4*

This hotel not far from the centre of Nijmegen feels like it's in the middle of the countryside, situated as it is in woodland. Rooms are all ensuite (though bathrooms can be bit cramped) and decorated in suitably rustic style, with autumn colours and heavy woods. There's a pleasant café downstairs. **www.sionshof.nl**

OOIJ Hotel Oortjeshekken   €

Erlecomsedam 4, 6576 JW **Tel** *(024) 663 1288* **Fax** *663 3004* **Rooms** *13*   **Road map** *D4*

This lovely little hotel offers affordable boutique-style accommodation. All the rooms are beautifully turned out, with painted wood-panelling and vintage furniture. All come with views: over the river, garden or meadows beyond. One room has a terrace. There's a similarly funky café and restaurant. Breakfasts are good. **www.oortjeshekken.nl**

VORDEN Hotel/Restaurant de Gravin van Vorden   €

Stadionsweg 24, 7251 EM **Tel** *(0575) 546 111* **Rooms** *16*   **Road map** *D4*

In a town at the heart of the peaceful Achterhoek region, this hotel offers comfortable, country-style accommodation. Rooms are decorated in rustic tones enlivened with bold modern pictures. There's also a large suite, and a bridal suite with Jacuzzi. The lounge has inviting leather sofas and a log fire. **www.hotelbloemendaal.nl**

NORTH BRABANT

'S-HERTOGENBOSCH Hotel All-In
Gasselstraat 1, 5211 KJ **Tel** *(073) 613 4057* **Fax** *613 4057* **Rooms** *5*   **Road map** *C4*

This one-star, family-run, family-orientated hotel in the city centre is within walking distance of all the major sights and activities. Rooms are plain but the period building they are in is a fine example of Art Deco architecture, with authentic flourishes throughout the interior. **http://home.wanadoo.nl/hotelallin/index.html**

BERGEN OP ZOOM Hotel Old Dutch
Stationsstraat 29–31, 4611 CB **Tel** *(0164) 271 888* **Fax** *271 889* **Rooms** *11*   **Road map** *B5*

The Old Dutch offers straightforward accommodation useful for late arrivals or early starts as it sits directly opposite the railway station. There's little variation between rooms: all of them are plainly but pleasantly furnished in unfussy style, and are spotlessly clean. Those on the front can be noisy. There's also a bar. **www.hotel-olddutch.nl**

DEURNE Plein Vijf
Markt 5, 5751 BE **Tel** *(0493) 327 040* **Fax** *327 041* **Rooms** *25*   **Road map** *D5*

This hotel is nicely situated near the De Peel nature reserve, with lots of cycling and walking opportunities. The big rooms come with flatscreen TVs as standard, and are decorated with bright murals and designer furniture. There are also larger themed suites, such as Tuscany or Japan. **www.pleinvijf.nl**

EINDHOVEN Corso
Vestdijk 17, 5611 CA **Tel** *(040) 244 9131* **Fax** *245 7399* **Rooms** *8*   **Road map** *C5*

Those looking for an unusual place to lodge might try this theatre, restaurant and hotel in one. Accommodation is nothing special, and bathroom facilities are shared, but it's a good enough bet for groups and backpackers, with rooms sleeping up to eight. The restaurant has cheap daily specials for residents. **www.theatermetsmaak.nl**

ERP Hotel Het Tramstation
Molentiend 12, 5469 EK **Tel** *(0413) 335 000* **Rooms** *8*   **Road map** *D5*

This 19th-century building in the lush countryside to the north-east of the province has been both farm and tram station in its time. Now it's a sweet café-restaurant with rooms above. Cheaper accommodation shares bathroom facilities, pricier has baths. The rooms are plain, neat and no-nonsense, but comfortable. **www.hoteltramstation.nl**

ETTEN-LEUR Herberg het Witte Paard
Oude Bredaseweg 15, 4872 AB **Tel** *(076) 503 8041* **Fax** *503 7530* **Rooms** *27*   **Road map** *B5*

This country hotel is part of a pleasant 19th-century building, halfway between Breda and Etten. Rooms are in a modern annexe, decorated with bright carpets and curtains, with compact bathrooms. Breakfast and service are both good, and the lovely attached café has been brought back to its original 1828 glory. **www.hotelhetwittepaard.nl**

GEMERT De Hoefpoort
Ridderplein 37, 5421 CG **Tel** *(0492) 392 008* **Rooms** *10*   **Road map** *C5*

A lot of thought has gone into this little hotel in a village to the north of the province. Rooms, named after places of local historical interest, are individually decorated with flair: wrought-iron furniture, bright colours, vintage wood. The owners will even arrange romantic champagne breakfasts and package deals. **www.hoefpoort.nl**

HELMOND Golden Tulip West Ende
Steenweg 1, 5707 CD **Tel** *(0492) 524 151* **Fax** *543 295* **Rooms** *70*   **Road map** *C5*

This imposing white building has the look of a country house, but was actually built for use as a factory in 1880. Now that industrial past has given way to impressive modern-day rooms, swagged with tasteful fabrics. Furniture is rustic, and bathrooms are good. The staff are helpful, and there's a restaurant. **www.goldentulipwestende.nl**

KAATSHEUVEL Hotel Restaurant de Joremeinshoeve
Lage Zandschel 1, 5171 TD **Tel** *(0416) 274 527* **Fax** *282 095* **Rooms** *11*   **Road map** *C5*

This big, thatched house in the middle of a dunes nature reserve used to be a farm until the present owners converted it into a hotel and restaurant. Popular with cyclists (ask about special cycling packages), rooms are snug. Two have cupboard beds; the most expensive has a whirlpool bath. **www.joremeinshoeve.nl**

ROOSENDAAL Hotel Merks
Brugstraat 55-57, 4701 LC **Tel** *(0165) 533 169* **Fax** *555 536* **Rooms** *29*   **Road map** *B5*

A pleasant, family-run hotel with restaurant, conveniently situated for the town centre and railway station. Rooms are perhaps spartanly furnished, but it's cheap and staff are accommodating, providing packed lunches for cyclists and early breakfasts for business travellers. The old-fashioned restaurant serves cheap meals. **www.hotel-merks.nl**

ZUNDERT De Roskam
Molenstraat 1, 4881 CP **Tel** *(076) 597 2357* **Fax** *597 215* **Rooms** *25*   **Road map** *B5*

At the heart of Van Gogh's village, this family hotel offers a pleasant affordable place to stay. Rooms are bright and fresh, with pine furniture and prints by Zundert's famous son adorning walls. The guests' lounge, with welcoming armchairs and fire, is cosy. There's also a restaurant and a terrace café. **www.hotel-de-roskam.nl**

Key to Price Guide *see p392* **Key to Symbols** *see back cover flap*

LIMBURG

ARCEN De Maas Parel
Schans 3-5, 5944 AE **Tel** *(077) 473 1296* **Fax** *473 1335* **Rooms** *23*   **Road map** *D5*

A mid-range hotel above an unpretentious restaurant. Rooms, in standard and larger deluxe sizes, are pleasantly decked out with armchairs and framed prints. For longer stays, there's a bigger apartment with its own kitchen. Value-for-money packages range from multiple days to culinary arrangements for cyclists. **www.maasparel.nl**

EPEN Appartementen Hotel Gueldal
Wilhelminastraat 21, 6285 AS **Tel** *(043) 455 1282* **Fax** *455 2636* **Rooms** *7*   **Road map** *D6*

Small, cosy hotel with seven modern apartments, sleeping either two or four people. All have fully-equipped kitchens and a balcony or terrace; there is also a lovely garden to sit in. A great location for walking and cycling. No bookings are taken for single nights; there is an extra charge for a buffet breakfast. **www.appartementen-hotelgeuldal.nl**

HERKENBOSCH Landgoed Kasteel Daelenbroeck
Kasteellaan 2, 6075 EZ **Tel** *(0475) 532 465* **Fax** *536 030* **Rooms** *18*   **Road map** *D5*

Excellent service is the key to this 15th-century castle hotel in the rolling Limburg hills. Accommodation, situated in a separate annexe, comes with private terraces. One room is split-level, and another is in a tower. All are decorated in an unfussy, upmarket style. There's also a restaurant, bar and lovely terrace. **www.daelenbroeck.nl**

HOUTHEM De Herberg
Vroenhof 148, 6301 KJ **Tel** *(043) 604 0277* **Fax** *604 2779* **Rooms** *12*   **Road map** *D5*

This simple, honest guesthouse offers a well-priced stay in a country location convenient for Maastricht, Valkenburg and the bordering countries. Rooms are pleasant and fresh, with bright floral decor. Some are ensuite, others share bathrooms. There are reductions for large groups. The hotel is attached to a restaurant. **www.herberghouthem.nl**

LANDGRAAF Hotel Winselerhof
Tunnelweg 99, 6372 XH **Tel** *(045) 546 4343* **Fax** *535 2711* **Rooms** *49*   **Road map** *D6*

This grand country estate house has been converted into an indulgent hotel. Rooms in the main building are big, come with lovely old-fashioned bathrooms, and are individually decorated in rustic style. The larger suites are arranged around a courtyard. Breakfast, in the conservatory restaurant, comes with a glass of Prosecco. **www.chateauhotels.nl**

MAASTRICHT De Hofnar
Capucijnenstraat 35, 6211 RP **Tel** *(06) 4968 8189* **Rooms** *3*   **Road map** *C6*

A good bet for visitors looking for cheap, neat and clean accommodation in the city centre, this B&B is just a few hundred metres from the main square. The building is a cute cottage on a charming street; accommodation is modern and bright. One room is split-level. Ten rooms also available at Keizer Karelplein. **www.hofnarmaastricht.nl**

MAASTRICHT Hotel Les Charmes
Lenculenstraat 18, 6211 KR **Tel** *(043) 321 7400* **Fax** *321 7400* **Rooms** *15*   **Road map** *C6*

From the gas-lit cobbled street to the chandeliered lounge, an old-world charm pervades this friendly, small-scale hotel. Rooms are spacious and individually decorated in a quirky, stylish way, with claw-footed baths in the white-tiled bathrooms. Breakfasts, eaten in the lounge or conservatory, are truly delicious. **www.hotellescharmes.nl**

MAASTRICHT Kruisherenhotel
Kruisherengang 19–23, 6211 NW **Tel** *(043) 329 2020* **Fax** *323 3030* **Rooms** *60*   **Road map** *C6*

The most stunning hotel in the country fuses elements from an original Crusaders' chapel with up-to-the-minute design and architecture. Steel and glass pierce ancient stone, the rooms have enormous church windows, and the walls are covered in contemporary art murals. One of a kind, it's as much gallery as hotel. **www.chateauhotels.nl**

ROOSTEREN Hotel Terborch
Kasteel Terborchstraat 1, 6116 BV **Tel** *(046) 449 1005* **Rooms** *10*   **Road map** *D5*

Budget-class accommodation in the Netherlands seldom looks this cosy. Rooms in this small hotel are painted white, and furnished with old-fashioned, dark wood furniture, creating a nostalgic feel. All are ensuite and, though bathrooms look dated, it doesn't seem to matter. There's even a mini-gym and sunbed! **www.bamby.nl/hotelterborch**

VALKENBURG Hotel Limburgia
Grendelplein 19, 6301 BS **Tel** *(043) 601 0080* **Rooms** *17*   **Road map** *D6*

Few Valkenburg hotels are more central than this, right on the scenic main square, and convenient for all the tourist sights. Rooms here are nothing fancy, but are reasonable value, spacious and comfortably furnished in standard style, with comfortable armchairs and big beds. Nightly rates drop for longer stays. **www.hotel-limburgia.nl**

VALKENBURG Château St. Gerlach
Joseph Corneli Allée 1, 6301 KK **Tel** *(043) 608 8888* **Fax** *604 2883* **Rooms** *112*   **Road map** *D6*

This landmark hotel is one of the most glamorous destinations in the country. A medieval château and country estate, it cries out decadence, with gilded surfaces, art and sculpture everywhere. Rooms, with all the expected facilities, range from large to enormous suites. There's a Kneipp spa and Michelin-starred restaurant, too. **www.chateauhotels.nl**

WHERE TO EAT

The Dutch are innovative people, and this quality comes out in their cooking. There is a growing number of chefs who are demonstrating an artistic approach to their profession; in recent years the number of ethnic restaurants has been growing, particularly in larger towns. Whereas previously you would find only one Chinese, one Italian and one Indonesian restaurant in these towns, now you can also enjoy dishes from countries as varied as Spain, Turkey, Greece, Morocco, Israel, Lebanon, Ethiopia, India, Thailand, Japan, Korea and Vietnam.

Chef

Among the cafés and bars you will find *eetcafés*, cafés where you can order meals. Not only will you be able to enjoy your meal in a livelier atmosphere but you will find that a lot of the food served here comes close in quality to that of established restaurants. Bars where you can have traditional snacks such as a *broodje kroket* (a deep-fried croquette in a bun) are now rarer, giving way to healthier options. The restaurants listed on pages 410–23 have been selected on the basis not only of the quality of food served but also of the atmosphere and service.

Eating out is an increasingly popular pastime in the Netherlands

TYPES OF RESTAURANT

The Netherlands boasts a wide variety of restaurants, and as the Dutch are eating out with increasing frequency, this means that the range of restaurants they can choose from is increasing as well. Because of the historical ties with Indonesia, Indonesian ("Indisch") restaurants are numerous in the Netherlands. Amsterdam is one of the best places in Europe to try the diverse flavours of that country. For purists, much of the cooking may lean too heavily towards the Chinese style, but it is still possible to sample genuine Indonesian recipes. Chinese restaurants and pizzerias have also spread far and wide across the country.

Traditional Dutch cooking is best described as frugal. As a maritime nation, the Netherlands does have large numbers of fish restaurants,

particularly along the coast. There is an overwhelming number of restaurants serving French cuisine. Their numbers are increasing steadily, and quality is also improving constantly. The chefs frequently add some local ingredients to the French recipes, such as fennel or asparagus. This means that in the Netherlands you can eat wild duck on endive *stamppot* (mashed potato and cabbage), a combination which is as yet unheard of in France. Nobody looks askance at tuna tartare, deep-fried celeriac or green asparagus and guacamole. It is in areas such as these that Dutch chefs are showing increasing inventiveness.

There has been an increase in the number of ethnic restaurants in the country.

The quality varies, and the range of foods on offer is vast, from Vietnamese to Lebanese, Thai to Greek, Indian to Turkish, Moroccan to Japanese. Indeed, it is difficult to find a country whose cuisine is not represented by some restaurant in the Netherlands. There is also an infinite variety in the range of food, contents, presentation and price. The majority of ethnic restaurants are situated in larger towns and cities, but even in the countryside their numbers are steadily increasing.

EETCAFÉS

Eetcafés (eating cafés) are a popular phenomenon in Dutch eating. Initially, some cafés and bars sold snacks to

Inter Scaldes in Kruiningen, one of the best restaurants in the country

An *eetcafé*, one of the many in Holland serving increasingly refined meals

go with their drinks, such as an appetizer, a sandwich or a meatball. These snacks have since been refined to a growing extent. Bars and cafés have gradually evolved into *eetcafés* where you can enjoy sandwiches at lunch time and cheap, often very decent, meals in the evenings. They vary from very simple dishes such as soups, sandwiches, salads, omelettes and French fries to exceptionally good three-course menus. Many such cafés are now concentrating increasingly on the food aspect. The prices charged at these cafés are in many cases much lower than those in traditional restaurants.

VEGETARIAN RESTAURANTS

Most restaurants have a number of vegetarian dishes on their menus. This applies both to Dutch/French restaurants and to ethnic restaurants. There are also an increasing number of restaurants which cater exclusively to vegetarian diners.

OPENING HOURS

The Netherlands has not had a tradition of lunching, but this is also gradually changing, with increasing numbers of restaurants now opening at lunch time. In the evenings the majority of restaurants open at 6pm; the kitchens usually stop serving food at 10pm or 10:30pm. Also – and in particular in the large

towns and cities – there is a growing number of night restaurants, with the kitchens staying open until after midnight. This allows you to round off a visit to the theatre, movies or café with a late dinner.

Traditionally, many restaurants do not open on Mondays, though this is also changing.

A snack bar, ideal for a quick but satisfying bite to eat

RESERVATIONS

Anybody wishing to eat in one of the country's more renowned restaurants would do well to book, and sometimes booking a few days in advance is advisable. It can get crowded in cafés and other informal restaurants in the evenings, but reservations are usually accepted only for large groups if at all.

TIPPING

A service charge of 15 per cent is included on the bill at most Dutch bars, cafés and restaurants. However, it is customary to round up the amount. The tip should be left as change rather than included on a credit-card payslip.

ETIQUETTE

The atmosphere at most Dutch restaurants is fairly informal, and you can generally wear what you like; smart casual or semi-formal dress is suitable almost everywhere. There are some exceptions, however: in some very upmarket restaurants dressing smartly is considered very important. It is illegal to smoke in all restaurants.

PRICES

Most Dutch restaurants display a menu giving the prices of various dishes or set meals on the wall or the front door so that you can get an idea of whether the prices suit you or not before going in. The prices are given inclusive of VAT (BTW) and service. Prices can vary markedly, and a restaurant can be found in each price class: you can find many establishments where you can eat for less than €22.50; in top restaurants, however, you should not be surprised if your bill comes to €70, excluding wine. The cost of drinks is invariably extra and the mark-up levied by a restaurant, especially on cheap wine, can be high.

TRAVELLERS WITH DISABILITIES

Most restaurants at ground floor level are accessible for wheelchairs. Toilet facilities, however, tend to pose a problem, with many of them reached via steep stairs and therefore not easily accessible.

DRINKS

In recent times a growing number of restaurants has been paying more attention to the wine list: in many of them, you can choose from a range of outstanding, often French, wines to accompany your meal. The list of often exotic aperitifs available is also growing in many establishments. However, beer is the drink of preference in most Dutch cafés and bars, and all have a wide selection of local and imported brews.

The Flavours of The Netherlands

The typical Dutch menu offers good, solid fare. Pork, hams and all kinds of sausages are popular, while the North Sea provides plenty of fresh fish, especially cod, herring and mackerel, as well as its own variety of tiny brown shrimps. Leafy green vegetables, such as cabbage, endive (chicory) and curly kale make regular appearances, frequently mashed with the ubiquitous potato. Sauerkraut arrived from Germany long ago and is now considered a native dish. The world famous Gouda and Edam cheeses are sold at various stages of maturity, and with flavourings such as cloves, cumin or herbs.

Edam cheese

ingredients, ideas and people from former colonies to settle. Dutch chefs branched out and tried new flavours, and as such, "fusion" food has long been a feature of Amsterdam's menus. From its street-corner fish-stalls to its cafés and top-flight gourmet restaurants, eating out in Amsterdam can be full of surprises. Over 50 national cuisines are represented, offering a sometimes bewildering variety of choice and good value for money.

THE MELTING POT

Amsterdam has long had a reputation for religious and political tolerance. Refugees who found a safe haven there brought along their own styles of cooking. In the 16th century, Jews fleeing persecution in Portugal and

Sampling pickled herring at one of Amsterdam's many fish-stalls

AMSTERDAM'S CULINARY INFLUENCES

Traditional Dutch cuisine may be simple, wholesome and hearty, but the variety of food on offer in Amsterdam is huge and influenced by culinary styles from across the globe. The Netherlands was once a major colonial power and its trading ships brought back exotic

Bami goreng (fried noodles with chicken and pork)

Steamed rice

Prawn crackers

Fried tofu with sambal oelek (chilli sauce)

Gado gado (vegetable salad with peanut sauce)

Satay ayam (chicken satay)

Selection of typical rijsttafel dishes

LOCAL DISHES AND SPECIALITIES

Dining out in the Netherlands is almost guaranteed to come up with some curious quirks. Cheese, ham and bread are standards at breakfast, but you may also find *ontbijtkoek* (gingerbread) and *hagelslag* (grains of chocolate) to sprinkle over bread. Ham and cheese are also lunchtime staples, often served in a bread roll with a glass of milk, though more adventurous sandwiches and salads are also common nowadays. In Amsterdam, pancake houses provide both sweet and savoury snacks throughout the day. The evening is the time when Amsterdam's eateries have the most to offer. The soups and mashed vegetables of Dutch farmhouse cooking sit alongside spicy Indonesian delights, as well as innovative cuisine from some of Amsterdam's fine chefs.

Brown shrimp

Erwtensoep *is a thick pea and smoked sausage soup, which is often served with rye bread and slices of bacon.*

Baskets of wild mushrooms at an organic market

INDONESIAN LEGACY

The Dutch began colonizing Indonesia in the 17th century and ruled the south-east Asian archipelago right up until 1949. Indonesian cuisine has had a marked influence on eating habits in The Netherlands. Ingredients once regarded as exotic have crept into Dutch dishes. It is now common-place to spice up apple pies and biscuits with cinnamon, which is sometimes even used to flavour vegetables. Coconut and chillis are very popular flavourings, too, and sampling a *rijsttafel* (see below) is considered one of the highlights of any trip to the country.

Antwerp were some of the first foreigners to make their home in the city. Today, Amsterdammers count as their own such Jewish specialities as *pekelvlees* (salt beef), pickled vegetables (often served as salad) and a variety of sticky cakes, now found mostly in the more old-fashioned tea-rooms.

The 20th century saw an influx of immigrants from Turkey and several North African countries. Large Arab and Turkish communities have become established in Amsterdam. As a result, restaurants with menus that feature Middle-Eastern style stuffed vegetables, succulent stews and couscous, are almost everywhere. *Falafel* (fried chickpea balls) are readily available from road-side take-aways and are now one of the city's favourite

late-night snacks. Ethiopians, Greeks, Thais, Italians and Japanese are among other waves of immigrants to make their culinary mark, and most recently traditional British fare has become popular.

Gouda on offer in an Amsterdam cheese shop

THE RIJSTTAFEL

Dutch colonialists in Indonesia often found that the modest local portions failed to satisfy their hunger. To match their larger appetites, they created the *rijsttafel* (literally "rice-table"). It consists of around 20 small spicy dishes, served up with a shared bowl of rice or noodles. Pork or chicken *satay* (mini kebabs with peanut sauce) and *kroepoek* (prawn crackers) usually arrive first. A selection of curried meat and vegetable dishes follows, with perhaps a plate of fried tofu and various salads, all more or less served together. A sweet treat, such as bananas fried in batter, rounds it all off.

Shrimp croquettes *are shrimps in a creamy sauce, coated in breadcrumbs and deep-fried.*

Stamppot *is a hearty dish of curly kale or endive (chicory) and crispy bacon mixed with mashed potato.*

Nasi goreng, *an Indonesian-style dish of egg-fried rice with pork and mushrooms, is also popular for a* rijsttafel.

Choosing a Restaurant

The restaurants in this guide have been selected across a range of price categories for their location, good value and exceptional food. The restaurants are listed area by area; entries are alphabetical within each price category. For Amsterdam street map references, see pp150–7 and for Road Map references, see the back inside cover.

PRICE CATEGORIES
The following price ranges are for a three-course meal for one, including half a bottle of wine, plus all unavoidable extra charges, such as cover, service and tax.

€ Under €30
€€ €30–€40
€€€ €40–€50
€€€€ Over €50

AMSTERDAM

OUDE ZIJDE Bird
€

Zeedijk 72–74, 1011 HB **Tel** *(020) 620 1442*   **Map** *2 E4*

The best Thai eatery in town is spacious, with authentic decor and impeccable service from the staff. It is also great value for money. Bird is renowned for its sublime red- and green-curry sauces, which are combined with fish, beef, chicken, pork and tofu. Alternatively, pop over to the tiny, typically Thai snack bar opposite. Closed lunch.

OUDE ZIJDE Café Bern
€

Nieuwmarkt 9, 1011 JR **Tel** *(020) 622 0034*   **Map** *2 E5*

This cheap and cheerful brown bar-restaurant specializes in Swiss cheese fondues, served alongside simple salads and desserts. It is particularly popular with locals, many of whom eat at the bar, so advance reservations are recommended. A wide range of spirits and house wines is available. Closed lunch.

OUDE ZIJDE De Jaren
€€

Nieuwe Doelenstraat 20–22, 1012 CP **Tel** *(020) 625 5771*   **Map** *5 A2*

This huge, high-ceilinged grand café serves simple soups and sandwiches on the ground floor, and heartier meat, fish and vegetarian dishes in the first-floor restaurant (which also features a large salad bar). Both areas have pleasant outdoor terraces. On the downside, when things get busy (and they often do), service can be slow.

OUDE ZIJDE Éenvistwéévis
€€

Schippersgracht 6, 1011 TR **Tel** *(020) 623 2894*   **Map** *5 C1*

Located near Kilimanjaro (see below), this small, charming restaurant is a paradise for fish lovers. The chef transforms the catch of the day – be it plaice, sea bass, oysters or tuna – into simple, no-frills dishes, not drowned in unnecessary sauces. A modest pavement terrace allows al fresco dining in summer. Closed lunch; Mon.

OUDE ZIJDE Kilimanjaro
€€

Rapenburgerplein 6, 1011 VB **Tel** *(020) 622 3485*   **Map** *5 C1*

This warm and friendly pan-African restaurant specializes in dishes from across the vast continent. Additional delights include the Alligator cocktail, Mongozo beer (served in a bowl) and Ethiopian coffee, which comes with popcorn. In warm weather, there is an outdoor terrace. Closed Mon; lunch.

OUDE ZIJDE Hemelse Modder
€€€

Oude Waal 11, 1011 BZ **Tel** *(020) 624 3203*   **Map** *2 E4*

This spacious, modern and gay-friendly restaurant, on one of the city's oldest canals, offers international cuisine with strong French and Italian influences, and an eclectic wine list. The pièce de résistance, however, is its charming terrace at the back. It is wise to book outdoor tables in advance. Closed Mon.

OUDE ZIJDE Blauw aan de Wal
€€€€

Oudezijds Achterburgwal 99, 1012 DD **Tel** *(020) 330 2257*   **Map** *2 E5*

This stylish restaurant is hidden at the end of a tiny alley. Refined palates will enjoy the imaginative Mediterranean fusion delights and excellent wine list. Blauw's reputation means that advance reservations are necessary, especially to eat on its peaceful terrace in summer. Closed lunch; Sun.

OUDE ZIJDE In De Waag
€€€€

Nieuwmarkt 4, 1012 CR **Tel** *(020) 422 7772*   **Map** *2 E5*

In De Waag is set in a castle-like building dating from 1488. Above the restaurant, which is lit entirely by candles, is where Rembrandt made sketches for *The Anatomy Lesson of Dr Tulp*, his first group portrait. On the menu are eclectic, if a little expensive, meat and fish dishes and vegetarian options. Desserts are also divine. Book ahead.

OUDE ZIJDE Vermeer (NH Barbizon Palace Hotel)
€€€€

Prins Hendrikkade 59–72, 1012 AD **Tel** *(020) 556 4885*   **Map** *2 E3*

Set within four adjoining 17th-century buildings, this Michelin-starred restaurant produces rich gastronomic delights from France. Start the adventure in the intimate cocktail lounge, then enjoy dishes such as seared lobster with cranberries, and turnips flavoured with lemon verbena. Inspired wine list. Closed Sat lunch; Sun.

Key to Symbols *see back cover flap*

NIEUWE ZIJDE Keuken van 1870

Spuistraat 4, 1012 TS **Tel** *(020) 620 4018*

€

Map *2 D3*

Something of an Amsterdam institution, this former soup kitchen (dating from 1870) still maintains its policy of providing cheap meals – though its patrons these days are office workers, students and pensioners. The set daily changing menu of "homely Dutch cooking" (meat and vegetable dishes) is cheap. Closed lunch; Sun.

NIEUWE ZIJDE Brasserie Harkema

Nes 67, 1012 KD **Tel** *(020) 428 2222*

€€

Map *4 F1*

A classic Parisian brasserie with a stylish New York sensibility, Harkema serves haute cuisine at affordable prices. It is immensely popular, especially in the evenings, so it is wise to book ahead. Feast on delights such as sautéed venison steak on toast with fried chanterelle mushrooms, followed by chocolate tart with a Bastogne biscuit base.

NIEUWE ZIJDE Catalá

Spuistraat 299, 1012 VS **Tel** *(020) 623 1141*

€€

Map *1 C5*

A tapas bar close to Spui square, Catalá serves all the Spanish dishes you'd expect. The interior is rustic and authentic, but a seat on the pavement terrace in summer is a great spot for people-watching. It's also practically next door to Harry's – one of the finest cocktail bars in Amsterdam.

NIEUWE ZIJDE 1e Klas

Stationsplein 15, 1012 AB **Tel** *(020) 625 0131*

€€€

Map *2 E3*

The former first-class waiting room on platform 2B of Centraal Station is now a grand café-restaurant exuding Art Nouveau elegance throughout its stunning interior. The menu offers a wide range of dishes, from standard fare, such as soup and salads, to first-class fare in the form of traditional French dishes. Breakfast is served from 8:30am.

NIEUWE ZIJDE Kapitein Zeppos

Gebed Zonder End 5, 1012 HS **Tel** *(020) 624 2057*

€€€

Map *4 F1*

Tucked down a tiny alley, lit by fairy-lights, this bar-restaurant (with Belgian ceramic-tile tables and eclectic ornaments) was once a coach stable, then a cigar factory. The kitchen turns out delicious French-Mediterranean cuisine, with Italian, Moroccan and Spanish influences. Ideal for a romantic evening.

NIEUWE ZIJDE Supperclub

Jonge Roelensteeg 21, 1012 PL **Tel** *(020) 344 6400*

€€€€

Map *1 C5*

Remove your shoes and recline on cushioned beds at this restaurant-club. DJs spin upbeat lounge music as you graze on culinary delights from the open kitchen – all spread out over five courses. Fine wines, video art, massage and offbeat performances complete this assault on the senses. There is also a lounge bar downstairs. Closed lunch.

CENTRAL CANAL RING Wagamama

Max Euweplein 10, 1017 MB **Tel** *(020) 528 7778*

€

Map *4 E2*

Fast food but relaxed service are the norm at this Japanese noodle restaurant with a designer canteen-style interior. Good for a quick lunch or dinner meal. Service is fast and food is fresh. Practically next door to the Paradiso music venue, and close to the cinemas and theatres on Leidseplein, it's a good place to start your night out.

CENTRAL CANAL RING Balthazar's Keuken

Elandsgracht 108, 1016 VA **Tel** *(020) 420 2114*

€€

Map *1 B5*

A clutter of pots and pans hangs from the open kitchen here. In fact, it is so cosy, you will feel as though you're eating at the home of owners Karin and Alain, not least because there is no menu: guests are simply given a weekly changing, three-course international meal. Closed lunch; Mon, Tue, Sat & Sun.

CENTRAL CANAL RING Los Pilones

Kerkstraat 63, 1017 GC **Tel** *(020) 320 4651*

€€

Map *4 E1*

A small cantina run by two Mexican brothers who serve authentic dishes. Los Pilones offers some of the best Mexican food in the whole of Amsterdam. Expect the occasional unusual combination such as *enchiladas* with a chocolate sauce. The pièce de résistance is their huge range of tequilas (around 35). Closed lunch; Mon.

CENTRAL CANAL RING Mayur

Korte Leidsedwarsstraat 203, 1017 RB **Tel** *(020) 623 2142*

€€

Map *4 E2*

Authentic tandoori dishes cooked in a wood-fired clay oven are the speciality of this spacious restaurant just off the Leidseplein. Preparation of food is also given special attention: meats are marinated for 24 hours in yoghurt and spices, resulting in dishes that are spicy but not eye-wateringly hot. Closed lunch.

CENTRAL CANAL RING Envy

Prinsengracht 381, 1016 HL **Tel** *(020) 344 6407*

€€€

Map *1 B5*

The menu here consists of tiny Italian delicacies that can be chosen individually, at your leisure. The Envy chefs expertly combine flavours in an open kitchen by the tall window of this narrow, designer warehouse space. An absolute must for foodies, this is one of Amsterdam's finest offerings. Closed lunch Mon & Tue.

CENTRAL CANAL RING Nomads

Rozengracht 133, 1016 LV **Tel** *(020) 344 6401*

€€€

Map *1 A5*

This first-floor restaurant is inspired by Arabic nomad culture. Kick off your shoes and lounge on beds in a scene straight out of Arabian Nights, while Eastern food is served from bronze platters. DJs at weekends. Late-opening kitchen (11:30pm) and bar (1am weekdays; 3am weekends). Closed lunch.

CENTRAL CANAL RING Proeverij 274

Prinsengracht 274, 1016 HH **Tel** *(020) 421 1848*   **Map** *1 B5*

Popular with both locals and visitors to the city, this warm and romantic two-floored restaurant serves classic international dishes made with organic ingredients. Book the round table by the door for a delightful view over the canal. Groups of up to 25 people can be catered for in the downstairs basement. Closed lunch.

CENTRAL CANAL RING Blue Pepper

Nassaukade 366, 1054 AB **Tel** *(020) 489 7039*   **Map** *4 D1*

Flawless and inspired contemporary Indonesian cuisine (with Chinese and Filipino influences), with extraordinary combinations of flavours. The *rijsttafel* (rice table – a selection of small dishes) created by the Javanese chef is utterly unique. No wonder this small, chic restaurant is adored by foodies. Impressive wine list. Closed lunch.

CENTRAL CANAL RING Vinkeles

Keizersgracht 384, 1016 GB **Tel** *(020) 530 2010*   **Map** *4 E1*

The intimate gourmet restaurant at this stunning boutique hotel offers international cuisine with an inspired choice of traditional and contemporary dishes. Service is attentive and the wine menu eclectic. Outdoor dining is on offer in the beautiful courtyard when the weather is good. A must for the discerning diner. Closed Sat lunch; Sun.

EASTERN CANAL RING Zushi

Amstel 20, 1017 AA **Tel** *(020) 330 6882*   **Map** *5 A2*

A large, bright, high-ceilinged modern sushi restaurant where you can take your sushi straight from the oval conveyor belt, while chefs in the middle of the belt prepare additional goodies. Each plate is colour-coded according to price. Wash the *wasabi* down with Japanese beers like Sapporo, Kirin or Asahi.

EASTERN CANAL RING Bazar

Albert Cuypstraat 182, 1073 BL **Tel** *(020) 675 0544*   **Map** *5 A5*

Eastern-style restaurant within a former church located halfway up the bustling Albert Cuyp street market. On the menu is a mouth-watering choice of North African, Moroccan, Iranian and Turkish dishes for breakfast, lunch or dinner (during the week, it opens at 8am; 9am at weekends). Great for vegetarians.

EASTERN CANAL RING Bouchon du Centre

Falckstraat 3; 1017 VV **Tel** *(020) 330 1128*   **Map** *5 A4*

You will feel like you are having dinner at a friend's house here. Hostess-chef Hanneke Schouten creates a fixed three-course meal using produce she has bought fresh from the market and specialist shops. The cuisine is tradition-al, but with a twist. Organic wines are chosen to match the food. Closed Sun–Tue; last orders 6:30pm.

EASTERN CANAL RING De Waaghals

Frans Halsstraat 29, 1072 BK **Tel** *(020) 679 9609*   **Map** *4 F3*

A superb vegetarian restaurant that will leave even the most hardened of carnivores sated. Each month, the menu focuses on a different country. Organic produce is used wherever possible; even the beer is locally brewed and the wines organic. In summer, ask for a table in the charming garden at the back. Book ahead. Closed lunch; Mon.

EASTERN CANAL RING Rose's Cantina

Reguliersdwarsstraat 38–40, 1017 BM **Tel** *(020) 625 9797*   **Map** *4 F2*

A sprawling, long-established Mexican restaurant with a terrific atmosphere and delicious food (though a limited choice for vegetarians). Its success is due to a combination of friendly service, great value and a classic menu: choose fillings for your *taco, enchilada* or *quesadilla*. Great cocktails, too. Small patio terrace at rear. Closed lunch.

EASTERN CANAL RING Garlic Queen

Reguliersdwarsstraat 27, 1017 BJ **Tel** *(020) 422 6426*   **Map** *4 F2*

A small, quaint restaurant with a dark interior located on Amsterdam's trendy gay street. Its novel speciality is garlic. Every dish contains it – from the starters to the desserts – yet it complements rather than overwhelms the flavours. Friendly service and a pleasant, relaxed ambience complete the experience. Closed Mon & Tue.

EASTERN CANAL RING Beddington's

Utrechtsedwarsstraat 141, 1017 WE **Tel** *(020) 620 7393*   **Map** *5 B3*

One for discerning taste buds and those in search of slow-paced dining in sober, stylish surroundings. From the open kitchen, British owner/chef Jean Beddington produces seamless French and Asian fusion, with a sprinkling of British sensibility. Delightful desserts and friendly service. Closed lunch; Mon & Sun.

MUSEUM QUARTER Café Toussaint

Bosboom Toussaintstraat 26, 1054 AS **Tel** *(020) 685 0737*   **Map** *4 D1*

This absolute gem is well worth the five-minute stroll from the busy Leidseplein across to this quiet street. It is a small but charming café with an open kitchen where healthy international fare, such as sandwiches, soups and tapas (with plenty for vegetarians), is created. Cosy and romantic at night, with a peaceful terrace and no mobile telephones.

MUSEUM QUARTER Pompa

Willemsparkweg 6, 1017 HD **Tel** *(020) 662 6206*   **Map** *4 D3*

In an area short of restaurants – let alone inexpensive ones – this tapas bar is a real find, especially after an evening at the nearby Concertgebouw, when most restaurants are filled to the brim. Split-level, warm and friendly, this eatery has a broad, value-for-money menu offering Mediterranean dishes and tapas; great salads, too.

Key to Price Guide *see p410* **Key to Symbols** *see back cover flap*

MUSEUM QUARTER Vertigo

Vondelpark 3, 1071 AA **Tel** *(020) 612 3021*   **Map** *4 D2*

Resembling a wine cellar, this spacious and comfortable international restaurant is within Amsterdam's historic Filmmuseum, at the top of the Vondelpark. Warm and candlelit in the winter, it has one of the city's most popular terraces in summer, when they also sell picnics that you can take into the park.

MUSEUM QUARTER Brasserie van Baerle

Van Baerlestraat 158, 1071 BG **Tel** *(020) 679 1532*   **Map** *4 E4*

This French-style brasserie is particularly popular with Dutch celebrities, especially for lunch and Sunday brunch (when it opens at 10am). Mouth-watering dishes include grilled sea bass with home-made crab mayonnaise and a roast-pepper dressing. Exceptional wine list and gorgeous garden terrace. Booking recommended. Closed Sat lunch.

MUSEUM QUARTER Pulpo

Willemsparkweg 87, 1071 GT **Tel** *(020) 676 0700*   **Map** *4 D3*

Just east of the Vondelpark, near the Museumplein, is this popular, relaxed and unpretentious restaurant. The Mediterranean cuisine is occasionally imbued with subtle African and Middle Eastern hints, such as stewed lamb with artichoke, nutty bulghur wheat and chilli yoghurt. Delicious desserts. Dinner only; closed Sun.

MUSEUM QUARTER Le Garage

Ruysdaelstraat 54–56, 1071 XE **Tel** *(020) 679 71 76*   **Map** *4 E4*

A favourite haunt of Dutch celebrities is this elegant bistro with red plush seating and mirrors. The food is French-international, and organic ingredients are used whenever possible. Le Garage is renowned for its three-course menu and superb wine list featuring classic and lesser-known wines from all over the world. Closed Sat & Sun lunch.

MUSEUM QUARTER The College Hotel

Roelof Hartstraat 1, 1071 VE **Tel** *(020) 571 1511*   **Map** *4 E5*

Head to this training hotel for catering students before (for breakfast) or after a day's shopping on nearby PC Hooftstraat. The renovated gymnasium of an 1895 school building is home to an elegant gourmet restaurant where classic Dutch dishes are given a contemporary twist. Closed Sun.

PLANTAGE Plancius

Plantage Kerklaan 61a, 1018 CX **Tel** *(020) 330 9469*   **Map** *6 D2*

A gay-friendly restaurant in a former fire station opposite the main entrance to Artis Royal Zoo. Although the designer decor is stark, it is comfortable and friendly. The menu is French-oriented, with an accent on meat and fish, but there are also tempting vegetarian options. On Saturdays and Sundays they also serve breakfasts.

PLANTAGE La Rive (Amstel Hotel)

Professor Tulpplein 1, 1018 GX **Tel** *(020) 520 3264*   **Map** *5 B4*

This Michelin-starred restaurant within the Amstel Hotel is one for connoisseurs. Outstanding cuisine from its modern French-Mediterranean kitchen is matched by an excellent wine list. Reserve the chef's table in the kitchen (four to eight people) for an unusual twist to your dining experience. Dress code is elegant. Closed Sat lunch; Sun.

WESTERN CANAL RING De Bolhoed

Prinsengracht 60–62, 1015 DX **Tel** *(020) 626 1803*   **Map** *1 B3*

A charming vegetarian restaurant with a delightful canalside terrace, great for sunny afternoons and balmy evenings. Chefs whip up imaginative international dishes from mostly organic ingredients. The daily vegan dish is superb. Plates overflow, but be sure to leave room for the delicious desserts. Service can be slow. Reservations recommended.

WESTERN CANAL RING Foodism

Oude Leliestraat 8, 1015 AW **Tel** *(020) 627 6424*   **Map** *1 C4*

Down a small street in the Jordaan, minutes from the Dam, this bright and endearing restaurant serves anything from New York-style breakfasts to hearty soups and sandwiches for lunch, and wild-basil pasta for dinner. Or pop in for a mid-afternoon coffee and cake. No alcohol. Opens 11:30am (12:30pm Sun); closed Mon & Tue evenings.

WESTERN CANAL RING Chez Georges

Herenstraat 3, 1015 BX **Tel** *(020) 626 3332*   **Map** *1 C4*

This restaurant is a veritable tour de force of Burgundian cuisine. It is a must for gourmands, who will delight in owner/chef Georges' superb meat and fish dishes (opt for the five-course or seven-course menus). It is also great value for money, though the fine wines could push up the price. Book ahead. Closed lunch; Wed & Sun.

WESTERN CANAL RING De Gouden Reael

Zandhoek 14, 1013 KT **Tel** *(020) 623 3883*   **Map** *1 C1*

This 1648 building used to be a herring warehouse and then a 19th-century *jenever* (Dutch gin) bar. Located in one of the most picturesque parts of Amsterdam, this low-key bar-restaurant is popular with lovers of French and Alsatian cuisine. There's a good wine list, and great waterfront views from the small terrace. Dinner only.

WESTERN CANAL RING Spanjer & Van Twist

Leliegracht 60, 1015 DJ **Tel** *(020) 639 0109*   **Map** *1 C4*

Close to the Anne Frank Huis, this split-level café-restaurant opens at 10am for breakfasts and offers a seasonally changing menu of soups, sandwiches and other dishes. It features a reading table and a charming canalside terrace. The kitchen closes at 10:30pm. Snacks served until closing time.

WESTERN CANAL RING Lof

Haarlemmerstraat 62, 1013 ES **Tel** (020) 620 2997   **Map** 2 D3

Lof is a firm favourite of many of the city's most discerning diners. The daily changing offerings revolve around seasonal fish, meat and game. There is no menu: the staff come to your table and simply describe what is on offer to you. For intimate, lingering dining, book the small backroom. Closed lunch; Mon.

WESTERN CANAL RING Stout!

Haarlemmerstraat 73, 1013 EL **Tel** (020) 616 3664   **Map** 2 D3

A hip restaurant offering creative international fusion fare, with inspired combinations of flavours. The speciality dish (Plateau Stout; for a minimum of two people) allows you to sample ten small, varied dishes. The restaurant is also renowned for its wine list.

WESTERN CANAL RING Toscanini

Lindengracht 75, 1015 KD **Tel** (020) 623 2813   **Map** 1 C3

Despite its huge size, this Italian restaurant gets booked up quickly. Formerly a coach house, then a blacksmith's forge, the venue retains its original 19th-century glass roof. Chefs create regional dishes in the open kitchen, while the wine list affords the chance to drink both classic and lesser-known wines from Italy. Closed lunch; Sun.

WESTERN CANAL RING Bordewijk

Noordermarkt 7, 1015 MV **Tel** (020) 624 3899   **Map** 1 C3

Renowned for its superb French cuisine with Italian and Asian influences, and for service that will make you feel truly pampered, Bordewijk is one of the best restaurants in town. The chef will come to your table in person to describe the day's menu. Book ahead. Closed lunch; Mon & Sun.

WESTERN CANAL RING Christophe

Leliegracht 46, 1015 DH **Tel** (020) 625 0807   **Map** 1 C1

This canalside establishment makes for an exceptional and intimate dining experience. The inventive, pure, full-flavoured dishes have earned the restaurant a well-deserved Michelin star every year for more than a decade. Closed lunch; Mon & Sun.

FURTHER AFIELD Amsterdam

Watertorenplein 6, 1051 PA **Tel** (020) 682 2666

Within a former water-pumping house dating from 1897, this huge, industrial-style restaurant near the Westerpark serves simple, well-priced European food – from steak and fries to grilled wild-boar cutlets. There is a relaxing grass terrace at the back, which makes it great for families. The kitchen is open until 11:30pm on Friday and Saturday.

FURTHER AFIELD Gare de L'Est

Cruquiusweg 9, 1019 AT **Tel** (020) 463 0620

Within the former coffee house of an old railway station built in 1901, this unique, romantic restaurant is hugely popular with locals and those who have wandered through the redeveloped Eastern Docklands area, where Gare de L'Est is located. Reservations for the daily changing, four-course global dinners are a must. Closed lunch.

FURTHER AFIELD Star Ferry

Piet Heinkade 1, 1019 BR **Tel** (020) 788 2090

Named after the Hong Kong ferry company, and located within the architecturally stunning Muziekgebouw aan 't IJ, this spacious, glass-walled café-restaurant specializes in Asian-influenced international cuisine. There are incredible views across the busy waterfront behind Centraal Station, but avoid the unshaded terrace on hot days.

FURTHER AFIELD De Odessa

Veemkade 259, 1019 CZ **Tel** (020) 419 3010

Head to this enchanting Ukrainian fishing boat as the sun sets and enjoy cocktails on the deck, while snacking on oysters. De Odessa's international menu of mainly fish and meat dishes is well presented and reasonable – but the draw is the experience itself. DJs play on the lounge-style deck below. Closed lunch; Mon & Tue in winter.

FURTHER AFIELD Fifteen

Jollemanhof 9, 1019 GW **Tel** (0900) 343 8336

British celebrity chef Jamie Oliver's open-plan restaurant is situated within a renovated waterfront warehouse. Book ahead for the set four-course modern Italian tasting menu (with vegetarian options), or just turn up for pasta, risotto or ravioli in the cheaper trattoria. The waiting staff and sommelier are very attentive. Closed Sun lunch.

FURTHER AFIELD Wilhelmina-Dok

Noordwal 1, 1021 PX **Tel** (020) 632 3701   **Map** 2 F2

Take the ferry from behind Centraal Station across the River IJ to this spacious 1950s-style restaurant with a waterfront terrace offering splendid views of Amsterdam's skyline. With its great-value Mediterranean food, reasonable wine list and extensive bar, it is ideal for groups and informal business lunches.

FURTHER AFIELD Yamazato (Okura Hotel)

Ferdinand Bolstraat 333, 1072 LH **Tel** (020) 678 8351   **Map** 4 F5

This Michelin-starred restaurant serves traditional Japanese specialities. For less adventurous palates, its sushi bar has more than 20 types of freshly prepared sushi and sashimi. Authenticity extends throughout – from the food to the tatami room, private-dining spaces and kimono-clad Japanese waiting staff. Also open 7:30–9:30am for breakfast.

Key to Price Guide see p410 **Key to Symbols** see back cover flap

TERSCHELLING/WEST TERSCHELLING Amsterdamsche Koffijhuis €

Willem Barentszstraat 17, 8881 BP **Tel** *(0562) 442 700* **Road Map** *C1*

This simple, friendly place decorated with dark wood, polished brass and potted plants looks like it could have come from another era. Prices are also refreshingly old-fashioned, but the food is up-to-date: tapas, vegetarian meals from South Africa and *tacos*. More nostalgic dishes include *liverworst* and huge plates of steak and chips. Closed Jan.

TEXEL/OUDESCHILD t Pakhuus €€€€

Haven 8, 1792 AE **Tel** *(0222) 313 581* **Road Map** *B2*

Light pours through the glass ceilings in this beautifully converted warehouse overlooking the working harbour on the eastern side of Texel. The decor of abstract paintings, fresh flowers and white linen combines the same elements of modern and classic as the menu. Local seasonal ingredients, seafood and lamb in particular, are specialities.

GRONINGEN

ADUARD Herberg Onder de Linden €€€€

Burgemeester van Barneveldweg 3, 9831 RD **Tel** *(050) 403 1406* **Road Map** *D1*

This beautiful 18th-century inn deep in the countryside has been a gourmet destination since 1991. The kitchen applies current trends to fresh local ingredients, resulting in dishes like asparagus with free-range egg, *pata negra* and chervil or chicory in caramel sauce. For warm weather, there's a lovely garden terrace. Closed lunch; Sun–Tue.

GRONINGEN Wagamama €

Vismarkt 54, 9711 KV **Tel** *(050) 313 0783* **Road Map** *D1*

This branch of the UK noodle bar chain is popular with students for its cheap and nourishing meals. The formula is healthy fast food in sleek surroundings. Not a place to linger over a romantic dinner for two, the long tables and benches are shared, and once you've eaten *ramen, gyoza* and seaweed salad, it's time to pay and go.

GRONINGEN De Pauw €€€

Gelkingestraat 52, 9711 NE **Tel** *(050) 318 1332* **Road Map** *D1*

White walls, linen and furnishings, and plenty of polished silverware add up to a classic eating experience at this restaurant in the city centre. Both starters and puddings are chosen from a trolley; mains range from retro (lamb cutlets with spring vegetables) to modern (quail and pigeon with *tarte tatin* and pine kernel *mousseline*). Closed lunch.

HAREN Villa Sasso €€€€

Meerweg 221, 9752 XC **Tel** *(050) 309 1365* **Road Map** *E2*

With a large terrace on the Paterswolder lake and well-spaced tables, this is a relaxing place for coffee, lunch or dinner. Local ingredients are transformed into fashionable versions of classics: asparagus as mousse and in tempura, or lamb stew. Set menus are good value, and lunch is a scaled-down version of dinner. Closed Mon & Sun; Sat lunch.

FRIESLAND

APPELSCHA Het Volle Leven €€

Oude Willem 5, 8426 SM **Tel** *(0516) 430 091* **Road Map** *D2*

In a welcoming farmhouse in the middle of the countryside, chef and owner Yt van der Ploeg cooks up outstanding vegetarian food. Everything is organic and many of the ingredients are harvested from the land outside the same day. The daily changing, no-choice set menu might include beetroot *carpaccio* and roast vegetable lasagne. Closed lunch.

DRACHTEN Koriander €€€€

Burgermeester Wuiteweg 18, 9203 KK **Tel** *(0512) 548 850* **Road Map** *D2*

A light, modern dining room with exposed brickwork and restored wood is the setting for the kitchen's beautifully presented cooking. Local ingredients figure large on the short menu – fish from Wergae, for example – and combine with Mediterranean herbs and flavours. Puddings and cheeses are a speciality. Closed Mon & Sun.

JOURE t Plein €€€€

Douwe Egbertsplein 1a, 8501 AB **Tel** *(0513) 417 070* **Road Map** *D2*

This stylish restaurant decked out in stark black and white, with ornate touches such as carved mirrors and fresh flowers, is a stylish spot for lunch or dinner. It's a favourite with regulars for the menu filled with local recipes, like *skinkespek* and *Fryske sûkerbôle*. Book the table in the kitchen to watch the action. Closed Mon & Sun.

LEEUWARDEN Eetcafé Spinoza €

Eewal 50–52, 8911 GT **Tel** *(058) 212 9393* **Road Map** *D2*

Unpretentious, good value *eetcafé* with a philosophical theme – there's a second branch in the town called Descartes. The menu offers simple, hearty favourites from around the world, christened with humorous names: "Italy v. Portugal" combines sardines with pasta, while "chop chop" is stir-fried beef and vegetables. Closed lunch.

PIAAM De Nynke Pleats   🚶♿🔧   €€€
Buren 25, 8756 JP **Tel** *(0515) 231 707*   **Road Map** *C2*

This converted 18th-century farmhouse in the countryside makes a pleasant stop for lunch, dinner, or just a coffee and snack. There's a terrace with rustic views, but indoors, the chandeliered barn is an equally impressive setting for the fresh, well-priced local specialities like Frisian onion soup, or local cheese with pea mousse. Call for opening times.

SLOTEN Het Bolwerk   🚶♿🔧   €€
Voorstreek 116, 8556 XV **Tel** *(0514) 531 405*   **Road Map** *C2*

This attractive restaurant in an 18th-century townhouse has low, beamed ceilings and simple decor. It's popular for its good prices and ample, filling portions of classic Dutch food served all through the day. Lunchtime might bring a big plate of local cheeses, with warming dishes like duck in a raspberry beer sauce for dinner.

DRENTHE

ASSEN Pacific Plaza   🚶♿🔧   €
Transportweg 2, 9405 PR **Tel** *(0592) 462 463*   **Road Map** *D2*

Those seeking a light, healthy alternative to meat and dairy-heavy Dutch food will appreciate this restaurant's pan-Asian dishes. Food is good quality, fresh and tasty. Japanese *teppenyaki* (cooked at the table) and sushi sit alongside Chinese standards like *char sui* pork. A wide range of set menus make it particularly good for groups.

DE SCHIPHORST De Havixhorst   🚶🔧   €€€€
Schiphorsterweg 34–36, 7966 AC **Tel** *(0522) 441 487*   **Road Map** *D3*

A landmark restaurant, both for food and the château it's housed in. Attention to detail are keywords here, from presentation to service. Inventive *amuse bouche* excite the tastebuds, followed with the likes of monkfish with poached egg and vandouvan curry, and chocolate tart with sweet woodruff mousse and cardamom. Reservations only.

DWINGELOO Hof van Dwingeloo   🍽🚶♿🔧   €
Drift 1, 7991 AA **Tel** *(0521) 593 094*   **Road Map** *D2*

At the heart of a much-visited, attractive village, this informal café-restaurant with a large outside terrace overlooks a pretty pond. Inside, the decor is traditional Dutch, as is the family-friendly menu: pancakes, croquettes and *satay* for lunch, beefsteak, ribs and sweet waffles for dinner. Snacks and drinks available all day. Closed Tue (except school hols).

EMMEN De Kamer   🚶🔧   €€
Marktplein 7, 7811 AM **Tel** *(0591) 618 180*   **Road Map** *E2*

This attractive restored farmhouse in the town centre is now home to a restaurant and art gallery in one. This theme carries through to the menu, with dishes given artistic names: "watercolour soup" is tomato soup with sour cream and basil, while "in fire and flame" is pork medallions in wine-caramel sauce.

NORG Bospaviljoen De Norgerberg   🍽🚶🔧   €
Langeloërweg 63, 9331 VA **Tel** *(0592) 614 266*   **Road Map** *D2*

This café-restaurant in a forest is equally good as a resting place after exploring, or a destination in itself. Outside there's a large terrace, inside is rather romantic, with lots of candles. The food is hearty but made with finesse: *schnitzel* and guinea-fowl *confit* are typical. Child- and senior-sized portions available. Closed Sep–May: Mon & Tue.

WESTERVELDE De Jufferen Lunsingh   ♿🔧   €€€
Hoofdweg 13, 9337 PA **Tel** *(0592) 612 618*   **Road Map** *D2*

This restaurant in a tall, white, shuttered building looks rather French in appearance, and the Gallic influence carries onto the menu of very local ingredients – they breed their own cattle and sheep. Although smart, the restaurant is also very walker-friendly: you are invited to explore their acres of land and they even provide picnics and bikes.

OVERIJSSEL

ALMELO Dock 19   ♿🔧   €€€
Haven Noordzijde 19, 7607 ER **Tel** *(0546) 578 819*   **Road Map** *E3*

This restaurant is highly thought of for its modern, New York-style interior with velvet walls and picture windows, as well as its fusion food. Begin with a delicious cocktail and move onto meals that embrace world cuisine on one plate, such as beef *sashimi* with olive *tapenade* and Ceylon curry. Closed Mon & Sun.

DEVENTER Engel en Bengel   🍽🔧   €
Grote Overstraat 55–57, 7411 JB **Tel** *(0570) 614 754*   **Road Map** *D3*

A kitsch and colourful little place that's quickly become a local favourite for both its bright flowery interior and honest, fairly priced food. Dishes include standards like *carpaccio*, trout cooked in foil and several old-fashioned Dutch dishes like liquorice and aniseed ice cream. Closed Mon; Tue–Fri lunch.

Key to Price Guide *see p410* **Key to Symbols** *see back cover flap*

ENSCHEDE De Fusting Downtown €
Zuiderhagen 16.18, 7511 GL **Tel** *(053) 436 7787* **Road Map** *E3*

There are two branches of this popular *eetcafe* in Enschede, and this one is right in the town centre, on one of the main shopping streets. Those refuelling post-spending spree will appreciate the hearty fare and cheap prices. The menu includes soups, sandwiches, salads and tapas. Closed Mon; Sun lunch.

HOLTEN Bistro de Holterberg €
Forthaarsweg 1, 7451 JS **Tel** *(0548) 363 849* **Road Map** *D3*

Set in a pretty village in a nature reserve, this informal bistro affords great views from the large terrace (40 km/ 25 miles on a clear day). Inside it's cosy, with a roaring fire. Customers also come for the unpretentious local and international menu, where shrimp croquettes sit alongside salmon with pasta and pesto. Closed lunch; Mon.

ZWOLLE De Librije €€€€
Broerenkerkplein 13, 8011 TW **Tel** *(038) 421 2083* **Road Map** *D3*

One of the best restaurants in the country, people come from all over the Netherlands (and beyond) for the culinary experience created by husband-and-wife team Jonnie and Thérèse Boer. It's one of the few Michelin-starred places that offers a gourmet vegetarian set menu. Sweet-toothed diners will delight in the soufflés, a house speciality.

FLEVOLAND

ALMERE Waterfront €€€
Esplanade 10, 1315 TA **Tel** *(036) 845 5777* **Road Map** *C3*

This restaurant overlooking the Gooimeer is part of the town's municipal theatre, serving dinner only on performance nights and every Thu–Sat. Locals are delighted by its sleek interior and the fashionable fusion food such as tuna with seaweed and *wasabi* or rabbit stewed with cherry beer. Some diners might find the portions on the small side.

ALMERE-HAVEN Brasserie Bakboord €€€€
Veerkade 10, 1357 PK **Tel** *(036) 540 4040* **Road Map** *C3*

This modern, glass-fronted restaurant in the harbour is unsurprisingly popular with yachters and pleasure cruisers, who relax on the lovely terrace's wicker chairs, and dine on well-executed classics which are rather difficult to get in the region: lobster thermidor, oysters, and roast duck breast and duck liver are washed down with good wines.

URK De Kaap €
Wijk 1–5, 8321 EK **Tel** *(0527) 681 509* **Road Map** *C3*

This fish specialist and *eetcafé* at the heart of an ancient fishing village is decked out in an appropriately nautical style, with model boats, lamps and anchors. The menu (available in Braille) lists lots of seafood and fish dishes: smoked eel is popular. There are also hearty steaks and schnitzels.

GELDERLAND

AALST De Fuik €€€€
Maasdijk 1, 4926 SJ **Tel** *(0418) 552 247* **Road Map** *C4*

This destination restaurant is built directly over a tributary of the Maas, giving beautiful views from the terrace and outside balcony. Dining here is a full-on gourmet experience, with Dutch ingredients transformed into French-style classics such as trio of *foie gras* or halibut with smoked beetroot. Cheese is a speciality. Closed Mon; Sat lunch.

APELDOORN Restaurant Jules Verne €€€
Raadhuisplein 3, 7311 LJ **Tel** *(055) 521 7394* **Road Map** *D3*

On a busy square at the heart of the city, Jules Verne will take you around the world on a plate of fusion food: *tempura* prawns with *ratatouille* and pesto is one example. Vegetarians are well-served here. Set menus range from four to six courses and the changing monthly four-course menu is good value.

ARNHEM Arnhems Proeflokaal €
Spijkerstraat 3, 6828 DA **Tel** *(026) 351 8485* **Road Map** *D4*

This cheerful and unpretentious *eetcafé* offers a real slice of Dutch life, from the low brass lamps and dark wood furnishings, to the simple, filling and very cheap – but seldom boring – food. It's usually busy all day with locals enjoying the likes of smoked chicken salad and vegetable soup with chorizo from the daily changing menu. Closed lunch; Mon.

DOESBURG De Waag €€
Koepoortstraat 2–4, 6981 AS **Tel** *(0313) 479 617* **Road Map** *D4*

The oldest Dutch café has also been voted among the best 100 in the country. This "beer-house", bar and restaurant is situated in a gorgeous medieval building overlooking a square. The café is upstairs, while there's more formal dining in the basement. Food includes local favourites (mustard soup, Belgian *waterzooi*) and innovations (tempura salmon).

HARDERWIJK t'Nonnetje
🏠   €€€

Vischmarkt 38, 3841 BG **Tel** *(0341) 415 848*   **Road Map** *C3*

Diners uniformly sing the praises of "the little nun", an atmospheric restaurant on a beautiful town square near the harbour. The set and à la carte menus both feature plenty of fish and Dutch ingredients. Wadden Sea cockles and Kamper lamb are treated with the latest techniques creating delicious and surprising results. Closed lunch; Sun.

NIJMEGEN Het Heimwee
🏠   €€€

Oude Haven 76–80, 6511 XH **Tel** *(024) 322 2256*   **Road Map** *D4*

Choose from set menus based on daily changing, fresh ingredients in this handsome townhouse restaurant overlooking the old harbour. Helpful staff talk diners through the choices, which may include poached egg with samphire and truffles. Meats come with sophisticated additions like apple chutney and morelle jus. Closed lunch; Mon.

NORTH BRABANT

'S-HERTOGENBOSCH Brasserie Pilkington's
🏃 ♿ 🏠   €

Torenstraat 5, 5211 KK **Tel** *(073) 612 2923*   **Road Map** *C4*

Visitors who sit beneath the shady trees or inside among the teapots and jam jars may think they're at an English country house. From English breakfast through to ploughman's lunch, high tea with scones and Earl Grey, and onto dinners of shepherd's pie, Pilkington's keeps the Union Jack flying. Closed Mon dinner.

BREDA Landgoed Wolfslaar
🏃 ♿ 🏠   €€€€

Wolfslaardreef 100–102, 4834 SP **Tel** *(076) 560 8000*   **Road Map** *B5*

In the countryside on the outskirts of the city, Wolfslaar is a 17th-century villa whose restaurant is in the former coach house. The chef's native province, Limburg, influences the menu, with stews, asparagus and root vegetables. Service is outstanding and the restaurant's fine cuisine has been awarded a Michelin star. Closed Sat lunch; Sun.

EINDHOVEN Taj Mahal
♿   €€

Geldropseweg 27–29, 5611 SC **Tel** *(040) 211 9440*   **Road Map** *C5*

Good Indian food is often difficult to come by in the Netherlands, which is why this restaurant is popular with an international crowd of regulars, particularly British expats. Chicken *tikka masala*, lamb *jalfrezi* and butterfly prawns are all consumed with nostalgic delight. There are also filling, value-for-money set dinners. Closed lunch.

EINDHOVEN Avant-Garde van Groeningen
♿   €€€€

Frederiklaan 10d, 5616 NH **Tel** *(040) 250 5640*   **Road Map** *C5*

Soothing beiges, browns, leather and marble create an opulent background for the kitchen's creations at this upmarket restaurant. Innovation and creativity are at the top of the chefs' agenda, resulting in lobster cooked in vanilla oil with *sabayon*, salsify *confit*, and fried, spiced pineapple with coconut curry sorbet. Closed Sat lunch; Sun.

OSS Buitengewoon
🏃 ♿ 🏠   €€

Kerkstraat 12, 5341 BK **Tel** *(0412) 643 248*   **Road Map** *C4*

The name of this restaurant translates as "unusual" and, run as it is by youngsters with learning difficulties, it probably is. There's nothing unusual about the well-made bistro-style food, however, and regulars enjoy sophisticated dishes like taleggio and mushroom lasagne. Discount with De Lievenkamp theatre ticket. Closed dinner Mon & Tue; lunch Sun.

SLEEUWIJK Boven de Rivieren
🏠   €€

Hoekeinde 24, 4254 LN **Tel** *(0183) 307 353*   **Road Map** *C4*

This restaurant in an attractive yacht harbour actually floats on the water and, although it looks rather shed-like outside, the light interior is stylishly decked out in deep reds. Lunch might consist of tapas or salad, while dinner offers plenty of simple fish dishes or grilled meat served with seasonal vegetables. Closed Mon.

TILBURG Breexz
🏃   €

Spoorlaan 47, 5038 CB **Tel** *(013) 542 5255*   **Road Map** *C5*

This bright and modern brasserie in the city's railway station attracts more than just commuters: many residents also head to what's considered the trendiest restaurant in Tilburg. There's a simple dinner menu of pastas, steaks and stir-fries, as well as more sophisticated finger-food like crab cakes and *yakitori* chicken, to accompany cocktails.

UDEN 't Raadhuis
♿ 🏠   €€€

Markt 1a, 5401 GN **Tel** *(0413) 257 000*   **Road Map** *C4*

This classy restaurant is situated in the former town hall (*raadhuis*). While you can order à la carte, the speciality here is seasonal, themed set menus of four or more elegant courses: the gastronomic *keukenmenu* has seven. When in season, the asparagus menu is a must. There's a large terrace for outdoor lunching. Reservations recommended.

WILLEMSTAD Frascati
🏠   €

Voorstraat 50, 4797 BH **Tel** *(0168) 476 080*   **Road Map** *B4*

This unpretentious little trattoria, near the yacht harbour in a fortified village, serves honest home-style Italian cooking. Alongside decent versions of *vitello tonnato*, and a wide range of tasty pasta and pizza, there are a few interesting takes on Dutch dishes, such as an *uitsmijter* made with *brioche*, duck liver and quail's eggs. Closed Mon; Tue–Fri lunch.

Key to Price Guide *see p410* **Key to Symbols** *see back cover flap*

LIMBURG

BEEK De Lindenboom
€€
Burgemeester Janssenstraat 13, 6191 JB **Tel** *(046) 437 1237*   **Road Map** D6

This long-standing restaurant has reinvented itself as a crisp, slick place selling fusion food created with ingredients from around the world: Scottish salmon and Breton potatoes rub shoulders with North Sea cod and Limburg abbey-raised pork. Three hundred wines are available, one hundred by the glass. Closed Mon, Tue; lunch Sat, Sun.

EPEN Panorama Restaurant Gerardushoeve
€€
Julianastraat 23, 6285 AH **Tel** *(043) 455 1722*   **Road Map** D6

Perched on the edge of a hillside, the lovely covered terrace here probably has the best view in the country, overlooking Dutch, Belgian and German landscapes. At lunch, Limburg bread is used to make sandwiches, and local influences carry through to dinner. In season, asparagus features in many dishes. Closed dinner Mon–Thu in Jan.

GULPEN l'Atelier
€€€€
Markt 9, 6271 BD **Tel** *(043) 450 4490*   **Road Map** D6

This restaurant on a pretty market square is valued by customers for its good service, good wine and accessible French food. Set menus offer particular value for money, providing a whirlwind tour of the kitchen's craft and incorporating the best local ingredients, such as grotto-aged cheese. Closed Tue–Wed; Sat lunch.

HEERLEN Geleenhof
€€€€
Valkenburgerweg 54, 6419 AV **Tel** *(045) 571 8000*   **Road Map** D6

This lovely country house with a shady, tree-lined courtyard offers quality Limburg cuisine with Mediterranean flourishes. The menu is short and reflects the season's harvest, and always offers a fish, meat and vegetarian choice for each course. The locally grown asparagus features large in springtime. Closed Mon, Tue; lunch Sat, Sun.

MAASTRICHT Rekko
€
Vrijthof 10, 6211 LC **Tel** *(043) 321 9956*   **Road Map** C6

There are few cheap and cheerful places to eat in Maastricht, so this *eetcafé* on the main square is welcome for its all-day kitchen and affordable prices. It opens early for breakfast and continues through lunch and dinner and onto evening snacks and nibbles. The menu holds no surprises, just honest food of the salads, steak and chicken sort.

MAASTRICHT Ginger
€€
Tongersestraat 7, 6211 LL **Tel** *(043) 326 0022*   **Road Map** C6

Those on the look out for a light alternative to the heavy Bourgandische local fare will welcome the clean, healthy flavours at this trendy pan-Asian restaurant. Thai, Korean and Japanese-style rice and noodle dishes predominate, and the range for vegetarians goes beyond just tofu. There are cocktails, wines and beers to drink. Closed lunch Sat & Sun.

MAASTRICHT Eetkamer de Bissjop
€€€
Luikerweg 33, 6212 ET **Tel** *(043) 459 9202*   **Road Map** C6

The walls of this little restaurant hang with paintings that are all for sale – it also doubles as an art gallery. The menu changes weekly, and consists of five courses; diners choose as many or few as they want, from the likes of tomato *bouillon* with wild garlic, John Dory with marinated fennel and chocolate mousse with advocaat. Closed lunch; Mon, Tue.

MAASTRICHT Au Coin des Bons Enfants
€€€€
Ezelmarkt 4, 6211 LJ **Tel** *(043) 321 2359*   **Road Map** C6

This upmarket restaurant has long been a favourite among Maastricht's elite and epicures; in fact, people travel from Belgium and Germany to indulge in its delicacies. Calf's tongue stuffed with veal kidneys and *foie gras*, Aquitaine caviar, Bresse pigeon – all these opulent ingredients are present. Particularly interesting puddings. Closed Tue–Wed.

ROERMOND L'Union
€€
Markt 21, 6041 EL **Tel** *(0475) 317 187*   **Road Map** D5

On an attractive square lined with bars and restaurants and overlooked by the cathedral, l'Union is a safe bet for a decent lunch or dinner. There's a large terrace on the square. Inside looks like a French bistro, with food to match: *bouillabaisse*, mixed grill, salmon mousse. Coffee comes with a glass of advocaat and whipped cream. Closed Mon.

SCHINNEN Aan Sjuuteeänjd
€€€€
Dorpsstraat 74, 6365 BH **Tel** *(046) 443 1767*   **Road Map** D6

Customers travel from all over the region to taste the outstanding, affordable cuisine from Limburg born-and-bred chef, Jean Thoma. He recreates the recipes of his home with modern twists: trout *"zure zult"* (brawn), chicken *pot-au-feu* with Limburg wine and unusual puddings. Closed Tue–Wed; lunch Sat & Sun.

VENLO Grand Café Dante
€
Parade 5e, 5911 CA **Tel** *(077) 321 1651*   **Road Map** D5

This attractive, split-level restaurant in a red-brick town house also has a walled garden for summer eating. The international menu offers well-executed standards such as spicy chicken *satay* with Indonesian pickles and fries, warming pasta dishes and meal-sized salads. Try the creamy home-made *tiramisu* for dessert. Closed Mon.

SHOPPING IN THE NETHERLANDS

Throughout the Netherlands you will find a huge range of shops and markets. Many towns will have large retail chains, but you will also find unique independent shops selling clothes, everyday goods and knick-knacks. Large specialized shops such as furniture stores, factory outlets and

Children's clothes

garden centres are usually on the outskirts of towns and sometimes grouped together in retail parks with parking facilities, child-care facilities and a cafeteria. Most are open, and at their busiest, on public holidays. Recent fashion items can often be picked up cheaply at street markets and second-hand shops.

Shop selling antiques and engrossing curios

MARKETS

Practically every town and village holds a general market at least once a week. There are also specialized markets, for example, the farmers' markets, where you can buy fresh farm produce, as well as antique markets and book fairs. Famous specialized markets include the cheese markets of Alkmaar, Edam and Gouda. Then there are also flea markets, where traders and individuals alike sell second-hand goods.

The Netherlands' biggest flea market takes place on Koninginnedag (Queen's Day) (see p32), when practically half of the country tries to get rid of unwanted goods on the street. Fairs are also popular and are held twice a year. Most markets start at 9:30am and shut at 4pm or 5pm, while some are open either in the mornings or the afternoons only.

ANTIQUES

Antique collectors will find plenty to occupy themselves with in the Netherlands. If you are fortunate, you may

strike it lucky in second-hand shops or at flea markets, but likely your best bet is to go to an authentic antique dealer. Many antique dealers specialize in a particular period or a field – prints or clocks, for instance. If you prefer buying antiques at auctions, you would probably do best to visit the branches of the international auctioneers **Sotheby's** or **Christie's**. In smaller auction houses too, interesting pieces often go under the hammer. Another way of buying antiques is to visit the antique markets and fairs that are held regularly throughout the country.

Amsterdam's Nieuwe Spiegelstraat is the place for antique collectors. Vendors include antique dealers specializing in ceramics, glass, antique prints, paintings and nautical memorabilia.

Haarlem, Middelburg and 's-Hertogenbosch have large numbers of antique shops; these are often located in old farmhouses. The most common pieces on sale are pine or oak furniture. The **MECC** in Maastricht and the **Brabanthallen** in 's-Hertogenbosch are the venues of annual antique fairs, such as the renowned TEFAF, the world's biggest art and antique fair. Antique dealers from around the world come here to trade.

Antique dealer's shop sign

FASHION

The Dutch are spending more and more of their incomes on good-quality fashionable clothing. Besides internationally renowned couturiers, many up-and-coming fashion designers set up their own boutiques. Their clothes are often handmade and fairly pricey. More affordable clothes are available at the larger fashion retailers, both home-grown and international. A typical Dutch way of being fashionable is to combine a new and expensive garment with second-hand clothes.

To see the designs of the most famous couturiers, it is best to go to Amsterdam. On the PC Hooftstraat you will find clothes by Hugo Boss, Armani and Yves Saint-Laurent. Classical English clothing and shoes are to be found in the shops on the Haagse Noordeinde in The Hague. Chains such as Vera Moda sell everyday and durable clothing.

One of the country's many antique and second-hand shops

A trendy clothing boutique featuring the very latest in Dutch fashion

RETAIL STORES AND SHOPPING CENTRES

The most upmarket retail store in the Netherlands is the **Bijenkorf**, which offers contemporary furniture, the latest names in fashion, a huge book department and all major cosmetics brands. The Vroom & Dreesmann department stores are slightly smaller and offer lower prices than the Bijenkorf. One step lower on the prices scale is Hema, which offers a wide and remarkably trendy range of things such as lighting accessories and household goods. At most shopping centres you will find the same names, although some centres are reserved for more exclusive shops. One of these is the **Magna Plaza** in Amsterdam, where you will find upmarket boutiques and jewellers' shops. De Groene Passage in Rotterdam is a covered shopping centre dedicated to the environment, selling items ranging from organic meat to New Age books. **La Vie** in Utrecht

has a good range of shops; in The Hague, **De Passage** is the prime shopping centre. Batavia Stad Outlet Shopping centre in Lelystad is a shopping village built to resemble a 17th-century town. Here manufacturers of expensive brands sell end-of-line products, in particular clothes, at heavy discounts. The designer outlet park in Roermond is a similar place to find bargains.

FURNITURE

The Netherlands' top furniture designer, Jan des Bouvrie, has his own shop in a converted arsenal in Naarden called Studio het Arsenaal. At Van Til Interior in Alkmaar you can buy designer furniture. In Amsterdam-Zuidoost, you can spend a day viewing furniture in the 75 shops of the Villa Arena. Woonthemacentrum De Havenaer in Nijkerk and Palazzo Lelystad also offer interesting collections. You will find "meubelboulevards", shopping streets of furniture stores, throughout the country.

AUCTION AND SALES HOUSES

The famous British auction houses **Sotheby's** and **Christie's** have branches in Amsterdam, where international collections

in particular are auctioned. The **Eland De Zon Loth Gijselman** in Diemen, as well as antiquities and art, also auctions furniture and estates. **Holbein** in Rijssen sells art and antiques, the **Veilinghuis de Vonst** in Zwolle specializes in stamps and coins.

GARDEN CENTRES

Dutch garden centres sell plants, seeds, bulbs, soil, compost, and garden furniture. For more unusual plants go to specialist growers, of which there are many in the Netherlands. Garden centres are usually on the edge of towns or just outside them. They are usually open for business on Sundays and public holidays.

An abundance of flowers at a Dutch garden centre

CHOCOLATE

Verkade and Droste are the Netherlands' best-known chocolate makers, and you can find their products everywhere. Many towns now have specialized confectioners' shops. The renowned Belgian confectioner **Leonidas** has numerous outlets in the country. **Puccini Bomboni** produce exceptional chocolates, sold individually.

TEA AND COFFEE

The Netherlands has been a tea and coffee importer for centuries, and you can find specialist tea and coffee shops everywhere; many still roast their own coffee. **Simon Levelt** always has at least 25 varieties of coffee and 100 tea blends on sale. **Geels & Co**, an old family business, has a roasting house and museum.

Magna Plaza (see p90), open for Sunday shopping

What to Buy in Holland

In the cities and tourist resorts, souvenir shops are not difficult to find. But if you are looking for something out of the ordinary, either for yourself or as gifts, you can often find something in more specialized shops, or even in a supermarket. Flowers and Delftware never fail to delight. For other things worth taking home, for example, local delicacies such as Dutch cheese and *speculaas* or drinks such as *jenever* gin, see page 426.

Souvenir Dolls
Dutch national costume is hardly worn in the Netherlands any more, except by souvenir dolls such as this trio from Volendam.

Miniature Houses
Painted miniature pottery houses (often Delft blue) are a popular souvenir. Some are designed to be filled with jenever *gin, while others are purely ornamental.*

Painted Wooden Clogs
The traditional wooden clog has come to symbolize Holland. They can be bought in all colours and sizes. They can also be ordered via the internet at http://www.woodenshoes.com

Dutch bulbs

Red Coral
Necklaces of red coral are often part of traditional costume in places such as Volendam. However, they also add a nice touch when worn with modern clothing.

Gouda Pipes
Long-necked clay pipes from Gouda, known as Grouwenaars (see p239), have been made here since the beginning of the 17th century and make a nice gift for smokers and non-smokers alike.

Flowers
Bulbs and cut flowers are available all the year round in the innumerable flower shops, flower stalls and garden centres to be easily found throughout the Netherlands.

Prints of Dutch windmills

Reproductions of maps of Amsterdam and Russia

Old Maps and Prints
Amsterdam in particular has made its mark in the field of cartography. Many antique shops sell atlases and books of prints.

Inlaid diamond necklace

Diamond brooch

Diamond's
Diamonds were cut in Amsterdam as early as the 16th century, and the town continues to be one of the main diamond centres of the world. Many jewellers sell uncut diamonds and second-hand diamond rings.

Diamonds of different colours

Delftware mugs

Modern Delftware
Modern blue Delftware items decorated with windmills or other images of Holland are available in the form of tea sets, sculptures, vases and even royal Delft ashtrays. When buying, make sure that there is a certificate of authenticity (see p28) to go with it.

Makkum Pottery
This colourful earthen-ware, primarily tiles, plates and bowls, is still produced by the Tichelaar factory (see p29) at Makkum in Friesland.

Speculaas
These biscuits, flavoured with cinnamon, cloves and ginger, are eaten mainly around St Nicholas' day.

Speculaas

A distinctive Edam cheese

Edam Cheese
The world-famous Edam cheese (see p174) has an excellent taste and makes a good souvenir.

Speculaas Board
Mould your own speculaas *biscuits in these biscuit moulds, or use them for attractive wall ornaments.*

Zeeland Butter Candies
These butter-flavoured sweets from Zeeland, made of glucose sugar syrup and butter, are delicious.

Butter candies

Haagse Hopjes
These coffee-flavoured sweets were first made at the end of the 18th century at the inspiration of a Baron Hop of The Hague.

Hopjes

Dutch Beer
The Dutch are renowned beer-drinkers. In addition to the three brands depicted here, there are countless other varieties available.

Jonge grain jenever

Sonnema herenburg

Zwarte Kip advocaat

Zaans Mustard
This coarse mustard is made at De Huisman mustard plant on the Zaanse Schans (see p175).

Spirits
Renowned Dutch spirits include jenever, *a kind of gin sold in glass or stoneware bottles (there is* jonge *and* oude *clear jenever, as well as that with herbs),* berenburg *(see p297), the Frisian distilled herbal drink and* advocaat, *made of brandy and eggs.*

Gingerbread

Gingerbread
This scrumptious bread comes in a variety of regional variations, and is excellent at breakfast or even as a snack – especially with a thick layer of butter.

Liquorice Drops
The ubiquitous liquorice drops are sold either salted or sweet.

DIRECTORY

ANTIQUES

Amsterdam Antiques Gallery
Nieuwe Spiegelstraat 34,
Amsterdam. **Map** 4 2F
Tel 020-6253371.

A Votre Servies
Vughtstraat 231,
's-Hertogenbosch. **Road Map** C4. *Tel 073-6135989.*

Brabanthallen
Diezekade 2,
's-Hertogenbosch. **Road Map** C4. *Tel 073-6293911.*
Spring antique fairs.

De Tijdspiegel
Nieuwstraat 17,
Middelburg. **Road Map** A5. *Tel 0118-627799.*

EH Ariëns Kappers
Nieuwe Spiegelstraat 32,
Amsterdam. **Map** 4 2F
Tel 020-6235356.

Emmakade 2 Antiek
Emmakade 2,
Leeuwarden. **Road Map** D1. *Tel 058-2153464.*

Jan de Raad Antiquiteiten
Postelstraat 64,
's-Hertogenbosch. **Road Map** C4. *Tel 073-6144979.*

Le Collectionneur
Damplein 5,
Middelburg. **Road Map** A5. *Tel 0118-638595.*

Le Magasin Antiek & Curiosa
Klein Heiligland 58,
Haarlem. **Road Map** B3. *Tel 023-5321383.*

MECC
Forum 100,
Maastricht. **Road Map** C6. *Tel 043-3838383.*
TEFAF in March.

Paul Berlijn Antiques
Amsterdamse Vaart 134,
Haarlem. **Road Map** B3. *Tel 023-5337369.*

RETAIL STORES AND SHOPPING CENTRES

De Bijenkorf
Galerij 152,
Amstelveen. **Road Map** B3. *Tel 0900–0919.*
Dam 1,
Amsterdam. **Map** 2 D3. *Tel 0900–0919.*
Ketelstraat 45,
Arnhem. **Road Map** D4. *Tel 0900–0919.*
Wagenstraat 32,
The Hague. **Road Map** B4. *Tel 0900–0919.*
Piazza 1,
Eindhoven. **Road Map** C5. *Tel 0900–0919.*
Coolsingel 105,
Rotterdam. **Road Map** B4. *Tel 0900–0919.*
Sint-Jacobsstraat 1a,
Utrecht. **Road Map** C4. *Tel 0900–0919.*
www.bijenkorf.nl

De Passage
Passage,
The Hague. **Road Map** B4. *Tel 070-3463830.*

La Vie Shoppingcentre
Lange Viestraat 669,
Utrecht. **Road Map** C4. *Tel 030-2341414.*

Magna Plaza
Nieuwez. Voorburgwal 182,
Amsterdam. **Map** 1 4C
Tel 020-6269199.

FURNITURE

Studio het Arsenaal
Kooltjesbuurt 1,
Naarden-Vesting. **Road Map** C3. *Tel 035-6941144.*

Van Til Interieur
Noorderkade 1038,
Alkmaar. **Road Map** B3. *Tel 072-5112760.*

Villa Arena
Arena Boulevard,
Amsterdam-Zuidoost.
Tel 0800-8455227.
www.villaarena.nl

Woonthemacentrum De Havenaer
Ampèrestraat,
Nijkerk. **Road Map** C3. *Tel 033-2462622.*

AUCTION AND SALES HOUSES

Christie's
Cornelis Schuytstraat 57,
Amsterdam. **Map** 3 4C
Tel 020-5755255.

De Eland De Zon Loth Gijselman
Industrieterrein Verrijn
Stuart, Weesperstraat
110–112, Diemen. **Road Map** C3. *Tel 020-6230343.*

Holbein Kunst- en Antiekveilingen
Jutestraat 31, Rijssen. **Road Map** D3. *Tel 0548-541577.*

Sotheby's
De Boelelaan 30,
Amsterdam.
Tel 020-5502200.

Veilinghuis de Vonst
Voorstraat 23,
Zwolle. **Road Map** D3. *Tel 038-4211045.*

CHOCOLATES

Huize van Wely
Beethovenstraat 72,
Amsterdam. **Map** 4 D5. *Tel 020-6622009.*
Hoofdstraat 88,
Noordwijk (ZH). **Road Map** B3. *Tel 071-3612228.*

Leonidas
Damstraat 15,
Amsterdam. **Map** 2 5D
Tel 020-6253497.
Bakkerstraat 2,
Arnhem. **Road Map** D4. *Tel 026-4422157.*
Passage 26,
The Hague. **Road Map** B4. *Tel 070-3649608.*
Fonteinstraat 3,
's-Hertogenbosch. **Road Map** C4. *Tel 073-6143626.*
Pottenbakkersingel 2,
Middelburg. **Road Map** A5. *Tel 0118-634750.*

Puccini Bomboni
Staalstraat 17,
Amsterdam. **Map** 5 A2
Tel 020-6265474.
Singel 184,
Amsterdam. **Map** 1 4C
Tel 020-4278341.

TEA AND COFFEE

Abraham Mostert
Schoutenstraat 11,
Utrecht. **Road Map** C4. *Tel 030-2316934.*

Geels & Co
Warmoesstraat 67,
Amsterdam. **Map** 2 4D
Tel 020-6240683.

Het Klaverblad
Hogewoerd 15,
Leiden. **Road Map** B3. *Tel 071-5133655.*

In de drij swarte mollen
Hinthamerstraat 190,
's-Hertogenbosch. **Road Map** C4. *Tel 073-6871411.*

Koffiebrander Blanche Dael
Wolfstraat 28,
Maastricht. **Road Map** C6. *Tel 043-3213475.*

Simon Levelt koffie- en theehandel
Prinsengracht 180,
Amsterdam. **Map** 1 4B
Tel 020-6240823.
Veerstraat 15,
Bussum. **Road Map** C3. *Tel 035-6939459.*
Zwanestraat 38,
Groningen. **Road Map** D1. *Tel 050-3114333.*
Gierstraat 65,
Haarlem. **Road Map** B3. *Tel 023-5311861.*
Botermarkt 1–2,
Leiden. **Road Map** B3. *Tel 071-5131159.*
Vismarkt 21.
Utrecht. **Road Map** B3. *Tel 030-2314495.*

Beurstraverse 69,
Rotterdam. **Road Map** B4. *Tel 010-4136034.*
Oude Gracht 136,
Utrecht. **Road Map** C4. *Tel 030-2317738.*

ENTERTAINMENT IN
THE NETHERLANDS

Cultural life in the Netherlands is not confined to the Randstad. Outside the big cities there is also plenty to do. There is a theatre or a cultural centre in just about every town, where theatre groups, cabaret artists, orchestras and rock bands perform. There is also a growing number of entertainment complexes, such as the Miracle Planet Boulevard centre in Enschede. You can find out what's on either by contacting the

Engelenbak theatre logo

relevant venue or through the local VVV (tourist) offices; another option is the AUB Ticketshop *(see p149)* in Amsterdam. Here you can usually book tickets centrally, or obtain more information about performances. You can also get tickets and information via the Uitlijn (0900-0191). The major national dailies publish a list of events each week. Most cities publish a weekly *uitkrant*, or entertainment guide, while the internet is another source of information.

THEATRE

The Netherlands boasts a large number of theatres, most located in Amsterdam. That city's top theatre is the Stadsschouwburg *(see p149)*, where many touring theatre companies put on performances. The Netherlands' largest theatre company, Amsterdam Theatre Group, is based here and is now directed by Ivo van Hove.

The annual highlight for opera, theatre and dance is the Holland Festival. The best in international cultural offerings is to be had during the Amsterdam Festival. During the International Theatre School Festival in June, experimental drama is performed at venues such as **De Brakke Grond** *(see p149)* and **Frascati**. The **Soeterijn**, on the other hand, specializes in theatre from developing countries. The theatre company frequently wins prizes under the inspired leadership of Theu Boermans. De Dogtroep is a company that stages spectacular street theatre, while the Theatergroup Hollandia has also won great acclaim with its performances in large halls and aircraft hangars. The musical dramas of Orkater can be seen in various parts of the country at different times of the year, but mainly at the Stadsschouwburg and **Bellevue**. **De la Mar** stages big box-office hits, comedy and concerts by Dutch solo artists and groups. Youth-

focused theatre is put on in **De Krakeling**. For years now the performances by the **Toneelschuur** in Haarlem have won critical acclaim. The De Appel group stages both experimental and repertory theatre at the **Appeltheater** in The Hague. Throughout the Netherlands there are numerous excellent theatre groups. Het Zuidelijk Toneel of Eindhoven in the south always packs theatre halls, as do the Theater van het Oosten from Arnhem in the east of the country and the Noord Nederlands Toneel from Groningen in the north.

Every year in May, the Festival aan de Werf in Utrecht presents an appealing smorgasbord of theatre and cabaret performances.

MUSICALS AND CABARET

The Netherlands' most outstanding musical theatres are the **Fortis Circustheater** of The Hague, the **Beatrix Theater** in Utrecht and the Koninklijk Theater Carré *(see p149)* in Amsterdam. These stage Dutch versions of big box-office hits such as *Les Misérables* and *Miss Saigon*.

De Kleine Komedie *(see p149)*, a magnificent 17th-century building on the Amstel river opposite the Muziektheater, is a favourite

Scene from the musical *Oliver!* at the Theater Carré

venue for cabaret groups. Stand-up comedy has also gained popularity mainly through this venue. Other comedy venues in Amsterdam are **Comedy Café, Toomler** and **Boom Chicago** *(see p149)*.

DANCE

The Netherlands is the proud home of two world-famous ballet troupes: the Nationale Ballet and the Nederlands Dans Theater (NDT). The Nationale Ballet is based in the Musiektheater *(see p149)*, which is commonly known among Amsterdam theatregoers as the "Stopera". This contemporary building can accommodate 1,600 people and is a significant centre both for dance and for opera. The foyer affords a spectacular view of the river Amstel.

The Nederlands Dans Theater, which is based in the **Lucent Danstheater** in The Hague, puts on works primarily by its former artistic

Noord Nederlands Toneel staging Anton Chekhov's *The Seagull*

director Jiří Kylian, who was succeeded by Marianne Sarstadt in 1999. Under the direction of the company's present choreographer Ed Wubbe it has staged sold-out performances with live music. Introdans of Arnhem performs an exciting combination of jazz, flamenco and ethnic dance. The country's biggest choreographers use the Holland Festival as a platform to present their new creations to the public. During the Internationale Theaterschool Festival, which

De Dogtroep performing lively and spectacular street theatre

also takes place in June, the proportion of dance performed is growing. The festival venue is the Nes, one of Amsterdam's oldest streets. Julidans is the name given to a summer dance festival in Amsterdam in which contemporary dance by various international dance companies is performed.

FILM

Going to the movies continues to be a popular pastime in the Netherlands, and you will find at least one or more cinemas in almost every town. Amsterdam alone has more than 45 cinemas. Foreign-language films are shown in the original language with subtitles. The most magnificent cinema in Amsterdam is Tuschinski, an Art Deco masterpiece built from 1918–21, with a stylish foyer and generous seating *(see p115)*. The major premieres are held here: if you want to see famous faces, the best time is Wednesday evenings at the cinema entrance. There is a list of all films that are showing at the box office of every cinema, and such lists are also displayed in cafés and restaurants. Cinema programmes change every Thursday, so you will find a list of films that are on in Wednesday's evening papers and in Thursday's morning papers. *De Filmkrant* is a

much-respected movie magazine that is published every Monday, which in addition to the week's film listings also provides background information on major films. Major film events in the Netherlands are the Nederlands Film Festival, which is held in Utrecht in September and October, where Dutch films are premiered. The IDFA (International Documentary Film Festival Amsterdam) is the biggest of its kind, held every year in November/December. The renowned International Film Festival in Rotterdam takes place each January.

ORCHESTRAL, CHAMBER AND CHOIR MUSIC

The Concertgebouw *(see p149)* in Amsterdam is traditionally the most important venue for concert music. The Grote Zaal hall is famous for its acoustics, and its resident musicians are the Koninklijk Concertgebouworkest. During summer the orchestra puts on special concerts. The Beurs van Berlage *(see p149)*, formerly the stock exchange, has for some time now been the home of the Nederlands Philharmonisch Orkest. Many of the country's better orchestras and choirs perform here.

De Ysbreker is situated in a magnificent building on the Amstel, and since 1979 has been the prime venue in Amsterdam for modern classical music.

The Golden Calf

The Amsterdamse Koninklijk Concertgebouworkest performing

An outstanding orchestra is the Rotterdams Philharmonisch Orkest, which since 1995 has been conducted by the Russian conductor Valeri Gergjev. The orchestra is based in **De Doelen** in Rotterdam. The Residentie Orkest, whose history goes back almost 100 years, performs regularly at the **Anton Philipszaal** in The Hague and is not to be confused with the **Muziekcentrum Frits Philips** in Eindhoven, where the Brabants Orkest is based.

The Gelders Orkest makes regular appearances in the **Musis Sacrum** concert hall in Arnhem. Another venue offering a rich programme of music is the **Muziekcentrum Vredenburg**.

CHURCH MUSIC

Of the many organs in the Netherlands, that of the **Grote Kerk** in Elburg is probably the best known. Every year it is used in the national amateur organist competition. The instruments in the **Oude Kerk** and the **Nieuwe Kerk** are the most famous of Amsterdam's 42 church organs. Organ concerts can also be heard at the **Waalse Kerk** and also on Tuesdays at lunch time in the **Westerkerk**.

The programme of the 17th-century **Engelse Kerk** contains a wide variety of music, ranging from Baroque to modern. In the **Domkerk** in Utrecht, concerts are performed on a regular basis.

OPERA

Established in 1988 in Amsterdam, the **Muziektheater** is the home of the Nederlandse Opera. One of Europe's most modern opera theatres, its stage has been graced by many established international companies, although it is also used for experimental works. The Stadsschouwburg *(see p112)* on the Leidseplein is also host to a great deal of opera, although if experimental opera is your thing, the Westergasfabriek is probably the best venue. The **Twentse Schouwburg** in Enschede, in conjunction with the Nationale Reisopera, organizes the Twents Opera Festival each year in July and August.

ROCK AND POP

Two venues in particular have established themselves as the most important rock venues in the Netherlands: **Ahoy'** in Rotterdam and Vredenburg in Utrecht, although international rock stars now perform in many parts of the Netherlands. With a capacity of over 5,000, the easily accessible **Heineken Music Hall** is Amsterdam's prime rock venue. It has been used for concerts by megastars such as the late Michael Jackson and the Rolling Stones. However, for locals, there are only two real rock venues: **Paradiso** and **De Melkweg**. Paradiso, in a former church near the Leidseplein, enjoys the greatest respect. The Melkweg (Milky Way), which is also near the Leidseplein, owes its name to the fact that the building in which it is located used to be a dairy. The programme in both of these respected venues changes constantly, and all rock and pop enthusiasts will eventually find something to their taste.

Every Sunday in summer there are free open-air concerts in the Vondelpark, often with renowned bands on the line-up. Programmes are displayed at the entrances to the park. In June the world's largest free pop festival, the Haagse Zuiderpark Parkpop, is held in The Hague. Another annual festival which attracts visitors from near and far is the Pinkpopfestival in Landgraaf (Limburg).

JAZZ

The foremost venue of the jazz scene in Amsterdam is the **Bimhuis**. Although the casual visitor might find the atmosphere a tad pretentious, the music here is of top quality, and the Bimhuis enjoys a reputation that goes far beyond the country's borders. There are good jazz cafés to be found all over Amsterdam, most of them featuring local jazz bands.

Hans Dulfer

Around the Leidseplein are the **Alto Jazz Café** and **Bourbon Street**, which is open until 4am on weekdays and until 5am on weekends. Alto is best on Wednesdays, when the "godfather" of Amsterdam jazz, Hans Dulfer, performs. His daughter Candy, who has gained international renown, sometimes plays in **De Heeren van Aemstel**. **De Engelbewaarder** is a venue for Sunday jazz. Meanwhile, in Rotterdam, the annual North Sea Jazz Festival takes place in the Congresgebouw. **Dizzy** jazz café has become a household name among jazz-lovers in Rotterdam, hosting over 100 jazz concerts every year.

DIRECTORY

THEATRES

Appeltheater
Duinstraat 6–8, The
Hague. **Road Map** B4.
Tel 070-3502200.

Arsenaaltheater
Arsenaalplein 7, Vlissingen.
Road Map A5.
Tel 0118-430303.

Bellevue
Leidsekade 90, Amsterdam.
Map 4 D1.
Tel 020-5305301/02.

Chassé Theater
Claudius Prinsenlaan 8,
Breda. **Road Map** B5.
Tel 076-5303132.

Compagnietheater
Kloveniersburgwal 50,
Amsterdam. **Map** 2 D5.
Tel 020-5205320.

Concordia
Oude Markt 26, Enschede.
Road Map E3.
Tel 053-4300999.

De Flint
Conickstraat 60,
Amersfoort. **Road Map**
C4. *Tel 033-4229222.*

De Harmonie
Ruiterskwartier 4, Leeu-
warden. **Road Map** D1.
Tel 058-2330233.

De Krakeling
Nwe Passeerdersstraat 1,
Amsterdam. **Map** 4 D1.
Tel 020-6253284.

De la Mar
Marnixstraat 404,
Amsterdam. **Map** 4 D1.
Tel 0900-3352627.

Frascati
Nes 63, Amsterdam. **Map**
2 D5. *Tel 020-6235723.*

Orpheus
Churchillplein 1,
Apeldoorn. **Road Map**
D3. *Tel 0900-1230123.*

Soeterijn
Linnaeusstraat 2,
Amsterdam. **Map** 6 E3.
Tel 020-5688500.

Stadsschouwburg
Leidseplein 26, Amsterdam.
Map 4 E2.
Tel 020-6242311.

't Spant
Kuyperlaan 3, Bussum.
Road Map C3.
Tel 035-6913949.

**Theater aan het
Vrijthof**
Vrijthof 47, Maastricht.
Road Map C6.
Tel 043-3505555.

Toneelschuur
Lange Begijnestr 9,
Haarlem. **Road Map** B3.
Tel 023-5173910.

Transformatorhuis
Haarlemmerweg 8–10,
Amsterdam. **Map** 1 A1.
Tel 020-6279070.

MUSICALS AND CABARET

Beatrix Theater
Jaarbeursplein 6, Utrecht.
Road Map C4.
Tel 030-2447044.

Boom Chicago
Leidseplein 12, Amsterdam.
Map 4 E2.
Tel 020-5300232.

Comedy Café
Max Euweplein 43–45,
Amsterdam. **Map** 4 E2.
Tel 020-6383971.

Fortis Circustheater
Circusstraat 4, The Hague.
Road Map B4.
Tel 070-4167600.

Toomler
Breitnerstr. 2, Amsterdam.
Map 3 C5.
Tel 020-6755511.

DANCE

Lucent Danstheater
Spuiplein 150, The Hague.
Road Map B4.
Tel 070-8800300.

**Rotterdamse
Schouwburg**
Schouwburgplein 25,
Rotterdam. **Road Map** B4.
Tel 010-4118110.

**Schouwburg
Arnhem**
Koningsplein 12, Arnhem.
Road Map D4.
Tel 026-4437343.

ORCHESTRA, CHAMBER AND CHOIR MUSIC

Anton Philipszaal
Spuiplein 150, The Hague.
Road Map B4.
Tel 070-8800300.

**Concertgebouw
De Vereeniging**
Keizer Karelplein,
Nijmegen. **Road Map** D4.
Tel 024-3228344.

De Doelen
Schouwburgplein 50,
Rotterdam. **Road Map** B4.
Tel 010-2171717.

De Ysbreker
Weesperzijde 23,
Amsterdam. **Map** 5 C4.
Tel 020-6939093.

Musis Sacrum
Velperbuitensingel 25,
Arnhem. **Road Map** D4.
Tel 026-4437343.

**Muziekcentrum
Frits Philips**
Heuvelgalerie, Eindhoven.
Road Map C5.
Tel 040-2655600.

**Muziekcentrum
Vredenburg**
Vredenburgpassage 77,
Utrecht. **Road Map** C4.
Tel 030-2314544.

CHURCH MUSIC

Domkerk
Domplein, Utrecht.
Road Map C4.
Tel 030-2310403.

Engelse Kerk
Begijnhof 48,
Amsterdam. **Map** 1 C5.
Tel 020-6249665.

Grote Kerk
Van Kinsbergenstraat,
Elburg. **Road Map** D3.
Tel 0525-681520.

Nieuwe Kerk
Dam, Amsterdam. **Map** 2
D5. *Tel 020-6386909.*

Oude Kerk
Oudekerksplein 23,
Amsterdam. **Map** 2 D4.
Tel 020-6258284.

Waalse Kerk
Walenplein 157,
Amsterdam.
Tel 020-6232074.

Westerkerk
Prinsengracht 281,
Amsterdam. **Map** 1 B4.
Tel 020-624776.

OPERA

**Muziektheater
Amsterdam**
see p149. **Map** 5 B2.

**Twentse
Schouwburg**
Langestraat 49, Enschede.
Road Map E3.
Tel 053-4858585.

ROCK AND POP

Ahoy'
Zuiderparkweg 20–30,
Rotterdam. **Road Map** B4.
Tel 010-2933300.

**Heineken Music
Hall**
Arena Boulevard 590,
Amsterdam.
Tel 0900-3001250.

Melkweg
Lijnbaansgracht 234 a,
Amsterdam. **Map** 4 E2.
Tel 020-5318181.

Paradiso
Weteringschans 6–8,
Amsterdam. **Map** 4 3F.
Tel 020-6264521.

JAZZ

Alto Jazz Café
Korte Leidsedwarsstraat
115, Amsterdam.
Map 1 B4.
Tel 020-6263249.

Bimhuis
Piet Heinkade 3,
Amsterdam.
Tel 020-7882188.

Bourbon Street
Leidsekruisstraat 6–8,
Amsterdam. **Map** 4 2E.
Tel 020-6233440.

De Engelbewaarder
Kloveniersburgwal 59,
Amsterdam. **Map** 2 5D.
Tel 020-6253772.

**De Heeren van
Aemstel**
Thorbeckeplein 5,
Amsterdam. **Map** 5 A2.
Tel 020-6202173.

Dizzy
's-Gravendijkwal 129,
Rotterdam. **Road Map** B4.
Tel 010-4773014.

Amusement and Theme Parks

The Netherlands offers a great variety of amusement and theme parks. Whether you want to see frolicking dolphins, take a white-knuckle ride, go back to Roman times or spend the day splashing in a swimming pool, there is something for everyone. And because the Dutch weather doesn't always play along, most parks have attractions indoors. Listed below is a sample of the parks to be found in the country.

Hellendoorn Adventure Park

AQUA ZOO FRIESLAND

This watery domain near Leeuwarden shows beavers, minks, polecats, storks and other animals in their natural surroundings. Otters are a highlight here, having disappeared from the Netherlands due to pollution of their freshwater habitat. A path winds its way through the entire terrain, leading at one point through a glass tunnel that provides visitors with a close-up of the otters' underwater antics.

ARCHEON

This open-air archaeological park brings the past to life in captivating fashion. Visitors wander from prehistoric times, the Roman period and the Middle Ages, aided by the re-creations of actors. You can see how the hunter-gatherers lived and how farmers tilled their fields. You then explore a Roman town complete with bath-house, temple and theatre, followed by a medieval city with working craftsmen. The hands-on fun includes a trip in a prehistoric canoe.

HET ARSENAAL

A large attraction with a maritime theme has been set up at Het Arsenaal in Vlissingen. First visitors watch a naval review with models of famous ocean liners, including the *Titanic*. For those hooked on adrenaline there is a shipwreck simulator and a scary pirate cave on a treasure island. In Onderwaterwereld you can observe sharks, lobsters and other creatures of the deep. The 64-m (210-ft) tower of Het Arsenaal gives a fine view of the Westerschelde estuary.

AVONTURENPARK HELLENDOORN

This place offers a vast range of attractions, including the Canadian River log-ride with a 12-m (39-ft) drop in a tree trunk, the Sungai Kalimantan rafting-ride, the Tornado and Rioolrat (underground) rat ride, a monorail over a dinosaur park and Montezuma's Revenge (prepare to get wet!). Younger children will enjoy Dreumesland (Dreamland) with its play castle and much more.

BURGERS' ZOO

This unusual park allows you to see animals from all over the world in their natural environments, which have been carefully re-created here.

In Burger's Desert, in a vast hall with 20-m (65-ft) ceilings, you can wander through a rocky cactus desert with birds and an oasis. There is also a dense tropical jungle and a safari park with giraffes, rhinoceroses and lions. In the ocean section, you can stand on a tropical coral beach and peer through the glass at an undersea world.

DOLFINARIUM

Frolicking dolphins and seals always draw large crowds, but the Dolfinarium does one better with its Lagune, a large bay where dolphins, sea lions and fish live. On the Roggenrif you can mingle with the seals and stroke sharks, while in Fort Heerewich you learn how stranded dolphins are cared for. An underwater show and a 3D film provide additional excitement.

DUINRELL

Nestled in the sandy woodlands of the Wassenaar region, this park has rides such as the Waterspin, toboggan runs, a frog roller coaster and a monorail. In summer there are elaborate shows such as the *Music Laser Light Show*. For the little ones there is a fairytale wonderland, a large playground and numerous kids' shows. A big draw is the Tikibad, an indoor pool with spectacular slides, a surf pool and a water ballet show.

Suspension bridge through the tropical rainforest in Burgers' Bush

ECOMARE

Located on the island of Texel, this is an information centre for the tidal flats of the West Frisian islands and the North Sea. There is a display about the creation of Texel, its habitat and the local fauna. The Waterzaal is full of aquariums, plus a basin of rays for petting. There's also a centre for stranded seals and seabirds.

DE EFTELING

This theme park in Kaatsheuvel draws on the world of fantasy. In the fairytale forest you may bump into Little Red Riding Hood, Snow White or Sleeping Beauty. The Fata Morgana is a simplified take on the Arabian Nights; here you can view the

Stranded seals recovering their health in EcoMare on Texel

The splash ride in Duinrell

entire park from a 45-m (148-ft) Flying Temple.

Extreme thrills are provided by the Python, the Pegasus and the underground Vogel Rok roller coasters and many other rides. It's worth checking the website for "busy" days.

If a day isn't enough, you can stay in the Efteling Hotel.

LINNAEUSHOF

This playground claims to be Europe's largest, with more than 350 different pieces of equipment, including a super slide, cable rides, a skate-rail, trampolines, a climbing wall, pedaloes and 360-degree swings. In the "spider's web", you risk tumbling into the water as you climb nets to the pirates' crow's nest.

Toddlers have their own special playground with a huge sandpit and road village where they can ride tricycles and toy aeroplanes. For wet weather there's an indoor playground.

NOORDWIJK SPACE EXPO

This sprawling display about the wonders of outer space is a treat for all ages. Some of its rockets and satellites are the real thing (as is the piece of moon rock 4 billion years old), but the replicas, such as a model lunar module, are convincing. You can visit a space station and watch multimedia presentations. Children will especially like the treasure hunt and weight-free simulator.

VERKEERSPARK ASSEN

This park offers an enormous circuit of roads, roundabouts and traffic lights where children aged between 6 and 12 can drive around and learn to deal with various traffic situations. Someone keeps an eye on participants from the traffic control tower. There's a play area and suitable rides for toddlers, while older children can ride motorized jeeps and "bouncy bikes".

DIRECTORY

Aqua Zoo Friesland
De Groene Ster 2, 8926 XE Leeuwarden. **Road map** D2. *Tel 0511-431214.* ☐ *10am–5pm daily (longer in summer).* **www**.aquazoo.nl

Archeon
Archeonlaan 1, 2408 ZB Alphen a/d Rijn. **Road map** B4. *Tel 0172-447744.* ☐ *Apr–Oct: 10am–5pm Tue–Sun.* **www**.archeon.nl

Het Arsenaal
Arsenaalplein 1, 4380 KA Vlissingen. **Road map** A5. *Tel 0118-415400.* ☐ *call ahead.* **www**.arsenaal.nl

Avonturenpark Hellendoorn
Luttenbergerweg 22, 7447 PB Hellendoorn. **Road map** D3. *Tel 0900-1236555.* ☐ *Apr–Aug:*

10am–5pm daily (7pm Jul–mid Aug); Sep–Oct: 10am–5pm Sat & Sun. **www**.avonturenpark-helendoorn.nl

Burgers' Zoo
Anton van Hooffplein 1, 6816 SH Arnhem. **Road map** D4. *Tel 026-4424534.* ☐ *Apr– Oct: 9am–7pm daily; Nov– Mar: 9am–5pm.* **www**.burgers-zoo.nl

Dolfinarium Harderwijk
Strandboulevard Oost 1, 3841 AB Harderwijk. **Road map** C3. *Tel 0341-467467* ☐ *mid-Feb–Jun & Sep–Oct: 10am– 5pm daily; Jul– Aug: 10am–6pm.* **www**.dolfinarium.nl

Duinrell
Duinrell 1, 2242 JP Wassenaar. **Road map** B4. *Tel 070-5155258.* ☐ **Theme park:** *Apr–Oct: 10am– 5pm daily (mid-Jul–Aug to 6pm).* **Tikibad:** *call ahead.* **www**.duinrell.nl

EcoMare
Ruyslaan 92, 1796 AZ De Koog, Texel. **Road map** B2. *Tel 0222-317741.* ☐ *9am–5pm daily.* **www**.ecomare.nl

De Efteling
Europalaan 1, 5171 KW Kaatsheuvel. **Road map** C4. *Tel 0416-288111* ☐ *Apr–Oct: 10am–6pm daily (later in summer).* **Winter Efteling:** *open around Christmas.*

www.efteling.nl

Linnaeushof
Rijksstraatweg 4, 2121 AE Bennebroek. **Road map** B3. *Tel 023-5845362.* ☐ *Apr–Sep: 10am–6pm daily.* **www**.linnaeushof.nl

Noordwijk Space Expo
Keplerlaan 3, 2201 AZ Noordwijk. *Tel 0900-87654321.* ☐ *10am–5pm Tue–Sun (also Mon in school hols).* **www**.spaceexpo.nl

Verkeerspark Assen
De Haar 1–1a, 9405 TE Assen. **Road map** D2. *Tel 0592-350005.*
☐ *Apr–Oct: 9:30am–5pm daily. Open days vary in some weeks so check ahead.*

Sports Holidays

With its abundance of water, the Netherlands lends itself to all kinds of watersports such as boating, sailing and canoeing; however, there are also plenty of opportunities for sporting activities on dry land, whether you want to kick a ball about or play golf or tennis, or even go riding. Most *VVV-gidsen (see p440)* tell you where there are golf courses and tennis courts in the locality, and they give the addresses of angling clubs, stables, boatyards, sailing schools and so on.

Ramblers in the Heuvelrug of Utrecht

Holland offers much in the way of watersports, such as canoeing

WATERSPORTS

The favourite places in the Netherlands for watersports are the Frisian seas, the coastal lakes, the Plassengebied (lakelands), the southwest river delta, and the lakes of the Vechtplassen, the Maasplassen, the IJsselmeer and, of course, the North Sea. Everywhere there are abundant marinas and watersports centres, often with equipment for hire. The ANWB publishes the *Wateralmanakken*, available at ANWB and VVV offices and in bookshops, which give details of sailing regulations, bridge and lock opening times, port information and so on. The *ANWB/VVV waterkaarten* (navigation charts) are also used by many people. You can obtain information on sailing and surfing organizations at institutions such as the **Commissie Watersport Opleidingen** (watersports training commission) and the ANWB. Surfers will find plenty to do on the North Sea and IJsselmeer coast (surfing beaches, equipment hire), and it is also possible to surf on many inland waters, including the Reenwijkse Plassen, the Randmeren and the Frisian lakes. For further information on sailing, boating and windsurfing, ask at the **Koninklijk Nederlands Watersport Verbond** (royal watersports association). Good places for diving include the Oosterschelde and Grevelingenmeer; for more information apply to the Dutch underwater-sports association, the **Nederlandse Onderwatersport Bond**.

For canoeing, your first port of call should be the **Nederlandse Kano Bond** (canoeing association). Dozens of round trips in various craft organized in lakes, rivers and the sea are also available. The local VVV tourist office will be able to direct you further.

RAMBLING AND CYCLING

Ramblers' guides and maps can be obtained in many places, including the VVV, ANWB and bookshops. The VVV also provides information on walking tours and local events. The *Er op Uit!* booklet published by the Dutch Railways contains rambling routes from one station to another. The majority of them are 15 to 20 km (9 to 12 miles), though some two-day hikes are also described. You will find route maps at the station where the hike begins. Around 30 long-distance hiking trails have been marked out in the Netherlands. These routes, which

---

SAILING

Sailing courses suitable for all ages and experience levels are widely available along the Dutch coast for practically all types of vessel. Taking lessons at a CWO registered sailing school will give you an internationally recognized CWO sailing certificate. More experienced sailors can explore the North Sea, the IJsselmeer (watch out for strong winds), the Waddenzee (where you have to watch the shallows) or the Westerschelde (which has strong tidal currents). However, you can also go for a more relaxing experience on the Vinkeveense Plassen lakes. Cruises are also widely available. Hollands Glorie (tel. 010-4156600) offers cruises on traditional sailing craft on waterways such as the IJsselmeer, the Waddenzee and the Frisian lakes.

Yachting on the Oosterschelde

Sailing dinghy

Golfers on the Lauswolt Estate in Friesland

are at least 100 km (62 miles) in length, follow mainly unmetalled tracks. A popular hiking trail is the Pieterpad (LAW 9), stretching 480 km (300 miles) from Pieterburen in Groningen to the Sint-Pietersberg at Maastricht. **Wandelplatform-LAW** publishes guides to the routes, with and without accommodation details. Many natural areas are criss-crossed by footpaths and cycle tracks, among them the Nationaal Park Hoge Veluwe *(see p339)*. You can find out about accessibility of various areas and about enjoyable routes or excursions at VVV or ANWB tourist information offices, at the Staatsbosbeheer (forestry commission) (tel. 030-692 6213) or the Vereniging Natuurmonumenten *(see p260)*. For details on cycling, see pages 456–7.

GOLF AND TENNIS

The Netherlands has some 160 golfing clubs, all members of the Nederlandse Golf Federatie (**NGF**). Many clubs also provide opportunities for non-members to play, although some may require proof of golfing

Riding on Ameland

proficiency. Many of them also offer training courses. Golf courses in the Netherlands are in dunelands, woodland and polderland.

In many areas you will find tennis clubs with outdoor and indoor courts. Most bungalow parks have tennis courts for the use of residents.

FISHING

Fishing is a popular sport in the Netherlands. In the inland waterways you can angle for bream, carp and pike, while flatfish and mackerel can be caught along the coast and in the sea. Local angling associations will give you information on when and where to fish. Don't forget to obtain a fishing permit (which is compulsory for inland waters). The permits are available at post offices, VVVs or angling associations. Sometimes you also need a permit for a particular lake or river. Along the coast, angling trips are organized on the North Sea and in the Waddenzee.

HORSE RIDING

There are many stables where you can hire horses for pony-trekking. Some stables hire out horses only if you have a riding permit or if you are on a guided tour (information is available from the **SRR**). For some nature reserves which allow riding you will need to get a riding permit from the organization managing the area, and you will have to keep to the bridleways. Beach riding is an unforgettable experience, but keep an eye on the signs, because some sections of beach – especially in summer – are closed to horses.

SURVIVAL GUIDE

PRACTICAL INFORMATION

The Netherlands is relatively small and has a dense road and motorway network with good public transport so getting around is quick and easy. Whether you are going to Amsterdam, the Veluwe, Maastricht or Zandvoort, you can get there from anywhere in the country very quickly by car or by train. The flat landscape

The logo of the Amsterdam Tourist Board

with its many canals and dykes means that holidaymakers have plenty of opportunity to explore the countryside by bicycle *(see pp456–7)* or by boat *(see p455)*. Another option is to take a trip by steam train. The best place to find out what's available in your area – and in the country as a whole – is the local VVV (tourist information) office.

VVV and ANWB offices, which often share the same premises

TOURIST INFORMATION

The best source of information for tourists is the local or regional **VVV** office. Many towns and places of interest have VVV offices where you can drop in and ask for advice and brochures about places of interest, local events, walks, cycle routes and excursions in the town or region. In addition, they can provide maps and books about other parts of the Netherlands. The VVV-*gidsen* series in Dutch is very practical, with information and facts about individual provinces and regions.

At VVVs you can also book domestic excursions, hotels, short breaks and theatre tickets anywhere in the country. Annual museum cards and CJPs are also on sale here. Smaller VVV outlets, although providing comprehensive information about their local area, do not provide other services.

ANWB offices in the Netherlands also have a

ANWB logo

selection of cycling, rambling and motoring guides, tickets, camping guides and road atlases. ANWB members have access to specialized membership information about various subjects and holiday offers. In many cases the VVV and the ANWB share the same premises. If you are travelling to the Netherlands from abroad you can obtain information in advance from the **Netherlands Board of Tourism (NBT)** in your own country.

LANGUAGE

The Dutch have been linguists for centuries, and most students learn English, some German and French. English is certainly very widely and fluently spoken in Amsterdam. However, it's always appreciated if you can handle a few niceties: greeting a Dutch person with "Dag" ("good day"), for example, before asking whether they speak English. The Phrase Book on pages 479–80 is a useful place to start.

ENTERTAINMENT

Many VVV-*gidsen* guides have an annual review of events in a particular region or province. For up-to-date information on events, exhibitions, performances and films, it is worth looking in the entertainment supplements issued by daily papers *(see p146)*, or ask at the local VVV office. Plays, concerts, special events and festivals are usually advertised on billboards or in cafés. Special regional and local entertainment guides are also a good source of information; for example, the monthly *Uitkrant* tells you what's on in Amsterdam in the way of theatre, while the weekly *Uitloper* is Utrecht's entertainment guide. These guides are distributed at many sites free of charge.

Tickets for concerts and events are available not only at the box office of the venue itself but also via the national **Ticket Service** and at VVV offices. Some towns also have their own booking bureau; for instance, in Amsterdam you can book your tickets at the AUB *(see p149)*, and in The Hague you can get your tickets at the Bespreekbureau Haagsche Courant (tel. 070-3656806).

Revellers at a music festival in Amsterdam

◁ The hard-working Dutch taking time out to relax

Museum Card

MUSEUM CARD

The Annual Museum Card (*Museumjaarkaart*) has quickly risen to huge popularity. It costs €39.95 for people over the age of 25, and €19.95 for under-25s. It gives the holder free entry to over 440 museums in the country. However, you usually have to pay a supplement for special exhibitions. The card is available at all participating museums and at VVVs, and requires a passport photograph. It can also be ordered from the **Stichting Museum-jaarkaart** (also available over the Internet).

TRAVELLERS WITH DISABILITIES

Most public buildings have good facilities for travellers with disabilities. Museums, art galleries, cinemas and theatres generally are wheel-chair-accessible. Only some establishments in very old buildings are less accessible, but there are always staff who are able to lend a hand. If you require assistance it's a good idea to phone in advance. Accessibility information for hotels is given on page 387.

In Amsterdam and other major cities, all main pedestrian crossings are equipped with sound for the blind. For disabled people travelling by train, the NS has issued a pack entitled *Gehandicapten*. This contains information on Dutch railway stations and what facilities they have, and also lists the stations (there are approximately 150 of them) where people in wheelchairs can get assistance when boarding and alighting from trains. Many trains have wheelchair-accessible doors, and most new double-decker trains have wheelchair-accessible toilets. If you need help, it's best to contact the **Bureau Assistentieverlening Gehandicapten** three hours before travelling.

Wheelchair-accessible tourist office

OPENING HOURS

Although until recently just about every shop in the country was open from 9am to 6pm, today there is an increasing variety in shop opening hours. Many retail stores and supermarkets are open until 7pm or later. In the cities, shops tend to stay open longer. Many towns have a "shopping evening" (*koopavond*) once a week, when most shops remain open until 9pm: Thursday in Amsterdam and The Hague, Friday in Utrecht. In an increasing number of towns shops open on Sundays at least once in the month. Many shops have half-day closing one day a week, usually Monday, but varying from one region to another.

Banks are usually open on weekdays from 9am to 5pm, and VVVs are also open on Mondays to Fridays from 9am or 10am to 5pm (sometimes on *koopavond* until 9pm). On Saturdays they close early or even all day, and most are closed on Sundays. Some VVVs are closed during the winter.

Many museums are shut on Mondays, and open from 10am to 5pm for the rest of the week. On Sundays and public holidays they tend to open later. Practically all museums are closed on Christmas and New Year's Day. Open-air museums and small museums tend to close for the winter.

DIRECTORY

TOURIST INFORMATION

Amsterdam Tourist Board
Leidseplein 1, Stationsplein 10 and Centraal Station, platform 2.
Tel 0900-4004040.

ANWB Main Office
Wassenaarseweg 220, 2596 EC The Hague.
Tel 088-2692222. Information line: 0800-0503.

Netherland Board of Tourism
PO Box 458, 2266 KA Leidschendam.
Tel 070-370 5705.
www.holland.com

In the UK:
Imperial House, 7th Floor, 15–19 Kingsway, London WC2B 6UN.
Tel 020-7539 7950.

VVV The Hague
Hofweg 1.
Tel 0900-3403505.

VVV Maastricht
Kleine Staat 1.
Tel 043-3252121.

VVV Rotterdam
Coolsingel 5.
Tel 0900-4034065.

VVV Utrecht
Domplein 9.
Tel 0900-12UTRECHT/ 0900-128873248.

ENTERTAINMENT

Ticket Service
Tel 0900-3001250.
www.ticketmaster.nl

MUSEUM CARD

Stichting Museumjaarkaart
Postbus 5020, 2900 EA Capelle a/d IJssel.
Tel 0900-4040910.
www.museumjaarkaart.nl

TRAVELLERS WITH DISABILITIES

Bureau Assistentie-verlening Gehandicapten
Postbus 2429, 3500 GK Utrecht. *Tel* 030-2305522 (Mon–Fri).

Flower seeds and bulbs, freely exported items (with certificate)

VISAS AND CUSTOMS

Travellers from other EU countries can travel freely in and out of the Netherlands provided they have a valid passport or European identity card. For a stay lasting up to three months, travellers from Australia, New Zealand and North America need only a valid passport.

EU residents may bring an unlimited quantity of goods into the country provided they are for their personal use. For tobacco and alcohol, the following quantities are considered limits for personal use: 800 cigarettes, 400 cigars, 1 kg of tobacco, 10 litres of spirits, 20 litres of liqueurs, 90 litres of wine (or 60 litres of fortified wine) and 110 litres of beer. Duty will be charged on quantities exceeding these specified limits.

For travellers from outside the EU, the limits are 200 cigarettes, 100 cigarillos, 50 cigars or 250 g of tobacco, 2 litres of unfortified wine plus 1 litre of spirits or 2 litres of fortified wine or liqueur wine or spirits, 50 g of perfume, 0.25l of eau de toilette and other items up to a value of €175. Residents of other EU countries may no longer import goods on which VAT has not been paid. If you are entering or leaving the EU, you can take non-VAT paid goods with you. More details are available from the **Customs Helpline** (*Douanetelefoon*), which gives precise information on customs regulations. Travellers from outside the Netherlands may be able to obtain information at the local embassy.

TIME

Like all its neighbouring countries, the Netherlands is on Central European Time, which is 1 hour ahead of Greenwich Mean Time in winter and 2 hours ahead in the summer. Summer time starts on the first weekend in April and continues until the last week of October.

Sydney is 9 hours ahead in winter (8 hours in summer), Johannesburg 1 hour (the same as the Netherlands in summer), New York is 6 hours behind, Los Angeles 9 hours behind.

TIPPING

Taxi drivers expect a tip of around 10 per cent, except on longer journeys. Although a service charge is included on restaurant bills,

Customers showing their appreciation with a tip

it is customary to round the bill up slightly *(see p407)*.

In hotels you may if you like leave something for the chambermaid after a longer stay, even though it is not generally the rule.

PUBLIC TOILETS

There is a limited number of public conveniences in the Netherlands. In some cities you will find toilets where you have to insert money into a slot to open the door. Popping into a café to use the toilets there is accepted practice in the Netherlands; some establishments have an attendant who should be paid a small amount. Large retail stores and stations also have toilets, and you generally need to pay a small fee to use these. The latter also have nappy-changing facilities for babies. On motorways you will find toilets at all service stations.

ELECTRICITY

In the Netherlands the electrical voltage is 220/230 volts. Dutch plugs are of the two-

Standard continental plug

pin type, and adapters are available for visitors from countries with different plugs (for example, Great Britain).

TELEVISION AND RADIO

The television programmes on offer in the Netherlands are undergoing a great deal of development at the moment. The traditional system was to have a large number of broadcasting networks, each with their own political or religious leanings, being given a certain amount of air-time on each of the three public TV stations (Nederland 1, 2 and 3). More recently, however, commercial television stations have emerged to compete with Hilversum (the town where the Netherlands' main networks are based, *see pp190–1*).

As well as national TV networks, the Netherlands has a number of regional and local providers, such as Omrop Fryslân, Omroep Flevoland, Omroep Gelderland and the Amsterdam local network AT5. In addition, large numbers of foreign programmes can be received on cable TV, the range varying depending on the local cable company.

The Netherlands has five national radio stations, each of them with their own "personality": Radio 1 deals mainly with current affairs and sport, Radio 2 broadcasts light music and various information programmes, Radio 3 rock and pop and Radio 4 classical music. 747 AM is a news channel.

NEWSPAPERS AND MAGAZINES

The Netherlands has five national morning newspapers *(De Telegraaf, de Volkskrant, Algemeen Dagblad, NRC Next* and *Trouw)* and two national evening papers *(Het Parool* and *NRC Handelsblad)*. These tend to focus on the west of the country. Regionally the more popular papers are the *Nieuwsblad van het Noorden, Friesch Dagblad, Tubantia, De Gelderlander, Utrechts Nieuwsblad, Provinciale Zeeuwsche Courant, Brabants Dagblad* and *Dagblad De Limburger*, which contain information on local holiday activities and events. The more famous Dutch weekly news magazines include *HP/De Tijd, Elsevier* and *Vrij Nederland*.

The major bookshops in the large cities (as well as the main railway stations) sell many major international newspapers and magazines.

PETS

If you bring your dog or cat to the Netherlands from abroad, you need to be able to prove that your pet has been immunized against rabies. This is shown by a valid pet's passport provided by your veterinarian which indicates when the animal was last vaccinated.

Cat in a travel basket

A selection of newspapers available

EMBASSIES AND CONSULATES

If you are visiting from abroad and your passport happens to be lost or stolen, you should report the loss immediately either to your consulate or embassy. Most embassies are situated in the administrative capital, The Hague. A number of countries, including the UK, USA, France, Germany and Italy, also have consulates, and these tend to be located in Amsterdam.

DIRECTORY

EMBASSIES AND CONSULATES

Australia
Embassy:
Carnegielaan 4,
2517 KH The Hague.
Tel 070-3108200.
www.australian-embassy.nl

Belgium
Embassy:
Lange Vijverberg 12,
2513 AC The Hague.
Tel 070-3123456.

Canada
Embassy:
Sophialaan 7,
2514 JP The Hague.
Tel 070-3111600.
www.dfait-maeci.gc.ca/~thehague

France
Embassy:
Smidsplein 1,
2514 BT The Hague.
Tel 070-3125800.
Fax 070-3125824.

Germany
Embassy:
Groot Hertoginne-laan 18–20,
2517 EG The Hague.
Tel 070-3420600.
Fax 070-3651957.
www.duitse-ambassade.nl

Consulate:
Honthorststraat 36–38,
1071 DG Amsterdam.
Tel 020-5747700.
Fax 020-6766951.

Great Britain
Embassy:
Lange Voorhout 10,
2514 ED The Hague.

Tel 070-4270427.
Fax 070-4270345.
www.britain.nl

Consulate General:
Koningslaan 44,
1075 AE Amsterdam.
Tel 020-6764343.
Fax 020-6761069.

Ireland
Embassy:
Dr Kuyperstraat 9,
2514 BA The Hague.
Tel 070-3630993/4.
Fax 070-3617604.

New Zealand
Embassy:
Carnegielaan 10,
2517 KH The Hague.
Tel 070-3469324.
Fax 070-3632983.

South Africa
Embassy:

Wassenaarseweg 36,
2596 CJ The Hague.
Tel 070-3105920.
www.zuidafrika.nl

United States
Embassy:
Lange Voorhout 102,
2514 EJ The Hague.
Tel 070-3109209.
Fax 070-3104688.
www.usemb.nl

Consulate:
Museumplein 19,
1017 DJ Amsterdam.
Tel 020-5755309.
Fax 020-5755310.
www.usemb.nl

CUSTOMS HELPLINE

Tel 0800-0143.
◻ 8am–10pm Mon–Thu,
8am–5pm Fri.

Personal Security and Health

If you keep to a few basic safety rules, you should have a trouble-free stay in the Netherlands. Obviously it is better not to carry large amounts of cash or valuables around, and not to keep passports, cheques and credit cards together in one place. Visitors from abroad can always insure themselves against losses of money and personal items from theft. It is also a good idea to insure yourself against medical expenses. For those who do find themselves in trouble on holiday, the country has efficient emergency services and facilities.

The police logo

EMERGENCIES

The national **emergency number** for the police, fire brigade and ambulance is 112. This number must only be dialled in emergencies. For less urgent help, it is best to contact the nearest police station, hospital or a local doctor. If your car breaks down, members of the ANWB can call out the roadside assistance service of the **ANWB Wegenwacht** 24 hours a day, 7 days a week, using the roadside emergency phones or by dialling a toll-free phone number. The same also applies to members of associated organizations, such as the **AA** and **RAC**, as long as you have a letter showing you are entitled to compensation for the costs of repair and recovery (up to a certain limit).

PERSONAL BELONGINGS AND SAFETY

It is as true of the Netherlands as elsewhere in Europe that opportunity makes the thief. When in busy shopping streets or on public transport, do not leave your wallet in your back pocket, and if you need to go to the lavatory on the train or when in a restaurant, take your handbag or wallet with you. Do not leave any valuables in your car, and always make sure it has been properly locked. Large cities, particularly Amsterdam, have a big problem with bicycle theft, so a decent lock is a good investment. Muggings are rare, but at night it is better to avoid unlit areas and parks. Women can visit cafés in the evening without risk.

REPORTING CRIME

Dutch police officers

If you have been the victim of theft or a mugging, report it to the nearest police station (some smaller municipalities do not have their own police station). You will need to make a verbal report describing any loss and, if necessary, injury. Many insurance companies require you to report within 24 hours of the incident taking place. If your passport is stolen, you should report this to your embassy (see p443) as well as to the police.

MEDICAL TREATMENT AND INSURANCE

Minor medical problems can usually be dealt with at a pharmacy, though the prescription of drugs is very strict. The majority of drugs are available only on prescription. Pharmacies – which are recognizable by their snake symbol – are open on weekdays from 8:30 or 9am to 5:30 or 6pm.

If the pharmacy is closed, you will find on the door a list of the nearest pharmacies that are open. Local newspapers also give details of duty doctors, pharmacies and other health services in the town or region. In an emergency you can get treatment in hospitals, which are open 24 hours a day.

Visitors from abroad who will be carrying prescription drugs with them should ask their doctor for a medical passport. This is a document stating your condition and the medication you require for it. The passport can be shown at the customs as evidence that you are bringing the medication in for your personal use.

Travellers from European Union countries can apply for a European Health Insurance Card (EHIC). You can do this online or at post offices in the UK before you leave. It will enable you to claim for state health service treatment in EU countries.

Fire engine

Police car

Ambulance

It is also a good idea to purchase comprehensive medical insurance if it is not included in your travel insurance.

MOSQUITOES

Attracted by the canals, mosquitoes can be a real irritant. Residents and regular summer visitors deal with them in various ways. Burning coils, ultra-violet tubes, mosquito nets, repellent sprays and anti-histamine creams and tablets are available from large pharmacies and supermarkets.

LOST PROPERTY

If you lose any valuables, you can check at the police station to see whether anyone has handed them in. Local police stations usually keep articles that have been handed in before passing them on to the central police station for the district. If you lose your passport you must also inform your consulate *(see p443)*. If you lose something on a train, inform the station first. Small stations keep lost

A crowded street festival: a place to be wary of pickpockets

SPOED-EISENDE HULP OPNAME

Oprijden tot de slagboom

Emergency room sign

property for one day. After that they are taken to the nearest main station, and finally to the **Central Lost Property Office** *(Centraal Bureau Gevonden Voorwerpen)* in Utrecht. By filling in a search form (available at railway stations), you can describe the items you have lost. If you lose something on a bus, tram or metro, you should contact the office of the local or regional transport organization (look for "openbaar

vervoer" (public transport) in the Yellow Pages). **Schiphol** Airport has a special lost property number.

DRUGS

Although the use of soft drugs is officially illegal in the Netherlands, the police will not take action if you have a small quantity of hashish or marijuana in your possession. It is worth remembering that not every restaurant or café owner will take kindly to tourists lighting up on the premises. People caught with hard drugs will be prosecuted.

DIRECTORY

EMERGENCY NUMBERS

Ambulance, Fire Brigade, Police
Tel 112.
For the deaf and hard of hearing **Tel** *0800-8112.*

SAFETY

Police
Non-urgent matters:
Tel 0900-8844 (you will be connected to the nearest police station).
For the deaf and hard of hearing **Tel** *0900-1844.*

Police Amsterdam-Amstelland
Head office:
Elandsgracht 117,
1016 TT Amsterdam.
Tel 0900-8844.

HOSPITALS IN MAJOR CITIES

Amsterdam:

Academisch Medisch Centrum
Meibergdreef 9.
Tel 020-5669111.

Onze Lieve Vrouwe Gasthuis
1ste Oosterparkstraat 297.
Tel 020-5999111.

Sint Lucas Andreas Ziekenhuis
Jan Tooropstraat 164.
Tel 020-5108911.

Slotervaart Hospital
Louwesweg 6.
Tel 020-5129333.

VU Medisch Centrum
De Boelelaan 1117.
Tel 020-4444444.

The Hague:

Bronovo Hospital
Bronovolaan 5.
Tel 070-3124141.

MCH Hospital Westeinde
Lijnbaan 32.
Tel 070-3302000.

Rotterdam:

Erasmus Medisch Centrum
Sgravendijkval 230.
Tel 010-4639222

Utrecht:

Academisch Hospital Utrecht
Heidelberglaan 100.
Tel 030-2509111.

LOST PROPERTY

Central Lost Property Office
2de Daalsedijk 4,
3551 EJ Utrecht.
Tel 030-2353923
(8am–8pm Mon–Fri,
9am–5pm Sat).

Schiphol – Lost Property
Tel 0900-SCHIPHOL /
0900-72447465.

ROADSIDE ASSISTANCE

ANWB Wegenwacht
Tel 0800-0888
(toll-free).

AA
Tel 00–800–0852840.

RAC
Tel 00–800–55005.

Banking and Local Currency

Cash is still the most popular form of payment in the Netherlands, though cash cards and other forms of plastic money are becoming increasingly common. Many hotels, shops and restaurants accept major credit cards in payment. Other means of payment are traveller's cheques (with identification), and, occasionally, US dollars (particularly at antique and souvenir shops). In 2002, the Netherlands began to use the euro. The best place to change money is at a bank. You can take an unlimited amount of currency into the Netherlands, and you can withdraw limited amounts of cash at an ATM.

Cash machine with logos

BANK OPENING HOURS

Banks are generally open on Mondays to Fridays from 9am to 4 or 5pm. Some banks remain open longer on *koopavond*, or shopping evening, often a Thursday.

These bureaux can still be found at the now unguarded border crossing points, at Amsterdam Schiphol Airport and at major railway stations. Most GWK bureaux are open daily and have extended opening hours.

GWK *(grenswisselkantoor)*, the Netherlands' official exchange bureau

CHANGING MONEY

Foreign currency can be changed at banks, post offices and American Express offices. A small commission is charged on these transactions.

In small bureaux de change (often open outside business hours), located throughout the major cities and in larger towns, you can exchange money from non-Eurozone countries, though often at unfavourable rates.

The Netherland's official bureaux de change, GWK *(grenswisselkantoor)*, is a privatized state enterprise, which gives reasonable rates of exchange and charges relatively low commissions, as well as providing various other services for travellers.

BANK AND CREDIT CARDS

You can use your bank card to withdraw money at any Dutch bank displaying your card's logo, but usually there is a substantial commission charge. You can also use bank cards to withdraw cash at ATMs 24 hours a day. These machines usually also accept Eurocard/MasterCard, American Express, Diners Club and Visa cards. When a foreign card is inserted, most ATMs will offer a choice of languages, and so should be simple to use. ATMs are plentiful and can be found outside post offices, banks and GWK offices, and within main railway stations.

Shops, restaurants and hotels post signs stating whether you can pay by credit card, switch card or chipknip/chipper (top-up cards available from Dutch banks or the Postbank). Most payphones *(see pp448–9)* accept credit cards for calls.

Credit cards are increasingly becoming an accepted means of payment in the Netherlands, but always check first as not all businesses (in particular taxis) accept them, especially outside major towns and cities.

CHEQUES

The advantage of traveller's cheques is that you are protected against loss and theft. You can also use traveller's cheques to pay at hotels and restaurants, although often you will not be given change from them if the value of the cheque is greater than that of the bill.

It is usually best as well as more convenient to obtain traveller's cheques in euros before you leave home.

THE HISTORY OF DUTCH CURRENCY

Before the introduction of the guilder, the Dutch national currency unit before the euro, duiten, stuivers, rijders, schellings and ducats made out of various metals were used. Until 1847 there was a double standard where the value of the coin was equal to the value of the gold or silver in it. Silver coins were minted until 1967, when nickel or bronze coins were minted. Gold and silver coins from earlier centuries are now valuable collector's items.

THE EURO

The euro (€) is the common currency of the European Union (EU). It went into general circulation on 1 January 2002, initially for 12 participating countries. The Netherlands was one of those 12 countries. EU members using the euro as sole official currency are known as the Eurozone. Several EU members have opted out of joining this common currency. Euro notes are identical throughout the Eurozone countries, each including designs of fictional architectural structures and monuments. The coins, however, have one side identical (the value side) and one side with an image unique to each country. Both notes and coins are exchangeable in each of the participating euro countries.

Bank Notes

Euro bank notes have seven denominations. The €5 note (grey in colour) is the smallest, followed by the €10 note (pink), €20 note (blue), €50 note (orange), €100 note (green), €200 note (yellow) and €500 note (purple). All notes show the 12 stars of the European Union. Not all businesses in the Netherlands accept the €200 and €500 notes.

€5 note

€10 note

€20 note

€50 note

€100 note

€200 note

€500 note

€2 coin

€1 coin

50 cents

20 cents

10 cents

Coins

The euro has eight coin denominations: €2 and €1; 50 cents, 20 cents, 10 cents, 5 cents, 2 cents and 1 cent. The €2 and €1 coins are silver and gold in colour; cent coins are gold or bronze. Prices are rounded off to the nearest 5 cents; the 2- and 1-cent coins are no longer in use.

5 cents

2 cents

1 cent

Communications

Before 1989, telephone and postal services in the Netherlands were part of the same state-run company,

PTT. This has now been separated into two companies – KPN Telecom and TNT Post. Both services are among the most forward-looking and efficient in Europe. For some years, Telfort public telephones have also been appearing beside the KPN boxes. The Telfort telephones are mostly found at train stations.

KPN kiosk

USING THE TELEPHONE

You will find the green KPN telephone kiosks in the streets, in post offices and outside many railway stations. Most KPN telephone kiosks take both phonecards and most major credit cards (the logo on the telephone will tell you which credit cards are accepted). If you use a credit card, you need to remove it from the slot before speaking (phonecards are only removed when you have finished your call), and you have to pay a surcharge of €1.15. In KPN booths, locals can also use their bank or giro card to make phone calls, if these are fitted with a "chip-per" or "chipknip" (which means you can top them up).

ANWB members can also use KPN telephone kiosks to call the roadside assistance patrol (see p445).

There are no longer any solely coin-operated pay-phones. KPN phone boxes accept only KPN phone-cards or special kiosk-cards, available at some train stations. KPN phonecards can be purchased at post offices, tobacconists, train stations and department stores, as well as at the GWK, and come in various denominations.

At train stations you will often find Telfort phone boxes, painted blue and orange. These accept Telfort phone-cards, available at ticket windows and in the Wizzl station shops and also at the GWK. Telfort phones also accept coins (10, 20 and 50 cent, €1 and €2) but do not give change, credit cards (with a €1.15 surcharge) and special kiosk-cards.

Instructions on how to use KPN and Telfort telephones can be found in the booths in Dutch, English and other west European languages.

MOBILE PHONES

There are four main GSM frequencies (Global System for Mobile Communications) in use, so if you want to ensure your phone will work while you are away you should have a quad-band phone. Tri-band phones from the EU will usually work in the Netherlands, but USA mobile phones may not. Contact your service provider for clarification. Check your insurance policy to see if you are covered in case your phone gets stolen, and keep your network operator's helpline number handy.

To use your mobile phone abroad, you may need to en-able the "roaming" function on it. It is also more expensive to make and receive calls while abroad, despite efforts to decrease roaming charges. A cheaper option is often to purchase a local SIM card to use in your phone. You can only do this if your handset is "sim free" or unlocked. KPN

Storefront of an Amsterdam telephone shop

FINDING THE RIGHT NUMBER

• Directory enquiries for phone and fax numbers in Holland dial 0900-8008 or 118 (only one number per call on either service).
• Directory enquiries for phone and fax numbers abroad dial 0900-8418, or visit www.detelefoon gids.nl.
• National or international calls through the operator dial 0800-0410.
• Collect calls in Holland or abroad dial 0800-0101.
• National dialling codes are: Australia 61, New Zealand 64, South Africa 27, the United Kingdom 44, and the USA and Canada 1.

Hotspots gives Internet access for smart phones; send an SMS to: HOTSPOTS, number 4222 and you can log on for 15 minutes for a small fee, which is charged to your phone.

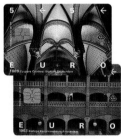

Colourful selection of Dutch pictorial phonecards

PHONING ABROAD

From the Netherlands you can direct-dial almost all destinations abroad. First you need to dial the international number 00, followed by the country number, and then the local number without the first digit (usually a 0), and finally the individual number. Many country codes are listed in telephone booths. Telephone directories have more detailed lists. Directories for the whole of the country are available. Calls made from hotel rooms are usually expensive.

Internet access at OBA (Amsterdam Public Library)

INTERNET

Faster than a letter and cheaper than a phone call, sending and receiving email has never been easier or more convenient. As most people in the Netherlands have either ADSL or a cable connection at home, the number of Internet cafés has decreased. Also, more and more hotels offer Wi-Fi for guests with laptops, though this is not always free, so check before you run up a hefty bill.

However, in most tourist areas you'll still find plenty of places to read and send email. Most are bars, cafés and coffee (smoking) shops, offering PCs with Internet services. Opening hours vary, but cafés are often open late into the night. Not all offer headsets, so using Skype or other VoIPs to make cheap phone calls is not always possible. The website www.easy internetcafe.com has up-to-date addresses of Internet cafés worldwide, plus useful reviews from customers.

A recent development are modern and trendy coffee bar franchises, like Coffee Company and Bagel and Beans, offering Wi-Fi for customers who bring their laptop. You either buy minutes or go online for a limited time for each beverage you order, using the code on your receipt to gain access.

Visitors to Amsterdam will find www.iamsterdam.com worth a look. Financed by Amsterdam city council, it offers listings and reviews in English about cultural events in the city, plus useful information on things like doctors and dentists. It also has information for expats living in the city. *Time Out Amsterdam* is a monthly listings magazine, also in English, aimed at tourists and available from newsagents in the city centre of the capital. Apart from comprehensive listings about what's on, it also offers reviews and features.

POSTAL SERVICES

Post offices in the Netherlands can be recognized by the TNT logo. In addition to buying stamps, sending telegrams and sending mail, you can also change money and traveller's cheques, make phone calls and send faxes. Larger post offices also have photocopy services and sell stationery. Smaller municipalities sometimes have only a sub post office (in a supermarket, for example) providing only basic services. There are no longer post offices in most villages.

SENDING MAIL

Most TNT postboxes have two slots. The right slot is for local mail (post codes are given above the slot), the left one is for other destinations. A sign on the

Slot for all other destinations

Slot for local destinations

Dutch TNT postbox

box indicates when the mail is collected (a red sign means 5pm or 6pm, a blue board means 7pm). There is no Saturday mail collection.

Postcards and letters weighing less than 20 g (1 oz) cost €0.44 (or one "Nederland 1" stamp) to send to destinations within the Netherlands; those sent to European destinations cost €0.77, or one "Europe 1" stamp; these new "standard" stamps are widely available in small shops, for example those selling postcards. For heavier letters or to post to other parts of the world, visit a post office – but be prepared for queues. Most post offices are open from 9am to 5pm weekdays; some also open on Saturdays until 1pm.

Postcards and letters weighing less than 20 g (1 oz) to destinations within Europe are sent by priority mail. For other international mail which you want to send priority, pay extra for a priority sticker at the post office. Important documents may be sent by insured or registered mail. Urgent mail can be sent by TNT's courier service.

POSTE RESTANTE

If you do not know where you'll be staying, you can have mail sent to *Poste Restante*, addressed to the Central Post Office. You will need some sort of identification with a photograph, such as a passport or a driving licence, to pick up your mail.

DIRECTORY

TNT

Tel 0800-1234 (customer service for domestic and international deliveries).

www.tnt.com/nl

TNT Post Klantenservice

(Customer service)

Postbus 99180,

8900 NA Leeuwarden.

Tel 058-2333333 (for information on postcodes and complaints).

◯ 8am–8pm Mon–Fri,

9am–4pm Sat.

www.tntpost.nl

TRAVEL INFORMATION

A lmost every major European airport has direct flights to Schiphol, but this modern international airport southwest of Amsterdam also has direct connections with other airports around the world, including many in the United States. The Netherlands also has efficient rail links with neighbouring countries. Major stations are served by international trains, including the Thalys, the high-speed train from Paris. The country's comprehensive road network makes the Netherlands ideal for exploring by car or by public transport *(see pp454–5).* Many packages and special-interest holidays are on offer, so it's worth shopping around.

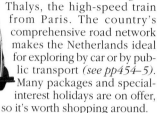

The Parking Hopper at Schiphol

Car-hire counter at Schiphol

BY AIR

Schiphol airport handles some 175,000 flights a year by many international carriers. To increase this volume further, there are serious plans to expand the airport. KLM (Royal Dutch Airlines) and its airline partners have flights to Amsterdam from over 350 cities worldwide. Northwest Airlines offers non-stop flights from Boston, Detroit and Washington, Delta Air Lines from Atlanta and New York (JFK) and United Airlines from Newark. There are many flights a day from the UK and the Irish Republic. Low-cost airline easyJet serves Amsterdam from Luton, and bmi british midland from East Midlands and London Heathrow. To get the lowest fare, generally you must book well in advance.

SCHIPHOL AIRPORT

Schiphol has only one terminal. The airport signs are colour-coded, with yellow signs indicating transfer desks and gates, green ones amenities such as coffee bars, restaurants and shops. Lounge South is designated for passengers travelling to countries in the Schengen agreement. At Schiphol Plaza you can find shops, book hotels, hire a car or buy a railway ticket. Beneath it are the platforms of Schiphol railway station. From the car park there are transfer buses to take you to the terminal. The long-stay car park is served by an automatic bus, the Parking Hopper, that takes you to the transfer bus.

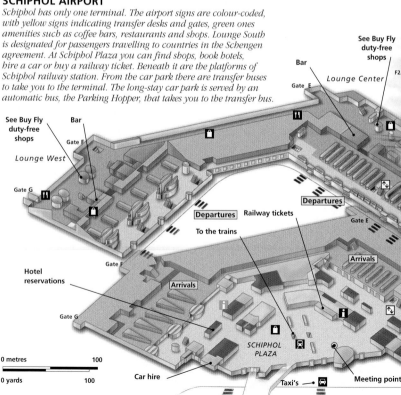

See Buy Fly duty-free shops

Bar

Lounge Center

Gate E

F2/F

See Buy Fly duty-free shops

Bar

Gate F

Lounge West

Gate G

Departures

Railway tickets

To the trains

Departures

Gate E

Gate F

Arrivals

Hotel reservations

Gate G

Arrivals

SCHIPHOL PLAZA

0 metres   100

0 yards   100

Car hire

Taxi's

Meeting point

Planes at Amsterdam Schiphol Airport

SHOPPING

If you are leaving the country by plane, you will find the large See Buy Fly shopping centre when you leave customs control. Although travellers to other EU member states are not permitted to buy duty-free goods at the airport *(see p442)*, it is still possible to find some bargains with the low See Buy Fly prices; only alcohol and tobacco is sold here at the same price as in local shops. Passengers to destinations outside the EU can still purchase duty-free alcohol and tobacco. The centrally located Schiphol Plaza is open to everyone, but the goods stocked here are not sold at See Buy Fly prices.

GETTING TO AND FROM SCHIPHOL

Every major city in the Netherlands can be reached by train from Schiphol Station. The journey to Amsterdam Centraal Station takes 20 minutes. Schiphol is also on the night-train network of the Western Netherlands *(see p454)*. In addition, the airport has good bus connections with many towns. KLM runs a bus service (the KLM Hotel Shuttle), linking the airport with some 20 hotels in central and south Amsterdam. There are also

Watch shop at Schiphol

abundant taxis waiting at the airport. Ask for a quote before getting in as tourists are often overcharged.

REGIONAL AIRPORTS

Eindhoven, Maastricht, Rotterdam and Groningen are all served by domestic flights, with flights between Eindhoven and Schiphol, Maastricht and Schiphol, Groningen and Rotterdam and Eindhoven and Rotterdam. There are direct international flights between Rotterdam and Eindhoven and Manchester and London, and between Maastricht and Munich, Berlin and London.

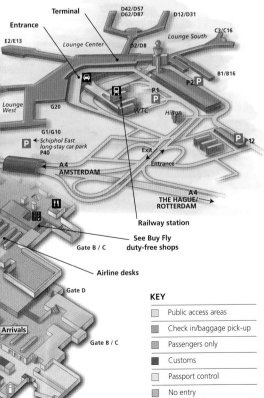

Terminal

Entrance

E2/E13

Lounge Center

D42/D57
D62/D87

D12/D31

C3/C16

Lounge South

D2/D8

B1/B16

P2

P1

Lounge West

G20

WTC

Hilton

G1/G10

Schiphol East long-stay car park
P40

P12

Exit

A4
AMSTERDAM

Entrance

A4
THE HAGUE/ROTTERDAM

Railway station

See Buy Fly duty-free shops

Gate B / C

Airline desks

Gate D

Arrivals

Gate B / C

KEY

	Public access areas
	Check in/baggage pick-up
	Passengers only
	Customs
	Passport control
	No entry

Information screens at Schiphol

BY RAIL

The Netherlands can easily be reached by train from most European countries, although visitors from further afield may have to change trains several times en route. Eurostar runs from London via the Channel Tunnel; passengers for Amsterdam must change at Brussels.

There are direct trains from a number of European stations. For example, Brussels, Paris, Berlin, Zurich, Vienna and (seasonally) Milan have direct rail links to Amsterdam Centraal Station (CS) and Utrecht CS. From Brussels and from Antwerp there are trains to Amsterdam all day, stopping at Roosendaal, Rotterdam, The Hague and Schiphol, including five journeys daily by the Thalys high-speed train from Paris.

Many other towns, particularly those in the border regions of Belgium and the Netherlands, can easily be reached by train. Hook of Holland is connected by trains which connect with ferries from the UK port of Harwich.

SPECIAL TICKETS

Tourists from other EU countries can purchase cards in their countries that will entitle them to special reductions. An Interrail card for people aged 26 and under, along with a slightly dearer version for the over-26s, allows travellers to use the entire European rail network at a

The Thalys high-speed train

Ferries serve Rotterdam, Hook of Holland and IJmuiden

discount. A Eurodomino card allows 3, 5 or 8 days of unlimited travel in the country of your choice and is available at a reduction for under-26s. Eurail Selectpass offers unlimited travel on the national rail networks of any three to five bordering countries out of 18 European nations, including the Netherlands.

BY COACH

For travellers from many European countries the cheapest way to reach the Netherlands is by coach. Most long-distance coaches have toilets and make regular stops. In summer in particular there are large numbers of coaches from other countries serving a whole range of towns in the Netherlands. **Eurolines** offers a very extensive network of coach connections. It has coaches running from many European cities to the Netherlands at least once per week. Dozens of points in the Netherlands (depending on the point of departure and route) are served by them. From Brussels and Antwerp there are coaches to places such as Breda, Rotterdam, The Hague, Utrecht and Amsterdam.

A Eurolines coach

FERRIES

A number of ferry companies serve routes between Britain and the Netherlands. **P&O North Sea Ferries** sails between Hull and Rotterdam/Europoort, while **Stena Line** sails between Harwich and Hook of Holland (by seacat). **DFDS Seaways** serves Newcastle and IJmuiden. Other convenient ferry ports for visitors from Great Britain are Zeebrugge (from Hull) and Oostende (from Dover) in Belgium, and Calais and Boulogne (from Folkestone and Dover) in France. Crossing times by ferry range from 16 hours (Newcastle–IJmuiden) to 75–90 minutes (Dover–Calais). Ticket prices depend on the speed of crossing. In summer it is a good idea to book in advance.

MOTORING IN HOLLAND

The Netherlands' good system of roads makes all parts of the country easy to reach by car. Beware, however, in the Randstad region: you may have to put up with traffic jams during the rush hour.

To drive in the Netherlands you need to have a valid national driving licence, but many car-hire firms prefer to see an international driving licence. In addition, if in your own car, you will need to have your vehicle log book and insurance papers with you.

Roads in the Netherlands are divided into three categories. Provincial roads are designated with the letter "N" before the road number, national motorways are designated with an "A" before the number and international highways have the letter "E" before the number. All Dutch motorways are equipped with emergency telephones from which motorists can call the **ANWB** road assistance service *(see p444)* if their car breaks down. A non-member can pay for the ANWB's services, or become a temporary ANWB member. Unless otherwise sign-posted, the maximum speed for cars in Holland is 120 km/h (75 mph) on motorways, 100 km/h (62 mph) on major roads, 80 km/h (50 mph) on secondary roads and 50 km/h (30 mph) in built-up areas. At unmarked junctions, give way to traffic coming from the left, except for trams, which always have right of way (except when you are driving along a

Emergency phone

road which has right of way). In built-up areas motorists must give way to buses that are leaving bus stops.

Finding somewhere to park is often a problem in the cities. As clamping is prevalent and theft rife, it is often best to look for a car park rather than to try to find street parking. When you enter a car park, take a ticket from the machine at the barrier, and pay at the payment machine before leaving. Avoid out-of-order street meters as you could get fined or your car clamped. You may not park on yellow lines, and on yellow broken lines you may not park even to load or unload. If you stop on a blue line, you will need to have a parking disc.

CAR HIRE

To hire a car you need to be at least 21 years old and have a valid driving licence. Some hire companies also require at least one year's driving experience. The main international car-hire companies such as Avis, Budget, Europcar and Hertz have offices at Schiphol and in all major cities. Local car-hire firms are often substantially cheaper. When hiring a car without a credit card, you may have to pay a hefty deposit.

One way of taking your bike along

DIRECTORY

SCHIPHOL AIRPORT

Information and services
Tel 0900-SCHIPHOL/ 0900-72447465.
www.schiphol.nl

REGIONAL AIRPORTS

Eindhoven Airport
Tel 040-2919818.

Groningen Airport Eelde
Tel 050-3097070.

Maastricht Aachen Airport
Tel 043-3589999/ 3589898.

Rotterdam Airport
Tel 010-4463444/ 4463454.

AIRLINES

Aer Lingus
Tel 020-5174747.
Tel 0818-365000 (Eire).
www.aerlingus.com

bmi british midland
Tel 020-3469211.
Tel 0870-6070555 (UK).
www.flybmi.com

British Airways
Tel 020-3469559.
Tel 0870-8509850 (UK).
www.ba.com

Delta Air Lines
Tel 1-800-2414141 (US).
www.delta-air.com

easyJet
Tel 0870-6000000 (UK).
Tel 0900-2658021 (NL).
www.easyjet.com

KLM & KLM Cityhopper
Tel 020-4747747.
Tel 0870-5074074 (UK).
www.klm.nl

Martinair
Tel 020-6011444/ 020-6011767.

Northwest Airlines
Tel 1-800-2252525 (US).
www.nwa.com

Transavia
Tel 020-73654997 (UK).
www.transavia.com

United Airlines
Tel 1-800-5382929 (US).
www.united.com

RAILWAYS

Public transport travel information
Tel 0900-9292.
www.ov9292.nl

International public transport information
Tel 0900-9296 (Netherlands).

In the UK:
European Rail Ltd.
Tel 020-73870444.
www.europeanrail.com

BUS COMPANIES

Eurolines Nederland
Amstelbusstation
Julianaplein 5,
1097 DN Amsterdam.
Tel 020-5608788.
www.eurolines.nl

Rokin 10,
1012 KR Amsterdam.
Tel 020-4217951.

Eurolines (UK)
Tel 01582-456654 (UK).
www.national express.co.uk

FERRIES

DFDS Seaways
Tel 0870-2520524.
www.dfdsseaways.co.uk

P&O North Sea Ferries
Tel 0870-5980333.
www.poferries.com

Stena Line
Tel 0900-8123/ 0174-315800.
Tel 08705-707070 (UK).
www.stenaline.co.uk

BY CAR

ANWB
Tel 0800-0503 (Head office).

CAR HIRE FIRMS AT SCHIPHOL

AVIS
Tel 020-6556050.

Budget Rent a Car
Tel 020-6041349.

Europcar
Tel 020-3164190.

Hertz
Tel 020-5020240.

Public Transport

The Netherlands has a comprehensive and efficient public transport system. Major cities can be easily reached by train, while towns and villages are served by local buses. The Randstad in particular gets fairly snarled up in the morning and evening rush hour. If

Dutch Rail-ways logo

you need to travel at that time, the best thing to do is to leave the car and take the train. The luxury Interliner long-distance coaches connect destinations without fast rail links.

Dieren–Apeldoorn steam train

STEAM TRAINS

There are many places in the Netherlands where you can take a ride in a steam train. There is, for example, the 22-km (14-mile) Dieren–Apeldoorn line, the 16-km (10-mile) Kerkrade–Schin op Geul, (the "million line", *see p368*), the 15.5-km (9.5-mile) Goes–Oudelande, around the Valkenburgse Meer lake and through the Hoogoventerrein at IJmuiden (21 km/13 miles), departing from Beverwijk Station, *see p188*). A steam train runs the 20 km (12 miles) between Hoorn and Medemblik in summer *(see p178*). Check with the VVV, as schedules vary.

Interliners cover an expanding number of routes

BY BUS

The Netherlands has a good network of local buses and inter-city coaches. Booklets are available giving detailed information on routes, time-tables and fares, although it is also possible to get information from **Openbaar Vervoer Reisinformatie** (0900-9292).

Interliners are luxury long-distance coaches. They usually follow direct routes between places and stop less frequently than local buses *(streek-bussen)*. In the evenings they do not operate as late as the local buses. The timetables for buses are based on the railway timetable. Tickets are available from the driver or in advance at Interlinerverkoop-punten (Interliner sales offices) and at many railway and bus stations. They can also be ordered by telephone from **Interliner Services** at 0900-8998998. Interliner stops are green and have an information display.

BY TRAM

There are trams in Amsterdam, Rotterdam, Utrecht and The Hague. They generally run from 6am to midnight. On Sundays they start one or one-and-a-half hours later. Tram stops display the name of the stop, the tram numbers that stop there and show the

other stops on the route. Tram shelters display maps of the tram network.

You can board or alight from any door, unless there is a conductor on the tram, when the rear door is for boarding only. Tram stops are normally announced, but if you aren't sure where to get off, you can always ask the driver to call out the stop.

BY TRAIN

The Dutch national railway company, Nederlandse Spoorwegen, or simply NS, runs a busy network which is considered one of the best in the world. Trains are clean and generally run on time, and tickets are reasonably priced. Timetables are displayed on yellow boards in stations. Rail tickets are available at ticket offices, Wizzl station shops and from ticket machines in stations, or, with a substantial supplement, from the conductor aboard the train. Dutch Railways has a wide variety of fare discounts on offer, including *Railrunner* tickets for children, and other offers for people regularly

using the same route. Combined season tickets for the train and local or urban transport are also available. For information it is best to ask at ticket offices, or telephone 0900-9292.

Many railways in Friesland, Groningen and the Achter-hoek are run by NordNed and Syntus. NS cards are also valid on these lines. Night trains run on the Utrecht CS-Amsterdam CS-Schiphol-Leiden Centraal-The Hague CS-Delft-Rotterdam CS lines.

An NS double-decker train speeding past tulip fields

METRO

Amsterdam and Rotterdam are the only towns in the Netherlands with a metro. Both networks are fairly extensive. Amsterdam's metro has three lines, two of which begin at the Centraal Station, and the third at Station Sloterdijk. They go as far as Gaasperplas and Gein. From Centraal Station there is also a suburban tram to Amstelveen. The Rotterdam metro system comprises two lines which cross one another, the north-south line going from Centraal Station to Spijkenisse, and the west-east line from Marconiplein to Capelle, with a branch to Ommoord-Zevenkamp. The first metro leaves the terminus at around 6am (around 7:45am on Sundays), and the last train arrives at its destination at approximately 0:15 or 0:30am.

Always swipe your *OV-chipkaart* to validate your journey

TRAM, BUS, METRO AND TRAIN TICKETS

To travel on buses, trams and metro systems throughout the Netherlands you must have an *OV-chipkaart*: a "smart-card" that works much like a pay-as-you-go phone card, deducting the cost of each trip from the available credit. It can also be used for train journeys, although separate train tickets are still available.

Disposable, one-time-use cards for durations of either 1 (€2.60) or 2 hours (€5), or one to seven days (€7–29), are available from metro and train stations, and from tram and bus drivers. For €7.50 you can buy a reloadable pass, usable for five years, which you top up as necessary. These are available from stations, Tourist Board offices and newsagents, and can be topped up at ticket offices (only Dutch bank card holders can use the automated ticket machines). In order to validate a journey, users need to hold the *OV-chipkaart* in front of the grey card reader at metro or platform gates and on boarding a bus or tram; remember to swipe again on disembarking, or you will be charged the full fare to the terminus. Children under 4 travel free; seniors and 4–11-year-olds can claim a discount if they buy their cards in advance.

Visitors to Amsterdam arriving at Schiphol can buy the "Amsterdam All-in-One" tickets, which include a return train ticket to the airport plus a 24/46/72/96-hour metro, tram and bus pass for the city.

TAXIS

If you need a taxi, the best thing is to either go to a taxi-stand or phone a Taxicentrale: numbers can be found in the phone directory and in the Yellow Pages. It is less common to hail a taxi in the street, although it can be done. Taxis are metered and after an initial charge, the fare depends on the distance travelled and the time. Taxis cost more at night.

A treintaxi

RAIL TAXIS

Around 100 Dutch railway stations operate a rail taxi, or *treintaxi*, service which enables you to travel cheaply to a destination in the same or nearby district. A ticket costs €3.80 at the station or €4.80 from the driver and is valid whatever the length of the journey. The taxi will also take other passengers to their destinations, and so will usually take a roundabout route.

Rail taxis operate from 7am (8am on Sundays and public holidays) until just after the arrival of the last train. You can book by phoning 0900-TREINTAXI/8734682. At the station, book by pressing the button on the blue-yellow column. Information on places covered by the service is given in the NS leaflet *Treintaxi-stations op een rijtje*.

SPECIAL OUTINGS

The *Museumboot* in Amsterdam is a river boat that stops near almost all the main sights of the capital (tel. 020-5309010). In the summer it departs every half hour from opposite the Centraal Station from 10am to 5pm, and in other seasons operates every 55 minutes. Tickets are available at the Centraal Station VVV office, or at one of the boat stops. An all-day *Museumboot-dagkaart* (day ticket) gives you reductions of 10 to 50 per cent on admission to most museums. Another boat, the *Artis Express*, takes you from Centraal Station to Artis Royal Zoo. This boat also runs every half hour (tel. 020-5309010). A boat tour of the canals of Amsterdam, Utrecht, Leiden and Delft gives you an entirely different view of the inner cities. Most of the boats have transparent roofs which are opened in fine weather. Tours in horse-drawn trams are available in some towns in Holland, such as Delft (April to September, departing from the Markt). In Gouda you can take a sightseeing tour in a horse-drawn carriage from late June to August (departing at the Agnietenkapel, behind the Waag). Details are available from the local VVV office. The *OV-chipkaart* cannot be used on the Museumboot.

The *Museumboot* in Amsterdam

Cycling

The flat landscape of the Netherlands makes it a boon for cyclists. At least 85 per cent of the population has a bicycle. However, there is no shortage of maps and guidebooks with interesting cycling routes. You can use the LF-routes *(see p457)* to plan your own daytrip or cycling holiday. Another possibility is to take part in an organized cycle tour, where you are awarded a souvenir medal at the end.

Guides showing cycling routes

ROAD SAFETY

The large number of cycle paths and cycle lanes, often equipped with traffic lights for cyclists, make cycling in the Netherlands a safe and enjoyable activity. However, it's worth keeping a look-out for mopeds, which frequently make use of cycle paths. Cycling in the peaceful countryside and cycling in the busy city are two quite separate experiences. In Amsterdam particularly, the traffic is fairly chaotic – mostly because of the large number of cyclists, who tend to ignore the traffic regulations. If you are unaccustomed to this, it's worth taking extra care. Front and rear lights, a rear reflector and reflective strips or reflective circles are compulsory at night. Many cyclists ride without this equipment, often leaving them almost invisible.

CYCLE HIRE

There are plenty of cycle hire shops in the Netherlands. You can either go to private cycle hire places or hire a bike from some 100 railway stations with a *Rijwielshop* or *Fietspoint*. Cycle hire usually costs around €5.40 per day. Cycle hire shops also offer weekly tariffs that work out relatively cheaper. Many of them require a deposit, which can range from €30 to €145, and often

Sign for the Rijwiel cycle hire shop, found at nearly 100 railway stations

want proof of identity. Tandems are also sometimes available, though they cost more, and their lack of manoeuvrability does not make them very suitable for use in city traffic.

If you are planning to make a train journey and hire a cycle from your destination, it is worth buying a *huurfietskaartje* (cycle hire ticket) when setting out. It is a good idea to reserve the bicycle by telephone in advance.

The NS publishes a special pamphlet, *Fiets en Trein*, which lists stations where you can hire bicycles. The VVV and ANWB can also direct you to cycle hire shops.

SECURITY

Even if your bicycle is equipped with a rear-wheel lock, it's a good idea – particularly in the big cities – to secure your bicycle to a post or a bicycle rack by the front wheel. Cycle hire shops will often provide you with a lock for the bike, especially in cities where bicycle theft is a problem. At many railway stations you can leave your bicycle in a secure bicycle-park for around €1.00. Do not leave any luggage on your bicycle if you park it somewhere, not even in a guarded bicycle park.

BICYCLES AND PUBLIC TRANSPORT

For an additional payment you can take your bicycle on the train, except during rush hours (Sep–Jun: 6:30–9am and 4:30–6pm Mon–Fri). To do this, you need to buy a *Dagkaart fiets* (bike ticket) from a train or metro station in addition to your ordinary train ticket. These tickets cost €6.00 and are valid for the whole day regardless of the length of your journey. Places for bicycles on trains are marked with stickers on the carriage. Folding cycles, when folded, may be taken on trains free of charge. Bicycles may be taken on metros and suburban (fast) trams, provided that you have a bike ticket, but they are not allowed on buses and city trams.

An organized cycling tour on the Zaanse Schans

CYCLING TOURS

If you want to get from point A to point B by the quickest possible route, just follow the white-and-red ANWB cycle route signposts. Maps and guides for cyclists describing routes of various lengths are available from the VVV, the ANWB and many bookstores. They often contain a variety of local background information, as well as the addresses of cycle hire shops and places to stay, such as *pensions*, camping sites and hiking huts *(see also p391)*. Useful examples are the regional *ANWB/VVV Toeristenkaarten*, which suggest some particularly enjoyable routes, and the *Dwarsstap-fiets-mappen*, which give descriptions of cycle routes, often in the area surrounding big cities, and also contain topographical maps. The regional *ANWB/VVV-fietsgiden* have maps and provide descriptions of hundreds of enjoyable cycling trips of around 25 km (15 miles), from the *Amelandroute* to the *Maasdalroute* in Limburg. Many of these routes are marked with hexagonal signs. Around 45 railway-based routes are also offered under the name *NS-Fietstocht*. Maps of the route are on sale at the relevant railway stations. NS publishes a booklet, entitled *Er op Uit!*, describing these routes. Long-distance tours of at least

Cyclists on tour stopping to enjoy an ice cream

200 km (125 miles) in length (for example, the 230-km/143-mile *Elfstedenroute* in Friesland) are described in guides such as the *ANWB/VVV Lange Fiestronde*. These routes are also signposted. Another organization, the **Stichting Landelijk Fiets-platform**, or national cycling association *(see p437)*, has a network of some 6,000 km (3,730 miles) of numbered National Cycle Routes (*Landelijke Fiestroutes*, or *"LF"*). These often follow quiet byroads and cycle tracks and are described in two of the *LF-basisgidsen*. Some are marked with square signs, such as LF-15, which is the *Boerenlandroute* (farmland route) from Alkmaar to Enschede. Guides to individual routes are also available. The *Fietsideeënkaart*, a map available from the VVV and ANWB, also provides brief descriptions of LF and other

Cycle lane sign

marked cycling routes around the country. To take part in an organized cycle tour, contact organizations such as **Cycletours** or the **Fietsvakantiewinkel** *(see p437)*, some of the main VVV offices and the ANWB (members only). These organizations can arrange cycle tour packages, including accommodation and luggage transfer. For information on cycling in nature reserve areas, see page 437.

CYCLING EVENTS

Meimaand Fietsmaand is the year's biggest bicycle event: a whole month (May) packed with bicycle rides, meets and races throughout the Netherlands. In 2010, about 570,000 cyclists participated. Information on the various routes and events can be found at the national cycling association's website: www.fietsplatform.nl. Local cycle touring clubs organize regular non-competitive tours through picturesque or interesting areas, although you have to pay a fee to join. For further information, apply at the Dutch cycle tour society (Nederlandse Toer Fiets Unie, or **NFTU**, *see p437*). In addition, dozens of local tours lasting several days are organized locally, such as the *Drentse Rijwielvierdaagse* in July. Participants can often choose between routes of lengths varying from 25 to 100 km (15 to 60 miles) per day. You will find an overview of these in the NFTU pamphlet *Fiestmeerdaagsen*, available from the VVV.

The ferry at Wijk near Duurstede, which carries bicycles

Index

Acknowledgments

Dorling Kindersley would like to thank the following people for their help in preparing this guide:

For Dorling Kindersley
TRANSLATION FROM DUTCH Mark Cole (Linguists for Business)
DESIGN AND EDITORIAL ASSISTANCE Jo Cowen, Jacky Jackson, Ian Midson, Conrad van Dyk, Stewart Wild
DTP DESIGNERS Jason Little, Conrad van Dyk
MANAGING EDITOR Helen Townsend
PUBLISHING MANAGER Jane Ewart

For International Book Productions
PROOFREADER Maraya Radhua

Main Author
Gerard ML Harmans graduated in biology and philosophy at the Vrije Universiteit (Amsterdam), and then chose to work in publishing. He edited an encyclopaedia for Het Spectrum before setting up an independent business with Paul Krijnen in 1989 called *de Redactie*, boekverzorgers.

Other Contributors
All contributors were selected from *de Redactie*, boekverzorgers in Amsterdam. The team of authors, translators and editors share a broad field of expertise. Every member of the team made an invaluable contribution.

Anneliet Bannier graduated in translation studies from Amsterdam University. She works as a translator and sub-editor on travel guides. She lives in Zaanstreek.

Hanneke Bos is an editor and translator in the fields of linguistics, cultural history and travel literature.

Jaap Deinema, from Eindhoven, is an expert in the field of the Netherlands. He has made numerous contributions to travel guides. He was responsible for the ATO/VVV edition *Infopocket Amsterdam*.

Jérôme Gommers, born in Paris, is a freelance author and lover of the Dutch landscape and its poetry. Among other things, he has conducted a comprehensive study of the construction and development of the Noordoostpolder.

Ron de Heer studied philosophy in Amsterdam. For ten years he has been working as a translator/editor, primarily of travel guides, novels and culinary publications.

Marten van de Kraats writes and translates texts in the fields of travel and automation. Every year he edits the Dutch edition of the Rough Guide Travels on the internet, the best-selling internet book on Holland and Belgium.

Paul Krijnen is a social geographer who has specialized in medieval mark organizations of the Netherlands, such as the Erfgooiers. His great passion is the Dutch borderlands.

Frans Reusink studied Dutch language. After working as a copywriter, he has been active as a photographer, written travel reports for magazines, and edited travel guides.

Theo Scholten is a Dutch scholar. He has worked on many literary publications but is currently active in non-fiction as an editor and translator. He has made previous contributions to travel guides on Belgium and France.

Ernst Schreuder, a Frisian editor, won the Elfsteden Cross for completing the Tocht der Tochten in 1986 and 1997. Travel and travel guides are his occupation and his hobby.

Catherine Smit studied Dutch language and letters at Utrecht and has contributed as editor and translator to many books, including travel guides.

Jacqueline Toscani graduated in European Studies from Amsterdam University. Since 1992 she has been working as an editor and translator of travel guides, including many titles from the Capitool and Marco Polo series. In the latest series she was co-author of the *Vakantieplanner (holiday planner)*.

Willemien Werkman is a historian and, after studying the history of the Vecht estates, has devoted herself to translation and editing.

Additional Contributors
Paul Andrews, Hedda Archbold, Christopher Catling, Jaap Deinema, Marlene Edmunds, Adam Hopkins, Marten van de Kraats, David Lindsey, Fred Mawer, Alison Melvin, Robin Pascoe, Catherine Stebbings, Richard Widdows, Stewart Wild. Other contributions were taken from the *Eyewitness Travel Guide Amsterdam* by Robin Pascoe and Christopher Catling, which previously appeared in a translated and revised edition *(Capitool Reisgids Amsterdam)* published by *de Redactie*, boekverzorgers.

Additional Illustrations
Peter de Vries, Mark Jurriëns, Hilbert Bolland, Gieb van Enckevort, Armand Haye and Stuart Commercial Artists: Jan Egas and Khoobie Verwer.

Additional Photography
Ian O'Leary

Editorial and Design Assistance
Louise Abbot, Willem de Blaauw, Frank Bontekoning, Lucinda Cooke, Emer FitzGerald, Willem Gerritze, Martine Hauwert, Peter Koomen, Catherine Palmi, Ron Putto, Sadie Smith, Susana Smith, Inge Tijsmans, Sylvia Tombesi-Walton, Pascal Veeger, Erna de Voos, Willeke Vrij, Gerard van Vuuren, Martine Wiedemeijer

Picture Research
Harry Bunk; Corine Koolstra; Dick Polman; *de Redactie*, boekverzorgers; Rachel Barber; Ellen Root

Special Assistance
John Bekker; Wim ten Brinke; Bert Erwich; Niek Harmans; Frits Gommers; Hans Hoogendoorn; Cathelijne Hornstra; Petra van Hulsen; Frank Jacobs; Chris de Jong; Nina Krijnen; Mies Kuiper; Louise Lang; Frank van Lier; Bas de Melker; Miek Reusink; Dick Rog; Joske Siemons; Erika Teeuwisse; Wout Vuyk, Douglas Amrine.

Picture Credits
t = top; tl = top left; tlc = top left centre; tc = top centre; tr = top right; trc = top right centre; c = centre; cl = centre left; cla = centre left above; clb = centre left below; ca = centre above; cr = centre right; cra = centre right above; crb = centre right below; bc = bottom centre; b = bottom; bl = bottom left; br = bottom right.

Every effort has been made to trace the copyright holders. Dorling Kindersley apologizes for any unintentional omissions and would be pleased, in such cases, to add an acknowledgment in future editions.

The publishers are grateful to the following museums, photographers and picture libraries for permission to reproduce their photographs:

4CORNERS IMAGES: SIME/ Pavan Aldo 147br; VAN ABBEMUSEUM, EINDHOVEN: © Pablo Picasso *Lady in Green*, 1909, 1999 c/o Beeldrecht Amstelveen 364tl; AKG, LONDON: 64bl, 101tr, 122ca, 217tr; ALAMY IMAGES: Ingolf Pompe 2 148bl; Bertrand Collet 409tl; Keith Erskine 146br; f1 online 11tl; Michiel Fokkema 11br; Owen Franken 409c; Peter Horree 12tr, 13cr, 13tr; David Noble 10cra; Werner Otto 13bl; Paul M Thompson 364bl; Raymond Wijngaard 12bl. ALGEMEEN RIJKSARCHIEF, THE HAGUE: 57cra; AMSTERDAM TOURISM & CONVENTION BOARD: 107br, 110tl, 440br, 440tc, 455cl; AMSTERDAMS HISTORISCH MUSEUM: 47cra, 47crb, 64/65c, 65bl, 66cla, 92tl, 92cl, 92bc, 93tl, 93rb, 93cr, 93br, 110b, 114bl; AFF/ANNE FRANK FOUNDATION, AMSTERDAM: 108cl, 108b, 109br, 109cr (Miep Gies); ANP: 17b, 72tr, 135tl, 59cra; ANWB AUDIOVISUELE DIENST: 23tr, 30clb, 35br, 48bl, 59tl, 136tr,

136cla, 136b, 137tl, 137tr, 137br, 138br, 141tr, 163tr,
166bl, 166br, 167b, 168bl, 169bl, 180bl, 185b, 188tl,
188bl, 191tl, 207ca, 207b, 210tr, 218tl, 220c, 224t, 224br,
230tl, 230tr, 230bl, 232br, 239tr, 245tr, 249bc, 251tr, 251c,
251bc, 252bc, 253 tl, 279tr, 289br, 315bl, 332tr, 338bl,
353bl, 356br, 360tr, 361cra, 361crb, 366, 377br, 378cr,
390cl, 390b, 438t, 438cla, 438br, 439b, 440cla, 440clb,
442r, 442c, 442br, 443tr, 444c, 445bl, 447c; ARCHEOLOGISCH
INSTITUUT VU/F KORTLANG, AMSTERDAM: 42/43c; ARDEA:
Duncan Usher 10tc; ARMANDMUSEUM, AMERSFOORT: 206bl;
THE ART ARCHIVE: Museo del Prado Madrid *The Surrender
of Breda* (1635) Diego Velazquez 363br; ATLAS VAN STOLK:
41clb, 47bl, 48br, 49tr, 52/53c, 53tl, 53cr, 54cl, 55tl. B&U
INTERNATIONAL PICTURE SERVICE: 101bl, 105br, 163bl,212cl;
AART DE BAKKER: 349t, 349br, 370tr, 373t, 373cr, 376tr,
424cla; BONNEFANTENMUSEUM, MAASTRICHT: 374tl, 374tr, 374cl,
374bl, © Rene Daniels *Platte Gronden*, 1986, 1999 c/o
Beeldrecht Amstelveen 374br; 375tl, 375cra, 375bl, 375br;
Boijmans-van Beuningen Museum, Rotterdam: 234cl;
HENK BRANDSEN: 45bc, 306cla, 307tl, 307tr, 307ca;
BRIDGEMAN ART LIBRARY: Christie´s London, *Grote Markt,
Haarlem,* Gerrit Berkheyde 182l; Stapleton Collection
19th-century Delft tile 226tl; Private collection *Self-
portrait* © Kazimir Malevitch 129br; QUINTA BUMA: 34t;
HARRY BUNK: 33cl, 69tr, 138clb, 139rb, 139cr, 143tl, 146t,
202b, © Ossip Zadkine *De verwoeste stad* 1947, 1999 c/o
Beeldrecht Amstelveen 230cl; 231cra, 231crb, 231bc, 232tl,
237cr, © Mari Andriessen *Cornelius Lely,* 1983, 1999 c/o
Beeldrecht Amstelveen 326bc; 407lb, 424t, 425bl, 446c,
448c; CEES BUYS: 23tl, 47ca, 191c, 244bc, 280clb, 283c,
287b, 299c, 302, 304cla, 309tl, 315cr, 317t, 320tl, 321tr,
321bl, 325tr, 325cr, 339br, 367b, 381ca, 381crb, 388clb;
GEORGE BURGGRAAFF: 1, 18t, 21bl, 28tr, 32cr, 32clb, 42cl,
166tr, 168tr, 168cla, 189tl, 197ca, 200cla, 216tr, 237tl, 246tr,
246br, 249crb, 254tr, 255tr, 255br, 258cr, 260clb, 261cra,
261br, 278br, 281tr, 297cr, 301cl, 314cl, 317br, 318ca,
318cl, 319cr, 319crb, 325br, 333bl, 336br, 343bl, 343tr,
345br, 353tl, 353tr, 358br, 361ca.

CATHARIJNECONVENT, UTRECHT: 45cra, 46tl, 50bl, 52tr, 201cra,
351tl; CENTRAAL MUSEUM, UTRECHT: Ernst Moritz 202br; 204tl,
204cla, 205tl, 205tr, 205br; CLEVELAND MUSEUM, CLEVELAND:
50/51c; COBRA MUSEUM, AMSTELVEEN: © Karel Appel
Foundation, Karel Appel *Questioning Children* 1949,
1999 c/o Beeldrecht Amstelveen 189br. HET CONCERT
GEBOUW: Hans Samson 146cla; CORBIS: Arcaid/ Alex Bartel
148tr; Dave Bartruff 408cl. JAN DERWIG: 99tr, 141b; JURJEN
DRENTH: 2/3, 16, 28cla, 30lb, 30/31c, 32ca, 35bl, 43crb,
53bl, 60/61, 67tr, 68tr, 68cla, 68bl, 68br, 69cra, 69cr, 74b,
79bl, 86tr, 108tr, 116, 118tr, 386br, 407c, 136clb, © Hildo
Krop *Berlage,* 1999 c/o Beeldrecht Amstelveen 142bl;
144cl, 145cr, 146cr, 147tr, 160/161, 163 tr, 166cl, 166/167c,
169br, 170, 171b, 173cr, 174bl, 192, 193b, 194clb, 196bl,
197b, 198cl, 198br, 199br, 200bc, 201bc, 203tl, 203br, 208,
209b, 210cla, 210clb, 211bl, 213clb, 219crb, © Peter
Struycken *Lichtkunstwerk NAI* 1994, 1999 c/o Beeldrecht
Amstelveen 233t; 236tr, 237tr, 237br, 240ca, 243b, 244tl,
246bc, 247bc, 249tl, 252tl, 252cr, 256/257, 259crb, 263bl,
264, 266tr, 266br, 267tl, 267br, 270/271c, 272cra, 275br,
276/277, 277b, 282b, 284tr, 284clb, 286tr, 287tr, 290, 292tr,
292br, 297ca, 299tr, 304b, 305cr, 307cra, 310bl, 312, 313b,
320br, 323b, 324tl, 324clb, 330, 338cla, 341tl, 345tl, 348tr,
352tl, 352cl, 352bl, 353cr, 353co, 354, 355b, 358tl, 358c,
362tr, 363tr, 364c, 365bc, 369cr, 371c, 372bl, 376cr, 380br,
382/383, 386tl, 386tr, 391tr, 406cl, 432/433, 444tl, 446cra,
446bl, 448bl; DRENTS MUSEUM, ASSEN: 42br, 308bl, *Badende
kinderen bij stroompje* c.1935 © von Duelman-
Krumpelmann 309br, 311br; DRO-VORM: Mirande
Phernambucq 142cla, 143br. DUTCH NATIONAL BALLET:
Angela Sterling 146tc.

ROBERT ECKHARDT: 288bl, 368c; JOOP VAN DE ENDE PRODUCTIES:
428br; ESCHER IN HET PALEIS, THE HAGUE: 218cla; MARY EVANS

PICTURE LIBRARY: 40bc.GERT FOPMA: 271br, 273bl; FOTO
NATURA: 164bl (B van Biezen), 291b (J Vermeer), 309tr
and 310t (F de Nooyer), 328t (J Sleurink); FRANS HALS
MUSEUM, HAARLEM: 65tc, 186t, 186cl, 186br, 187tl, 187tr,
187cr, 187bl; FRIES MUSEUM, LEEUWARDEN: 44tl.

GEMEENTEARCHIEF AMSTERDAM: 99tl, 99cl, 100clb, 101br,
102bl, 103tr, 103cr, 104tr, 105tr, 105cr; GEMEENTEMUSEUM,
THE HAGUE: © Piet Mondrian/Holtzman Trust *Victory
Boogie-Woogie* (unfinished), 1942-44, 1999 c/o Beeldrecht
Amstelveen 224cl; GETTY IMAGES: Louis-Laurent Grandadam
10bl; Vincent Jannink 343bl; Martin Rose 148cr. GRONINGER
MUSEUM, GRONINGEN: 259tr, 284tl, 284cla, 284bc, 284br,
285tl, 285tr, 285bl.TOM HAARTSEN, J HOLTKAMP COLLECTION:
28br, 28/29c; VANESSA HAMILTON: 101c; ROBERT HARDING
PICTURE LIBRARY: 14bl; MARTINE HAUWERT: 447tl; JAN DEN
HENGST: 3c, 91br; HOLLANDSE HOOGTE: 303b, 428t, 429tr,
429b; P. Babeliowsky 295tl, 295cra; Gé Dubbelman 296bc;
B. van Flymen 32br, 300cra, 300bl; Vincent van den
Hoogen 364cr; Rob Huibers 206br; Jaco Klamer 317c; M.
Kooren 18tl, 18tl, 33c, 34cr, 35tr, 41cro, 41br, 59bc; M.
Pellanders 59br; Berry Stokvis 181bc; Lex Verspeek 178bl;
G. Wessel 274tl, 294c, 295br; HORTUS BOTANICUS, LEIDEN:
214cla; HULTON GETTY COLLECTION: 66t.

ICONOGRAFISCH BUREAU: 103tl; INTERNATIONAAL
BLOEMBOLLENCENTRUM: 31cr, 212br, 213tl, 213clb, 213cl,
213clo, 213bl; INTERNATIONAAL INSTITUUT VOOR SOCIALE
GESCHIEDENIS, AMSTERDAM: 55crb. WIM JANSZEN: 256cl, 262cl,
266cl; WUBBE DE JONG: 59clb, 109tl; JOODS HISTORISCH
MUSEUM, AMSTERDAM: 67br; JOPIE HUISMAN MUSEUM,
WORKUM: 298cla.

HUGO KAAGMAN: © Hugo Kaagman *Delft blue plane-tail
decoration* 1996-1997, 1999 c/o Beeldrecht Amstelveen
29tr; ANNE KALKHOVEN: 283bl, 311tr, 344tl; JAN VAN DE KAM:
19b, 37tr, 37cra, 37crb, 37br, 169tr, 169cra, 169crb, 260tl,
260cl, 260bc, 261tr, 261cr, 262tl, 262cla, 262cra, 262br,
262bl, 263tl, 263tlc, 263trc, 263tr, 263crb, 263cro, 263br,
268tl, 268tr, 269tl, 269tc, 269tr, 269cra, 269crb, 269bc,
269clb, 269bl, 269br, 269tl, 269tr, 269clb, 269bl, 270br,
271ca, 271cra, 271tr, 274br, 278cl, 293tr, 314b, 323, 328c,
328br, 332br, 333crb, 342tl, 346/347, 348br, 350tr, 350cla,
350clb, 350br, 350/351c, 351tr, 351crb, 351bl, 357ca, 358tr,
358cla, 359ca, 359cr, 360clb, 365cl, 368cla, 369tr, 371bl,
372tl, © Joep Nicolas, *Pieke* 1995-1996, 1999 c/o
Beeldrecht Amstelveen 372tr; 372cla, 372br, 373br, © Mari
Andriessen *Maastreechter Gees* 1961-1962, 1999 c/o
Beeldrecht Amstelveen 376tl; 376bl, 377cl, 378bl, 379cr,
380tr, 380cla, 380crb, 381bc; KLOMPENMUSEUM: 309bl; S
KONINKLIJKE BIBLIOTHEEK, THE HAGUE: 52cl; KONINKLIJK
INSTITUUT VOOR DE TROPEN, AMSTERDAM: 56tr,56/57c; KONINKLIJK
PALEIS, AMSTERDAM/RVD: 65cr, 88cla, 88clb, 89tr, 89crb;
CORINE KOOLSTRA: © Suze Boschma-Berkhout *Bartje,* 1999
c/o Beeldrecht Amstelveen 308c; PETER KOOMEN: 178tr;
RENÉ KREKELS, NIJMEGEN: 23crb; KRÖLLER-MÜLLER MUSEUM,
OTTERLO: © Jean Dubuffet *Jardin d´Émail* 1973-4, 1999
c/o Beeldrecht Amstelveen 338tr; 338br, 339c.

ANDRIES DE LA LANDE CREMER: 265b, 278tr; LEEUWARDER
COURANT: Niels Westra 294bl; FRANS LEMMENS: 30c, 322,
391tr; CLAUDE LÉVESQUE: 352/353c.

MAURITSHUIS, THE HAGUE: 8/9, 222tr, 222c, 222bl, 223tc,
223crb, 223cro, 223co, 227tl; ARNOLD MEINE JANSEN: 242,
MULTATULI MUSEUM, AMSTERDAM: 57tr; MUSÉE DE LA CHARTREUSE,
DOUAI: 50cr; MUSEUM BOERHAAVE, LEIDEN: 50bc, 51tl, 51clb;
MUSEUM BOIJMANS-VAN BEUNINGEN, ROTTERDAM: 234-5 all;
MUSEUM BREDIUS, THE HAGUE: 220bl; MUSEUM LAMBERT VAN
MEERTEN, DELFT: 229tr; MUSEUM DE FUNDATIE, PALEIS A/D
BLIJMARKT: Gerlinde Schrijver 316bl; MUSEUM NAIRAC,
BARNEVELD: 337br; MUSEUM HET REMBRANDTHUIS, AMSTERDAM:
75bc, 80br; MUSEUM SCHOKLAND: 326tr, 326cra.

NATIONAL GALLERY, LONDON: 241tr; NATURA ARTIS MAGISTRA: 139cra; NEDERLANDS ARCHITECTUUR INSTITUUT: 105cl, 142/143c; NEDERLANDS SCHEEPVAARTMUSEUM, AMSTERDAM: 48tl, 65bc, 132bl, 132cla, 132tl, 133b, 133crb, 133t; NIEDERSÄCHSISCHE STAATS- UND UNIVERSITÄTSBIBLIOTHEK, GÖTTINGEN: 44/45c; FLIP DE NOOYER: 268/269c; NORTH SEA JAZZ FESTIVAL/ROB DREXHAGE: 33br. ONZE-LIEVE-VROUWEBASILIEK, MAASTRICHT: 377tr. PALEIS HET LOO, NATIONAAL MUSEUM, APELDOORN: E. Boeijinga 334tr; A. Meine Jansen 334cla, 335tl, 334bl; R. Mulder 334cla; OPENBARE BIBLIOTHEEK AMSTERDAM: 449tl; DE PAVILJOENS, ALMERE: © Robert Morris Observatorium, 1977, 1999 c/o Beeldrecht Amstelveen 329br; PAUL PARIS: 24tr, 66br, 67bl, 70, 168/169c, 169tl, 190br, 194tr, 245br, 253br, 263cl, 268cla, 279cra, 282tr, 286clb, 288tr, 293br, 299br, 301br, 305tr, 306clb, 307br, 315tr, 331b, 348bl, 368tr; DICK POLMAN: 266tl, 274c; ROBERT POUTSMA: 20bl, 67tl, 142tr, 142br, 143tr, 143cr, 144cr, 144br, 162cl, 175tl, 276, 340cr, 384ca, 424br, 425tl, 426c; PROJECTBUREAU IJBURG: 167t; PTT MUSEUM, THE HAGUE: 50tl.

RANGE PICTURES: 48cla; HERMAN REIS: 19c, 20c, 21tr, 25cl, 52bl, 211br, 236b, 237tr, 270cla, 272br, 311cl, 319bl, RIJKSMUSEUM, AMSTERDAM: 26tr, 26cl, 26bl, 26/27c, 27tr, 27cr, 27bl, 38, 40tr, 53t, 53crb, 57tl, 64cla, 66c, 122cl, 122bc, 123t, 123c, 123br, 124tr, 124bl, 125tr, 125b, 195bl; RIJKSMUSEUM MUIDERSLOT, MUIDEN: 51cr; RIJKSMUSEUM VAN OUDHEDEN, LEIDEN: 42tl, 42clb, 43t, 43bc, 44bc, 44crb, 214ca; RIJKSMUSEUM VOOR VOLKENKUNDE, LEIDEN: 56bl, 57crb; RIJKSWATERSTAAT: 246clb, 247tl, 247cr, 272tl; MARNIX RUEB: 220tl.

HERMAN SCHOLTEN: 25bl, 172l, 175bl, 178tl, 180cr, 190tl, 195t, 199tr, 202cla, 206tr, 221b, 231tc, 240b, 246cla, 248tl, 248tr, 248cl, 249cra, 254c, 254bl, 258b, 280cla, 280b, 281br, 283tr, 292cl, 296tr, 296cl, 324tr, 324c, 333br, 356cla, 357tr; 373bc, 378tl; SCHOOLMUSEUM, ROTTERDAM/WOLTERS- NOORDHOFF, GRONINGEN: 46/47c, 49tl, 54/55c; SCIENCE CENTER NEMO: 136br, 136cla, 136clb, 136tr, 137br, 137cra; SINGER MUSEUM: Particuliere Collection 191bl; SINT-JAN, DEN BOSCH: E Van Mackelenbergh 360cla, 360bc, 361tl; SPAARNESTAD FOTOARCHIEF: 55tr, 57b, 58clb, 58br, 59cla, 99bc, 143bl; SPOORWEGMUSEUM, UTRECHT: 201crb; SPL: Earth Satellite Corporation 14cl; STEDELIJK MUSEUM, AMSTERDAM: © Gerrit Rietveld Steltman chair 1963, 1999 c/o Beeldrecht Amstelveen 66bl; 128tr, © Marc Chagall Portrait of the Artist with Seven Fingers 1912, 1999 c/o Beeldrecht Amstelveen 128cla; © Gerrit Rietveld Red Blue Chair c.1918, 1999 c/o Beeldrecht Amstelveen 128bl; © Piet

Mondrian/Holtzman Trust Composition in Red, Black, Blue, Yellow and Grey 1920, 1999 c/o Beeldrecht Amstelveen 128br; 129tl, © Karel Appel Foundation Man and Animals 1949, 1999 c/o Beeldrecht Amstelveen 129ca; © Jasper Johns Untitled 1965, 1999 c/o Beeldrecht Amstelveen 129bc; 129br, Tanzende 1911 © Ernst Ludwig Kirchner 129tl; STEDELIJK MUSEUM DE LAKENHAL, LEIDEN: 46cl, 104br, 216b; STEDELIJK MUSEUM, ZWOLLE: 316tr; STICHTING LEIDENS ONTZET: 35tl; STICHTING PAARDENREDDINGBOOT AMELAND: 275t; STICHTING VESTING BOURTANGE: 289tr; STICHTING4-STROMENLAND, TIEL: 34bl; STUDIO PUTTO, DERIJP: 18bl, 20c, 30/31b, 33tr, 41bl, 41crb, 44br, 84tr, 113bl, 173tr, 173cr; STUDIOPRESS: Guy van Grinsven 174tr.

TONY STONE IMAGES: 100tr, 179cla, 213tl; SVEN TORFINN: 359tl, 359br; TPG NEDERLAND: 448crb, 449bc; HANS TULLENERS: 99tr, 100cr, 102c. VAN GOGH MUSEUM, AMSTERDAM: 126cla, 126clb, 127t, 127tr, 127cr; GERARD OP HET VELD: 30tr, 142c, 298tr, 336cr, 341bl, 342br, 356bc, 365tr, 368bl, 369br, 371tr, 379tr, 379bl; 385b; VERENIGING DE FRIESCHE ELF STEDEN 292rb; GOVERT VETTEN: 18tr, 56tl, 68cl, 69bl, 81br, 120clb, 142/143c, 195br, 196t, 260cla, 385b, 424c, 436br; VOLKSKRANT: Wim Ruigrok 22tr; SIETSKE DE VRIES, AMSTERDAM: 30cl; WILLEKE VRIJ: 31tr. WACON-IMAGES/RONALD DENDEKKER: 147tl; PIM WESTERWEEL: 162cr, 163cr, 164crb, 195cra, 259cra, 259b, 262clb, 329tr, 341cr, 349cr, 362bl; WEST-FRIES MUSEUM, HOORN: 56cla; WL/DELFT HYDRAULICS: 164br. ZEEUWS MUSEUM, MIDDELBURG: Anda van Riet 250bl; 250crb, 250tl; ZUIDERZEEMUSEUM, ENKHUIZEN: 165tr, photo Petra Stavast © Hugo Kaagman The Blue Fishvendor (www.kaagman. nl) stencils and spraypaint 177tl.

FRONT ENDPAPER LEFT: JURJEN DRENTH tl, tc, tr, cl, bl, br; JAN VAN DER KAM cr; ARNOLD MEINE JANSEN bc.

FRONT ENDPAPER RIGHT: ANWB AUDIOVISUELE DIENST bc; CEES BUYS cra; JURJEN DRENTH c, br; ROBERT POUTSMA tr.

JACKET
FRONT - MASTERFILE: Minden Pictures. BACK - ALAMY IMAGES: Arterra Picture Library/van der Meer Marica tl; Blaine Harrington III bl; Robert Harding Picture Library Ltd/Roy Rainford clb; DORLING KINDERSLEY: cla; Spine - MASTERFILE: Minden Pictures t.

All other images © Dorling Kindersley. For further information see: www.dkimages.com

SPECIAL EDITIONS OF DK TRAVEL GUIDES

DK Travel Guides can be purchased in bulk quantities at discounted prices for use in promotions or as premiums. We are also able to offer special editions and personalized jackets, corporate imprints, and excerpts from all of our books, tailored specifically to meet your own needs.

To find out more, please contact:
(in the United States) **SpecialSales@dk.com**
(in the UK) **travelspecialsales@uk.dk.com**
(in Canada) DK Special Sales at **general@ tourmaline.ca**
(in Australia)
business.development@pearson.com.au

Phrase Book

In Emergency

Help!	**Help!**	Help
Stop!	**Stop!**	Stop
Call a doctor	**Haal een dokter**	Haal uhn **dok**-tur
Call an ambulance	**Bel een ambulance**	Bell uhn ahm-bew-**luhns**-uh
Call the police	**Roep de politie**	Roop duh poe-**leet**-see
Call the fire brigade	**Roep de brandweer**	Roop duh **brahnt**-vheer
Where is the nearest telephone?	**Waar is de dichtstbijzijnde telefoon?**	Vhaar iss duh **dikhst**-baiy-zaiyn-duh tay-luh-**foan**
Where is the nearest hospital?	**Waar is het dichtstbijzijnde ziekenhuis?**	Vhaar iss het **dikhst**-baiy-zaiyn-duh **zee**-kuh-houws

Communication Essentials

Yes	**Ja**	Yaa
No	**Nee**	Nay
Please	**Alstublieft**	Ahls-tew-**bleeft**
Thank you	**Dank u**	Dahnk-ew
Excuse me	**Pardon**	Pahr-**don**
Hello	**Hallo**	Hallo
Goodbye	**Dag**	Dahgh
Good night	**Slaap lekker**	Slaap **lek**-kah
morning	**Morgen**	**Mor**-ghuh
afternoon	**Middag**	**Mid**-dahgh
evening	**Avond**	**Ah**-vohnd
yesterday	**Gisteren**	**Ghis**-tern
today	**Vandaag**	Vahn-**daagh**
tomorrow	**Morgen**	**Mor**-ghuh
here	**Hier**	Heer
there	**Daar**	Daar
What?	**Wat?**	Vhat
When?	**Wanneer?**	Vhan-**eer**
Why?	**Waarom?**	Vhaar-**om**
Where?	**Waar?**	Vhaar
How?	**Hoe?**	Hoo

Useful Phrases

How are you?	**Hoe gaat het ermee?**	Hoo ghaat het er-**may**
Very well, thank you	**Heel goed, dank u**	Hayl ghoot, dahnk ew
How do you do?	**Hoe maakt u het?**	Hoo maakt ew het
See you soon	**Tot ziens**	Tot zeens
That's fine	**Prima**	**Pree**-mah
Where is/are?	**Waar is/zijn?**	Vhaar iss/zayn…
How far is it to…?	**Hoe ver is het naar…?**	Hoo vehr iss het naar…
How do I get to…?	**Hoe kom ik naar…?**	Hoo kom ik naar…
Do you speak English?	**Spreekt u engels?**	Spraykt ew **eng**-uhls
I don't understand	**Ik snap het niet**	Ik snahp het neet
Could you speak slowly?	**Kunt u langzamer praten?**	Kuhnt ew **lahng**-zahmer praa-tuh
I'm sorry	**Sorry**	Sorry

Useful Words

big	**groot**	ghroaht
small	**klein**	klaiyn
hot	**warm**	vharm
cold	**koud**	khowt
good	**goed**	ghoot
bad	**slecht**	slekht
enough	**genoeg**	ghuh-**noohkh**
well	**goed**	ghoot
open	**open**	open
closed	**gesloten**	ghuh-**slow**-tuh
left	**links**	links
right	**rechts**	rekhts
straight on	**rechtdoor**	rekhht dohr
near	**dichtbij**	dikht baiy
far	**ver weg**	vehr vhekh
up	**omhoog**	om-**hoakh**
down	**naar beneden**	naar buh-**nay**-duh
early	**vroeg**	vroohkh
late	**laat**	laat
entrance	**ingang**	**in**-ghahng
exit	**uitgang**	**ouht**-ghang
toilet	**wc**	vhay say
occupied	**bezet**	buh-**zett**
free (unoccupied)	**vrij**	vraiy
free (no charge)	**gratis**	**ghraah**-tiss

Making a Telephone Call

I'd like to place a long-distance call	**Ik wil graag interlokaal telefoneren**	Ik vhil ghraakh **inter**-loh-kaahl tay-luh-foe-**neh**-ruh
I'd like to call collect	**Ik wil "collect call" bellen**	Ik vhil "collect call" **bel**-luh
I'll try again later	**Ik probeer het later nog wel eens**	Ik pro-**beer** het laater nokh vhel ayns
Can I leave a message?	**Kunt u een boodschap doorgeven?**	Kuhnt ew uhn **boat**-skhahp **dohr**-ghay-vuh
Could you speak up a little please?	**Wilt u wat harder praten?**	Vhilt ew vhat **hahr**-der **praah**-tuh
Local call	**Lokaal gesprek**	Low-**kaahl** ghuh-**sprek**

Shopping

How much does this cost?	**Hoeveel kost dit?**	Hoo-**vayl** kost dit
I would like	**Ik wil graag**	Ik vhil ghraakh
Do you have…?	**Heeft u…?**	Hayft ew…
I'm just looking	**Ik kijk alleen even**	Ik kaiyk alleyn **ay**-vuh
Do you take credit cards?	**Neemt u credit cards aan?**	Naymt ew credit cards aan
Do you take traveller's cheques?	**Neemt u reischeques aan?**	Naymt ew **raiys**-sheks aan
What time do you open?	**Hoe laat gaat u open?**	Hoo laat ghaat ew opuh
What time do you close?	**Hoe laat gaat u dicht?**	Hoo laat ghaat ew dikht
This one	**Deze**	**Day**-zuh
That one	**Die**	Dee
expensive	**duur**	dewr
cheap	**goedkoop**	ghoot-**koap**
size	**maat**	maat
white	**wit**	vhit
black	**zwart**	zvhahrt
red	**rood**	roat
yellow	**geel**	ghayl
green	**groen**	ghroon
blue	**blauw**	blah-ew

Types of Shops

antique shop	**antiekwinkel**	ahn-**teek**-vhin-kul
bakery	**bakker**	**bah**-ker
bank	**bank**	bahnk
bookshop	**boekwinkel**	**book**-vhin-kul
butcher	**slager**	slaakh-er
cake shop	**banketbakkerij**	bahnk-**et**-bahk-er-aiy
cheese shop	**kaaswinkel**	**kaas**-vhin-kul
chip shop	**patatzaak**	pah-**taht**-zaak
chemist (dispensing)	**apotheek**	ah-poe-**taiyk**
delicatessen	**delicatessen**	daylee-kah-**tes**-suh
department store	**warenhuis**	**vhaar**-uh-houws
fishmonger	**viswinkel**	**viss**-vhin-kul
greengrocer	**groenteboer**	**ghroon**-tuh-boor
hairdresser	**kapper**	**kah**-per
market	**markt**	mahrkt
newsagent	**krantenwinkel**	**krahn**-tuh-vhin-kul
post office	**postkantoor**	**pohst**-kahn-tor
shoe shop	**schoenenwinkel**	**sghoo**-nuh-vhin-kul
supermarket	**supermarkt**	**sew**-per-mahrkt
tobacconist	**sigarenwinkel**	see-**ghaa**-ruh-vhin-kul
travel agent	**reisburo**	**raiys**-bew-roa

Sightseeing

art gallery	**gallerie**	ghaller-ee
bus station	**busstation**	**buhs**-stah-shown
bus ticket	**strippenkaart**	**strip**-puh-kaahrt
cathedral	**kathedraal**	kah-tuh-**draal**
church	**kerk**	kehrk
closed on public holidays	**op feestdagen gesloten**	op **fayst**-daa-ghuh ghuh-**slow**-tuh
day return	**dagretour**	**dahgh**-ruh-tour
garden	**tuin**	touwn
library	**bibliotheek**	bee-bee-yo-**tayk**
museum	**museum**	mew-**zay**-uhm
railway station	**station**	stah-**shown**
return ticket	**retourtje**	ruh-**tour**-tyuh
single journey	**enkeltje**	**eng**-kuhl-tyuh
tourist information	**VVV**	fay fay fay
town hall	**stadhuis**	staht-**houws**
train	**trein**	traiyn

Staying in a Hotel

Do you have a vacant room?	Zijn er nog kamers vrij?	Zaiyn er nokh kaa-mers vray
double room with double bed	een twees persoonskamer met een twee persoonsbed	uhn tvhay-per soans-kaa-mer met uhn tvhay-per-soans beht
twin room	een kamer met een lits-jumeaux	uhn kaa-mer met uhn lee-zjoo-moh
single room	eenpersoons-kamer	ayn-per-soans-kaa-mer
room with a bath	kamer met bad	kaa-mer met baht
shower	douche	doosh
porter	kruier	krouw-yuh
I have a reservation	Ik heb gereserveerd	Ik hehp ghuh-ray-sehr-veert

Eating Out

Have you got a table?	Is er een tafel vrij?	Iss ehr uhn tah-fuhl vraiy
I want to reserve a table	Ik wil een tafel reserveren	Ik vhil uhn tah-fuhl ray-sehr-veer-uh
The bill, please	Mag ik afrekenen	Mukh ik ahf-ray-kuh-nuh
I am a vegetarian	Ik ben vegetariër	Ik ben fay-ghuh-taahr-ee-er
waitress/waiter	serveerster/ober	Sehr-veer-ster/oh-ber
menu	de kaart	duh kaahrt
cover charge	het couvert	het koo-vehr
wine list	de wijnkaart	duh vhaiyn-kaart
glass	het glas	het ghlahss
bottle	de fles	duh fless
knife	het mes	het mess
fork	de vork	duh fork
spoon	de lepel	duh lay-pul
breakfast	het ontbijt	het ont-baiyt
lunch	de lunch	duh lernsh
dinner	het diner	het dee-nay
main course	het hoofdgerecht	het hoaft-ghuh-rekht
starter, first course	het voorgerecht	het vohr-ghuh-rekht
dessert	het nagerecht	het naa-ghuh-rekht
dish of the day	het dagmenu	het dahgh-munh-ew
bar	het cafe	het kaa-fay
café	het eetcafe	het ayt-kaa-fay
rare	rare	'rare'
medium	medium	'medium'
well done	doorbakken	dohr-bah-kuh

Menu Decoder

aardappels	aard-uppuhls	potatoes
azijn	aah-zaiyn	vinegar
biefstuk	beef-stuhk	steak
bier, pils	beer, pilss	beer
boter	boater	butter
brood/broodje	broat/broat-yuh	bread/roll
cake, taart, gebak	"cake", taahrt, ghuh-bahk	cake, pastry
carbonade	kahr-bow-naa-duh	pork chop
chocola	show-coa-laa	chocolate
citroen	see-troon	lemon
cocktail	cocktail	cocktail
droog	droakh	dry
eend	aynt	duck
ei	aiy	egg
garnalen	ghahr-naah-luh	prawns
gebakken	ghuh-bah-ken	fried
gegrild	ghuh-ghrillt	grilled
gekookt	ghuh-koakt	boiled
gepocheerd	ghuh-posh-eert	poached
gerookt	ghuh-roakt	smoked
geroosterd brood	ghuh-roas-tert broat	toast
groenten	ghroon-tuh	vegetables
ham	hahm	ham
haring	haa-ring	herring
hutspot	huht-spot	hot pot
ijs	aiyss	ice, ice cream
jenever	yuh-nay-vhur	gin
kaas	kaas	cheese
kabeljauw	kah-buhl-youw	cod
kip	kip	chicken
knoflook	knoff-loak	garlic
koffie	coffee	coffee
kool, rode of witte	coal, roe-duh off vhit-uh	cabbage, red or white
kreeft	krayft	lobster
kroket	crow-ket	ragout in bread-crumbs, deep fried
lamsvlees	lahms-flayss	lamb

lekkerbekje	lek-kah-bek-yuh	fried fillet of haddock
mineraalwater	meener-aahl-vhaater	mineral water
mosterd	moss-tehrt	mustard
niet scherp	neet skehrp	mild
olie	oh-lee	oil
paling	paa-ling	eel
pannekoek	pah-nuh-kook	pancake
patat frites	pah-taht freet	chips
peper	pay-per	pepper
poffertjes	poffer-tyuhs	tiny buckwheat pancakes
rijst	raiyst	rice
rijsttafel	raiys-tah-ful	Indonesian meal
rode wijn	roe-duh vhaiyn	red wine
rookworst	roak-vhorst	smoked sausage
rundvlees	ruhnt-flayss	beef
saus	souwss	sauce
schaaldieren	skaahl-deeh-ruh	shellfish
scherp	skehrp	hot (spicy)
schol	sghol	plaice
soep	soup	soup
stamppot	stahm-pot	sausage stew
suiker	souw-ker	sugar
thee	tay	tea
tosti	toss-tee	cheese on toast
uien	ouw-yuh	onions
uitsmijter	ouht-smaiy-ter	fried egg on bread with ham
varkensvlees	vahr-kuhns-flayss	pork
vers fruit	fehrss frouwt	fresh fruit
verse jus	vehr-suh zjhew	fresh orange juice
vis	fiss	fish/seafood
vlees	flayss	meat
water	vhaa-ter	water
witte wijn	vhih-tuh vhaiyn	white wine
worst	vhorst	sausage
zout	zouwt	salt

Numbers

1	een	ayn
2	twee	tvhay
3	drie	dree
4	vier	feer
5	vijf	faiyf
6	zes	zess
7	zeven	zay-vuh
8	acht	ahkht
9	negen	nay-guh
10	tien	teen
11	elf	elf
12	twaalf	tvhaalf
13	dertien	dehr-teen
14	veertien	feer-teen
15	vijftien	faiyf-teen
16	zestien	zess-teen
17	zeventien	zayvuh-teen
18	achtien	ahkh-teen
19	negentien	nay-ghuh-teen
20	twintig	tvhin-tukh
21	eenentwintig	aynuh-tvhin-tukh
30	dertig	dehr-tukh
40	veertig	feer-tukh
50	vijftig	faiyf-tukh
60	zestig	zess-tukh
70	zeventig	zay-vuh-tukh
80	tachtig	tahkh-tukh
90	negentig	nayguh-tukh
100	honderd	hohn-durt
1000	duizend	douw-zuhnt
1,000,000	miljoen	mill-yoon

Time

one minute	een minuut	uhn meen-ewt
one hour	een uur	uhn ewr
half an hour	een half uur	uhn hahlf ewr
half past one	half twee	hahlf tvhay
a day	een dag	uhn dahgh
a week	een week	uhn vhayk
a month	een maand	uhn maant
a year	een jaar	uhn jaar
Monday	maandag	maan-dahgh
Tuesday	dinsdag	dins-dahgh
Wednesday	woensdag	vhoons-dahgh
Thursday	donderdag	donder-dahgh
Friday	vrijdag	vraiy-dahgh
Saturday	zaterdag	zaater-dahgh
Sunday	zondag	zon-dahgh